W9-BLL-499

PROPERTY OF
BARNEY WELLS

# HEBREW-ENGLISH
# LEXICON

# HEBREW-ENGLISH
# LEXICON

### CONTAINING

## ALL THE HEBREW AND CHALDEE WORDS
## IN THE OLD TESTAMENT SCRIPTURES,
## WITH THEIR MEANINGS IN ENGLISH

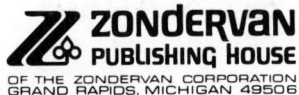

**ZONDERVAN**
**PUBLISHING HOUSE**
OF THE ZONDERVAN CORPORATION
GRAND RAPIDS, MICHIGAN 49506

*Published by special arrangement with*
SAMUEL BAGSTER & SONS, LTD.,
London

Zondervan Edition 1970
Second printing 1971
Third printing 1972
Fourth printing 1973
Fifth printing 1974

Library of Congress Catalog Card Number: 72-106438

Catalog Number: 6264

*Printed in the United States of America*

# PREFACE

THE best modern authorities have been consulted in the preparation of the present work; and we have endeavoured to give the results of their researches in as condensed and convenient a form for reference as possible.

The arrangement is that of Leopold's "Lexicon Manuale," which is itself taken altogether from the larger lexicons of Gesenius and Winer.

The valuable analytical Index which Leopold, from the same authorities, prints separately as an appendix, we have incorporated with the lexicon itself, in alphabetical order; thus making, it is hoped, a useful addition to his already copious collection of references.

To economise the student's time as far as possible, the meaning in English accompanies the reference wherever it has been found practicable to express it by a single word; in the hope of combining, in some degree, the advantages of the alphabetical with those of the radical arrangement, upon which the lexicon of Leopold is formed.

All fictitious roots have been discarded: i. e. words

occurring in no language, but which ought to be the roots whence certain Hebrew nouns have been derived, according to the analogy of the Hebrew grammar.

We are well aware of the advantage which these invented words afford to the arrangement under roots; but it is obvious, nevertheless, that nothing of this nature can compensate for the evil which arises from the presentation of a falsity to the mind of a beginner. The only words not occurring in the Bible which will be found in this lexicon are roots from the cognate languages, bearing a fair similarity of meaning to the Hebrew compounds which are arranged with them. In the many cases in which no such resemblance is to be found, the simplest form of the Hebrew compound has been printed in the larger character by which radical words are denoted.

The proper names are arranged as Leopold has given them, under the roots whence, according to the analogy of the Hebrew grammar, they would appear to be derived. This, however, is merely for the convenience of finding them in the lexicon. The derivations which he has added have been all but invariably discarded. A high authority in Hebrew lexicography having questioned the necessity, or even propriety, of inserting the proper names in the lexicon at all, it is right to explain that they have been retained in order to relieve the beginner in Hebrew from the necessity of resorting to the very expedient whereby that author proposes to dispense with them, namely, by referring him to an approved version. The compiler of the present work has found a frequent appeal to translations to interfere so fatally with his own progress in the acquisition of a language, that he has felt it his duty to bestow much care and pains upon them, making many additions to Leopold, so as to put the student in possession of the whole of the proper names that occur in the Hebrew Bible, even though in so many instances no better account of them can be given, than that they are names of persons or places.

As to the meanings (which form of course the really important part of the work), but very little use has been made of the Latin renderings of Leopold, which are only of any value when they repeat those of the authors upon whose labours his lexicon is founded. Leopold's authorities themselves, as well as others, to whose works he had probably no access, have been consulted upon every word. The concordance of Noldius and Fürst have also been appealed to in all cases of difficulty arising from variations of opinion among the authorities consulted; and thus from the passages themselves it has been endeavoured to form a judgment of the words which best expressed the sense of the sacred text. For this purpose, the racy idiomatic English of Professor Lee's renderings has been freely taken advantage of; this obligation to him is thankfully acknowledged.

The lexicon is specially designed to put into the hands of the English student, in a compressed and compendious form, the contributions of modern philology to the interpretation of the Hebrew Scriptures. There are many words the meaning of which the researches of the learned have not succeeded hitherto in elucidating. In such cases it has been deemed the best course to give the rendering in the Authorised English Version only. The speculations which may have been indulged in by interpreters, ancient or modern, as to their meaning, are of little value in themselves, while to the beginner they are worse than worthless; they are moreover known to the proficient, and the student will readily find them in the larger lexicons. We give a single instance. The word אַבְרֵךְ Gen. 41:43 is rendered by our translators "bow the knee," assuming it to be an anomalous Hiphil form of the denominative from בֶּרֶךְ "knee." This, though somewhat forced, is at any rate more feasible than the modern interpretation, which, assuming with considerable probability that it is an Egyptian word or phrase, declares that it is equivalent to ⲁⲡⲉⲣⲉⲕ, which is to be translated "bow the head." Such however is by no means the case. The general meaning of the word ⲁⲡⲉ or ⲁⲫⲉ is "the top or summit of a thing." It does not appear to be used of the head at all in the Coptic Bible, but rather of the crown or scalp. The Egyptian word for the head, as a member of the body, is ⲭⲱ. The word ⲣⲉⲕ means "to bow," but the construction of the supposed phrase is althogether foreign to the idiom of the language. Nor does it appear in any degree probable from the remains of it, which are very copious, that ⲁⲡⲉⲣⲉⲕ or ⲁⲫⲉⲣⲉⲕ would be a more intelligible direction to an Egyptian to bow the head than "crown bow" would be to an Englishman. The phrase repeatedly occurs in the Coptic Bible, and is written **ⲡⲉⲕϫⲱ.** It is to be regretted that biblical difficulties are too often dealt with in this loose unsatisfactory manner.

In the English meanings throughout, it has been endeavoured to counteract the blasphemous attempt of one of the great modern schools of sacred hermeneutics to vulgarise and debase the word of God by quaint and burlesque interpretations. On the other hand, it has been deemed expedient to avoid the equally fallacious principle of another class of interpreters, who elevate into authoritative glosses the renderings of writers confessedly ignorant of Hebrew, for no better reason than that they wrote some twelve or fifteen centuries ago.

We have striven to give the student the benefit of the labours of both schools, without leading him into the errors of either.

It is only needful further to explain that wherever a word or meaning is accompanied by one, or in some instances by two references, it is denoted that such word or meaning occurs in those places only in the Hebrew Bible.

# ABBREVIATIONS OF GRAMMATICAL TERMS
## USED IN THE LEXICON

| | | | |
|---|---|---|---|
| m. | masculine | Niph. | Niphal form of verb |
| f. | feminine | Hiph. | Hiphil form of verb |
| s. | substantive | Hith. | Hithpael form of verb |
| pa. | particle | | |
| part. | participle | Pi. | Piel form of verb |
| denom. | denominative; that is, a verb derived immediately from a noun (*de nomine*) | Pu. | Pual form of verb |
| | | Po. | Poel *or* Polel form of verb |
| patron. | patronymic: a proper name derived from that of the father of the individual | Hoth. | Hothpael form of verb |
| | | Ith. | Ithpael form of verb |
| | | imp. | imperative mood |
| sing. | singular | const. | construct state of noun |
| pl. | plural | emph. | emphatic state of noun |

# HEBREW-ENGLISH
# LEXICON

# LEXICON.

אב

**אָב** m (const. אֲבִי and אַב, Gen. 17:4, 5; with suff. אָבִי, אָבִיךָ, אֲבִיכֶם; pl. אָבוֹת).—I. *a father.*—II. *a progenitor, ancestor*; used generally for any senior male relative.—III. *an originator, inventor,* Gen. 10:21, &c.—IV. *a head, chief,* or *ruler*; applied to kings, prophets, priests, &c.; אָב לְפַרְעֹה *a father,* that is, *a counsellor to Pharaoh,* Gen. 45:8.

**אַב** m. Ch. (with suff. אֲבוּךְ, אֲבִי, אֲבוּהִי, pl. אֲבָהָן), *a father.*

**אָבַב** not used.

**אֵב** m., *greenness, freshness,* אִבִּים *green herbs.*

**אֵב** m., Ch. *fruit;* אִנְבֵּה for אִבֵּהּ, *his fruit.*

**אָבִיב** m.—I. *a green ear of corn,* Lev. 2:14.—II. *shooting into the ear,* spoken of barley, Ex.9:31. Hence חֹרֶשׁ הָאָבִיב *the month Abib,* the name of the month in which the barley shoots into ear, corresponding partly with our March, partly with April, otherwise called נִיסָן.

**אֲבַגְתָא** p.n., one of the chamberlains of King Ahasuerus, Est. 1:10.

אבה

**אָבַד** (inf. אֲבֹד, אֲבֹד, fut. יֹאבַד and יֹאבֵד).—I. *strayed, lost.*—II. *was ruined, perished* (const. with לְ or מִן); part. אֹבֵד *one about to perish, a wretch;* Pi. אִבַּד, and Hiph. הֶאֱבִיד *made to stray, dispersed, laid waste, ruined, destroyed.*

**אֲבַד** Ch. (fut. יֵאבַד), *perished;* Aph. הוֹבֵד *destroyed;* Hoph. הוּגַד *was destroyed.*

**אֹבֵד** m., *perishing, ruin.*

**אֲבֵדָה** f., *something lost,* the grave · see following word.

**אֲבַדּוֹן** *extermination, destruction, the grave,* the place where the body decays after death, opposed to שְׁאוֹל the place of the soul after death, Pro. 15:11, &c.; see the word.

**וָאַבְּדָךְ, אַבְּדָךְ** for (וָאֲאַבְּדָךְ), Pi. fut. with suff.

**אַבְדָן** m., *extermination, ruin,* Est. 9:5; אָבְדָן the same, Est. 8:6.

**אָבָה** (fut. יֹאבֶה), in Kal only, *desirous, willing;* const. mostly with the neg. לֹא and with or without לְ.

**אֵבֶה** m., *a reed, rush;* אֳנִיּוֹת אֵבֶה *vessels made of reeds,* Job 9:26

אָבוּא for אָבוּ pret..pl.

אֶבְיוֹן m., *wishing, desiring;* hence, *destitute, poor, miserable.*

אֲבִיּוֹנָה f., *desire,* Eccl. 12:5.

אֲבוֹי (lit. *misery*), *alas!* Pro. 23:29.

אָבוֹשׁ fut.; see בוֹשׁ.

אֲבָחָה ,אָבָה f.; אַבְחַת חֶרֶב, *the resting, descent of the sword;* according to others, *the threatening of the sword,* or, *the drawn sword.* Ezek. 21:20.

אֲבַטִּיחִים m. pl., *melons,* Nu. 11:5; see בַטִּיחַ.

אָבִי for אָבִיא Hiph. fut. 1 pers.; see בוֹא, 1 Ki. 21:29; Mic. 1:15.

אֲבִי (*my father*), p. n., the mother of King Hezekiah, 2 Kings 18:2.

אֲבִידָה for אַאֲבִידָה Hiph. fut. 1. pers.; see אבד.

אֲבִיאֵל (*the divine Father*), p.n.—I. the grandfather of Saul, 1 Sa. 9:1.—II. one of David's generals.

אֲבִיאָסָף ,אֶבְיָסָף (*father of gathering, collector*), p.n., one of the Korahites.

אֲבִינַיִל ,אֲבִיגַל (*she whose father rejoiceth,* or, *the dancer*), p. n.—I. the wife of Nabal, afterwards of David.—II. the sister of David, 1 Chron. 2:16.

אֲבִידָן (*the father of judgment, the judge*) p. n., one of the princes of Benjamin, Nu. 1:11, &c.

אֲבִיָּהוּ ,אֲבִיָּה (*he whose father is Jehovah*), see אֲבִים; p.n.—I. of a man. —II. of a woman

אֲבִיהוּא p. n., a son of Aaron.

אֲבִיהוּד (*the father of glory,* πατροκλος), p. n. of a man

אֲבִיחַיִל (*the father of artifices, he who is skilful*), p.n. of a man.

אֲבִיחַיִל (*the same*), p. n. of a woman.

אֲבִיטוֹב (*father of goodness*), p. n. of a man.

אֲבִיטַל (*father of dew, vigorous*), p.n., a wife of David.

אֲבִים (*the sailor*), p. n. of a man; the same as אֲבִיָּהוּ, and probably an error of some transcriber.

אֲבִימָאֵל p. n. of a man.

אֲבִימֶלֶךְ (*father of a king*), p. n.— I. a king of the Philistines, Gen. c. 20, perhaps the common name of the kings of that country.—II. name of a man, Jud. 8:31, &c.

אֲבִינָדָב (*father of willingness*), p. n. of a man.

אֲבִינֹעַם (*father of pleasantness*), p.n. of a man.

אַבְנֵר ,אֲבִינֵר (*father of light*), p.n., one of Saul's generals.

אֲבִיעֶזֶר (*father of help*), p.n. of a man.

אֲבִי־עַלְבוֹן m. (*violator*), p.n. of a man.

אַבִּיר ,אַבִּיר *mighty;* see אבר.

אֲבִירָם m. (*father of pride, a proud one*), p. n. of a man.

אֲבִישַׁג f. p. n., one of David's concubines, 1 Kings 1:15, &c.

אֲבִישׁוּעַ (*father of salvation*), p. n. of a man.

אֲבִישׁוּר (*father of song, singer*), p. n. of a man, 1 Chron. 2:28.

אֲבִישַׁי ,אֲבִישָׁי (*father of gifts, generous*), p. n. of a man.

אֲבִישָׁלוֹם (*father of peace*), the grandfather of Abijam king of Judah, 1 Kings 1ﬁ: 2.

אֶבְיָתָר (*a father of excellence, he who excels*), Abiathar, the son of Ahimelech, a high priest in David's time, 1 Sa. 22:20.

אָבַךְ Hith. only. יִתְאַבְּכוּ "they swell with a rolling motion like volumes of smoke," Isa. 9:17.

I. אָבַל (fut. יֶאֱבַל), mourned, lamented; const. with עַל; Hiph. הֶאֱבִיל made or caused to mourn; Hith. הִתְאַבֵּל grieved, betook himself to mourn; const. with אֶל or עַל.

אָבֵל m. (const. אֲבֶל-אָבֶל; pl. אֲבֵלִים), אֲבֵלָה f. mourning; אֵבֶל m. (with suff. אֶבְלִי) the same, grief, howling.

אָבֵל מִצְרַיִם (the mourning of Egypt), p.n., a place beyond Jordan, where the children of Israel mourned for their father when they carried him forth to his burial, Gen. 50:11.

II. אָבֵל not used (Arab. fresh, green, grass).

אָבֵל a grassy place, field; hence the following names of places.—I. א' הַגְּדוֹלָה the greater Abel, a district of the Philistines, 1 Sa. 6:18.—II. א' בֵּית-מֵעֲכָה a large city in the land of the tribe of Manasseh, called א' מַיִם, 2 Chron. 16:4.—III. א' הַשִּׁטִּים a place in the land of Moab.—IV. א' כְּרָמִים a village of the Ammonites.—V. א' מְחוֹלָה a village in the land of Issachar; hence the appellation מְחֹלָתִי; see the word.

III. אֲבָל adv., certainly, but, indeed.
אוּבַל, אֲבָל; see יבל.

אֶבֶן f., I. a stone, rock (pl. אֲבָנִים; אַבְנֵי); לְאֶבֶן like a stone; אֶבֶן יָד a stone which may be thrown with the hand; א' בָּרָד (אֲבָנִים גְּדֹלוֹת) hail stones.—II. precious stones, jewels; אַבְנֵי-אֵשׁ shining stones.

—III. a weight; אֶבֶן וָאֶבֶן divers weights.—IV. a plummet.

אֶבֶן עֵזֶר (stone of help), p. n. of a place, 1 Sa. 7:12.

אֶבֶן הָאֵזֶל (stone of departure), p. n. of a place.

אֶבֶן f. Ch. emph. state אַבְנָא; a stone. אֶבֶן m., dual אָבְנָיִם.—I. "potter's wheel," Jer. 18:3.—II. "upon the stools," Ex. 1:16; Eng. Ver. The true meaning is uncertain.

אֲבָנָה p. n., a river of Damascus, 2 Ki. 5:12.

אֲבֻנְם see בנט.

אֲבִינֵר p. n. of a man; see אֲבִנֵר.

אָבַס, part. אָבוּס fattened.

אֵבוּס m. (pl. אֲבוּסִים) a crib or stall in which animals are fed; מַאֲבוּס m., barn, granary, Jer. 50:26.

אֲבַעְבֻּעוֹת ulcers; see בּוּעַ.

אֶבֶץ p.n. of a city in the tribe of Issachar.

אִבְצָן (he who is shining, famous), p. n., a judge of Israel.

אָבָק m., fine dust, powder; אֲבָקָה f., אַבְקַת רוֹכֵל aromatic dust, powdered perfume; "powder of the merchant," Cant. 3:6, Eng. Ver.; נֶאֱבַק Niph. wrestled (because the ancient wrestlers covered their bodies with dust before they began to wrestle).

אָבַר Kal, not used, was strong; Hiph הֶאֱבִיר flew, soared.

אֵבֶר m., quill, wing-feather.
אֶבְרָה f., the same.
אַבִּיר, אָבִיר m.—I. mighty (an epithet of God).—II. strong, valiant, noble, אַבִּירִים strong bulls, or horses; אַבִּיר הָרֹעִים the prince of the shepherds.

אַבְרָם (exalted father), p. n., Abram; אַבְרָהָם (father of a multitude), p. n., the patriarch Abraham.

אַבְרֵךְ Gen. 41:43, "bow the knee," Eng. Ver. The true meaning is uncertain.

אַבְרְכָה Pi. fut. with suff.; see ברך.

אַבְישַׁי p. n., see אֲבִישַׁי.

אַבְשָׁלוֹם (father of peace), p. n., Absalom, the son of David.

אָגָא (fugitive), p. n. of a man.

אֶנְאָלְתִּי Hith. pret. 1. pers. for הִנְאָלְתִּי; see נאל.

אֲגָג p. n., a king of the Amalekites.

אֲגָגִי Agagite, a title of Haman, Est. 3:1.

אָגַד not used (Ch. and Arab. bound in a mass).

אֲגֻדָּה f.—I. a bunch or bundle (of hyssop).—II. a band or body of men; אֲגֻדָּתוֹ his church, people, Am. 9:6.—III. knots, bindings, Isa. 58:6.

אֱגוֹז m., a nut, Cant. 6:11.

אָגוּר (companion), p. n. of a woman.

אֲגֻרָה wages; see אגר.

אָגַל not used (Arab. gathered together, collected).

אֶגֶל m., אֶגְלֵי טַל drops of dew, Job 38:28.

אֶגְלַיִם (two fountains), p. n., a village of the Moabites, Isa. 15:8.

אָגַם not used (Arab. was hot).

אֲגַם Ch., was stagnant (of water); see עגם.

אֲגַם m. (pl. אֲגַמִּים, אֲגַמֵי).—I. a pool, pond, marsh.—II. flags, reeds.

אָגֵם m., sorrowful.

אַגְמוֹן m.—I. a reed, rush.—II. a rope of rushes.—III. a cauldron, kettle,

Job 41:12, this is however doubtful. See Lee in loco.

אַגָּן (Arab. a bason); אַגָּן m., אַגָּנָה f., (pl. אַגָּנוֹת), a bason or bowl.

אָגָף◌אַגַּף m., pl. אֲנַפִּים hosts, armies; see גף.

אָגַר (fut. יֶאֱגֹר), he laid up provision.

אֲגוֹרָה f., a small coin; ὀβολός, 1 Sa. 2:36; see גרה.

אִגְּרָא f. Ch. emph. state אִגַּרְתָּא; same as the following word.

אִגֶּרֶת f. (pl. אִגְּרוֹת), letter, edict.

אֲגַרְטָל a dish or bason, Ezr. 1·9.

אֶגְרוֹף the fist; see גרף.

אֵד mist, vapour; see אוד.

אָדַב Kal, not used, Hiph. he languished, was fatigued; לְהַאֲדִיב for לַאֲדִיב inf.).

אַדְבְּאֵל (the finger of God), p.n. of a man.

אֲדָדָה for אֶתְדָּדָה Hith. fut.; with suff. אֶדַּדֵּם; see דדה.

אָדָד (long-lived), p. n. of a man.

אַדּוֹ p. n. of a man.

אָדוֹן, אֲדֹנָי Lord; see אָדָן.

אֲדוֹרַיִם (two hills), p. n., a city of Judah.

אֲדוֹרָם p. n. of a man.

אֱדַיִן Ch. adv., then; בֵּאדַיִן at that very time; מִן אֱדַיִן from that time.

אֲדִיקֵם Hiph. fut. with suff. for אֲדִיקֵם; see דקק.

אַדִּיר great; see אדר.

אֲדַלְיָה (Jehovah's righteousness), p. n. of a man.

אָדַם was red, reddish brown; Pu. part. מְאָדָּם growing, turning red; Hiph be red; Hith. grow red.

דָּם m. (const. דַּם; with suff. דָּמוֹ, דָּם pl. דְּמֵי, דָּמִים).—I. blood; דָּם נָקִי

*innocent blood*; אִישׁ דָּמִים *a man of bloods*, i.e. *cruel.*—II. *slaughter, murder*; גֹּאֵל הַדָּם *avenger of blood*; אֵין לוֹ דָּם *blood is not on him*, i.e. *he has done no murder*; בֵּית הַדָּמִים *a bloody house.*—III. דַּם עֲנָבִים *blood of grapes, wine*; see דמה.

אָדָם m., *man* (in general); כָּל־אָדָם *all men*; אָדָם *a man*, as distinguished from a woman; בֶּן־אָדָם *mortal man.*

אָדָם p.n.—I. *Adam*, the first man.—II. *a city on Jordan*, Jos. 3:16.

אָדֹם, אָדֵם m., אֲדֻמָּה f., *red, reddish brown.*

אֱדֹם (*red*), p.n., one of the names of Esau.

אֱדֹם p.n., *the land of Edom*; אֲדֹמִי *an Edomite.*

אֹדֶם m., *a ruby*, or *carnelion.*

וְאָדֹם, אָדֹם Kal fut.; see דמם.

אֲדַמְדָּם m.; f. אֲדַמְדֶּמֶת; pl. אֲדַמְדַּמּוֹת *very red, glowing.*

אֲדָמָה f.—I. *ground, soil*; אֹהֵב א׳ *given to agriculture*, lit. *loving the ground.*—II. *fruit, produce.*—III. *region, country, the whole earth.*—IV. p.n. *a city of the tribe of Naphtali.*

אֲדָמָה p.n., one of the cities of the plain.

אֶדָּמֶה for אֶתְדַּמֶּה Hith. fut. 1. pers.; see דמה.

אֲדָמִים p.n. of a place.

אַדְמוֹנִי *red haired*, πυρράκης.

אֲדָמִי p.n., *a city of the tribe of Naphtali.*

אַדְמָתָא (*land*), p.n. of a man.

אֶדֶן m. (pl. אֲדָנִים)—I. *the base of a column.*—II *any foundation.*

אֲדוֹן, אֲדֹן p.n. of a man.

אָדוֹן m. (from אֱדֹן, pl. אֲדוֹנִים), *proprietor, master, lord.*

אֲדֹנָי m., *the Lord*, exclusively applied to God.

אֲדֹנִי בֶזֶק (*lord of Bezek*), p.n., a king of the Canaanites, Jud. 1:5.

אֲדֹנִי צֶדֶק (*righteous lord*), p.n., Canaanitish king of Jerusalem, Jos. 10:1.

אֲדֹנִיָּה (*the Lord is my Lord*), p.n. of a m.

אֲדֹנִיָּהוּ p.n. of a man.

אֲדֹנִיקָם (*the Lord confirmeth*), p.n. of a m.

אֲדֹנִירָם (*the Lord exalteth*), p. n. of a man, 1 Ki. 4:6.

אָדַר *does not occur in Kal*; Niph. part. נֶאְדָּר, with Jod parag. נֶאְדָּרִי, *it hath become glorious*; Hiph. (fut. יַאְדִּיר) *he made glorious.*

אַדִּיר *great, powerful, glorious, majestic.*

אַדִּיר m., *a prince*

אֶדֶר m.—I. *a cloak*; see אַדֶּרֶת—II. *amplitude, splendour.*

אַדֶּרֶת f. (with suff. אַדַּרְתּוֹ).—I. *a cloak*; שִׁנְעָר א׳ *a Babylonish garment*; שֵׂעָר א׳ *a hair cloak.*—II. *magnificence.*

אֲדַרְגָּזְרִין Ch. pl., *officers of the court at Babylon*, Dan. 3:2,3, the nature of their office unknown.

אָדָר p n.—I. *a place in the tribe of Judah.*—II. *of a man.*

אִדֶּר *threshing-floor*; see גרן.

אֲדָר m., *the twelfth month of the Hebrew year, corresponding with our February and March.*

אַדְרַזְדָּא Ch., *quickly, diligently.*

דַּרְכְּמוֹן, אֲדַרְכּוֹן, δαρεικὸς, *a Persian gold coin*

אֲדַרְמֶּלֶךְ (*the exalted Moloch*), p. n.—I. an idol of the Sepharvites, 2 Ki. 17:31.—II. a son of Sennacherib, Isa. 37:38, &c.

אֶדְרָע arm; see דרע.

אֶדְרָעִי (*planting*), p. n.—I. the city of Og, Deu. 1:4.—II. a city of the tribe of Naphtali.

אָדֹשׁ for הַדֹשׁ Niph. inf. abs.; see דרש.

אָדֹשׁ (inf. אָדוֹשׁ the same as דּוֹשׁ), *threshing*, beating out corn with the wheel, Isa. 28:28.

אָהַב, אָהֵב (inf. const. אֲהֹב, אַהֲבָה; imp. אֱהַב; fut. יֶאֱהַב; p. 1. אֹהַב and אָהַב), *loved, desired, delighted in*; part. אֹהֵב (pl. אֹהֲבִים, f. אֹהֶבֶת) *a friend*; Niph. part. pl. נֶאֱהָבִים *loved, amiable*; Pi. part. מְאַהֵב *lover*.

אֱהַב Kal fut. 1. pers.

אַהֲבָה f., *love, beloved*.

אֲהָבִים m. pl. (sing. אַהַב), *amours, loves, love-gifts*.

אֹהָבִים m. pl. (sing. אֹהַב), the same.

אֹהַד (*strength*), p. n., one of the sons of Simeon.

אֲהָהּ *ah! alas!* an exclamation of sorrow.

אַהֲוָא p. n.—I. of a country.—II. of a river.

אֵהוּד (*he who is powerful*), p. n. of a man.

אַהֲוֹדֶנּוּ(for אֹורֶנּוּ)Hiph. fut. 1. pers. with suff.; see ידה.

אֱהִי the same as אֵי *where?*

אֱהִי probably for אַיֵּה *where?* which see: Hos. 13:10.

אֱהִי fut. apoc. 1. pers.; see חיה.

אָהַל (fut. יֶאֱהַל, יַאֲהֵל), *pitched a tent, lived in tents*; Pi. fut. יַהֵל for יַאֲהֵל the same; יַאֲהִיל *shone*, Job 25:5; see הלל *to shine*.

אֹהֶל m. (with ה parag. אֹהֱלָה; with suff. אָהֳלֶךָ, אָהֳלֶךָ, Syr. אָהֳלִיךָ; pl. אֹהָלִים, Syr. אָהֳלִים).—I. *tabernacle, tent, habitation.*—II. p. n. of a man, 1 Chron. 3:20.

אָהֳלָה (*her tent*), p. n., allegorical name of Samaria, Eze. 23:4.

אָהֳלִיאָב (*tent of her father*), p. n. of a m.

אָהֳלִיבָה (*my tent with her*), p. n., allegorical name of Jerusalem, Eze. 23:4.

אָהֳלִיבָמָה (*my tent a high place*), p. n of a wife of Esau.

אֲהָלִים m. pl., אֲהָלוֹת f., ξυλαλόη, ἀγάλλοχον, *lign-aloes*, a perfumed wood.

אֶהֱמָיָה fut. with ה parag. for אֶהֱמֶה, see המה.

אַהֲרֹן p. n., *Aaron*, the brother of Moses; בְּנֵי א׳, בֵּית א׳ *Aaronites*.

אוֹ conj.—I. *or, either;* יָמִים אוֹ עָשׂוֹר *ten days at least.*—II. *for* כִּי; אוֹ כִּי *but if.*—III. אוֹ....אוֹ, *whether....or.*

אַו *desire*; see אוה.

אוּאָל p. n. of a man.

אוּב not used.

אוֹב m. (pl. אוֹבוֹת).—I. *a spirit of divination,* or *necromancy.*—II. νεκρόμαντις, *a necromancer*, one who calls up spirits from the abyss to foretel future events.—III. *th. art of necromancy.*

אוֹבוֹת I. *skins used as bottles for wine*, Job 32:19.—II. p. n. of a place in the wilderness.

אוֹבִיל (*he that causeth joy*), p. n. of a man, 1 Chron. 27:30.

אוּבַל ; see יבל.

אוּד not used (Arab. *bent, crooked*; also *wood*); etymology doubtful.

אֵד m., *smoke, mist*.

אוּד m., *smoking firebrand*.

אוֹדוֹת f. pl., *projects, means, cause*; עַל אוֹדוֹת (and אֶל for עַל) *because of*; עַל אֲדֹתִי *on my account*; עַל אֲדוֹתֶיךָ *because of thee*.

אוֹדְךָ, with נ epenth. אוֹדֶךָ Hiph. fut. 1. pers. with suff.; see ידה.

אֵיד m., *calamity, destruction.*

מְאֹד m.—I. *power, might, excess*; בְּכָל מְאֹדְךָ *with all thy might*; בִּמְאֹד מְאֹד *in great excess*; עַד מְאֹד and עַד לִמְאֹד *even to excess, exceedingly.*—II. adv. *exceedingly.*

אָוָה not used (Arab. *desired*); Pi. אִוָּה (fut. יְאַוֶּה), *desired, longed for*, const. with בְּ and לְ ; Hith. הִתְאַוָּה (fut. apoc. יִתְאָו), *desired, coveted, claimed*; וְהִתְאַוִּיתֶם לָכֶם *and claim for yourselves*, Nu. 34:10.

אַו or אָו m., *desire*, Pro. 31:4.

אַוָּה f.—I. *natural desire for food.*—II. *lust.*

מַאֲוַי m. (pl. מַאֲוַיִּים), *desires*, Ps. 140:9.

תַּאֲוָה f.—I. *desire, lust.*—II. *an object of desire*; see תאה.

אוֹחִילָה, Kri אוֹחִילָה Hiph. fut. 1. pers.; see חול.

אוֹי, אוֹיָה I. *alas!* expression of grief. —II. *ho!* expressing anger.

אוֹת com. (pl. אֹתוֹת).—I. *mark, memorial, warning.*—II. *sign, portent, miracle.*

אָת Ch. (pl. אָתִין), the same.

אִי m. (pl. אִיִּים).—I. *habitable land, continent, island.*—II. *shore, coast, countries on the coast*; אִיֵּי הַגּוֹיִם and אִיֵּי הַיָּם *isles of the Gentiles, isles of the West*, countries little known to the Hebrews.—III. אִיִּים *savage land animals*, Is. 13:22, hence:—IV. interj. *woe! horror!* see אוֹן.

אוֹיֵב *enemy*; see איב.

אוּנִי p. n. of a man.

אוּנָל p. n. of a city in Arabia; probably Senaar, the capital of Arabia Felix, Gen. 10:27.

אֱוִי p. n. of a king of Midian.

אוֹבִיל Hiph. fut. 1. pers.; see אכל.

אוֹבַל Kal fut. 1. pers.; see אכל.

אָוַל root not used; same as יאל.

אֱוִיל *a fool, an impious person.*

אֱוִיל־מְרֹדַךְ p. n., a king of Babylon, descendant of Nebuchadnezzar, 2 Ki. 25:27.

אֱוִילִי, same as אֱוִיל.

אִוֶּלֶת f. (with suff. אִוַּלְתִּי), *folly, sin.*

I. אוּל (Arab. *to dispose, govern aright*); root not used.

אוּל m.—I. *a prince.*—II. *administration.*—III. *body*, Ps. 73:4.

אוּלַי adv.—I. *perhaps, unless.*—II. p. n. of a river, Dan. 8:2.

אֻלָם, אֻלָּם (pl. אֻלַמִּים).—I. m., *an entrance hall, vestibule.*—II. pa. *but, nevertheless.*—III. p. n. of a man.

II. אוּל (Arab. *grew thick*, of fluids); root not used.

אַיִל m. (const. אֵיל ; pl. אֵילִים).—I. *a ram.*—II. *lintel, arch over a door or window.*

אֵיל m., strength, force.

אֱיָלוּת f., the same.

אַיָּל com., an antelope, gazelle.

אַיָּלָה f. (pl. אַיָּלוֹת; const. אַיְלוֹת), female antelope.

אַיֶּלֶת f., the same; אַיֶּלֶת הַשַּׁחַר the name of the tune to which the Psalm is to be sung, Ps. 22.

אַיִל m. (pl. אֵלִים, אֵילִים).—I. hero, mighty man.—II. the pine or terebinth (a tall thick tree).

אֵילִים p.n. of one of the stations of the Israelites in the wilderness, Ex.c.15.

אֵל (with suff. אֵלִי; pl. אֵלִים, אֵלִם).—I. hero, man of might.—II. power; יֶשׁ לְאֵל יָדִי it is in the power of my hand, i.e. I am able.—III. God (the true God); בְּנֵי אֵלִים the sons of God, i.e. the angels.—IV. an epithet denoting excellence; אַרְזֵי אֵל cedars of God, i.e. lofty, well grown.—V. an idol, false god.

אֵלָה f., terebinth; see אֵיל, אַלָּה, &c.

אֵלוֹן m.—I. oak, lofty tree; compare preceding word.—II. p.n. of a man.—III. of a city.

אֵילָם, אֵלָם m., a lintel; see אוּלָם I.

אִילָן m. Ch., a tree.

וָאֵלֵךְ, אוֹלִיךְ Hiph. fut. 1. pers.; see הָלַךְ, יָלַךְ.

אוֹמָר p.n. of a man.

אָוֶן or אָיֶן root not used; (Arab. time, a fit time).

אָוֶן m. (with suff. אוֹנִי, אוֹנֶךָ, אוֹנָם; pl. אוֹנִים).—I. vanity, falseness, that which is nothing, hence:—II. an idol; בֵּית אָוֶן house of idols; בִּקְעַת אָוֶן valley of idols (a valley near Damascus, now Un, Am. 1:5).—III. sin, wickedness.—IV. sorrow,

distress; בֶּן־אוֹנִי the son of my sorrow; לֶחֶם אוֹנִים bread of affliction; see אָנַן.

אוֹן m. (v th suff. like אָוֶן).—I. power.—II. manhood; רֵאשִׁית הָאוֹן first-born.—III. wealth, riches.

אַיִן const. אֵין I. non-existence; אֵין בַּבּוֹר he was not in the pit. אֵין יֹצֵא וְאֵין בָּא there was neither going out nor coming in; אֵין לִי I have not, lit. there is nothing to me; אֵין לָבוֹא "none might enter," Eng. Ver., Est. 4:2; אֵין דָּבָר, מְאוּמָה nothing; אֵין כֹּל absolutely nothing; אֵינֶנּוּ it is not.—II. with personal pronoun אֵינֶנִּי, אֵינֶךָ, אֵינֵךְ, אֵינֶנּוּ, אֵינָם, אֵינֶכֶם, אֵינָנָּה and אֵינֵימוֹ I am, was, not, shall not be, thou art not, &c.—III. with prepositions, בְּאַיִן in not being, before, without, כְּאַיִן like not being, nearly, Ps.73:2; לְאַיִן to him who has not, Is. 40:29; מֵאַיִן (poetic only), not, absolute negation; מֵאֵין יוֹשֵׁב no inhabitant, Jer. 33:10.

אִין same as אֵין, 1 Sa. 21:9.

אִי (perhaps from אַיִן), not, Job c. 22:

אִי־כָבוֹד (ignoble), p. n. of a man.

תְּאֵנָה f. (pl.תְּאֵנִים, fig (tree and fruit); יָשַׁב תַּחַת תְּאֵנָתוֹ he sat under his fig-tree, i.e. he lived peacefully and prosperously.

תַּאֲנִים m. pl., vexation, vanity, falsehood, Ezé. 24:12.

אוֹן I. (strength), p. n. of a man.—II. אוֹן, אֹן Heliopolis, a city of Lower Egypt.

אוֹנוֹ (strong), p. n. of a city in the tribe of Benjamin.

אוֹנָם (the same), p. n. of a man.

אוֹן (*vigorous*), p.n., one of the sons of Judah.

אוּפָן p. n., a country where gold was found (perhaps the same as the following word).

אוֹפִיר, אוֹפָר p. n., a country abounding in gold, gems, and perfumed wood.

אוֹפָן a wheel; see אפן.

אוּץ *pressed, was urgent upon*; const. with בְּ, לְ, מְ; Hiph. *pressed, hastened*; const. with בְּ, לְ.

אוֹצָר *treasure*; see אצר.

אוֹצָרָה Hiph. fut. 1. pers. with ה parag.; see רצא.

אוֹר I. *became light, shone, enlightened*.—II. *prospered*; imperat. אוֹרִי f. *shine thou*, Isa. 60:1. Niph. נָאוֹר (fut. יֵאוֹר), *become bright*; part. נָאוֹר *illustrious*. Hiph. הֵאִיר (fut. apoc. יָאֵר).—I. *enlighten, illuminate, kindle*.—II. ה' פְּנֵי עֵינֵי פ' *cheer up, exhilarate*, lit. *enlighten the eyes*, or *face*; ה' פָּנָיו (const. with עַל, לְ, בְּ, אֶת, אֶל).—III. *instruct, inform* (illuminate the mind), Ps. 119:130.

אוֹר m. (f. Job 36:32).—I. *light, brightness, lightning, luminary*; אוֹר חַיִּים *the light of life*; א' פָּנִים *light of the face*, i. e. *cheerfulness, good will*; pl. אוֹרִים *stars*, i. e. *luminaries*, Ps. 136:7.—II. metaph. *prosperity*.—III. *knowledge*.

אוּר I. *fire, the light of fire*.—II. p.n. of a man.—III. (אוּרִים וְתֻמִּים) LXX. δήλωσις καὶ ἀλήθεια, "Urim and Thummim," Eng. Ver., a part of the high-priest's breast-plate; meaning uncertain.—IV. אוּרִים

(*lights*), p. n. of a country.—V. אוּר כַּשְׂדִּים p.n., *Ur of the Chaldeans*, a place in Mesopotamia.

אוֹרָה f. (pl. אוֹרוֹת).—I. *light*, Ps. 139:12.—II. *prosperity, joy*, Est. 8:16.—III. טַל אוֹרוֹת *light reflecting dew*, Isa. 26:19; אוֹרוֹת *herbs*, 2 Kings 4:39.

אוֹרוּ imp. pl.; see ארר.

מָאוֹר m.—I. *light*; מְאוֹרוֹת *stars; luminaries*.—II. *candlestick*; מְנוֹרַת הַמָּאוֹר *the candlestick in the tabernacle*, lit. *place of light*.

מְאֻרָה f., *den, hole*, of a serpent, Isa. 11:8.

אֻרְוֹת *stables*; see ארה.

אוּרִי (*fiery*), p. n. of a man.

אוּרִיאֵל (*fire of God*), p. n. of a man.

אוּרִיָּה (the same), p. n.—I. the husband of Bathsheba.—II. a priest in the reign of Ahaz.

אוֹת *sign*; see אוה.

אוֹת or אָנָת; Niph. (fut. pl. p.1. נֵאוֹת p.3. יֵאוֹתוּ), *consenting to, agreeing*.

אוֹתִיּוֹת part. f. pl.; see אתה.

אָז adv., *then, at that time* (used with either tense); (מְן־אָז) מֵאָז.—I. *from that time, of old, before*.—II. *whence*; מֵאָז אַפֶּךָ *whence thine anger* (was kindled); מֵאָז בָּאתִי *whence I came*; with infin. מֵ' דַּבְּרָךְ *whereof thou hast spoken*.

אֲזַי *then*, Ps. 124:3,4,5.

אָזָא or אָזָה Ch., *he kindled*.

אָזַב, root not used; Arab. the same meaning.

אֵזוֹב m., *hyssop*.

אוֹזְבִּי p. n. of a man.

אֲזַד Ch., *went forth, departed*

אֵזוֹר *belt*; see אזר.

אָזִין for אַאֲזִין Hiph. fut. 1. pers.; see אזן.

אַזְכָּרָה *memorial*; see זכר.

אָזַל *he went away, departed*; מָאֻזָּל from אוּזָל *Uzal* (see the word), Ez. 27:19, taken by mistake for Pu. part. of this verb. See Rosenmüller on the passage.

Ch., the same.

אֵזֶל m., *departure*, 1 Sa. 20:19, {some call it a p. n.).

אֲזַל Ch. imp. for אָזַל, Syr. for אֵזֶל; see אזל.

אָזַן, Pi. אִזֵּן *attended to* and *investigated*, Ecc. 12:9. Hiph. הֶאֱזִין *heard, attended*; const. with לְ, אֶל, עַל, עַד: of God, *he hearkened, heard prayer*; of man, *he obeyed*.

מֹאזְנַיִם dual, *the balance*, lit. having two dishes, bilanx.

מֹאזְנַיִן Ch. the same.

אֹזֶן f. (with suff. אָזְנִי; dual אָזְנַיִם), *the ear*; בְּאָזְנֵי פ׳ *in the ears* (that is, the hearing), *of any one*.

אַזְנוֹת־תָּבוֹר p. n. of a city in the tribe of Naphtali.

אָזְנִי (*he who hearkens*), p. n. of a man, Nu. 26:16.

אֲזַנְיָה (*whom the Lord hears*), p. n. of a man.

אֶזֶן שֶׁאֱרָה p. n. of a place.

אֵזֶן m. (pl. אֲזֵנִים), "*weapons*," Deu. 23: 14, Eng. Ver.; meaning uncertain.

אֲזִקִּים *chains*; see זקק.

אָזַר (imp. אֱזֹר; fut. יֶאְזֹר; with suff. יַאְזְרֵנִי), *bound, girt, clothed himself*; trop. אָזְרוּ חַיִל *they clothed themselves with strength*; const. with

בְּ. Niph. part. נֶאְזָר *girded*: const. with בְּ. Pi. sense as Kal. Hith. *became bound, armed himself*.

אֵזוֹר m.—I. *a belt, girdle.*—II. *fetters*.

אֶזְרוֹעַ *arm*, same as זְרוֹעַ; see זרע.

אֶזְרָחִי, אֶזְרָח *native*; see זרח.

אָח m., (const. אֲחִי; with suff. אָחִי, אֲחִיכֶם אָחִיךָ; pl. אַחִים, אַחֵינוּ; with suff. אֶחָיו, אָחִיו, אַחֵינוּ; אֲחִיכֶם) —I. *a brother.*—II. *a relative.*—III. *a fellow countryman.* —IV. *a friend.*—V. any person or thing like another.—VI. a term of affection; אִישׁ מֵעַל אָחִיו *one from the other*; אִישׁ אֶל אָחִיו *one from the other*.

אָח Ch., *a brother*.

אַחֲוָה f., *fraternity*.

אָחוֹת f. (with suff. אֲחוֹתִי; pl. אֲחָיוֹת, with suff. אַחְיוֹתַי, אַחְיוֹתֵיכֶם).—I. *sister.*—II. used as אָח V., which see; אִשָּׁה אֶל אֲחוֹתָהּ *one from the other* (of persons or things fem.).

אָח interj., *alas!* exclamation of grief.

אָחַח not used; οἰμώζειν, *to howl*; whence is derived:—

אֹחִים m. pl., *howlings*, or *howling animals* (it is uncertain which), Isa. 13:21.

אָח f., *a pot* filled with hot coals to warm rooms in winter, Jer. 36: 22; 23.

אַחְאָב (*brother of the father*), p. n., *Ahab* king of Israel.

אָחָב p. n. of the same king

אַחְבָּן p. n. of a man.

אֶחָד const. אַחַד m., אַחַת with the pause, אֶחָת f.—I *one.*—II. *the first* (used with days of the month); בְּאֶחָד לַחֹדֶשׁ on the first day of the month; שְׁנַת אַחַת the first year.—III. alone, a single one; לֹא אֵין, אֶחָד not a single one, no one.—IV. a certain one (τις); it has the power of the ind. article a, an; הָעָם 'אֶ one of the people, a person ; 'נָבִיא א, προφήτης τις, a certain prophet.—V. the same one, the same ; אַחַת (פַּעַם) בְּאַחַת, at the same time, together; כְּאֶחָד כְּאִישׁ אֶחָד as one man, together; pl. אֲחָדִים the same, united into one, a few.

אֶחָד Hith., take hold of, unite thyself; see יָחַד.

חַד Ch., one, first, any one, same as אֶחָד.

אָחוּ m., the bulrush, reed, an Egyptian word ; Copt. άχι.

אֶחוּד (union), p. n. of a man.

אַחְוָה and אָחוֹת ; see אָח.

אַחְוָה ; see חוה.

אֲחֹתָי, אֲחִיָּה p. n. of a man ; patr. אֲחֹחִי.

אַחֻוֶּךָ, with נ epenth. אֲחַוְּךָ Pi. fut. 1. pers. with suff.; see חוה.

אֲחֻמַי p. n. of a man.

אָחוֹר after ; see אַחַר.

אָחַז (inf. c. אֱחֹז ; with pref. בֶּאֱחֹז, imper. אֱחֹז; fut. יֹאחֵז and יֶאֱחֹז).—I. seized (fear, terror); const. with בְּ.—II. caught (i.e. in hunting). —III. took hold of, seized; const. with בְּ of the part seized.—IV. held, kept.—V. joined, united.—VI. locked up, Neh. 7:3.—VII. covered, overlaid, veneered, 1 Ki. 6:10.—VIII. drew by lot. Niph.—I. was

caught, Ecc. 9:12.—II. was held, Gen. 22:13. Pi. מְאַחֵז shut up (same as Kal VI.), Job 26·9. Hoph. מָאֳחָז joined, united (same as Kal V.), 2 Chron. 9:18.

אָחָז p.n.—I. Ahaz, king of Judah.— II. of a man.

אֶחֱזֶה, אַחַז fut. apoc. in pause for אֶחֱזֶה; see חזה.

אֲחֻזָּה f., possession, tenure.

אַחְזַי p. n. of a man.

אֲחַזְיָהוּ and אֲחַזְיָה p.n.—I. of the son of Ahab king of Israel.—II. of the son of Joram king of Judah.

אַחְזָם p. n. of a man.

אֲחֻזַּת p. n. of a man.

אֲחַטֶּנָּה Pi. fut. 1. pers. with suff. for אֲהַטְאֶנָּה; see חטא.

אֲחִי p. n. of a man.

אֲחִידָה ; see חוד.

אֲחִיָּה (friend of God), p. n. of a man.

אֲחִיהוּד (friend of the Jews), p.n. of a m.

אֲחִיו p. n. of a man.

אֲחָיוֹת sisters; see אָחוֹת, in אָח.

אֲחִיחֻד and אֲחִיחֻר p. n. of a man.

אֲחִיטוּב (loving good), p. n. of a man.

אֲחִילוּד (brother's son), p. n. of a man.

אֲחִימוֹת (brother of death), p. n. of a m.

אֲחִימֶלֶךְ (brother of a king), p.n. of a m.

אֲחִימָן (brother of gifts), p. n. of a man.

אֲחִימַעַץ (brother of anger), p. n. of a m.

אָחְיָן (brotherly) p. n. of a man.

אֲחִינָדָב (brother of good will), p. n. of a man.

אֲחִינֹעַם (brother of delight), p.n. of a w.

אֲחִיסָמָךְ (brother of defence), p.n. of a m.

אֲחִיעֶזֶר (brother of help), p. n. of a man.

אֲחִיקָם (brother of enmity), p. n. of a m.

אֲחִירָם (exalted brother), p. n. of a m.

אֲחִירַע (evil brother), p. n. of a man.

אֲחִישַׁחַר (*brother of the morning*), p. n. of a man.

אֲחִישָׁר (*brother of song*), p.n. of a man.

אֲחִיתֹפֶל (*foolish brother*), p.n. of a m.

אָחֵל Hiph. fut. 1. pers., אָחֵל with dag. forte imp.; see חלל.

אַחְלָב (*fecundity*) p.n. of a place in the tribe of Asher.

אַחְלַי (*would that !*) p.n.—I. of a man.—II. of a woman.

אַחְלַי, אַחֲלַי *would that ! I wish !* see חלה.

אַחְלָמָה *amethyst*; see חלם.

אֲחַסְבַּי p. n. of a man.

אַחְמְתָא p.n., *Ecbatana*, a city of Media, Ezr. 6:2.

אָחַר root not used; fut. 1. pers. pl. אֶחַר, Gen. 32:5. Pi. אִחַר (fut. יְאַחֵר), *delayed, waited, deferred* (Arab. the same); see יָחַר.

אָחוֹר m. (pl. אֲחֹרִים).—I. *the but-end* of a spear, 2 Sa. 2:23.—II. *the west, westward.* Adv. *behind, after*; מֵאָחוֹר, לְאָחוֹר, בְּאָחוֹר, *behind*; לְאָחוֹר *hereafter*, Isa. 41:23.

אַחֵר m., אַחֶרֶת f. (pl. אֲחֵרִים, אֲחֵרוֹת).—I. *another*; אֱלֹהִים אֲ' *other gods, idols.*—II. p. n. of a man.

אַחַר *the hinder part.* Adv. of time and place, *behind, afterwards.* Prep. *behind, after*; הָלַךְ אַ' *follow*; אַ' הַדְּבָרִים הָאֵלֶּה *after these things, afterwards*; אַ' דִּבֶּר פ' *after he had spoken*; אַחֲרֵי cōnst. (with suff. אַחֲרַי, אַחֲרָיו, אַחֲרֶיךָ), *behind, after*; אַחֲרֵי כֵן אֲ' אֲשֶׁר *after, afterwards*; with prefixes מֵאַחֲרֵי *after something past, after that*; מֵאַחֲרֶיהָ *afterwards* מֵאַ' כֵן *behind him*; אֶל אַחֲרֵי *after*; עַל אַ' *behind*.

אַחֲרֵי Pi. pret. pl. for אֵחֲרוּ; see אָחַר.

אַחֲרוֹן m., אַחֲרוֹנָה f —I. *the hinder part, the back part.*—II. *the latter day, or time.*—III. *the west*; הַיָּם הָא' *the Mediterranean sea.*—IV. *posterity*; דּוֹר אַ' *the generation to come*; אַחֲרֹנִים *successors*; בָּאַחֲרוֹנָה, לָאַחֲרוֹנָה *afterwards.*

אָחֳרִי Ch. adj. f., *another.*

עַד־אָחֳרֵין Ch., *at last, at length.*

אַחֲרִית f.—I. *the last, the latter time*; אַ' הַיָּמִים *the latter days.*—II. *the end*; אַ' הַשָּׁנָה *end of the year.*—III. *posterity.*

אָחֳרָן Ch. m., *another.*

אֲחֹרַנִּית adv., *backwards.*

אַחְרַח (*after his brother ?*) p.n. of a man.

אַחַרְחֵל (*behind a wall*), p.n. of a man.

אֲחַשְׁדַּרְפְּנִים m. pl., *chief satraps, or doorkeepers,* officers of the Persian court. ־יִן Ch., the same.

אֲחַשְׁוֵרוֹשׁ a title common to all the kings of Persia. It is spelt *Chosroes* by the later Greek and Latin historians.

אֲחַשְׁרַשׁ the same.

אֲחַשְׁתָּרִי p.n. of a man; see next word.

אֲחַשְׁתְּרָנִים m. pl., *mules.*

אַחַת f., *one*; see אֶחָד.

אֲחַת Ch. Aph. imp.; see נחת.

אַחְתָּה Niph. fut. 1. pers. with ה parag.; see חתת.

אַט Hiph. fut. apoc. 1. pers. for אַטֶּה; see נטה.

אָטָד m., *black thorn*; rhamnus paliurus (Linn.).

אָטָד p.n., a place beyond Jordan, where was a threshing-floor; afterwards Abel-mizraim, Gen. 50:10, 11.

אֵטוּן m., linen (of Egypt) ὀθόνιον, probably an Egyptian word, Pro. 7:16.

אָטַם not used; (Arab. uttered a low sound).

אֵט m. (pl. אִטִּים).—I. necromancers, enchanters.—II. gentle, soft. Adv. לְאַט, לָאַט, אַט softly, slowly; לְאִטִּי at my convenience.

אָטַם shut up, closed. Hiph. the same; יַאֲטֵם אָזְן he closes (his) ear.

אָטַר with עַל shut; fut. יֵאָטַר, Ps. 69:16.

אִטֵּר maimed; אִ׳ יַד יְמִינוֹ lit. having his right hand bound (left-handed).

אֵטֶר (he that halteth), p. n. of a man.

אִי ; see אֱוָה and אַיִן.

אַי where? with suff. אַיֶּכָּה where art thou? אַיּוֹ where is he? אַיָּם where are they? also with pronouns and adverbs, אֵי זֶה who? what? where? אֵי מִזֶּה whence? אֵי לָזֹאת wherefore? why? with ה demonst. אַיֵּה where?

אֵיכָה where? how?

אֵיךְ (apoc.) how?

אֵיכֹה (Kri אֵיכוֹ) where? 2 K. 6:13.

אֵיכָכָה how?

אַיִן always in comp.; מֵאַיִן whence? (for another meaning see אַיִן).

אֵיפֹה where? how?

אָן (contract. from אַיִן), where? whither? מֵאָן whence? עַד־אָן until; with the paragogic ה, אָנָה whither? whereunto? where? עַד־אָנָה how long? אָנָה וָאָנָה hither and thither, 1 K. 2:36, 42.

אָיַב hated, was an enemy, Ex. 23:22. אֹיֵב m., enemy, אֹיֶבֶת f., the same. אֵיבָה f. enmity.

אֵיד calamity; see אוּד.
אַיֵּה where? see אַי.

אַיָּה f.—I. name of a bird of prey; "vulture, kite," Eng. Ver.; LXX. ἰκτίν; Vulg. vultur.—II. p. n. of a man.

אִיּוֹב (miserable), p.n., Job, the patriarch.

אִיזֶבֶל p. n., Jezebel, the wife of Ahab.

אַיֵּכָה, אֵיךְ ; see אַי.

אִי־כָבוֹד (where is the glory? i.e. without glory); p. n. of a man.

אַיֶּכָּה where art thou? אַי with suff. and כ epenth.

אַיִל, אֵיל, אֵיל, &c.; see אוּל.

אֵילוֹן (oak), p. n.—I. of a city.—II. of a man.

אַיָּלוֹן (place of hinds), p. n. of a city.

אֵילְכָה for אֵלְכָה Kal fut. 1. pers. with ה parag.; see יָלַךְ, הָלַךְ.

אֵילִם (grove of oaks), p. n. of a place.

אֵילַת (tree), אֵילוֹת (trees), p.n., Elath, a city on the eastern gulf of the Red Sea, now Akabah.

אַיֶּלֶת a gazelle; see אוּל.

אָיַם root not used, was terrible; Ch Pa. frightened.

אָיֹם, אֵימָה m., terrible, Hab. 1:7.

אֵימָה f. (pl. אֵימוֹת ; with ה parag אֵימָתָה) terror; pl. אֵימִים, אֵמִים.—I. terrible things.—II. idols, Jer. 50:38.—III. p. n. of one of the tribes of the Moabites.

אַיִן ; see אַיִן and אַי.
אֵינֵימוֹ they are not; see אַיִן with suff.
אֱיָעֵר (helpless), p.n. of a man.

אֵיפָה, אֵפָה f., Ephah, a corn measure, capacity unknown; אֵיפָה וְאֵיפָה divers measures; אֵי שְׁלֵמָה just measure.

אֵיפֹה ; see אֵי.

אֵיפֹוא same as אֵפֹוא.

אִישׁ m. (pl. אֲנָשִׁים ,אַנְשֵׁי; see אֱנוֹשׁ; three times אִישִׁים).—I. *a man*, as distinguished from a woman.—II. *a husband.*—III. *a male.*—IV. used collectively for the inhabitants of a country; אִישׁ יִשְׂרָאֵל *the Israelites.*—V. used to denote the qualifications of men; אִ׳ מִלְחָמָה *a warrior*; אִ׳ אֱמֶת *a faithful man*; אִ׳ שָׂדֶה *a husbandman.*—VI. *any one*; אִישׁ...אִישׁ *one...another.*—VII. *every man*; opposed to אָח, רֵעַ עָמִית; וַיֵּלְכוּ אִישׁ לִמְקֹמוֹ *they went every one to his place*; כָּל־אִישׁ *every one.*—VIII. *every thing*, Ex. 25:20.—IX. impers., כֹּה אָמַר הָאִישׁ *thus it was said.*

אִישׁ, Hith. הִתְאֹשֵׁשׁ (ἀνδρίζεσθαι, 1 Cor. 16:13); pl. הִתְאֹשָׁשׁוּ *become ye men*, i. e. be courageous, Isa. 46:8.

אִישׁוֹן m., lit. *little man*, i. e. the small image of one's self seen in the eye of another.—I. אִ׳ בַּת עַיִן עֵין *pupil of the eye*; hence:—II. אִ׳ חֹשֶׁךְ לַיְלָה lit. *pupil*, i. e. *middle, of the night, midnight*,

אִשָּׁה or אֵשֶׁת f. (with suff. אִשְׁתִּי, אִשְׁתֵּךְ and אִשְׁתְּךָ), I.—*woman.*—II. *wife.*—III. *concubine.*—IV. opposed to אָחוֹת and רֵעוּת, like אִישׁ.—V. *any one, every one.*—VI. applied to men by way of reproach.

אִישׁ־בֹּשֶׁת p. n. of a son of Saul.

אִישְׁהוֹד (*man of vigour*), p.n. of a man.

אִישַׁי (*manly*), p. n. of a man.

אִיתַי Ch., same as יֵשׁ *he is*; אִיתָיִךְ

אִיתוֹהִי *he is*; אִיתָנָא *thou art*; אִיתֵיכוֹן *ye are*; אִיתֵינָא *we are*.

אִיתַי p. n. of a man.

אִיתִיאֵל (*God with me*), p. n. of a man.

אִיתַם for אַתֶּם Kal fut. 1. pers.; see תמם.

אִיתָמָר (*place of palm trees*), p. n. of one of the sons of Aaron.

אֵיתָן p. n. of a man; see יתן.

אַךְ adv., *only, alone, except*; אַךְ שָׂמֵחַ *only* (i. e. nothing else but) *rejoicing*, Deu. 16:15; אַךְ חֹשֶׁךְ *only* (nothing but) *darkness*, Ps. 139:11; אַךְ טָרֹף טֹרָף *he is only torn in pieces*, i. e. nothing else has happened to him, Gen. 44:28.

אַכַּד (*fortress*), p. n. of a city built by Nimrod, Gen. 10:10.

אָכוֹת Kal fut. 1. pers., see כתת.

אַכְזִיב p. n.—I. of a city in the tribe of Asher, Greek ἐκδιππα, now *Zib.*—II. of a city in the tribe of Judah.

אַכְזָר ,אַכְזְרִיּוּת see כזר.

אָכִישׁ (*Ethiopian*), p. n. of a king of the Philistines.

אָכַל (inf. אָכוֹל; const. אֲכֹל; with pref. לֶאֱכֹל; with suff. אָכְלְךָ, אָכְלוֹ; imper. אֱכֹל; with ה parag. אָכְלָה; fut. יֹאכַל and יֹאכֶל).—I. *ate.*—II. *devoured*, spoken of men or things; joined to the accusative with בְּ, מִן: אָכַל לֶחֶם *feasted*; בְּלֶחֶם and אָכַל לֶחֶם פּ׳ אִ׳ לֶחֶם עַל שֻׁלְחַן פּ׳ *to be the guest inmate, of any one*; אָכַל לִפְנֵי יְהֹוָה *ate that which was offered in sacrifice*; אָכַל בִּשַׂר פּ׳ *ate his flesh*, i. e. injured him, Ps. 27:2; Niph נֶאֱכַל, part. f. נֶאֱכֶלֶת *is, may be*, *eaten.* **Pu.** אֻכַּל *devoured, consumed.* **Hiph.** הֶאֱכִיל (fut. יַאֲכִיל; inf. הַאֲכִיל) *gave, made, caused, to eat, devour.*

אֲכַל **Ch.,** *the same.*

אֹכֶל m., *food;* with suff. אָכְלוֹ.

אָכְלָה f., *meat, food,* Gen. 1:29, 30.

אֲכִילָה f., *meat, feast,* 1 K. 19:8.

מַאֲכָל m., *food, that which may be eaten;* עֵץ מ׳ מַאֲכָל *fruit tree;* צֹאן מ׳ *cattle to be slaughtered for the table.*

מַאֲכֹלֶת מַאֲכֹלֶת f., *food.*

מַאֲכֶלֶת f., *slaughtering knife,* lit. *devourer;* pl. מַאֲכָלוֹת.

אֻכָל (*eaten, consumed*), p. n. of a man.

אֲכַל, וְאֵכַל Pi. fut. apoc. 1. pers.; see כלה.

אֲכַלֶּה Ex. 33:3, Pi. fut. 1. pers. with suff. for אֲכַלְךָ; see כלה.

אָכֵן *truly;* see כּוּן.

אַכֶּנּוּ Hiph. fut. 1. pers. with suff.; see נכה.

אָכַף *compel, bow down to,* Pro. 16:26.

אֶכֶף m. (with suff. אַכְפִּי), *palm of the hand,* Job 33:7.

אֶכֹּף for אֶכֹּף Niph. fut. 1. pers.; see כפף.

אָכַר *root not used;* (Arab. *digged*).

אִכָּר m., *ploughman, husbandman.*

אַכְשָׁף (*city of magicians*), p. n. of a city in the tribe of Asher.

אַל *not,* &c.; see אלל.

אֵל *God;* see אול.

אֶל, אֵל prep. (with suff. אֵלֶיךָ, אֵלַי, אֵלֵינוּ, אֲלֵיכֶם, אֵלֶיהָ, אֵלָיו, אֲלֵיהֶם, אֲלֵיהֶן; pl. poet. אֵלֵימוֹ, poet. אֱלֵי).—I. *sign of the dative,* like לְ.—II. *to, towards.*—III. *unto,*

*at.*—IV. *of, concerning.*—V. *in, into* —VI. *among.*—VII. *by, through.*— VIII. *for, on account of;* the original meaning is *to, towards,* variously modified by the context; אֶל־פִּי יְהֹוָה *according to the command* (*mouth*) *of God;* אֶל־אַמָּה *a cubit,* i. e. *according to the measure of a cubit,* Gen. 6:16; וַיֹּאמֶר אֶל־שָׂרָה *he said concerning* (*relative to*) *Sarah;* וַיֵּלֶךְ אֶל־נַפְשׁוֹ *he went, having regard to his life,* i. e. *to save his life;* אֶל־בְּאֵר הַמַּיִם *near* (i. e. *towards*) *the well;* יֵשֶׁב אֶל־הַשֻּׁלְחָן *he sat at* (i. e. *to*) *the table.* —IX. used with other particles; אֶל־מֵחוּץ לְ *behind me;* אֶל־אַחֲרֵי *without;* אֶל־תַּחַת *a pleonasm, same as* תַּחַת.

אֵל, with article הָאֵל, אֵלֶּה pron., *these, those;* אֵלֶּה־וְאֵלֶּה οἱ μὲν— oἱ δέ, *these—those;* **Ch.,** *the same.*

אֵלָא (*terebinth*), p.n. of a man; see אלה.

אֶלְגָּבִישׁ m., *hail;* see גבש.

אַלְגֻּמִּים name of a tree; see אלמנים.

אֶלְדָּד (*beloved of God*), p. n. of a man.

אֶלְדָּעָה (*called of God*), p.n. of a man.

אָלָה I. *lay under a curse, imprecate.* —II. *howl,* see אלל. **Hiph.** *swore, execrated, laid under a curse;* fut. apoc. וַיֹּאֶל.

אָלָה f.—I. *oath, imprecation;* בֹּא בְאָלָה *come into the terms of the oath, agree by oath,* Neh. 10:30; הֵבִיא בְאָלָה *make one swear,* Eze.17:13; נָשָׂא אָלָה בְּ *lay an oath upon any one.*—II. *curse, cursing;* הָיָה לְאָלָה *he was for a curse;* נָתַן לְאָלָה *he gave over unto cursing*

תַּאֲלָה f., *cursing.*

אֱלָהּ m. Ch., *God.*

אֱלוֹהַּ m., *God* (pl. אֱלֹהִים).—I. *God,* the true God.—II. *false gods,* idols; followed by the verb in the sing., very rarely in the pl.; אִישׁ אֱ' *a man of God;* בְּנֵי אֱ' *sons of God,* i. e. they that loved and served God; with pref. בֵּאלֹהִים, כֵּאלֹהִים; const. אֱלֹהֵי לֵאלֹהִים.

אַלָּה *gazelle;* see אַיָּל.

אֵלָה *terebinth;* see אַלָּל.

אֲלֻוּ Ch., *behold!* same as אֲרֻו.

אִלּוּ for אִם־לוּ, *otherwise, unless,* Ecc. 6:6, Est. 7:4.

אֱלוּל m.—I. *vanity;* same as אֱלִיל, see אַלָּל.—II. *Elul,* the sixth month of the Hebrew year, answering nearly to our September, Neh. 6:15.

אַלּוֹן *oak;* see אַיָּל אַלָּל the same; in אַלָּל.

אַלּוּף *friend;* see אַלָּה.

אֱלוּשׁ (*lion's den*), p. n., one of the encampments of the Israelites.

אֶלְזָבָד (Θεοδῶρος), p. n. of a man.

אָלַח Niph. נֶאֱלַח *was corrupt, base.*

אֶלְחָנָן (*gift of God*), p. n. of a man.

אֱלִיאָב (*who has God for his father*), p. n. of a man.

אֱלִיאֵל (*strong in God*), p. n. of a man.

אֱלִיאָתָה or אֱלִיָּתָה (*to whom God comes*), p. n. of a man.

אֶלְדָּד (*beloved of God*), p. n. of a prince of the Benjamites.

אֶלְדָּע (*known of God*), p. n. of a man.

אַלְיָה f. (Arab. the same), the fat tail of the sheep in the East.

אֵלִיָּה, אֵלִיָּהוּ (*the Lord he* IS *God*), p. n., Elijah ('Hλίας), the prophet.

אֵלִיהוּא, אֵלִיהוּ (the same), p. n. of one of Job's friends.

אֶלְיְהֹעֵינַי, אֶלְיוֹעֵינַי (*mine eyes* ARE *unto the Lord*), p. n. of a man.

אֱלִיַּחְבָּא (*hidden of God*), p. n. of one of David's generals.

אֶלְיַחְרֻף (*God* IS *his avenger*), p. n. of a man.

אֱלִיל *vanity;* see אַלָּל.

אֱלִימֶלֶךְ (*God* IS *king*), p. n. of a man.

אֵלֶּן, אִלֵּין pron. pl. Ch., *these, those*

אֶלְיָסָף (*increased of God*), p. n. of a prince of the Gadites.

אֶלְיָעֶזֶר (*holpen of God*), p. n. of a man.

אֶלְיָעֵינַי (*God is mine eye,* i. e. directs me), p. n. of a man.

אֶלְיָעָם (*people of God*), p. n. of a man.

אֱלִיפַז (*God is precious*), p. n.—I. of a son of Esau.—II. of one of Job's friends.

אֱלִיפָל (*my God is strong*), p. n. of a man.

אֱלִיפְלֵהוּ (*whom God makes famous*), p. n. of a man.

אֱלִיפֶלֶט (*God is his help*), p. n. of a m.

אֱלִיצוּר (*God* IS *his rock*), p. n. of a man.

אֶלְצָפָן or אֱלִיצָפָן (*whom God protects*), p. n. of a man.

אֱלִיקָא p. n. of a man.

אֶלְיָקִים (*whom God makes strong*), p. n.—I. of the house-steward of Hezekiah.—II. of a king of Judah, afterwards changed to יְהוֹיָקִים (*Jehovah makes strong*).

אֱלִישֶׁבַע (*vowed to God*), p. n., Elishebah ('Ελισάβετ), the wife of Aaron.

אֱלִישָׁה p. n. of a place on the shores of the Mediterranean.

אֱלִישׁוּעַ (*whose salvation is God*), p. n. of a son of David.

אֶלְיָשִׁיב (*whom God pardons*), p.n. of a man.

אֱלִישָׁמָע (*whom God hears*), p.n. of a m.

אֱלִישָׁע (*whose salvation is God*), p.n., *Elisha* (Ἐλισσαῖος), the prophet.

אֱלִישָׁפָט (*God is the judge*), p.n. of a m.

אֱלִיאָתָה p.n.; see אֱלִיאָתָא.

אֵלֶּךְ pron. m. pl. Ch.; same as Heb. אֵלֶּה *those*, Dan. 3:12, 13

אֵלֵךְ with ה parag. וָאֵלְכָה, אֵלְכָה Kal fut. 1. pers.; see ילך, הלך.

אלל root not used (Arab. *passed away quickly*).

אַל s., *nothing*, Job 24:25.; adv. *not*; with the fut. אַל־תִּירָאוּ *fear not*; אַל־נָא *do not* (I beseech you), Gen. 19:18.

אֱלִיל *vain things, vanity*; אֱלִילִים *idols*, lit. *vain things*.

אַלְלַי *woe is me!* see ילל.

אַלָּה f., *terebinth*, Jos. 24:26; see אוּל.

אַלּוֹן m.—I. *oak.*—II. p.n. of a man; see אוּל.

אָלַם not used in Kal either in Heb. or Arab. Niph. נֶאֱלַם *was dumb, silent*, lit. *tongue-tied*. Pi. *bound*, like sheaves of corn, Gen. 37:7.

אֹלֶם m., *silence*; אֶלֶם צֶדֶק *is justice silent?* Ps. 58:2; יוֹנַת אֵלֶם *the dove of silence*, title to Ps. 56.

אִלֵּם m., *dumb person*; pl. אִלְּמִים.

אֲלֻמָּה f. (pl. אֲלֻמִּים and אֲלֻמּוֹת), *a sheaf of corn*.

אַלְמֹן m., *widowhood*, Isa. 47:29.

אַלְמָן m., *a widower*, Jer. 51:5.

אַלְמָנָה f., *a widow*.

אַלְמְנוֹת for אַרְמְנוֹת *palaces*, Isa. 13:22.

אַלְמָנוּת f., *widowhood*; pl. אַלְמְנֻתִים.

אַלְמֹנִי m., *some one, a certain one*, lit. *one not to be named*; always joined with פְּלֹנִי, which see.

אָלֵם and אֵלֶם; see אוּל.

אַלְמֻגִּים a resinous and odoriferous wood, not the produce of Canaan; perhaps *the red sandal-wood*, 1 Ki. 10:11, &c.; in 2 Chron. 2:7, it is transposed to אַלְגּוּמִּים.

אַלְמוֹדָד p.n. of one of the descendants of Shem, Gen. 10:26.

אַלַּמֶּלֶךְ (*the king's oak*), p.n. of a place in the tribe of Asher.

אַלְמֹנִי, אַלְמָנָה, אַלְמָנוּת, אַלְמָן, אַלְמֹן; see אָלַם

אֶלְנַעַם (*God is his delight*), p.n. of a man.

אֶלְנָתָן (*given of God*), p.n. of a man.

אֶלָּסָר p. n. of a city.

אֶלְעָד (*God is his help*), p.n. of a man.

אֶלְעָדָה (*whom God adorns*), p.n. of a m

אֶלְעוּזַי (*God my strength*), p.n. of a m.

אֶלְעָזָר (*God is his helper*), p.n. of a m.

אֶלְעָלֵא, אֶלְעָלֵה p.n. of a town in the tribe of Reuben.

אֶלְעָשָׂה (*made of God*), p.n. of a man.

אָלַף *learnt*; fut. יֶאֱלַף. Pi. אִלֵּף *taught*. Hiph. part. f. מַאֲלִיפוֹת (from אֶלֶף), *producing a thousand*, Ps. 144:13.

אֶלֶף m., *a thousand*; dual אַלְפַּיִם *two thousand*; pl. אֲלָפִים *thousands*; שְׁלֹשֶׁת אֲלָפִים *three thousand*, אַרְבָּעִים אֶלֶף *forty thousand*, מֵאָה אֶלֶף *a hundred thousand*, אֶלֶף אֲלָפִים *a thousand thousands*, אַלְפֵי רְבָבָה 10,000,000; אֶלֶף s.— I. *a chiliad* (a troop of 1000 soldiers); שַׂר הָאֶלֶף, χιλίαρχος, *commander of a chiliad.*—II *a nation*

*tribe* (i.e. *many persons*).—III. pl.
אֲלָפִים *oxen*; see below.—IV. p. n.
of a city in the tribe of Benjamin,
Jos. 18:28.

אֲלַף, אֶלַף Ch., *a thousand.*

אַלּוּף adj., *familiar, tame*, Jer. 11:19.
s.—I. *a friend.*—II. *an ox* (*a
tame animal*).—III. *head of a tribe
or family*, φύλαρχος.

אֶלְפֶּלֶט (*God the deliverer*), p. n. of a m.

אֶלְפַּעַל (*God who performeth*), p. n. of
a man.

אֶלְצָפָן p. n. of a man; see אֱלִיצָפָן·

אָלַץ (Syr. *he urged*). Pi. אִלֵּץ *pressed,
urged on*, Jud. 16:16.

אַלְקוּם m., Prov. 30:31, מֶלֶךְ אַלְקוּם
עִמּוֹ *a king who is irresistible*,
" against whom there is no rising
up," Eng. Ver.; meaning uncertain.

אֶלְקָנָה (*for whom God cared*), p. n. of
a man.

אֶלְקֹשִׁי p. n. of a people.

אֶלְתּוֹלַד p. n. of a city; same as תּוֹלַד·

אֶלְתְּקֵה, אֶלְתְּקֵא p. n. of a city of the
Levites in the tribe of Dan.

אֶלְתְּקֹן p. n. of a city in the tribe of Judah.

אֵם f. (with suff. אִמִּי; pl. אִמּוֹת).—I.
*a mother.*—II. *a grand-mother.*—
III. *a step-mother.*—IV. *metropolis,
chief city;* אֵם הַדֶּרֶךְ *mother*, i.e.
*head of two ways*, Ez. 21:26.—V.
*nation, entire people.*

אַמָּה f.—I. *fore arm*, hence:—II. *a
cubit*, measure of 21·888 inches;
dual אַמָּתַיִם *two cubits;* עֶשֶׂר
אַמּוֹת *ten cubits;* שְׁלֹשׁ מֵאוֹת אַמָּה
*three hundred cubits.*—III. *a basis
or pedestal*, Isa. 6:4.—IV. p. n. of
a hill, 2 Sa. 2:24.

אַמָּה f. Ch., *cubit.*

אַמָּה f. (pl. אַמִּים, אַמּוֹת), *families,
tribes.*

אֻמָּה f. Ch., the same.

אִם cond. pa.—I. *surely, truly*, this is
its radical meaning, hence:—II.
*if;* אִם...אִם *whether...or;* עַד־אִם,
אִם־אֲשֶׁר־עַד *whilst, until.*—III. *if?
whether?* אִם, הֲ...אִם, וְאִם...הֲ
*whether?...or?*—IV. used as an
asseveration אִם has the power of
denial, אִם־לֹא of affirmation;
אִם־אֶעֱשֶׂה *let me be accursed if
I do it*, i.e. I will not do it.—V.
in comp. הַאִם same as הֲלֹא *is not?*
אִם־לֹא *unless.*

אֶמְאָסְאֵךְ Hos. 4:6; perhaps for
אֶמְאָסְאֵךְ i. e. אֶמְאַסְאֵךְ Kal fut. 1.
pers. with suff.; see מָאַס·

אָמָה f. (with suff. אֲמָתִי; pl. אֲמָהוֹת;
const. אַמְהוֹת), *maid-servant;* בֶּן־
אָמָה *servant.*

אֲמָהוֹת pl.; see אָמָה·

אֻמָּה, אַמָּה; see אֵם·

אָמוֹן, אֲמוֹנָה, אָמֻן; see אמן·

אָמוֹץ (*strong*), p. n. of the father of
Isaiah, Isa. 1:1.

אָמִי p. n. of a man.

אֵמִים p. n. of one of the giant races in
Canaan.

אָמִיץ *strong*; see אמץ·

אָמִיר *top*; see אמר·

אמל root not used; *was sick.* Pul.
אֻמְלַל *sick, wasting, declining.*

אֻמְלָה f., *pained, sick*, Eze. 16:30.

אֻמְלַל m., *wasting with disease*, Ps.
6:3.

אֻמְלָל m. (pl. אֻמְלָלִים), *wasted, feeble
men*, Neh. 3:34.

אָמָם p. n. of a city.

אָמַן I. *was true, faithful*; part. אֱמוּנִים *the faithful.*—II. *nursed, brought up*; part. אֹמֵן *foster-father, nurse.* Niph. נֶאֱמַן—I. *was sure.*—II. *was enduring, durable*; בַּיִת נֶאֱמַן *an enduring house.*—III. *was faithful.*—IV. *was carried* (as a child), Isa. 60:4. Hiph. הֶאֱמִין *confided, entrusted, believed, relied on,* followed by בְּ, לְ with inf.

אָמַן Ch. Aph. הֵימִן *entrusted.*

אָמָן m., *artificer*, Cant. 7:2.

אֹמֶן m.—I. *a true thing, truth*; אֱלֹהֵי א' *the God of truth.*—II. *formula of acquiescence, Amen, so be it.*

אֵמוּן m.—I. *constant, unvarying*, Pro. 8:30.—II. same as הָמוֹן *the multitude*, Jer. 52:15.—III. p. n. of an Egyptian idol *Amoun* in נֹא אָמוֹן, which see.—IV. p. n. of a king of Judah.

אָמוֹן m.—I. *a faithful, true, sincere one.*—II. *educated, brought up,* Lam. 4:5.

אֹמֶן m., *faith*; adv. *truly.*

אָמְנָה f., *beam, lintel*, 2 Kings 18:16.

אֲמֻנָה I. f. of אָמוּן; וַיְהִי יָדָיו אֱמוּנָה *his hands were made steady, true.*—II. *faithfulness.*—III. *truth.* Pl. אֱמוּנוֹת.

אֲמָנָה f.—I. *covenant, contract*, Neh. 11:23.—II. p. n. of a river near Damascus.—III. of a region.

אָמְנָה I. adv., *truly, indeed.*—II. f., *education, nursing*, Est. 2:20.

אֻמְנָם, אָמְנָם adv., *certainly, verily*; הַאֻמְנָם *indeed?* 1 Kings 8:27.

אֶמֶת f. (with suff. אֲמִתּוֹ).—I. *per-*

manency, durability.— II. *truth*, especially religious truth; used for truthfulness in God, and piety in man.

אֲמִינוֹן, אַמְנוֹן (*faithful*), p. n. of a son of David.

אָמֵץ (imp. אֱמַץ; fut. יֶאֱמַץ), *was powerful, courageous*; with מִן *prevailed, was mightier than.*—Pi. I. *strengthen*, Job 4:1.—II. *repair* (a house), 2 Chro. 24:13.—III. *fasten, secure*, Pro. 8:28.—IV. *encourage.*—V. א' לֵב פ' *harden the heart.* Hiph. *strengthen, confirm.* Hith. *acquired power, took courage.*

אַמִּיץ *strong, prevailing.*

אֹמֶץ m., *vigour*, Job 17:9.

אָמֹץ m., *powerful, vigorous* (of horses) pl. אֲמֻצִּים Zec. 6:3.

אַמְצָה f., *strength*, Zec. 12:5.

אָמֹצִי (*strong*), p. n. of a man.

אֲמַצְיָהוּ, אֲמַצְיָה (*strengthened of God*), p. n., *Amaziah* king of Judah.

מַאֲמַצִּים m. pl.; מַאֲמַצֵּי כֹחַ *confirmers of power*, Job 36:19.

אָמַר I. *he said* (to any one, with אֶל, לְ; of any one, with לְ and accus.); sometimes same as דִּבֶּר *he spoke*; inf. לֵאמֹר *saying.*—II. *commanded*—III. *he thought*, lit. *he spake inwardly*, Gen. 44:28, Ex. 2:14, &c. &c. בְּלִבְכֹבוּ, בְּלִבּוֹ. Niph. *was said of* or *concerning any one* (with לְ); impers. יֵאָמֵר *it is said*; with לְ *it is said to some one.* Hiph. *made declared*, "avouched," Eng. Ver., Deu. 26:17, 18. Hith. *were declared, published, made famous*

אֲמַר Ch., *he said, commanded.*

אֵמֶר m.—I. same as דִּבֶר *a discourse,*

speech; אִמְרֵי אֵל the words of God.
—II. an appointment, declaration,
Job 20:29; with suff. אִמְרִי; pl.
אֲמָרִים.

אֹמֶר m., enunciation, expression, saying; same as דָּבָר a thing, a
matter.

אִמֵּר (tall), p. n. of a man.

אִמַּר Ch., a lamb, Ezr. 6:9, 17, &c.

אִמְרָה f., word, declaration, discourse;
pl. אֲמָרוֹת.

אֶמְרָה f., the same.

אָמִיר m., the pod which contains
the fruit of the palm tree, Isa.
17:6.

מַאֲמָר m., edict, command, Ezr. 1:
15, &c.

מֵאמַר m. Ch., the same.

אִמְרִי (eloquent), p. n. of a man.

אֱמֹרִי the Amorite; LXX.᾿Αμορῥαῖος.

אֲמַרְיָה and אֲמַרְיָהוּ p. n. of a man.

אַמְרָפֶל p. n. of the king of Shinar,
Gen. 14:1, 9.

אֶמֶשׁ yesterday, lit. the day before
last night.

אֱמֶת truth; see אמן.

אַמְתַּחַת sack; see מתח.

אֲמִתַּי (truth-teller), p. n. of the father
of the prophet Jonah, Jon. 1:1.

אָן, אָנָה, אֶן; see אי.

אֹן Heliopolis; see און.

אֲנָא, אֲנָה Ch., pers. pron. I.

אָנָּא interj., gently, I pray, &c.

אֲנָבָּה Ch., for אִבָּה; see אב in אבב.

אֲנַדְרַע; see יָנְדַּע.

אָנָה he suffered, Isa. 3:19. Pi. אִנָּה
he caused pain, Ex. 21:13. Pu.
was made to suffer, Pro. 12:21,
Ps. 91:10. Hith. part. מִתְאַנֵּר

affecting irritation, seeming to be
irritated, followed by לְ.

אֲנָחֲרָה p. n. of a city.

אֲנִיָּה f., suffering, pain, Isa. 29:2.

תַּאֲנִיָּה f., the same, Lam. 2:5.

אֳנִי com., a ship; collectively, a fleet.

אֳנִיָּה f., a ship.

תַּאֲנָה f., sexual impulse, Jer. 2:24.

תֹּאֲנָה f. opportunity, revenge, Jud. 14:4.

אֲנוּ com., we, Jer. 42:6; see אֲנַחְנוּ.

אִנּוּן m., אִנִּין f. pron. pl. Ch., these,
those.

אֱנוֹשׁ p. n.; see אנש.

אָנַח Niph. נֶאֱנַח he sighed (the things
sighed for preceded by מִן עַל).

אֲנָחָה f., sighing, sobbing.

אֲנִי I; see אָנֹכִי.

אֲנִיָּה, אֲנִיָּה, אֲנִי; see אנה.

אֲנִיעָם (mourning of the people), p. n. of
a man.

אֲנָךְ m.—I. lead.—II. a plummet, Am.
7:7, 8.

אָנֹכִי (contr. אֲנִי; with the pause אָנִי),
pers. pron. I; pl. אֲנַחְנוּ, sometimes
נַחְנוּ (אֲנוּ Jer. 42:6), we.

אָנַן. Hith. הִתְאוֹנֵן he groaned, Nu.
11:1, Lam. 3:39.

אָנַס urge, force, Est. 1:8.

אֲנַס Ch., the same; trouble, Dan. 4:6.

אָנַף (fut. יֶאֱנַף), breathe through the
nose, snort; hence was irritated,
angry (with בְּ). Hith. הִתְאַנֵּף
became angry.

אַף m. (with suff. אַפִּי).—I. nose;
גְּבַהּ אַף disdainful, haughty, lit. turned
up of nose, Ps. 10:4.—II. anger;
dual אַפַּיִם I. nostrils by synecd.—
II. face, countenance; לְאַפֵּי same

**as** לִפְנֵי **in the right of, before;** מָנָה אַחַת אַפַּיִם **one of two persons,** i. e. a double portion, 1 Sa. 1:5.— III. **anger,** אֶרֶךְ אַ' **slow to anger;** קְצַר אַ' **quick to anger, hasty.**

אַף **also; see in its place.**

אַנַף Ch., dual, **nostrils, face.**

אֲנָפָה f., name of an unclean bird, "heron," Eng. Ver.; LXX. χαρα-δριός; Lev. 11:19, Deu. 14:18.

אָנַק **cry out for pain; inf.** אֲנֹק; **fut.** יֶאֱנַק. Niph. נֶאֱנַק **lament.**

אֲנָקָה **const.** אֶנְקַת f.—I. **crying out for pain.**—II. **name of a reptile** so called from its cry, Lev. 11:30.

אָנַשׁ **root not used.** (אֲנַס Ch., **compress, compel**). Part. אָנוּשׁ m., אֲנוּשָׁה f. **incurable** (of a wound), **grievous, mortal, unlucky** (of a day), **malignant** (of a disposition); Niph. **he became mortally sick,** 2 Sa. 12:15.

אֱנוֹשׁ m.—I. **man** (as mortal and miserable).—II. **mankind.**—III. **plebeian, low person; pl.** אֲנָשִׁים (const. אַנְשֵׁי; with suff. אֲנָשֶׁיךָ, אֲנָשֵׁיהֶם), **man, men; see** אִישׁ.— IV. אֱנוֹשׁ p. n. of a son of Seth.

אֱנָשׁ אֱנָשׁ Ch., **man.**

אַנְתָּה Ch., pers. pron. m., **thou.**

אָסָא (**healing**), p. n. of a king of Judah.

אָסוּךְ **cup; see** סוּךְ.

אָסִיר, אָסוּר, אַסִּיר **bound; see** אסר.

אָסִיף **harvest; see** אסף.

אָסָם m., pl. אֲסָמִים **store-houses, granaries;** LXX. ταμεῖα.

אָסַן **root not used;** (Arab. **death, destruction**).

אָסֹן m., **injury, death by accident.**

אָסְנָה p. n. of a man.

אָסְנַפַּר p. n. of an Assyrian general

אָסְנַת (**belonging to Neith**), p. n. of the wife of Joseph.

אָסְעָרֵם Syr. for אֲסָעֲרֵם Pi. fut. 1. pers. with suff.; see סער.

אָסַף (inf. אֲסֹף; const. אֱסֹף; with suff. אָסְפְּךָ; fut. יֶאֱסֹף, with suff. יַאַסְפֵנִי; 1. pers. אֶאֱסֹף and אֹסֵף).— I. **collected, gathered** (with אֶל and עַל before the place in which). —II. **take away, take off, destroy** אָ' נַפְשׁוֹ **he deprived himself of life.** Niph. נֶאֱסַף I. **was gathered, received.**—II. **was taken away, ceased.**—III. **perished,** Hos. 4:3, (with עַל, לְ, אֶל; נֶאֱסַף אֶל־עַמּוֹ, אֶל־אֲבוֹתָיו, עַמָּיו, was gathered to his people, fathers,** i. e. was buried; used in this sense alone נֶאֱסַף Nu. 20:26.—Pi. I. **gather, receive.**— II. **close the rear of a march,** Nu. 10:25, Jos. 6:9, 13. Pu. **was gathered.** Hith. הִתְאַסֵּף **gather themselves together,** Deu. 33:5.

אָסָף (**collector**), p. n. of a man.

אֹסֶף m., **ingathering, harvest of fruits.**

אָסִיף m., **harvest of apples.**

אֲסֵפָה f., **collection, gathering,** Isa. 24:22.

אֲסֻפִּים m. pl., **collection of stores or money, storehouses.**

אֲסֻפּוֹת f. pl., **the same.**

אֶסְפְּךָ Kal fut. 1. pers. with suff. 1 Sa. 15:6; Kal part. with suff. 2 Ki. 22:20; see אסף.

הָאסַפְסֻף m., with the article אֲסַפְסֻף **mixed multitude,** Nu. 11:4.

אָסְפַּרְנָא Ch. adv., **exactly, carefully, quickly.**

אַסְפָּתָא p. n. of a son of Haman.

אָסַר (fut. יֶאְסֹר and יַאֲסֹר).—I. *he tied, bound*, followed by לְ; א הַמֶּרְכָּבָה *yoking the horses to the chariot*.— II. מִלְחָמָה א *he kept together the battle*, i. e. made his troops attack closely and, continuously. — III.. אָסַר אִסָּר עַל־נַפְשׁוֹ *he bound himself by an oath*; part. אָסוּר *captive, prisoner*. Niph. *becoming bound*. Pu. *taken, reduced to bondage.*

אֵסוּר m., *chain*; pl. אֲסוּרִים; בֵּית הָאֵסוּר *prison*.

אֵסוּר Ch., the same.

אָסוּר m., *a captive.*

אָסִיר m.—I. *captive.*—II. p. n. of a man.

אֱסָר m., *an obligation.*

אֱסָר m. Ch., the same.

אִסָּר m., the same.

מוֹסֵר m.; see in its place.

אֵסַר־חַדֹּן p. n., *Esar-haddon* king of Assyria, the successor of Sennacherib; LXX. Ἀσορδάν.

אָסְרֵם Kal fut. 1. pers. with suff.; see יסר

אֶסְתֵּר (*star*), p. n., *Esther* queen of Persia; her name before was הֲדַסָּה Est. 2: 7.

אָע m. Ch., same as Heb. עֵץ *wood*.

אַף *nose*; see אנף.

אַף part., also, *moreover, nay, indeed*; אַף כִּי אָמַר *indeed, truly*; hath (God) *indeed said*, Gen. 3: 1.

אַף Ch., the same.

אַפְאֵיהֶם Hiph. fut. 1. pers. with suff.; see פאה.

אָפַד *he put on the Ephod*, Ex. 29: 5, Lev. 8: 7 (with לְ of the person, and בְּ of the thing).

אֵפוֹד m.—I. *Ephod*, a garment worn

by the priesthood; א נָשָׂא *he wore the ephod*, i. e. he fulfilled the priest's office.—II. perhaps the name of an idol, Jud. 8: 27, &c.

אֲפֻדָּה f., *made like an ephod*; probably the dress of an idol.

אָפֹד p. n. of a man.

אַפֶּדֶן *camp*; see פדן.

אָפָה *baking*. Niph. *baked.*

אֹפֶה m., *a baker*; pl. אֹפִים.

אֹפָה f., the same; pl. אֹפוֹת.

מַאֲפֶה m., *bakemeat.*

אֵפוּ Syr. for אֵפוֹא imp. pl. of the verb אפה.

אֵפוֹ, אֵפוֹא pa., οὖν, δή), *now, then*; אִם כֵּן א *if then it be so*; אַיֵּה א *where then?* מָה א *what then!* דְּעוּ א γινώσκετε οὖν *know then!*

אֵפוֹד *ephod*; see אפד.

אָפִיחַ p. n. of a man.

אַפַּיִם p. n. of a man.

אָפִיק *swelling*; see אפק.

אָפַל root not used (Arab. *set as the sun*).

אָפֵל, אֲפֵלָה f.—I. *concealed*.—II. *very dark.*

אֹפֶל m., *obscure.*

אֹפֶל m., *thick darkness*; more intense than חֹשֶׁךְ.

אֲפֵלָה f., *darkness*; חֹשֶׁךְ א *thick darkness.*

מַאְפֵל m., *darkness.*

מַאְפֵּלְיָה f., *extreme darkness*, Jer 2: 31.

אֶפְלָל (*judgment*), p. n. of a man.

אָפַן root not used; same as פָּנָה *turn, roll.*

אוֹפָן m., *wheel*; const. אֹפַן; pl אֹפַנִּים.

אֹפֶן season (περίοδος); דָּבָר עַל־אָפְנָיו *a word in season*, Pro. 25:11.

אֶפֶס m.—I. *termination, extremity*; אַפְסֵי אֶרֶץ *ends of the earth*; dual אֲפָסַיִם *two extremities*, i.e. of both feet; *the soles* or *ankles*, Eze. 47:3.—II. *deficiency, wanting*; בְּאֶפֶס *without*, lit. *in there not being*, followed by the genitive of the thing; אֶפְסִי עוֹד אִ/ *until there is none*; בְּאֶפֶס *besides me*; מֵאֶפֶס *without*; *of, from nothing*; אֶפֶס כִּי *except, unless*.

אֶפֶס דַּמִּים p. n. of a town in the tribe of Judah, 1 Sa. 17:1; see פַּס דַּמִּים.

אֶפְעֶה m., *an adder*, Isa. 41:24; see פָּעָה.

אֶפְעֶה *adder*; see פָּעָה.

אָפַף *enclose, hem in*; pret. pl. אָפְפוּ; with suff. אֲפָפוּנִי.

אָפַק Kal, root not used; (Arab. *visited many countries*). Hith. הִתְאַפֵּק I. *went on, proceeded*.—II. *restrained himself from proceeding*, Gen. 45:1, &c.; LXX. ἀνέχομαι, ἐγκρατεύομαι.

אָפִיק m. adj.—I. *mighty, eminent man*, Job 12:21.—II. *river, torrent*.—III. *the bosses of a shield*, Job 41:7.—IV. *swellings of the sea*.—V. p. n. of a city in the tribe of Asher, Jud. 1:31, same as:—

אֲפֵק p.n.—I. of a city in the tribe of Asher.—II. of a city in the tribe of Issachar.

אֲפֵקָה p. n. of a town in the mountains of Judah, Jos. 15:53.

אָפַר root not used; (Arab. *casting away*).

אֵפֶר m.—I. *ashes*.—II. *any thing worthless*.

אוֹפִיר p. n. of a kingdom; see in its place.

אְפֵר m. (transpos. of פְּאֵר), *a tiara, crown*, 1 Ki. 20:38, 41.

אֶפְרֹחַ *chicken*; see פרח.

אַפִּרְיוֹן m., LXX. φορεῖον, *car, sedan*, Cant. 3:9, 10.

אֶפְרַיִם p.n.—I. *Ephraim*, the younger son of Joseph.—II. the tribe that descended from him.—III. afterwards, the kingdom formed by the ten tribes that revolted from the house of David.

אֶפְרָת, אֶפְרָתָה p.n.—I. of a city in the tribe of Judah: called also בֵּית־לֶחֶם.—II. same as אֶפְרַיִם, Ps. 132:6.

אֶפְרָתִי I. *an Ephraimite*.—II. an inhabitant of Ephratah.

אֲפַרְסָיֵא p. n. of an unknown people, Ezr. 4:9.

אֲפַרְסְכָיֵא p.n., as above, Ezr. 5:6.

אֲפַרְסַתְכָיֵא p. n. of the inhabitants of a city in Assyria, Ezr. 4:9.

וָאֶפֶת, אֵפֶת Niph. fut. apoc. 1. pers. for אֶפְתָּה; see פתה.

אַפְּתֹם pa., *thus then, then moreover*, Ezr. 4:13.

אָצְבּוֹן p. n. of a man.

אֶצְבַּע *finger*; see צבע.

אַצִּיעָה Hiph. fut. 1. pers. with ה parag., see יצע.

אָצַל I. *holding back, withholding*, with מִן.—II. *laying up with one's self*, with לְ. Niph. *contracted*, Eze 42:6. Hiph. *withhold*; fut. וַיָּאצֶל Nu. 11:25.

אָצִיל m. (Arab. rooted, firm).—I. nobleman, Eze. 24:11.—II. end, extremity, Isa. 41:9.

אָצִיל m. joint, suture; אַצִּילֵי יָדָיִם the wrists.

אָצֵל p. n.—I. of a man.—II. of a place near Jerusalem, Zec. 14:5.

אֵצֶל prep., near; מֵאֵצֶל near; (אֶצְלוֹ) near him.

אֲצַלְיָה p.n. of a man.

אֹצֶם p.n. of a man.

אֶצְעָדָה bracelet; see צעד.

אָצַק Kal fut. 1. pers. of the verb; see יצק.

אָצַר treasured. Niph. laid up, Isa. 23:1,18. Hiph. הוֹצֵר appoint as treasurer, Neh. 13:13, with עַל; fut. with ה parag. אוֹצְרָה.

אוֹצָר m. (pl. אוֹצָרוֹת).—I. treasury. —II. treasure; בֵּית הָאֹ I. treasure-house.—II. warehouse.

אֶצֶר p.n. of a man.

אָצָרְךָ Kri, Jer. 1:5, Kal fut. 1. pers. with suff.; see יצר.

אֶקְדָּח carbuncle; see קדח.

אַקּוֹ m., gazelle, Deu. 14:5.

אֶקַּח Kal fut. 1. pers. of the verb לקח.

אֶקְחָה for אֶקָּחָה Isa. 56:12, Kal fut. 1. pers. with ה parag., from לקח.

אֶקְרָאָה Kal fut. 1. pers. with ה parag., from קרא.

אוֹר light; see יאר.

אֲרָא p. n. of a man.

אֵרֶא, וָאֵרָא Niph. fut. apoc., from ראה.

אֲרִאֵל, אֲרִאֵלִי name of Jerusalem; see ראה.

אָרַב lying in wait, ambush; with לְ, עַל; fut. יֶאֱרֹב. part. אוֹרֵב ambus-cader. Pi. part. pl. מְאָרְבִים lying in wait. Hiph. he places an ambush, 1 Sa. 15·5.

אֲרָב p. n. of a town in the tribe of Judah.

אַרְבִּי a native of Arabia.

אֶרֶב m., lying in wait, place of ambush, Job 37:8, 38:40.

אֹרֶב m., the same; with suff. אָרְבּוֹ.

אָרְבָּה f., the same; pl. אָרְבוֹת; const. אָרְבוֹת.

אַרְבֶּה m., a species of locust, from רָבָה was many.

אֲרֻבָּה f.—I. net or wicker work to cover windows: hence,—II. window.—III. pigeon-holes, Isa. 60:8. IV. applied to the visible heavens, Gen. 7:11, 8:2.—V. a chimney, Hos. 13:3.

אֲרֻבּוֹת (plots), p. n. of a place in the tribe of Judah.

מַאֲרָב m., ambush, ambuscade.

אַרְבֵּאל p. n. of a place, Hos. 10:14; see בֵּית.

אַרְבַּע p. n. of a giant.

אַרְבַּע four; see רבע.

אָרַג I. plaiting the hair, Jud. 16:13. —II. weaving, Isa. 59:5; part. אֹרֵג a weaver, f. אֹרְגָה.

אֶרֶג m.—I. texture, web, Job 7:6.— II. weaver's comb, Jud. 16:14.

אַרְגֹּב p. n.—I. of the district of Og. —II. of a man.

אַרְגְּוָן Ch., purple, same as אַרְגָּמָן.

אַרְגָּז bag; see רגז.

אַרְגָּמָן m., purple.

אַרְדְּ p. n. Ard, a son of Benjamin; אַרְדִּי patronymic of Ard.

**אַרְדֹּן** p. n. of a man.

**אָרָה** I. *pluck fruit*, Ps. 80:13.—II. *gather*.

**אֱרֶה** Nu. 22:6, imp. with ה parag.; see ארר.

**אֲוֵרוֹת** f. pl., *stables, stalls for beasts*, 2 Chron. 32:28.

**אַרְווֹת** f. pl., const. אֲרָיוֹת
**אַרְיוֹת** f. pl., const. אֲרָיוֹת —I. *stalls.*—II. *stable.*

**אֲרִי** m., *a lion*; pl. אֲרָיִים and אֲרָיוֹת. **אַרְיֵה** m., *a lion.*

**אַרְיֵה** m. Ch., *a lion*; pl. אַרְיָוָן.

**אֲרִיֵּךְ** Isa. 16:9, transpos. for אֲרַוֵּיךְ or אֲרַיֵּוֵךְ (same as ריה). Pi.fut. 1. pers. with suff.; see רוה.

**אֲרִיאֵל, אֲרִיאֵל** (*lion of God*).—I. a name of the altar of burnt-offering.—II. a name for Jerusalem.—III. p. n. of a man.

**אֲרִאֵל** (the same), p. n. of a man.

**אֲרִאֵלִי** (the same), p. n. of a man.

**אֶרְאֶלָם** m., "their valiant ones," Isa. 33:7, Eng. Ver.; probably for אֶרְאֶה לָהֶם *I will appear unto them* (Lee).

**אָרוֹן** com.—I. *ark, chest*; אֲרוֹן הַבְּרִית, אֱלֹהִים הָעֵדוּת, *the ark of the covenant.*—II. *coffin, mummy-case*, Gen. 50:26.

**אֲרוּ** Ch., *behold! see!*

**אַרְוַד** p. n., *Aradus*, a city and district on the coast of Phœnicia.

**אֲרוֹדִי, אֲרווֹדִי** p. n. of a man.

**אֲרוּכָה** *repairing*; see ארך.

**אֲרוּמָה** p. n. of a city.

**אֲרוֹמִים** *Syrians*; see ארם, אֲרַמִּי.

**אֲרוֹמָם** for אֶתְרוֹמַם Hith. fut. 1. pers.; see רום

**אָרַז** *was firm, closely packed*; part אֲרָזִים.

**אֶרֶז** m., *cedar*; pl. אֲרָזִים, const אַרְזֵי.

**אַרְזָה** f., *cedar wainscot*, Zep. 2:14.

**אָרַח** *he goeth to herd with*, Job 34:8; part. אֹרֵחַ *traveller.*

**אֹרֵחַ** (*wanderer*), p. n. of a man.

**אֹרַח** com. (with suff. אָרְחִי; pl. אֳרָחוֹת; const. אָרְחוֹת; with suff. אָרְחֹתָם and אָרְחֹ').—I. *way, road, path.*—II. *mode or manner*; אֹרַח יְהוָֹה *way of the Lord*, i. e. the way that pleases the Lord; אֹרַח חַיִּים *the way of life*, i.e. that leads to life; אֹרַח עוֹלָם *the old path*, i.e. the manners of ancient times.—III. *wayfaring man.*

**אֹרַח** m. Ch., the same; pl. אָרְחָן.

**אֹרְחָה** f.—I. *step, progress.*—II. *travelling company, caravan.*

**אֲרֻחָה** f.—I. *fixed portion, ration.*—II. *portion generally.*

**אֲרִיאֵל, אֲרָיוֹת, אֲרָיֵה, אֲרִי** p. n.; see ארה.

**אֲרִידַי** p. n. of a son of Haman, Ἀριδαῖος.

**אֲרִידָתָא** (*strong*), p. n. of a man.

**אַרְיוֹךְ** p. n.—I. of a king of Ellasar, Gen. 14:1.—II. of a Chaldean.

**אֲרִיסַי** p. n. of a son of Haman.

**אָרַךְ** (fut. יֶאֱרַךְ; pl. יַאַרְכוּ), *was long, became* or *was made long*; אָרְכוּ לוֹ הַיָּמִים *he had tarried there many days*, Gen. 26:8. Hiph. הֶאֱרִיךְ trans. *make long, prolong*; הֶאֱרִיךְ יְמֵי פ' *lengthen his days, prolong life*; הֶאֱרִיךְ נַפְשׁוֹ *was long suffering, patient.*

**אֲרֻכָּה, אֲרֻכָה** f.—I. *lengthening out.*

—II. *repairing, restoring, healing;* (Arab. the same).

אֲרַךְ Ch. (part. אָרֵיךְ), *becoming, suitable.*

אָרֵךְ (const. אֲרֶךְ), *long;* א הָאֵבֶר *with long pinions,* Ecc. 7:8; א אַפַּיִם *slow to anger;* א רוּחַ μακρόθυμος, *long-suffering.*

אֶרֶךְ p.n. of a city of Shinar, Gen. 10:10; hence אַרְכְּוָיָא *an inhabitant of Erech;* אַרְכִּי *the same.*

אֹרֶךְ m., *length* (of time and space); with suff. אָרְכּוֹ.

אָרֹךְ m., אֲרֻכָּה f., *long, lasting long.*

אַרְכָא אַרְכָה f. Ch., *time, duration.*

אַרְכֻּבָּה *the knee,* Dan. 5:6; see ברך.

אֲרָם f. (const. אֲרַם), p.n., *Aramea;* the region of Damascus and Syria to the Orontes and Mesopotamia; א נַהֲרַיִם אֲרָם *Mesopotamia;* פַּדַּן אֲרָם *Padan Aram;* א צוֹבָה part of *Syria;* א דַּמֶּשֶׂק *Syria of Damascus;* א מַעֲכָה the region beyond Jordan at the foot of Anti-Libanus; א בֵּית־רְחוֹב part of *Syria;* see רְחֹב.

אֲרַמִּי m., *Syrian* (f. אֲרַמִּיָה; pl. אֲרַמִּים and אֲרוֹמִים).

אֲרָמִית adv., *in Syriac, in the language of Syria.*

אַרְמוֹן m. (pl. const. אַרְמְנוֹת), *palace.*

אַרְמֹנִי p.n. of one of the sons of Saul.

אֹרֶן m., *the mountain ash,* Isa. 44:14; LXX. πίτυς; Vulg. *pinus.*

אֹרֶן p.n. of a man.

אֲרָן p.n. of a man.

אַרְנֶבֶת f., *the hare,* Lev. 11:6, Deu. 14:17; (Arab. the same).

אַרְנוֹן (*sounding,* see רָנַן), p.n., *Arnon,*

a river which bounded the land of Israel to the east.

אַרְנָן p.n. of a man.

אֲרַוְנָה (אֲרַנְיָה 2 Sa. 24:15). p.n., *Araunah,* the Jebusite.

אַרְעָא, אֲרַע m. Ch.—I. *the earth.*—II. an epithet: *low, inferior* followed by מִן.

אַרְעִית f. Ch., *low, mean.*

אַרְפַּד p. n. of a city of Syria.

אַרְפַּכְשַׁד p.n. of a son of Shem.

אֶרֶץ f., sometimes m. (with art. הָאָרֶץ; with suff. אַרְצוֹ; pl. אֲרָצוֹת).—I. *earth.*—II. *the world.*—III. *the ground;* אַרְצָה *on the ground.*—IV. *region, province.* Pl. אֲרָצוֹת I. *lands, countries.*—II. *heathen nations.*

אַרְצָא p.n. of a man.

אֲרַק f. Ch., *the earth,* Jer. 10:11.

אָרַר (imp. אֹר; with ה parag. אָרָה; pl. אוֹרוּ; fut. יָאֹר), *denounce, curse.* Niph. part. pl. נְאָרִים *denounced, cursed.* Pi. אֵרֵר *denounce, bring on a curse;* part. pl. מְאָרְרִים. Hoph. fut. יוּאָר *is made accursed.*

מְאֵרָה f., *cursing.*

אֲרָרָט p.n., *Ararat,* a mountain in Armenia.

אֲרָרִי same as הֲרָרִי *Ararite.*

אָרַשׂ. Pi. אֵרֵשׂ, אֵרַשׂ (with accusative אִשָּׁה) *espouse a wife* by entering into a contract under a fine; with בְּ of the sum mulcted. Pu. pret. f. מְאֹרָשָׂה אֹרָשָׂה *espoused;* part. f.

אָרַשׁ root not used; (Arab. *he desired*)

אֲרֶשֶׁת f., *petition;* LXX. δίησις, Ps 21:3.

אַרְתַּחְשַׁשְׁתָּא, אַרְתַּחְשַׁסְתָּא, אַרְתַּחְשַׁשְׁתְּא } *Arta-xerxes*, king of Persia.

אִשְׂרָאֵל (same as אִסְרָאֵל), p. n. of a m.

אִשְׂרִיאֵל p.n. of a man; ־ִי *patronymic* of above.

אֵשׁ f., sometimes m. (with suff. אִשּׁוֹ, אִשָּׁם אִשְּׁכֶם).—I. *fire.*—II. *lightning;* אֵשׁ אֱלֹהִים *lightning.*—III. *heat of the sun,* Joel 1:19, 20.—IV. *appearance of God.*—V. *God's fierce anger.*—VI. *ardour of mind.*—VII. *great tribulations.*

אֵשׁ com. Ch., emph. state אֶשָּׁא *fire.*

אִשֶּׁה m.(const. אִשֵּׁה; pl. אִשִּׁים, אִשֵּׁי).—I. *burnt-offering.* — II. *incense-offering.*

אֵשׁ אִשְׁתָּם f.(אִשְׁתָּם Jer. 6:29), for אֵשׁ תָּם *(by) fire is consumed.*

אַשְׁבֵּל p. n. of a son of Benjamin, patronymic of the same.

אַשְׁבָּן p.n. of a man.

אֶשְׁבֵּעַ p. n. of a son of Saul.

אֶשְׁבַּעַל p. n. of a son of Saul.

אָשַׁד root not used; (Arab. *he rushed*).

אֶשֶׁד m., *bed of a river* or *brook;* אֶ׳ הַנְּחָלִים *bed of the torrents,* Nu. 21:15.

אַשֵׁדָה *foot, base of a mountain;* pl. אַשְׁדֹת; const. אַשְׁדֹּות.

אַשְׁדּוֹד (from שָׁדַד), p.n. *Ashdod* (Ἄζωτος), a city of the Philistines; אַשְׁדּוֹדִי *an Ashdodite;* ־ִית I. *a woman of Ashdod.*—II. *in the language of Ashdod.*

אִשָּׁה *woman;* see אֱנֹשׁ.

אֲשִׁיָּה f., *foundation,* Jer. 50:15; from שׁוּת.

אַשּׁוּר, אַשּׁוּרִי, אַשּׁוּר *footstep;* see אָשַׁר.

אַשְׁחוּר p. n. of a man.

אֲשִׁימָא p.n. cf a god of the Hamathites.

אֲשֵׁרָה *erection;* see אֲשֵׁרָה.

אָשִׁישׁ *foundation,* Isa. 16:7, see אָשׁ, perhaps for אִישֵׁי *men,* as Jer 48:31.

אֲשִׁישׁ, אֲשִׁישָׁה *food;* see אָשַׁשׁ.

אֶשֶׁךְ m., *testicles,* Lev. 21:20.

אֶשְׁכֹּל *Eshcol;* from שָׁכַל.

אַשְׁכִּים Ch. Hiph. inf. abs.; from שָׁכַם

אַשְׁכְּנַז p. n. of a people of North Asia

אֶשְׁכָּר *a rich gift,* Eze. 27:15, Ps. 72:14; from שָׂכַר.

אֵשֶׁל m., *the tamarisk,* a middle-sized thorny tree; tamarix orientali (Linn.).

אָשַׁם and אָשֵׁם and אָשׁוֹם (fut. יֶאְשַׁם).—I. *was guilty, sinned* (when against any one, with לְ; when in any thing, with בְּ and לְ).—II. *was conscious of guilt.*—III. *suffered for sin,* Ps. 34:22, &c. Niph. *suffered the consequences of sin,* Joel 1:18; Hiph. *bring on the consequences of guilt,* Ps. 5:11.

אָשֵׁם m., *guilty.*

אָשָׁם m.—I. *guilt,* i.e. the consequence of sin.—II. *a sacrifice to expiate it.*

אַשְׁמָה, לְאַשְׁמָה f.—I. (inf. of אָשַׁם), בָּהּ *to trespass therein,* Lev. 5:26; לְאַשְׁמַת הָעָם *so that the people trespass.*—II. *guilt, trespass.*—III. *a trespass-offering,* Lev. 6:5.

אַשְׁמַנִּים m., *"desolate places,"* Eng. Ver., Isa. 59:10; meaning uncertain.

אַשְׁמֻרָה f., *the three watches into which the night was divided;* root שָׁמַר

אֶשְׁנָב m., *a latticed window*, Jud. 5:28, Pro.7:6.

אַשְׁנָה p. n. of two cities in the tribe of Judah.

אֶשְׁעָן (*a prop*), p. n. of a city in the tribe of Judah.

אַשָּׁף m. Heb. and Ch. (pl. אַשְׁפִים), an *enchanter*.

אַשְׁפָּה f., *quiver*; בְּנֵי אַ *sons of the quiver, arrows*, Lam. 3:13.

אַשְׁפֹּת f. pl., *dung, dung heap*.

אַשְׁפַּתֹּת f. pl., the same.

אַשְׁפְּנַז p. n. of one of the eunuchs of Nebuchadnezzar.

אַשְׁפָּר *measure, cup*, 2 Sa. 6:10, 1 Chron. 6:3.

אַשְׁקְלֹון p. n. of a city of the Philistines.

אָשַׁר *went straight on, walked along.* —Pi. I. *guide, lead aright.*—II. *consider, pronounce good, happy*; Pu. אֹשַׁר אֻשַּׁר.—I. *was guided.*—II. *was esteemed happy.*

אָשֵׁר p. n. of one of the sons of Jacob;

אָשֵׁרִי I. *an Asherite.*—II. p. n. of a city near Sichem, Jos. 17:7.

אֶשֶׁר m., *happiness*; only in the const. pl. as אַשְׁרֵי הָאִישׁ *blessed is the man*, Ps. 1:1; אַשְׁרֶיךָ *blessed art thou*, Deu. 33:29.

אֹשֶׁר m., *happiness*, Gen. 30:13; with suff. אָשְׁרִי.

אָשׁוּר f.—I. *a step.*—II. *wood of the box tree*, Eze. 27:6.

אַשּׁוּר f.—I. *step*, Job 31:7.—II. p.n.f., *Assyria, kingdom of*; m., *an Assyrian*; דֶּרֶךְ אַ *into Assyria; the way of Assyria.*—III. אַשּׁוּרִים a race of Ishmaelites, Gen. 25:3.

אֲשׁוּרִי p. n. of a man.

אַשַׁרְנָא m. Ch., *wall, building*, Eze.5:3.

תְּאַשּׁוּר m., *the box tree*, Isa. 41:19, 60:13.

אֲשֶׁר I. relat. pron. of every gender and number; *he who, she who, it which*, &c.—II. note of the relative when it comes before pronouns and adverbs; אֲשֶׁר הוּא חַי *he who lives*; אֲ אֶת־עָפָר *which is dust*; אֲ לֹו, לָה *to whom*, sing.; אֲ לָהֶם, לָהֶן, *to whom, which*, pl.; אֲ אֹתֹו *whom, which*, sing אֲ אֹתָם, אֹתָן, *whom, which*, pl.; אֲשֶׁר־לְשֹׁנֹו *whose tongue*; אֲ בֹּו, בָּהּ *in whom, which*; אֲ בְּאַרְצָם *in whose land*; אֲ מִמֶּנּוּ *from whom*; אֲ שָׁם *where*; אֲ מִשָּׁם *whence*; אֲ שָׁמָּה *whither*; אֲ תַּחַת כְּנָפָיו *under whose wings.*—III. precedes pron. of the 1. and 2. pers.; אֲ מְכַרְתֶּם אֹתִי *(ye) who have sold me*; אֲ בָּחַרְתִּיךָ *thee whom I have chosen.*—IV. compounded with preps.; אֶת־אֲשֶׁר *him whom*; בַּאֲשֶׁר *where; according to, as if, because, when*; מֵאֲשֶׁר *from thence, whence.*—V. preceded by adverbs; בַּעֲבוּר, אַחַר, תַּחַת, עַל, עַד, יַעַן connecting them with the following words.—VI. אֲשֶׁר לְ note of the genitive; אֲשֶׁר לְאָבִיהָ הַצֹּאן *her father's cattle*; אֲשֶׁר conj. ὅτι, *because, that*; ἵνα with fut.; *since, when*, ὅτε; ὡς *as*, with כֵּן.

שֶׁ with dag. forte (sometimes שְׁ) same as אֲשֶׁר relat. pron. and in its other significations; שֶׁשָּׁם *where*; שֶׁל *of, whose*; בְּשֶׁ *because*; כְּמְעַט שֶׁ *almost*; עַד שֶׁ *until*. For שֶׁ and שְׁ; see Noldii Concordantiæ, and Prof. Lee's Grammar

בְּשֶׁל because, on account of; בִּשְׁלִי for my sake; בְּשַׁלְמִי on whose account? בְּשֶׁל אֲשֶׁר whatever.

אֲשַׂרְאֵלָה (from אֲשֶׁר and אֵל), p. n. of a man.

אֲשֵׁרָה, אֲשֵׁירָה (probably m. of עֲשְׁתֹּרֶת), p. n. of a deity of the Syrians; pl. אֲשֵׁרִים and אֲשֵׁרוֹת images of this idol.

אַשְׁרְנָא buildings; see אֲשֶׁר.

אָשַׁשׁ root not used. Hith. הִתְאֹשֵׁשׁ be men; see אִישׁ.

אָשִׁישׁ m. pl., const. אֲשִׁישֵׁי foundations; see in its place.

אֲשִׁישָׁה f., cake, pancake; pl. ־ים and אֲשִׁישׁוֹת.

אֻשִּׁין m. pl. Ch., foundations.

אֵשֶׁת woman; see אִשָּׁה.

אֶשְׁתָּיוּ Ch. pret. pl. with א prosthet., from שׁתה.

אֶשְׁתָּאֹל p. n. of a town of the Danites.

אֶשְׁתַּדּוּר Hith. of שׁדר.

אֶשְׁתּוֹן p. n. of a man.

אֶשְׁתְּמֹעַ and אֶשְׁתְּמֹה p. n. of a town in the tribe of Judah.

אָת sign; see אוה.

אֵת m., ploughshare; pl. אִתִּים and אֵתִים 1 Sa. 13:21; with suff. אֵתֵיכֶם.

אֵת, אֶת note of:—I. the accus. —II. the nom. with verbs passive and neuter; יִקָּרֵא אֶת־שְׁמָךְ thy name shall be called; with suff. אֹתְךָ, אֹתִי me, אוֹתְךָ (with pause אֹתָךְ) with ה parag. (אוֹתְכָה) אֹתְךָ m., אֹתָךְ f., thee; אֹתוֹ him; אֹתָהּ her; אֹתָנוּ us; אֶתְכֶם, אֶתְכֶם, אוֹתְכֶם you;

אוֹתָם them, m.; אֹתָן with ה parag. אֹתָנָה, אֶתְהֶן them, f.

III. אֶת, אֵת prep. with, by, one; besides, towards; אֶת־פְּנֵי before some one; with suff. אִתִּי with me; אִתְּךָ (with pause אִתָּךְ) m., אִתֵּךְ f., with thee; אִתּוֹ with him; אִתָּהּ with her; אִתָּנוּ with us; אִתְּכֶם, אִתְּכֶן with you; אִתָּם with them (sometimes אֹתִי, אֹתוֹ, &c.); מֵאֵת denotes separation, from; מֵאִתִּי, מֵאוֹתָךְ from me; מֵאִתְּךָ from thee, &c.

אֶתְבַּעַל p. n. of a king of Sidon.

אַתָּה (sometimes אַתְּ m.; אָתְּ, with pause אָתָּ, sometimes אַתִּי f.), pers. pron. thou; אַתֶּם m., אַתֵּן, אַתֵּנָה f., ye.

אָתָה (אָתָא Isa. 21:12), came; pret. pl. אָתָנוּ; imper. pl. אֵתָיוּ; fut. וַיֶּאֱתָה, תֵּאתֶה, וַיֵּאת; pl. יֶאֱתָיוּ. Hiph. imper. pl. הֵתָיוּ bring ye.

אֲתָה Ch., came. Aph. הַיְתִי brought. Hoph. was brought.

אִתּוֹן m., entrance, Eze. 40:15.

אֶתְוַדַּע Hith. fut. 1. pers., from ידע.

אַתּוּן com. Ch., furnace, Dan. 3:6, 11, 15.

אַתִּיק, אָתוּק m., gallery, Eze. 41:3, 15.

אִתַּי p. n. of a man.

אָתַיוּ Syr. for אֵתָיוּ which is for אֵתוּ imp. pl., from אתה.

אֵתָיוּ for אֲתָאנוּ pret. pl. 1. pers., from אָתָה. אֲתָא.

אַתֵּן, אַתֵּם you; see אַתָּה.

אֵתָם p. n. of a place in the desert.

אֶתְמוֹל, אֶתְמוֹל, אֶתְמוֹל yesterday; same as תְּמוֹל.

אָתַן root not used (Arab. *stepping shortly, she-ass*).

אָתוֹן f., *she-ass.*

אֶתְנָה, אֶתְנַן *gift;* see יתן.

אֶתְנִי (*gift*), p.n. of a man.

אֶתְקֶנְךָ Kal fut. 1. pers. with suff. and נ epenth., from נתק.

אֲתַר m. Ch., *place;* אֲתַר דִּי *in that place, where;* בָּאֲתַר *after;* בָּאתְרָךְ *after thee.*

אֲתָרִים m., *places;* or p.n. according to others Nu 21:1.

## ב

בְּ prep.—I. of place: *in, among, with, near, before;* never motion either to or in a place.—II. of time: *in, within.*—III. used of the means or instrument: *by, with.*—IV. of the cause: *for, because.*—V. of the rule: *according to.*—VI. *by* (in an oath).—VII. often prefixed to the inf. of verbs, translated by *in* or *when;* with suff. בִּי; בְּךָ m. (with the pause בָּךְ); בָּךְ f., בּוֹ, בָּהּ; בָּנוּ, בְּכֶם and בְּהֶן, בָּם and בְּהֶם, בָּהֶם.

בֹּא imp. with ה parag.; בָּאִי, בָּאִים part. pl.; בָּאָה inf. with suff.; בָּאת and בָּאת pret. f. 2. pers., from בוא.

בֹּאָה *entrance;* see בוא.

בְּאֹשׁ *wicked;* see באש.

בָּאַר, Pi. בֵּאֵר.—I. *dig, cut upon or into, define well;* with עַל.—II. *make clear, publish,* Deu. 1:5.

בְּאֵר f. (pl. const. בְּאֵרוֹת).—I. *well, cistern.*—II. p.n. of one of the stations in the desert.—III. p.n. of

a town in the tribe of Judah. בְּאֵר אֵלִים (*the well of heroes*), p.n. of a well. בְּאֵר לַחַי רֹאִי (*the well of the living God that seeth me*), p.n. of a well in the desert. בְּאֵר שֶׁבַע (*well of the oath*), p.n. of a city in the tribe of Simeon. בְּאֵרוֹת p.n. of a city in the tribe of Benjamin; בְּאֵרֹתִי בְּאֵרֹתִי, epithet of an inhabitant of Beeroth. בְּאֵרֹת בְּנֵי יַעֲקָן (*wells of the sons of Iaachan*), p.n of a station in the desert.

בְּאֵר often, בּוֹר m.—I. *well of water; well of bitumen,* Gen. 14:10.—II. *pit* or *dungeon* in which prisoners were kept; בֵּית הַבּוֹר *prison house.*—III. *grave, sepulchre;* יוֹרְדֵי בוֹר *they that go down into the pit,* i. e. the dead; עַד בוֹר *even to the grave;* with ה *den, place,* בֹּרָה, pl. בֹּרוֹת, בְּאֵרוֹת.

בְּאָרָא p.n. of a man.

בְּאֵרָה p.n. of a man.

בְּאֵרִי p.n.—I. of the father of Hosea.—II. of the father-in-law of Esau.

בָּאַשׁ (fut. יִבְאַשׁ) *emitted an ill savour, stank.* Niph. *became fetid, in ill odour,* i.e. hateful; (with בְּ, אֶת). Hiph. הִבְאִישׁ *rendered, made bad,* i. e. *odious;* (with בְּ); int. *stank,* Ex. 16:24; *did wickedly, became bad;* (with עִם), 1 Chron. 19:6.

בְּאַשׁ Ch., *was evil;* (with עַל), Dan. 6:15.

בְּאֹשׁ m.—I. *stench;* with suff. בָּאְשׁוֹ, בָּאְשָׁם.—II. *evil, affliction.*

בָּאְשָׁה f., *poisonous herb,* probably hemlock, Job 31:40.

בְּאֻשִׁים m. pl., *wild, sour grapes,* Is. 5:2, 4.

בָּאֵשׁ m. Ch., *bad, wicked;* f. emph. בָּאִשְׁתָּא.

בָּאתַר *after;* see אָתַר.

בָּבַח *pupil of the eye;* see בּוּב.

בֵּבָי p.n. of a man.

בָּבֶל p.n.f.—I. *Babylon;* with ה, signifying place, בָּבֶלָה.—II. *the kingdom of Babylon.*

בָּבְלָיָא Ch. *Babylonish;* pl. const. בָּבְלָיֵא.

בַּג m., לְבַג, Eze. 23:7, a wrong reading; Kri לְבַז "*for a spoil,*" Eng. Ver.

בָּגַד (fut. יִבְגַּד, יִבְגּוֹד; inf. בָּגוֹד; const. בְּגוֹד; with suff. בִּגְדוֹ), *dissembled, acted perfidiously, cheated,* with בְּ and מִן; part. בֹּגֵד *a perfidious person.*

בֶּגֶד m. (f. Lev. 6:20; with suff. בִּגְדִי, בִּגְדוֹ, pl. בְּגָדִים; const. בִּגְדֵי, בִּגְדוֹתָיךְ, Ps. 45:9).—I. *wrapper, coverlet.*—II. *cloak, garment.*—III. *dissimulation, perfidy.*—IV. *rapine, violence.*

בֹּגְדוֹת f. pl., *great perfidy,* Zep. 3:4.

בָּגוֹד m., בָּגוֹדָה f., *perfidious,* Jer. 3: 7, 10.

בֻּגְוַי p.n. of a man.

בִּגְלַל *because;* see גלל.

בִּגְתָא p.n. of a eunuch of Ahasuerus.

בִּגְתָן p.n. of a eunuch of Ahasuerus.

בַּד m., *fine linen;* בַּדִּים *linen garments;* see also בַּד under בדד.

בָּדָא *originated, innovated;* part. with suff. בֹּדְאָם Syr. for בֹּדְאָם.

בָּדַד, part. בּוֹדֵד *separate, solitary person.*

בַּד m., *being alone, separate, apart;* pl בַּדִּים.—I. *shoots, branches.*—II.

*staves of wood.*—III. *limbs, members of the body.*—IV. *defences,* i. e. *princes,* Hos. 11:6, &c.—V. *lies,* Is. 16:6, &c.

לְבַד adv., *alone, separate, only;* אָנֹכִי לְבַדִּי *I alone;* אַתָּה לְבַדְּךָ *thou alone;* לְבַדְּךָ *to thee alone;* לְבַדּוֹ *he alone;* מִלְבַד מִן and מִלְבַד אֲשֶׁר *besides;* מִלְבַד אֲשֶׁר *beside that which;* לְבַד עַל *the same.*

לְבָדָד m., *separate, alone, solitary;* and בָּדָד adv. *apart, separate.*

בְּדַד p.n. of the father of Hadad king of Edom.

בְּדֵי same as בְּ; see דַּי.

בְּדֵיָה p.n. of a man.

בָּדַל Niph. *was separated;* with לְ it signifies, *unto something;* with מִן, *from something;* with אֵל, *he separated himself unto one thing alone.* Hiph. הִבְדִּיל I. *made, caused division,* const. with מִן and מֵעַל—II. *distinguished, divided,* with בֵּין...לְ, בֵּין, בֵּין...לְבֵין, וּבֵין.—III. *designed,* with לְ.

בְּדַל m., בְּדַל אֹזֶן *portion of the ear,* Amos 3:12.

בְּדִיל m., *tin;* אֶבֶן הַבְּדִיל *the weight at the plumb-line, the plummet.*

מִבְדָּלוֹת f. pl., *separations, separate places,* Jos. 16:9.

בְּדֹלַח m. *bdellium,* a translucent and odoriferous gum; according to Lee, a precious stone, either *the crystal* or *the beryl,* Gen. 2:12, Num. 11:7.

בְּדָן p.n.—I. of a judge, perhaps the same as בָּרָק, 1 Sam. 12:11.—II. of another man, 1 Chron. 7:17.

בָּדַק (Arab. *tear, rend*); inf. בְּדוֹק

*repairing injury, decay,* 2 Chron. 34:10.

בֶּדֶק *injury, decay in a building;* with suff. בִּדְקֶךָ.

בִּדְקַר p. n. of a man.

בְּדַר Ch. same as Heb. בָּזַר; Pa. imper. בַּדַּרוּ *sprinkle.*

בָּהָה (Arab. *void*).

בֹּהוּ m., *emptiness, destitution.*

בַּהַט m., *marble,* Est. 1:6.

בָּהַל Niph. נִבְהַל.—I. *was terrified, astonished.*—II. *cast down, ruined,* with לְ *at,* מ *from.* Pi. בִּהֵל.—I. *cause to hurry, hasten.*—II. *astonish, confound, ruin;* fut. יְבַהֵל. Pu. part. מְבֹהָל *hurried, gotten too speedily.* Hiph. הִבְהִיל same as Pihel.

בְּהַל Ch., Pa. *affrighted.* Ithp. part. *alarmed.*

בֶּהָלָה f., *fear, terror, ruin;* pl. בֶּהָלוֹת.

בְּהִילוּ f. Ch., *hurry, haste,* Ezr. 4:23.

הִתְבַּהֲלָה f. Ch., *haste.*

בָּהַם root not used; (Arab. *was dumb*).

בְּהֵמָה f. (const. בֶּהֱמַת; with suff. בְּהֶמְתְּךָ).—I. *cattle.*—II. *wild beast,* בֶּהֱמַת יַעַר, הָאָרֶץ, הַשָּׂדֶה *wild beasts;* pl. בְּהֵמוֹת; const. בַּהֲמוֹת, Job 40:15, name of some stupendous quadruped.

בֹּהֶן m.—I. *the thumb.*—II. *the great toe;* pl. בְּהֹנוֹת.

בֹּהַן (*thumb*), p.n. of a son of Reuben; אֶבֶן בֹּהַן p. n. of a place in the tribe of Judah.

בָּהַק root not used; (Arab. *was shining*).

בֹּהַק m., LXX. ἀλφός, *a white scurf, cicatrix on the skin,* Lev. 13:39.

בָּהַר root not used; Ch. *he shone.*

בָּהִיר m., *breaking through the clouds* (of light), Job 37:21.

בַּהֶרֶת f., *the white spot covered with hair which was the sure symptom of leprosy;* pl. בֶּהָרֹת, Lev. c. 13

בֶּהָרֵן for בְּהֵהָרֵן Niph. inf. with the pref. בְּ from הרן.

בְּהַשַּׁמָּה for בְּהַשַּׁמָּה Hoph. inf. with suff. and pref. from שמם.

בּוֹא (fut. יָבֹא, יָבוֹא; part. pl. בָּאִים, בָּאֵי), *entered, came or went in,* to, for, &c., with לְ, בְּ, אֶל; יָצָא וּבָא same as הָלַךְ, *he went in and out,* i. e. *he lived familiarly;* with בּוֹא לִפְנֵי הָעָם *to go before, lead the people;* בּוֹא בְרִית *he entered into covenant;* בּוֹא אֶל אִשָּׁה with *had connection with a woman;* בָּאָה שֶׁמֶשׁ *the sun was setting;* const. also with עַד, עַל, לְ, אֶל; בּוֹא בַיָּמִים *advanced in years;* with אֵת, עִם *went with, had intercourse with,* Ps. 26:4, Pro. 22:24. Hiph. הֵבִיא (with suff. הֱבִיאוֹ; imper. הָבִיא, הָבֵא; fut. יָבִיא, וַיָּבֵא) *caused, made, induced to enter, come in;* with עַל, לְ, אֶל. Hoph. הוּבָא *brought in.*

בָּאָה f., *entrance.*

מָבוֹא m., *entrance, porch;* מְבוֹא הַשֶּׁמֶשׁ *place of sunset.* Pl. מְבוֹאִים, const. מְבוֹאֵי and מְבֹאוֹת.

מוֹבָא m., *entrance,* 2 Sa. 3:25, Ez. 43:11.

תְּבוּאָה f.—I. *income.*—II. *store.*—III. *profit.*—IV. *produce;* pl. תְּבוּאוֹת

תְּבוּאָה f., Job 22:21; תְּבוּאָתְךָ from בּוֹא, fut. Kal with ה parag.

בּוּב Niph. part. נָבוּב.—I. proud, insolent, Job 11:12.—II. hollow.

בָּבָה f., apple of the eye, pupil; בָּבַת עַיִן pupil, Zec. 2:12.

בּוּז (fut. יָבוּז), despised, neglected; with ל comp. בזה בזון.

בּוּז m.—I. contempt.—II. p. n. of a brother of Abraham, and of the nation he founded in Arabia Deserta; בּוּזִי a Buzite.—III. p. n. of a man, 1 Chron. 5:14.

בּוּזָה f., contempt, contemptible thing.

בָּנִי p. n. of a man.

בּוּךְ Niph. נָבוֹךְ confused, perplexed, Ex. 14:3, Est. 3:15.

מְבוּכָה f., confusion, perplexity, Isa. 22:5; Mic. 7:4.

בּוֹכִיה Kal, part. from בכה.

בּוּל increase, same as יְבוּל; see יבל.

בּוּן and בִּין.—I. distinguished, discerned.—II. perceived, understood, with בְּ, עַל, אֶל, לְ; part. בָּנִים prudent persons; pret. בַּנְתָּ בָּן and בִּינוֹתִי, בִּין; fut. יָבִין. Niph. נָבוֹן became discerning; part. נָבוֹן wise; נָבוֹן דָּבָר wise in word, eloquent. Pil. בּוֹנֵן made him discerning, Deu. 32:10. Hiph. הֵבִין. — I. taught, explained, with לְ, אֶל, בְּ.—II. understood, was wise; part. מֵבִין skilful, learned; imper. הָבֵן and הָבִין; with suff. הֲבִינֵנִי fut. יָבִין, וַיָּבֶן. Hith. הִתְבּוֹנֵן same as Niph.; with עַד, בְּ, אֶל.

בֵּין const. בֵּין s.—I. interval, midst; dual בֵּינַיִם אִישׁ man of two intervals, i. e. between the two armies,

1 Sam. 17:4.—II. prep. between among, within; בֵּין, לְ...בֵּין...וּבֵין, בֵּין...לְבֵין between...and (whether... or, Lev. 27:12); with suff. בֵּינִי, בֵּינְךָ; with pause בֵּינֶךָ, בֵּינוֹ; with suff. pl. בֵּינֵיכֶם, בֵּנֵינוּ and בֵּינֵינוּ, בֵּינֶיךָ; fem. בֵּינֵיהֶם; אֶל־בֵּין־בֵּינוֹתָם בֵּינוֹתֵינוּ among; אֶל־בֵּנוֹת לְ the same; מִבֵּין from between; מִבֵּינוֹת the same; עַל־בֵּין up among; לְ בְּבֵין in the midst.

בֵּין Ch., among; pl. with suff. בֵּינֵיהוֹן.

בִּינָה f., intelligence, discernment, prudence; Ch. the same.

תָּבוּן m., תְּבוּנָה f., understanding, prudence; pl. תְּבוּנוֹת.

בּוּנָה (intelligence), p. n. of a man.

בּוּנִּי from בָּנָה, p. n. of a man.

בּוּס (fut. יָבוּס and יָבֻס; part. pl. בּוֹסִים) trampled, trod upon, despised. Pil. בּוֹסֵם trod down (profaned holy place). Hoph. part. מוּבָס trodden down. Hith. part. f. מִתְבּוֹסֶסֶת become trodden down, Eze. 16:6, 22.

מְבוּסָה f., treading upon.

תְּבוּסָה f., destruction, 2 Chron. 22:7.

בּוּעַ root not used; Ch. was boiling.

אֲבַעְבֻּעוֹת f. pl., spots on the skin.

בּוּץ root not used; (Arab. fine linen).

בּוּץ, בֵּץ m., βύσσος, linen, fine linen

בֵּיץ m., or בֵּיצָה f., pl. בֵּיצִים eggs.

בּוֹצֵץ (shining), p. n. of a rock near Gibeah.

בּוּק root not used; (Arab. heavy rain see בקק).

בּוּקָה f., emptiness, devastation, Neh 2:11.

מְבוּקָה f., emptiness; the same.

בּוֹר well, same as בְּאֵר; see בָּאַר

בּוּר (same as בָּרַר), *explored.*

בּוֹשׁ (pret. בּוֹשׁ, בּוֹשׁוּ, בֹּשְׁתְּ, בּשְׁנוּ; fut. יֵבוֹשׁ (אֵבוֹשׁ) *ashamed, put to shame, blushed,* with מִן and לְ; עַד־בּוֹשׁ *until they were ashamed.* Pil. בּוֹשֵׁשׁ *put to a stand, delayed,* Jud. 5.28, Ex. 32:30. Hiph. הֵבִישׁ and הוֹבִישׁ (from cognate יָבֵשׁ) *brought to shame, confusion;* part. מֵבִישׁ *bringing, causing shame, wicked.* Hith. הִתְבֹּשֵׁשׁ *become ashamed,* Gen. 2:25.

בּוּשָׁה f., *shame, ignominy.*

בָּשְׁנָה f., the same, Hos. 10:6.

בֹּשֶׁת f.—I. *shame, blushing.*—II. *ignominy.*—III. *an idol.*

מַבֻשִׁים m., pl. מְבֻשִׁים *secret parts,* Deu. 25:11.

בֹּשְׁכֶם Po. inf. with suff. from בֹּשׁ

בּוּת Ch.; בָּת *passed the night,* Dan. 6:19.

בַּיִת m. (const. בֵּית; with suff. בֵּיתְךָ, בֵּיתוֹ; pl. בָּתִּים, const. בָּתֵּי), *habitation.*—I. *temple* of God or idols. —II. *palace.*—III. *house, tent, cave;* אֲשֶׁר עַל בַּיִת *mayor of the palace;* בֶּן יָלִיד *or, household-slave).*—IV. *sepulchre.*—V. *receptacle* of anything; בָּתֵּי נֶפֶשׁ *perfume boxes,* Isa. 3:20.—VI. *family, race.* With ה parag. בַּיְתָה, const. בֵּיתָה, adv. *inwards;* מִבַּיִת, מִבֵּית לְ, בֵּית לְ *within;* מִבַּיְתָה לְ, לְמִבֵּית לְ *within.*

בַּיִת m. Ch., *house, palace, temple.*

בִּיתָן m., *great house, palace,* Est. 1: 5; 7: 7, 8.

The p.n. of many towns are compounds of בַּיִת; בֵּית אָוֶן in the

tribe of Benjamin; בֵּית־אֵל between Jerusalem and Sichem; בֵּית הָאֱלִי *a Bethelite;* ב׳ אֵצֶל in Samaria; ב׳ אַרְבֵּאל *Arbela* in Galilee; בַּעַל מְעוֹן, ב׳ בַּעַל מְעוֹן and בֵּית מְעוֹן in the tribe of Reuben; ב׳ בָּרָה (*ferry-house*) Βηθαβαρά, near Jordan; ב׳ בִּרְאִי in the tribe of Simeon; ב׳ גָּדֵר in the tribe of Judah; ב׳ הַגִּלְגָּל same as גָּלְגָּל, see גָּלָל; ב׳ גָּמוּל (see גְּמָל) in the land of Moab; ב׳ דָּגוֹן, ב׳ דִּבְלָתַיִם see דִּבְלָתַיִם (*temple of Dagon*), in the tribe of Judah, also in the tribe of Asher; ב׳ הָרָם and הָרָן in the tribe of Gad; ב׳ חָגְלָה (*place of partridges*), town of the Benjamites in the tribe of Judah; ב׳ חָנָן (*house of mercy*), in the tribe of Judah or Dan; ב חוֹרוֹן two towns in the tribe of Ephraim; ב׳ הַיְשִׁימוֹת town of the Reubenites on the shore of the Red Sea; ב׳ כַּר a strong place of the Philistines in the tribe of Judah; ב׳ הַכֶּרֶם (*house of vineyards*), in the tribe of Judah; ב׳ לְבָאוֹת (*place of lionesses*), in the tribe of Simeon; ב׳ לֶחֶם (*house of bread*) Βηθλεὲμ, in the tribe of Judah, see אֶפְרָתָה; another town in the tribe of Zebulun; ב׳ הַלַּחְמִי *a Bethlehemite;* ב׳ מִלּוֹא; ב׳ לְעַפְרָה, see עָפְרָה; ב׳ מַעֲכָה see מִלּוֹא a town at the foot of Hermon; ב׳ הַמֶּרְחָק (from רָחַק) on the banks of Kedron; ב׳ הַמַּרְכָּבוֹת (*house of chariots*), in the tribe of Simeon; ב׳ נִמְרָה (*place of pure water*) in the tribe of Gad; עֶרֶן 'ב (plea-sant place), a town near Damascus; עַזְמָוֶת 'ב see עַזְמָוֶת 'ב הָעֵמֶק (house of the valley), in the tribe of Asher; עֲנוֹת 'ב (place of echo), in the tribe of Judah; עֲנָת 'ב (the same), in the tribe of Naphtali; עֵקֶד הָרֹעִים 'ב (place where shepherds bind their sheep), near Samaria; הָעֲרָבָה 'ב (place in the desert), on the confines of Judah and Benjamin; פֶּלֶט 'ב (place of flight), in the tribe of Judah; פְּעוֹר 'ב (see פְּעוֹר), in the land of Moab, not far from Jordan; פָּצֵץ 'ב (place of dispersion), in the tribe of Issachar; צוּר 'ב (house of the rock), in the mountains of Judah; רְחֹב 'ב (see רְחֹב, אֲרָם), a city of Syria; שָׁן 'ב, שֵׁאָן 'ב (house of sleep), in the tribe of Manasseh, beyond Jordan; הַשִּׁטָּה 'ב (see שִׁטָּה), a town on Jordan; שֶׁמֶשׁ 'ב (house of the sun), name of several towns: a. of the Levites in the tribe of Judah; בֵּית־הַשִּׁמְשִׁי inhabitant of....; β. in the tribe of Naphtali; γ. in the tribe of Issachar or Zebulon; δ. same as אוֹן in Egypt; תַּפּוּחַ 'ב, תּוֹנַרְמָה 'ב, see תִּנְרְמָה (place of apple trees), in the tribe of Judah.

בַּז from בָּזוּ for בָּז, Zec. 4:10; see בּוּז. בָּז בְּזָה spoiled; see בזז.

בָּזָא, בְּזָא Isa. 18:2, have spoiled.

בָּזָה same as בּוּז despised, spurned; const. with עַל, לְ. Niph. part. נִבְזָה despised; pl. נִבְזִים. Hiph. inf. הַבְזוֹת make despised, Est. 1:17.

בָּזֹה inf., despised, Isa. 49:7.

בִּזָּיוֹן m., great contempt, Est. 1:18.

בִּזְיוֹתְיָה (despised of the Lord), p. n. of a town in the tribe of Judah.

נִבְזֶה contemptible, 1 Sa. 15:9.

בָּזַז took the spoil or prey; part. pl. בֹּזְזִים spoilers; pret. pl. בְּזָזְנוּ, בָּזֹזוּ and בַּזּוֹנוּ; inf. בֹּז; fut. יָבֹזּוּ. Niph. נָבֹז, and Pu. בֻּזַּז were spoiled, Jer. 50:37.

בַּז m. (with suff. בִּזָּה), spoil; הָיָה לְבַז was for a spoil; נָתַן לְבַז gave for a spoil.

בִּזָּה f., booty.

בָּזָק m., lightning, Eze. 1:14.

בֶּזֶק p. n. of a town to the southward of Bethshan, Βεζέκ.

בָּזַר (fut. יָבְזֹר), dispersed, Dan. 11:24; Pi. בִּזַּר the same, Ps. 68:31.

בִּזְתָא p. n. of a eunuch of Ahasuerus.

בָּחַל was greedy, niggard; with בְּ, Zec. 11:8. Pu. part. f. מְבֹחֶלֶת coveted, gotten by covetousness, Pro. 20:21.

בָּחַן (imper. בְּחַן; with suff. בְּחָנֵנִי; fut. יִבְחָן).—I. tried, tested (metals with fire).—II. tried (men with affliction).—III. tried (God.... the heart). Niph. be tried.

בֹּחַן m., examination, trial, Isa. 28:16, Eze. 21:18.

בַּחַן m., watch-tower, Isa. 32:14.

בָּחוֹן m., mound, watch-tower, Isa. 23:14.

בָּחוּן m., trial, experiment.

בָּחַר (fut. יִבְחַר), chose; with בְּ, לְ, עַל; בָּחַר לוֹ he chose for himself; with מִן preferred; part. בָּחוּר

*chosen, excellent.* Niph. *chosen;*
part. נִבְחָר *elect, excellent;* with
מִן *better.*

בָּחִיר m., *elect;* (ἐκλεκτὸς τοῦ Θεοῦ
*the elect of God*).

בָּחוּר m., *a youth;* pl. בַּחוּרִים *youths,*
liable to be chosen (balloted) for
military service.

בְּחוּרִים m. pl., *youth.*

בְּחוּרוֹת f. pl., the same.

בַּחֻרִים p. n. of a town in the tribe of
Benjamin; בַּחֲרוּמִי and בָּרְחֻמִי
an inhabitant of Bachurim.

מִבְחָר, מִבְצָר m.—I. *the choice, the
best.*—II. p. n. of a man.

מִבְחוֹר m., the same, 2 Ki. 3:19; 19:23.

בָּטָא and בָּטָה *speaks wrongfully,
falsely,* Pro. 12:18; part. בּוֹטֶה.
Pi. בִּטֵּא *spake falsely.*

מִבְטָא m., *rashness in speaking;*
מ' שְׂפָתָיִם, Nu. 30:7,9.

בָּטַח (inf. בְּטוֹחַ; with suff. בִּטְחֲךָ;
imper. בְּטַח; fut. יִבְטַח; pl. f.
תִּבְטַחְנָה), *trusted in, to, on;* with
בְּ, אֶל, לְ, עַל, Job 6:20; impers.
*was for a confidence;* part. בָּטוּחַ
*trusted, was confident, incautious;*
part. בּוֹטֵחַ *secure, confiding.* Hiph.
הִבְטִיחַ *made to confide, trust;* with
אֶל and עַל.

בֶּטַח m., *confidence, security;* בֶּטַח and
לָבֶטַח adv. *confidently, securely,
safely.*

בֶּטַח p.n. of a town of Aram Zobah,
2 Sam. 8:8.

בִּטְחָה f., *confidence,* Isa. 30:15.

בִּטָּחוֹן m., the same, Isa. 36:4, Ecc. 9:4.

בַּטֻּחָה f., the same; pl. בַּטֻּחוֹת, Job
12:6.

מִבְטָח m. (with suff. מִבְטָחִי, מִבְטַחֲךָ;
pl. מִבְטַחִים; (מִבְטַחִים), *trust, confidence;* metonym. *he in whom
trust is reposed.*

אַבְטִיחִים see טבח.

בָּטֵל *cease, fail,* Ecc. 12:3.

בְּטֵל Ch., *ceased,* Ezr. 4:24. Pa.
בַּטֵּל *caused to cease, hindered.*

בֶּטֶן f. (with suff. בִּטְנִי).—I. *belly.*—
II. *womb;* פְּרִי בֶטֶן *fruit of the
womb, offspring;* מִבֶּטֶן, מִן־הַבֶּטֶן,
מִבֶּטֶן אִמִּי ἐκ γαστρὸς, the same.—
III. ἡ κοιλία *the inner man, seat of
thought, feelings.*—IV. the project-
ing part of the chapter of a column, 1 Ki. 7:20.—V. p.n. of a
town in the tribe of Asher.

בָּטְנִים m. pl., *nuts,* Gen. 43:11. Pistachia vera (Lin.), a tree abounding in Palestine, but unknown in
Egypt.

בְּטֹנִים p. n. of a town in the tribe of
Gad.

בִּי pa. of supplication, (always with
אֲדֹנָי or אֲדֹנָי), *Lord, I pray thee;
ah, Lord!*

בִּינָה, בֵּן, בִּין *understand;* see בּוּן.

בֵּיצִים *eggs,* see בּוּץ.

בִּיקְרוֹתַיִךְ f. pl., with suff., pref., and
dag. euphon. see יָקַר.

בַּיִר *well;* same as בְּאֵר.

בִּירָה f.—I. *palace.*—II. *the temple.*

בִּירָה f. Ch., the same.

בִּירָנִיּוֹת f. pl., *palaces;* sing. never
occurs.

בַּיִת, בֵּיתָן, *house, &c.;* see בּוּת

בָּכָה (fut. יֵבְךְּ, יִבְכֶּה; inf. בְּכוֹ and
בְּכֹה).—I. *wept.* — II. *mourned;*

with אֶת, בְּ, עַל, לְ, אֶל. Pi. *deplored*, with עַל.

בְּכָא m.—I. *the Baka shrub, Amyris Gileadensis* (Linn.); pl. בְּכָאִים —II. עֵמֶק הַבָּכָא (*valley of weeping*), p. n. of a valley in Palestine, Ps. 84:7.

בֶּכֶה m., *weeping*, Eze. 10:1.

בְּכֹ' inf. abs. from בכה.

בְּכִית and בְּכוּת f., *weeping*, Gen. 50:4.

בְּכִי m. (with pause בֶּכִי; with suff. בִּכְיִי).—I. *weeping.*—II. *dropping of water in wells*, Job. 28:11.

בֹּכִים p. n. of a town near Gilgal.

בָּכַר Kal, root not used; (Arab. *early*). Pi. בִּכֵּר.—I. *brought forth early fruits.*—II. *was the first-born*, Deu. 21:16. Pu. passive of Pi., Lev. 27:26. Hiph. *brought forth her first-born*, Jer. 4:13.

בְּכוֹר m., *first-born* בְּכֹרוֹת pl., *the first-born of brutes*, Gen. 4:4, Deu. 12:17. Trop. בְּכוֹר מָוֶת *the worm*, Job 18:13; בְּכוֹרֵי דַלִּים *the first-born of the poor, the poorest.*

בְּכוֹרָה f., *primogeniture.*

בְּכוֹרַת p. n. of a man, 1 Sa. 9:1.

בְּכִירָה f., *eldest, first-born daughter.*

בֵּכְרוּ (same as בֵּכֶר הוּא), p. n. of a man.

בִּכְרִי (*my first-born*), p. n. of a man.

בֶּכֶר m., *a young camel*, Isa. 60:6; f. בִּכְרָה *a young she-camel*, Jer. 2:23.

בֶּכֶר, בְּכִי p. n.—I. of a son of Ephraim.—II. of a son of Benjamin.

בִּכּוּר m., pl. בִּכֻּרִים and בִּכּוּרִים *first-fruits*; יוֹם הַבִּכּוּרִים *feast of first-fruits, Pentecost*, Nu. 28:26.

תְּאֵנֵי בַכּוּרוֹת f., *the early fig*; בַּכּוּרָה *early figs.*

בְּכוֹרַת p. n. of a man.

בַּל; see בלה.

בֵּל *Bel*, same as בַּעַל.

בַּלָּא *destroy*; see בָּלָה.

בֵּלְאדָן (*whose lord is Baal*), p. n. of a king of Babylon; see מְרֹדַךְ.

בָּלַג Kal, root not used (Arab. *opened, shone*).—Hiph. הִבְלִיג with עַל I. *made to rise*, Am. 5:9.—II. *made glad*, Ps. 39:14.

בִּלְגָּה (*joy*), p. n. of a priest.

מַבְלִיגִית f., *exhilaration*, Jer. 8:18.

בִּלְדַּד p. n. of one of Job's friends.

בָּלָה (fut. יִבְלֶה).—I. *grew old.*—II. *perished*; with מֵעַל *worn off*, spoken of clothes. Pi. בִּלָּה *made cold.*

בְּלָא Ch. form. Pa. *destroy, make to disappear*, Dan. 7:25; see בלה Pi.

בָּלֶה m., בָּלָה f., *old, effete, worn out*, Jos. 9:4,5, Eze. 23:43.

בָּלָה p. n. of a city.

בְּלֹאִים and בְּלוֹיִם m. pl., *old, worn*, Jer. 38:11,12.

בְּלוֹ m. Ch., *custom, tax.*

תַּבְלִית f., *destruction*, Isa. 10:25.

בָּל m. Ch., *the heart, mind*, Dan. 6:15.

בַּל (*wanting*); adv., *not, nothing.*

בְּלִי I. *loss, destruction*, Isa. 38:17.—II. *wanting, without* (written בִּבְלִי and בְּלִי); בְּ רַעַת *without knowledge*; לְבְלִי *without*; מִבְּלִי *from want of.*—III. adv., same as לֹא *not*; הֲמִבְּלִי אֵין *is it not because there is not?* מִבְּלִי אֲשֶׁר לֹא *excepting that not*, Ecc. 3:11; עַד בְּלִי *until the ceasing of*, Mal. 3: 10; עַל בְּלִי *because not*, Gen. 31:20

בְּלִימָה (compounded of בְּלִי and מָה), *nothing*, Job 26:7.

בְּלִיַּעַל (compounded of בְּלִי and יַעַל). —I. *uselessness.*— II. *wickedness, sin;* אִישׁ בְּ׳ *a wicked man.*—III. *injury, destruction;* נַחֲלֵי בְּ׳ *destructive torrents,* i.e. overwhelming oppressions, Ps. 18:5.

בַּלְעֲדֵי and בִּלְעֲדֵי (compounded of בַּל and עֲדֵי).—I. *besides, without.*—II. *not concerning, nothing to;* בִּלְעֲדָי *nothing to me;* מִבַּלְעֲדֵי the same.

בְּלִי *consumption;* used only with the parag. jod, בִּלְתִּי.—I. *without.* —II. *besides, except.*—III. adv., *not;* with suff. בִּלְתִּי *besides me,* בִּלְתְּךָ *besides thee;* לְבִלְתִּי *not, that it may not,* with a verb; מִבִּלְתִּי with inf., *because it is not;* עַד־בִּלְתִּי *until it is not.*

בָּלָה. Pi. בִּלָּה same as בִּהֵל, *harassing,* Ezr. 4:4.

בַּלָּהָה f.—I. *terror.*—II. *calamity.*

בִּלְהָה p.n.—I. of the handmaid of Rachel.—II. of a town in the tribe of Simeon.

בִּלְהָן p. n. of a man.

בְּלוֹ, בְּלוֹאִים; see בָּלָה.

בֵּלְטְשַׁאצַּר p.n., Chaldee name of Daniel.

בְּלִיַּעַל, בְּלִימָה ,בַּל; see בָּלָה.

בָּלַל (fut. יָבֹל).—I. *suffused,* Ps. 92:3. —II. *confounded,* const. with בְּ. Hith. *become confounded,* Hos. 7: 8, with בְּ.—III. *from* בְּלִיל; *gave fodder,* Jud. 19:21.— IV. *fade, wither,* Isa. 64:5.

בְּלִיל m., *fodder for cattle,* lit. *mixture.*

תֶּבֶל m., *unnatural intercourse,* Lev. 18:23, 20:12.

תְּבַלֻּל m., *a disease in the eye,* Lev. 21:20; תְּ׳ בְּעֵינוֹ *confused* (i. e. indistinct for vision) *in his eye.*

בָּלַם *bound, bridled,* Ps. 32:8.

בָּלַס *pluck figs,* Am. 7:14.

בָּלַע I. *swallowed.* — II. *destroyed* · עַד־בִּלְעִי רֻקִּי *untii I have swallowed my spittle;* i. e. in a moment, Job 7:19. Niph. *be swallowed up, lost;* with הַיִן מִן *immersed in wine,* Isa. 28:7. Pi. as Kal; כְּבַלַּע *as in a moment).* Pu. *was swallowed up.* Hith. as Niph., Ps. 107:27.

בֶּלַע m.—I. *swallowing up.*—II. *destruction;* with suff. בִּלְעוֹ.—III. p.n. of a town on the Dead Sea.—IV. of a man; בַּלְעִי m., *inhabitant of Bela.*

בַּלְעֲדֵי, בִּלְעֲדֵי *besides;* see בָּלָה.

בִּלְעָם (*stranger*).—I. p. n. of the prophet Balaam.—II. same as יִבְלְעָם.

בָּלַק *make waste,* Isa. 24:1. Pu. part. f. מְבֻלָּקָה, *desolate,* Nah. 2:11.

בָּלָק p.n. of a king of Moab.

בֵּלְאשַׁצַּר and בֵּלְשַׁאצַּר p.n. of the last king of the Chaldees (Nabonnedus or Labynetus).

בִּלְשָׁן p.n of a man.

בִּלְתִּי *not;* see בֶּלֶת under בָּלָה.

בָּמָה f. (pl. בָּמוֹת, const. בָּמֳתֵי [בָּמוֹתֵי Kri] with suff. בָּמוֹתֶיךָ (בָּמֳתֵי). —I. *high place for idolatrous worship;* רָכַב עַל בָּמֳתֵי אָרֶץ *he rode upon the high places of the earth,* i.e. he conquered. — II. *places for true worship.*—III. *fortresses, places of strength;* דָּרַךְ עַל בָּ׳ *he rode upon the high places,* i. e. he

subdued.—IV. *waves of the sea,*
Job 9:8.—V. *clouds,* Isa. 14:14.
בָּתֵּי הַבָּמוֹת same as בָּמוֹת *idol
temples;* בַּהֲגֵי הַבָּמוֹת *idolatrous
priests.*

בָּמוֹת and בַּעַל בָּמוֹת p.n. of a town
in Moab on the Arnon.

בִּמְהָל (*son of circumcision*), p.n. of a m.

בְּמוֹ same as בְּ; see מָה, מוֹ.

בָּמָתִי pl. const. from בָּמָה.

בָּנָה (inf. בְּנֹה; const. בְּנוֹת; fut. יִבְנֶה
וַיִּבֶן).—I. *built, really.*—II. *built,*
metaphorically, i. e. raised, increased in family; const. with
עַל, בְּ, לְ, אֶת־דָּהָר בְּ *he built
upon the hill,* 1 Ki. 16:24; בְּ
בַּיִת לְ *he raised up a house to.*
—Niph. I. *was built.*—II. *was raised
up,* as a house, family.

בְּנָא בְּנָה Ch., *built.* Ithp. *was built.*

בֵּן m. (const. בֶּן, sometimes בֶּן; with
suff. בִּנְךָ, בְּנוֹ, בְּנִי; pl. בָּנִים, בְּנֵי,
בְּנֵי).—I. *son*; בְּנֵי בָנִים *grandsons, posterity*; בְּנֵי עַמּוֹן *Ammonites*; אִישׁ
מִבְּנֵי יִשְׂרָאֵל *an Israelite*; בְּנֵי צִיּוֹן
*inhabitants of Zion*; בְּנֵי נְבִיאִים
*sons,* i. e. *disciples of the prophets.*—
II. used metaphorically; בֶּן־עַוְלָה
*son of perverseness,* i. e. perverse
person; בֶּן־מָוֶת *son of death,* i.e.
a person guilty of a capital crime;
בֶּן־קֶשֶׁת *son of the bow,* i.e. arrow,
Job 41:20.—III. used with numerals; בֶּן־שְׁמוֹנִים שָׁנָה *one eighty
years old, octogenarian*; בֶּן־שָׁנָה
*yearling.*—IV. *the young of brutes*;
בֶּן־יוֹנָה *young dove.*—V. *young
shoots of trees*; בֶּן־פֹּרָת *twig of a
fruit tree.*

בֵּן p. n. of a Levite, 1 Chron. 15:18.

בֵּן m. Ch., *son*; pl. בְּנִין, בְּנֵי.

בֶּן־אוֹנִי (*son of my sorrow*), p.n. given
to Benjamin by his mother.

בֶּן־הֲדַד p.n. of the kings of Damascus.

בֶּן־גֻּבִּי p. n. of a man.

בֶּן־חַיִל (*strong*), p. n. of a man.

בֶּן־חָנָן (*son of mercy*), p. n. of a man.

בָּנִי (*built up*), p. n. of a man.

בֻּנִּי (*built up*), p. n. of two men.

בְּנֵי בְרַק p. n. of a town in the tribe
of Dan.

בְּנֵי יַעֲקַן p.n. of a place.

בִּנְיָה f., *building*, Eze. 41:13.

בְּנָיָה (*built up of God*), p.n. of a man.

בְּנָיָהוּ the same.

בִּנְיָמִין (*son of my right hand*), p. n.,
Benjamin, the son of Jacob;
אִישׁ־יְמִינִי, בֶּן־הַיְמִינִי, בֶּן־יְמִינִי and
יְמִינִי a Benjamite; pl. בְּנֵי יְמִינִי;
אֶרֶץ־יְמִינִי *land of the Benjamites.*

בֶּן־יָמִין I. same as בִּנְיָמִין.—II. p. n.
of a man, 1 Sa. 9:1.

בִּנְיָן m., *building,* Eze. 40:5.

בְּנִינוּ (*our son*), p.n. of a man.

בָּנוּ for בָּאנוּ Kal pret. pl. 1. pers., from
בּוֹא.

בִּנֹתֶךָ for בְּנוֹתְךָ Kal inf. with suff.,
from בנה.

בַּת f. (with suff. בִּתִּי; pl. בָּנוֹת; const.
בְּנוֹת).—I. *daughter.*—II. *niece.*—
III. the female inhabitants of any
place; בְּנוֹת צִיּוֹן *the daughters of
Zion,* Isa. 3:17; בְּנוֹת יִשְׂרָאֵל
*daughters of Israel.*—IV. used for
the inhabitants of any place col-
ectively; בַּת צֹר *the Tyrians,* Ps.
15:12; בַּת מִצְרַיִם *the Egyptians.*
—V. בְּנוֹת הָעִיר smaller cities

dependent upon larger ones. —VI.
used with numerals in the age of
women: בַּת תִּשְׁעִים שָׁנָה a woman
of ninety (see בֶּן III.).—VII. used
metaph.: בְּנוֹת הַשִּׁיר daughters of
song, i.e. singers; בַּת עַיִן pupil of
the eye (see בֶּן II.).—VIII. applied
to the produce of animals, trees, or
places; בַּת הַיַּעֲנָה female ostrich, &c.

בַּת f. Ch., the same; pl. בָּתִּין.

בַּת־רַבִּים (daughter of multitudes),
p. n. of the gate of Heshbon.

בַּת־שֶׁבַע (daughter of an oath), p. n.
of the wife of Uriah.

בַּת־שׁוּעַ the same.

מִבְנֶה m., building, Eze. 40:2.

תַּבְנִית f.—I. model, πρωτότυπον.—II.
form, resemblance.—III. building.

בָּנַט, Pers. bando; Sansc. bandha;
Eng. band.

אַבְנֵט m., a girdle (a foreign word).

בְּנַס Ch., was angry, Dan. 2:12.

בְּנֵא, בְּנָעָה p. n. of a man.

בְּסוֹדְיָה (in the council of the Lord),
p. n. of a man.

בְּסַי p. n. of a man.

בָּסַר root not used; (Arab. unripe date).

בֶּסֶר m., unripe, sour grape, Job 15:33.
בֹּסֶר m., the same.

בָּעָא see בעה.

בָּעַד root not used; (Arab. after).

בַּעַד prep., after, behind, as to time
or place; with suff. בַּעֲדִי and בַּעֲדֵנִי,
בַּעַדְךָ, בַּעֲדוֹ, בַּעֲדֵנוּ and בַּעֲדֵינוּ,
בַּעַדְכֶם; מִבַּעַד לְ behind, Cant.
4:1, &c.

בָּעָה I. pressed forward, ran over, Isa.
64:1.—II. requested, importuned;

fut. pl. תִּבְעָיוּן; imp. pl. בְּעָיוּ. Niph
—I. become obtruded, swelled out
Isa. 30:13.—II. being sought, Obad
v. 6.

בְּעָה and בְּעָא Ch., requested, prayed
with מִן and מִן קֳדָם.

בָּעוּ f. Ch., petition, Dan. 6:8, 14.

בְּעִי m., prayer, Job 30:24.

בָּעוֹן habitation; same as מָעוֹן.

בְּעוֹר p. n. of the father of Balaam.

בֹּעַז p. n.—I. the husband of Ruth.—
II. name of one of the pillars in
Solomon's temple.

בָּעַט I. trample upon, kick at: hence,
—II. despise, reject.

בְּעִי building; see בָּעָה.

בְּעָיוּ Kal imper. pl. with pause, from
בעה.

בְּעִיר beast; see בער.

בָּעַל I. possess, govern.—II. marry a
wife; part. pl. majest. בְּעָלַיִךְ thy
husband; בְּעֻלָה and בְּעֻלַת־בַּעַל
married. — III. (with בְּ) despised,
Jer. 3:14; 31:32. Niph. be married

בַּעַל m. (suff. בַּעֲלָה, בַּעֲלִי,
בַּעֲלֵיהֶם)
—I. lord.—II. husband.—III. owner,
possessor, that wherein any one
excels; בַּעַל הַחֲלֹמוֹת בְּ dreamer; בַּעֲלֵי
שְׁכֶם the Shechemites, &c.; pl.
בְּעָלִים (const. בַּעֲלֵי; with suff. בְּעָלָיו,
בְּעָלֶיהָ) often used of one only.—
IV. הַבַּעַל p. n., Baal, name of a
Phenician god; הַבְּעָלִים statues of
Baal.—V. p. n. of a man.—VI.
compounded in the names of many
towns: בַּעַל גָּד a town on the
borders of Palestine, to the north;
בְּ בַּ׳ הֲמוֹן at the foot of Lebanon; בַּ׳
חָצוֹר in the tribe of Ephraim

ב' חָרְמָה one of the peaks of Mount Hermon; a town near it; ב' מְעוֹן and בֵּת מְעוֹן in the tribe of Reuben; ב' פְּרָצִים (place of slaughter) where the Philistines were routed by David; ב' צָפוֹן in Egypt; ב' שְׁלִשָׁה in Mount Ephraim; ב' תָּמָר (place of palms) not far from Gibeah; בַּעֲלֵי יְהוּדָה Jews.

בְּעֵל m. Ch., lord.

בַּעֲלָה f.—I. lady.—II. used collectively (like בַּת) a city.—III. p.n. of a city in the north of Judah; otherwise קִרְיַת־בַּעַל and קִרְיַת יְעָרִים.—IV. another city in Judah; otherwise בָּלָה and בִּלְהָה.

בַּעֲלַת p.n. of a city in the tribe of Dan.

בַּעֲלוֹת p.n. of a city in the tribe of Judah.

בַּעְלְיָדָע (whom Baal knows), same as אֶלְיָדָע

בְּעַלְיָה (in whom the Lord rules), p.n. of a man.

בַּעַל חָנָן (the Lord of grace), p.n. of a king of Edom.

בַּעֲלִים p.n. of a king of the Ammonites.

בַּעֲנָא (son of misery), p.n. of a man.

בַּעֲנָה (the same), p.n. of a man.

בָּעַר injure, consume.—I. by fire.—II. with anger.—III. burn.—IV. that which injures, is brutish (from בְּעִיר); part. בֹּעֲרִים cattle, beasts. Niph. become brutish. Pi. בִּעֵר.—I. injured, destroyed.—II. consumed with fire, with בְּ, מִן and אַחֲרֵי. Pu. part. f. מְבֹעֶרֶת burnt. Hiph. same as Pi.

בְּעִיר m.—I. beast, cattle generally.—II. beast of burden.

בַּעַר m., stupid, brutish.

בְּעֵרָה f., burning, Ex. 22:5.

בַּעֲרָא p.n. of a man.

תַּבְעֵרָה p.n. of a place in the desert.

בַּעֲשֵׂיָה (work of God), p.n. of a man.

בַּעְשָׁא p.n. of a king of Israel, son of Ahijah.

בְּעֶשְׁתְּרָה an idol; see עַשְׁתֹּרֶת.

בָּעַת Niph. נִבְעַת was terrified. Pi. בִּעֵת.—I. alarmed.—II. excited, came suddenly upon; fut. יְבַעֵת; part. f. with suff. מְבַעְתֶּךָ.

בְּעָתָה f., terror, Jer. 8:15; 14:19.

בִּעוּתִים m. pl., terrors, Ps. 88:17.

בֵּץ, בָּצָה mud; see בצץ.

בְּצֹאתָיו for בְּצֹאתָיו pl. with suff. from בִּצָּה or בֵּץ.

בְּצִי (same as בֵּסִי), p.n. of a man.

בָּצִיר vintage; see בצר.

בָּצָל m., onion, Nu. 11:5.

בַּצְלִית, בַּצְלוּת p.n. of a man.

בָּצַע I. cut off parts, pieces.—II. acquire gain. Pi. בִּצַּע I. cutting off (as the weaver his web from the loom): hence,—II. finish, complete.—III. acquired filthy lucre, Eze. 22:12.

בֶּצַע m. (with suff. בִּצְעָם).—I. gain.—II. filthy lucre; מַה־בֶּצַע what gain?

בָּצֵץ root not used; (Arab. run slowly).

בֹּץ m., mud, mire, Jer. 38:22.

בִּצָּה f., the same; pl. with suff. בְּצֹאתָיו for בְּצֹאתָיו.

בָּצֵק swelled (of the foot), Deu. 8:11, Neh. 9:21.

בֶּצֶק m., *dough* ( from its swelling in fermenting).

בָּצְקַת p. n. of a town in the tribe of Judah.

בָּצַר I. *cut, cropped off:* hence,—II. *pruned the vine.*— III. *gathered the vintage,* Ps. 76:13; part. בֹּצֵר *vintage-gatherer;* trop. *remorseless enemy;* part. בְּצוּרָה *inaccessible,* lit. *cut off from access;* בְּצֻרוֹת *hidden, incomprehensible,* Jer. 33:3. Niph. *cut off, prohibited,* with מִן. Pi. *fortified* (of cities).

בָּצִיר m., *vintage;* adj., same as בָּצוּר *fortified,* Zec. 11:2.

בֶּצֶר m., *gold;* perhaps *wealth,* Job 36:19.

בֶּצֶר m.—I. the same, Job 22:24, 25. —II. p. n. of a city in the tribe of Reuben.—III. p. n. of a man.

בָּצְרָה f.—I. *fold for cattle,* Mic. 2: 12.—II. p. n. of a city of Edom, Βόστρα.—III. of a city of Moab.

בִּצָּרוֹן m., *fortified place,* Zec. 9:12.

בַּצֹּרֶת f., and pl. בַּצָּרוֹת *withholding of rain, drought,* Jer. 14:1; 17:8.

מִבְצָר m.—I. *fortification;* עִיר מ׳ *fortified town;* pl. מִבְצָרִים and מִבְצָרוֹת—II. p. n. of a chief of the Edomites.

בְּקַבֻּק, בַּקְבֻּק, &c.; see בקק.

בָּקַע with בְּ—I. *cut, cleft, divided.*— II. *laid open,* i. e. subdued, took (of fortified places).—III. *let go* (as young birds from eggs, or water from a dam).—Niph. I. *became cleft, destroyed.*— II. *laid open, subdued.*—III. *let go* (as young birds or water). Pi. same

as Kal. Pu. pass. of Pi. Hiph. I. *cause to be subdued* —II. *sent forth,* with אֶל. Hoph. *was broken up,* Jer. 39:2. Hith. as Niph. I., Jos. 9:13, Mic. 1:4.

בֶּקַע m., *fissure,* Isa. 22:9, Am. 6:11. בֶּקַע m. (*cutting*), half a shekel, Gen. 24:22, Ex. 38:26.

בִּקְעָה f., *valley, plain;* pl. בְּקָעוֹת; בִּקְעַת הַלְּבָנוֹן *valley of Lebanon,* between Anti-Libanus and Hermon, κοίλη Συρία, Cœle-Syria, Jos. 11:37, 12:7; בִּקְעַת אָוֶן, see אָוֶן.

בָּקַק I. *threw, cast off, out* (as fruit from a tree); with אֶת־עֵצָה *I will cast off* (*deprive of*) *counsel,* Jer. 19:7.—II. *make empty, void,* Isa. 24:1. Niph. נָבַק (inf. הִבּוֹק, fut. יִבּוֹק) *become void,* Isa. 19:3; 24:3. Pi. fut. יְבַקְקוּ *make empty, void,* Jer. 51:2.

בַּקְבֻּק I. *bottle, narrow-necked vase;* the word expresses the sound of a fluid issuing from it.—II. p. n. of a man.

בַּקְבֻּקְיָה p. n. of a man.

בַּקְבַּקַּר p. n. of a man.

בֻּקִּי p. n. of a man.

בֻּקִּיָּהוּ p. n. of a man.

בָּקַר *cut, laid open;* not in use: hence, Pi.—I. *look, inquire after.*—II. *observe.*—III *care for,* with לְ and בֵּין...?

בַּקַּר Pa. Ch., *inquired.* Ithpa. *was sought.*

בַּקָּרָה f., *inquiring after, seeking,* Exr. 34:12.

בִּקֹּרֶת f., *observation, chastisement,* Lev. 19·20.

בָּקָר (from the plough which *cleaves* the earth).—I. *oxen* used in ploughing, Job. 1 : 14.—II. *oxen* generally; בֶּן בָּקָר *milch cows*; בֶּן בָּקָר *steer*; seldom pl. בְּקָרִים *oxen*.

בֹּקֵר m., *herdsman*, Am. 7 : 14.

בֹּקֶר m. (pl. בְּקָרִים).—I. *dawn, morning*; לַבֹּקֶר, בַּבֹּקֶר, בַּבֹּקֶר *in the morning*; לַבְּקָרִים, בַּבֹּקֶר בַּבֹּקֶר *every morning*; עַד הַבֹּקֶר לִבְקָרִים *to-morrow morning*. — II. לַבֹּקֶר *early, soon*, Ps. 49 : 15, &c.

בָּקַשׁ. Pi. בִּקֵּשׁ *sought, sought out, after* or *into*, with עַל, מִן, לְ or אֶל *according to the sense*; ב' אֶת־יְהֹוָה or ב' אֶת־פְּנֵי יְהֹוָה *he sought the Lord*; נֶפֶשׁ פ' ב' *the soul, life of any one, to injure destroy it*; דָּם פ' ב'...*his blood.*

בַּקָּשָׁה f., *petition*, Est. 5 : 3; 7 : 3, Exr. 7 : 6.

בַּר, בֹּר, בַּר *son*, &c.: see ברא and ברר.

בָּרָא (inf. בְּרֹא; with suff. בְּרַאֲךָ; imp. בְּרָא; fut. יִבְרָא).—I. *created, formed, made.*—II. same as בָּרָה *he ate.* Niph. *was created, born, produced.* Pi. בֵּרֵא.—I. *cut, as with a sword or axe.*—II. *make, form.* Hiph. הִבְרִיא *fatten*, 1 Sa. 2 : 29.

בְּרִיאָה f., *a wonderful, new thing.*

בַּר m., *son*; with suff. בְּרִי; another meaning, see in ברר.

בַּר m. Ch.—I. *son.*—II. *grandson*; with suff. בְּרֵהּ.

בְּרָאיָה (*created of God*), p. n. of a m.

בְּרֹאדַךְ see מְרֹאדַךְ.

בַּרְבֻּרִים *fed beasts*; see ברר.

בָּרָד *hailed*, Isa. 32 : 19.

בָּרָד m., *hail.*

בָּרֹד m. (pl. בְּרֻדִּים), *spotted*, "grisled," Eng. Ver.

בֶּרֶד p. n.—I. of a place in the wilderness of Shur.—II. of a man.

בָּרָה I. *ate.*—II. same as בַּר *chose.* Pi. inf. בָּרוֹת *eating.* Hiph. *give food.*

בָּרִיא m., בְּרִיאָה f., *fat*; see another meaning above.

בְּרִי m., בְּרִיָה f., *fat*, Eze. 34 : 20.

בִּרְיָה f., *food*, 2 Sa. 13 : 5, 7, 10.

בָּרוּת f. *food*, Ps. 69 : 22.

בְּרִית f.—I. *any agreement*; בַּעֲלֵי ב' *united in covenant*, Gen. 14 : 13.—II. the covenant made by God with the patriarchs, and ratified in the person of Jesus Christ.—III. the sign of that covenant (circumcision), Gen. 17 · 13; מַלְאַךְ הַבְּרִית μεσιτης, *the angel of the covenant, Messiah*; בַּעַל בְּרִית a name of Baal.

בָּרוּךְ *blessed*; see ברך.

בְּרוֹמִים *costly clothing*; see ברם.

בְּרוֹשׁ m.—I. *fir-tree*; עֲצֵי בְרוֹשִׁים *instruments of fir-wood*, 2 Sa. 6 : 5.—II. *staves of lances made of fir-wood*, Nah. 2 : 4.

בְּרוֹת m. the same, Cant. 1 : 17.

בֵּרוֹתַי, בֵּרוֹתָה p. n. of a city in Syria of Zobah.

בָּרוֹת *eating*; see ברה.

בִּרְזִית p. n. of a woman.

בַּרְזֶל m. (with suff. בַּרְזִלּוֹ).—I. *iron.*—II. *hard as iron.*—III. *instrument of iron.*

בַּרְזִלַּי p. n. of a man.

בָּרַח (fut. יִבְרַח; part. m. בֹּרֵחַ, f. בֹּרַחַת). —I. *pass on.*—II. *fly*, with מִן

בְּרַח לֶךָ imper. ;אַחֲרֵי ,מִפְּנֵי ,מֵאֵת *flee away.*—IV. *pass through*, Ex. 36:33. Hiph. *made to pass, fly.*

בָּרַח ,בָּרִיחַ m.—I. *a fugitive.*—II. p. n. of a man.

בְּרִיחַ m.—I. *transverse bar.*—II. *bars* or *bolts* for fastening the gates of a city; בְּרִיחֶהָ, Isa. 15:6, "her fu-gitives" as above, not "her princes" i. e. bars, defences.

מִבְרָח m., *fugitive*, Eze. 40:2.

בַּר, בָּרִיא ,בְּרִיָה; see ברה.

בְּרֵי (same as בְּאֵרִי *my well*), p.n. of a man.

בְּרִיאָה; see ברא.

בְּרִיעָה p. n. of a man.

בְּרִית *covenant;* see ברה.

בֹּרִית *soap;* see ברר.

בֶּרֶךְ f., *knee;* dual בִּרְכַּיִם *both knees.*

בֶּרֶךְ ,בְּרַךְ f. Ch., the same.

בָּרַךְ (fut. יְבָרֵךְ; inf. abs. בָּרוֹךְ).—I. *knelt.*—II. *worshipped, blessed;* בָּרוּךְ יְהֹוָה and בָּרוּךְ לַיהוָה *blessed of the Lord;* בָּרוּךְ יְהוָֹה *blessed be the Lord.* Niph. *be blessed.* Pi. בֵּרֵךְ ,בָּרַךְ *pronounced, made, blessed,* with לְ, בְּשֵׁם יְהוָֹה. Pu. בֹּרַךְ *be* or *become blessed.* Hiph. הִבְרִיךְ *made kneel down,* Gen. 24: 11. Hith. הִתְבָּרֵךְ *be made blessed,* Gen. 22:18, &c.; *account oneself blessed,* Deu. 29:18, &c.

בְּרַךְ Ch., *knelt.* Pa. *blessed.*

בָּרוּךְ p. n. of the friend of Jeremiah.

בֶּרֶכְאֵל (*blessed of God*), p.n.of a man.

בְּרָכָה f. בְּרָכָה Gen. 27:38; const. בִּרְכַּת; pl. בְּרָכוֹת, const. בִּרְכוֹת).—I. *blessing,* ascription of praise to God.—II. the same received

from God.—III. *favour, present*—IV. p. n. of a man.

בְּרֵכָה f., *pool, fish-pond.*

בֶּרֶכְיָה and בֶּרֶכְיָהוּ (*blessed of the Lord*), p.n. of a man.

אַבְרֵךְ; see in its place.

אַרְכֻּבָּה f. Ch., *knee.*

בְּרַם Ch. pa. of confirmation, *but.*

בָּרַם *root not used;* (Arab. *garment adorned with gems*).

בְּרוֹמִים m. pl., *costly raiment,* Eze. 27:24.

לִבְרָם ,בָּרַם Kal inf. with pref. and suff. from ברר.

בָּרְנֵעַ (*fountain of delight*), p. n. of a place in the wilderness, written קָדֵשׁ־בַּ׳, which see.

בֶּרַע p. n. of a king of Sodom.

בִּרְעָה p. n. of a man.

בָּרָק *lightened*, Ps. 144:6.

בָּרָק m. (pl. בְּרָקִים).—I. *lightning.*—II. *glitter of a sword.*—III. p. n. of the captain who defeated the Canaanites, Jud. 4:6, &c.

בָּרֶקֶת f., *carbuncle.*

בַּרְקָנִים m. pl., *threshing waggons,* having sharp iron teeth, Jud. 8: 7, 16.

בַּרְקוֹס p. n. of a man.

בָּרַר I. *examined, tested,* Ecc. 3:18.—II. *separated, selected, chose,* Eze. 20:38, with מִן and לְ; part. בָּרוּר *pure, chaste.* Niph. נָבַר *became pure;* part. נָבָר *pure* Pi. *purify,* Dan. 11:35. Hiph. *make clean, polish.* Hith. *become, appear pure.*

בָּרָה f.—, בַּר m.—I. *beloved,* Cant. 6:9. —II. *pure, clean.*—III. *empty void,* Pro. 14:4.

בַּר, בָּר m.—I. *corn*, purified from the chaff.—II. *growing corn*; see another meaning in ברא.

בָּר m., *field, open plain*, Job 39:4.

בַּר m. Ch., the same.

בֹּר m.—I. *pureness.*—II. same as בֹּרִית.

בֹּרִית f., *soap*, Jer. 2:22, Mal. 3:2.

בַּרְבֻּרִים m., *stalled cattle*, 1 Ki. 5:3.

בִּרְשַׁע p. n. of king of Gomorrah.

בְּשׂוֹרָה, בְּשׂוֹר *good news*; see בשׂר.

בָּשָׂם m. (Anyrum opobalsamum), *the balsam tree*, an aromatic shrub.

בֶּשֶׂם and בֹּשֶׂם m. (pl. בְּשָׂמִים).—I. *the odour of perfumes.*—II. *the perfumes themselves.*

בָּשְׂמַת I. p. n. of the wife of Isaiah.—II. of the daughter of Solomon.

מִבְשָׂם p. n. of a man.

בָּשַׂר Pi. בִּשֵּׂר I. *announce, declare.*—II. *tell glad tidings.* Hith. *was, became informed*, 2 Sa. 18:31.

בְּשׂרָה and בְּשׂוֹרָה f.—I. *good tidings*, 2 Sa. 18:22, 27.—II. *the reward of good tidings*, 2 Sa. 4:10.

בְּשׂוֹר p. n. of a river near Gaza.

בָּשָׂר m.—I. *flesh.*—II. *body.*—III. כָּל־בָּשָׂר *all living creatures.*—IV. עַצְמִי וּבְשָׂרִי *my bone and flesh, kinsman*; also בְּשֵׂר *kinsman*, Lev. 15:2, &c.—V. *secret parts* (male).

בְּשַׂר m. Ch.—I. *flesh.*—II. *mankind.*

בָּשַׁל I. *ripened*, Joel 4:13.—II. *boiled, cooked*, Eze. 24:5. Pi. *boiled, cooked*; part. pl. מְבַשְּׁלִים *cooked*, Eze. 46:24. Pu. *was cooked.* Hiph. *matured, ripened*, Gen. 40:10.

בָּשֵׁל m., בְּשֵׁלָה f., *cooked.*

מְבַשְּׁלוֹת f. pl., *boilers*, Eze. 46:23.

בְּשֶׁלְמִי, בְּשֶׁלִּי; see שֶׁל in אֲשֶׁר.

בִּשְׁלָם p. n. of a man.

בָּשָׁן p. n., *Batanea*, the region beyond Jordan, between Hermon and the brook of Jabbok.

בָּשְׁנָה *shame*; see בּוּשׁ.

בֹּשֶׁם. Po. בּוֹשֵׁם same as בּוֹסֵם *trampling on, injuring*, Am. 5:11.

בֹּשֶׁת *shame*; see בּוּשׁ.

בַּת *daughter*; see בנה.

בַּת *measure*; see בתת.

בָּתָה and בַּתָּה; see בתת.

בְּתוּאֵל p. n.—I. of the father of Laban.—II. same as בְּתוּל name of a place.

בְּתַיָה p. n. of a man.

בָּתִּים *houses*; see בַּיִת, בּוּת.

בָּתַל root not used; (Arab. *separated*).

בְּתוּלָה f. (pl. בְּתֻלוֹת, בְּתוּלוֹת).—I. *a virgin.*—II. used for *nation, city, people*, like בַּת, which see.

בְּתוּלִים m. pl., *tokens of virginity.*

בָּתַק Pi. בִּתֵּק *cut, pierce*, Eze. 16:40.

בָּתַר Pi. בִּתֵּר *dissect, cut in two*, Gen. 15:10.

בֶּתֶר m. (with suff. בִּתְרוֹ).—I. *part, piece.*—II. *separation*, Cant. 2:17.

בְּתַר Ch., same as בָּאתַר *after*; see אָתַר.

בִּתְרוֹן p. n. of a place on Jordan.

בָּתַת root not used; (Arab. *cut, cleft*).

בַּת m. (f. Isa. 5:10), *Bath*; a liquid measure, the tenth part of a Homer.

בַּת m. Ch., the same.

בָּתָה f., *desolation, excision*, Isa 5:6.

בַּתָּה f. (pl. בָּתּוֹת), Isa. 7:19, *clefts, fissures.*

# ג

גָּאָה (fut. יִגְאֶה).—I. *grew high* (as a plant), Job 8:11; (as water,) Exr. 47:5.—II. *becoming lofty, powerful, proud.*

גֵּא m., *proud,* Isa. 16:6.

גֵּאֶה m.—I. *elevated.*—II. *proud, arrogant;* pl. גֵּאִים.

גַּאֲוָה f., *pride, arrogance,* Pro. 8:13.

גַּאֲוָה f.—I. *excellency, majesty.*—II. *pride, arrogance.*

גְּאוּאֵל (*the divine majesty*), p. n. of a man.

גָּאוֹן m.—I. *excellency, glory.*—II. *pride;* pl. גְּאוֹנִים.

גֵּאוּת f.—I. *ascent,* Isa. 9:17.—II. *sublimity, excellency.*—III. *pride, arrogance.*

גֵּאֶיוֹן m., *proud,* Ps. 123:4.

גֵּוָה f. (for גַּאֲוָה).—I. *elevation, victory,* Job 22:29.—II. *pride,* Job 33:17.

גֵּוָה f. Ch., *the same,* Dan. 4:34.

גֵּאָיוֹת *valleys;* see גַּיְא.

גָּאַל (fut. יִגְאַל).—I. *redeem by paying value for.*—II. *retribute, avenge.*—III. *pollute;* part. גֹּאֵל *redeemer, avenger, relative,* to whom the duty of avenging the death of any one was assigned; part. pass. גְּאוּלִים גְּאוּלֵי *redeemed, set at liberty.* Niph. נִגְאַל, נְגֹאַל *was redeemed, liberated, polluted.* Pi. גֵּאֵל *polluted,* Mal. 1:7. Pu. *was polluted.* Hiph. אֶגְאַלְתִּי *contaminate,* Isa. 63:1. Hiph. *polluted himself,* Dan. 1:8.

גֹּאֶל m., *pollution;* pl. const. גֹּאֲלֵי Neh. 13:29.

גְּאֻלָּה f.—I. *relationship.*—II. *right, duty of redemption.*—III. *price of redemption.*—IV. *thing redeemed.*

מֹגָאֵל m., *next of kin after the Goel.*

גֹּב *locust;* see גּוֹב.

גָּבָא root not used; (Arab. *gathered together*).

גֶּבֶא m., *cistern, pit.*

גָּבַב root not used.

גַּב m. (with suff. גַּבִּי; pl. גַּבִּים, גַּבּוֹת).—I. *back.*—II. *defence, mound.*—III. *vaults.*—IV. *arch of the eyebrow,* Lev. 14:9; גַּב מָגֵן *the boss of a shield,* Job 15:26.

גַּב m. Ch., *back.*

גֹּב m. Ch., *well;* emph. גֻּבָּא.

גּוֹב m., *locust;* pl. גּוֹבַי.

גֹּב m. (pl. גֹּבִים), *locusts.*

גָּבַהּ (fut. יִגְבַּהּ; inf. גָּבְהָה).—I. *was high, lofty,* with עַל; when with מִן *was higher than.*—II. *exalted;* גָּבַהּ לִבּוֹ *his heart was lifted up:* or merely גָּבַהּ *lifted up.* Hiph. *raise, exalt.*

גָּבֹהַּ m. (const. גְּבֹהַּ; f. גְּבֹהָה).—I. *high, tall.*—II. *haughty, proud.* Subst. *height,* 1 Sa. 16:7.

גָּבֵהַּ; const. גְּבַהּ m.—I. *high.*—II. *arrogant, proud.*

גֹּבַהּ m. (with suff. גָּבְהוֹ; pl. const. גָּבְהֵי).—I. *height.*—II. *majesty,* Job 40:10.—III. *arrogance;* גֹּבַהּ אַף *insolence,* Ps. 10:4.

גַּבְהוּת m., *pride,* Isa. 2:11, 17.

גְּבוּלָה, גְּבוּל *border;* see נבל.

גְּבוּרָה *mighty;* see נבר.

גִּבֵּחַ m., *bald,* Lev. 13:41.

גַּבַּחַת f.—I. *baldness.*—II. *loss of knap* (in cloth), Lev. 13:55.

גַּב p. n. of a man.

גֵּבִים (see גֵּב), p. n. of a place not far from Jerusalem.

גְּבִינָה cheese; see נבן.

גָּבִיעַ cup; see נבע.

גְּבִיר, גְּבִירָה master; see נבר.

גָּבִישׁ see נבש.

גָּבַל limited; with בְּ and אֶת. Hiph. set bounds to.

גְּבָלִי p. n. of a Phenician city; an inhabitant of Gebal.

גְּבָל p. n. of a mountainous district beyond Jordan, Ps. 83:8.

גְּבוּל, גְּבֻל m.—I. limit, boundary.—II. space or country limited.

גְּבוּלָה, גְּבֻלָה f., pl. גְּבוּלוֹת boundaries, lands.

גְּבֻלוֹת f., artificial work, device, Ex. 28:22; 37:15.

מִגְבָּלָה f. (pl. מִגְבָּלוֹת), the same, Ex. 28:14.

גָּבֵן root not used; (Syr. curdled).

גְּבִינָה f., cheese, 2 Sa. 16:2.

גִּבֵּן m., hunchback, Lev. 21:20.

גַּבְנֻנִּים m. pl., risings, mounds; הַר גַּבְנֻנִּים a hill of mounds, i. e. made up of other hills.

גָּבִיעַ m. (with suff. גְּבִיעִי; pl. גְּבִיעִים).—I. a cup or vase.—II. flower, the calix of an artificial flower.

גֶּבַע p. n. of a town in the tribe of Benjamin.

גִּבְעָא p. n. of a man.

גִּבְעָה f., a hill; pl. גְּבָעוֹת.

גִּבְעַת אֱלֹהִים p.n. of a place.

גִּבְעַת בְּנֵי בִנְיָמִין p.n. of a city in the tribe of Benjamin.

גִּבְעַת פִּינְחָס p. n. of a city.

גִּבְעַת שָׁאוּל p. n. of a hill.

גִּבְעָתִי inhabitant of Gibeah.

גִּבְעוֹן p. n. of a city in the tribe of Benjamin.

מִגְבָּעָה f. (pl. מִגְבָּעוֹת), the mitre or bonnet of the priests.

גִּבְעֹל flowering (of flax), Ex. 9:31.

גָּבַר and גָּבֵר (fut. יִגְבַּר).—I. was powerful, mighty.—II. conquered, (prevailed), with מִן or עַל. Pi. made strong. Hiph.—I. was powerful, Ps. 12:5.—II. confirm, Dan. 9:27. Hith. became powerful, victorious.

גֶּבֶר m.—I. man, husband, hero; pl. גְּבָרִים; לִגְבָרִים manfully.—II. p. n. of a man, 1 Ki. 4:19.

גְּבַר m., Ch. the same; pl. גֻּבְרִין.

גֶּבֶר m. (same as Ch.), man, Ps.18:26.

גְּבִיר m., lord, Gen. 27:29, 37.

גְּבִירָה f., lady, queen.

גְּבֶרֶת f. (with suff. גְּבִרְתִּי), the same.

גִּבּוֹר, גִּבֹּר m.—I. mighty, brave.—II. renowned; גִּבּוֹר חַיִל renowned for wealth, rich.

גִּבָּר m. Ch.—I. brave, strong, heroic.—II. p.n. same as גִּבְעוֹן, Ezr. 2:20.

גְּבוּרָה f.—I. power.—II. courage.—III. acts of courage, power; גְּבוּרוֹת יְהֹוָה acts of God, i. e. miracles.

גְּבוּרָה f. Ch. the same.

גַּבְרִיאֵל p.n. of an archangel.

גָּבַשׁ root not used; (Arab. congelation).

גָּבִישׁ m., crystal (lit. ice), Job 28:18.

גִּבְּתוֹן p. n. of a town of the Philistines in the tribe of Dan.

גָּג m. (with suff. גַּגּוֹ; pl. גַּגּוֹת).—I. roof of a house.—II. covering, grate of the altar.

גַּד; see גדד.

גִּדְבְּרִין m. pl. Ch., *treasures*, Dan. 3:
2,3; same as גִּזְבָּר.

גְּדוֹרָה p. n. of a place in the Arabian
desert.

גָּדַד *assault, attack* (as an army).
Hith. הִתְגּוֹדֵד I. *cutting, making incisions.* — II. *attacking, assembling
to attack.*

גְּדַד Ch., *cut down* (of a tree), Dan.
4:11, 20.

גְּדוּד m. (pl. גְּדוּדִים, גְּדוּדוֹת). — I.
*cutting*, Jer. 48:37. — II. *furrow*,
Ps. 65:11. — III. *section, detach-
ment of an army.*

גַּד m., *coriander seed*, Ex. 16:31, Nu.
11:7.

גָּד m., *good fortune*; בְּגָד *prosperously*, Gen. 30:11.

גָּד nom., p.n. of an idol, Isa. 65:11.

גָּד p. n. *Gad.*—I. one of the sons of
Jacob.—II. the tribe descended
from him; גָּדִי *a Gadite.*

גַּדִּי p.n. of a man, Nu. 13:11.

גַּדִּיאֵל p. n. of a man.

גָּדָה root not used; (Syr. *leaping*).

גְּדִי m., *a kid*; pl. גְּדָיִים; const. גְּדָיֵי.

גְּדִיָּה f., pl. גְּדִיוֹת *female kids*,
Cant. 1:8.

גָּדָה f., const. pl. גְּדוֹת *banks of a
river.*

גְּדִי, גְּדוּד; see גדד.

גְּדוֹלָה, גְּדִילִים, גָּדוֹל *great*; see גדל.

גְּדוּפָה, גְּדוּף *reproach*; see גדף.

גְּדִיָּה, גְּדִי; see גדה.

גָּדִישׁ *heap*; see גדש.

גָּדַל and גָּדֵל (fut. יִגְדַּל), *was or
grew great* (in anything), with
עַד, מִן, לְ, בְּ, אֶת. Pi. גִּדֵּל, גִּדֵּל I.
*made* or *pronounced great*: hence,

— II. *trained, educated.* Hiph. I.
*became great.*— II. *made great
high*; הִגְדִּיל אֶת פִּיו *he spake insolently.* Hith. *showed himself great.*

גָּדֵל m., pl. const. גְּדֻלֵי, *great ones,*
Eze. 16:26.

גָּדוֹל m. (const. גְּדוֹל and גְּדָל; f.
גְּדוֹלָה), *great* (in anything); גְּדוֹלִים
*nobles*; גְּדֹל חֶסֶד *great in mercy*;
עוֹד הַיּוֹם גָּדוֹל *it is yet high day,*
i. e. early, Gen. 29:7; pl. גְּדֹלוֹת
*great* (i. e. proud) *things*, Ps. 12:4.

גֹּדֶל m. (with suff. גָּדְלוֹ, גָּדְלֶךָ), *greatness, magnificence, pride.*

גְּדוּלָה f.—I. *great* (act or deed).
—II. *greatness*; pl. גְּדֹלוֹת *great
things.*

גְּדִילִים m. pl., *platted chain-work*, 1 Ki.
7:17.

גִּדֵּל p. n. of a man.

גְּדַלְיָהוּ, גְּדַלְיָה *Gedaliah*, p.n. of a man.

גִּדַּלְתִּי p. n. of a man, 1 Ch. 25:4, 29.

מִגְדָּל (pl. מִגְדָּלִים, מִגְדָּלוֹת).—I. *tower,
castle.*—II. *pulpit*, Neh. 8:4.—III.
*artificial mound,* in a garden covered
with sweet flowers, Cant. 5:13.

מִגְדּוֹל, מִגְדָּל p.n. of a city in Egypt.

מִגְדַּל־אֵל p.n. of a fortress in the tribe
of Naphtali.

מִגְדַּל־גָּד p. n. of a place in the tribe
of Judah.

מִגְדַּל עֵדֶר p.n. of a place near Bethlehem.

גָּדַע I. *cut off* or *down.*—II. *broke.*
Niph. *became cut off, down.* Pi.
*broke.* Pu. *was cut down*, Isa. 9:9.

גִּדְעֹם p. n. of a place in the tribe of
Benjamin.

גִּדְעוֹן p. n. of a judge of Israel.

גִּדְעֹנִי p. n. of a man.

גָּדַף Pi. גִּדֵּף blasphemed.

גִּדּוּף m., pl. גִּדּוּפִים, גִּדּוּפוֹת re-proaches, Isa. 43:28; 51:7.

גְּדוּפָה f., reproach, Zep. 2:8.

גָּדַר walled, fenced up; part. גֹּדֵר fencer.

גָּדֵר com. (const. גֶּדֶר; with suff. גְּדֵרוֹ; pl. גְּדֵרִים).—I. wall, fence. —II. fenced place.

גְּדֵרָה f.—I. wall.—II. fence, hurdle.— III. same as בֵּית גָּדֵר p.n. of a town in the tribe of Judah; גְּדֵרָתִי a Ge-derite.—IV. גְּדֵרוֹת and גְּדֵרוֹתַיִם p.n. of places in the tribe of Judah.

גְּדֶרֶת f., a fence, Eze. 42:12.

גֶּדֶר p.n. of a city of the Canaanites.

גְּדֹר p.n. of a town in the tribe of Judah.

גְּדֵרִי an inhabitant of בֵּית גָּדֵר.

גָּדַשׁ root not used; Ch. heaped up.

גָּדִישׁ m.—I. sepulchral mound.—II. heap of corn.

גֵּה for זֶה, Eze. 47:13.

גֵּהָה raise up, Hos. 5:12.

גֵּהָה f., relief, healing, Pro. 17:22.

גָּהַר bowed, bent downwards.

גַּו, גֵּו, גֵּוָא; see נוה.

גּוּב cut, cleft; part. גָּבִים ploughers.

גֵּב m.—I. board, plank.—II. well; see another meaning in גֵּבָה.

גּוֹב (cistern), p.n. of a place; see another meaning in גֵּבָה.

גּוֹג p.n. of the king of Magog; see מָגוֹג.

גּוּד, יְגוּדֶנּוּ, see גָּדַד; shall rush upon him, Gen. 49:19; Hab. 3:16.

גֵּוָה root not used.

גֵּו, גֵּוָא m. Ch., middle.

---

גֵּו m. Ch.—I. middle; with suff. גַּוֵּהּ. —II. Heb. back; with suff. גֵּוִי.

גֵּו m.—I. back.—II. middle; with suff. גֵּוִי.

גֵּוָה f., a body, Job 20:25; see another meaning under גֵּאָה.

גְּוִיָּה f.—I. body, person.—II. dead body, carcase of men or animals.

גּוֹי m. (with suff. גּוֹיִי; pl. גּוֹיִם, גּוֹיֵי, with suff. גּוֹיֶךָ, גּוֹיֵיהֶם).—I. gene-rally people, Israelites as well as foreigners.—II. specially, foreign nations.—III. multitudes of locusts, Joel 1:6; of animals, Zep. 2:14.

גַּיְא com. (const. גֵּיא; pl. גֵּיאוֹת, גֵּיאָיוֹת), valley.

גַּיְא, גֵּיא the same.

גַּי m. (const. גֵּי), the same.

גֵּאָיוֹת f. pl., valleys.

גּוּז pass over, Ps. 90:10; fut. apoc. וַיָּגָז, Nu. 11:31.

גּוֹזָל young bird; see גזל.

גּוֹזָן p.n., a district in North Mesopo-tamia, between the rivers Chaboras and Saocoras, the Γαυζανῖτις of Ptolemy.

גּוּחַ break forth; see גִּיחַ.

גְּוִיָּה, גֵּו; see נוה.

גּוּל rejoice; see גִּיל.

גּוֹלָן, גּוֹלָה; see גלה.

גּוּמָץ pit; see גמץ.

גּוּנִי p.n. of a man.

גָּוַע (fut. יִגְוַע; inf. גּוֹעַ; const. גְּוַע and גָּוַע), expire, die.

גּוּף Kal, root not used; (Arab. shut up). Hiph. fut. pl. יָגִיפוּ let (them) shut, Neh. 7:3.

גּוּפָה f., dead body; (Arab. the same).

גּוּר I. sojourned, dwelt, with בְּ, עִם.

אָת; part. גָּר *dwelling with*; גָּרַת
בֵּיתָהּ *her inmate.*—II. *avoided,*
*feared,* with מִן and מִפְּנֵי—III.
*congregated, come together,* with
עַל; see גֵּרָה. Hith. הִתְגּוֹרֵר—I.
*withdraw.*—II. *dwell,* 1 Ki. 17:20.
—III. *violent destroying,* Jer. 30:23.

גֵּר (גֵּיר, 2. Ch. 2:16), m., *sojourner,*
*stranger.*

גֵּרוּת f., *sojourning, residing,* Jer. 41:
17.

גּוּר m.—I. *lion's whelp*; גּוּר אַרְיֵה,
Gen. 49:9, &c.—II. *jackall,* 2 Sa.
4:3.

גֹּר m. the same; f. pl. גֹּרוֹת.

גּוּר בַּעַל (*dwelling of Baal*), p. n. of a
town in Arabia.

מָגוּר m.—I. *sojourning.*—II. *residence,*
*habitation.*—III. *human life; so-*
*journ on earth.*

מָגוֹר m., *fear, terror*; pl. מְגוּרִים.

מְגוֹרָה f., *fear*; pl. מְגוֹרוֹת.

מְגוּרָה f.—I. *granary.*—II. *fear, ter-*
*ror*; pl. מְגוּרוֹת.

מַמְּגֻרָה f. (pl. מַמְּגֻרוֹת), *granaries,*
Joel 1:17.

גּוֹרָל *lot*; see גרל.

גּוּשׁ m., *clod,* Job 7:5.

גִּישָׁן p. n. of a man.

גֵּז *fleece*; see גזז.

גִּזְבָּר *treasurer,* Ezr. 1:8; pl. גִּזְבְּרִין,
Ezr. 7:21, and גְּדָבְרִין, Dan. 3:2, 3.

גָּזָה (Arab. *bring forth*); part. גֹּחִי,
lit. " *he who brought me forth,*" Ps.
71:6.

גָּזִית f.—I. lit. *cutting, hewing*: hence,
—II. *hewn stones.*

גָּזַז (fut. יָגֹז; inf. גֹּז and גְּזֹז).—I. *shear,*
*cut off hair, wool, &c.*; part. גֹּזְזִים

*shavers.*—II. *drive away* (of quails),
Nu. 11:31. Niph. pret. pl. נָגֹזּוּ
*were cut off.*

גֵּז m. (pl. const. גִּזֵּי).—I. *shearing of*
*sheep*: hence,—II. *the fleece.*—III.
*young grass after mowing.*

גִּזָּה f., *fleece,* Jud. 6:39, 40.

גָּזֵז (*barber*), p. n. of a man.

גָּזַל I. *cut off.*—II. *snatch away, injure.*
Niph. *was taken away,* Pro. 4:16.

גָּזֵל m., const. גְּזֵל *rapine, plunder.*

גְּזֵלָה f., the same.

גּוֹזָל m., *young pigeon,* Gen. 15:9;
Deu. 32:11.

גָּזָם root not used; (Arab. *destruction*)

גָּזָם m., *a species of locust.*

גַּזָּם p. n. of a man.

גִּזּוֹנִי m., *an inhabitant of Gizon.* .

גָּזַע root not used. (Arab. *cutting off*)

גֶּזַע m. (with suff. גִּזְעָם), *stock; trunk*
*of a tree.*

גָּזַר I. *cut off, down.*—II. *in two parts*
*divided.* — III. *decided, as judg-*
*ment.* Niph. *was cut off,* with
מִן; *was decided,* Est. 2:1.

גְּזַר Ch., *decided, determined* the fate
of others by astrology; part. pl.
גָּזְרִים *soothsayers.*

גֶּזֶר I. *division, section*; pl. גְּזָרִים.—
II. p. n. of a city on the western
frontier of the tribe of Ephraim,
Γάζηρα.

גְּזֵרָה (גְּזֵירָה) f., *place cut off, separated,*
Lev. 16:22.

גְּזֵרָה f. Ch., *decision,* Dan. 4:14, 21.

גִּזְרָה f.—I. *cut, polish* (of precious
stones), Lam. 4:7.— II. *insulated,*
*separated* (of a certain enclosure
of the temple), Eze. 41:42.

מְגֵזְרָה f., *axe*, 2 Sa. 12:31.

גִּזְרִי inhabitant of *Gezer*.

גָּחוֹן *belly*; see גחן.

גֵּחֲזִי, גֵּיחֲזִי p. n. of a servant of the prophet Elisha.

גָּחַל root not used; (Arab. *to burn*).

גֶּחָל m. (pl. גֶּחָלִים, גַּחֲלֵי).—I. *burning coals.*—II. *thunderbolts.*

גַּחֶלֶת f., the same; with suff. גַּחַלְתִּי.

נַחַם p. n. of a man.

גָּחַן root not used; Ch. גְּחַן *bowed down.*

גָּחוֹן m., *belly of a serpent*, Lev. 11:42; with suff. גְּחֹנְךָ, Gen. 3:14.

גַּי, גַּיְא, גֵּי, גֵּי; see גוה.

נַחַר p. n. of a man.

גִּיד m., *sinew, nerve.*

גִּיחַ and גּוּחַ (fut. יָגִיחַ; part. גָּח).—I. *drew out.* — II. *extended, elongated.* Hiph. *drew out.*

גִּיחַ or גּוּחַ Ch. Aph. *rushed forth.*

גִּיחַ p. n. of a place near Gibeon, 2 Sa. 2:24.

גִּיחוֹן I. p. n. of a river of Paradise, Gen. 2:13.—II. of an aqueduct near Jerusalem; otherwise שִׁלֹּחַ.

גִּיל and גּוּל (fut. יָגִיל) *leap, exult, rejoice*, with בְּ, עַל, לְמַעַן.

גִּיל m., *exultation, rejoicing.*

גִּיל m. Ch., *equal in age, rank, &c.*, Dan. 1:10.

גִּילָה f., *exultation.*

גִּילְנִי; see גלה in נלה.

גֵּינַת; see נגן.

גִּיר (גֵּר) m., *burnt lime-stone*, Isa. 27:9.

גִּיר m. Ch., *plaster of lime*, Dan. 5:5.

גֵּיר *stranger*, same as גֵּר; see גור.

גִּישׁ *clod*, same as גֻּשׁ.

גִּישָׁן p. n. of a man.

גַּל for גֹּל Kal imper. from גָּלַל Ps. 119: 12. Pi. imper. apoc. from גָּלָה, Ps. 119:18.

גְּלָא Ch., *reveal*; see גלה.

גָּלַב root not used; (Arab. *drew, shaved*).

גַּלָּב m., *barber*, Eze. 5:1.

גִּלְבֹּעַ p. n., *Gilboa*, hills in the tribe of Issachar.

גֻּלְגֹּלֶת, גֻּלְגֹּל, גַּלְגַּל; see גלל.

גֶּלֶד m., *skin*; with suff. גִּלְדִּי *my skin*, Job 16:15.

גֻּלָּה *bowl*; see גלל.

גָּלָה (fut. יִגְלֶה, יֶגֶל; inf. גָּלֹה, גְּלוֹת).—I. *laid bare, disclosed, opened.*—II. *depopulated* a country, i. e. *led into captivity, migrated*; part. m. גֹּלֶה, f. גֹּלָה *migrated, gone into captivity*; גָּלוּי *opened, proclaimed, published* (of an edict). Niph. נִגְלָה (fut. יִגֶל, יִגָּלֶה; inf. abs. נִגְלֹה, נִגְלוֹת).—I. *was uncovered, exposed, revealed.*— II. *migrated, went into captivity*, Isa. 38:12; part. f. pl. נִגְלֹת *revealed*, Deu. 29:29. Pi. גִּלָּה (fut. יְגַל, יְגַלֶּה).—I. *uncovered, made naked.*— II. *had carnal connexion with*, with אֶת and עַל. Pu. גֻּלָּה *was uncovered*; part. f. מְגֻלָּה *openly said.* Hiph. הֶגְלָה, הִגְלָה *led captive* (fut. יַגֵּל, וַיַּגְלֶה). Hoph. הָגְלָה *was made captive.* Hithp. הִתְגַּלָּה *made himself naked*; fut. apoc. וַיִּתְגַּל, Gen. 9:21.

גְּלָא Ch., *revealed.* Piel גַּלִּי *revealed.* Aph. הַגְלִי *carried captive*, Ezr. 4:10, 12.

גָּלֹה p. n. of a city in the mountains

of Judah; its inhabitants were styled גִּילֹנִי.

גּוֹלָה, גֹּלָה f.—I. *captivity.*—II. *captive, troop of captives.*

גּוֹלָן p.n. of a city of Batanea, Γαυλών. גָּלֻת f., *captive;* as גּוֹלָה.
גָּלוּת f. Ch., the same.

גִּלָּיוֹן m., *tablet, book,* Isa. 8:1; pl. גִּלְיוֹנִים *mirrors,* Isa. 3:23. Writing tablets and mirrors were both, in ancient times, plates of metal.

גָּלְיַת p. n., *Goliath,* the giant whom David slew.

גָּלִיל, גְּלִילָה, גַּלִּים, גַּלְגַּלִּים; see גלל.
גִּלּוּם; see גלם.

גָּלַח Pi.—I. *shaved head* or *beard.* II. *devastated by war,* Isa. 7:20. Pu. *was shaven,* Ju. 16:17, 22; Jer. 41:5. Hithp. *shave himself.*

גִּלֹה p. n. of a city.
גָּלְיַת, גִּלָּיוֹן; see גלה.

גָּלַל (sing. p. 1. גַּלּוֹתִי, pl. גַּלּוּ; inf. גֹּל, גָּלֹל; imp. גַּל, גֹּל).—I. *roll* (as a stone).—II. with מֵעַל *roll away,* used metaphorically of things morally heavy. — III. with עַל, אֶל *commit to,* lit. *roll upon;* גּוֹל עַל יְיָ דַּרְכֶּךָ *commit thy way unto the Lord,* Ps. 37:5. Niph. נָגֹל *were rolled up,* Isa. 34:4; *rolled away,* Am. 5:24. Pil. גִּלְגֵּל *roll off,* Jer. 51:25. Hithpal. *roll, rush in violently,* Job 30:14. Hiph. הֵגֵל *roll,* Gen. 29:10. Po. גּוֹלֵל *roll about in,* Isa. 9:4. Hithpo. הִתְגּוֹלֵל *rolled in, weltered in,* 2 Sa. 20:12.—II. *fall upon,* with עַל, Gen. 43:18.

גָּלָל m.—I. *dung.* — II. בְּגָלַל *because, for the sake of;* בְּגְלָלְךָ *for thy sake.*—III. p. n. of a man.

גָּלָל m. Ch., *great, heavy,* (of stones)

גֵּלֶל m. (with suff. גֶּלְלִי; pl. גְּלָלִים; const. גֶּלְלֵי) *dung.*

גְּלָלַי, גָּלָל p.n. of a man.

גִּלּוּלִים m. pl., *idols.*

גָּלִיל m.—I. *that which can be turned on hinges,* 1 Ki. 6:34.—II. *ring,* Cant. 5:14.—III. *circuit, tract of country;* הַגָּלִיל and הַגָּלִילָה p.n. of a region in the tribe of Naphtali, *Galilee.*

גְּלִילָה f. *circuit, region.*

גַּל m. (pl. גַּלִּים).—I. *a heap* (of stones, &c.). — II. *spring, fountain.*—III. pl. *waves, breakers.*

גַּלִּים p.n. of a town in the tribe of Benjamin; 1 Sa. c. 25; Jos. c. 10.

גֻּל m., *oil jar,* Zec. 4:2.

גֻּלָּה f.—I. same as גַּל (pl. גֻּלּוֹת) *well,* Jos. 15:10; Jud. 1:15.—II. const. גֻּלַּת *oil jar* or *vessel.* — III. *vase-like ornaments,* or *flowers on the capitals of columns.*

גַּלְגַּל m.—I. *wheel;* pl. גַּלְגַּלִּים.—II. *whirlwind.*—III. *chaff* (as driven by the wind).

גַּלְגַּל m. Ch., *wheel,* Dan. 7:9.

גִּלְגָּל m. —I. *cart wheel,* Isa. 28:28. —II. p.n. of a city between Jericho and Jordan.

גֻּלְגֹּלֶת f.—I. *skull.*—II. used in numbering men, as we say, *head of cattle;* with suff. גֻּלְגָּלְתּוֹ; pl. with suff. גֻּלְגְּלֹתָם.

מְגִלָּה f., *volume, roll, book.*

מְגִלָּה f. Ch., the same.

גָּלַם *wrapped together* (as a mantle) 2 Ki. 2:8.

גְּלוֹם m., *cloak, mantle,* Eze. 27:24.

גֹּלֶם m., *embryo, foetus*, Ps. 139:16.

גַּלְמוּד m., *hard, barren, fruitless.*

גָּלַע. Hithp. הִתְגַּלַּע *intermeddle, be impudent.*

גִּלְעָד I. p.n., *Gilead*, the son of Machir, grandson of Manasseh: hence,—II. p.n. of a hill and town near Lebanon.—III. of a region beyond Jordan; גִּלְעָדִי *a Gileadite.*

גַּלְעֵד (*heap of witness*), p.n. of the heap of stones erected by Laban and Jacob, Gen. 31:47, 48.

גִּלְשׁ "appear," Cant. 4:1; 6:5, Eng. Ver.; meaning uncertain.

נַם; see גמם.

גָּמָא. Pi. *drink in*, Job 29:24. Hiph. *give to drink*, Gen. 24:17.

גֹּמֶא m., *the paper reed*; תֵּבַת גֹּמֶא *an ark of reeds*, and כְּלִי גֹ *a boat of reeds.*

גֶּמֶד m., *pruning knife, short-sword*, Ju. 3:16.

גְּמָדִים m. pl., *short-swordsmen*, Eze. 27:11.

גִּמְזוֹ p. n. of a town in the tribe of Judah.

גָּמַל (fut. יִגְמֹל).—I. *recompense, repay*, with לְ and עַל.—II. *mature, ripen.* — III. *wean as a child.* Niph. *was weaned.*

גְּמוּל *recompence, retribution*, either of good or bad actions.

גְּמוּל p. n. of a man.

גְּמוּלָה f., *recompence, retribution.*

גְּמַלִיאֵל (*God my restorer*), p.n. of a man.

תַּגְמוּל m., *retribution, kindness*, Ps. 116:12.

גָּמָל com., *camel*; pl. גְּמַלִּים.

גְּמַלִּי p. n. of a man.

גָּמַם (Arab. *filled up, desired*).

גַּם *moreover, also*; הֲגַם *is it not also!* גַּם...גַּם *and...also*; גַּם כִּי *but if, although.*

מְנַמָּה f., *desire, object*, Hab. 1:9.

גָּמֵץ (Syr. *a well*).

גּוּמָץ m., *a well or pit*, Ecc. 10:8.

גָּמַר (fut. יִגְמֹר).—I. *bring to pass.*—II. *finish, fail.*

גְּמַר Ch., *complete, learned*, Eze. 7:12.

גְּמַרְיָה and גְּמַרְיָהוּ p.n. of a man.

גֹּמֶר p. n.—I. of a northern race of people, perhaps the *Cymri.*— II. of the wife of Hosea.

גַּן *garden*; see גנן.

גָּנַב *he stole, with or without violence*; with לֵב, Gen. 31:20, 26, 27, "*stole away unawares.*" Niph. *stolen.* Pi. *secretly*, Ex. 22:11. Pu. *steals, was stolen.* Hith. *stole themselves away.*

גַּנָּב m., *a thief.*

גְּנֵבָה f., *stolen thing*, Ex. 22:2, 3.

גְּנֻבַת p. n. of a man.

גִּנָּה, גַּנָּה; see גנן.

גָּנַן root not used; (Arab. *covered*).

גֶּנֶז m., pl. גְּנָזִים; const. גִּנְזֵי *treasures.*

גְּנַז or גַּנַז m. Ch., pl. גִּנְזִין *treasures.*

גִּנְזַךְ m., *treasury*, 2 Ch. 28:11.

גָּנַן *guard, protect*, with עַל, אֶל. Hiph. the same.

גַּן com. (with suff. גַּנִּי, pl. גַּנִּים) *garden.*

גַּנָּה f., *a garden*; pl. גַּנּוֹת.

גִּנָּה f., the same.

נִינַח p. n. of a man.

גִּנְּתוֹן גִּנְּתוֹ p. n. of a man.

גֵּן m. (suff. מָגִנִּי, pl. מָגִנִּים) shield, fig., *God the protector*, Gen. 15:10; מָגִנֵּי־אָרֶץ *shields of the earth*, i.e. princes, Ps. 47:10., &c.

מְגִנָּה f., with לֵב *veiling, covering of heart*, Lam. 3:65.

גָּעָה *lowed* (as oxen), Job 6:5.

גֹּעָה p. n. of a place near Jerusalem.

גָּעַל *loathed, abhorred.* Niph. *was rejected, cast away*, 2 Sa. 1:21. Hiph. *cast* (brought forth prematurely), Job 21:10.

גֹּעַל m., *loathing*, Eze. 16:5.

גַּעַל p. n. of a man.

גָּעַר (fut. יִגְעַר) *rebuked, reproved*, with בְּ.

גְּעָרָה f., *chiding, reproof.*

מִגְעֶרֶת *rebuke, calamity*, Deu. 28:20.

גָּעַשׁ *shook, trembled*, Ps. 18:8. Pu. גֹּעַשׁ *was shaken*, Job 34:20. Hithp. *was moved.* Hithpo. the same, Jer. 25:16.

גַּעַשׁ p. n. of a mountain in the tribe of Ephraim.

גַּעְתָּם Kal. inf. const. from נגע.
גַּעְתָּם p.n. of the son of Eliphaz.

גַּף body; see גפף.

גֶּפֶן com.—I. *climbing plant.*—II. *vine.*

גָּפַף root not used; (Arab. *troop of men*).

גַּף m.—I. *person, self*; בְּנַפּוֹ *with himself only*, i.e. *alone*, Ex. 21:3,4.— II. *back*, i.e. *hillock*, Pro. 9:3.

גַּף m. Ch., pl. גַּפִּין *wings.*

גֹּפֶר m., name of a tree; probably, the *pitch-pine*, Gen 6·14.

---

גָּפְרִית f., *brimstone.*

גֵּר; see גּוּר and נֵּר.

גֵּר, גּוּר; see גּוּר.

גֵּרָא (same as גֵּרָה), p. n. of a man.

גָּרַב root not used; like *scratch, scurf*, and many other words in all languages, an imitation of the noise made in *scratching*, &c.

גָּרָב m., *scurf, scurvy.*

גָּרֵב p. n. of one of David's generals.

נַּרְנְּרוֹת, נַּרְנַּר, see גרר.

גִּרְנָּשִׁי p. n. of a nation of Canaanites.

גָּרַד Hithp.inf. הִתְנָּרֵד *scrape, scratch*, Job 2:8; see גָּרַב.

גָּרָה Pi. גֵּרָה *produce, kindle strife.* Hithp. *prepare to contend, contend with*; const. with בְּ.

תִּגְרָה f., *attack, stroke*, Ps. 39:11.

גָּרוֹן m., *throat*; see גרר.

נָּרוֹן גֵּרָה; see גרר.

גֵּרוּת *sojourning*; see גּוּר.

גֹּרֶן same as גַּרַן. Niph. pret. נִגְרַזְתִּי *I am cut off*, Ps. 31:23; 88:6.

גַּרְזֶן m., *axe.*

גִּרְזִי (גִּרְזִי) p. n. of a nation of Canaanites.

הַר גְּרִזִים p n. of a mountain, *Gerizim.*

גָּרַל root not used; (Arab. *was gravelly, sandy*).

גּוֹרָל m. (pl. גּוֹרָלוֹת).—I. *lot*, lit. the *pebble* by which it was determined. —II. הִפִּיל, הִשְׁלִיךְ, יָרָה, יָדָה, נָתַן הַגּוֹרָל *determined by lot*, הָיָה לוֹ גּוֹרָל, עָלָה עָלָיו גּוֹרָל i.e. יָצָא the lot fell.—III. *the thing obtained by lot.*

גָּרֹל (const. גְּרָל) Pro 19:19; keri גָּדֹל *great.*

גֶּרֶם m. (pl. גְּרָמִים).—I. bone.—II. powerful, Gen. 49:14.—III. framework, pulpit, 2 Ki. 9:13.

גְּרֶם m. Ch., bone.

גֵּרֶם cut, spoil, Zep. 3:3. Pi. fut. יְגָרֵם shall destroy.

גַּרְמִי p. n. of a man.

גֹּרֶן root not used; (Arab. place for drying dates).

גֹּרֶן f. (pl. גְּרָנוֹת; const. גָּרְנוֹת).—I. open place at the gate of a city, court of justice.—II. threshing-floor.—III. corn of the floor, Job 39:12. גֹּרֶן הָאָטָד p. n. of a place beyond Jordan; see אָטָד.

גָּרַם pained, overwhelmed, Ps. 119:20. Hiph. fut. וַיַּגְרֵם and brake, destroyed, Lam. 3:16.

גֶּרֶשׂ m. (with suff. גִּרְשָׂהּ), thrashed; perhaps, ground corn, Lev. 2:14, 16.

גָּרַע I. took away.—II. shaved, took away the beard, Jer. 48:37. Niph. (fut. יִגָּרַע) was taken away. Pi. draws off; fut. יְגָרַע Job 36:27.

מִגְרָעוֹת f. pl., ledges, steps in buildings, 1 Ki. 6:6.

גָּרַף swept away (as a flood), Jud. 5:21. אֶגְרוֹף m., fist.

מַגְרֵפָה f., furrow, Joel 1:17.

גָּרַר he drew, dragged; fut. יָגֹר. Niph. fut. יַגֹּר chew the cud. Po. sawed, 1 Ki. 7:9. Hithpo. swept away, Jer. 30:23.

גֵּרָה f.—I. the cud.—II. Gerah, a weight equal to the twentieth part of a shekel.

גַּרְגַּר m., berry, Isa. 17:6.

גַּרְגְּרָה f., throat, front of the neck.

גָּרוֹן m. (const. גְּרוֹן), throat.

מְגֵרָה f., saw.

גְּרָר p. n. of a city of the Philistines.

גֶּרֶשׂ flower; see נרס.

גָּרַשׁ put forth, cast forth. Niph. was cast, driven, out. Pi. גֵּרֵשׁ expel Pu. גֹּרַשׁ was expelled.

גֶּרֶשׁ m., produce, fruit, Deu. 33:14.

גְּרֻשָׁה expulsion.

מִגְרָשׁ m.—I. suburbs.—II. pastures, open places.—III. lands, surrounding the cities of the Levites; pl. מִגְרָשׁוֹת, מִגְרָשִׁים.

גֵּרְשֹׁם p. n. of the son of Moses.

גֵּרְשׁוֹן (Gershon), p. n. of a man; גֵּרְשֻׁנִּי a Gershonite.

גַּשׁ, גְּשָׁה, גֶּשׁ Kal imp., from נגשׁ.

גְּשׁוּ Kal imp. pl., from נגשׁ.

גְּשׁוּר (bridge), p. n. of three places.—I. the country of the Canaanites to the east of Jordan.—II. of a district in South Palestine.—III. of a district in Syria. גְּשׁוּרִי a Geshurite.

גָּשַׁם Kal, root not used; (Arab. fatness). Hiph. part. pl. מַגְשִׁמִים cause to rain, Jer. 14:22.

גֶּשֶׁם m., heavy shower; pl. גְּשָׁמִים, גִּשְׁמֵי.

גֶּשֶׁם m., the same; with suff. גִּשְׁמָהּ.

גֶּשֶׁם m., body.

גֶּשֶׁם, גַּשְׁמוּ p. n. of a man.

גֹּשֶׁן (Goshen), p. n.—I. of the country bordering on Egypt, which was inhabited by the Israelites during the first captivity.—II. of a town in the tribe of Judah.

נִשְׁפָּא p. n. of a man.

גָּשַׁשׁ Pi. fut. with ה parag. נְגַשְׁשָׁה we feel, grope about, Isa. 59:10.

גָּשַׁת Kal inf. with suff. גִּשְׁתּוֹ, from נגשׁ.

גַּת f.—I. the vat in which grapes were trodden; pl. גִּתּוֹת.—II. p. n. of a city of the Philistines in the country of Goliath. גַּת הַחֵפֶר p. n. of a town in the tribe of Zebulun; גַּת רִמּוֹן p. n. of cities of the Levites in Dan and Manasseh; גִּתִּי a Gittite.

גִּתַּיִם p. n. of a town in the tribe of Benjamin.

גִּתִּית f., probably the name of a musical instrument; occurs in the titles of certain psalms.

גֶּתֶר p. n. of a people of Syria, Gen 10:23.

# ד

דָּא pron. Ch. f. and neuter, this; דָּא לְדָא together.

דָּאַב same as דּוּב was languid.

דְּאָבָה f., pining away, Job 41:14.

דְּאָבוֹן m., extreme languor, fainting; const. דַּאֲבוֹן, Deu. 28:65.

דָּאַן fish, same as דָּג; see דָּנָה.

דָּאַג I. grieve, be anxious, with לְ.— II. fear, with מִן.

דֹּאָן (Syr. דֹּוֵין), p. n. of a prince of the Edomites.

דְּאָגָה f., anxiety, alarm.

דָּאָה flew; fut. וַיֵּדֶא יִדְאֶה.

דָּאָה f., name of a bird, kite, Lev. 11: 14; LXX. γὺψ; Vulg. milvus; corresponding passage, Deu. 14:13, רָאָה

דֹּאר p. n., same as דּוֹר.

דֹּב bear; see דבב.

דָּבָא root not used; (Arab. produced, multiplied).

דֹּבֶא riches, power; LXX. ἰσχύς, Deu 33:25; with suff. דָּבְאֶךָ.

דָּבַב crept, flowed softly (of wine) Cant. 7:10.

דֹּב, דֻּבִּים m. (pl. דֻּבִּים) a bear.

דֹּב m. Ch., the same.

דִּבָּה f.—I. calumny.—II. calumniator, Pro. 25:10.

דְּבוֹרָה bee; see דבר.

דְּבַח Ch., sacrificed, Ezr. 6:3; see זבח

דְּבַח m. Ch., sacrifice, Ezr. 6:3.

מַדְבַּח m. Ch., altar, Ezr. 7:17.

דִּבְיוֹנִים m. pl., pigeons' dung, 2 Ki. 6:25.

דְּבִיר oracle; see דבר

דָּבַל root not used; (Arab. pressed together).

דְּבֵלָה f. (const. דְּבֶלֶת; pl. דְּבֵלִים) παλάθη, cake of dry figs.

דִּבְלָתַיִם, דִּבְלָה, בֵּית דִּ׳ p. n. of a city of the Moabites.

דִּבְלַיִם p. n. of a man.

דָּבַק and דָּבֵק (fut. יִדְבַּק; inf. דָּבְקָה).—I. adhered, cleft to.—II. reached, attained, with בְּ, לְ, אֶל. Pu. fut. pl. יְדֻבָּקוּ made to adhere. Hiph. (fut. יַדְבִּיק, וַיַּדְבֵּק) joined, caused to stick, attained. Hoph. part מֻדְבָּק stuck to, Ps. 22:16.

דְּבַק Ch., adhered, Dan. 2:43.

דָּבֵק m., adhering; pl. דְּבֵקִים.

דֶּבֶק m., solder, for joining metals; pl. דְּבָקִים rivets (for armour).

דָּבַר not used in the pres. pret.; part. דֹּבֵר speaking; דָּבָר spoken; inf. דָּבְרְךָ thy speaking. Piel דִּבֵּר, (fut. יְדַבֵּר) he spoke, uttered words to or with any one, with לְ, עַל, אֶת, עִם, אֶל; concerning any one, with עַל, אֶל, בְּ; against any one, with עַל, בְּ; by any one, with בְּיָד; דִּבֵּר used idiomatically; דִּבְּרִים לַעֲשׂוֹת he threatened; ד' דְּבָרִים he uttered words; ד' שָׁלוֹם, with אֶת or עִם he spoke friendly with any one; with בְּ the same; ד' לְאִשָּׁה he asked her in marriage. Pu. was spoken. Niph. became, i.e. set about speaking, with עַל, בְּ. Hiph. subdued (with his word); fut. יַדְבֵּר. Hithp. part. מִדַּבֵּר speaking.

דָּבָן m. (const. דְּבַר; pl. דְּבָרִים, דִּבְרֵי).—I. word; בַּעַל אִישׁ דְּבָרִים eloquent man.—II. thing.—III. thing, matter, subject in hand; דְּבַר יוֹם בְּיוֹמוֹ the thing (duty) of the day in its day; אַחַר הַדְּבָרִים הָאֵלֶּה after these things, μετὰ ταῦτα: אֵין ד' לֹא דָבָר nothing; there is nothing; בַּעַל ד' he who pleads a cause; דְּבַר and דִּבְרֵי because; עַל דְּבַר אֲשֶׁר because of.

דֶּבֶר m., pestilence; pl. דְּבָרִים.

דְּבִיר m.—I. the oracle, i.e. the place in the temple whence the responses were given.—II. p. n. of a city in the tribe of Judah.

דֹּבֶר m., fold, pasture, Mic. 2:12.

דִּבְרָה f., cause for adjudication; עַל דִּבְרַת because; with שֶׁ because that; עַל דִּבְרָתִי according to, after the order of, Ps. 110:4.

דִּבְרָה f. Ch., cause.

דְּבוֹרָה f.—I. a bee; pl. דְּבֹרִים.—II. p. n. of a woman who judged Israel.

דֹּבְרוֹת f. pl., floats, rafts, 1 Ki. 5:23.

דַּבְּרוֹת f. pl., sayings, Deu. 33:3.

מִדְבָּר m.—I. any large plain used for pasture.—II. a desert or wilderness; מִדְבַּר הַ the desert of Sinai. —III. speech, address, Cant. 4:3.

דְּבַשׁ m. (with suff. דִּבְשִׁי).—I. honey of bees.—II. honey dew, collected in large quantities in Palestine.

דַּבֶּשֶׁת f.—I. the hunch, or more probably, the pack-saddle of a camel. —II. p.n. of a place, Jos. 19:11.

דָּגָה multiplied, Gen. 48:16.

דָּג (דָּאָג) m., fish; pl. דָּגִים, דָּגִין. דָּגָה const. דְּגַת f., a fish, fish in general.

דָּגוֹן m., p. n. of an idol of the Philistines, probably in the form of a fish.

דָּגָן (const. דְּגַן) m.—I. bread.—II. corn.

דָּגַל part. דָּגוּל.—I. marked, signalised, Cant. 5:10.—II. fut. נִדְגֹּל we will set up our banner, Ps. 20:6. Niph. part. pl. נִדְגָּלוֹת having banners, i.e. an army, Cant. 6:4, 10; see next word.

דֶּגֶל m. (with suff. דִּגְלוֹ; pl. דְּגָלִים, דִּגְלֵי), standard, banner.

דָּגָן com.; see דָּגָה.

דָּגַר hatch, brood over eggs, Isa. 34: 15; Jer. 17:11.

דַּד m., dual דַּדַּיִם, דַּדֵּי the two breasts of a woman.

דָּדָה. Hith. fut. אֶדַּדֶּה I will proceed gently, submissively, joyfully.

דְּדָן (pl. דְּדָנִים), p. n. of the inhabitants of a district in the north of Arabia.

דְּדָנִים m. pl., p. n. of a people.

דְּהַב m. Ch., gold.

מַדְהֵבָה f., an epithet of Babylon, lit. place of gold, Isa. 14:4.

דְּהָיֵא p. n. of a people who were colonised in Samaria, Ezr. 4:9.

דָּהַם. Niph. part. נִדְהָם reduced, impotent, Jer. 14:9.

דָּהַר, part. דֹּהֵר charging, attacking, Nah. 3:2.

דַּהֲרָה f., charge of cavalry; pl. דַּהֲרוֹת, Jud. 5:22.

תִּדְהָר m., name of a tree; Vulg. ulnus; the elm or box.

דּוֹב same as דֹּב bear; see דבב.

דּוּב same as דָּאַב wasting. Hiph. part. pl. מְדִיבוֹת things wasting, Lev. 26:16.

דּוּג and דִּיג (from דָּג) he shall fish, Jer. 16:16.

דַּיָּג, דַּוָּג m., a fisher.

דּוּגָה f., fishing, Am. 4:2.

דּוּד I. root not used; Ch. was agitated.—II. same as יָדַד he loved.

דּוּד m.—I. a pot or caldron; pl. דְּוָדִים.—II. basket; pl. דּוּדִים.

דּוּדָאִים m. pl.—I. baskets.—II. mandrakes, plants used as philtres or love potions.

דּוֹד m. (pl. דֹּדִים).—I. love.—II. offices of love.—III. beloved.—IV. uncle.

דּוֹדָה f., aunt.

דָּוִד, דָּוִיד p. n., David king of Israel.

דָּוָה I. was sick.—II. was unclean, polluted; inf. דְּוֹתָהּ her uncleanness (i. e. the menses), Lev. 12:2.

דָּוֶה m., דָּוָה f., sick, unclean.

דְּוַי m., sickness, disease, Ps. 40:4.

דַּוָּי m., habitual (chronic) disorder.

דְּוֹת inf. of דָּוָה, which see.

מַדְוֶה m., consuming disease.

דּוּחַ. Hiph. הֵדִיחַ I. expel, Jer. 51:34.—II. dispel, i. e. scour clean.

דָּוִיד p. n., same as דָּוִד; see דּוּד.

דּוּךְ same as דָּכַךְ beat, pounded, Nu. 11:8.

מְדֹכָה f., mortar, Nu. 11:8.

דּוּכִיפַת f., LXX. ἔποψ; Vulg. upupa; the hoopoe, Lev. 11:19; Deu. 14:18.

דּוּם root not used, same as דָּמַם was silent.

דּוּמָה f.—I. silent.—II. death.—III. the grave.—IV. p. n. of a people of Arabia.

דּוּמִיָּה f.—I. remaining, abiding.—II. quietness, silence.

דּוּמָם m., very quiet, silent.

דּוּמֶשֶׂק p. n., same as דַּמֶּשֶׂק.

דּוּן; see דִּין.

דּוֹנַג, דּוֹנָג m., wax.

דּוּץ (fut. יָדוּץ) leaps, exults, Job 41:14.

דּוּק Ch., grind small, Dan. 2:35.

דָּיֵק m., entrenchment, foss, dyke, used in sieges.

דּוּר I. dwell, reside, Ps. 84:11.—II. encircle, place round, Eze. 24:5.

דּוּר Ch., dwell.

**דּוּר** m.—I. *a circle*, Isa. 29:3.—II. *a ball*, Isa. 22:18.

**דּוֹר, דֹּר** m. (lit. *circle of years*).— I. *age, generation.*—II. *race of men*; עַד דֹּר, לְדֹר דֹּר, לְדֹר וָדֹר, דֹּר וָדֹר, מִדֹּר דֹּר וָדֹר *from generation to generation, for ever*; pl. דּוֹר דּוֹרִים *eternity*; דּוֹרוֹת *generations of men, posterity.*—III. *habitation* (see דּוּר); with אֲבוֹת *sepulchre*, Ps. 49:20.

**דָּר** m. Ch., *age, generation.*

נְפוֹת דּוֹר and נָפַה דּ׳, דֹּאר, דּוֹר p.n. of a city not far from Mount Carmel.

**מְדוֹר** m. Ch., *habitation.*

**מְדֹר** m. Ch., the same.

**מְדוּרָה** f., *pile of fire.*

**תְּדִירָא** f. Ch., *a revolution*; בִּתְדִירָא *continually*, Dan. 6:17, 21.

**דּוּרָא** p.n. of a valley or plain in Babylonia.

**דּוּשׁ** and דִּישׁ (fut. יָדֹרשׁ).—I. *tread, trample on.*—II. *tread out corn.*—III. metaphorically, *conquer enemies.* Niph. נָדֹרשׁ *was trampled down*; inf. abs. הִדּוּשׁ (as it were). Hoph. fut. יּוּדַשׁ *is trodden*, Isa. 28:27.

**דּוּשׁ** Ch., *is trodden*, Dan. 7:23.

**דַּיִשׁ** m., *time of treading out corn*, Lev. 26:5.

**מְדוּשָׁה** f., with suff. מְדֻשָׁתִי *my treading out*, Isa. 21:10.

**דּוּהָ** see דָּוָה.

**דָּחָה** *drive, urge on to fall*; inf. abs. דָּחֹה; part. f. דְּחוּיָה *impelled.* Niph. *urged* or *impelled*; part. pl. נִדְחֵי, נִדְחִים. Pu. pl. דֹּחוּ *are driven.*

**דְּחִי** m. (with pause דֶּחִי), *impulse, being driven on.*

**דַּחֲוָה** Ch. f., pl. דַּחֲוָן Dan. 6:19 "instruments of music," Eng Ver.; meaning uncertain.

**מַדְחֵה** m., *driving out, ruin*, Prov 26:28.

**דָּחַח** Niph. fut. pl. יִדָּחוּ, same as דָּחָה Niph., *is urged, impelled.*

**דְּחַל** Ch., part. דְּחִיל *fearful.* Pa *affright*, Dan. 4:2.

**דֹּחַן** m., *millet*, Eze. 4:9.

**דָּחַף**, part. pl. דְּחוּפִים *hurried, hastened.* Niph. *was hurried.*

**מַדְחֵפוֹת** f. pl.; לְמַדְ *swiftly, hastily*, Ps. 140:12.

**דָּחַק** *press upon*, Joel 2:8; part. דֹּחֵק *oppressor*, Ju. 2:18.

**דַּי** m. (const. דֵּי, with suff. דַּיִי), *a sufficiency, enough*; דֵּי הָשִׁיב *as much as shall restore*, Lev. 25:28; דַּיָּם *sufficient for them*; דֵּי חֲלֵב *enough of milk*, Pro. 27:27; בְּדַי *same as* בְּ; כְּדֵי *as (it were) enough*; מִדֵּי *same as* מִן; מִדֵּי שָׁנָה בְּשָׁנָה *from year to year, yearly.*

**דִּי** Ch.—I. the relative pron. *who, which, what*, like אֲשֶׁר.—II. *of*, like the *de* of the modern European languages.— III. conj. like אֲשֶׁר *that.*—IV. same as כִּי, ὅτι. כְּדִי *when, as*; מִן דִּי *from the time when*; עַד דִּי *until.*

**דִּי זָהָב** (*enough of gold*); p.n. of a place in the desert near Sinai, Deut. 1:1.

**דִּיבוֹן** p.n.—I. of a town of the Moabites.—II. of a place in the tribe of Judah; same as דִּימוֹנָה.

**דַּיָּג**, דַּיָּן *fishermen*; see דּוּג.

**דִּיָה** root not used; Ch. דְּהָא *was black.*

דַּיָּה f., *black vulture, turkey buzzard;* LXX. ἰκτίνος, Vulg. milvus, Deut. 14:13, &c.

דְּיוֹ m., *ink,* Jer. 36:18.

דִּימָן same as דִּיבוֹן p. n. of a town of Moab.

דִּימוֹנָה p. n. of a town in the tribe of Judah.

דִּין and דּוּן (pret. and part. דָּן; inf. and imper. דִּין; fut. יָדִין).—I. *judged.*—II. *pleaded, defended.*—III. *punished,* with בְּ.—IV. *contend with one,* with עִם.—V. *govern,* with בְּ. Niph. part. נָדוֹן *contend,* 2 Sa. 19:10.

דִּין and דּוּן Ch., the same.

דִּין (דּוּן Job 19:29.) m.—I. *judgment.*—II. *cause for judgment* (דָּן and דִּין עָשָׂה *he pleaded a cause*).—III. *litigation, strife.*

דִּין m. Ch.—I. *judgment.*—II. *court of judgment.*—III. *punishment.*

דִּינָה p. n. of the daughter of Jacob.

דִּינָיֵא Ch., p. n. of a people of Assyria.

דַּיָּן m., *a judge;* Ch. pl. דַּיָּנִין *judges.*

דָּן p. n., *Dan.*—I. a son of Jacob and his tribe.—II. a city in the north of Palestine.

דָּנִיֵּאל, דְּנִיֵּאל p. n., *Daniel.*

מָדוֹן m.—I. *dispute, contention;* pl. מִדְיָנִים, מְדָנִים.—II. אִישׁ מָדוֹן *man of height, stature* (see מִדָּה), 2 Sa. 21:20.—III. p. n. of a city of the Canaanites.

מָדָן m. (pl. מְדָנִים).—I. *strifes, disputes.*—II. p. n. of the son of Abraham and Keturah.

מָדְיָנִי (pl. מִדְיָנִים) *Midianite;* see מִדְיָנִים

מְדִינָה f., lit. *jurisdiction:* hence,—I. *province.*—II. *region, country.*

מְדִינָה f. Ch., the same.

דִּיפַת p. n. of a son of Japhet, 1 Ch 1:6, a wrong reading for רִיפַת Gen. 10:3.

דָּיֵק *dyke;* see דּוּג.

דָּיִשׁ *tread;* see דּוּשׁ.

דִּישׁוֹן m.—I. a species of deer, Deut. 14:5.—II. p. n. of a son of Seir and of a district called after him.

דַּךְ *poor;* see דכך.

דָּךְ Ch. pron., *this, he;* fem. דָּךְ *she.*

דָּכָא. Pi. דִּכָּא.—I. *beat small, break*—II. *trample on.*—Pu. *was broken, contrite.* Hith. fut. יַדַּכְּאוּ *shall be broken.* Niph. part., *beaten, oppressed,* Isa. 57:15.

דַּכָּא m.—I. *crushed.*—II. *humbled, dejected.*

דָּכָה *is broken,* Ps. 10:10. Niph. *broken, afflicted.* Pi. דִּכִּיתָ *thou hast broken.*

דָּכִי m., with suff. דָּכְיָם, *their beating, dashing,* Ps. 93:3.

דָּכַךְ root not used, same as דָּכָה and דּוּךְ.

דַּךְ (with pause דָּךְ m.), *poor, mean, afflicted,* Pro. 26:28; יִשְׁנָא דַכִּין *makes hateful those whom it has afflicted.*

דַּכָּה f., *bruising,* θλάσις, Deu. 33:2.

דִּכֵּן Ch. pron., *this.*

דְּכַר Ch., same as זָכָר *male.*

דְּכַר m. Ch., *a ram;* pl. דִּכְרִין.

דִּכְרוֹן m. Ch. (emph. state דָּכְרוֹנָה *memorial, record,* Ezr. 6:2.

דָּכְרָן m. Ch. the same, Ezr. 4:15.

דַּל poor; see דָּלָה דלה and דלל.

דִּלֵּג leaping, skipping. Pi. the same, with עַל.

דָּלָה I. draw (water from a well). Pi. draw up out of prison, Ps. 30:2. —II. totter, vacillate, be lame; דָּלְלוּ for דָּלְיוּ Pro. 26:7.

דַּל m. for דֶּלֶת door, Ps. 141:3.

דֶּלֶת gate, door; dual דְּלָתַיִם folding, double doors or gates; דַּלְתֵי שָׁמַיִם the doors of heaven (clouds?); דַּ' פָּנִים doors of the face (jaws), Job 41:6; דַּ' בֶּטֶן doors of the womb. Pl. דְּלָתוֹת; const. דַּלְתוֹת f. (m. Neh. 13:19). —I. doors.—II. leaves, valves of gates.—III. leaves of a book, Jer. 36:23.

דְּלִי m., bucket, Isa. 40:15.

דְּלִי m., dual דָּלְיִם (with suff. דָּלְיָו), his drawings up or forth, Nu. 24:7.

דָּלִית f., pl. דָּלִיּוֹת boughs, branches.

דְּלָיָהוּ, דְּלָיָה p. n. of a man.

דַּלָּה poverty; see דלל.

דָּלַח disturb, render muddy (of water), Eze. 32:2, 13.

דָּלְיוּ for דָּלוּ Pi. imp. pl., from דלה.

דָּלַל wasted, reduced, weakened. Niph. (fut. וַיִּדַּל) is wasted, reduced.

דַּל m. (pl. דַּלִּים; f. דַּלָּה, pl. דַּלּוֹת), poor, weak.

דַּלָּה f.—I. thin thread, Isa. 38:12.— II. smallness, poverty.—III. hair of the head, Cant. 7:6; pl. דַּלּוֹת.

דְּלִילָה p. n. of the concubine of Samson.

דִּלְעָן p. n. of a town in the tribe of Judah.

---

דָּלַף I. dropped.—II. shed tears.

דֶּלֶף m., rain drop.

דַּלְפוֹן p. n. of the son of Haman.

דָּלַק (fut. יִדְלַק).—I. burning, consu-ming.—II. applied metaphorically to strong mental affections, with אַחֲרֵי. Hiph. kindled, inflamed.

דְּלַק Ch., burnt, Dan. 7:9.

דַּלֶּקֶת f., burning fever, Deu. 28:22.

דְּלָתוֹת, דְּלָתַיִם, דֶּלֶת; see דלה.

דָּם; see אדם.

I. דָּמָה was like to, resembled, with אֶל, לְ. Niph. was assimilated, with כְּ. Pi. דִּמָּה.—I. assimilated, compare, with לְ, אֶל.—II. imagined, thought, meditated. Hithp. fut. אֲדַמֶּה same as Niph., Isa. 14:14.

II. דָּמָה same as דָּמַם.—I. silent, quiet.—II. ruined, destroyed. Niph. was silent, ruined. Pi. exterminate, destroy.

דְּמָה Ch., be similar, like.

דְּמוּת f., similitude, likeness; בִּדְמוּת (also without כְּ) as, like.

דְּמִי m., silence, rest.

דֳּמִי m., the same.

דִּמְיוֹן m., same as דְּמוּת likeness, Ps. 17:12.

דָּמַם (pret. pl. דַּמּוּ; imp. and inf. דֹּם; fut. יִדֹּם; pl. יִדְּמוּ) was dumb, quiet, inactive, in consequence of some strong affection of the mind, with לְ; דֹּ' לַיהוָה to wait silently upon the Lord. Po. דּוֹמַמְתִּי made silent, Ps. 131:2. Hiph. הָדַם reduced to silence, ruined, Jer. 8:14. Niph. נָדַם (fut. יִדְּמוּ, תִּדְּמִי) became silent, destroyed.

דִּמָּה f., cut off, ruined, Eze. 27:32.

דְּמָמָה f., *silence*, 1 Ki. 19:12.

דֹּמֶן m., *dung*.

דִּמְנָה p.n. of a town in the tribe of Zebulun.

מַדְמֵן p. n. of a town of Moab.

מַדְמֵנָה f.—I. *dung-hill*, Isa. 25:10.— II. p. n. of a town in the tribe of Benjamin.

מַדְמַנָּה p. n. of a town in the tribe of Judah, Jos. 15:31.

דֶּמַע m., lit. *tear* (with suff. דִּמְעֲךָ Ex. 22:29), *juice of the grape, olive, &c.*

דִּמְעָה f. (pl. דְּמָעוֹת)—I. *tear*.—II. *weeping.*

דּוּמֶשֶׂק, דַּרְמֶשֶׂק, דַּמֶּשֶׂק p. n. —I. *Damascus*, a city of Syria.— II. *a Damascene* (supp. אִישׁ), Gen. 15:2.

דְּמֶשֶׂק or מֶשֶׂק *damask*, silk cloth made at Damascus.

דֵּן, see דִּין.

דֵּן Ch. pron., *this, that*; emph. דְּנָה; כִּדְנָה *thus*; עַל דְּנָה *thereupon*; אַחֲרֵי דְנָה *afterwards.*

דַּנָּה p.n. of a town in the tribe of Judah.

דִּנְהָבָה p.n. of a town in Edom.

דָּנִיֵּאל p.n.; see דִּין.

דַּנַּנִּי Kal pret. with suff. and נ epenth., from דִּין.

דֵּעַ, דֵּעָה *knowledge*; see ידע.

דְּעֵה Kal imp. with ה parag., from ידע.

דְּעוּאֵל p. n. of a man.

דָּעַךְ.—I. *put out, extinguish.*—II. *made worse.* Niph. נִדְעֲכוּ *are extinguished*, Job 6:17. Pu. דֹּעֲכוּ *the same*, Ps. 118:12.

דַּעַת *knowledge*; see ידע.

דָּפָה root not used; (Arab. *slaying*).

דֳּפִי (with pause דֹּפִי m.) *stroke, destruction*, Ps. 50:20.

דָּפַק.—I. *beat, drive* (as cattle), Gen. 33:13.—II. *knock at a door*, Cant. 5:2. Hith. *knocked*, Judg. 19:22.

דָּפְקָה p.n. of one of the stations of the Israelites in the desert.

דַּק, דַּקָּה, דֹּק; see דקק.

דִּקְלָה p.n. of a district of Joktan in Arabia, Gen. 10:27.

דָּקַק (fut. יָדֹק, with suff. יְדִקֶּנּוּ) *beat or grind small.* Hiph. הֵדַק (fut. with suff. אֲדִיקֵם for אֲדִקֵּם; inf. הָדֵק, also הַדֵּק adv., *as fine as dust*, Ex. 30:36), *reduce to powder.* Hoph. fut. יוּדַק *is ground, powdered*, Isa. 28:28.

דְּקַק Ch., *pounded.* Aph. *made small*; see דוּק.

דַּק m., דַּקָּה f., *small, thin, impalpable*; דַּק s., *small dust.*

דֹּק m., *thin, fine cloth*, Isa. 40:22.

דָּקַר (fut. יִדְקֹר) *pierce, run through.* Niph. fut. יִדָּקֵר *shall be thrust through*, Isa. 13:15. Pu. part. מְדֻקָּרִים.—I. *they who are thrust through.*—II. *slain by want*, Lam 4:9.

דֶּקֶר p.n. of a man.

מַדְקָרוֹת f. pl., *piercings of the sword*, Pro. 12:18.

דַּר *marble*; see דרר.

דֹּר, דָּר *race*; see דוּר.

דָּרָא root not used; (Arab. *excite evil*).

דֵּרָאוֹן m., *abhorring, contempt*, Dan 12:2.

דְּרָאוֹן m. *abomination*, Isa. 66 : 24.

דָּרַב root not used ; (Arab. *point*.)

דָּרְבָן m. *goad*; βούκεντρον, 1 Sa. 13 : 21.

דָּרְבֹנוֹת f. pl. *goads*, Ecc. 12 : 11.

דָּרַג root not used ; (Arab. *step, stair*).

מַדְרֵגָה f. *steep place, precipice*.

דְּרוֹר, דַּרְדַּר, דָּרוֹם, דַּרְדַּע ; see דרר.

דָּרְיָוֶשׁ p. n. of the kings of Persia.—
—I. *Darius* the Median (Cyaxares II.).—II. *Darius* Hystaspes.—III. *Darius* Nothus.

דָּרַךְ I. *tread* (as grapes), with בְּ, עַל.
—II. *bend a bow*, by placing the left foot upon it; חִצִּים 'ד *he shot arrows from the bent bow*.—III. *tread down, destroy*.—IV. *enter, pass in*, with עַל, בְּ.—V. *walk in state*.—Hiph. I. *caused to proceed, led*.—II. *bent as a bow*.—III. *trod down*.—IV. *took possession of*.

דֶּרֶךְ com. (with suff. דַּרְכִּי; pl. דְּרָכִים, דַּרְכֵי; dual דְּרָכַיִם).—I. *way, road*; עֵץ 'ד *way to the tree*; הַמֶּלֶךְ 'ד *king's highway*.—II. *journey*; 'ד הַיּוֹם *a day's journey*.—III. *mode, manner, custom*; יְהוָֹה 'ד *God's dealings*.—IV. *the fruits of one's ways*, Isa. 10 : 24, &c.

מִדְרָךְ m., *foot-prints*, Deu. 2 : 5.

דַּרְכְּמֹן drachm, same as אֲדַרְכֹּן.

דַּרְמֶשֶׂק *Damascus*, same as דַּמֶּשֶׂק.

דְּרָע com. Ch., *arm*, Dan. 2 : 32.

אֶדְרָע com. Ch., *arm*, Ezr. 4 : 23.

דַּרְקוֹן p. n. of a man.

דָּרַר root not used; (Arab. *flew, went, round*).

דְּרוֹר m.—I. *swallow or wild pigeon*.

—II. *spontaneously flowing myrrh*, Ex. 30 : 23, hence:—III. *liberty*; בְּ and לְ 'ד קָרָא *he proclaimed liberty to any one, he manumitted his slave*; שְׁנַת הַדְּרוֹר *the year of Jubilee*, in which all Hebrew slaves were free, Lev. 25 : 10.

דַּר m., some unknown kind of *marble*, Ezr. 1 : 6 ; LXX. πίννινος λίθος.

דַּרְדַּע p. n. of a man.

דַּרְדַּר m., *brambles*.

דָּרוֹם m., the country south of Judea.

דָּרַשׁ I. *he sought, enquired for, into*, &c., with בְּ, לְ, אֶל, אֶת.—II. *enquired about, concerning*, with עַל; used especially of asking supernatural counsel : with מֵעִם before the person asked; with בְּ, אֶל, לְ before the being from whom the oracle is asked.—III. *demanded, asked, required* : with מִן before the person from whom the demand is made; דָּרַשׁ דָּם with מִן or מֵעִם or מִיָּד *required the blood of one slain*, i. e. avenge his death.—IV. *promoted, sought to accomplish*; רָעַת פ' 'ד *sought to do him evil*. —V יְהוָֹה 'ד *sought the Lord*, in acts of worship.—VI. *cared for*. Niph. *was sought, enquired after*.

דְּרִיוֹשׁ m., *seeking*, Ezr. 10 : 16.

מִדְרָשׁ m., *book, commentary*, 2 Chron. 13 : 22.

דָּשָׁא *became grassy*, Joel 2 : 22. Hiph. *sent forth grass*, Gen. 1 : 11, 12.

דֶּשֶׁא m., *tender herb, first blades of grass*.

דָּשֵׁן *grew fat*, Deu. 31 : 20.—Pi. דִּשֵּׁן

I. made, considered fat.—II. anointed.—III. from דֶּשֶׁן removed ashes. Pu. was made fat, satisfied. Hothpa. pret. הַדַּשְׁנָה made fat (of a sword), Isa. 34:6.

דָּשֵׁן m., fat, fruitful.

דֶּשֶׁן m. (with suff. דִּשְׁנִי).—I. fatness of meat.—II. fertility.—III. ashes, specially those of burnt-offerings, &c. which were used for manure.

דָּת f. (pl. דָּתֵי, דָּתִים), edict, mandate, law.

דָּת f. Ch., law, edict.

דְּתָבָר m. Ch., judges or lawyers, Dan. 4:12, 20.

דִּתְאָה emph. דְּתָאָה Ch. m., same as Heb. דֶּשֶׁא grass.

דֹּתָיִן p.n. of a place north of Samaria.

דָּתָן p.n. of one of the accomplices of Korah.

## ה

ה (הָ, הַ).—I. def. art. ὁ, ἡ, τὸ the.—II. demon. pron. this; הַיּוֹם this day.—III. relat. pron. who, which; הֶחָלְכוּא who went, Jos. 10:24; הָעֲלֶיהָ that which is above her.—IV. sign of the vocative; הַמֶּלֶךְ O King! הַבַּעַל O Baal! 1 Ki. 18:26.

הֲ (הַ, הָ) pref., sign of an interrogation; הֲשֹׁמֵר אָחִי אָנֹכִי am I my brother's keeper, Gen. 4:9.

הָא (Ch.) behold!

הָאָח aha! exclamation of joy or scorn.

הָאֲנִיחוּ for הַזְּנִיחוּ Hiph. pret. pl., from זנח.

הַב with ה parag. הָבָה; pl. הָבוּ Kal imper., from יהב.

הָבֵא, הָבִיא Hiph. imper., from בוא.

הֵבָאת Hoph. pret. f., from בוא.

הֹבֵאישׁ for הוֹבִישׁ Hiph., from באשׁ.

הַבְהָבִים gifts; see יהב.

יַהֲבוּ Hos. 4:18, pret. pl. for הֵבוּ, from יהב.

הִבּוֹק Niph. inf., from בקק.

הָבִי Ruth 3:15, Kal imp. f., from יהב, or Hiph. imp. f. for הָבִיא, from בוא.

הֶבֵל (fut. יֶהְבַּל) act vainly, sinfully. Hiph. cause to act vainly, Jer. 23:16

הֶבֶל m. (with suff. הֶבְלִי; pl. הֲבָלִים, הַבְלֵי).—I. vanity, instability, deception.—II. idols.—III. abortions, Ecc. 6:4, and thence, men in general.—IV. adv., vainly, in vain.—V. p.n., Abel, the son of Adam.

הָבֵל m., vanity.

הָבְנִים (הוֹבְנִים) ebony, Eze. 27:15.

הָבַר (Arab. that which cuts); הֹבְרֵי שָׁמַיִם they who cut, divide the heavens, astrologers, Isa. 47:13; Vulg. augures coeli; LXX. ἀστρολόγοι τοῦ οὐρανοῦ.

הָבֵר Hiph. inf. from בור.

הָגַג root not used; (Syr. imagined).

הָגִין m., deep, ardent meditation.

הָגָה (fut. יֶהְגֶּה; inf. הָגֹה).—I. murmur, coo, growl.—II. meditate.—III. declare one's meditations, with בְּ.—IV. discern, separate. Po. inf. הֹגוּ utter, speak. Hiph. part. pl. מַהְגִּים mutterers, i. e. enchanters, Isa. 8:19.

הֶגֶה m.—murmur, whisper.—II. thunder.

הָנֻת f., *meditation*, Ps. 49:4.

הָנִין m., *a musical stringed-instru-*
הָנִיּן }    *ment* or *the sound of one.*

חֹנֵן 2 Sa. 20:13, for הוֹנָה Hiph. from
ינה *he removed*

חָנוֹ Kal inf. abs. from II. הנה.

חֹנוֹ Po. inf. from הנה.

הָגִין m., הֲנִינָה f., *straight, commodi-*
*ous*, Eze. 42:12.

הָנְלָת (Syr. for הָנְלָתָה) Hoph. pret. f.,
from נלה.

הָגָר p. n. of the mother of Ishmael.

הַגְרִיאים, הַגְרִים p. n. of a people eastward of Gilead.

הֵד *shout*; see הדד.

הַדָּבְרִין m. pl. Ch., title of certain officers in the court of Babylon;
"counsellors," Eng. Ver.

הָדַד root not used; (Arab. *shouting*).
הֵידָד *shouting* (of bodies of men).
הֵד m., *shouting*, Eze. 7:7.
הֲדַד p. n. of a king of Edom.
הֲדַדְעֶזֶר p.n. of a king of Syria.
הֲדַדְרִמּוֹן p. n. of a town not far
from Megiddo.

הָדָה *guided* (his hand), Isa. 11:8.

הֹדּוּ (for הֹנְדּוּ Hindu), p. n. *Hin-*
*dustan*, India.

הֲדוֹרָם p. n. of an Arab tribe, descended from Joktan, Gen. 10:27.

הַדִּי, חֻרִי p. n. of a man.

הָדַךְ *break down, overturn*, Job 40:12.

הָדַם root not used; (Arab. *destruc-*
*tion*).
הֲדֹם m., *footstool.*
הַדָּם m. Ch., *piece, fragment.*
הֲדַס m., *myrtle*; pl. הֲדַסִּים.

הֲדַסָּה p.n. the former name of Esther

הָדַף (fut. יֶהְדֹּף), *thrust out, drive*
*back.*

הָדַר (fut. יֶהְדַּר), *honoured, dignified*
(in dress), Isa. 63:1; with פְּנֵי פ
*take the part of any one.* Niph.
*was honoured*, Lam. 5:12. Hith.
*was glorious*, Pro. 25:5.
הֲדַר Ch. Pa. *honoured.*
הָדָר m., *glorious, honourable, dignified.*
הֶדֶר m., *honour*, Dan. 11:20.
הֲדָרָה f. (const. הַדְרַת), *honourable* (in
apparel).

הַדְּשָׁנָה Hothp. pret. f., from דשׁן.

הָהּ *ah!* exclamation of grief.

הֹהּ same as הוֹי *alas!*

הוּא pers. pron. m.—I *he, it.*—II.
*this, the same.*
הֲוָא Ch., *was*; same as הָוָה.
הֱוֵא for הֲוֵה imp., from הוה.
הוּבַד Hoph. pret., from אבד.
הוֹבַד Ch. Aph. inf., from אבד.
הוֹבִישׁ Hiph., from בושׁ and יבשׁ.
הוֹד *glory*; see with its comp. in
נהד.

הוֹדָה Hiph. pret. הוֹדוּ; imp. pi.
הוֹדוֹת; inf. from ידה.

הָוָה.—I. *fell, descended.*—II. *existed,*
*was*; part. הֹוֶה; imper. הֱוֵא הֲוֵה,
f. הֱוִי; fut. יֶהְוָא (for יֶהְוֶה יְהוּ).
הֲוָא הֲוָה Ch., *was.*

הַוָּה f.—I. *intense desire, lust.*—II. *ac-*
*cident, injury, ruin.*

הֹוָה f., *accident, injury.*

הַיָּה f., same as הַוָּה *calamity.*

יְהֹוָה *Jehovah*, the name whereby God
would be known to the Hebrews,
Ex. 3:14. Written with prefixes

(like אֲדֹנָי), בִּיהוָֹה, לַיהוָֹה, מֵיהוָֹה; with אֲדֹנָי it is written יֱהוָֹה (like אֱלֹהִים).

יָהּ an abbreviated form of יְהוָֹה.

יֵהוּא p. n.—I. *Jehu*, king of Israel.—II. of a man.

יוֹאָחָז, יְהוֹאָחָז p. n.—I. a king of Israel, the son of Jehu.—II. a king of Judah, the son of Josiah.

יוֹאָשׁ, יְהוֹאָשׁ p. n.—I. a king of Judah, the son of Ahaziah.—II. a king of Israel, the son of Joash.

יְהוֹזָבָד p.n. of a man.

יְהוֹחָנָן, יוֹחָנָן (the Lord is merciful), Ἰωάννης, p.n. of a man.

יְהוֹיָדָע, יוֹיָדָע p.n. of a man.

יְכָנְיָהוּ, יוֹיָכִין, יְהוֹיָכִין p. n. of a king of Judah, the son of Jehoiakim.

יְהוֹיָקִים, יוֹיָקִים (the Lord confirmeth), p.n. of a king of Judah, the son of Josiah.

יְהוֹיָרִיב p.n. of a man.

יְהוֹנָדָב, יוֹנָדָב (the Lord's gift), p. n. of a man.

יְהוֹנָתָן, יוֹנָתָן (the Lord giveth, Θεόδωρος), p. n. of a man.

יְהוֹעַדָּה (the Lord adorneth), p.n. of a man.

יְהוֹעַדָּן p.n. of a woman.

יְהוֹצָדָק, יוֹצָדָק (the Lord is righteous), p.n. of a man.

יְהוֹרָם, יוֹרָם (the Lord is exalted), p. n.—I. a king of Judah, the son of Jehosaphat.—II. a king of Israel, the son of Ahab.

יְהוֹשֶׁבַע (the Lord hath sworn), p.n. of a son of king Joram.

יְהוֹשֻׁעַ (the Lord saveth), p.n. of a man, Joshua.

יְהוֹשָׁפָט (the Lord judgeth), p. n.—I.

of a king of Judah, the son of Asa.—II. of many men.

יוֹאָב p.n. of a man.

יוֹאָח p.n. of a man.

יוֹאֵל (the Lord he is God), **p. n. of a** man.

יוֹזָבָד p.n. of a man.

יוֹזָכָר p.n. of a man.

יוֹכֶבֶד p.n. of the mother of Moses.

יוֹעֵד (the Lord is witness), p.n. of a man.

יוֹעֶזֶר (the Lord helpeth), p.n. of a m.

יוֹעָשׁ p.n. of a man.

יוֹתָם p.n.—I. of a king of Judah, the son of Uzziah.—II. of a man.

הוֹחָם p.n. of a king.

הוֹי, הוֹ interj. of exhortation, threatening, grief, with עַל, אֶל and לְ.

הוּךְ Ch., proceed, go; fut. יְהָךְ; inf. מְהָךְ.

הֻכָּה for הֻכְּבָה Hoph., from נָכָה.

הֻלֶּדֶת, הֻלֶּדֶת Hoph. inf., from ילד.

הֻלְּלוּ for הֻלְּלוּ Pu. pret. pl., from הלל.

הוֹלְלוֹת, הוֹלֵלוּת; see הלל.

הוּם pret. הָם perturb, harass, Deu. 7:23. Niph. was moved, excited; fut. f. וַתֵּהֹם. Hiph. heave, swell, be tumultuous.

מְהוּמָה f., perturbation, tumult, vexation.

תְּהוֹם com. (pl. תְּהֹמוֹת), the deep, the ocean; from its tossing and roaring.

הוֹמָה, הוֹמִיָה part. f., from המה.

הוֹמָם p.n. of a man.

הוּן Kal, root not used; (Arab. was light). Hiph. made light of, despised, with inf. and לְ.

הֹון m.—I. *wealth, plenty.*— II. adv. *enough,* Pro. 30:15, 16.

הִין m., a liquid measure containing twelve logs (לג).

הֹור, הֹ־עַד *"thy progenitors,"* Eng. Ver., Gen. 49:26, from הרה.

הֹשַׁבֹותִים Zec. 10:6. Hiph. pret. 1. pers., with suff., for הֹשַׁבְתִּים, from ישב.

הֹשָׁמֵעַ *(the Lord heareth),* p. n. of a m.

הֹשֵׁעַ p.n., name of Joshua, afterwards changed to יהֹושֻׁעַ.

הֹושַׁעְיָה *(the Lord saveth),* p.n. of a m.

הֹות Po. fut. תְּהֹוֵתְתִי *attack unjustly,* Ps. 62:4.

הֻתַּל Pu. or Hoph., from התל.

הָזָה *doze, sleep idly,* Isa. 56:10.

הַזְדָה Ch. Aph. inf., from זוד.

הִזְדַּמִּנְתּוּן Ch. Ithp., from זמן.

הִזִּילוּ Hiph. pret. pl., from זלל.

הִזַּכּוּ for הִתְזַכּוּ Hithp. imper. pl., from זכה.

הִזָּרֹותֵיכֶם for הִזָּרֹותְכֶם Niph. inf., with suff., from זרה.

הֶחְבֵּאתָה Jos. 6:17. Hiph. pret. fem., with ה parag., for הֶחְבִּיאָה, from חבא.

הֶחְדַלְתִּי Jud. 9:9, 11, 13. for Kal pret. 1.pers., with ה interrog., from חדל.

הֶחֱטִי הֶחֱטִי Hiph. pret.for inf. for הַחֲטִיא, from חטא.

הֶחֵל Hiph. pret., Eze. 20. Niph.inf , with suff. and pref. לְהֵחַלֹּו, Lev. 21:4; see חלל.

הַט Hiph. imp. apoc., from נטה.

הִטַּמְּא Hothp., from טמא.

הִטַּתּוּ Hiph.pret.3. pers. fem. with suff., from נטה.

הַטֹּתָהּ Hiph. inf. with suff., from נטה.

הִי *lamentation;* see נהה.

הִיא pers. pron. f., *she, this;* see הוא; with art. הַהִיא *the same, this very* (*woman, &c.*); Ch. the same.

הַיָּדֹות f. pl., Neh. 12:8; wrong reading for הֹודֹות *dignities;* see in נתד.

הֵידָד *shouting;* see הדד.

הָיָה (inf. abs. הָיֹה; const. הֱיֹות, with pref. בִּהְיֹות; imper. הֱיֵה, f. הֱיִי, pl. הֱיוּ; fut. יִהְיֶה, apoc. יְהִי).—I. *came to pass,* וַיְהִי, with כְּ and ו *and it came to pass that.*—II. *was,* i.e. *existed;* never used as the logical copula, *is, was;* const. with לְ *there was to any one,* i.e. *he had;* with לְ and the inf. *was about to, intent upon;* with כְּ *was the same as;* with עִם *was, had communication with.* Niph. *came to be, took effect, had been,* Dan. 2:1; 8:27.

הַיָּה *ruin;* see הוה.

הֵיךְ Ch., same as אֵיךְ *how?*

הֵיכָל m. (pl. הֵיכָלֹות, הֵיכָלִים)—I. *any great and splendid building, temple, palace,* &c.—II. *the temple of Jehovah* built by Solomon.

הֵיכַל m. Ch.—I. *palace.*—II. *temple.*

הֵילִיכִי Hiph. imp. f., from ילך, הלך.

הֵילֵל *glorious;* see הלל.

הִים *swell;* see הום.

הֵימָן p. n. of a man.

הֵימִן Ch. Aph. pret., from אמן.

הֵימִיר for הֵמִיר Hiph., from מור.

הִין *light;* see הון.

הֵיתִי Ch. Aph. pret.; הַיְתָיָה inf., הֵיתָיַת Hoph. pret. f. 3. pers.; הֵיתָיוּ pl., from אתה.

הַךְ Hiph. imp. apoc., from נכה.

הַכֻּם Hiph. pret. pl.,with suff.,from נכה.

הַכּוֹת Hiph. inf., from נכה.

הִכּוֹגֵן for הִתְכּוֹגֵן Hithpo., from כּוּן.

הָכִיל Eze. 21:33, for הַאֲכִיל Hiph. inf., from אכל (others make it Hiph., from כּוּל).

הַכֵּיגִי Hiph imp., with suff. for הַכְּבֵּיגִי from נכה.

הִכְּךָ Hiph. pret. with suff., from נכה.

הִכְלַמְנוּ for הִכְלַמְנוּ Hiph. pret. pl. 1. pers., from כלם.

הִכָּם Hiph. pret. with suff., from נכה.

הֲכִנֻּנוּ for הֲכִינֹנוּ Hiph. pret. pl. 1. pers., from כּוּן.

הִכַּנִי Hiph. pret. with suff., from נכה.

הָכֵר, fut. תָּהְכְּרוּ ye contemn, Job 19:3.

הַכָּרָה astonishment; see נכר.

הַל, the הַ inter. and the pref. לְ written thus, for reverence sake, in the phrase הַל יְיָ Deu. 32:6.

הָלָא. Niph. part. f. נַהֲלָאָה removed, cast away, Mic. 4:7.

הָלְאָ removed, הָלְאָה pa., thence, farther, onward; denotes time and place.

הַלְאָת for הֶלְאֲתָה Hiph. pret. f., from לאה.

הַלּוֹ Kal inf. with suff., from הלל.

הַלּוּלִים great praise; see הלל

הַלָּז, הַלָּזֶה, הַלֵּז; see זֶה.

הָלַךְ and יָלַךְ (part. הוֹלֵךְ; pl. הֹלְכִים; f. הֹלֶכֶת, הֹלְכָה; inf. הָלוֹךְ; const. לֶכֶת, הֲלוֹךְ; with suff. לֶכְתְּךָ; imper. לֵךְ; with ה parag. לְכָה; fut. יֵלֵךְ; וַיֵּלֶךְ; poet. אֶהֱלָךְ, יַהֲלֹךְ; (תְּהֲלָךְ).— I. walked, went, proceeded; const. with many particles which modify the sense, e. g. with אַחֲרֵי followed; with אֶת, עִם

accompanied; with בְּ walked with i. e. brought, Hos. 5:6.—II. made way, progress; וַיֵּלֶךְ הָלֹךְ וְגָדֵל increased continually.—III. proceeded, went on.—IV. went off, disappeared, i. e. died, Gen. 15:2; Ps. 39:14. Niph. נֶהֱלַכְתִּי I set about departing, Ps. 109:23. Pi. הִלֵּךְ went, proceeded. Hiph. הוֹלִיךְ and הֵילִיךְ.—I. cause to go, lead, conduct.—II. let perish, Ps. 125:5. Hith. הִתְהַלֵּךְ become walking, proceed, go on, go about.

הֵלֶךְ m.—I. going, travel, 2 Sa.12:4. —II. a stream, 1 Sa. 14:26.

הֲלַךְ Ch., walked, proceeded. Aph. the same.

הֲלָךְ m. Ch., proceeds of the state, taxation.

הֲלִיךְ m.; הֲלִיכָה f.; pl. הֲלִיכוֹת.—I. step.—II. way.—III. procedure.

מַהֲלָךְ m.—I. walk.—II. journey.

תַּהֲלוּכָה f., procession, Neh. 12:31.

הַהֹלְכוּא, הַהֹלְכֻא who went, Jos.10:24. Kal pret. pl. with א parag. and ה relat., from הלך

הָלַל shone. Pi. הִלֵּל.—I. praised. — II. gloried.—III. pronounced vain-glorious, foolish, mad; const. with לְ (הַלְלוּ־יָהּ [without dag. forte] praise ye the Lord). Pu. הֻלַּל was praised; part. מְהֻלָּל praised, to be praised. Hiph. הֵלֵל shone. Hith. began to glory, boast. Po. fut. יְהוֹלֵל make a fool, shame. Poal part. מְהוֹלָל mad. Hithpo. became mad.

הֵילֵל m., Lucifer, i. e. the morning star, Isa. 14:12.

הוֹלֵלָה f. (pl. הוֹלֵלוֹת), glory, folly.

הוֹלֵלוּת f., folly, Ecc. 10:13.

הִלּוּלִים m. pl.—I. great praise, subject of praise, Lev. 19:24.—II. songs of, feasts of, joy, Ju. 9:27.

הִלֵּל p. n. of a man.

מַהֲלָל m., praising, Pro. 27:21.

מַהֲלַלְאֵל (the praise of God), p.n. of a m.

תְּהִלָּה f.—I. praise.—II. hymn of praise; pl. תְּהִלּוֹת praises; pl. m. תְּהִלִּים the book of Psalms.

תְּהִלָּה f., folly, emptiness, Job 4:18.

הָלַם struck, beat.

הֲלֹם adv., hither; עַד־הֲלֹם thus far.

הֶלֶם (blow), p.n. of a man.

הַלְמוּת f., workman's hammer, Jud. 5:26.

יַהֲלֹם m., name of a gem, adamant.

מַהֲלֻמוֹת f. pl., beatings, stripes.

הָם or הָם p.n. of an unknown place, Gen. 14:5.

הֵמָּה, הֵם pers. pron. m. pl., these, they; with the art. הָהֵם, הָהֵמָּה; הִמּוֹן Ch., these, they.

הַמְדָּתָא p. n. of a man.

הָמָה (inf. const. הָמוֹת; fut. יֶהֱמָה; part. m. הֹמֶה; f. הוֹמָה).—I. ferment (as wine).—II. moved (as the bowels with mental emotions).— III. roar, rage, murmur, moan; part. f. pl. הוֹמִיּוֹת noisy, i.e. full of people, Pro. 1:21.

הָם or הֹם, pl. הָמִים; with suff. and pref. מֵהֲמֵהֶם their riches, Ezr. 7:11.

הֶמְיָה f., sound of the lute, Isa. 14:11.

הָמוּ m. (f. Job 31:34).—I. emotion, lit. moving the bowels.—II. musical sounds.—III. multitude of men, &c.

הָמוֹן m., abundance; with suff. הֲמֹנְכֶם, Eze. 5:7.

---

הֲמוֹנָה the mystical name of a city, Eze. 39:16; see preceding verse.

הֵמִין for הֵימִין Hiph., from ימן.

הֲמִתִּיו 1 Sa. 17:35, for הֲמִתְּיו הַמַתִּיו, Hiph. pret. 1. pers. with suff., from מות.

הֻמְבְּכוּ for הוּמַבְּכוּ Hoph. pl., from מבך.

הָמַל root not used; (Arab. rain continually).

הֲמֻלָּה הֲמוּלָה f., commotion, rushing of wings.

הָמֵם (fut. יָהֹם, וַיָּהָם; inf. const. with suff. הֻמָּם).—I. put in motion, agitated.—II. dispersed, put to the rout.

הֵמָן p. n. of a man.

הֲמָן multitude; see in הָמָה.

הַמְנִיךְ or הַמְנוּךְ Ch., collar, bracelet, Dan. c. 5.

הֵמַס Niph. inf., from מסס

הֵמַסִיו Ch. for הִמְסוּ Hiph. pl., from מסה

הָמָס m., pl. הַמָסִים slight noises, Isa. 64:1.

הָמַר root not used; (Arab. poured water).

מַהֲמֹרוֹת f. pl., torrents, floods, Ps. 140:11.

הֲמִרוֹתָם Hiph. inf. with suff. and dag. euphon., from מרה.

הֲמִתָּה Hiph. 2. pers. with ה parag., הֲמִתִּי 1.pers.—הֲמִתִיהָ 1. pers. with suff., הֲמִתָּם 2.pers. pl., from מות.

הֵנָּה, הֵן pers. pron. f. pl., they, them; with art. הָהֵנָּה; adv., here, hither; הֵנָּה וָהֵנָּה hither and thither, מִמְּךָ וָהֵנָּה from thee hitherwards, עַד הֵנָּה thus far.

הֵמּוֹן pers. pron. m. pl. Ch., *he*; f. הֵמִּין *she*.

הֵנָּה, הִנֵּה, הֵן, הֵן interj., *behold! lo!* with suff. הִנְנִי, הִנְנִי *behold me! lo I am here!* הִנְּךָ *behold thou art,* &c.

הֵן Ch., *if, whether;* הֵן...הֵן *either... or.*

הַנַּח Hiph. imp., from נוח.

הִנִּיחַ Hiph. הֻנַּח Hoph., from נוח.

הֲנָחָה *rest;* see נוח.

הִנֹּם p. n.; גֵּי בֶן־הִנֹּם *the valley of the sons of Hinnom* (where Molech was worshipped).

הֵנַע p. n. of a city in Mesopotamia.

הַנְעַל Ch. Aph. pret., הַנְעָלָה inf., from עלל.

הֲנָפָה Ch. for הֵנִיף Hiph. inf., from נוף.

הַסָּה Pi. imp. הַס; with pause הָס *hush! be silent!* pl. הַסּוּ. Hiph. (fut. apoc. וַיַּהַס), *made to be silent,* Nu. 13:30.

הִסִּית for הֵסִיתָ Hiph., from סות.

הַעַל Hiph. imper. apoc., from עלה.

הֶעֱלָה for הֶעֱלָה Hiph., from עלה.

הֹעֲלָה for הָעֲלָה Hoph., from עלה.

הֲפֻנּוֹת *remission;* see פונ.

הַפֹּדֶךְ part. with suff. and art., from פדה.

הָפַךְ (fut. יַהֲפֹךְ; inf. הָפוֹךְ; const. הֲפֹךְ; with suff. הָפְכִי).—I. *turn over.* — II. *subvert, ruin.* — III. *change, pervert, convert.* Niph. נֶהְפַּךְ *was turned,* &c.; with לְ, עַל *to* or *into, was ruined.* Hoph. הָהְפַּךְ *turned upon, against,* Job 30:15. Hith. part. מִתְהַפֵּךְ *becomes turned about;* f. מִתְהַפֶּכֶת *the*

same; fut. f. תִּתְהַפֵּךְ *becomes changed,* Job 38:14.

הֶפֶךְ, הֵפֶךְ m., *perversion,* Eze. 16:34

הֲפֵכָה f., *subversion,* Gen. 19:29.

הַפַכְפַּךְ m., *turning, tortuous,* Pro 21:8.

מַהְפֵּכָה f., *overthrow, subversion.*

מַהְפֶּכֶת f., *imprisonment, stocks* בֵּית הַמַּהְפֶּכֶת *prison-house.*

תַּהְפֻּכָה f. (pl. תַּהְפֻּכוֹת), *perversion, perverseness.*

הַפְרְכֶם Hiph. inf. with suff., from פרך.

הִצְטַיֵּד Hith. denom., from צִיד or צוד.

הַצָּלָה *deliverance;* see נצל.

הֶצֶן m., *an armament, force,* Eze 23:24.

הַר m. (with art. הָהָר; pl. הָרִים; with art. הֶהָרִים), aff. הָרְרִי, הֲרָרִי; pl. הַרְרֵיהָ; also const. הָרֵי, הֲרֵי.—I. *mountain.*—II. *mountainous district.* — III. *fastness, stronghold.*—IV. *strong men,* Isa. 41:15; with ־ה affix (הָרָה), *towards the mountain.*

הָרָרִי *a mountaineer,* 2 Sa. 23:33.

הָרָרִי the same, v. 11, a title of Shammah.

הֹר p. n.—I. of the mountain in Edom where Aaron was buried.—II. of a mountain in Palestine.

הַר חֶרֶם p. n. of a mountain in the tribe of Dan, Jud. 1:35.

הָרָא p. n. of a region in Syria.

הַרְאֵל p. n. of the altar of burnt-offering, Eze. 43:15; elsewhere אֲרִיאֵל which see in ארה.

הַרְבֵּה Hiph. imp. apoc., from רבה.

הָרַג (fut. יַהֲרֹג; inf. הָרוֹג; const. הֲרֹג, with לְ, בְּ, *kill, slay,* generally with violence. Niph. *was slain.* Pu. הֹרָג *slain.*

הֶרֶג m., הֲרֵגָה f., } *slaughter, slaying.*

הָרָה (inf. abs. הָרֹה, הָרוֹ; fut. f. תַּהַר, (וַתַּהַר).— I. *conceived, became pregnant,* with לְ, אֶת; part. f. הוֹרָה; inf. הֹרוֹ; *she that conceiveth.*— II. *conceive in the mind, devise.* Pu. הֹרָה *conceived,* Job 3:3.

הָרָה adj. f., *pregnant;* pl. הָרוֹת.

הָרִיָּה adj. f., pl. with suff. הָרִיּוֹתָיו *her pregnant women.*

הֵרוֹן הֵרָיוֹן } m., *conception.*

הַרְהֹר m. Ch., *imaginations,* Dan. 4:2, from Pa. Ch. הַרְהֵר.

הֹרָם p.n. of a king of Canaan.

הֹרֵם p. n. of a man.

הֵרְמוּ Niph. imp. pl., from רמם.

הַרְמוֹן m. (same as אַרְמוֹן) *palace,* Am. 4:3.

הָרָן p.n. of a man.

הֹרֵנִי Hiph. pret. with suff., from ירה.

הָרַם (inf. הָרוֹם; fut. יַהֲרֹם (נַהֲרֹם *broke down.*— 1. *houses, &c.*— 2. *men,* i. e. *put down, reduced.*— 3. *teeth,* Ps. 58:7. Niph. *was broken down.* Pi. *destroyed;* as Kal

הֶרֶם m., עִיר הַהֶרֶם p.n. of an unknown city in Egypt, Isa. 19:18; " city of destruction," Eng. Ver.; some read חֶרֶם which see.

הֲרִיסָה f., *broken down,* Am. 9:11.

הֲרִיסוּת f., *ruin,* Isa. 49:19.

הֶרֶף Hiph. imp. apoc., from רפה.

הָרְצָת Ch. for הִרְצָתָה Hiph. pret. f. 3. pers., from רצה.

הַר, הֲרָרִי, הֲרָרָי; see הַר.

---

Hiph. הָשִׁיב, הָשֵׁב with pause for הָשֵׁב imp. from שׁוּב.

Hoph. הֻשְׁפָה (in some editions הֻשְׁמָה) inf. with suff., from שׁמם.

הָשֵׁם p. n. of a man.

הַשְׁמָעוֹת *hearing;* see שׁמע.

הוֹשַׁע Ps. 39:14, Hiph. imp., from שׁעה Isa. 6:10, Hiph. imp., from שׁעע.

הִשְׁתַּחֲוֶה Hithp., from שׁחה.

הִשְׁתַּמְּשׁע Hithpa., from שׁעע.

הִתְאֹשֵׁשׁוּ Hithp., from אישׁ.

הֲתָבוּתָךְ Ch. Aph. inf. with suff., from תּוּב.

הִתְגָּר Hithp. imp. apoc., from גרה.

הִתְוַדֵּה Hithp., from ידה.

הִתְחַל Hithp. imp. apoc., from חלה.

הָאֵתָיו for הֶאֱתָיו which is for הִתְיוּ Hiph. imp. pl., from אתה.

הַתָּמִךְ for הַתָּמֵךְ Hiph. inf. with suff., from תמך.

הִתּוּךְ *melting;* see נתך.

הֲתָךְ p. n. of a Persian eunuch.

הָתַל, הִתֵּל Pi.; (inf. הָתֵל; fut. יְהַתֵּל, pl. תְּהָתֵלּוּ, יְהָתֵלּוּ) *deluded, deceived.* Hoph. הוּתַל *deceived.*

הֲתֻלִּים m. pl., *mockeries,* Job 17:2.

מַהֲתַלּוֹת f. pl., *delusions,* Isa. 30:10.

הָתֵל Pi.; see התל.

הִתְנַבּוֹת Hithp. inf., from נבא.

הִתְנַבִּית Hithp. pret., from נבא.

ו

וְ, וּ, וָ conj., used to connect together words, phrases, sentences, &c.; it may be interpreted in modern languages by any of the particles which are applied to the same use: such as *and, but, if, moreover, &c.* according to the context.

וֶדָן p.n. of a place in Arabia.

וָהֵב Num. 21:14, probably p.n. of a place or well.

וָו m., pl. וָוִים hooks or pins at the top of the pillars of the tabernacle.

וָזָר loaded; see יזר.

וַיְזָתָא p.n. of a son of Haman.

וָלָד, וֶלֶד see ילד.

וַנְיָה p.n. of a man.

וָפְסִי p.n. of a man.

וְשְׁנִי p.n. of a man.

וַשְׁתִּי p.n. of the wife of Ahasuerus.

## ז

זְאֵב m.—I. a wolf.—II. p.n. of one of the princes of Midian.

זֹאת demonst. pron. f. of זֶה this, that.

זֹה for זֹאת this.

זוּ for זֹה relat. pron. this, Ps. 132:12.

זָבַב root not used; (Arab. fly).

זְבוּב m., fly or bee; בַּעַל זְבוּב (fly-god), p.n. Baalzebub, the idol of the Ekronites.

זָבַד hath given, endowed, Gen. 30:20.

זֶבֶד a gift, Gen. 30:20.

זָבָד p.n. of a man.

זַבְדִּי p.n. of a man.

זַבְדִּיאֵל (gift of God), p.n. of a man.

זְבַדְיָה (given of the Lord), p.n. of a man, Ζεβεδαῖος.

זְבַדְיָהוּ p.n. of a man.

זָבוּד p.n. of a man.

זַבּוּד p.n. of a man.

זְבִידָה, וְבוּדָה p.n. of a woman.

זְבֻב fly; see זבב.

זְבוּלֻן, זְבֻל, זְבֻל; see זבל.

זָבַח (inf. const. זְבֹחַ; fut. יִזְבַּח), slaughtered for sacrifice. Pi. זִבֵּחַ sacrificed.

זֶבַח m. (with suff. זִבְחִי; pl. זְבָחִים [זִבְחֵי, זְבָחוֹת]).—I. slaughter of men or animals.—II. the thing slaughtered.—III. sacrifice.—IV. that which is offered in sacrifice.—V. p.n. of a king of Midian.

מִזְבֵּחַ m. (const. מִזְבַּח; with suff. מִזְבַּחֲךָ, מִזְבְּחִי; pl. מִזְבְּחוֹת), altar; הַמִּזְבֵּחָה toward the altar.

זַבַּי p.n. of a man.

זָבַל, fut. with suff. יִזְבְּלֵנִי he will dwell with me, Gen. 30:20.

זְבֻל, זְבוּל m.—I. habitation, place of residence.—II. p.n. of a man.

זְבֻלֻן, זְבֻלֻן, זְבוּלֻן (residence), p.n. of a son of Jacob; זְבוּלֹנִי a Zebulonite.

זְבַן Ch., gaining (time), Dan. 2:8.

זְבִינָא p.n. of a man.

זָג m., the transparent skin of the grape, Nu. 6:4.

זֵד, זָדוֹן; see זוד.

זֶה demonst. pron., he, it, this, that; with art. הַזֶּה this; זֶה...זֶה the one...the other; זֶה אֶל זֶה the one to the other; כָּזֶה וְכָזֶה thus and thus; sometimes same as אֲשֶׁר that; זֶה פַעֲמַיִם these two times; בָּזֶה in this place, here, there; מִזֶּה hence; מִזֶּה וּמִזֶּה from this and that part; מַה־זֶּה what is this? אֵי־זֶה where? לָמָּה־זֶּה why?

זוּ com., this; sometimes for אֲשֶׁר

הַלָּזֶה m.,
הַלֵּזוּ f.,   } this.
הַלָּז com.,

זָהָב m. (const. זְהַב, זֲהַב).—I. *gold*; with a numeral preceding, supply שֶׁקֶל : עֲשָׂרָה זָהָב *ten shekels of gold.*—II. perhaps *fair weather*, Job 37:22.

זָהֵר root not used; (Syr. *splendour*).
זִו m. (*beauty of flowers*), the second month of the Hebrew year, which probably began on the thirty-first day after the sun had entered Aries.
זִיו m. Ch., *majesty, splendour.*

זָהַם. Pi. זִהַם *abhorred,* Job 33:20.
זֹהַם p. n. of a man.

זָהַר. Hiph. הִזְהִיר I. *enlighten, give light.*—II. *admonish, warn,* with מִן of the thing to be avoided. Niph. נִזְהַר *was admonished.*
זְהַר Ch., part. זָהִירִין *admonished, cautioned.*
זֹהַר m., *brilliancy.*

זֶה *this;* see זֹאת.
זֹה the same; see זֶה.
זֹהַ; see זֹהַ.

זוּב.—I. *issue, flow,* as water, blood, &c.—II. *abound, overflow.*—III. *waste away, expire;* part. זָב; f. זָבָה; const. זָבַת.
זוֹב m., *issue, discharge of blood,* &c.

זוּד, זִיד.—I. *boil, seethe,* Gen. 25:29.—II. *swell, behave* or *act insolently,* with אֶל or עַל (fut. with נ parag. (יְזִידוּן), Deu. 17:13.
זוּד Ch. Aph., *was proud, haughty,* Dan. 5:20
זֵד m., *proud, haughty.*
זֵידוֹן m., *overflowing, overwhelming,* Ps. 124:5.

זָדוֹן const. זְדוֹן m., *pride, haughtiness, insolence.*
נָזִיד m. (part. Niph. for נָזוּד), any viand prepared by boiling.
זָוָה root not used; (Arab. *angle, corner*).
זָוִית or זָוִיָּה f. (pl. זָוִיּוֹת), *angle, corner* of a building, &c.
מָזֶו m. (pl. מְזָוִים), *vault for corn, matadore,* Ps. 144:13.
זוּן, זִין root not used; (Arab. *abundance, riches*).
זִין m.—I. *abundance,* Isa. 66:11.—II. זִיז שָׂדַי *wealth* (i.e. cattle) of the fields, Ps. 50:11; 80:14.
זִיזָא p. n. of a man.
זִיזָה p. n. of a man.
מְזוּזָה f., *doorpost, jamb.*
זוּזִים p. n. of a race of giants.
זוֹחֵת p. n. of a man.
זוּל, part. זָלִים *removing, pouring forth, casting out,* Isa. 46:6.
זוּלָה const. זוּלַת f. (lit. *removal, rejection*), prep. *besides;* with suff. זוּלָתִי *besides me;* זוּלָתְךָ *besides thee,* &c.; with י parag. זוּלָתִי *besides.*
זוּן Hoph. part. מוּזָנִים *fed, fattened,* Jer. 5:8.
זוּן Ch. Hithp. *nourished, fed,* Dan 4:9.
מָזוֹן m., *food, meat.*
מָזוֹן m. Ch., *meat.*
זוֹנָה; see זנה.
זוּנָה for זָנָה, Pu.; see זנה
זוּע *moved, was agitated.* Pil. part. מְזַעֲזֵעַ *vexing,* Hab. 2:7.
זוּע Ch., part. pl. זָאֲעִין Dan. 5:19

(נְזָעִים) id. 6:27. *moving, in commotion.*

זְוָעָה f., *agitation, commotion.*

זְעָיָה f., *vexation.*

זֵעָה f., *sweat (as the result of motion)*, Gen. 3:19.

זַעַן p.n. of a man.

זִיע p.n. of a man.

זוּר (pret. זָר, זֹר; fut. יָזוּר, וַיָּזַר).—I. *compressed, squeezed.*—II. (same as סוּר *departed) departed, receded, was strange, abominable, adulterous;* part. זָר *a stranger, a barbarian, an enemy;* f. זָרָה *strange woman, harlot.* Niph. נָזֹרוּ *been receding, falling off,* Isa. 1:4. Hoph. part. מוּזָר *made separate,* Ps. 69:9.

זוּרֶה m., *pressed together, broken,* Is. 59:5.

מָזוֹר m., *compression of a wound by bandages;* יָשִׂימוּ מ' *they make a binding* (wound), Obad. 7.

זָחַח. Niph. *be removed, separated;* fut. יִזַּח.

זָחַל *withdrew, hesitated, delayed,* Job 32:6; part. pl. זֹחֲלֵי עָפָר *fearful things (serpents of the dust).*

זִיד, זֵידוֹן *pride;* see זוּד.

זִיו *splendour;* see זהה.

זִיז, זִיזָא, זִיזָה; see זוז.

זִיף p.n.—I. *of a town and desert in the tribe of Judah;* זִיפִי *a Ziphite.*—II. p. n. of a man.

זִיקוֹת *ornaments,* &c.; see זנק.

זַיִת const. זֵית m.—I. *olive tree.*—II. *olive;* הַר הַזֵּיתִים *Mount of Olives,* near Jerusalem.

זֵיתָן p. n. of a man.

זָכָה *same as* זָכַךְ *was pure.* Pi. זִכָּה

*cleanse, purify.* Hitnp. imp. הִזַּכּוּ (for הִתְזַכּוּ) *be, become, clean,* Isa. 1:16.

זְכוּ f. Ch., *purity, innocence,* Dan. 6:23.

זָכַךְ *was pure, clean.* Hiph. הֵזַךְ *have cleansed,* Job 9:30.

זַךְ m., זַכָּה f.—I. *pure, free from dregs.*—II. *innocent, upright.*

זְכוּכִית f., *glass or crystal,* Job 28:17

זַכַּי p. n. of a man.

זָכַר (fut. יִזְכֹּר).—I. *remember.*—II. *meditate upon, call to mind,* with לְ, בְּ, part. זָכוּר *remembered.* Niph. נִזְכַּר.—I. *be remembered, recollected.*—II. *be born a male,* from זָכָר, Ex. 34:19. — Hiph. הִזְכִּיר *record, commemorate, make mention of;* part. מַזְכִּיר לְבֹנָה *bringing a memorial or praise-offering of frankincense,* Isa. 66:3; מַזְכִּיר s., *recorder,* ἱστοριογράφος.

זֵכֶר, זֶכֶר m. (with suff. זִכְרוֹ).—I. *memory.*—II. *memorial.*

זָכָר m., *male.*

זָכוּר m., *male.*

זַכּוּר p.n. of a man.

זִכָּרוֹן m. (const. זִכְרוֹן; pl. זִכְרֹנִים, זִכְרֹנוֹת—) *memorial, record.*

זִכְרִי p.n. of a man.

זְכַרְיָהוּ, זְכַרְיָה (*whom the Lord remembers*), Ζαχαρίας, p. n. of a m.

אַזְכָּרָה f., *an offering for a memorial,* Lev. 2:2, &c.

זָלַג *root not used.*

מַזְלֵג m., *a fork with three teeth.*

מִזְלָגָה f., pl. מִזְלָגוֹת *the same.*

זָלַל, part. זוֹלֵל *acting basely, profligately, obscenely.* Hiph. הֵזִיל *debase, defile.* Niph. נָזַל; pl. נָזְלוּ, גְזוֹלוּ *were debased.*

זֵלוּת f., *baseness, lightness,* Ps. 12:9.

זַלְזַלִּים m. pl., *tender branches,* Isa. 18:5.

זַלְעָפָה, זִלְעָפָה f.—I. *poisonous wind,* Simoon.—II. *great excitement.*— III. *hunger, famine.*

זִלְפָּה p. n. of the hand-maid of Leah.

זַמְזֻמִּים, זַמָּה, זִמָּה; see זמם.

זְמִיר, זָמִיר, זְמוֹרָה; see זמר.

זַמֹּתִי, Ps. 17:3, for זַמּוֹתִי; see זמה or זמם.

זָמַם (pret. זָמַמְתִּי, fut. pl. יָזְמוּ), *intended, determined;* part. זֹמֵם *determines, plots against.* Ps. 37:12.

זָמָם m., *determination, project,* Ps. 140:9.

זִמָּה f.—I. *intention, imagination.*— II. *sin,* specially adultery.—III. p.n. of a man.

זִמָּה f., pl. with suff. זִמֹּתִי *my meditation* (Gesenius), Ps. 17:3.

זַמְזֻמִּים p. n. of a race of giants, same as זוּזִים, which see.

מְזִמָּה f., *thought, intention, purpose* (for good or evil).

זָמַן Kal, root not used; (Arab. *appointed time*). Pu. part. מְזֻמָּנִים עִתִּים, עִתִּים מְזֻמָּנוֹת *stated times.*

זְמַן Ch. Pa. *appointed, concerted,* or Hith. הִזְדַּמֵּן *according to Ketib,* Dan. 2:9.

זְמָן m., *appointed time;* pl. זְמַנִּים.

זְמַן, זִמַן m. Ch. (pl. זִמְנִין), *appointed time;* זְמָנִין תְּלָתָה *thrice, three times.*

זָמַר (fut. יִזְמֹר), *cut, prune.* Niph. *was cut.* Pi. זִמֵּר *he sang,*

*with* בְּ; *celebrated the praises of,* with לְ.

זֶמֶר m., *mountain goat,* Deu. 14:5.

זָמִיר m., *pruning time,* Cant. 2:12.

זָמִיר m., *song, hymn;* pl. זְמִירוֹת.

זְמוֹרָה f., *branch, bough;* pl. זְמֹרִים.

זָמְרָת, זִמְרָת, const. זִמְרָה f., *song, praise, music;* זִמְרַת הָאָרֶץ *the cropping, gathering of the earth,* Gen. 43:11.

זִמְרִי p. n. of a man.

זִמְרָן p. n. of a son of Abraham.

זְמָר m. Ch., *sound* (of musical instruments).

זַמָּר m. Ch., *singer,* Ezr. 7:24.

מִזְמוֹר m., *psalm* or *hymn.*

מְזַמֶּרֶת f., pl. מְזַמְּרוֹת *psalteries.*

מַזְמֵרָה f., pl. מַזְמֵרוֹת *pruning instruments.*

זַן, with pause זָן m. (pl. זְנִים), *kind, species.*

זַן m. Ch., the same.

זָנָב m. (pl. זְנָבוֹת; const. זַנְבוֹת), *tail* of an animal.

זִנֵּב Pi., *cut off, smite the rear of an army,* lit. *tail it.*

זָנָה I. *play the whore.*—II. *become, be idolatrous,* with אַחֲרֵי, בְּ, אֶל, מֵעַל, תַּחַת, מִתַּחַת, מֵאַחֲרֵי, מִן; part. f. זוֹנָה *harlot.* Pu. זֻנָּה *committed fornication.* Hiph. הִזְנָה *caused to commit whoredom.*

זְנוּן m., pl. זְנוּנִים.—I. *whoredom.*— II. *idolatry.*

זְנוּת f., *idolatry;* pl. זְנֻתִים.

תַּזְנוּת f., the same; pl. תַּזְנוּתִים.

זָנַח I. *stank,* Hos. 8:5.—II. *rejected, loathed.* Hiph. הִזְנִיחַ.—I. *stank,* Isa. 19:6.—II. *rejected*

זָנוֹד p. n. of two towns in the tribe of Judah.

זָנַק. Pi. fut. יְזַנֵּק strikes, restrains, Deu. 33:22.

זִק f., pl. זִקִּים Pro. 26:18, " firebrands," Eng. Ver.; arrows tipped with fire; see זקק.

זִיקָה f., pl. זִיקוֹת Isa. 50:11, "sparks," Eng. Ver.; sparkling ornaments, (Lee); meaning uncertain.

זַעֲוָה זַעֲוָה, זְוָעָה; see זוע.

זָעִיר little; see זער.

זָעַךְ. Niph. נִזְעֲכוּ " are extinct," Eng. Ver.; are swift (Lee).

זָעַם (imp. זַעֲמָה; fut. אֶזְעֹם), was indignant, angry, with עַל, אֶת. Niph. part. נִזְעָמִים became indignant, angry, Pro. 25:23.

זַעַם m. (with suff. זַעְמְךָ וְזַעְמִי), indignation, anger.

זָעַף I. was indignant, enraged, with עַל, עִם.—II. part. pl. זֹעֲפִים mentally excited, wretched, σκυθρωποί.

זָעֵף m., indignant.

זַעַף m. (with suff. זַעְפּוֹ).—I. anger.—II metaphorically, the raging of the sea.

זָעַק (fut. יִזְעַק; imp. זְעַק; inf. זְעֹק) cry out, shout for help, with אֶל of the person implored; with עַל, לְ of the cause of suffering. Niph. was crying out. Hiph. הִזְעִיק summoned, proclaimed.

זְעַק Ch., called to, Dan. 6:21.

זַעַק m., } a cry, shout for help.
זְעָקָה f., }

זָעַר root not used; (Syr. was little).

זָעִיר m., a little.

זְעֵירָה f. Ch., the same, Dan. 7:8.

מִזְעָר m., a little (of time or number).

זִפְרוֹן p. n. of a town in the north of Palestine, Nu. 34:9.

זֶפֶת f., pitch.

זִק f., זִקִּים; see זנק and זקק.

זָקָן com.—I. the beard.—II. the chin.

זָקֵן was old; fut. יִזְקַן. Hiph. grew old.

זָקֵן m. (const. זְקַן; pl. זְקֵנִים, זִקְנֵי), old, aged, with מִן; pl. heads of tribes or families; f. pl. זְקֵנוֹת old women, Zec. 8:4.

זֹקֶן m., age, old age, Gen. 48:10.

זִקְנָה f., old.

זְקֻנִים m. pl., the same.

זָקַף erected, lifted up.

זְקַף Ch. part. זְקִיף lift up, hang a criminal.

זָקַק pour out, melt, fuse. Pi. זִקַּק fuse as metals, Mal. 3:3. Pu. fused, purified.

זֵק m., pl. זִקִּים bonds, fetters; see also in זנק.

אֵזֵק m., pl. אֲזִקִּים fetters, Jer. 40:1, 4.

זָר, זָרָה; see זור.

זֵר; see זרר.

זָרָא part. from זור strange, abominable, Num. 11:20.

זָרַב. Pu. fut. יְזֹרְבוּ they are bound, oppressed, Job. 6:17.

זְרֻבָּבֶל p. n.; see זרה.

זֶרֶד p. n. of a valley in the land of Moab.

זָרָה spread, disperse. Niph. was dispersed. Pi. זֵרָה—I. disperse.—II. discern, sift. Pu. זֹרָה was dispersed, spread out.

זְרֻבָּבֶל p. n. of the leader of the Jews on their return from Babylon.

זֶרֶת f., *a span*, a measure of 10·944 inches.

מִזְרֶה m., *winnowing fan*.

מְזָרִים m., Job 37 : 9, probably the name of some northern constellation.

מַזָּרוֹת Job 38 : 32, probably the same; but see more under נזל.

זְרוֹעַ, זְרֹעַ *seed*; see זרע.

זַרְזִיף *shower*; see זרף.

זַרְזִיר *firm*; see זרר.

זָרַח (fut. יִזְרַח; inf. וְזְרֹחַ).—I. *rise as the sun.*—II. *give light, glory.*—III. *be white*; hence, *have leprosy.*

זֶרַח m.—I. *rising.*—II. p. n. of one of the sons of Judah, and others; זַרְחִי *a Zarchite.*

יְזְרַחְיָה, זְרַחְיָה p. n. of a man.

אֶזְרָח m., *indigenous, home born*, a tree not transplanted, Ps. 37 : 35.

אֶזְרָחִי (יִזְרָח) p. n., *an Ezrachite.*

מִזְרָח m., *the east*, the quarter of heaven whence the sun rises; מִזְרָחָה (and without ה affix) *towards the east.*

זָרַם *overwhelm*, Ps. 90 : 5. Po. *made to pour down*, Ps. 77 : 18.

זֶרֶם m., *inundation*, of rain or otherwise.

זִרְמָה f., *effusion, emission*, Eze. 23 : 20.

זֹרֶם Pi. pret. with suff.; see זרה.

זָרַע (fut. יִזְרַע; inf. זְרֹעַ; imp. זְרַע). I. *sowing* (as seed, &c.).—II. *planting.*—III. metaphorically of righteousness, wickedness, &c. Niph. *was sown, was propagated, was dispersed*, Eze. 36 : 9. Pu. זֹרָעוּ *shall they be sown*, Isa. 40 : 24.

Hiph. part. מַזְרִיעַ *producing seed*; fut. תַּזְרִיעַ, Lev. 12 : 2.

זֶרַע m. (with suff. זַרְעֲךָ; pl. זְרָעִים, (זַרְעִי).—I. *seed.*—II. *seed time.*—III. *semen* (of animals).—IV. *issue, progeny.*

זְרַע m. Ch., the same.

זְרֹעַ f., sometimes m. (pl. זְרֹעִים, זְרֹעֹת, (זְרֹעֵי).—I. *arm.*—II. *fore-leg of an animal.*—III. *strength, power, violence.*

זֵרֻעַ m., *seed corn*; pl. זֵרֻעִים.

זֵרֹעִים and זֵרֹעֹנִים m. pl., *legumes, vegetables.*

אֶזְרוֹעַ f., same as זְרֹעַ *arm.*

יִזְרְעֶאל p. n.—I. of a town in the tribe of Issachar; m. יִזְרְעֵאלִי; f. יִזְרְעֵאלִית, יִזְרְעֵלִית *a Jezreelite.*—II. of a town in the tribe of Judah.—III. of a man.

מִזְרָע const. מִזְרַע m., *sown field*, Isa. 19 : 7.

זָרַף root not used.

זַרְזִיף m., *copiously raining*, Ps. 72 : 6.

זָרַק (fut. יִזְרֹק) *scatter, sprinkle*; with עַל of grey hairs, Hos. 7 : 9. Pu. זֹרַק *was sprinkled*, Nu. 19 : 13, 20.

מִזְרָק m., *bowl* or *cup*; pl. מִזְרָקִים, מִזְרָקוֹת.

זֵר m., *border, moulding.*

זָרִיר m., *firm, compact*, Pro. 30 : 31

זֶרֶשׁ p. n. of the wife of Haman.

זֶרֶת *span*; see זרה.

זַתּוּא p. n. of a man.

זֵתָם p. n. of a man.

זֵתַר p. n. of a eunuch of Ahasuerus.

## ח

חָבָא Kal, root not used. Niph. נֶחְבָּא *became, was, hidden*; with

אֵל, בְּ, followed by inf. with לְ נֶחְבֵּאתָ לִבְרֹחַ, in secret; thou fleddest secretly. Pu. חֻבָּא same as Niph., Job 24:4. Hiph. הֶחְבִּיא hide, conceal. Hoph. הָחְבָּא same as Niph., Isa. 42:22. Hithp. הִתְחַבָּא was, lay, hidden.

מַחֲבֵא m., hiding-place, Isa. 32:2.

מַחֲבֹא m., pl. מַחֲבֹאִים the same, 1 Sa. 23:23.

חָבַב part. חֹבֵב loving, cherishing, Deu. 33:3.

חֹב m., with suff. חֻבִּי my bosom, Job 31:33.

חֹבָב p. n. of the father-in-law of Moses.

חָבָה same as חָבָא hide, be in conceal-ment; imp. f. חֲבִי. Niph. inf. הֵחָבֵה lay hidden.

חֲבָיָה p.n. of a man.

חֶבְיוֹן covering, vail, Hab. 3:4.

חוֹבָה p.n.of a place near Damascus, Gen. 14:15.

נַחְבִּי p. n. of a man.

חַבּוּרָה, חַבֹּר; see חבר.

חָבַט (fut. יַחְבֹּט) beat off, threshed out. Niph. is beaten out, Isa. 28:27.

I. חָבַל 1. bind; part. חֹבְלִים binders, bands, Zec.11:7.—2. bind by pledge, pledge; inf. חֲבֹל; imp. חֲבֹל; fut. יַחְבֹּל. יַחְבָּל. Pi. חִבֵּל brought forth with pain.

I. חָבַל inflicting pain, oppressing. Niph. suffer pain, loss, Pro.13:13. Pi. injure, corrupt. Pu. חֻבַּל in-jured, destroyed.

חֲבַל Ch. Pa. injure, destroy. Ithp. perish.

חֵבֶל m.—I. the throes of child-bearing,

ὠδίς.—II. pains generally, Job 21 17; pl. חֲבָלִים, חֶבְלֵי.

חֶבֶל m. (f. Zep. 2:6, with suff. חֶבְלִי; pl. חֲבָלִים, חֶבְלֵי, חֶבְלֵי)—I. rope, cord.—II. measuring line.—III. tract of land, region, inheritance. — IV. snare, gin.— V. company, band of men, I Sa. 10:5, 10.

חֲבֹל m., } pledge, deposit. חֲבֹלָה f., }

חַבָּל m. Ch., } injury, hurt. חֲבָל m. Ch., }

חֲבוּלָא f. Ch., corrupt thing, Dan 6: 23.

חֹבֵל m., mast of a ship, Pro. 23:34.

חֹבֵל m., sailor.

תַּחְבֻּלוֹת, תַּחְבּוּלוֹת f.pl.—I.guidance, direction.—II. rule of action.—III. wisdom.

חֲבַצֶּלֶת f., bulbous-rooted flower, lily.

חֲבַצִּנְיָה p. n. of a man.

חָבַק embrace, fold together, with לְ. Pi. חִבֵּק embraced.

חִבֻּק m., folding of the hands.

חֲבַקּוּק p. n. of a prophet; LXX. Ἀμβακούμ.

חָבַר I. joined, attached, assembled, with אֶל.—II. charm, bind with a spell. Pi. חִבֵּר bind, join, with עִם Pu. חֻבַּר was joined, with אֶל, לְ, Ps. 94:20. Hiph. fut. אַחְבִּירָה I might compose, put together, with עַל, Job 16:4. Hithp. be joined.

חָבֵר m., companion; pl. חֲבֵרִים חֲבֵרֵי

חַבֶּרֶת f., associate.

חֲבַר m. Ch., companion.

חֶבְרָה f. Ch., the same.

חָבֵר m., pl., חֲבֵרִים *associates*, Job 40:30.

חֶבֶר m.—I. *association.*—II. *incantation*, Isa. 47:9,12; pl. חֲבָרִים.—III. p. n. of a man; חֶבְרִי *Heberite*, Nu. 26:45.

חֶבְרָה f., *association.*

חֹבֶרֶת f., *coupling*, Ex. 26:4, 10.

חָבוֹר p.n. of a river in Mesopotamia, *Chaboras.*

חַבּוּרָה, חַבֻּרָה f., *closing, seam, scar of a wound*; with suff. חַבֻּרָתִי; pl. חַבֻּרוֹתַי with suff.

חֶבְרוֹן p. n.—I. of a town in the tribe of Judah.— II. of a man; חֶבְרֹנִי *a Hebronite.*

חֲבַרְבֻּרוֹת f. pl., *spots of the leopard*, Jer. 13:23.

מַחְבֶּרֶת f., *joining, seam*; with suff. מַחְבַּרְתּוֹ.

מְחַבְּרוֹת f. pl.—I. *binders, beams of timber*, 2 Chron. 34:11.—II. *iron cramps*, 1 Chron. 22:3.

הִתְחַבְּרוּת f., *league*, Dan. 11:23.

חָבַשׁ (inf. חֲבוֹשׁ; fut. יַחְבֹּשׁ).—I. *bind, gird*, with לְ, עַל.—II. *govern, restrain*. Pi. חִבֵּשׁ *restrain*, Job 28:11, with מִן Pu. חֻבַּשׁ *was bound up.*

חָבִית m., pl. חֲבִתִּים *pancakes*, 1 Chron. 9:31.

מַחֲבַת f., *frying pan.*

חָגָב.—I. *locust.*—II. p. n. of a man.

חֲגָבָה p.n. of a man.

חָגַג (fut. יָחֹג), *feasting, revelling*, specially, keeping the festivals prescribed by law.

חָג m. (const. חַג; with art. הֶחָג;

with suff. חַגִּי; pl. חַגִּים), *festival under the law.*

חָגָא f., *refuge*, Isa. 19:17.

חַגַּי p. n. of the prophet *Haggai*; LXX. Ἀγγαῖος.

חַגִּי p. n. of a son of Gad.

חַגִּיָּה p. n. of a man.

חַגִּית p.n. of one of the wives of David.

חָגָה root not used; (Syr. *a rock*).

חֲגָוִים, חֲגָוֵי m. pl., *fastnesses, clefts.*

חֲגוֹרָה, חֲגוֹר *girdle*; see חגר.

חָגְלָה p. n. of a woman.

חָגַר (fut. יַחְגֹּר).—I. *gird, attire*; with עַל of the part of the body attired; with בְּ of the object put on; part. חָגוּר *girt.*—II. *withhold, restrain.*

חֲגוֹר m., חֲגוֹר m., חֲגוֹרָה f., *girdle, belt*; pl. חֲגֹרוֹת.

מַחֲגֹרֶת f., *girding*, Isa. 3:24.

חַד Ch., *a, an, once*; see אֶחָד, also חדד.

חָדַד *are keen, fierce*; pret. חַדּוּ Hab. 1:8. Hiph.fut. יָחַד *sharpens*, Pro. 27:17. Hoph. הוּחַד *sharpened*, Eze. 21:14—16.

חַד m., חַדָּה f., *sharp.*

חַדּוּדִים, חַדּוּדֵי m. pl., *very sharp*, Job 41:22.

חֲדַד p.n. of a son of Ishmael.

חָדִיד p. n. of a town of the Benjamites.

חָדָה (fut. apoc. יַחְדְּ), *rejoice*, Ex. 18:9. Pi. fut. with suff. תְּחַדֵּהוּ *make glad*, Ps. 21:7. Hiph. יַחְדְּ *delight, make glad*, Pro. 27:17.

חֶדְוָה f. Ch., *joy, gladness.*

חֲרִין m. pl. Ch., Dan. 2:32, same as Heb. חָזֶה breast.

חָדַל and חֲדֵל (inf. חֲדֹל; in.p. חֲדָל; fut. יֶחְדַּל) cease, desist, forbear, fail, with מִן.

חָדֵל m., ceasing, wanting, failing.

חֶדֶל with pause חָדֶל m., leisure, Isa. 38:11.

חַדְלִי Jud. 5:7, with pause and with dag. euphon. for חֲדֵלִי, חָדֵלִי pret. pl., from חדל.

חַדְלַי p. n. of a man.

חֲדַלְתִּי; see הֶחְדַּלְתִּי.

חֵדֶק root not used; (Arab. melongena spinosa, a thorny shrub).

חֵדֶק and חֶדֶק, with pause חָדֶק m., a species of thorn, Pro. 15:19.

חִדֶּקֶל a river of Mesopotamia, perhaps the Tigris.

חָדַר, part. f. חֹדֶרֶת enclosing, laying siege to, Eze. 21:19.

חֶדֶר m. (const. חֲדַר; with suff. חַדְרוֹ; pl. חֲדָרִים, חַדְרֵי), chamber, inner apartment; fig. חַדְרֵי־תֵמָן the chambers of the south, i. e. the south; חַדְרֵי בָטֶן the inner parts of the body; חַדְרֵי מָוֶת the tomb.

חַדְרָךְ p. n. of a part of Syria, near Damascus, Zec. 9:1.

חָדַשׁ . Pi. חִדֵּשׁ renew, restore. Hith. is renewed, Ps. 103:5.

חָדָשׁ m., new, recent, fresh; f. חֲדָשָׁה (pl. חֲדָשׁוֹת).

חֹדֶשׁ m. (with suff. חָדְשׁוֹ; pl. חֳדָשִׁים, חָדְשֵׁי)—I. new moon: hence,—II. certain feasts regulated by the moon.—III. month which began with the new moon; חֹדֶשׁ יָמִים a whole month.—IV. p. n. of a

woman; חָדְשִׁי the son of Hodash.

חֲדַת m. Ch., new.

חוֹב . Pi. חַיֵּב render due, forfeit, Dan 1:10.

חוֹב m., debt, Eze. 18:7.

חוֹבָה p. n.; see חָבָה.

חוּג circumscribe, Job 26:10.

חוּג m., sphere, globe.

מְחוּגָה f., compasses, Isa. 44:13.

חוּד propose a riddle, problem.

חִידָה f., parable, riddle.

אֲחִידָה f. Ch., the same, Dan. 5:12.

חָוָה . Pi. חִוָּה shew, declare. חַוִּי, חַוָּה, חַוָּא. Pa. Ch., shew, declare. Aph. the same.

אַחְוָה f., shewing, argument, Job 13:17.

אַחֲוָיָה f. Ch., the same, Dan. 5:12.

חַוָּה f., pl. חַוּוֹת villages of huts; see also under חוי.

חַיָּה f., crowd of men, 2 Sa. 23.11, 13; Ps. 68:11; see also under חוי.

חוּן root not used; (Arab. shore, coast)

מָחוֹז m., haven, harbour, Ps. 107:30

חוֹנִי p. n. of a man.

חוֹחַ m. (pl. חֲחִים, חוֹחִים).—I. thorn or bramble generally.—II. fish hook, Job 40:26.—III. a ring with spikes put round the necks of captives, 2 Ch. 33:11.

חָח m.—I. hook or ring put into the nose of animals, e.g. the camel.—II. a nose jewel, worn as an ornament.

חוּט Ch. Aph., join in one thread, Exr. 4:12.

חוּט m., *thread*; מֵחוּט וְעַד שְׂרוֹךְ־נַעַל *from a thread to a shoe-latchet*, Gen. 14:23, i. e. nothing whatever.

חִוִּי p. n., *the Hivites*, a people of Canaan.

חֲוִילָה p. n. of an unknown district where there was gold.

חוּל and חִיל חֹל (fut. יָחִיל, יָחוּל; apoc. וַתָּחָל, וַתָּחֶל; imp. f. חֹלִי; pl. חִילוּ).—I. *feel, be in pain*.—II. *tremble as a woman in labour*.— III. *bring forth*, Isa. 54:1.—IV. *precipitate, fall upon*.—V. *be strong, durable*.—VI. *waited*; see יָחַל. Hiph. fut. יָחִיל.—I. *shake*, Ps. 29:8. —II. *exult*, Job 20:21. Hoph. fut. יוּחָל *shall be brought forth*, Isa. 66:8. Pil. חוֹלֵל—I. *dance in a circle*, Jud. 21:23.—II. *humble*, Job 26:5.— III. *bring forth*.—IV. *wait*, Job 35: 14. Pul. חוֹלָל *was born*. Hithpo. הִתְחוֹלֵל.—I. *was tormented*.—II. *fell upon*.—III. *waited*, Ps. 37:7. Hithpal. הִתְחַלְחַל *was pained*, Est. 4:4.

חוֹל m.—I. *sand*.—II. *measure, number*, Job 29:18.—III. *weight*.—IV. *abundance*.

חוּל p. n. of a son of Aram, Gen. 10:23.

חַיִל m. (const. חֵיל; with suff. חֵילוֹ; pl. חֵילִים).—I. *strength, power*; עָשָׂה חַיִל *aid valiantly*.—II. *an army*; אַנְשֵׁי ח׳ or בְּנֵי חַיִל *soldiers*; שַׂר הֶחָיִל *general*.—III. *riches, wealth*; עָשָׂה חַיִל *acquired wealth*. —IV. *virtue, integrity*.—V. חֵיל הָעֵץ *strength* (i. e. fruit) *of the tree*, Joel 2:22.

חַיִל m. Ch.—I. *strength*.—II. *army*.

חֵיל and חֵל m.—I. *army*.—II. *outwork space before a fortification*.

חִיל m. } —I. *pain*.—II. *trembling,*
חִילָה f. }    *fear*, Ex. 15:14.

חֵילָה Ps. 48:14, same as חֵיל *fortification*; others read חֵילָה.

חַלְחָלָה f., *great, grievous pain*.

מָחוֹל m.—I. *dance, dancing*.—II. p. n. of a man.

מְחֹלָה f., *dance*.

חוּם root not used; (Arab. *was black*).

חוּם m., *black*.

חוֹמָה f., *a wall*; const. חוֹמַת; pl. חוֹמוֹת; dual חֹמָתַיִם.

חוּם (fut. יָחֹם, יָחוּם; 1. pers. אָחוּם) *spare, pity, grieve for*; often with עַיִן *the eye*.

חוֹף *shore*; see חפף.

חֻפִּים, חֻפָּם p. n. of a son of Benjamin; חוּפָמִי *a Chuphamite*.

חוּץ root not used; (Arab. *surrounded*).

חוּץ m. (pl. חֻצוֹת, חִצוֹת).—I. *open place, court, garden*.—II. *out-fields, lands* (without a city).—Adv. I. *without*, opposed to *within*; חוּצָה, הַחוּצָה *without*; בַּחוּץ the same; לַחוּץ, לַחוּצָה *to the without*; מֵחוּץ the same; with לְ *besides*; מֵהַחוּץ *without*, Eze. 41:25; מִן הַחוּץ *without*; מִחוּצָה the same, Eze. 40:40, 44; אֶל־הַחוּץ the same, Eze. 41:9; אֶל הַחוּץ the same, Eze. 34:21; חוּץ מִן אֶל מֵחוּץ לְ the same; *more than*, Ecc. 2:25.

חַיִץ m., *a wall*, Eze. 13:10.

חִיצוֹן m., חִיצוֹנָה f., *outer, exterior*; לַחִיצוֹן *without*; הַמְּלָאכָה הַחִיצוֹנָה *outward business*, i. e. civil, opposed to sacred, 1 Ch. 26:29.

חוק חלק same as חֵיק.

חָוַר, fut. pl. יֶחֱוָרוּ shall be white, pale, Isa. 29:22.

חוֹר, חֹר, חֹחֹר m.—I. white linen.—II. nobles.—III. cavern, aperture, hole; pl. חֹרִים, חֹרִי, חוֹרִי; see also חרר.

חִוָּר m. Ch., white, Dan. 7:9.

חֹרִי m., white bread, Gen. 40:16.

חֹרִי (τρωγλοδύτης) p. n., a Horite, i.e. dweller in a cave, a Canaanitish nation.—II. p. n. of a man.

חֹרִי p. n. of a man.

חָרִי same as הָרִי p. n. of a man.

חִירָם, חֻרָם p. n.—I. of a king of Tyre.—II. of a man.

חַוְרָן p. n. of a country beyond Jordan, Eze. 47:16, 18.

חֹרֹנַיִם p. n. of a city of the Moabites; חֹרֹנִי a Horonite.

חוֹרִים white, &c.; see חֹר in חרר.

חוּשׁ and חִישׁ (fut. יָחִישׁ; apoc. וַתָּחַשׁ; imp. חוּשָׁה).—I. hasten (part. חָשִׁים hasting).—II. felt, enjoyed, Ecc. 2:25, with לְ. Hiph. הֵחִישׁ—I. hasten, accelerate.—II. stumble, fail.

חוּשָׁה p. n. of a man; חֻשָׁתִי a Cushathite.

חוּשַׁי p. n. of one of David's companions.

חֻשִׁים p. n. of a man.

חִישׁ adv., hastily, Ps. 90:10.

חוֹתָם seal; see חתם.

חָזָה (inf. חָזוּת; imp. חֲזֵה; fut. יֶחֱזֶה; apoc. תַּחַז, אֶחַז).—I. saw visions.—II. saw with pleasure.—III. look at, regard, with בְּ; look for, search out, choose, with מִן; part. חֹזֶה;

subst. const. חֹזֵה, חֹזֵה; pl. חֹזִים—I. prophet, seer.—II. agreement, Isa. 28:15.

חֲזָא, חֲזָה Ch., he saw.

חָזֶה m., breast of an animal cut up const. חֲזֵה; pl. חָזוֹת.

חֵזוּ m. Ch., vision.

חֲזוֹ p. n. of a man.

חִזָּיוֹן m., vision, revelation.

חָזוּת f.—I. vision, revelation.—II. matter of vision.—III. agreement, Isa. 28:18.

חָזוֹת f., vision, 2 Ch. 9:29.

חֱזוֹת f. Ch., appearance, Dan. 4:8, 17;

חִזָּיוֹן m. const. חֶזְיוֹן; pl. חֶזְיוֹנוֹת dream, vision.

חֶזְיוֹן p. n. of a man, 1 Ki. 15:18.

מַחֲזֶה m., vision.

מֶחֱזָה f., window, 1 Ki. 7:4, 5.

מַחֲזִיאוֹת p. n. of a man.

חֲזָאֵל p. n. of a king of Syria.

חֲזִיאֵל p. n. of a man.

חֲזָיָה p. n. of a man.

יַחֲזִיאֵל p. n. of a man.

יַחְזֵיָה p. n. of a man.

חָזַז root not used; (Arab. pierced).

חֲזִיז or חָזִיז m., thunder-bolt, Zec. 10:1.

חֲזִיר m., hog, swine.

חֲזִיר p. n. of a man.

חָזַק (fut. יֶחֱזַק) was strong, firm, powerful, unyielding, applied to persons, mind, or things: const. with בְּ in; עַל, אֶל on, to; מִן more than; לְ to, for. Pi. חִזַּק made strong, firm. —I. with יָד 1. strengthened the hand.—2. supported.—II. with לֵב 1. hardened the heart.—2. restored, healed Hiph. הֶחֱזִיק I. take fast hold of, obtain, retain, with בְּ, לְ, עַל.—II. applying strength to, repairing, confirming, prevailing. Hith. הִתְחַזֵּק became, waxed strong, received strength, &c.; with לִפְנֵי oppose, resist; with בְּ or עִם assist, aid.

חָזֵק m., becoming strong; הוֹלֵךְ וְחָ׳ waxing strong.

חָזָק m., strong, mighty, unyielding, prevailing, used either in a good or bad sense.

חֵזֶק m., strength; with suff. חִזְקִי Ps. 18:2.

חֹזֶק m., the same; with suff. חָזְקִי.

חֶזְקָה f. (same as חֵזֶק inf., see חָזַק), בְּחֶזְקָתוֹ when he gained strength, with בְּ; בְּחֶזְקַת־הַיָּד when the hand of God impelled.

חָזְקָה f.—I. force, vehemence; בְּחָזְקָה with power, vehemently.—II. repairing an edifice, 2 Ki. 12:13.

חִזְקִי p. n. of a man.

יְחִזְקִיָּהוּ, יְחִזְקִיָּה, חִזְקִיָּהוּ, חִזְקִיָּה p. n., Hezekiah, king of Judah, and others; LXX. Ἐζεκίας.

יְחֶזְקֵאל (the Lord strengthens), p. n., Ezekiel the prophet; LXX. Ἰεζεκιήλ.

חָח, חַחִים hook; see חוֹחַ.

חָטָא (inf. חֲטֹא, חֲטוֹא; fut. יֶחֱטָא).—I. err, wander from.—II. sin; with בְּ, לְ, or עַל by, against.—III. miss the mark, fall short of, with מִן; part. m. חוֹטֵא, חֹטֵא; pl. חֹטְאִים; f. חֹטֵאת. Pi. חִטֵּא expiate, cleanse, free from sin. Hiph. הֶחֱטִיא I. miss the mark.—II. cause to sin. Hith. I. be, become erring, Job 41:17.—II. be cleansed from sin.

חֵטְא m. (with suff. חֶטְאִי; pl. חֲטָאִים, חֲטָאֵי), sin, wickedness.

חֵטְא or חֲטִי m. Ch., sin, Dan. 4:24.

חֲטָאָה f., sin.

חַטָּא m., sinner; חַטָּאָה f., Am. 9:8.

חֲטָאָה f., sin, Gen. 20:9.

חֲטָאָה f., sin, Ex. 34:7; Isa. 5:18.

חֲטָאָה f., sin, Nu. 15:28.

חַטָּאת f. (const. חַטַּאת; pl. חַטָּאוֹת; const. חַטֹּאות).—I. sin.—II. sin-offering.—III. idol.—IV. punishment of sin, Zec. 14:19; Pro. 10:16.

חֲטָאָה Ch. (Kri) חֲטָיָא (Ketib), sin-offering, Ezr. 6:17.

חֲטֹר־חָטָא Kal inf. const., from חָטָא.

חָטַב (fut. יַחְטֹב) cutting wood. Pu. part. f. מְחֻטָּבוֹת hewn stones, Ps. 144:12.

חֲטֻבוֹת f. pl., striped, variegated, Pro. 7:16.

חִטָּה f., wheat; pl. חִטִּים; Ch. חִטִּין and חִנְטִין grains of wheat.

חַטּוּשׁ p. n. of a man.

חֲטִיטָא p. n. of a man.

חַטִּיל p. n. of a man.

חָטַם (lit. ring a camel through the nose, which is the mode of bitting that animal); fut. אֶחֱטָם־לָךְ I will restrain my anger against thee, Isa. 48:9.

חָטַף (fut. יַחְטֹף) rob, take by violence.

חֲטִיפָא p. n. of a man.

חֹטֶר m., stick, rod, Pro. 14:3; Isa. 11:1.

חַי, חִיאֵל see חיי.

חִידָה riddle; see חוד.

חָיָה (inf. חָיֹה, חָיֹה; const. חֲיוֹת; imp. חֲיֵה; fut. יִחְיֶה; apoc. יְחִי) he lives in health, safety, vigour, &c.; with

מן recovered after sickness. Pi. חיה.—I. giving, preserving, restoring life.—II. strengthen, make effectual; חיה זרע preserve seed, Gen. 7:3. Hiph. הֶחֱיָה give, preserve life.

חיה or חֲיָא Ch., he lived; imp. חֲיִי. Aph. part. מַחֵא giving life.

חָיָה m., not used; f. חָיָה; pl. חָיוֹת lively, strong, Ex. 1:19.

יְחַוְאֵל p.n. of a man.

מִחְיָה f.—I. means of living, food.—II. crude, raw, i.e. unsound, diseased, Lev. 13:10, 24; see also in חוה.

חָיַי lived; pret. m. חַי, וָחַי; f. וְחָיְתָה Ex. 1:16.

חַי m. (const. חֵי; pl. חַיִּים, חַיֵּי; with suff. חַיֶּיךָ), s. living, alive; חַי יְהֹוָה as the Lord liveth and וְחֵי נַפְשְׁךָ thy soul liveth; adj. (f. חַיָּה; pl. חַיּוֹת) living, alive, safe, reviving; כָּעֵת חַיָּה according to the time of life; metaphorically, living (i. e. springing) water; living (i.e. fresh) meat.

חַי m. Ch., living; pl. חַיִּין, חַיֵּי, s. life.

חַיָּה f. (const. חַיַּת; חַיָּתוֹ; with suff. חַיָּתוֹ; pl. חַיּוֹת).—I. life.—II. animal, wild beast; see also in חוה.

חַוָּה (same as חַיָּה life), p. n. Eve the first woman; LXX. ʼEva, Vulg. Heva; see also in חוה.

חַיְוָא f. Ch., living creature.

חַיּוּת f., life.

חַיְתוֹ const. state with ו parag. for חַיַּת from חַיָּה; see in חַיֵּי.

יְחִיאֵל p.n. of a man; יְחִיאֵלִי one of the family of Jehoel.

חִיאֵל p.n. of a man.

חַיִל, חַיִל, חֵיל, חֵילָה; see חול.

חֵלְאָם, חֵילָם p.n. of a city not far from the Euphrates.

חֵלָן same as חֹלָן.

חֵין; see חנן.

חִיצוֹנָה, חִיצוֹן, חִיצֹן; see חוץ.

חֵיק and חֵק m., the bosom.—I. in a conjugal sense.—II. in a dishonest sense, Pro. 5:20.—III. in a moral sense, the feelings, affections.—IV. bosom, lappet of a garment.—V. hollow place in a chariot, 1 Ki. 22:35; in the altar, Eze. 43:13, &c.

חִירָה p.n. of a man.

חִישׁ hastily; see חוּשׁ.

חֵךְ, חַכָּה palate; see חנך.

חָכָה waiting, with לְ, Isa. 30:18. Pi. חִכָּה the same.

חַכֵּי for חַכֵּה Pi. inf. of חָכָה.

חַכְלִילִי m., brightened with wine (of the eyes), Gen. 49:12.

חַכְלִלוּת f., fierceness of eyes, Pro. 23:29.

חֲכִילָה p.n. of a hill in the wilderness of Ziph.

חֲכַלְיָה p.n. of a man.

חָכַם (fut. יֶחְכַּם) was wise, intelligent, taught. Pi. made wise, taught. Pu. part. מְחֻכָּם made wise. Hiph. part. f. מַחְכִּימָה making wise, Ps. 19:8. Hithp. account oneself wise, cunning.

חָכָם m. (f. חֲכָמָה).—I. wise.—II. teacher of wisdom.—III. intelligent, clever; חֲכָמִים wise men (of soothsayers, &c.); קִינָה חֲכָמוֹת (i.e. קִינָה) women skilled in lamenting at funerals, Jer. 9:16.

חַכִּים m. Ch., wise man, magician.

חָכְמָה f., wisdom.

חָכְמָה f. Ch., *wisdom.*

חַכְמוֹת, חָכְמוֹת f., the same.

חַכְמוֹנִי p.n. of a man.

חָל same as חִיל pain; see חול.

חֹל *profane;* see חלל.

חֵלָא same as חָלָה *sick, weak, afflicted.*

חֶלְאָה f.—I. *refuse, filth, scum,* Eze. 24:6.—II. p.n. of a woman.

חֲלָאִים *diseases;* see חלי in חלה.

חָלָב m. (const. חֲלֵב; with suff. חֲלָבִי), *new milk* or *cream.*

חֵלֶב and חֶלֶב m. (with suff. חֶלְבּוֹ; pl. חֲלָבִים, חֶלְבֵּי).—I. *fat, fatness, the best of any thing;* ח' הָאָרֶץ *the fatness of the earth;* ח' חִטָּה *the best of the wheat.*—II. *hardness, impenitency,* Ps. 17:10, &c.—III. p. n. of a man.

חֶלְבּוֹן p.n. of a town in the tribe of Asher.

חֶלְבּוֹן p.n. of a city in Syria, Χαλυβών.

חֶלְבְּנָה f., *galbanum,* an odoriferous gum, Ex. 30:34.

חָלֶד root not used; (Arab. *duration*).

חֶלֶד m. (with suff. חֶלְדִי), *time, duration;* מְתִים מֶחָלֶד *men of time,* i.e. of this world, Ps. 17:14.

חֹלֶד m., *a mole.*

חֻלְדָּה p. n. of a prophetess; LXX. Ὀλδά.

חֶלְדַי p.n. of a man.

I. חָלָה (fut. apoc. וַיֶּחַל), *was sick, weak, afflicted,* with עַל. Niph. נֶחְלָה *became sick, weak, afflicted;* part. נַחְלֶה (f. נַחְלָה), *diseased, infirm.* Pi. חִלָּה *afflicted;* with suff. חִלּוֹתִי *my sickness.* Pu. חֻלָּה

*afflicted, infirm,* Isa. 14:10. Hiph. הֶחֱלִי (for הֶחֱלָה) *afflicted, made sick, infirm.* Hoph. הָחֳלָה *wounded.* Hith. *feigned sickness;* imper. apoc. הִתְחָל, fut. apoc. וַיִּתְחַל.

חַלּוֹתִי Ps. 77:11. Pi. inf. with suff., from I. חלה.

חֱלִי with pause חֹלִי m. (with suff. חֶלְיוֹ; pl. חֲלָיִים). *disease, sickness, evil, inconvenience.*

חֱלִי m., *ornament, necklace;* pl. חֲלָאִים.

חֶלְיָה f., the same.

אַחֲלַי m., *prayer;* אַחֲלֵי, אַחֲלִי *would that!*

מַחֲלֶה m.,   } *sickness, disease.*
מַחֲלָה f.,   }

מַחְלָה p. n. of a woman.

מַחְלוֹן p. n. of a man.

מַחְלִי p. n. of a man.

מַחֲלֻיִים m., pl. מַחֲלֻיִים *circumstances of disease,* 2 Chron. 24:25.

מַחֲלַת m., a title of Ps. 53 and 88; meaning uncertain.

מַחֲלַת p. n. of a woman.

תַּחֲלֻאִים m., pl. תַּחֲלֻאִים, תַּחֲלוּאָ *diseases.*

II. חָלָה Kal not used; (Arab. *was sweet*). Pi. חִלָּה, with פְּנֵי *make propitious, conciliate favour, satisfy;* imp. apoc. חַל, fut. apoc. וַיְחַל.

חַלּוֹן, חַלָּה; see חלל.

חֲלוֹם *dream;* see חלם.

חֹלוֹן p. n. of a town in the land of Moab.

חֲלוֹף *passing away;* see חלף.

חֲלוּשָׁה *defeat;* see חלש.

חֶלַח p.n. of a province in the kingdom of Assyria (Καλαχηνη).

חַלְחָלָה *pain;* see חול.

חָלַט. Hiph. fut. וַיַּחְלְטוּ 1 Ki. 20:33, "did hastily catch," Eng. Ver.; "hasted greatly" (Lee).

חֲלִי .חָלָה see ; חֲלִי חָלִיל pipe; see חלל

חֲלִיפָה change; see חלף.

חֲלִיצָה spoil; see חלץ.

חָלַד root not used; (Arab. *intense blackness*).

חֶלְכָּה with pause m., *very miserable*, Ps. 10:8,14; pl. חֵלְכָּאִים, v. 10.

חָלַל *pierced, wounded*, Ps. 109:22. Niph. נֶחַל *profaned, became common, prostituted*; inf. הֵחַל; fut. תֵּחַל יֵחַל. Pi. חִלֵּל—I. *wounded*, Eze. 28:9.—II. *profaned, made common, violated* (a covenant).—III. *played upon the flute*, 1 Ki. 1: 40, from חָלִיל. Pu. part. מְחֻלָּל *profaned*. Po. חוֹלֵל *wounding*. Poal. part. מְחוֹלָל *wounded*. Hiph. הֵחֵל—I. *make profane, violate, loose, set free*.—II. *begin*; pret. 1. pers. הַחִלֹּתִי; inf. with suff. הַחֵלָּם *their beginning*; fut. יָחֵל *shall begin*; fut. יַחֵל *shall loose*. Hoph. הוּחַל *was begun*, Gen. 4:26.

חָלִיל m., *pipe*; pl. חֲלִילִים; חָלִילָה int. *profane! fie!* with לְ of the pers. and inf. with מִן; ח' לְךָ מֵעֲשׂוֹת *that be far from thee to do so*.

חָלָל (const. חֲלַל m.).—I. *pierced, wounded, slain*.—II. *profane, common*; f. חֲלָלָה *prostitute*, Lev. 21:7, 14.

חֹל m., *profane, common*.

חַלָּה const. חַלַּת f., *cake* (pierced with holes).

חַלּוֹן com., *window*, (i. e. *opening*); pl. חַלּוֹנִים.

מְחִלָּה f., pl. מְחִלּוֹת *caves, holes of the earth*, Isa. 2:19.

תְּחִלָּה f., *beginning*; בַּתְּחִלָּה *at first, formerly*.

חָלַם (fut. יַחֲלֹם)—I. *dream*.—II. *be fat*, Job 39:4. Hiph.—I. *make stout, strong*, Isa. 38:16.—II. part. מַחְלְמִים *causing to see visions*, Jer. 29:8.

חֲלוֹם m., *a dream*; pl. חֲלֹמוֹת.

חֵלֶם m. Ch.—I. *dream*.—II. p. n. of a man.

חֶמְאָה f., Job 6:6, "egg," Eng. Ver., *cheese*, (Lee).

חַלָּמִישׁ m., *flint, stone striking fire*.

אַחְלָמָה f., *a precious stone*; LXX ἀμέθυστος.

חֹלֹן p. n.—I. of a town in the tribe of Judah; same as חִילֵן.—II. חֹלוֹן in the land of Moab; same as חֹרוֹן.

חָלַף (יַחֲלֹף)—I. *pass by, away*.—II. *put away*. Pi. חִלֵּף *change* (as clothes). Hiph. הֶחֱלִיף.—I. *change* (as clothes).—II. *renew*.

חֲלַף Ch., *pass by or away*.

חֵלֶף prep. *for, instead of*, Nu. 18:21, 31.

חֲלוֹף m.; בְּנֵי ח' *children of those passed away, orphans*, Pro. 31:8.

חֲלִיפָה f., *change, renewal* (of clothes, troops, &c.).

מַחֲלָף m., *knife for sacrifice*, Ezr. 1:9.

מַחְלְפוֹת pl. f., *locks of hair*, Jud. 16: 13, 19.

חָלַץ (יַחֲלֹץ)—I. *deliver, free*.—II. *give the breast*, Lam. 4:3.—III. *gird, arm for battle*, with מִן, חֲלוּץ הַנַּעַל *without sandals*. Niph. —I. *was delivered*.—II. *was armed*

Pi. *deliver, set free;* חֲלִיץ *girt, armed, ready;* חֲלוּץ צָבָא *host armed;* חֲלוּצֵי־מוֹאָב *warriors of Moab.* Hiph. יַחֲלִיץ *make strong,* Isa. 58:11.

חֲלִיצָה f., *spoil,* Jud.14:19; 2 Sa.2:21.

חֲלָץ m., dual חֲלָצַיִם *loins.*

חֶלֶץ p. n. of a man.

מַחֲלָצוֹת f. pl., *dress of honour, mantle.*

חָלַק (fut. יַחֲלֹק).—I. *apportioned, divided land, wealth, spoil.*— II. *was smooth, fallacious,* with עִם. Niph. *was divided, distributed.* Pi.—I. *divided, distributed,* with אֶת.—II. *dispersed,* with לְ. Pu. *was divided.* Hiph. — I. *make smooth, flattering.*—II. *taking portion,* Jer. 37:12. Hithp. *dividing, apportioning,* Jos. 18:5.

חָלָק m., *smooth, slippery, fallacious, flattering.*

חֵלֶק m. (with suff. חֶלְקִי; pl. חֲלָקִים).—I. *part, portion, lot of land, field.*—II. *portion of the sacrifice.*—III. *prey;* חֶלְקֵי נַחַל Isa.57:6, "*smooth stones;*" Eng. Ver. *river gods* (Lee); חֵלֶק with אֶת, עִם, בְּ, *my portion is with,* &c.—IV. *smoothness.*—V. p. n. of a son of Gilead; חֶלְקִי son of *Chelek.*

חֲלָק m. Ch., *part, portion.*

חָלָק m., pl. חַלֻּקִים *smooth stones,* 1 Sa. 17:40.

חֶלְקָה f.—I. *slipperiness.*—II. *flattery.*—III. *portion;* pl. חֲלָקוֹת *slippery ways,* Ps. 73:18.

חֶלְקָה f., *division, divided part,* 2 Chron. 35:15.

חֲלָקוֹת f. pl. Ch., *blandishments,* Dan. 11:32.

חֶלְקֵי pl. const. with dag. euphon., from חֵלֶק.

חֶלְקַי p. n. of a man.

חִלְקִיָּהוּ, חִלְקִיָּה p.n.—I. of a man.—II. the high priest in Josiah's reign.—III. the father of Jeremiah the prophet.— IV. the father of Eliakim.

חֲלַקְלַקּוֹת *very slippery ways, devices*

מַחֲלֹקֶת f. (with suff. מַחֲלֻקְתּוֹ; pl. מַחֲלְקוֹת).— I. *appointment, distribution, order, course.*—II. p. n. of a place; סֶלַע הַמַּחְלְקוֹת.

מַחֲלֹקָה f. Ch., *distribution, order,* Ezr 6:18.

חָלַשׁ (fut. יַחֲלֹשׁ) *grow feeble,* Job 14:10; (fut. יַחֲלֹשׁ) *discomfit, reduce,* with עַל, Ex. 17:13.

חַלָּשׁ m., *weak person,* Joel 4:10.

חֲלוּשָׁה f., *discomfiture,* Ex. 32:18.

חָם m. (with suff. חָמִיהָ, חָמִיךְ) *father-in-law;* see also in חמם.

חָמוֹת f., *mother-in-law.*

חֹם *hot;* see חמם.

חָמָא root not used; (Arab. *curdled, of milk*).

חֲמָאָה (Syr. חֵמָה) *cheese, curd.*

חֵמָה f., the same; see also in יחם.

מַחֲמָאוֹת f. pl., Ps. 55:22; read מֵחֶ׳ *than butter.*

חָמַד (fut. יַחְמֹד) *desired, coveted;* part. (חֲמֵדוֹת pl. m. חֲמוּדִים, f. חֲמוּד) *desirable thing.* Niph. part. נֶחְמָד *desirable.* Pi. *greatly desired,* Cant. 2:3.

חֶמֶד m., חֶמְדָּה f., *desire, that which is desirable;* חֶמְדַּת כָּל גּוֹיִם *the desire of all nations,* i. e. Messiah, Hag. 2:7.

חֲמוּדוֹת, חֲמֻדוֹת f. pl., *desirable things.*

חֶמְדָּן p. n. of a man.

מַחְמָד m. (pl. מַחֲמַדִּים) *desirable, desirable things.*

מַחֲמַדִּים m. pl., the same, Lam. 1:7, 11.

חָמוֹן, חַמּוּאֵל, חֶמָּה; see חמם.

חֶמְאָה same as חֶמְאָה *butter;* see also in יחם.

חֲמוּטַל p. n. of the wife of Josiah.

חָמוּץ *sour;* see חמץ.

חָמוּק *surround;* see חמק.

חֲמוֹר *ass;* see חמר.

חָמוֹת *mother-in-law;* see חָם.

הֹמֶט m., kind of *lizard,* Lev. 11:30; LXX. σαύρα.

חֲמִישִׁי *fifth;* see חָמֵשׁ.

חָמַל (fut. יַחְמֹל; inf. חֶמְלָה) *bear with, forbear with,* with עַל; *spare,* with עַל, אֶל.

חֶמְלָה f., *clemency.*

מַחְמָל *support, comfort,* Eze. 24:21.

חָמַם (fut. יַחֹם, יָחֹם; inf. חֹם, with suff. חֻמּוֹ).—I. *be, grow hot;* כְּחֹם הַיּוֹם *in the heat of the day;* חַם לוֹ *he becomes warm.* — II. *hot with lust.* Niph. *became hot, inflamed;* fut. יֵחַם, יֵחָם; part. pl. נֶחָמִים. Pi. *warms, hatches,* Job 39:14. Hithp. *becomes warm,* Job 31:20.

חָם m.—I. *warm, growing hot;* pl. חַמִּים—II. p. n. of a son of Noah. —III. perhaps Egypt (Copt. χημι), Ps. 78:51, &c.; see also חָם in its place.

חֹם m., *heat;* לֶחֶם חֹם *hot bread,* i.e. new.

חַמָּה f., const. חַמַּת *heat;* see in יחם.

חַמָּה f.—I. *heat, glow,* Ps. 19:7.—II. *the sun.*

חַמּוּאֵל p. n. of a man.

חַמּוֹן p. n.—I. of a town in the tribe of Asher.—II. of a town in the tribe of Naphtali.

חַמָּן m., pl. חַמָּנִים *sun-images;* probably the *Amoun* of Egypt; Greek ἀμουν.

חָמַס (fut. יַחְמֹס), *doing violence, injury, wrong,* with עַל. Niph. *violated,* Jer. 13:22.

חָמָס m. (const. חֲמַס; with suff. חֲמָסִי; pl. חֲמָסִים), *violence, injury, that which is obtained by violence.*

תַּחְמָס m., *ostrich;* LXX. γλαύξ Vulg. noctua.

חָמֵץ (fut. יַחְמַץ; with pause יֶחְמָץ; inf. חֲמֹצָה), *fermented, leavened;* part. חָמוּץ *scarlet;* part. חֹמֶץ Hiph. part. f. מַחֲמֶצֶת *fermented* Hith. *was excited, perturbed,* Ps. 73:21.

חָמֵץ m., *leavened, fermented.*

חֹמֶץ m., *vinegar.*

חָמוּץ m., *injured, oppressed,* Isa. 1:17.

חָמִיץ m., "clean provender," Isa. 30:24, Eng. Ver.; "a salt, sour plant of the desert, much relished by the camel" (Lee).

חָמַק *withdrew, disappeared,* Cant. 5:6. Hith. *loiter, act undecidedly,* Jer. 31:22.

חַמּוּק m., חֲ' יְרֵכַיִךְ Cant. 7:2; probably *large beads,* strung together and worn as a girdle; such girdles are often represented in the tombs of Egypt.

חָמַר (fut. pl. יֶחְמְרוּ), *fermented, was excited* Poal. חֳמַרְמַר *excited, become inflamed.* (From חֵמָר) Hiph. fut. with suff. וַתַּחְמְרָה *she cemented it with pitch,* Ex. 2:3.

חֵמָר m., *mineral pitch,* ἄσφαλτος.

חֶמֶר m., *wine.*

חֲמַר m., *the same.*

חֹמֶר m. (pl. חֳמָרִים).—I. *clay, earth, mire.*—II. *heap, mound of earth.*—III. *measure of capacity,* containing ten baths.

חֲמוֹר, חֲמֹר m.—I. *an ass.*—II. *a heap,* Jud. 15:16, same as חֹמֶר; dual חֲמֹרָתָיִם.—III. p.n. of a man.

חָמְדָן, חַמְרָן p.n. of a man.

יַחְמוּר m., *goat or gazelle of a brown colour.*

חֹמֶשׁ m., *the abdomen;* see also in חָמֵשׁ.

חָמֵשׁ const. חֲמֵשׁ f., חֲמִשָּׁה, חֲמֵשֶׁת m., *five;* pl. חֲמִשִּׁים *fifty;* with suff. חֲמִשָּׁיו, חֲמִשֵּׁיךְ; שַׂר חֲמִשִּׁים *captain of fifty.*

חִמֵּשׁ Pi. *divided into fifth part,* Gen. 41:34.

חֹמֶשׁ m., *fifth part,* Gen. 47:26.

חֲמִישִׁי, חֲמִשִּׁי m., *fifth;* f. חֲמִישִׁית, חֲמִשִׁית; pl. with suff. חֲמִשִׁיתָיו *the fifth part of it.*

חֲמֻשִׁים m. pl., *compact in battle array;* Aquila ἐνωπλισμένοι; Vulg. armati.

חֵמֶת m., *bottle, skin for holding liquids;* const. חֵמַת, חֶמַת.

חֲמָת p.n., *Hamath* in Syria, north of Palestine; חֲמָתִי *a Hamathite.*

חֲמַת דֹּאר p.n. of a town in the tribe of Naphtali.

חֲמָדָד, חֵן; see חנן.

חָנָה (fut. יֶחֱנֶה; apoc. וַיִּחַן).—I. *declined* (of the day), Jud. 19:9.—II. *pitch a tent, encamp;* with עַל *encamp against;* with לְ *defended.*—III. *dwell, reside,* Isa. 29:1.

חָנוּת f., pl. חֲנֻיוֹת *wells* used as dungeons, Jer. 37:16.

חֲנִית f., *spear, lance;* pl. חֲנִיתִים, חֲנִיתֹת.

מַחֲנֶה m. (f. Gen. 32:9).—I. *camp.*—II. *army, body of people.*—III. *flock of cattle, locusts, &c.;* const. מַחֲנֵה; pl. מַחֲנִים (מַחֲנֵים) מַחֲנוֹת. מַחֲנֵה־דָן (*camp of the Danites*), p.n. of a place in the tribe of Judah.

מַחֲנַיִם (*two troops*), p.n. of a town in the tribe of Gad.

תַּחֲנוֹת f. pl., *camp,* 2 Ki. 6:8.

תַּחַן p.n. of a man; תַּחֲנִי *son of Tachan.*

חֲנִינָה, חֲנִיאֵל, חָנוּן, חַנּוּן, חַנָּה; see חנן.

חָנִיךְ, חֲנוֹךְ; see חנך.

חָנַט I. *ripened,* Cant. 2:13.—II. *embalmed, mummified,* Gen. 50:2, 2, 26.

חֲנֻטִים m. pl., *mummy, embalmed body.*

חִטָּה, חִטִּים, חֲנְטִין *wheat;* see חִטָּה.

חָנַךְ *adapt, fit to certain ends.*—I. *teach a child,* Pro. 22:6.—II. *dedicate a temple.*

חֵךְ m. (with suff. חִכִּי).—I. *palate, taste.*—II. *moral perception,* Pro. 8:7.

חַכָּה f., *fish-hook.*

חָנִיךְ m., *trained men,* Gen. 14:14.

חֲנוֹךְ p.n. of a man; חֲנֹכִי *the son of Chanoch.*

חֲנֻכָּה f., *dedication.*

חֲנֻכָּה Ch., the same.

חִנָּם in vain; see חנן.

חֲנַמְאֵל p. n. of a man.

חֲנָמָל m., *frost.*

חָנַן (fut. יָחֹן, יֶחֱנַן; וַיָּחָן; with suff. יְחֻנְּךָ, יָחָנְּנִי; תֶּחֲנַם; with נ epenth. יְחֻנֶּךָ; inf. abs. חָנוֹן; const. חֲנַן; with suff. חֲנַנְכֶם, חָנְנָה; imper. with suff. חָנֵּנִי, חָנֳנֵי; pl. חָנֳנֵי, חַנּוּנוּ), *being, acting favourably, graciously, kindly.* Niph. נֵחַן *was pitiable,* Jer. 22:23. Pi. fut. יְחַנֵּן *be favourable, gracious to.* Po. חוֹנֵן the same, Pro. 14:21. Hoph. fut. יֻחַן *be favoured, find favour.* Hith. הִתְחַנֵּן *implore, supplicate favour,* with לְ, אֶל, לִפְנֵי; inf. with suff. הִתְחַנְּנוּ.

חֲנַן Ch., *show favour.* Hith. *implore favour.*

חֲנַנְאֵל p. n. of a fortress of Jerusalem.

חֲנָנִי p. n. of a man.

חֲנַנְיָה ('Aνανίας), p. n. of a man.

חֵן m. (with suff. חִנּוֹ).—I. *grace, favour;* מָצָא חֵן בְּעֵינֵי פ׳ *found favour in his sight;* נָתַן חֵן בְּעֵינֵי פ׳ *gave favour in the sight of him.*—II. *elegance, grace of deportment.*—III. *worth, value.*—IV. *prayer for grace,* Zec. 12:10.—V. p. n. of a man.

חֲנָדָד p. n. of a man.

חִין m., *destructiveness,* Job 41:4.

חַנָּה f. (pl. חֲנּוֹת).—I. *entreaty for favour, showing favour.*—II. p. n. of a woman, ʹAννα.

חָנָן p. n. of a man.

חַנּוּן m., *very gracious.*

חֲנִיאֵל p. n. of a man.

חֲנִינָה f., *grace, favour,* Jer. 16:13.

חִנָּם adv.—I. *freely, for nothing.*—II. *in vain.*—III. *for nothing, undeservedly.*

תְּחִנָּה f.—I. *favour, mercy.*—II. *prayer for favour, prayer.*

תַּחֲנוּנִים m. pl., *prayers for mercy, supplications.*

תַּחֲנוּנוֹת f. pl., the same.

חָנֵס p. n. of a city in Egypt ('Hρα κλέους πόλις).

חָנֵף (fut. יֶחֱנַף, *was heathenish, profane, ungodly.* Hiph. הֶחֱנִיף the same.

חָנֵף m., *profane, ungodly;* חֲנֵפִים חַנְפֵי.

חֹנֶף m., *heathenism,* Isa. 32:6.

חֲנֻפָּה f., the same, Jer. 23:15.

חָנַק. Niph. fut. וַיֵּחָנַק *hanged himself,* 2 Sa. 17:23. Pi. part. מְחַנֵּק *suffocating,* Nah. 2:13.

מַחֲנָק m., *suffocation,* Job 7:15.

חָסַד. Pi. חִסֵּד *accuse of baseness, impiety,* Pro. 25:10. Hith. (fut. תִּתְחַסָּד) *show thyself merciful,* 2 Sa. 22:26; Ps. 18:26.

חֶסֶד m. (with suff. חַסְדּוֹ; pl. חֲסָדִים חֲסָדֶי).—I. *favour, kindness, mercy;* עָשָׂה חֶסֶד with עִם, עַל, לְ, אֶת, *he showed mercy to him.*—II. *goodness, benevolence.*—III. *shame, disgrace, incest,* Lev. 20:17.—IV. p. n. of a man.

חֲסַדְיָה p. n. of the son of Zerubbabel.

חָסִיד m., *gracious, confident;* חֲסִידֵי יְהֹוָה *they that trust in the Lord.*

חֲסִידָה f., *stork,* supposed by the ancients to be pious to its parents.

חָסָה (fut. אֶחֱסֶה אֶחְסֶה), *trust, confide in,* with בְּ.

חֹסָה p. n. of a man.

חָסוּת f., *confidence,* Isa. 30:3.

חָסָיָה for חָסְתָה Kal pret. f.; pl. חֲסָיוּ for חָסוּ, from חסה.

מַחְסֶה, מַחֲסֶה m. (with suff. מַחְסִי), *refuge.*

מַחְסֵיָה p. n. of a man.

חָסַל *crop off, devour,* Deu. 28:38.

חָסִיל m., *kind of locust,* LXX. βροῦχος.

חָסַם (fut. יַחְסֹם), *bind, tie up, stop* (the mouth).

מַחְסוֹם m., *bridle, curb,* Ps. 39:2.

חָסַן Niph. fut. יֵחָסֵן *was strong, powerful,* Isa. 23:18.

חֲסַן Ch. Aph. *confirm, make strong.*

חֲסֵן m. Ch., *might, power.*

חֹסֶן m., *strength, power, wealth.*

חָסוֹן m., *strong, powerful.*

חָסִין m., *mighty,* Ps. 89:9.

חֶסֶף m., *potter's clay.*

מַחְסְפַּס m., *scaly, having scales,* Ex. 16:14.

חָסֵר (inf. חֲסוֹר; fut. יַחְסַר יַחְסְרוּ), *want, lack, be in need.* Pi. *diminish, make to want.* Hiph. הֶחְסִיר *cause to fall short.*

חָסֵר m., *wanting, destitute of,* with מִן; חֲסַר־לֵב *without heart* (i. e. *sense), foolish.*

חֶסֶר m., *deficiency, want.*

חֹסֶר m., the same.

חֶסְרָה (תַּרְחֵם) p. n. of a man.

חֶסְרוֹן m., *much want,* Ecc. 1:15.

חַסִּיר m. Ch., *deficient,* Dan. 5:27.

מַחְסוֹר m. (with suff. מַחְסֹרוֹ; pl. מַחְסֹרִים) *want, lack, need.*

חָפָא same as חָפַר. Pi. *acted secretly, clandestinely,* 2 Ki. 17:9.

חָפָה *covered, veiled.* Pi. חִפָּה *overlaid, cased* (with gold). Pu. חֻפָּה "*defence;*" Eng. Ver., Isa. 4:5 see חָפַף. Niph. נֶחְפָּה *covered, overlaid,* with בְּ, Ps. 68:14.

חָפַז (fut. יֶחְפֹּז).—I. *affright, alarm.*—II. *hurry.* Niph. נֶחְפַּז *was hurried.*

חִפָּזוֹן m., *haste, hurry.*

חָפַן root not used ; (Arab. a measure containing two hands full).

חֹפֶן m., dual חָפְנַיִם, חָפְנַיִם *both hands closed so as to contain something.*

חָפְנִי p. n. of the son of Eli.

חָפַף *cover, protect,* Deu. 33:12, with עַל.

חֹף, חוֹף m., *shore of the sea.*

חַף m., *pure, faultless,* Job 33:9 (lit. *protected).*

חֻפָּה f.—I. *defence;* see חפף.—II. *bridal chamber.*—III. p. n. of a man.

חֻפִּים p. n. of a man.

חָפֵץ (fut. יַחְפֹּץ יַחְפָּץ).—I. *delight, be pleased with,* with לְ and בְּ.—II. *bend, move.*

חָפֵץ m., *willing, delighting, acquiescing;* אִם חָ׳ אַתָּה *if thou wilt;* חָ׳ רֶשַׁע *delighting in wickedness.*

חֵפֶץ m. (with suff. חֶפְצִי).—I. *pleasure, delight.* — II. *wish, desire, will.*—III. *costly, precious.*—IV. *business, concern, affair;* pl. חֲפָצִים *precious things.*

חֶפְצִי־בָהּ *my delight (is) in her.*—I. a mystic title of Christ's true church, Isa. 62:4. — II. p. n. of the mother of Manasseh, 2 Ki. 21:1.

חָפַר (fut. יַחְפֹּר).—I. *dig* (as a well, &c). —II. *search out, investigate;* חָפֵר (fut. יֶחְפַּר) *blush, be ashamed, confounded.* Hiph. הֶחְפִּיר.—I. *blush.* —II. *cause to blush, put to shame.*

חֵפֶר p. n.—I. of a city of Canaan.— II. of a man; חֶפְרִי *a Hepherite.*

חֲפָרַיִם p. n. of a town in the tribe of Issachar.

חֲפַרְפָּרוֹת (digger), *a mole,* Isa. 2:20; probably wrong reading for חֲפַרְפָּרוֹת *moles.*

חָפְרַע p. n., *Pharaoh Hophra* king of Egypt; LXX. Ουαφρη.

חָפַשׂ *search, investigate.* Niph. *shall be sought out,* Obad. v. 6. Pi. חִפֵּשׂ *search diligently.* Pu. חֻפַּשׂ *is searched.* Hithp. הִתְחַפֵּשׂ (from another root), *was clothed, bound, equipped, accoutred.*

חֵפֶשׂ m., *search, enquiry,* Ps. 64:7.

חָפַשׁ Pu. חֻפְּשָׁה *she was freed,* Lev. 19:20.

חֹפֶשׁ m. בִּגְדֵי ח' *clothes of liberation,* i.e. *spread out to exhibit for sale,* Eze. 27:20.

חֻפְשָׁה f., *freedom,* Lev. 19:20.

חָפְשִׁי m. (pl. חָפְשִׁים), *free from servitude, evil,* &c.; בְּמֵתִים ח' *free from the dead,* Ps. 88:6, i.e. *free from the evils of life.*

חָפְשׁוּת חָפְשִׁית f., *freedom from business, servitude,* &c. בֵּית ח' *retreat, place of retirement,* 2 Ki. 15:5.

חֵץ *arrow;* see חצץ.

חָצַב and חָצֵב (fut. יַחְצֹב) *cut, hew out wood, stone, metal,* &c.; part.

חֹצֵב s., *hewer;* applied to lightning, 1 Chron. 22:2, 15. Niph. *was engraven,* Job 19:24. Pu. *hewn,* Isa. 51:1. Hiph. *cause to cut to pieces.*

מַחְצֵב m., *hewing* (of stones).

חָצָה (fut. יֶחֱצֶה; apoc. וַיַּחַץ) *divide, apportion,* Ps. 55:24; לֹא־יֶחֱצוּ יְמֵיהֶם *shall not live out half their days.* Niph. *was divided.*

חֲצוֹת const. חֲצוֹת f., *middle.*

חֵצִי with pause חֵצִי m. (with suff. חֶצְיוֹ) *half, part, portion of any thing;* see also in חצץ.

חֲצִי הַמְּנֻחוֹת p. n. of a man; patron. חֲצִי הַמְּנַחְתִּי

מֶחֱצָה f., *half,* Nu. 31:36, 43.

מַחֲצִית f., the same.

חָצִיר, חֲצוֹצְרָה, חָצוֹר; see חצר.

חֹצֶן root not used; (Arab. *bosom*).

חֹצֶן m.—I. *bosom, chest.*—II. *bosom of garment,* perhaps, *girdle,* Neh. 5:13; with suff. חָצְנֵנוּ.

חֹצֶן m., the same; with suff. חָצְנִי.

חֲצַף Ch. Aph. *was urgent, pressing,* Dan. 2:15; 3:22.

חָצִין part. חֹצֵץ *rushing on,* Pro. 30:27. Pi. part. pl. מְחַצְּצִים *persons taking part* (in conversation), Jud. 5:11. Pu. *are cut, decided,* Job 21:21.

חָצָץ m.—I. *gravel.*—II. *arrow,* i.e lightning, Ps. 77:18.

חֵץ m. (with suff. חִצִּי; pl. חִצִּים, חִצֵּי).—I. *arrow;* בַּעֲלֵי־חִצִּים *bowmen.*—II. metaph. *lightning.*

חַצְצוֹן־תָּמָר and חַצְצֹן p. n. of a place in the tribe of Judah.

חֲצֹצְרָה *trumpet;* see חצר.

חָצַר root not used.—I. (Arab. *surrounding*).—II. (Arab. *field*).

חָצֵר com. (pl. חֲצֵרִים, חֲצֵרוֹת).—I. *enclosure, area, court.*—II. *village;* חֲצַר־אַדָּר (*threshing-floor of Addar*), p. n. of a town in the tribe of Judah; ח׳ סוּסִים, ח׳ סוּסָה p. n. of a town in the tribe of Simeon; ח׳ עֵינָן, ח׳ עֵינוֹן a town in the north of Palestine; ח׳ שׁוּעָל a town in the tribe of Simeon; חֲצַר הַתִּיכוֹן a town on the borders of Syria; חֲצֵרוֹת p. n. of a station in the desert.

חָצוֹר p. n.—I. of a town in the tribe of Naphtali.—II. of a town in the tribe of Benjamin.—III. of a region of Arabia.

חֶצְרוֹן p. n.—I. of a son of Reuben.—II. of a son of Perez; patron. חֶצְרוֹנִי.

חֶצְרַי p. n. of a man.

חַצַרְמָוֶת (*court of death*), p. n. of a district in Arabia.

חָצִיר m.—I. *enclosure* (habitable place).—II. *grass;* see root II.

חֲצֹצְרָה, חֲצוֹצְרָה f., *trumpet;* from this word comes Pi. מְחַצְּרִים or Hiph. מַחְצְרִים (ketib מַחֲצֹצְרִים, מְחַצְּרִים) *persons blowing with trumpets.*

חֵק *bosom;* see חֵיק.

חֹק, חָק־, חָקָה; see חקק.

חָקָה. Pu. part. מְחֻקֶּה *engraven, carved.* Hith. with עַל *impressed, furrowed,* Job 13:27.

חֲקוּפָא p. n. of a man.

חָקַק *carve, engrave, inscribe;* part. חֹקֵק *legislator,* Jud. 5:9. Pu. part. כִּחְקָק *statute,* Pro. 31:5. Po. *decide, decree,* Pro. 8:15; part. מְחֹקֵק *lawgiver.* Hoph. fut. יֻחָקוּ *engraven, inscribed,* Job 19:23.

חֵקֶק m., pl. const. חִקְקֵי־.—I. *impressions, imaginations,* Jud. 5:15.—II. *decrees,* Isa. 10:1.

חֹק, חָק־ m. (with suff. חֻקֵּךְ, חֻקֵּךְ; pl. חֻקִּים, חֻקֵּי־, חֻקֵּי).—I. *statute, law.*—II. *custom, privilege.*

חֻקָּה f.—I. *statute.*—II. *custom.*

חָקַר (fut. יַחְקֹר; inf. חֲקֹר), *search, investigate, try.* Niph. נֶחְקַר *that may be searched.* Pi. חִקֵּר like Kal, Ecc. 12:9.

חֵקֶר m., *investigation, search, enquiry.*

מֶחְקָר m., pl. const. מֶחְקְרֵי *depths* (of the earth), Ps. 95:4.

חָוָר חָרָר; see חַר, חֹר.

חָרָא root not used; (Arab. *dung*).

חֲרָא or חֲרֵא m., pl. חֲרָאִים *dung,* Isa. 36:12.

חַר or חֹר m., the same; pl. const. חֲרֵי־. מַחֲרָאָה f., *draught-house,* 2 Ki. 10:27.

חָרַב (fut. יֶחֱרַב, יֶחְרַב).—I. *dry, be dry.*—II. *desolate, ruin.* Niph. נֶחֱרַב *was ruined.* Pu. חֹרַב *been dried.* Hiph. הֶחֱרִיב I. *dry up.*—II. *ruin.* Hoph. הָחֳרַב *was wasted, destroyed.*

חֲרַב Ch. Hoph. *t.,* הָחֳרָבַת *is wasted,* Ezr. 4:15.

חָרֵב m.—I. *dry.*—II. *desolate, devastated;* f. חֲרֵבָה; pl. חֲרָבוֹת.

חֶרֶב f. (with suff. חַרְבִּי; pl. חֲרָבוֹת). I. *sword.*—II. *sharp weapon* or *cutting instrument.*—III. *drought,* Deut. 28:22.

חֹרֶב m.—I. *drought.*—II. *heat.*—III. *desolation.*

חֹרֵב, חָרֵב (dry, desolate), p. n. of one
of the summits of Sinai.

חָרְבָּה f., pl. חֲרָבוֹת (const. חָרְבוֹת)
desolations.

חָרָבָה f., drought.

חֹרֶב m., pl. const. חַרְבֹנֵי great
droughts, Ps. 32:4.

חַרְבוֹנָא p. n. of a Persian eunuch.

חָרַג suffer pressure, trouble, Ps.18:46.

חָרְגֹּל m., the larva of the locust,
Lev. 11:22.

חָרֵד or חָרַד (fut. יֶחֱרַד), was timid,
fearful, trembling, with אֶל, לְ or
מִן. Hiph. affrighted.

חָרֵד m.—I. fearful, anxious, with
אֶל, בְּ.—II. trembling.

חֲרָדָה const. חֶרְדַּת f.—I. fear.—II.
trembling.—III. p. n. of a station
of the Israelites, Nu. 33:24.

חָרוֹד p. n. of a place in the mountain of Gilboa, Ju. 7:1; חֲרֹדִי a
Harodite, 2 Sa. 23:25.

חָרָה (inf. abs. חָרֹה; fut. יֶחֱרֶה; apoc.
יִחַר), was, became hot, angry;
חָרָה אַפּוֹ with בְּ, עַל, אֶל, his anger
was kindled against; חָרָה לוֹ he
was angry; חָרָה בְּעֵינָיו it grieved
him. Niph. נֶחֱרוּ were enraged,
angry; part. נֶחֱרִים angry. Hiph.
הֶחֱרָה.—I. made angry.—II. became warm, zealous, Neh. 3:20.
Hithp. fut. apoc. תִּתְחַר be thou
vexed.

חָרוֹן m.—I. אַף חֲ heat of anger.—
II. angry person, Ps. 58:10.

חֳרִי m.; אַף חֲ heat, burning.

תַּחְרָא m., "habergeon," Eng. Ver., Ex.
28:32, &c.; meaning uncertain.

תַּחֲרָה contend with, emulate, Jer.
12:5; 22:15.

חָרוּז m., pl. חֲרוּזִים necklace of precious stones, Cant. 1:10.

חָרוּל m., a thorny shrub; pl. חֲרֻלִים.

חָרוּץ fine gold; see חרץ.

חַרְחוּר heat; see חרר.

חָרַט (Arab. engraver).

חָרִיט m., pl. חֲרִיטִים pockets, purses.

חֶרֶט m.—I. graving tool, Ex. 32:4.
—II. writing style, Isa. 8:1.

חַרְטֹם m., pl. חַרְטֻמִּים.—I. the sacred
scribes of Egypt who engraved
hieroglyphics, ἱερογραμματεῖς.—
II. the wise men of Babylon, Dan.
1:20; 2:2.

חַרְטֻמִּין m. pl. Ch., same as חַרְטֻמִּים
wise men, magicians.

חֲרִי heat; see חָרָה.

חֹרִי bread; see חָוָר.

חֲרֵי pl. const. from חַר dung; see חרא.

חָרִיץ cutting; see חרץ.

חָרִישִׁי, חָרִישׁ; see חרש.

חָרַךְ (fut. יַחֲרֹךְ), roasts, Pro. 12:27.
חֲרַךְ Ch. Hith. was burnt, Dan. 3:27.

חֲרַכִּים m. pl., latticed windows, LXX.
δίκτυα, Cant. 2:9.

חָרַם. Kal not used; (Arab. forbidden, sacred). Hiph. הֶחֱרִים.—I.
devote to destruction.— II. apply
to sacred uses. Hoph. הָחֳרַם.—I.
was devoted to destruction, slain.
—II. was consecrated.

חֵרֶם m. (with suff. חֶרְמִי).—I. devo-
tion to destruction.—II. the thing
so devoted.

חָרֵם p. n. of a town in the tribe of
Naphtali.

חֵרֶם m with suff. חֶרְמִי; (pl. חֲרָמִים).
I. *a net.*— II. *allurements*, Ecc. 7:
26.

חָרֻם m. (Arab. *cut off, tear*), *flat-
nosed*, Lev. 21:18.

חָרֻם p. n. of a man.

חָרְמָה p. n. of a town of the Canaanites.

חֶרְמוֹן p. n. of a range of hills in
Anti-Libanus; חֶרְמוֹנִים *Hermonites*.

חֶרְמֵשׁ m. (from חָרַם and חָרַשׁ),
*sickle, reaping hook.*

חָרָן p. n.—I. of a city of Mesopotamia,
Χαρράν.—II. of a city of Arabia.
—III. of a man.

חֹרֹנַיִם p. n. of a place; see חַוּר.

חַרְנֶפֶר p. n. of a man.

חָרַשׂ, חָרַשׁ root not used; (Arab.
*scratching*).

חֶרֶס m., *the itch*, Deu. 28:27.

חֶרֶס m. (with ה parag. חַרְסָה), *the
sun*, Ju. 8:13; 14:18; עִיר הַחֶרֶס
prophetic name of a city in Egypt,
Isa. 19:18; see חֶרֶס.

חֶרֶשׂ m., *earthenware, potsherd*; כְּלִי
חֶרֶשׂ *earthen vase.*

חַרְסוּת f., *pottery*; שַׁעַר הַחַרְסוּת *the
potter's gate*, one of the gates of
Jerusalem.

חָרַף (fut. יֶחֱרַף).—I. *pluck* (the fruit
of), *eat up*, Isa. 18:6.—II. *strip of
honour, value; reproach.* Pi. חֵרַף
I. *reproach, blaspheme.*—II. *expose
to reproach*, Ju. 5:18. Niph. part.
f. נֶחֱרֶפֶת *deprived of all right, espoused*, Lev. 19:20.

חֹרֶף m.—I. *autumn.*—II. *youth*, Job
29:4, (the year was supposed to
begin in autumn).

חֶרְפָּה f. (pl. חֲרָפוֹת; const. חֶרְפוֹת)
—I. *reproach, contempt.*—II. *person* or *thing reproached.*

חָרִיף p. n. of a man; patron. חֲרִיפִי.

חֶרֶף p. n. of a man.

חָרַץ (fut. יֶחֱרַץ).—I. *was sharp, active,
courageous.*—II. *was decided, determined*; part. חָרוּץ.—I. *maimed,
rent*, Lev. 22:22.—II. *decided, determined.*—III. *punishment.* Niph.
part. f. נֶחֱרָצָה *decided, determined, decreed.*

חָרִיץ m.—I. *ditch, foss.*—II. *the sharp
spikes of a thrashing dray*; pl.
const. חֲרִצוֹת.—III. *sharpened, in-
structed.*— IV. *gold.*—V. *decree*;
pl. חֲרוּצִים; see חרץ.—VI. p. n. of
a man.

חָרִיץ m. (pl. const. חֲרִיצֵי).—I. *cut-
tings of cheese*, LXX. τρυφαλίς,
1 Sa. 17:18.—II. same as חָרוּץ
*spikes, sharp points.*

חַרְצָן m., pl. חַרְצַנִּים *sour grapes*,
Nu. 6:4.

חֲרַץ Ch., same as Heb. חָלָץ *loins*,
Dan. 5:6.

חַרְצֻבּוֹת f. pl.—I. *bonds, bandages*,
Ps. 73:4.—II. *grievous pains*, Isa.
58:6.

חָרַק (fut. יֶחֱרַק), *ground, gnashed the
teeth*; (with שִׁנַּיִם, בְּשִׁנַּיִם and עַל
*against*).

חָרַר.—I. *was hot.*—II. *was dry.* Niph.
נָחַר (fut. יֵחַר), *was hot, dry*;
נָחַר *became dry.* Pilp. inf. חַרְחַר
*make hot, kindle*, as fire, Pro
26:21.

חֲרֵרִים m. pl., *dry, parched places*,
Jer. 17:6.

חֹר m., pl. חֹרִים nobles, great men; see also חוּר.

חַרְחֻר m. — I. inflammation, fever, Deu. 28:22.—II. p. n. of a man.

חֶרֶשׂ potsherd; see חרס.

חָרַשׁ (fut. יַחֲרֹשׁ).—I. cut, plough the land.—II. engrave, sculpture, with עַל (חֹרֵשׁ ploughman).—III. (fut. יֶחֱרַשׁ) was dumb, silent, was deaf, with מִן. Niph. was ploughed. Hiph.—I. engrave, carve.—II. fabricate, devise evil, 1 Sa. 23:9.—III. be still, quiet. Hith. fut. pl. יִתְחָרְשׁוּ were silent, Ju. 16:2.

חָרִישׁ m., ploughing, tilling the land; חֲרִישׁוֹ his field.

חֲרִישִׁי m., חֲרִישִׁית f., very drying, Jon. 4:8.

חָרָשׁ m. (const. חֲרַשׁ; pl. חָרָשִׁים, חָרָשֵׁי), worker, artificer, in wood, stone, metal, &c.; חָרָשֵׁי מַשְׁחִית forgers of destruction, Eze. 21:36.

חֶרֶשׁ m.—I. cunning work; גֵּי חֲרָשִׁים valley of the mechanics, near Jerusalem). — II. silence, silently.—III. p. n. of a man.

חֹרֶשׁ m. wood, forest; pl. חֳרָשִׁים; בַּחֹרְשָׁה into the wood; חֹרְשָׁה in the wood.

חָרָשׁ m., artificer; cutting instrument (Gesen.), Gen. 4:22.

חֵרֵשׁ m., deaf; pl. חֵרְשִׁים.

חַרְשָׁא p. n. of a man.

חֲרֹשֶׁת f.—I. sculpture.—II. p. n. of a place in North Palestine.

מַחֲרֵשָׁה f., coulter, 1 Sa. 13:21; pl. מַחֲרֵשׁוֹת.

מַחֲרֶשֶׁת f. (with suff. מַחֲרַשְׁתּוֹ), ploughshare, 1 Sa. 13:20.

חָרַת same as חָרַשׁ; part. חָרוּת cut, engraven, Ex. 32:16.

חֶרֶת (same as חֹרֶשׁ), p. n. of a wood in the tribe of Judah.

חָשׂיף, חֲשׂוּפָא; see חשׁף.

חָשַׂךְ (fut. אֶחְשֹׂךְ, תַּחְשֹׂךְ).—I. withhold, keep back.—II. save, with מִן.—III. refuse.—IV. spare. חֹשֵׂךְ sparing, Pro. 13:24. Niph. fut. יֵחָשֵׂךְ is restrained, Job 16:6; יֵחָשֵׂךְ id. 21:30.

חָשַׂף (fut. יַחְשֹׂף), make bare, denudate, expose.—II. draw (as water)

חֲשׂוּפָא p. n. of a man.

חָשִׂיף m., flock, 1 Ki. 20:27.

מַחְשֹׂף m., laying bare, Gen. 30:37.

חָשַׁב (fut. יַחְשָׁב יַחְשֹׁב).—I. think, devise, meditate.— II. consider, esteem, reckon, impute, with inf. and לְ חֹשֵׁב artificer, deviser; with לֹא of no esteem. Niph. נֶחְשַׁב (fut. יֵחָשֵׁב) was thought, esteemed, computed, reckoned, with בְּ, כְּ, עִם, בְּ, עַל. Pi. חִשֵּׁב think, compute, esteem, reckon, with אֶל. Hithp. was accounted, Nu. 23:9.

חֲשַׁב Ch., considered, esteemed, Dan. 4:32.

חֵשֶׁב m., the belt, girdle of the ephod.

חֶשְׁבּוֹן m.—I. device, discovery. — II. p. n. of a city of the Amorites, Ἐσβοῦς.

חִשְּׁבוֹן m. pl., חִשְּׁבֹנוֹת warlike machines, 2 Chron. 26:15.

חֲשַׁבְדָּנָה p. n. of a man.

חַשּׁוּב p. n. of a man.

חֲשֻׁבָה p. n. of a man.

חֲשַׁבְיָה, חֲשַׁבְיָהוּ p. n. of a man.

חֲשַׁבְנָה, חֲשַׁבְנְיָה p. n. of a man.

מַחֲשָׁבָה, מַחֲשֶׁבֶת f. (pl. מַחְשְׁבוֹת; const. מַחְשְׁבוֹת).—I. *thought, design, project.*— II. *work of art, ingenuity.*

חָשָׁה *was silent.* Hiph. הֶחֱשָׁה, part. מַחְשָׁה *was or made silent.*

חֲשַׁח Ch., *persons, things wanting.*

חַשְׁחוּת f. Ch., *want, necessity,* Ezr. 7:20.

חֲשֵׁיכָה same as חֲשֵׁכָה *dark;* see חֹשֶׁךְ.

חָשַׁךְ (fut. יֶחְשַׁךְ) *be, become obscure, dark.* Hiph. הֶחֱשִׁיךְ *made dark, obscure;* fut. יַחֲשִׁיךְ.

חֲשֻׁכִים m., pl. חֲשֵׁכִים *obscure persons,* Pro. 22:29.

חֹשֶׁךְ m. (with suff. חֹשְׁכִּי).—I. *darkness.*—II. *ignorance.*—III. *calamity, misery, destruction.*

חֲשׁוֹךְ m. Ch., *darkness.*

חָשֵׁךְ m., pl. חֲשֵׁכִים *obscured, darkened.*

חֲשֵׁכָה, חֲשֵׁיכָה f., *obscurity, darkness.* חֶשְׁכָּה, חֶשְׁכָּה f., the same.

מַחְשָׁךְ m., I. *darkness.*—II. *adversity, trouble;* pl. מַחְשַׁכֵּי מַחֲשַׁכִּים.

חָשַׁל. Niph. part. נֶחֱשָׁלִים *debilitated, infirm persons,* Deu. 25:18.

חֲשַׁל Ch., *pounded to powder,* Dan. 2:40.

חַשְׁמַל *some brilliant white or pale yellow metal;* LXX. ἤλεκτρον.

חָשֻׁם p.n. of a man.

חֶשְׁמוֹן p.n. of a town in the tribe of Judah.

חַשְׁמוֹנָה p.n. of a station of the Israelites in the desert.

חַשְׁמַן m., pl. חַשְׁמַנִּים *rich, powerful men,* Ps. 68:32

חָשַׁן (Arab. *to adorn*).

חֹשֶׁן m., *breast-plate* of the high priest; called also חֹ. הַמִּשְׁפָּט.

חָשַׁק.—I. *desire, delight in,* with בְּ —II. *it pleased, seemed good,* with לְ and inf. Pi. חִשַּׁק *attached to,* Ex. 38:28. Pu. *was joined to,* Ex. 27:17.

חֵשֶׁק m. (with suff. חִשְׁקִי), *desire, delight.*

חֲשֻׁקִים, חֲשׁוּקִים m. pl.—the *tie-rods* or *poles* which passed through the upright pillars of the forecourt of the tabernacle.

חִשֻּׁקִים m. pl., *spokes of a wheel,* 1 Ki. 7:33.

חָשַׁר root not used; (Arab. *collected*)

חַשְׁרָה f., *collection of waters,* 2 Sam. 22:12.

חִשֻּׁרִים m. pl., *naves of wheels,* 1 Ki. 7:33.

חָשָׁשׁ m., *dry grass, hay.*

חֵת, pl. חִתִּים p. n. of a people of Canaan.

חָתָה (fut. יַחְתֶּה) *take up* and *remove* (as fire, coals, &c.), *lay hold of;* fut. with suff. יַחְתְּךָ *he will lay hold on thee,* Ps. 52:7.

מַחְתָּה f.—I. *shovel* or *pan* for removing hot coals.—II. *censer.*—III. *dishes* for receiving the snuffs of the lamps; LXX. ὑπόθεμα.

חִתִּית, חַתְחַת, חִתָּה, חַת; see חתת.

חָתַךְ. Niph. נֶחְתַּךְ *has been determined,* Dan. 9:24.

חָתַל. Pu. and Hoph. הָחְתֵּל לֹא חֻתָּלְתְּ, *thou wast not bandaged,* Eze. 16:4.

חִתּוּל m., *bandage for a wound,* Eze. 30:21.

חֲתֻלָּה f., *swaddling, bandage*, Job 38:9.

חָתֻלֹן p. n. of a place in Syria.

חָתַם (fut. יַחְתֹּם).—I. *seal, seal up.*— II. *conclude, finish*, with בְּעַד, בְּ. Niph. *was, became sealed.* Pi. *sealed, determined upon*, Job 24:16. Hiph. הֶחְתִּים *seal, shut up*, Lev. 15:3.

חֲתַם Ch., *sealed.*

חוֹתָם m. (with suff. חֹתָמְךָ).—I. *seal-ring.*— II. *seal.*— III. p. n. of a man.

חֹתֶמֶת f., *seal*, Gen. 38:25.

חָתָן, part. m. חֹתֵן *father-in-law, wife's father*; f. חֹתֶנֶת *mother-in-law, wife's mother*; with suff. חֹתַנְתּוֹ. Hith. הִתְחַתֵּן *became re-lated by marriage*, specially with a daughter, with אֵת, בְּ, לְ.

חָתָן m. (const. חֲתַן; with suff. חֲתָנוֹ; pl. חֲתָנִים).—I. *relative.*—II. *son-in-law.*—III. *bridegroom.*—IV. *re-lative by blood*, i. e. circumcision, חֲתַן־דָּמִים Ex. 4:25, 26.

חֲתֻנָּה f., *marriage*, Cant. 3:11.

חָתַף same as חָטַף; (Arab. *destruc-tion*;) fut. יַחְתֹּף *snatch away*, Job 9:12.

חֶתֶף m., אִישׁ ח' *man of rapine*, Pro. 23:28.

חָתַר (fut. יַחְתֹּר).—I. *dig, delve*, with בְּ *into.*—II. *row* (dig into water), Jon. 1:13.

מַחְתֶּרֶת f., *digging through*, i. e. breaking in.

חָתַת *be, become broken with shame, fear, &c.* Niph. נֵחַת (fut. יֵחַת;

pl. יֵחַתּוּ), same as Kal, with מִן, מִפְּנֵי. Pi. חִתֵּת I. *broken to pieces, shivered.*—II. *affrighted*, Job 7:14. Hiph. הֵחַת (pret. הַחְתַּתָּ, הַחְתַּתִּי), *break to pieces, ruin.*

חַת m.—I. *ruin*, Job 6:21.—II. p. n. of a man.

חַת m. (with suff. חִתְּכֶם; pl. חַתִּים) *broken, spoiled*, applied to persons or things.

חִתָּה f.—I. the same.—II. *fear*, Gen. 35:5.

חִתִּית f., *fear, terror, dread.*

חַתְחַת m., pl. חַתְחַתִּים *broken down with fear*, Ecc. 12:5.

מְחִתָּה f.—I. *stroke, injury, ruin.*—II. *fear, terror.*

## ט

טְאֵב Ch., *was glad*, Dan. 6:24.

טַאטֵא *debase*; see טוּא.

טָבְאֵל, טָבְ; see טוֹב.

טְבוּלִים m. pl. (Ethiop. טבלל *folded*) *turbans*, Eze. 23:15.

טַבּוּר m., *mountain, high place.*

טֶבַח (inf. const. טְבֹחַ; imp. טְבַח) *slaughter*, specially animals for eat-ing, also of men.

טַבָּח m.—I. *cook, butcher.*—II. *officer of state*, probably, *executioner*; שַׂר (רַב) טַבָּחִים *chief officer.*

טַבָּח m. Ch., *officer of state.*

טַבָּחָה f., *female cook.*

טֶבַח m. (with suff. טִבְחֹה).—I. *slaugh-ter of animals.* — II. *animals slaughtered.*—III. p. n. of a man.

טִבְחָה f., the same.

אֲבַטִּחִים (trans.) m. pl., *melons*, Nu. 11:5.

מַטְבֵּחַ m., *slaughter*, Isa. 14:21.

טִבְחָה (elsewhere בֶּטַח), p. n. of a city of Syria.

טָבַל I. *dip, plunge.* — II. *stain, dye.* Niph. *were dipped*, Jos. 3:15.

טְבוּלִים; *see in its place.*

טַבַלְיָהוּ p. n. of a man.

טָבַע *sank down* (as into mud). Pu. טֻבַּע *sank in, were immerged*, Ex. 15:4. Hoph. הָטְבַּע *were let in* (as pillars in their bases, &c.).

טַבַּעַת f. (pl. טַבָּעוֹת; const. טַבְּעוֹת). —I. *seal ring.*—II. *any ring.*

טַבָּעוֹת p. n. of a man.

טַבְרִמּוֹן; see טוֹב.

טִבָּת p. n. of a town in the tribe of Ephraim.

טֵבֵת m., the *tenth month* of the Hebrew year, Est. 2:16.

טָהֵר (fut. יִטְהַר) *was, became, clean, pure*, from disease, from legal uncleanness, from moral impurity. Pi. טִהֵר.—I. *cleanse, purify.*—II. *declare clean.* Pu. *was purified.* Hithp. הִטַּהֵר (pl. הִטַּהֲרוּ; imp. pl. הִטַּהֲרוּ) *was, became clean, purified.*

טָהוֹר (const. טְהָר־, טְהוֹר־; f. טְהֹרָה; pl. טְהֹרוֹת) *clean, pure.*

טֹהַר m.—I. *brightness, glory.* — II. *purification.*

טָהֳר m., \
טָהֳרָה f., } *the same.*

טְוָא Ch., root not used; (Syr. *fasted*.) טְוָת f. Ch., *fasting*, Dan. 6:19.

טוּא or טָוָא. Pil. טִאטֵא *humble, debase*; part. מְטַאטֵא *humbling, debasing*, Isa. 14:23.

טוֹב (pret. pl. טֹבוּ; fut. יִיטַב from

טוֹב לִי (יָטַב) *was good, agreeable; it pleases me*, Nu. 24:1; with בְּעֵינַי *the same.* Hiph. הֵטִיב *do well, liberally, make good*, Hos. 10:1; *make happy*, Ecc. 11:9.

טוֹב m. טוֹבָה f.—I. *good.*—II. *happy, prosperous.* — III. *valuable.* — IV. *handsome* (goodlike).—V. *kind.*— VI. used adverbially, *well, rightly;* s. m. and f. טוֹבָה.— I. *goodness* —II. *wealth.*—III. *prosperity, happiness;* לָטוֹב, לְטוֹבָה, with לְ *that it may be well with thee.*—IV. *beauty.* —V. p. n. of a country on the other side Jordan.

טָב m. Ch., *good, excellent.*

טָבְאֵל with pause טָבְאָל p. n. of a man, Syrian or Persian.

טַבְרִמּוֹן p. n., the father of Benhadad, king of Syria.

טוּב m.—I. *goodness.*— II. *wealth.*— III. *prosperity.* — IV. *beauty.*—V. *goodness* (of discernment). — VI. *God*, as the source of all good. טוּב אֶרֶץ *the best part of the land*, Gen. 45:18.

טוֹב אֲדֹנִיָּהוּ p. n. of a man.

טוֹבִיָּהוּ, טוֹבִיָּה p. n. of a man.

טָוָה *spin* (lit. *twine*), Ex. 35:25, 26.

מַטְוֶה m., *yarn*, Ex. 35:25.

טוּחַ I. *plaister, paint.* — II. *overlay.* Niph. inf. הִטּוֹחַ *was covered, plastered*, Lev. 14:43, 48.

טִיחַ m., *plastering*, Eze. 13:12.

טֻחוֹת f. pl.—I. *inward parts, viscera*, Ps. 51:8.—II. *the motive power of the heavenly bodies*, Job 38:36.

טוֹטָפוֹת *bandages;* see טפף.

טוּל. Hiph. הֵטִיל *cast forth, out, into.*

Hoph. הֻגְמַל *was, became cast out, forth, &c.* Pil. טִלְטֵל *cast out,* Isa. 22:17.

טַלְטֵלָה f., *entire casting out,* Isa. 22:17.

טוּף (Arab. *surrounded*).

טוֹטָפֹת f. pl., φυλακτήρια, *frontlets;* probably jewels worn on the forehead.

טוּר see טֻגָר and תִּגָּר.

טוּר m. (pl. טוּרִים, טֻרִים), *series, order, range.*

טִירָה f.—I. *any series of buildings.* —II. *palace.*—III. *certain chambers in the Temple.*

טוּר m. Ch., same as צוּר *mountain,* Dan. 2:35, 45.

טוּשׂ *fly swiftly,* Job 9:26.

טְוָת *fasting;* see טְוָא.

טָחָה (Arab. *expand*). Pil. part. מְטַחֲוֵי־ קָשֶׁת *archers,* Gen. 21:16.

טְחוֹת *viscera;* see טוּחַ.

טְחוֹרִים *hæmorrhoids;* see טָחַר.

טָחַן (fut. יִטְחַן).—I. *grind with a hand-mill.*—II. *oppress.*

טְחוֹן m., *hand-mill,* Lam. 5:13.

טַחֲנָה f., the same, Ecc. 12:4.

טַחַר (Syr. *arms*).

טְחוֹרִים m. pl., *emerods* (hæmorrhoids).

טִיחַ *plaster;* see טוּחַ.

טִיט m., *mud, mire.*

טִין m. Ch., *clay, potter's clay.*

טִירָה *row;* see טוּר.

טַל *dew;* see טְלַל.

טָלָא, part. טָלֻא *patched, having patches of various colours;* pl. טְלֻאִים, מְלָאוֹת. Pu. part. f. pl.

מְטֻלָּאוֹת *patched* (of shoes), Jos 9:5.

טָלָם, טְלָאִים; see טְלִי, טָלֶה.

טָלֶה (Syr. *an infant*).

טָלֶה const. טְלֵה m., *young lamb.*

טְלִי m.—I. the same; pl. טְלָאִים.— II. p. n. of a town; see טָלָם.

טַלְטֵל, טַלְטֵלָה; see טוּל.

טָלַל. Pi. טִלֵּל *covered, roofed,* Neh. 3:15.

טָלַל Ch. Aph. אַטְלֵל *takes shade,* Dan. 4:9.

טַל m. (with pause טָל, with suff. טַלָּם), *dew.*

טַל m. Ch., *dew.*

טָלָם p. n. of a town in the tribe of Judah; also טְלָאִים.

טַלְמוֹן p. n. of a man.

טָמֵא (fut. יִטְמָא; inf. with ה parag. טָמְאָה), *was unclean, polluted,* with בְּ. Niph. נִטְמָא *was polluted,* with בְּ. Pi. טִמֵּא.—I. *polluted, defiled.*—II. *pronounced unclean.* Pu. part. f. מְטֻמָּאָה *polluted.* Hith. הִטַּמֵּא *polluted,* with לְ. Hothp. pret. f. הֻטַּמָּאָה the same, Deu. 24:4.

טָמֵא m., *unclean, polluted;* f. טְמֵאָה.

טֻמְאָה f. (pl. const. טֻמְאֹת), *polluted, defiled.*

טָמָה same as טָמֵא. Niph. pl. נִטְמִינוּ *we are unclean, despised.*

טָמַן *conceal, hide in the earth.* Niph. *was hidden.* Hiph. *hide,* 2 Ki. 7:8.

מַטְמוֹן m. (pl. מַטְמֹנִים), *treasure, that which is laid up, hidden.*

טֶנֶא (with suff. טַנְאֲךָ) m., *basket.*

טָנַף. Pi. *soil*, Cant. 5:3.

טָעָה same as תָּעָה. Hiph. הִטְעָה *made to err*, Eze. 13:10.

טָעַם (fut. יִטְעַם).—I. *taste*.—II. *discriminate, judge*.

טְעַם Ch. Pa. *make to eat*.

טַעַם m.—I. *reason, judgment*.—II. *taste*.

טְעַם m. Ch., *edict*.

טְעַם m. Ch.—I. *taste*.—II. *judgment*. —III. *edict*.

מַטְעַמּים m., מַטְעַמּות f. pl., *dainty meats*.

טָעַן.—I. *load* (of beasts of burden), Gen. 45:17.-II. Pu. טֹעַן *pierced through*, Isa. 14:19.

טַעַת Kal. inf.; see נטע.

טַף *infant*; see טפף.

טָפַד. Pi. טִפַּח *spread out, extend* (from טֶפַח), spec. with the hand.

טֶפַח m.—I. *palm, hand-breadth*, a measure of about three and-a-half inches; pl. טְפָחות Ps. 39:6.—II. *coping stones of a building*.

טֹפַח m., *hand-breadth, measure*.

טִפֻּחִים m. pl., Lam. 2:20, *that which is stroked with the hand*.

מִטְפַּחַת f. (pl. מִטְפָּחות), *upper garment, mantle*.

טָפַל.—I. *lay on or over*.—II. *cover, conceal*.

טִפְסַר m., *prince, general*.

טַפְסַר m., the same; pl. טַפְסְרים.

טָפַף *tripping, mincing*, Isa. 3:16.

טַף m. (with pause טָף; with suff. טַפֵּנוּ), *child, infant*.

טְפַר m. Ch., *nails, claws*.

טִפֵּשׁ *fat, stupid*, Ps. 119:70.

טָפַת p. n. of a daughter of Solomon.

טָרַד *driving out*; part. טֹרֵד *perpetual, successive* (i. e. one driving out the other), Pro. 19:13; 27:15.

טְרַד Ch., *driving out, driven out*.

טָרָה root not used; (Arab. *was fresh*).

טָרִי m., טְרִיָה f., *fresh, moist*, Jud 15:15; Isa. 1:6.

טְרום ketib, same as טֶרֶם.

טָרַח. Hiph. *stretches out*, Job 37:11.

טֹרַח m. (with suff. טָרְחֲכֶם), *pressure, wearying*.

טָרַם root not used; (Arab. *cut off*).

טֶרֶם adv., *not yet*; בְּטֶרֶם and טֶרֶם *before that*; מִטֶּרֶם the same.

טָרַף (fut. יִטְרַף, יִטְרף), *tear in pieces, wound, injure*. Niph. *be torn in pieces*. Pu. טֹרַף the same. Hiph. *feed, provide for*.

טֶרֶף m., *prey, provision, food*.

טָרָף m., *leaf* (that which is plucked), Gen. 8:11.

טְרֵפָה f.—I. *any thing torn*.—II. *animal torn by a wild beast*.

טַרְפְּליָא Ch., p. n., a people so called, Ezr. 4:9; LXX. Ταρφαλαῖοι.

## י

יָאַב *desired, longed for*, with לְ.

יָאָה with לְ *it becometh*, Jer. 10:7.

יְאור same as יְאֹר.

יֵאֹתוּ Niph. fut. pl., from אות.

יַאֲזַנְיָה (*whom the Lord hears*), p. n. of a man.

(וַיְזַנְיָהוּ) יַאֲזַנְיָהוּ (contr. יְזַנְיָהוּ) p. n. of a man.

יָאִיר (the Lord enlightens, 'Ιάειρος), p. n. of a man; patron. יָאִירִי.

יָאַל I. same as אָל Niph. נוֹאַל was foolish.—II. same as אוּל Hiph. הוֹאִיל (fut. וַיּוֹאֶל.—1. undertook, began, with inf.—2. was willing, contented.

יָאֶל, וַיָּאֶל Hiph. fut. apoc., from אלה.

יוֹאֶל, וַיּוֹאֶל Hiph. fut. apoc., from II. יאל.

יָאֶר Hiph. fut. apoc., יָאֵר Niph. fut., from אור.

יָאֹר Kal fut., from ארר.

יְאֹר, יָאוֹר m., a river, specially the Nile; pl. יְאֹרִים rivers.

יָאַשׁ. Niph. נוֹאַשׁ was hopeless, desperate, with מִן; part. נוֹאָשׁ desperate, in vain. Pi. inf. יָאֵשׁ rendered hopeless, Ecc. 2:20.

יֹאשִׁיָּה p. n. of a man.

יֹאשִׁיָּהוּ ('Ιωσίας) p. n. of a man.

יָאַת וַיֵּאָת Kal fut. apoc., אֶתָיו fut. pl., אֶתָיִנִי fut. with suff.; see אתה.

יִתְרִי p.n. of a man (same as אֶתְנִי).

יָבֵא Hiph. fut. apoc.; see בוא.

יְבָאֵנִי for יְבִאֵנִי Kal fut. pl. with suff.; see בוא.

יָבַב Pi. יְבֵב cried out, Jud. 5:28

יוֹבָב p. n.—I. of a people in Arabia Felix.—II. of a king of Edom.—III. of a man.

וַיָּבֹא יְבֹא 2 Ki. 12:12, for וַיָּבֹא Kal fut.; see בוא.

יְבוּס p. n. of the Canaanitish inhabitants of Jerusalem; יְבוּסִי Jebusite.

יְבוּל produce; see יבל.

יָבוֹשׁ Kal fut., from בושׁ.

יְבֶחָר (chosen of the Lord), p. n. of a man.

יָבִין p. n. of two Canaanitish kings.

יָבַל וַיָּבֶל Kal fut. apoc.; see בכה.

יָבַל. Hiph. הוֹבִיל bare, carried, led. Hoph. הוּבַל was borne, carried, led. Ch. Aph. הֵיבֵל bring, Ez. 5:14; 6:5.

יְבוּל m. (with suff. יְבוּלָה).—I. produce (of the earth, &c.)—II. provision, wealth.

בּוּל m.—I. produce, increase.—II name of a month 1 Ki. 6:38, the eighth of the calendar, answering to our October.

מַבּוּל m. flood of Noah, deluge.

יָבָל m.—I. stream of water.—II. p. n of a son of Lamech.

יוֹבֵל com. (lit. a protracted note or sound), the Jubilee, a feast of the Jews announced by the sounding of horns; שְׁנַת הַיּוֹבֵל and יֹבֵל the year of Jubilee.

יוּבָל m.—I. canal, Jer. 17:8.—II. p. n. of a son of Lamech.

אָבֵל, אוּבָל m., a river, canal, Dan 8:2, 3, 6.

יַבֶּלֶת f., issue, running disease, Lev. 22:22; Vulg. papulas habens.

תֵּבֵל f., same as אֶרֶץ.—I. the world, the earth, specially the inhabited part of it.—II. the world's inhabitants, mankind.

יִבְלְעָם p. n. of a town in the tribe of Manasseh.

יָבָם m. husband's brother; יִבֵּם. Pi marry the brother's wife; see Deu. 25:5, 7.

יְבָמָה f. (with suff. יְבִמְתּוֹ) brother's wife; one married to her husband's brother.

יַבְנְאֵל p. n., two towns in the tribes of Judah and Naphtali.

יַבְנֶה p. n. of a town of the Philistines, Ἰαμνία, Ἰάμνεια.

יִבְנְיָה p. n. of a man.

יַבֹּק p.n. of a brook which runs into the river Jordan.

יֶבֶרֶכְיָהוּ (blessed of the Lord), p. n. of a man.

יִבְשָׂם p. n. of a man.

יָבֵשׁ (inf. const. יְבֹשׁ; fut. יִיבַשׁ; pl. (וַיִּיבְשׁוּ) was or became dry, arid. Pi. יַבֵּשׁ dry up. Hiph. הוֹבִישׁ. —I. dry up, make to wither.—II. was ashamed, confounded; see בּוֹשׁ

יָבֵשׁ m., יְבֵשָׁה f.—I. dry.—II. p. n. of a town in Gilead; called also יָבֵישׁ —III. p. n. of a man.

יַבָּשָׁה, יַבֶּשֶׁת f., dry land.
יַבֶּשֶׁת f. Ch., the same.
יַבֶּשֶׁת f., dried, Gen. 8:7.

וַיַּבְשֻׁהוּ for וַיְבַשֻּׁהוּ Pi. fut. with suff.; see יבשׁ.

יְבֹשֶׁת Kal inf. const.; see יבשׁ.

יִגְאָל (the Lord redeemeth), p. n. of a man.

יָגֵב same as נגב ploughed; part. יוֹגְבִים ploughmen.

יְגֵבִים m. pl., ploughed lands, Jer. 39:10.

יָנְבָּה with ה parag. יִגְבְּהָה p. n. of a town in the tribe of Gad.

יִגְדַּלְיָהוּ (let the Lord be magnified), p. n. of a man.

יָגָה. Niph. part. נוּגָה pained (perhaps cast out). Pi. יָגָּה afflict, pain, Lam. 3:33. Hiph. הוֹגָה.—I. afflicted.— II. removed, 2 Sa. 20:13.

וַיִּגֶה, יִגֶה for וַיִּגֶּה Pi. fut., from יגה
יָגוֹן m., affliction, grief.
תּוּגָה f., sorrow, grief.

יָגוּר (the Lord dwelleth there), p. n. of a town in the tribe of Judah.

יַגְלִי p. n. of a man.

וַיָּגֶל, יָגֵל Hiph. fut. apoc.; see נלה.

יָגַע (fut. יִיגַע; pl. יִיגְעוּ), labour to weariness; with בְּ and לְ, be wearied. Pi. יִגַּע fatigue, cause to labour to weariness. Hiph. הוֹגִיעַ same as Pi. with בְּ.

יָגֵעַ m., wearying, wearied.
יָגֵעַ const. יְגִיעַ m.—I. wearied, fatigued.—II. labour.—III. the fruit of labour, wealth.

יֶגַע m., wealth, Job 20:18.
יְגִיעָה f., hard labour, exertion, Ecc. 12:12.

יְגַר m. Ch., heap of stones, Gen. 31:47.

יָגֵר Niph. fut., from נגר.

יָגֹר (pret. יָגֹרְתִּי, יָגֹרְתָּ), fear, be afraid of, with מִפְּנֵי

יָגוֹר m., fearing, afraid of.

יָד com., generally f. (const. יַד; with suff. יֶדְכֶם, יָדִי; dual יָדַיִם, יְדֵי const. יְדֵי, with suff. יָדָיו (יְדֵיכֶם). —I. hand; with עִם, אֶת assist, aid; with אֶל, בְּ hand against, afflicting, troubling; with עַל upon him, inspiring, strengthening.—II. power, spirit or word of God, 1 Sa. 5:11, &c.—III. with prep. עַל יַד, לְיַד same as בְּ; בְּעַד יַד, אֶל יַד, עַל יְדֵי at hand, near.—IV. space, place; אִישׁ עַל יָדוֹ every man in his place.—V memorial, monument, 1 Sa. 15:12;

2 Sa. 18:18. — VI. *by means of.* Pi. יְדוֹת; const. יְדוֹת.—I. *tenons of planks.*—II. *axletrees of wheels,* 1 Ki. 7:32, 33.—III. *arms of a throne,* 1 Ki. 10:19. Used with pref. בְּיַד with (בְּיָדוֹ *with him*), *by, before, against;* מְיַד, מִידֵי *from, out of;* יָד לְיָד *hand in hand,* as striking a bargain, Pro. 11:21.

יַד com. Ch., *hand.*

יְדָא *put forth;* see ידה.

יָדָא וַיֵּרֶא fut. apoc.; see דאה.

יִרְאֲלָה p. n. of a place in the tribe of Zebulun.

יִדְבָּשׁ p. n. of a man.

יָדַד, same as דוד *loved.*

יָדִיד m., *beloved,* specially of God's children; pl. f., יְדִידוֹת.

יִדּוֹ p. n. of a man.

יְדִידָה p. n. of the mother of king Josiah.

יְדִידוּת f., *love,* Jer. 12:7.

יְדִידְיָה *beloved of the Lord,* a title of Solomon.

יָדָה.—I. *put forth* (as casting stones).—II. *uttering praise;* imp. pl. יְדוּ *they cast at her,* Jer. 50:14. Pi. *cast stones or lots;* fut. וַיַּדּוּ; inf. יְדּוֹת. Hiph. הוֹדָה (fut. יוֹדֶה, יְהוֹדֶה; with suff. אוֹדְךָ, אֲהוֹדֶנּוּ), *recount, commemorate* (God's mercies, with עַל); *praise, celebrate,* with לְ. Hith. הִתְוַדָּה *become known,* with עַל and לְ.

יְדָא Ch. Aph. *praise, celebrate.*

תּוֹדָה f.—I. *confession.*—II. *praise, thanksgiving.*—III. *company of persons giving thanks.*

וַיָּדוּ for וַיִּדּוּ, יָדוּ Pi. fut.; see ידה.

יָדַיִן יָדְכֶם; see יָד with suff.

יָדֹם Kal fut.; pl. יִדְּמוּ; see דמם.

יְהוּדָה p. n.—I. the patriarch *Judah.*—II. Afterwards applied to the kingdom of the house of David.—III. Ultimately to the whole of Palestine.—IV. p. n. of a man.

יְהוּד Ch., *the Jews,* the kingdom of Judah.

יְהוּדִי (pl. יְהוּדִים, יְהוּדִיִּים).—I. *a Jew;* f. יְהוּדִית *Jewess;* יְהוּדִית adv. *Hebrew,* the Hebrew tongue —II. p. n. of a man.

הִתְיַהֵד Hith. *became a Jew.*

יְהוּדִי Ch., *a Jew.*

יְהוּדִית; see יְהוּדִי p. n. of a wife of Esau.

יְהֻד p. n. of a town in the tribe of Dan.

הוֹדַוְיָה p. n. of a man.

הוֹדַוְיָהוּ p. n. of a man.

יָדוֹן p. n. of a man.

יַדּוּעַ p. n. of a man.

יְדִיתוּן, יְדֻתוּן, יְדֻתוּן p. n. of a Levite skilled in music; probably also a musical instrument invented by him.

יַדִּי p. n. of a man.

יְדִידְיָה, יְדִידוּת, יְדִידָה, יָדִיד; see ידד

יֶדְיָה p. n. of a man.

יְדִיעֲאֵל p. n. of a son of Benjamin.

יֶלְדָּף p. n. of a son of Nahor.

יָדַע (fut. יֵדַע, יֵירַע; inf. abs. יָדֹעַ; const. דַּעַת; with suff. דֵּעֲתָה; imp. דַּע, דְּעֶה; part. יוֹדֵעַ, יֹדֵעַ; f. יֹדַעַת).—I. *perceive, become informed, aware of, feel.*—II. *know carnally.*—III. *recognise, acknowledge.*—IV. *regard;* part. יֹדֵעַ *wise;* יִדֵּעַ *noted, illustrious.* Niph. נוֹדַע *known, apparent, recognised.* Pi

יְדַע made to know. Pu. part.
מְיֻדָּע known, familiar. Po. יוֹדֵעַ declared, indicated. Hiph. הוֹדִיעַ (imp. הוֹדַע; fut. יוֹדִיעַ; apoc. יוֹדַע), make known, show, confess, inform, teach. Hoph. הוֹדַע was, made known. Hith. הִתְוַדַּע made himself known; with אֶל.

יְדַע Ch., know, understand, perceive; fut. יִנְדַּע. Hoph. הֻגְדַּע made known, taught.

דֵּעַ m., pl. דֵּעִים } knowledge, science,
דֵּעָה f., pl. דֵּעוֹת } opinion.

דַּעַת f., knowledge, science, opinion.

יָדָע p.n. of a man.

יְדַעְיָה p.n. of a man.

יִדְּעֹנִי m. (pl. יִדְּעֹנִים), false prophet, soothsayer.

מַדָּע, מַדַּע m.—I. knowledge, experience.—II. mind.

מַדּוּעַ adv. interrog., why then? why indeed?

מַנְדַּע m. Ch.—I. knowledge.—II. intelligence.

מוֹדָע m., familiar, friend.

מוֹדַעַת f., the same.

יְדַשְּׁנָה Pi. fut. with ה parag.; see דשן.

יָהּ one of the names of God; probably an abbreviation of יְהֹוָה.

יָהַב I. give, allow.—II. appoint, place; imper. הַב; with ה parag. הָבָה; f. הָבִי; pl. הָבוּ.

יְהַב Ch., give, place. Ith. was given.

יְהָב m., burden; with suff. יְהָבְךָ Ps. 55:23.

הַבְהָבִים m. pl., gifts, Hos. 8:13.

יֶהְדַּי p.n. of a man.

יָהוּא for יָהוּ fut. apoc. pl., from הוה.

יֵהוּא p.n.; see הוה.

יְהוֹבֵד Ch. Aph. fut.; see אבד.

יְהוֹדָה for יוֹדָה Hiph. fut.; see ידה.

יְהוּדִית; יְהוּדִי, see ידה.

יְהוּד, יֶהְגֶּה, יֶהְגִּי, יָהוּד; see ידה.

יְהֹוָה the most sacred and unalienable name of God; see הוה.

יְהוֹשִׁיעַ for יוֹשִׁיעַ Hiph. fut.; see ישע.

וַיְהִי, יְהִי fut. apoc.; see היה.

יְהֵילִילוּ for יְיֵלִילוּ Hiph. fut.; see ילל.

יֵהָךְ Ch. fut.; see הוך.

יַאֲהֵל for יַאֲהֵל Pi. fut.; see אהל.

יָהִיר m., haughty, vain.

יַהֲלֹם; see הלם.

יֶהֱמָיוּן fut. pl. with נ parag.; see המה.

יַהַץ, יַהְצָה p.n. of a city of Moab.

יִתְהַלְּלוּ Pi. fut. pl. with dag. euphon. see התל.

יוֹב p.n. of a son of Issachar.

יוֹבָב; see יבב.

יוֹבֵל, יוּבַל; see יבל.

יֵאָכְלוּ Eze. 42:5, for יֵאָכְלוּ, Hoph. fut.; see אכל.

יֹלֶדֶת for יוֹלֶדֶת part. f.; see ילד.

יוֹם m.—I. day; הַיּוֹם this day, to-day, now; בַּיּוֹם this very day, immediately; בְּיוֹם with inf. on the day, when; כַּיּוֹם now, at present; כַּיּוֹם הַזֶּה as it is at this day; מִיּוֹם from the day since; יוֹם יוֹם, בְּיוֹם בְּיוֹם, יוֹם בְּיוֹם daily; dual יוֹמַיִם two days; pl. יָמִים, const. יְמֵי, sometimes יְמוֹת days, many days; מִקֵּץ יָמִים, מִיָּמִים after many days, some days, some time after; חֹדֶשׁ יָמִים i. e. יֶרַח an entire month; שְׁנָתַיִם יָ׳ two whole years.—II. duration, time; מִיָּמֶיךָ so long as thou livest; כָּל־הַיָּמִים פּ׳ all his days; בָּא בַּיָּמִים advanced in years.—III. anniversary; מִיָּמִים

יָמִימָה **annually;** לְיָמִים **the same, Jud. 17:10; זֶבַח יָמִים** ***annual sacrifice.***

יוֹם **m. Ch.,** ***day, period.***

יוֹמָם **adv.,** ***by day.***

יָוָן **p. n.** ***Javan*** **the founder of the Greeks, Ionians; בְּנֵי הַיְּוָנִים** ***Ionians, Greeks.***

יָוֵן ***mire, clay.***

יַיִן **m. (const. יֵין; with suff. יֵינִי).—I.** ***wine.*****—II.** ***intoxication.***

יוֹנָה **f. (pl. יוֹנִים).—I.** ***dove.*****—II. p. n. of a prophet; see also in ינה.**

יוֹנֵק, יוֹנֶקֶת; **see ינק.**

יוֹסֵף, יְהוֹסֵף **(from אָסַף or יָסַף).—I. p. n.** ***Joseph,*** **the son of Israel, Ἰωσήφ.—II. given afterwards specially to the tribes of his sons, and generally to the kingdom of Israel. —III. p. n. of a man**

יוֹסִפְיָה **p. n. of a man.**

יוֹעֵאלָה **p.n. of a man.**

יוֹצֵאת **for** יוֹצֵאת **part. f.; see יצא.**

יוֹר, וַיּוֹר **Hiph. fut. apoc; see ירה.**

יוֹרֶא **Pro. 11:25 (*shall be watered*), for** יֻרְוֶה **Hoph. fut., see רוה; or for** יוֹרֶה **Hoph. fut., see ירה.**

יוֹרֶה, יוֹרֵי ***teach;*** **see ירה.**

יוּשַׁב חֶסֶד **(*confirming mercy*), p. n. of a man.**

יוֹשִׁבְיָה **(*the Lord confirmeth*), p.n. of a man.**

יוֹשָׁה **p. n. of a man.**

יוֹשַׁוְיָה **p.n. of a man.**

יוֹתֵר, יוֹתֶרֶת; **see יתר.**

יוֹשַׁבְתְּי **Jer. 22:23, for** יוֹשֶׁבֶת**, part. f. with ׳ parag.; see ישב.**

יַז, יַזּ, וַיַּז, יָז, יִז **Kal fut. apoc; see נזה.**

יַז, וַיַּז **Hiph. fut. apoc.; see נזה.**

יְזִיאֵל **p. n. of a man.**

יִזַּח **Niph. fut.; see זחח.**

יִזִּיָּה **p. n. of a man.**

יִזְלִיאָה **p. n. of a man.**

יָזֹמּוּ **for** יָזֹמּוּ **Kal fut. pl.; see זמם.**

יָזַן. **(Arab.** ***weighed, was heavy*****). Pu. part.** מְיֻזָּנִים ***appointed, accoutred for war*** **(of horses), Jer. 5:8, Kri.**

יְזַנְיָה, יְזַנְיָהוּ; **see** יַאֲזַנְיָה

יִזְרַח, יִזְרַחְיָה; **see זרח.**

יֶזַע **m.,** ***sweat,*** **Eze. 44:18.**

יָזֵר, וַיָּזֵר **Kal fut. apoc; see זור.**

יִזְרְעֶאל **p. n.; see זרע.**

יָחַד **(fut. יֵחַד)** ***unite, be as one,*** **with** בְּ, אֶת**. Pi. יַחֵד** ***unite, make as one,*** **Ps. 86:11.**

יָחִיד **m.,** ***solitary one, only one;*** **f.** יְחִידָה.

יַחַד **m.,** ***union,*** **1 Chron. 12:17; adv. —I.** ***as one.*****— II.** ***singly, at once.*** **—III.** ***wholly, entirely, together,*** **יַחְדָּו יַחְדָּיו the same; the pron. is a pleonasm.**

יֵחַד. וַיִּחַד **Kal fut. apoc.; see חדה.**

יָחֵד **for** יָחֵד **Hiph. fut.; see חדד.**

יַחְדּוֹ **(*united*), p. n. of a man.**

יַחְדִּיאֵל **(*united with God*), p. n. of a man.**

יֶחְדְּיָהוּ **(*united to the Lord*), p.n. of a man.**

יַחֲזִיאֵל, יַחְזְיָה **p. n.; see חזה.**

יְחֶזְקֵאל, יְחִזְקִיָּה, יְחִזְקִיָּהוּ**, p. n.; see חזק.**

יֶחֱזָיוּן **fut. pl. with נ parag.; see חזה.**

יַחְזֵרָה **p. n. of a man.**

יְחִיאֵל, יְחִוּאֵל **p.n.; see חיה, חיי.**

יְחִי, וַיְחִי **fut. apoc.; see חיה.**

יְחִיתַן **Hiph. fut. with suff. ־ָן for ־ֵן because of the pause; see חתת.**

יָחִיד; see יחד

יָחַל Pi. יִחֵל.—I. *hope for, expect, wait.*—II. *cause to hope,* with לְ, אֶל. Hiph. הוֹחִיל same as Pi. with לְפְנֵי לְ. Niph. נוֹחַל (fut. יִיָּחֵל) same as Pi.

יָחֵל *he will begin;* יָחֵל *he will play,* Hiph. fut.; see חלל.

יָחִיל m., *one waiting,* Lam. 3:26.

יַחְלְאֵל p. n. of one of the sons of Zebulon; patron. יַחְלְאֵלִי.

יִחֲלוּ Pi. pret. pl. with dag. euphon., from יחל.

תּוֹחֶלֶת f., *expectation, hope.*

יָחַם (fut. יֶחַם, יֵחַם; pl. וַיֵּחֲמוּ; f. וַיֵּחַמְנָה).—I. *be in heat* (for sexual intercourse): hence,—II. *conceive.*—III. *be hot with anger.* Niph. part. pl. m. נֵחָמִים *heated with idol worship,* Isa. 57:5. Pi. (inf. יַחֵם; pret. f. with suff. יְחֵמַתְנִי) *conceived.*

יֶחֱמוּ for יֶחֱמוּ Pi. pret. pl., from יחם.

יֵחַמְנָה Gen. 30:38. for תֵּחַמְנָה Kal fut. pl. f., from יחם.

חֵמָה const. חֲמַת f.—I. *heat.*—II. *anger, fury.*—III. *venom of noxious creatures,* Deut. 32:33.

חֲמָא חֵמָא f. Ch., *heat, anger.*

יַחְמַי p.n. of a man.

יַחְמוּר *gazelle;* see חמר.

יְחֵמַתְנִי for יִחֲמַתְנִי Pi. pret. f. with suff.; see יחם.

וַיִּחַן יִחַן Kal fut. apoc.; see חנה.

יָחְנְךָ for יָחְנְךָ Kal fut. with suff.; see חנן.

יֶחֱסָיוֹן fut. pl. with ן parag.; see חסה.

יָחֵף m., *barefooted.*

יַחְצְאֵל יַחְצְאֵלִי p.n. of a man;

יָחַר same as אָחַר *tarrying,* 2 Sa. 20. 5; fut. וַיִּיחַר; וַיֹּחַר Kri Hiph. fut. Ch.; see אחר.

וַיִּחַר יִחַר Kal fut. apoc.; see חרה.

יַחַשׂ m., *generation, family;* סֵפֶר הַיַּחַשׂ *register of descent,* Neh. 7:5.

הִתְיַחֵשׂ Hiph. *being, becoming registered* (as to pedigree); ἀπογράφεσθαι; inf. s., *registration.*

יָחַת Kal fut. pl. יֵחַתּוּ with dag. euphon.; see נחת. Niph. fut.; see חתת.

וַיֵּט יֵט יֵט Kal fut. apoc.; see נטה.

וַיֵּט יֵט Hiph. fut. apoc.; see נטה.

יָטַב same as טוֹב (fut. יִיטַב, תִּיטְבִי) *be or seem, good, happy;* with לְ *it was well with him;* with בְּעֵינֵי, לִפְנֵי *it seemed good to him;* with לֵב *was glad* (did the heart good). Hiph. הֵיטִיב (fut. יֵיטִיב, יֵיטִיב) *do good, well to;* הֵיטַבְתָּ לִרְאוֹת *thou hast rightly seen,* Jer. 2:12; מֵיטִיב לְנַגֵּן *skilled in music;* with אֶל, לְ, עִם; inf. הֵיטֵב adv. *well, rightly.*

יְטַב Ch., *was good, happy;* with עַל *it pleased him.*

מֵיטָב m., *good, choice, best.*

יָטְבָה p.n. of a place.

יָטְבָתָה p. n. of a station of the Israelites in the desert.

יוּטָה, יָטָּה p.n. of a city in the tribe of Judah.

יְטוּר p.n. of a son of Ishmael and of the people descended from him. *the Itureans.*

יָדַע for יֵדַע Kal fut.; see ידע.

יֵיטִיב for יֵיטִיב Hiph. fut; see טב.

יָלִיל for יְיֵלִיל Hiph. fut.; see ילל.

יַיִן; see יַן.

יֵיף Kal fut. apoc.; see יָפֿה.

יַד 1 Sa. 4:13. for יָד *hand*.

וַיֵּף יַד Hiph. fut. apoc.; see נכה.

יְכַבְּדָנְנִי Pi. fut. with suff. and נ epenth; see כבד.

יְכוֹנְנֶנּוּ for יְכוֹנְנֶנּוּ Pil. fut. with suff.; see כּוּן.

יָכַח Hiph. הוֹכִיחַ.—I. *show, evince.*—II. *convince, chastise, punish,* with אֶת, אֶל, עִם, הוּכַח *was reproved,* Job 33:19. Niph. נוֹכַח *be contending.* Hith. הִתְוַכַּח same as Niph., with עִם Mic. 6:2.

תּוֹכֵחָה f., *reproof, punishment.*

תּוֹכַחַת f. (with suff. תּוֹכַחְתִּי; pl. תּוֹכָחוֹת).—I. *argument.*—II. *reproof, punishment.*

יָכִין p. n.; see כּוּן.

יָכֹל (fut. יוּכַל; inf. abs. יָכוֹל; const. יְכֹלֶת) *capable of, equal to,* any action, so as *to succeed, prevail, overcome,* with ל.

יְכֵל Ch. (part. יָכִיל, יָכֵל; fut. יוּכַל, תֻּכַּל) *was able, prevailed, overcame.*

יְכָלְיָהוּ, יְכָלְיָה (*the Lord who prevaileth*), p. n., the mother of king Uzziah.

יְהוּכַל p. n. of a man.

יֵכַל Kal fut. apoc.; see כלה.

יִכַּל Ch. fut.; see יכל.

יְכֹלֶת inf. const.; see יָכֹל.

יְכָנְיָה p. n.; see יְהוֹיָכִין in הוה.

יְכַסְיֵמוֹ Ex. 15:5, for יְכַסּוּמוֹ, Pi. fut. with suff.; see כסה.

יֻכַּתּוּ, יֻגְבַּת for יֻכַּתּוּ, יֻבָּת Hoph. fut.; see כתת.

יָכַתּוּ for יֻכַּתּוּ Hiph. fut. pl.; see כתת.

יָלַד, יָלֵד, יָלֹד (fut. יֵלֵד, יֵלַד; inf. abs. יָלֹד, לֵדָה; const. לֶדֶת, לַת; with suff. לִדְתָּהּ).—I. *bring forth.*—II. *beget* (part. יוֹלֶדֶת *mother*). Niph. נוֹלַד (fut. יִוָּלֵד), *was born.* Pi. יִלֵּד *aiding to bring forth,* Ex. 1:16; part. מְיַלֶּדֶת *midwife;* pl. מְיַלְּדוֹת. Pu. יֻלַּד *was born.* Hiph. הוֹלִיד *cause to bring forth, produce, beget.* Hoph. inf. הֻלֶּדֶת, יוֹם הֻלֶּדֶת אֶת־ *be born;* פַּרְעֹה Pharaoh's *birthday,* Gen. 40:20. Hith. הִתְיַלֵּד *recorded in the genealogies as begotten,* Nu 1:18.

וֶלֶד m., *son, progeny.*

וָלָד m., the same.

יֶלֶד m.—I. *lad, youth, child.*—II. *young of beasts,* Isa. 11:7.

יְלִיד m., *offspring, son;* יְלִיד בַּיִת *household slave.*

יִלּוֹד m., *offspring, son.*

יַלְדָּה f., *girl, female child.*

יַלְדּוּת f.—I. *birth,* Ps. 110:3.—II. *youth,* Ecc. 11:9, 10.

מוֹלָדָה p. n. of a town in the tribe of Judah.

מוֹלֶדֶת f. (pl. מוֹלָדוֹת).—I. *nativity, birth.*—II. *birth-place.*—III. *person born.*—IV. *relatives, members of the same family.*

מוֹלִיד p. n. of a man.

תּוֹלָד p. n. of a town in the tribe of Simeon; same as אֶלְתּוֹלַד.

תּוֹלְדוֹת f. pl.—I. *birth,* Ex. 28:10.—II. *posterity.*—III. *history;* סֵפֶר תּוֹלְדוֹת *genealogy,* Gen. 2:4; 6:9.

יַלֹן p. n. of a man.

יַלִּיזוּ Rabbinical, for יָלִיזוּ, Hiph. fut. pl.; see לוז.

יַלִּינוּ Hiph. fut. pl.; see II. לון.

יֵלֵךְ walk; see הָלַךְ.

יָלַל Hiph. הֵילִיל (fut. יְיֵלִיל, וַיֵּלִיל, יְהֵילִיל), wail, howl, cry, mourn.

יְלֵל m., howling, Deu. 32:10.

יְלָלָה const., יִלְלַת f., wailing, lamenting.

תּוֹלֵלִים m. pl., those who cause to lament, Ps. 137:3.

יֵלֶךְ Kal fut. apoc. in pause for יֵלֵךְ; see לון.

יָלַע retain, hold, Pro. 20:25.

יַלֶּפֶת f., itching scurvy, Lev. 21:20; 22:22.

יֶלֶק m., a hairy, winged locust.

יַלְקוּט bag; see לקט.

יָם, const. יַם־ יָם m.—I. the sea.—II. any large lake.—III. any large river; pl. יַמִּים; הַיָּם הַגָּדוֹל or הָאַחֲרוֹן the Mediterranean, i.e. Western Sea: hence יָם the west; רוּחַ יָם the west wind; יָמָּה westward; מִיָּם from the west; מִיָּם לְ from the west of a district; פְּאַת־יָם sea (that is western) quarter; יָם הַנְּחֹשֶׁת brazen sea, a large vessel for ablution in the temple of Solomon.

יְמוּאֵל p.n. of a son of Simeon.

יָמִים, יָמוֹת days; see יום.

וַיָּמַח, יָמַח Kal fut. apoc.; see מחה.

יָמִים m. pl., Gen. 36:24, perhaps hot springs; Vulg. aquæ calidæ.

יְמִימָה p.n. of one of Job's daughters.

יְמִינִי, יָמִין right hand; see ימן.

יִמְלָא p.n. of the father of Micaiah the prophet.

יְמַלֵּא for יְמַלֵּא Pi. fut.; see מלא.

יָמְלֵךְ p.n. of a prince of the Simeonites.

יָמַן Hiph. הֵימִין take the right hand or southward.

יָמִין m.—I. the right side, hand, leg, eye; יַד יְמִינוֹ his right hand; מִימִין, מִיָּמִין with לְ and suff. יָמִין at the right hand; יָמִין, לַיָּמִין, אֶל הַיָּמִין to, towards the right.—II. south; מִימָן southward of any where.—III. p.n. of a man.

יִמְנָה p.n. of a son of Asher.

יְמָנִי m., יְמָנִית f., right hand, side, &c. יְמִינִי a Benjamin; see בֶּן in בִּנְיָמִין.

תֵּימָן lit. right (because a man facing the rising of the sun would have his hand to the south).—I. the south.—II. the south wind; תֵּימָנָה towards the south.—III. p.n. of a city and district of the Edomites; תֵּימָנִי a Temanite.

יִמְנָע p.n. of a man.

יִמָּצוּ for יִמָּצְאוּ Niph. fut. pl., see מצא.

יָמַר same as מור. Hiph. הֵימִיר change, exchange, Jer. 2:11. Hith. הִתְיַמֵּר ye shall obtain rule, Isa. 61:6 (like Arab. word for commanded; whence "Emir"—Lee).

יֵמַר for יִמְרַר (was bitter) fut.; see מרר.

יִמְרָה p.n. of a man.

יִמְרוּךְ for יֹאמְרוּךְ Kal fut. pl. with suff.; see אמר.

יְמֹשׁ same as מָשַׁשׁ. Hiph. imp. הֲמִישֵׁנִי Kri, הֲמִשֵׁנִי Ketib, let me grope, feel, Jud. 16:26.

יַנְאֵץ Syr. for יִנְאַץ Hiph. fut.; see נאץ.

ינדע for ידע Ch. Pe. fut.; see ידע.

ינה oppress, ruin; (part. f. יונה). Hiph. הונה (fut. יונה) same as Kal; with מן drove away.

ינוח p. n., a town in the confines of Ephraim and Manasseh.

ינום p. n. of a place in the tribe of Judah.

ינח see נוח. Hiph. הניח (fut. יניח, ויּנּח).—I. gave rest to.—II. gave comfort to.—III. allowed to fall down.—IV. caused to rest upon, with ל. Hoph. הניח I. was placed, Zec. 5:11.—II. left, remaining, Eze. 41:9, 11.

יני for יניא Hiph. fut.; see נוא.

יניח Hiph. fut. ויּנּח fut. apoc.; see ינח.

ינק (fut. יינק) suck in; trop. enjoy; part: יונק sucking infant. Hiph. היניק suckle, give suck; part. f. מינקת, מינקת nurse; with suff. מנקתה, מנקתו; pl. מיניקות.

יונק m.—I. suckling.—II. sucker (young shoot).

יונקת f., the same.

יניקה f., the same; pl. יניקות.

ינשא Niph. fut. with א parag.; see נשא.

ינשוף ינשוף owl; see נשף.

יסב for יסב Kal fut.; see סבב.

יסב for יסב Hiph. fut.; see סבב.

יסד I. founded, established, placed.—II fixed, laid up. Niph. נוסד was plotting, laying the ground-work of, Ps. 2:2; was founded, Isa. 44:28. Pi. יסד cause to found, fix, establish. Pu. יסד was founded, Hoph. inf. הוסד was founded;

part. מוסד founded, secure, Isa 28:16, &c.

יסוד m., foundation; pl. יסודים, יסדות.

סוד m.—I. setting a fence about.—II. decree, counsel.—III. deliberation.—IV. consideration, prudence.—V. assembly for deliberation.—VI. secret.

סודי p. n. of a man.

יסד m., beginning, i. e. foundation of a building, Ezr. 7:9.

יסודה f., foundation, Ps. 87:1.

מוסד m., foundation, support, prop.

מוסדה f., the same.

מוסד m., foundation, support; pl מוסדות and מוסדים.

מסד m., foundation, 1 Ki. 7:9.

יסך was poured out, Ex. 30:32; see נסך.

יסכה p. n. of Lot's sister.

יסמכיהו p. n. of a man.

יסף (part. יוסף; pl. יוספים and Hiph יאסיף ויסף, יוסף, יוסיף; הוסיף; fut. ויאסף; part. מוסיף).—I. added, repeated, with ל, אל, על.—II. used as an auxiliary, with ל, אל, על before the inf. when it may mostly be translated by again. Niph. נוסף was added, repeated; part. f. pl. נוספות additions of calamity. יסף Ch., Hoph. הוסף was added.

יסר (fut. with suff. אסרם; part. יסר). Pi. יסר (fut. ייסר; inf. יסרה, יסר) chastised, corrected (as parents their children), with מן. Niph. נוסר was chastised; pl. נוסרו. Hiph. fut. איסרם I will chastise them, Hos. 7:12

יִפּוֹר will chastise, Job 40:2.

מוֹסֵר chains; see אָסַר.

מוּסָר m. — I. chastisement, discipline. —II. learning, doctrine.

מֹסָר m., the same, Job 33:16.

יָע shovel; see יָעֶה.

יַעְבֵּץ p.n.—I. of a man.—II. of a town in the tribe of Judah.

יָעַד (fut. יִיעַד) appoint, determine. Niph. נוֹעַד.—I. brought together, assembled, met.— II. agreed, with עַל ,אֶל ,לְ. Hiph. הוֹעִיד appoint. Hoph. הוּעַד appointed, fixed, Jer. 24:1.

עֵדָה const. עֲדַת f.—I. an assembly.— II. party, persons united for a purpose.—III. a family.—IV. the congregation of Israel.—V. עֵ דְּבוֹרִים swarm of bees, Jud. 14:8.

מוֹעֵד m. (pl. מוֹעֲדִים ,מוֹעֲדֵי).— I. coming together, congregation; אֹהֶל מוֹעֵד the tabernacle of the congregation.—II. time, season.—III. place appointed; see also מֹעָד.

מוֹעֵד m., assembly, host, Isa. 14:31.

מוֹעֵדָה f., pl. מוֹעֲדוֹת solemn feasts, 2 Chron. 8:13.

מוּעָצָה f., appointment; עָרֵי הַמּוּעָצָה appointed cities of refuge

וַיַּעַד ,יֵעַד Hiph. fut.; see עוּד.

יָעָה carry off, destroy, Isa. 28:17.

יָע m., pl. יָעִים shovels or fire-pans.

יְעִיאֵל ,יְעוּאֵל p.n. of a man.

יְעוּץ p.n. of a man.

יְעוּרִים m. pl., woods, Eze. 34:25; see יָעַר.

יְעוּשׁ p.n. of a man.

יָעַז Niph. part. נוֹעָז, Isa. 33:19; Vulg. impudens, powerful, formidable.

יְעֲזִיאֵל p.n. of a man.

יַעֲזִיָּה p.n. of a man.

יַעְזֵיר ,יַעְזֵר (the Lord helpeth) p. n. of a town beyond Jordan of the tribe of Gad.

יָעַט clothe, cover, Isa. 61:10.

יְעַט Ch. same as Heb., יָעַץ advise, counsel. Ith. consulted together, Dan. 6:8.

יָעֲטִין m. pl., councillors.

עֵטָא f., counsel, wisdom, Dan. 2:14.

וַיַּעַט ,יָעַט Kal fut.; see עוּט.

יָעִיר p.n. of a man.

יַעְקָן p.n. of a man.

יָעַל. Hiph. הוֹעִיל be profitable, advantageous, with לְ.

יָעֵל m.—I. ibex, mountain goat; pl. יְעֵלִים ,יַעֲלֵי.—II. p. n. of a judge of Israel.—III. p. n. of a woman. —IV. צוּרֵי הַיְּעֵלִים p. n. of a rock in the desert of Engaddi.

יַעֲלָה f.—I. female ibex.—II. p. n. of a man.

יַעְלָם p. n. of the son of Esau.

יַעֲמֹדְנָה Dan. 8:22. Kal fut. pl. f. for תַּעֲמֹדְנָה; see עָמַד.

יַעֲנִי ,יַעַן see ענה.

יַעַן perhaps from עָנָה cried.

יַעֵן pl. יְעֵנִים f., ostriches, Lam. 4:3.

בַּת הַיַּעֲנָה f. (pl. בְּנוֹת יַעֲנָה fe male ostriches.

יָעַף (fut. יִיעַף) lit. ran swiftly, was fatigued, wearied. Hoph. part. מֻעָף swift, Dan. 9:21.

יָעֵף m., weary, fatigued, Isa. 40:29; 50:4.

יָעַף m., flight, Dan. 9:21.

תּוֹעָפוֹת f. pl.— I. swiftness. — II

*wealth, treasure* (acquired by fatigue).

יָעַץ (fut. יִיעַץ) *advise, admonish, counsel self* or *others*, with עַל, אֶל; part. יֹעֵץ *counsellor.* Niph. נוֹעַץ *be advised, counselling, consulting,* with עִם, אֶל, אֵת. Hithp. יִתְיָעֲצוּ same as Niph.

עֵצָה const. עֲצַת f., *counsel;* בְּעֵצָה *deliberately;* see also עצה

מוֹעֵצָה f., pl. מוֹעֵצוֹת *counsels, devices.*

יַעֲקֹב, יַעֲקֹבָה p. n.; see עקב.

יַעְשָׁן see בְּנֵי־יַעְשָׁן.

יַעַר m.—I. *honey-comb* (const. יַעְרַת). —II. *wood, forest;* יַעְרָה *to the wood;* pl. יְעָרִים, יְעוֹרִים, יַעֲרוֹת—III. p.n.: יַעַר אֶפְרַיִם *grove of Ephraim;* קִרְיַת יְעָרִים *a city in the tribe of Judah;* יַעַר חָרֶת *the wood of Hereth* in the tribe of Judah.

וַיַּעַר, יָעַר Hiph. fut.; see עור.

יַעְרָה same as יְהוֹעַדָּה p. n. of a man.

יַעֲרֵי אֹרְגִים (*thickets,* perhaps abbreviated יָעִיר) p. n. of a man.

יַעֲשָׂיָה p. n. of a man.

יַעֲשַׂי p. n. of a man.

יַעֲשִׂיאֵל p. n. of a man.

יִפְדְיָה (*the Lord redeemeth*), p. n. of a man.

יָפֵר (fut. יִיפֶה, וַיִּיף) *was fair, beautiful.* Pi. *beautified,* Jer. 10:4. Pul. יֻפְּפָה *was very beautiful.* Hith. *beautify oneself.*

יָפֶה const. יְפֵה m.; יָפָה const. יְפַת f., *beautiful, excellent.*

יָפוֹ, יָפוֹא p.n., *Joppa,* a celebrated port on the Mediterranean, Ἰόππη.

יֳפִי m. (with pause יֹפִי; with suff. יָפְיוֹ), *beauty, excellence.*

יְפֵה־פִיָה f., *very beautiful,* Jer. 46:20

יְפֵיפִית Pul., Ps. 45:3, from יפה.

יָפַח same as פוח. Hith. *was panting in agony,* Jer. 4:31.

יָפֵחַ m.—I. *breathing out.*—II. *panting after, longing for.*

יַפְלֵט p.n. of a man; patron. יַפְלֵטִי.

יֻפֻּנֶּה p. n. of the father of Caleb and others.

יָפַע. Hiph. הוֹפִיעַ *exhibit brilliancy, shine forth.*

יִפְעָה f., *beauty, brilliancy,* Eze. 28: 7, 17.

יָפִיעַ p.n.—I. of a town in the tribe of Zebulun.—II. of a man.

יַפֵּר Hiph. fut. apoc.; see פרה.

יִפְתְּ Hiph. fut apoc.; see פתה.

יפת root not used.

מוֹפֵת m.—I. *sign, wonder.*—II. *intimation, portent* (τύπος).

יֶפֶת p.n., *Japheth,* son of Noah; LXX. Ἰάφεθ.

יִפְתָּח p. n.—I. a town in the tribe of Judah.—II. a judge of Israel (Ἰεφθά).

יִפְתַּח־אֵל p. n., a valley in the tribes of Zebulun and Asher.

יָצָא (fut. יֵצֵא; inf. abs. יָצֹא; const. צֵאת; imp. צֵא; with ה parag צֵאָה; part. m. יֹצֵא, f. יֹצֵאת, יָצֵאת, יֹצֵת).—I. *go out, go forth;* with מִן of the place whence; with בְּ of the place whither.—II. *issue* (from the womb), *be born.*—III *descended.*—IV. *go forth* (from captivity or into captivity).—V *shooting of a tree,* Isa. 11:1, also *grew, came forth* (of plants and flowers).—VI. *arose* (of

and stars).—VII. *issue a decree.*
There are many similar usages, all
modifications of the primary meaning *go forth.* Hiph. הוֹצִיא *cause
to come out, bring out;* with דִּבָּה
*brought up an evil report,* Nu. 14:
36. Hoph. הוּצָא *was brought
forth, out.*

יְצָא Ch., Shaph. שֵׁיצִיא *wrought out,
finished,* Ezr. 6:15.

יְצִיא m., *issue, child,* 2 Chron. 32:21.

מוֹצָא m.—I. *outgoing.*—II. *time of
outgoing.*—III. *place of outgoing.*
—IV. *the east.*—V. *that which
goeth out,* production, speech, &c.
—VI. p. n. of a man.

מוֹצָאָה f.—I. *going forth,* Mic. 5:1.—
II. *draught-house,* 2 Ki. 10:27.

תּוֹצָאוֹת f. pl.—I. *termination.*—II.
*escape,* Ps. 68:21.—III. *result,*
Pro. 4:23.

צֶאֱצָאִים m. pl.—I. *productions of the
earth.*—II. *offspring.*

יָצַב *same as* נָצַב. Hith. הִתְיַצֵּב I.
*was set up, stood fast,* with עַל,
לְפָנֵי.—II. *stood up against,* with
עַל.—III. *stood before, in presence
of,* with עִם, בִּפְנֵי, לִפְנֵי.

יְצַב Ch. Pa. *certify.*

יַצִּיב m. Ch., *firm, fixed, settled;*
מִן יַצִּיב adv., *surely.*

יָצַג הַצִּיג יָצַן; see נצג.

יִצְהָר p.n.; see צהר.

יִצְחָק p.n.; see צחק.

יְצַטַּבַּע Ch. Ithp. fut.; see צבע.

יְצְטַיְרוּ Hith. fut. pl.; see ציר.

יָצַע, part. יָצוּעַ *laid, placed,* s. *bed.*
Hiph. הִצִּיעַ *place, strew.* Hoph.
הֻצַּע *spread* (as a couch), Isa. 14:11.

יָצִיעַ *same as* יָצוּעַ.

מַצָּע m., *bed or couch,* Isa. 28:20.

יָצַק (fut. יָצַק, וַיִּצֹק; inf. const. צֶקֶת;
imp. יְצֹק, צַק).—I. *pour out.*—II.
*fuse* (as metal), with בְּ, עַל; part.
יָצוּק *hard* (like a cast of metal).
Hiph. הִצִּיק *put down, place, lay
out,* Jos. 7:23; 2 Sa. 15:24. Hoph.
הוּצַק *be, become poured out;* part.
מֻצָק *firm,* Job 11:15.

וַיִּצֶק יֶצֶק Kal fut., from יצק.

יִצֹּק Kal fut., from יצק.

יְצֻקָה f., *casting, cast,* 1 Ki. 7:24.

מוּצָק, const. מֻצַק m., *cast of brass,*
see also in צוק.

מוּצָקָה f., pl. מוּצָקוֹת *funnels* for
pouring the metal into moulds or
casts, Zec. 4:2.

מֻצֶקֶת f., with suff. מֻצַקְתּוֹ *its being
fused,* 2 Chron. 4:3.

I. יָצַר (fut. יָצַר, וַיִּצֶר, וַיִּיצֶר), *form,
fashion, make;* part. יוֹצֵר *moulder,
potter;* כְּלֵי יוֹצֵר *fictile vases;
creator.* Niph. נוֹצַר and Hoph.
הוּצַר *was formed, made.* Pu. יֻצַּר
the same.

יֵצֶר m. (with suff. יִצְרֵנוּ).—I. *figment,
any thing formed.*—II. *thought,
imagination.*—III. p. n. of a son
of Naphtali; patron. יִצְרִי.

וַיִּיצֶר, יִצֶר Kal fut., Gen. 2:19, from I. יצר.

יֻצָּרִים m. pl., *things formed, members,*
Job 17:7.

II. יָצַר *same as* צרר but intrans., *was
straitened, distressed, anxious;*
וַיֵּצֶר לוֹ *and he was in anxiety,*
Gen. 32:8.

יָצְרוּ, יִצֶר Kal fut. with suff., from
II. יצר.

וַיֵּצֶר יֵצֶר Kal fut., from II. יצר.

וַיֵּצַר יֵצַר Kal fut. apoc.; see צור.

יָצַת (fut. יָצַתּוּ, יִצַּת).—I. burn, Isa. 9:17, with בְּ.—II. was on fire. Niph. נִצַּת I. was on fire, burnt.— II. burnt with anger, with בְּ, 2 Ki. 22:13,17. Hiph. הִצִּית, הוֹצִית kindle, set fire to.

יִצַּתּוּ Kal fut. pl. with dag. euphon., from יצת.

יָצַתִי for יָצָאתִי; see יצא.

יָקָב root not used; (Arab. a tank).

יֶקֶב m. (with suff. יִקְבְּךָ).—I. wine or oil vat.—II. the trough in which grapes are trodden, Job 24:11.

יָקְבְצְאֵל p.n., same as קַבְצְאֵל.

יָקַד (fut. יִקַּד, יִיקַד) burnt (as fire). Hoph. הוּקַד became, was, burning.

יְקַד Ch., burning, Dan. 3:6, &c.

יְקוֹד m., the same, fire-brand, Isa. 10:16.

יְקֵדָה f. Ch., the same. Dan. 7:11.

מוֹקֵד m.—I. burning, Isa. 33:14.— II. fire-brand, Ps. 102:4.

מוֹקְדָה f., hearth where the burnt-offerings were consumed, Lev. 6:2.

יָקְדְעָם p.n. of a city in the tribe of Judah.

יָקָה root not used; (Arab. he obeyed).

יָקְהָה or יִקְּהָה, const. יִקְהַת f. obedience.

יָקֶה p.n. of a man.

יְקוּם whatever has been called into existence, Gen. 7:4, 23; Deut. 11:6; see קום.

יָקוֹשׁ יָקֻשׁ; see יקשׁ.

יְקוּתִיאֵל p.n. of a man.

יִפַּח Kal fut.; יֻפַּח Hoph. fut.; see לקח.

יָקְטָן p.n., a descendant of Shem, the son of Eber, Gen. 10:25, 26.

יָקִים p.n. of a man.

יַקְמְיָה p.n. of a man.

יָקְמְעָם p.n. of a man.

יָקְמְעָם p.n., a city of the Levites in the tribe of Ephraim; see also קִבְצַיִם.

יָקְנְעָם p.n. of a city in the tribe of Zebulun.

יָקַע (fut. יֵקַע; pret. נָקַע which see).— I. fell, became dislocated, Gen. 32: 26.—II. fell away (in mind, affection). Hiph. הוֹקִיעַ suspend, hang, ἀνασκολοπίζειν. Hoph. part. מוּקָעִים hanged, 2 Sa. 21:13.

יָקַץ (fut. וַיִּיקַץ, יָקַץ, יִיקַץ) awake out of sleep; see קוץ.

יָפַץ Kal fut.; see יקץ.

יָקַר (fut. וַיִּיקַר, יֵקַר, יִיקַר) became precious, prized, valued, with לְ, בְּעֵינֵי. Hiph. הוֹקִיר (lit. make precious). rare, scarce.

יָקָר m. יְקָרָה f.—I. precious, dear.— II. rare, scarce. — III. honorable, glorious.

יְקָר m., weight, value, honour, glory

יְקָר m. Ch. — I. costly things, Dan. 2:6.—II. honor, glory.

יַקִּיר m., precious, honored, Jer. 31:20.

יַקִּיר m. Ch., honored, grave.

יָקְרֶךָ Kal. fut. with suff. and dag. euphon.; see קרה.

יָקַשׁ, יָקֹשׁ (קֹשׁ נָקֹשׁ see) snaring, taking by means of snares; part. יוֹקֵשׁ a fowler. Niph. נוֹקֵשׁ was ensnared as a bird.

יָקוֹשׁ יָקֻשׁ m., fowler.

יוּקְשׁ m., pl. יֻקְשִׁים snared, Ecc. 9:12

יָקְשָׁן p. n. of a son of Abraham.

מוֹקֵשׁ m. (pl. מוֹקְשִׁים, מוֹקְשׁוֹת) *snares* or *traps* for birds or beasts; mostly used metaphorically, as מוֹקְשֵׁי מָוֶת *snares of death, &c.*

וַיָּקֶשׁ, יָקֹשׁ Kal fut. apoc.; see קשש.

יָקֹשׁ Hiph. fut. apoc.; see קשה

יָקְתְאֵל p. n.—I. a town in the tribe of Judah.—II. a city in Arabia.

יָרֵא (fut. יִירָא, יָרֵא; imp. יְרָא; inf. const. יְרֹא; with pref. לֵרֹא; with ה parag. יִרְאָה), *feared* God, man, anything; with ב, אֶת, ל, מִן, Niph. fut. תִּוָּרֵא *thou art to be feared,* Ps. 130:4; part. נוֹרָא *fearful, terrible, marvellous thing;* pl. נוֹרָאוֹת. Pi. יֵרֵא *alarm, cause to fear.*

יָרֵא const. יְרֵא m. (יִרְאָה const. יִרְאַת f.), *fearing God* or *man,* with מִפְּנֵי

יִרְאָה const. יִרְאַת f., *the same.*

יִרְאוֹן p. n. of a city in the tribe of Naphtali.

מוֹרָא m.—I. *fear.*—II. *reverence,* Mal. 1:6.—III. *object of fear, reverence.*—IV. *fearful, stupendous act.*

מוֹרָה same as מוֹרָא; see also in מָרָה.

וַיָּרֵא, יָרֵא Kal fut. apoc.; see ראה.

יִרְאוּ for יָרְאוּ Ps. 34:10, imp. pl.; see ירא.

יָרְאוּ Kal fut. pl., see ירא; יִרְאוּ Kal fut. pl., see ראה.

וַיִּרְאוּ, יָרְאוּ 2 Sa. 11:24, for יִירְאוּ, Hiph. fut. pl. apoc.; see ירה.

יְרָאִיָּה p. n. of a man.

יְרֻבֶּשֶׁת, יְרֻבַּעַל עָרֵב see ריב.

וַיִּרֶב, יָרֶב for יָאָרֶב, Hiph. fut.; see ארב.

יְרִבִּין Kal fut. pl. with ן parag.; see רבה.

יָרָבְעָם p. n., *Jeroboam,* the name of two of the kings of Israel.

יָרַד (fut. יֵרֵד, וַיֵּרֶד, יֵרַד; imp. רֵד, וַיֵּרֶד, רְדָה; inf. abs. יָרֹד, const. רֶדֶת, רָדָה).— *descended, went down,* κατέβη (used both of men and things in a great variety of acceptations). Hiph. הוֹרִיד *make descend, bring down, cast down* (of men and things); *subdued,* with תַּחַת. Hoph. הוּרַד *brought down, lowered.*

יֶרֶד p. n. of a man, 'Ιαρέδ.

יַרְדֵּן p. n. of the river *Jordan.*

מוֹרָד m., *descent, declivity;* מַעֲשֵׂה מוֹרָד *sloping,* perhaps *arched work,* 1 Ki. 7:29.

יִרְדֹּף Ps. 7:6, apparently a corruption, from רָדַף Kal fut. and יְרַדֵּף Pi. fut.; or possibly from two readings יָרִיד and יִרְדֹּף.

יָרָה (fut. יִירֶה; inf. יָרֹה; const. יְרוֹת, יְרוֹא; imp. יְרֵה).— I. *cast out, shoot,* as arrows, &c.; part. יוֹרִים *archers,* Pro. 26:18.—II. *cast, lay a foundation,* see יוֹרֶה. Niph. fut. יִיָּרֶה *shall be shot,* Ex. 19:13. Hiph. הוֹרָה (fut. יוֹרֶה, וַיּוֹר).—I. *cast forth, shoot,* as arrows, rain, &c. מוֹרִים *archers*); see מוֹרֶה.—II. *put forth,* as instruction, *teach,* with מִן, אֶל, ל, ב.

יוֹרֶה m. (part. Kal).—I. *the former rain,* i. e. of the autumn.—II. p. n. of a man; same as חָרִיף.

יוֹרַי p. n. of a man.

מוֹרֶה m. (part. Hiph.).—I. *teacher, doctor.*—II. *arrow, archer.*—III. *former rain.*— IV. p. n. אֵלוֹן or

אֵלוֹנֵי מֹרֶה the oaks of Moreh, near Sichem; גִּבְעַת־הַמּוֹרֶה hill of Moreh in the valley of Jezreel.

תּוֹרָה f.—I. instruction, direction.—II. law, enactment.—III. the law, as revealed to Moses and recorded in the Pentateuch.

יָרָה (fut. תִּירָה), was astounded with fear, Isa. 44:8.

וַיִּרְא יָרוּ Hiph. fut. pl.; see ירה.

לִירֹא יְרֹא for יְרֹ Kal inf.; see ירה.

יְרוּאֵל p. n. of a desert.

יָרֹחַ (same as יֶרַח), p. n. of a man.

יְרֹנֵן Kal fut. pl. with נ parag.; see רוה.

יָרֹן Pro. 29:6, Kal fut.; see רנן. Others refer it to רגן.

יָרוּץ for יָרֻץ Kal fut.; see רצץ.

יְרוּשָׁה יְרוּשָׁא p. n. of the mother of king Jotham.

יְרוּשָׁלַיִם יְרוּשָׁלֵם for יְרוּשָׁלֵם (the habitation of peace), p. n. of the principal city of Palestine, Ἱερουσαλήμ, Ἱεροσόλυμα.

יְרוּשָׁלֵם Ch., the same.

יָרֵחַ m., the moon.

יֶרַח m., (pl. יְרָחִים יַרְחֵי).—I. month, one revolution of the moon round the earth.—II. p. n. of a people and country, Gen. 10:26.

יְרַח m. Ch., month.

יְרִיחוֹ,יְרִיחוֹ,יְרֵחוֹ p. n., Jericho, a city in Palestine.

יְרֹחָם p. n. of a man.

יְרַחְמְאֵל p. n. of a man; patron. ־ִי.

יְרֹחָע p. n. of a woman.

יָרַט cast down to ruin, ruin.

מֹרָט m., "peeled" Eng. Ver.; "ruined" (Gesenius), Isa. 18:2, 7.

יְרִיאֵל p. n. of a man.

יְרִיבַי יָרִיב; see ריב.

יְדָיָהוּ יְדָיָה p. n. of a man.

יְרִיחוֹ יְרִיחוֹ p. n.; see יָרֵחַ.

יְרִיעוֹת יְרִיעָה shouting; see ירע.

יָרֵךְ m. (const. יֶרֶךְ; with suff. יְרֵכוֹ).—I. thigh; שׁוֹק עַל־יָרֵךְ hip and thigh, i. e. wholly, Ju. 15:8; יֹצְאֵי יָרֵךְ offspring, Ex. 1:5.—II. stem of the candlestick in the tabernacle; dual יְרֵכַיִם both thighs.

יַרְכָּה f., side, part, quarter; dual יַרְכָתַיִם const. יַרְכְּתֵי the two sides.

יַרְכָּה f. Ch., thigh.

יֵרַךְ Niph. fut., from רכך.

יַרְמוּת p. n. — I. a town in the tribe of Judah.—II. a town of Israel.

יְרֵמוֹת p.n. of a man.

יְרֵמַי p. n. of a man.

יִרְמְיָהוּ יִרְמְיָה (exalted of the Lord), p. n. Jeremiah, the prophet.

יָרַע same as רוע.—I. was in evil condition; fut. יֵרַע with לִי I am in affliction; with בְּעֵינֵי it was evil in the eyes of.—II. was grieved, pained.

I. יֵרַע Kal fut., from II. ירע Job 20:26; fut. apoc., from רעה.

יְרִיעָה f., veil, curtain of a tent.

יְרִיעוֹת (veiled), p. n. of a woman.

יִרְפְּאֵל p. n. of a place in the tribe of Benjamin.

יָרַק same as רָקַק spit.

יָרוֹק m., green herb, shoot, Job 39:8.

יֶרֶק m., green herb.

יֶרֶק m., freshness, green herbage.

יָרָקוֹן m.—1. *withering, wasting*; LXX. ᾦχρα.—II. *the smut in corn.*

יְרַקְרַק m.—I. *gold colour*, Ps. 68:14. —II. *greenish* or *yellowish*; pl. f. יְרַקְרַקוֹת.

יָרַשׁ, יָרֵשׁ (fut. יִירַשׁ, יִרַשׁ; inf. const. רֶשֶׁת; imp. יְרַשׁ, רַשׁ, רֵשׁ).—I. *possess, inherit.*—II. *dispossess others.*—III. *be, become poor*; יוֹרֵשׁ *heir.* Niph. *be, become poor.* Pi. יָרַשׁ *take into possession*, Deu. 28:42. Hiph. הוֹרִישׁ.—I. *cause to possess.*—II. *dispossess.*—III. *make poor, desolate.*

יְרֵשָׁה f., *possession*, Nu. 24:18.

יְרֻשָּׁה f., *the same.*

רֶשֶׁת f. (inf. *to take*; with suff. רִשְׁתּוֹ). —I. *net.* — II. *snare.* — III. *network.*

מוֹרָשׁ m. } *possession.*
מוֹרָשָׁה f. }

מוֹרֶשֶׁת גַּת p.n. of a district near Gath; מוֹרַשְׁתִּי *a Moreshethite.*

תִּירוֹשׁ, תִּירֹשׁ m., *new wine, must.*

יִשְׂחָק same as יִצְחָק p.n.; see צחק.

יְשִׂימָאֵל p.n. of a man.

יֻשַּׁם same as שׂוּם intrans. *was set, laid*; fut. יִישַׁם, וַאִישְׁמָה.

יִשְׂרָאֵל (*a prince with God*), p.n., *Israel*, the new name given by God to Jacob, afterwards applied to his descendants; m. יִשְׂרְאֵלִי, f. יִשְׂרְאֵלִית *an Israelite.*

יִשָּׂשׂכָר p.n. *Issachar*, the son of Jacob, and the tribe that descended from him.

יֵשׁ, יֶשׁ- (τὸ εἶναι), *is, are, was, were*; with suff. יֶשְׁךָ *thou art*; יֶשְׁנוֹ *he is*; יֶשְׁכֶם *ye are*; יֶשׁ לִי *I have*;

יֵשׁ אֲשֶׁר *it is, because that*; יֵשׁ וְיֵשׁ *it is, yea it is*, 2 Ki. 10:15.

יָשַׁב (fut. יֵשֵׁב; inf. יָשֹׁב; const. שֶׁבֶת; with suff. שִׁבְתִּי; imp. שֵׁב, שְׁבָה). —I. *sit, sit down*, with בְּ, עַל.— II. *lie in wait for.*—III. *have intercourse with*, with עִם.—IV. *remain.*—V. *dwell in.*—VI. *was inhabited*, with בְּ, עַל. Niph. נוֹשַׁב *was inhabited.* Pi. יִשֵּׁב *cause to remain*, Eze. 26:4. Hiph. הוֹשִׁיב *cause to sit, dwell, reside in* or *with, inhabit.* Hoph. הוּשַׁב *made, caused to dwell.*

יוֹשַׁבְתִּי; see יֹשַׁבְתִּי.

שִׁיבָה f., *residing*, 2 Sa. 19:33; see in שׁוּב.

יֹשֵׁב בַּשֶּׁבֶת p.n. of one of David's generals.

יַשׁוּבְאָב p.n. of a man.

יְשֵׁבוּ בְנֹב p.n. of a man.

יָשָׁבְקָשָׁה p.n. of a man.

מוֹשָׁב m. (pl. f. מוֹשָׁבוֹת; const. מֹשְׁבֵי m.).—I. *residence.*—II. *seat.*— III. *time of residing*, Ex. 12:40.— IV. *act of sitting.*—V. *inhabitants.*

תּוֹשָׁב m., *settler, sojourner.*

יִשְׁבַּח p.n. of a man.

יָשְׁבִי לֶחֶם p.n. of a man.

יָשָׁבְעָם p.n. of a man.

יִשְׁבָּק p.n. of a son of Abraham.

יָשׁוּב p.n. of a man; patron. יָשֻׁבִי.

יָשֻׁד for יָשֹׁד Kal fut.; see שׁדד.

יִשְׁוִי, יִשְׁוָה p.n. of a man.

יִשְׁוֹחָיָה p.n. of a man.

יְשׁוּעָה, יֵשׁוּעַ *salvation*; see ישע.

יֶשַׁח m., *baseness, hypocrisy*, Mic. 6:14.

יִשָּׁחוּ Niph. fut.; see שָׁחַח.

יַשְׁמְ Hiph. הוֹשִׁים extend, stretch out.

יִשַׁי p. n., Jesse, the father of David; LXX. 'Ιεσσαί.

יַשִּׁיא for יַשִּׁיא Hiph. fut.; see נשׁא.

יְשִׁיָּהוּ, יְשִׁיָּה p. n. of a man.

יָשִׂים for יָשִׂם Hiph. fut.; see שׂים.

יׁשָׁל Kal. fut. apoc., from III. שׁלה.

יָשֵׁם was desolate, laid waste; fut. תִּישְׁמֶנָה, תֵּשַׁם; see שָׁמֵם.

יְשִׁימוֹן m.—I. any great desert.—II. specially, the Desert of Sinai.

יְשִׁימוֹת f., desolations, Ps. 55:16.

בֵּית־הַיְשִׁימוֹת p. n. of a place near the Dead Sea.

יׁשָׁם for יָשֵׁם Kal. fut.; see שָׁמֵם.

וְיֵשַׁם Hiph. fut.; see שָׁמֵם.

יִשְׁמָא p. n. of a man.

יִשְׁמָעֵאל p. n.—I. Ishmael, the son of Abraham and Hagar. — II. of a man; יִשְׁמְעֵאלִים Ishmaelites.

יְשַׁמְעַיָה, יִשְׁמַעְיָהוּ p. n. of a man.

יִשְׁמְרַי p. n. of a man.

יָשַׁן, יָשֵׁן (fut. יִישַׁן) slept, slumbered, dozed. Niph. נוֹשַׁן grew old, dry. Pi. יִשֵּׁן made to sleep, Jud. 16:19.

יָשֵׁן m., old.

יְשֵׁנָה f.—I. the same.—II. p. n. of a town in the tribe of Judah.

יָשֵׁן m. יְשֵׁנָה f.—I. sleepy.—II. p. n. of a man.

שֵׁנָה f. — I. sleep. — II. dream, Ps. 90:5.

שְׁנָא f., sleep, Ps. 127:2.

שְׁנָא or שְׁנָה f. Ch., the same.

שְׁנָת f., sleep, Ps. 132:4.

יֶשְׁנוֹ compounded of יֵשׁ and suff. with נ epenth.

יׁשַׁע Hiph. הוֹשִׁיעַ (fut. יוֹשִׁיעַ, יְהוֹשִׁיעַ; apoc. יוֹשַׁע) deliver, set free, save, with מִן; לְ, מִיַּד. Niph. נוֹשַׁע was delivered, with מִן; part. נוֹשָׁע one saved, Zec. 9:9.

יֵשַׁע, יֶשַׁע m. (with suff. יִשְׁעִי, יִשְׁעֲךָ), deliverance, freedom, safety, salvation.

וַיּוֹשַׁע, יׁשַׁע Kal fut. apoc., from שָׁעָה.

יׁשַׁע Hiph. fut. apoc. יֹשַׁעֲכֶם fut. with suff., from ישׁע.

יִשְׁעִי p. n. of a man.

יְשַׁעְיָהוּ p. n., Isaiah the prophet; LXX. 'Ησαΐας; Vulg. Isaias.

יְשַׁעְיָה p. n. of a man.

יֵשׁוּעַ (same as יְהוֹשֻׁעַ, 'Ιησοῦς), p. n. of a man.

יְשׁוּעָה f., freedom, safety, salvation.

מוֹשָׁעוֹת f. pl., great salvation, Ps. 68: 21.

יָשְׁפֵה, יַשְׁפֶּה the jasper, a variegated gem.

יִשְׁפָּה p.n. of a man.

יִשְׁפָּן p. n. of a man.

יָשַׁר (fut. יִישַׁר, יֵישַׁר).—I. proceed, go right, i. e. directly onwards; יָשַׁר בַּדֶּרֶךְ he went straight on his way. —II. with בְּ, בְּעֵינֵי he was right, upright, good. Pi. יִשַּׁר make right, direct. Pu. part. made direct, plain, laid smooth, 1 Ki. 6:35. Hiph. made direct, straight forward, Pro. 4:25.; (imp. הַיְשַׁר) make direct, Ps. 5:9.

יָשָׁר m., יְשָׁרָה f., right, upright, righteous, true; יָשָׁר s., the book of right, i. e. right things, Deu. 6:18.

יֵשֶׁר p. n. of a man.

יֵשֶׁר m., *rectitude, integrity*.

יִשְׁרָה f., the same.

יֶשְׁאֵלָה p. n. of a man.

יְשֻׁרוּן m., a periphrastic title of Israel, applied to the whole people generally, lit. *entirely righteous*.

יִשְׁרֶנָה 1 Sa. 6:12, for תִּשְׁרֶנָה Kal fut. f. pl. 3. pers., from יָשַׁר.

מֵישׁוֹר m.—I. *a plain*.—II. *truth, righteousness*; adv. *righteously, truly*.

מֵישָׁרִים, מֵישָׁרִים m. pl.—I. *true men*. —II. *truth, righteousness*.—III. לְמֵישָׁרִים, בְּמֵישָׁרִים *truly, righteously*.

יָשֵׁשׁ m., 2 Chron. 36:17, *aged, elderly person*.

יָשִׁישׁ m., the same.

יְשִׁישַׁי p. n. of a man.

וַיִּשְׁתַּחוּ, יִשְׁתַּחוּ Hith. fut. apoc. sing. for יִשְׁתַּחֲוֶה; see שׁחה.

יִשְׁתָּעִין Kal fut. pl. with נ parag., from שׁעה.

יְשַׁקְשְׁקוּ Hith. fut. pl., from שׁקק.

יָת Ch., same as Heb. אֵת.

וַיֵּתֵא, יֵתֵא Kal fut. apoc. for יֶאְתֶּה, יֶאְתֶּה; see אתה.

יִתְאָו Hith. fut. apoc., from אוה.

יְתֵב Ch., same as יָשַׁב *sit*. Aph. *reside*, Ezr. 4:17.

וַיִּתְנַל, יִתְנַל Hith. fut. apoc., from נלה.

יָתֵד root not used; (Arab. *pin, nail*).

יָתֵד, const. יְתַד f. (pl. יְתֵדוֹת).—I. *pin, peg*.—II. *tent-pin*; hence *wise* (i. e. firmly fixed) *rulers*, Isa. 22: 23, 25.—III. *dibble, to bore holes in the earth*, Deu. 23:14.

וַיְתָו, יְתָו Pi. fut. apoc., from תוה.

יִתְוַכַּח Hith. fut., from יכח.

יִתְּגָר *abundance*; see תגר.

יִתְּזִין Ch. Ithp. fut., from זון.

יָתַח root not used; (Arab. *smote with a club*).

תּוֹתָח m., *club*; LXX. σφύρα, Job 41:21.

יִתְכַּם Hith. fut. apoc., from כסה.

יִתְלָה p. n. of a city of the Danites.

יָתַם root not used; (Arab. *was an orphan*).

יָתוֹם m., *orphan*.

יִתְּמוּ, וַיִּתַּמוּ, in pause יִתָּמּוּ Kal fut., from תמם.

יִתַּמּוּ Niph. fut. pl., from תמם.

יִתְמָה p. n. of a man.

יָתַן root not used; (Arab. *was enduring*).

אֵיתָן, אֵתָן m.—I. *mighty, irresistible, violent*; יֶרַח הָאֵיתָנִים *the month of the powerful*, i. e. Tisri, 1 Ki. 8:2.—II. *might, irresistibleness*.— III. p. n., perhaps the author of Ps. 89.

יַתְנִיאֵל p. n. of a man.

יִתְנָן p. n. of a city in the tribe of Judah.

יָתַר, part. יוֹתֵר *exceeding, redundant*. Hiph. הוֹתִיר I. *cause to remain, leave*.—II. *abound, be wealthy*. Niph. נוֹתַר *be left, remain*; part. m. נוֹתָר, f. נוֹתֶרֶת *that which is left*.

יֶתֶר m.—I. *excellence, abundance*, עַל־יֶתֶר *unto abundance*, Ps. 31: 24; adv., *abundantly, exceedingly*. — II. *residue, the rest of*. — III. *string* or *cord*.—IV. p. n. of a man: *patron*. יִתְרִי.

יִתְרָה f., *abundance, excess*.

**יֶתֶר, יוֹתֵר** (part. Kal).—I. *abundance, profit.*—II. adv., *more, further, moreover, excessively.*

**יוֹתֶרֶת** f.—I. *exceeding, redundant.*—II. *lobe, i.e. excess of the liver.*

**יַתִּיר** m. Ch.—I. *excellent, extraordinary;* **יַתִּירָה** adv., *very, exceedingly.*—II. Heb. p. n., a town in the tribe of Judah.

**יִתְרוֹ** p. n., the father-in-law of Moses, who was also called **יֶתֶר** and **חוֹבָב**.

**יִתְרוֹן** m., *gain, profit, good.*

**יִתְרְעָם** p. n. of a man.

**מוֹתָר** m.—I. *increase.*—II. *excellence,* Ecc. 3:19.

**מֵיתָר** m.—I. *bow-string,* Ps. 21:13.—II. *tent-cord.*

**יִתְּשֻׁם** Ch. Ithp. fut., from **שׂוּם**.

**יְתֵת** p. n. of a prince of Edom.

## כ

**כְּ, כָּ** pa. pref. signifying comparison, resemblance.—I. *as, as if, like;* **כְּ...כֵּן, כְּ...וּכְ, כְּ...כְּ** *as...so;* with suff. **כְּמוֹ, כָּכֶם, כָּהֶם;** see **כְּמוֹ**.—II. *according to* (κατά).—III. *nearly, almost;* **כַּיּוֹם הַזֶּה** *as on this day;* **כַּחֲצֹת הַלַּיְלָה** *about midnight.*—IV. with inf. (sometimes with part.) *when,* ὡς.

**כָּאַב** (fut. **יִכְאַב**) *be pained.* Hiph. I. *cause pain,* Eze. 13:22.—II. *mar, ruin,* 2 Ki. 3:19.

**כְּאֵב** m., *pain.*

**מַכְאוֹב** m. (pl. **ים-, וֹת-**).—I. *pain.*—II. *cause of pain.*—III. *sorrow.*

**כָּאָה**. Niph. *pained, enfeebled,* Dan. 11:30. Hiph. *pain, enfeeble the heart,* Eze. 13:22.

**כָּאֶה** m., *afflicted, helpless,* Ps. 10:10.

**כָּאר** Am. 8:8, for **כִּיאֹר**.

**כָּאֵרִי** Ps. 22:17; see **כּוּר**.

**כָּבֵד, כָּבַד** and **כָּבֹד** (fut. **יִכְבַּד**).—I. *be heavy, grievous.*—II. *be grave, respectable, honorable,* with **עַל, אֶל**. Niph. *became honorable, glorious;* part. **נִכְבָּדִים** *nobles,* **נִכְבָּדוֹת** *made glorious,* with **בְּ**. Pi. **כִּבֵּד** I. *make heavy, sullen, unrelenting.*—II. *make honourable, honour,* with **לְ**, **לְשֵׁם**. Pu. **כֻּבַּד** *was honoured.* Hiph. I. *made heavy, grievous, sullen.*—II. *made honorable, glorious.*—Hith. **מִתְכַּבֵּד** *fancying himself honorable,* Pro. 12:9.

**כָּבֵד** const. **כְּבַד**, **כְּבֵד** m.—I. *heavy.*—II. *rich.*—III. *numerous.*—IV. *stupid, sullen.*—V. *grievous.*—VI. *dense.*—VII. *slow of utterance.*—VIII. *hard to be understood.*—IX. *the liver.*

**כָּבוֹד** m., lit. *heaviness:* hence,—I. *glory, splendour, majesty.* — II. *abundance, wealth.*—III. *multitude.*—IV. *mind, soul.*—V. *honour,* **כְּבוֹד יְהוָֹה** *the glory of God,* LXX. δόξα Κυρίου.

**כָּבֹד**, f. **כְּבוּדָּה** *glorious, precious.*

**כֹּבֶד** m.—I. *weight.*—II. *abundance.*

**כְּבֵדוּת** f., *heavily,* Ex. 14:25.

**כָּבָה** *was extinguished.* Pi. *extinguished.*

**כָּבוּל** p. n.—I. a district of Galilee.—II. a town in the tribe of Asher.

**כַּבּוֹן** p. n., a town in the tribe of Judah.

**כַּבִּיר, כְּבִיר;** see **כבר**.

**כֶּבֶל** root not used; (Arab. *iron fetter*)

**כֶּבֶל** m., *footlock of iron*.

**כָּבַם כֹּבֵם** part. *fuller*. Pi. כִּבֵּם, כִּבֶּם *wash, cleanse* clothes and the like, not the body. Pu. כֻּבַּם *was washed*. Hothp. inf. הֻכַּבֵּם *to be washed*, Lev. 13:55, 56.

**כבע** root not used; see קבע, נבע. כּוֹבַע, כּוֹבַע m., *helmet*.

**כָּבַר** Hiph. *multiplied*, Job 35:16; part. *abundance*, Job 36:31.

**כְּבָר** p. n. of a river in Mesopotamia, *the Chaboras*.

**כְּבָר** adv., *already, now*.

**כַּבִּיר** m., *mighty, powerful, great*.

**כְּבִיר** m., *cushion or pillow* cased with goat skin, 1 Sa. 19:13, 16.

**כְּבָרָה** f., *sieve*, Am. 9:9.

**כִּבְרָה** f., an unknown measure of length; LXX. ἱππόδρομος.

**מִכְבָּר** m., *brazen lattice-work*.

**מַכְבֵּר** m., *carpet, coarse cloth*, 2 Ki. 8:15.

**כבש** root not used; same as כָּבַשׁ *subdue*.

**כֶּבֶשׂ** m., *a lamb*.

**כַּבְשָׂה, כִּבְשָׂה** f. (pl. כְּבָשֹׂת const. כִּבְשֹׂת) *a she-lamb*.

**כָּבַשׁ** I. *trample, tread under foot*; metaph. *shall trample on sling stones*, i.e. not be harmed by them, Zec. 9:15.—II. *subdue, humble*.—III. *force*, Est. 7:8. Niph. *be subdued, humbled*. Pi. *subdued*, 2 Sa. 8:11.

**כֶּבֶשׁ** m., *footstool*, 2 Chron. 9:18.

**כִּבְשָׁן** m., *smelting furnace*.

**כַּד** jar; see כדר.

---

**כָּדַד** root not used; (perhaps from Arab. *straitness*).

**כַּד** f. (with suff. כַּדֵּךְ; pl. m. כַּדִּים) *earthen jar, water vessel*.

**כִּידוֹד** m., *spark of fire*, Job 41:11.

**כַּדְכֹּד** m., *a precious stone*, perhaps the ruby.

**כְּדָי**, see דַּי; **כְּדִי**, see דִּי; **כִּדְנָה**, see דֵּן.

**כִּידוֹר** m., *attack, onset*, Job 15:24.

**כְּדָרְלָעֹמֶר** p. n. of a king of Elam.

**כֹּה** pa.—I. *so, thus, in this form, manner*, &c.; כֹּה...כֹּה *on this manner and on that manner*, 1 Ki. 22:20.—II. *here, hither*; כֹּה...וְלֹה *hither and thither*, Ex. 2:12; עַד כֹּה *yonder*, Gen. 22:5.—III. *now*; עַד כֹּה *until now*, Ex. 7:16; עַד כֹּה וְעַד כֹּה *so and so long*, i.e. a very short time, 1 Ki. 18:45. Ch., עַד כָּה *thus far*, Dan. 7:28.

**כָּהָה** (fut. יִכְהֶה; apoc. וַתִּכְהֶ).—I. *become weak, languid* (of the eyes).—II. of the mind or person, Isa. 42:4. Pi. כֵּהָה, כִּהָה *made weak, disheartened*.

**כֵּהֶה** f. כֵּהָה.—I. *expiring, fading* (of a lamp), Isa. 42:3.—II. of the eyes.—III. of a disease or eruption.—IV. אֵין כֵּהֶה *not weak*, i.e. vigorous, Nah. 3:19.

**כֵּהוֹת** Pi. inf., from כהה.

**כְּהַל** Ch., *able, adequate*.

**כָּהַן** Pi. כִּהֵן *act, officiate as priest*.

**כֹּהֵן** m. (pl. כֹּהֲנִים) *priest*; with הַמָּשִׁיחַ or הָרֹאשׁ or הַגָּדוֹל *the high priest*.

**כָּהֵן** m. Ch., *priest*.

כְּהֻנָּה f., priesthood, office of the priest.

כּוּב p. n., a country in the south, Eze. 30:5.

כּוֹבַע helmet; see כבע.

כָּוָה. Niph. תִּכָּוֶה was, became burnt.

כַּו m. Ch., pl. כַּוִּין windows, casements, Dan. 6:11.

כְּוִיָּה f., burning, branding, Ex. 21:25.

כִּי m. (for כְּוִי) branding, Isa. 3:24.

כִּי pa.; see further.

מִכְוָה f., inflamed part (of body), Lev. 13:24, 25, 28.

כּוּחַ root not used; (Arab. conquer in battle).

כֹּחַ, כּוֹחַ m.—I. strength, vigour, power, ability.—II. wealth; כֹּחַ הָאָרֶץ fruit of the earth, Gen. 4:12.—III. a kind of lizard (from its strength), Lev. 11:30.

כּוֹכָב m., star, constellation.

כָּל measured, Isa. 40:12. Hiph. הֵכִיל I. contain.—II. sustain. Pil. כִּלְכֵּל I. contain (as a vessel).— II. sustain (with food).—III. bear (with firmness). Pu. כָּלְכַּל were sustained.

כִּימָה the constellation of the pleiades.

כּוּמָז bracelet of gold beads.

כּוּן fashioned, set in order, Job 31:15. Pil. כּוֹנֵן dispose, prepare, fix, establish, with עַל, בְּ, אֶת. Pul. כּוֹנַן established, confirmed. Hiph. הֵכִין dispose, prepare, fix, establish. Hoph. הוּכַן was disposed, prepared. Niph. be, become disposed, set in order, fixed, established (of person or thing); part. נָכוֹן (f. נְכֹנָה) firm, established, sure;

שַׁחַר נָכוֹן the true dawn, as opposed to the false, or premature twilight in the East, Hos. 6:3; אֶל־נָכוֹן certainly, for certain. Hith. הִתְכּוֹנֵן, הִכּוֹנֵן same as Niph.

כֵּן adj.—I. substantial, true; pl. כֵּנִים. —II. part. really, truly: whence, —III. as, so, thus; אַחֲרֵי־כֵן, אַחַר כֵּן afterwards; בְּכֵן thus; לָכֵן therefore; עַל־כֵּן because; לָכֵן אֲשֶׁר because; עַד־כֵּן hitherto; see also in כבן.

כֵּן Ch., thus.

אָכֵן pa. (for הָכֵן inf. abs. Hiph. confirmed), surely, certainly, truly.

כּוּן p. n., a Phenician city, 1 Chron. 18:8, called in 2 Sa. 8:8, בֵּרֹתַי Berytus.

כַּוָּן m., small round cake, Jer. 7:18; 44:19.

כִּיּוּן p.n. of an idol, Am. 5:26, called Ρεμφαν, Acts 7:43, the planet Saturn.

יָכִין I. p. n. of a son of Simeon; patron. יָכִינִי.—II. one of the columns in the temple of Solomon.

מָכוֹן m.—I. place, establishment.— II. foundation.

מְכוֹנָה f.—I. basis.—II. p. n. of a town in the tribe of Judah.

מְכוּנָה f., place, Zec. 5:11.

תְּכוּנָה f.—I. presence.—II. arrangement.—III. furniture, stores.

כּוֹס f.—I. drinking cup; pl. כֹּסוֹת.— II. rough-billed pelican, Lev. 11: 17; Deu. 14:16; Ps. 102:7.

כּוּר root not used; (Arab. digging, piercing); כָּאֲרִי piercing, Ps 22:17.

כָּר m., *camel's pack-saddle*, Gen. 31: 34 ; see also כרר.

כָּרִי an officer of a certain rank, 2 Ki. 11:4,19; כָּרֵתִי Kri, 2 Sa. 20:23.

כּוּר m., *furnace for melting metals.*

כּוּר עָשָׁן (*smoking furnace*), p. n. of a city in the tribe of Simeon.

כֹּר m., a measure of capacity, containing 10 baths.

כִּיּוֹר m. (pl. כִּיֹּרִים, כִּיֹּרוֹת).—I. *a pot* or *brazier* for fire, Zec. 12:6.— II. *laver of brass.*—III. *chafing dish*, 1 Sa. 2:14. — IV. *pulpit*, 2 Chron. 6:13.

כִּירַיִם m. dual, *pots or jars*, Lev.11:35; LXX. χυτρόποδες.

כִּכָּר f. (for כִּרְכָּר).—I. *tract of country.* — II. כִּכָּר לֶחֶם *cake of bread*; pl. m. כִּכָּרוֹת *talent* (of gold or silver); dual כִּכָּרַיִם; const. כִּכָּרֵי; pl. f. כִּכְּרֵי, כִּכָּרִים.

כִּכָּר f. Ch., pl. כִּכְּרִין the same.

מְכוֹרָה, מְכֻרָה f., *place of origin, birth*, lit. *digging*; see Isa. 51:1.

מְכֵרָה f., *sword*, Gen. 49:5.

כּוּשׁ p. n.—I. *Ethiopia.*—II. name of a man, Ps. 7:1.

כּוּשִׁי m. (pl. כּוּשִׁיִּים; f. כּוּשִׁית).—I. *an Ethiopian.*—II. p. n. of a man.

כּוּשָׁן f., Hab. 3:7, same as כּוּשׁ *Ethiopia.*

כּוּשַׁן רִשְׁעָתַיִם p. n. of a king of Mesopotamia.

כּוּשָׁרָה f., *wealth*; see כשר.

כּוּתָה, כּוּת p.n. of a region whence the kingdom of Israel was colonised after its depopulation.

כָּזָב, part. כֹּזֵב *deficient, falling short*, Ps.116:11. Pi. כִּזֵּב—I. *lie, deceive.*

—II. *fail*, with לְ or בְּ. Hiph. *convict of falsehood*, Job 24:25. Niph. *was fallacious, false.*

כָּזָב m., *falling short of truth, lying, falsehood.*

כֹּזְבָא p.n., same as כָּזִיב.

כָּזְבִּי p.n. of a Midianitish woman.

כְּזִיב p. n. of a town in the tribe of Judah.

אַכְזָב m.,*deficient, deception, unstable*

אַכְזִיב p.n.—I. a town in the tribe of Judah.—II. a town in the tribe of Asher, on the Mediterranean. Ἐκδιππα.

כָּזַר root not used; (Arab. *muddy turbid*).

אַכְזָר m., *untractable, cruel, fierce.*

אַכְזָרִי *very cruel.*

אַכְזְרִיּוּת f., *great cruelty*, Pro. 27:4.

כֹּחַ *strength*; see כוח.

כָּחַד. Pi. כִּחֵד *keep back, conceal*, with מִן or לְ. Niph. I. *was concealed.*—II. *made useless, destroyed.* Hiph. I. *hold back.*—II. *bring to nought.*

כָּחַל *black* (the eyes) *with antimony*, Eze. 23:40.

כָּחַשׁ *fail, be deficient.* Pi. כִּחֵשׁ I. *withhold.*—II. *fail, deceive, deny, lie*, with בְּ and לְ. Niph. and Hith. *were, became liars*, with לְ.

כַּחַשׁ m.—I. *deficiency.*—II. *failure, falsehood.*

כֶּחָשׁ m., *lying*, Isa. 30:9.

כִּי pa.—I. *if, for*, at the beginning of a speech.—II. *because, therefore*, in the second member of a sentence: also,— III. *surely, without doubt*

It connects the hypothesis and condition of an entire sentence, and may be translated by almost any particle that is so used; הֲכִי whether? is not? עַל כִּי, יַעַן כִּי because; עַד כִּי until; כִּי עַל־כֵּן therefore; see also כֵּנָה.

כִּי אִם I. that.—II. if not, with oaths. —III. except, after a negative.— IV. but, only.

כִּיד m., ruin, destruction, Job 21:20.

כִּידוֹן m.—I. spear.—II. גֵּן כִּידוֹן (the plain of spears), p. n. of a district; see נָכוֹן.

כִּידוֹד sparks; see כדד.

כִּידוֹר attack; see כרר.

כִּיּוּן an idol; see כון.

כִּיּוֹר pot; see כור.

כִּלְי, בֵּילַי vessel; see נבל.

כִּלָּפוֹת axes; see כלף.

כִּימָה Pleiades; see כום.

כִּים bag; see נכם.

כִּיר pot; see כור.

כִּיתָרוֹן Syr. for פִּיתָרוֹן.

כָּכָה same as כֹּה thus; אֵיכָכָה how? see אֵיךְ in אֵי.

כִּכָּר, see כור.

כָּל, כֹּל all; see כלל.

כָּלָא restrain, confine, withhold (part. כָּלוּא, כָּלֻא shut up), with מִן; fut. יִכְלָה. Niph. restrained, withholden.

כֶּלֶא m. (with suff. כִּלְאוֹ), prison; בֵּית הַכֶּלֶא, בֵּית כֶּלֶא the same; pl. בָּתֵּי כְלָאִים.

כִּלָּה, כֶּלֶה f., all that, from כֹּל; see כלל.

כִּלְאַיִם dual, of two sorts or kinds, ἑτερογενῆ.

כֶּלֶא (כְּלִיא) m., prison.

מִכְלָה f. (pl. מִכְלָאוֹת), fold or pen for flocks.

כִּלְאָב p. n. of a son of David.

כְּלוּב m.—I. fruit-basket, Am. 8:1,2. —II. bird-cage, Jer. 5:27.—III. p. n. of a man.

כֶּלֶב m.—I. a dog.—II. bad, cruel man.

כָּלֵב p. n. of a man, Caleb; patron. כָּלִבִּי.

כָּלָה (fut. תִּכְלָה, יִכְלֶה; apoc. יִכֶל (וַתֵּכַל).—I. was completed, finished —II. was wasted, ruined, decayed. Pi. כִּלָּה I. complete, determine.— II. waste, ruin, destroy, with לְ. Pu. כֻּלָּה (fut. יְכֻלָּה), were completed.

כָּלָה, f. כָּלָה consuming, Deu. 28:32.

כָּלָה f., completion, destruction; עָשָׂה כָּלָה hath done even to destruction, altogether, with אֶת, בְּ; adv. כָּלָה, לְכָלָה completely, entirely.

כְּלִי m. (with pause כֶּלִי; pl. כֵּלִים, כְּלֵי).—I. vessel.—II. boat, Isa. 18:2.—III. musical instrument.—IV. arms, weapon.—V. implement of husbandry.—VI. clothing.

כְּלָיוֹת const., כִּלְיוֹת f. pl., the reins, kidneys, metaph. as the seat of sense, the feeling.

כִּלָּיוֹן const., כִּלְיוֹן m.—I. consumption, Isa. 10:22.—II. wasting of the eyes, Deu. 28:65.

כִּלְיוֹן p. n. of a man.

מִכְלֻלוֹת f. pl., with זָהָב, 2 Chron. 4:21. pure gold.

תִּכְלָה f., perfection; LXX. συντέλεια.

תַּכְלִית f.—I. extremity, Neh. 3:21.— II. boundary. — III. completeness perfection.

כְּלָה, פְּלִלוֹת; see כלל.

פְּלֻהִי p. n. of a man.

כֻּלְּהֶם for כֻּלָּם, from כֹּל; see כלל.

כֻּלְּהֶנָה for כֻּלָּנָה, from כֹּל; see כלל.

כָלוּ 1 Sa. 6:10, Kal pret. pl., from כלא.

כֶּלַח m.—I. wealth.—II. insolence, Job 30:2.

כֶּלַח p. n. of a city, Gen. 10:11.

כְּלִי, כִּלְיוֹת, כִּלְיָן; see כלה.

כִּלְכָּל p. n. of a man.

כָּלַל perfected, Eze. 27:4, 11.

כְּלַל Ch., finished, completed; Shaph. שַׁכְלֵל the same; passive אִשְׁתַּכְלַל was completed.

כָּלִיל m.—I. whole, entire; adv. wholly, entirely; כְּלִיל הָעִיר the whole city.—II. whole burnt-offering, i.e. offering entirely consumed, Deu. 33:10; Ps. 51:21.

כַּלָּה f.—I. daughter-in-law.—II. spouse.

כְּלוּלוֹת f. pl., espousals, Jer. 2:2.

כֹּל (כּוּל) Jer. 33:8;—I. the whole, all.—II. complete, entire.—III. all, every.—IV. many, most of; לֹא כֹל none: with suff. כֻּלָּנוּ all we; כֻּלְּכֶם all ye; כֻּלָּם, כֻּלָּהֶם all they; כֻּלְּהֶנָה, כֻּלָּנָה all they, f.; כֻּלּוֹ all of it, m., כֻּלָּהּ the same, f.; with adv. כָּל־עֻמַּת שֶׁ as long as, just as, Ecc. 5:15.

כֹּל, כָּל Ch., the same; כֹּלָּא adv., altogether, entirely.

מִכְלָל m., perfection, Ps. 50:2.

מִכְלוֹל m., the same (of clothing), Eze. 23:12, &c.

מִכְלָלִים m. pl., splendid garments, Eze. 27:24.

כָּלַם. Hiph. הִכְלִים, הָכְלִים put to

shame, make ashamed, injure. Hoph. was ashamed, confounded. Niph. was ashamed, confounded.

כְּלִמָּה f., shame, ignominy.

כְּלִמּוּת state of shame, Jer. 23:40.

כַּלְמָד p. n. of a region or city.

כַּלְנֵה, כַּלְנֶה, כַּלְנוֹ p. n. of a city on the river Tigris (Ctesiphon?).

כָּלַף root not used; (Arab. drove).

כִּלַּפּוֹת f. pl., axes or hammer, Ps. 74:6; LXX. λαξευτήρια.

כִּלָּתוּ Pi. pret. 3. pers. f. with suff., from כלה.

כְּלִתַנִי 1 Sa. 25:33, Kal pret. 2. pers. f. with suff., from כלא.

כָּמַהּ desired intensely even to fainting.

כְּמָהָם p. n. of a man.

כַּמָּה, כַּמֶּה, כְּמָה; see מָה.

כְּמוֹ, כְּמוֹ pa., same as כְּ thus, as, whether; with suff. כָּמוֹנִי as I am, כָּמֹכָה, כָּמוֹךָ as thou art, כָּמֹהוּ as he is; כָּמוֹהָ as she is; כָּמוֹנוּ as we are, sometimes for כָּכֶם, כָּהֶם; כְּמוֹכֶם, כְּמוֹהֶם as ye, they, are; כְּמוֹ...כְּמוֹ as...so.

כְּמוֹשׁ p. n., an idol of the children of Moab and Ammon; עַם כְּמוֹשׁ the Moabites.

כַּמֹּן m., the herb cummin, Isa. 28: 25, 27.

מִכְמַנִּים m. pl., treasures, Dan. 11:43.

כָּמַס laid, treasured, up, Deu. 32:34.

כָּמַר. Niph. נִכְמַר I. was affected (warmed with intense feeling, love, compassion).— II. was black with burning, Lam. 5:10.

כֹּמֶר m., pl. כְּמָרִים idolatrous priests.

כַּמְרִיר blackest, gloomiest thing, Job 3:5.

מַכְמֹר, מִכְמָר m., pl. מַכְמֹרִים net used by fishermen.

מִכְמֶרֶת, מִכְמֹרֶת f., net used by fisher-men.

כֵּן; see כּוּן and כָּנַן.

כָּנָה Kal not used; (Syr. named). Pi. כִּנָּה I. call by name.—II. flatter.

כְּנָת m. (man of the same name), companion, associate; pl. כְּנָוֹת (σύνδουλοι).

כְּנָת Ch., the same; pl. כְּנָוָן; with suff. כְּנָוָתְהֹ, כְּנָוָתְהֹון.

כַּנָּה; see כנן.

כַּגֵּד p. n. of a city (perhaps for כַּלְנֵה).

כִּנּוֹר m. (with suff. כִּנֹּרִי; pl. כִּנֹּרִים, כִּנֹּרוֹת), harp (κινύρα).

כִּנָּוֹת, כִּנָּוֹת from כְּנָת; see כנה.

כָּנְיָהוּ p. n. of a king of Judah; same as יְהוֹיָכִין.

כַּנֹּתֶךָ Hiph. inf. with pref. and suff. for כְּהַנְלֹתֶךָ; see נלה.

כָּנָּם; see כנן.

כְּנָאמָא Ch., "as it is said" (for Lee).

כַּנָּה f., stock, root, Ps. 80:16.

כְּנָנִי p. n. of a man.

כְּנָנְיָהוּ, כְּנַנְיָה p.n. of a man.

כְּנָנְיָהוּ p. n. of a man.

כֵּן m. (with suff. כַּנֹּו, כַּנֶּךָ.—I. place, station.—II. base, foot of the laver; see also כּוּן.

כֵּן m., lice; pl. כִּנִּים LXX. σκνίφες.

כִּנָּם for כַּנָּם same as כִּנִּים; see pre-ceding word, Ex. 8:12.

כָּנַס collect, gather together. Pi. like Kal. Hith. being collecting, com-prehending, Isa. 28:20.

---

מִכְנָם m., dual const. מִכְנְסֵי drawers, breeches of linen (for the priests).

כָּנַע. Hiph. הִכְנִיעַ humble, debase, bring down. Niph. נִכְנַע was hum-bled, debased.

כִּנְעָה f., package, bale of merchan-dise, Jer. 10:17.

כְּנַעַן I. p. n. of a son of Ham.—II. of the land inhabited by his pos terity.—III. m., a merchant.

כְּנַעֲנִי (f. כְּנַעֲנִיָה; pl. כְּנַעֲנִים.—I. a Canaanite.—II. a merchant.

כְּנַעֲנָה p. n. of a man.

כְּנַעֲיָה pl. with suff., from כְּנַעַן.

כָּנַף root not used; (Arab. put away). Niph. יִכָּנֵף put away, remove, Isa. 30:2.

כָּנָף f. (dual כְּנָפַיִם f.; pl. const. כַּנְפֵי כַּנְפוֹת m. and f.).—I. wing (of a bird, &c.).—II. wing (of an army). —III. skirt (of a garment).—IV. extreme part (of the earth or land). —V. by meton. person protected, i. e. wife &c.

כִּנֶּרֶת, כִּנְּרוֹת, כִּנְּרוֹת p. n., a city in the tribe of Naphtali, near the sea of Galilee (Γεννησαρέτ); יָם כִּנֶּרֶת the sea of Galilee.

כְּנַשׁ Ch., collect, Dan. 3:2. Hith. being assembled, Dan. 3:3, 27.

כַּסְדָּי Ch., same as כַּשְׂדִּי a Chaldean.

כָּסָה, part. כֹּסֶה covering, concealing, Pro. 12:16, 23; כָּסֻי covered, Nu. 4:6, 14. Niph. נִכְסָה being co-vered, concealed. Pi. כִּסָּה cover, conceal, with אֶל, אֵת, בְּ, לְ, עַל. Pu. כֻּסָּה, כֻּסָּה covered, was co-vered, with בְּ. Hith. same as Niph. Pu. with בְּ.

כֵּם m., כֵּ׳ יָהּ the throne of Jehovah, Ex. 17:16.

כָּסֶה, כֵּסֶא m., the new moon, Ps. 81:4; Pro. 7:20.

כִּסֵּא, כִּסֵּה m. (with suff. כִּסְאִי; pl. כִּסְאוֹת), regal chair, throne.

כְּסוּת f.—I. covering.—II. clothing.

סוּת f., a false reading for כְּסוּת garments, Gen. 49:11.

כְּסָתוֹת f. pl., Eze. 13:18, 20, LXX. προσκεφάλαια, cushions, probably ornaments.

מִכְסֶה m., covering.

מְכַסֶּה m., covering, Isa. 14:11.

כָּסַח, part. כָּסוּחַ cut off.

כַּסּוּחָה like filth, Isa. 5 : 25 ; see סוּחַ.

כָּסַל was a fool; fut. יִכְסְלוּ Jer. 10:8.

כְּסִיל m.—I. a fool.—II. the constellation Orion.—III. p. n. of a city in the tribe of Judah.

כְּסִילוּת f., foolish woman, Pro. 9:13.

כֶּסֶל m.—I. the loins.—II. the viscera; pl. כְּסָלִים.—III. expectation, confidence.—IV. foolishness.

כִּסְלָה f.—I. confidence.—II. folly.

כִּסְלֵו m., the ninth month of the Hebrew year, answering to our November and December.

כְּסָלוֹן p. n. of a town on the borders of the tribe of Judah.

כִּסְלוֹן p. n. of a man.

כְּסָלוֹת p. n. of a town in the tribe of Issachar.

כִּסְלוֹת־תָּבוֹר p. n. of a town at the foot of Mount Tabor.

כַּסְלֻחִים m. pl., p. n. a people so called.

כָּסַם adorn, Eze. 44:20.

כֻּסֶּמֶת f., a kind of corn, spelt, ζέα; pl. כֻּסְּמִים.

כָּסַם apportion, divide out, Ex. 12:4.

מֶכֶס m., fractional part, number.

מִכְסָה f., number.

כָּסַף desired intensely (lit. grew pale with desire), with לְ. Niph. become desirous, earnestly longing for, with לְ.

כֶּסֶף m. (with suff. כַּסְפִּי; pl. כְּסָפִים). —I. silver.—II. money; with numerals, the shekel of silver; אֶלֶף כ׳ 1,000 shekels.

כְּסַף m. Ch., silver.

כַּסְפְּיָא p. n. of a country.

כְּסָתוֹת ornaments; see כסה.

כִּסְּתַנִי Pi. pret. 3 pers. f. with suff., from כסה.

כְּעַן adv. Ch.—I. so, therefore.—II. but. —III. now; כְּעֶנֶת so on; see עתה.

כָּעַס (fut. יִכְעַס).—I. was angry.—II irritated. Pi. כִּעֵס irritate. Hiph הִכְעִיס.—I. was angry.—II. made angry, irritated.

כַּעַס m.—I. vexation, sadness.—II. anger; pl. כְּעָסִים excitements to anger.

כַּעַשׂ m., the same, in Job only.

כַּפָּה, כַּפּוֹת כַּף; see כפף.

כֵּף rock, Job 30:6; Jer. 4:29.

כִּפָּה avert, appease, Pro. 21:14; see כבה.

כְּפִירָה, כְּפִיר, כְּפוֹר see כפר.

כָּפַל doubled; part. כָּפוּל. Niph. be repeated, Eze. 21:19.

כֶּפֶל m., doubling, twofold; dual כִּפְלָיִם Job 11:6; Isa. 40:2.

כָּפַן became languid, Eze. 17:7.

כָּפָן m., hunger, Job 5:22; 30:3.

**כָּפַס** (Syr. *tie, join*).

**כָּפִיס** m., *tie-beam*; "*tenon*" (Lee); LXX. κάνθαρος.

**כָּפַף** *bend, bow down*, with distress. Niph. *bow myself down*, with לְ *before*, Mic. 6:6.

**כַּף** f.—I. *palm of the hand*.—II. *hand* (with suff. כַּפִּי; dual כַּפַּיִם *both hands*; pl. כַּפּוֹת).—III. *sole of the foot*.—IV. *foot of a beast*.—V. *bason* or *phial*.—VI. *receptacle for the stone in a sling*; כַּף־הַקֶּלַע *cup of the sling*, 1 Sa. 25:29.—VII. *bent palm branches*; כַּפּוֹת תְּמָרִים *bent palm branches*, Lev. 23:40.—VIII. כַּף־הַיָּרֵךְ *cup of the thigh joint*, Gen. 32:26, &c.

**כִּפָּה** f., *curved branch, branch*.

**כָּפַר**—I. generally *cover*.—II. specially, *pitch, smear with pitch*, Gen. 6:14, with בְּ. Pi. כִּפֶּר (fut. יְכַפֵּר) I. *cover, expiate for sin*, used of the sinner and the sin.—II. *appease anger*.—III. *avert calamity*, with עַל, לְ, בְּעַד, אֶת. Pu.—I. כֻּפַּר *was expiated*.—II. *was abolished*. Hith. *was expiated*; נִתְכַּפֵּר for נִכַּפֵּר Deu. 21:8.

**כְּפוֹר** m.—I. *vessel, covered cup*.—II. *hoar frost*, Ex. 16:14; Ps. 147:16.

**כְּפִיר** m.—I. *a young lion*.—II. metaph. *fierce, bold man*.—III. *village*, Neh. 6:2.

**כָּפָר** m., *village*.

**כְּפִירָה** p. n. of a city of the Hivites.

**כְּפַר הָעַמּוֹנִי** p. n., a town in the tribe of Benjamin.

**כֹּפֶר** m.—I. *pitch*, Gen. 6:14.—II. *a village*, 1 Sa. 6:18.—III. *expiation*,

lit. *covering for sin*, λύτρον.—IV. the *cypress tree*, Cant. 1:14

**כִּפֻּרִים** m. pl., *expiation*.

**כַּפֹּרֶת** f., the *covering of the ark*; *mercy-seat*; בֵּית הַכַּפֹּרֶת the *holy of holies*.

**כָּפַשׁ** Hiph. *overwhelmed, covered* Lam. 3:16.

**כְּפַת** Ch., *bound, tied*.

**כַּפְתּוֹר** p. n., a country of the Philistines; כַּפְתֹּרִים its inhabitants, Gen. 10:14.

**כַּפְתֹּרִים** m. pl.—I. *twisted capitals* or *columns*.—II. *ornamented bowls* of the golden candlestick, Ex. 25:36.

**כַּר**, see כּוּר; **כַּר**, see כּוּר and כָּרַר.

**כְּרָא** or **כְּרָה** Ch. Ithp. *was pained, afflicted*.

**כִּרְבֵּל** Pu. part. מְכֻרְבָּל *equipped clothed*, 1 Chron. 15:27.

**כַּרְבְּלָא** Ch., *a cloak*, Dan. 3:21.

**כָּרָה** *dig* (as a well, pit); with אָזְנַיִם *mine ears hast thou digged, opened*, Ps. 40:7. Niph. I. *was dug*.—II. *buy, purchase*, Deu. 2:6; Hos. 3:2.—III. *feast*, 2 Ki. 6:23.

**כֵּרָה** f.—I. *digging*, Zep. 2:6; pl. const. כָּרֹת.—II. *feast*, 2 Ki. 6:23.

**מִכְרֶה** m., *pit*, Zep. 2:9.

**כְּרוּב** m., pl. כְּרֻבִים, כְּרוּבִים—I. *cherub*; a symbolical figure over the mercy-seat; described Eze. 4:6.—II. p. n. of a man, Ezr. c. 2; Neh. c. 7.

**כְּרַז** Ch. Aph. *proclaim*, κηρύσσειν, Dan. 5:29.

**כָּרוֹז** m. Ch., *herald*, Dan. 3:4.

פְּרִי; see כָּגר.

פְּרִיתוּת, כְּרִית; see כרת.

כַּרְכֹּב m. (with suff. כַּרְכֻּבּוֹ) *brazier* (on the grating of the altar for containing the fire).

תַּכְרִיךְ m., *robe*, Est. 8:15.

כַּרְכְּמִישׁ p. n. of a city on the Euphrates, *Carchemish* (Κιρκήσιον).

כַּרְכֹּם m., *saffron*, Cant. 4:14.

כַּרְכַּס p. n. a Persian eunuch.

כִּרְכָּרוֹת; see כרר.

כֶּרֶם m. (f. Isa. 27:2, 3).—I. *vineyard.* —II. *olive yard.*—III. *orchard.*

כֹּרֵם m., *vine-dresser.*

כַּרְמִי p. n. of a man.

כַּרְמֶל m. (quasi כֶּרֶם־אֵל; with suff. כַּרְמִלּוֹ).—I. *well-cultivated plain, or-chard, field.*—II. *Carmel,* a very fruit-ful hill south of Asher, near the Me-diterranean; כַּרְמְלִי m.; כַּרְמְלִית f., *a Carmelite.*— III. גֶּרֶשׂ כַּרְמֶל and כַּרְמֶל *first fruits* (of the most fertile land), Lev. 2:14; 23:14.

כַּרְמִיל m., *crimson.*

כְּרָן p. n. of a man.

כָּרְסֵא m. Ch., same as כִּסֵּא *throne.*

כִּרְסֵב quadrilit. *devoured*, Ps. 80:14.

כָּרַע.—I. *bent his legs* (as an animal to lie down).—II. *bowed, lay down, crouched* (with לְ or לִפְנֵי before any one).—III. *was weak.* Hiph. *cause to bow down, depress, afflict.* כְּרָעַיִם f. dual, *both the legs* or *leg bones.*

כַּרְפַּס m., *cotton cloth, calico,* Est. 1: 6; (Arab. the same).

כָּרַר. Pil. כִּרְכֵּר *leap about, dance,* 2 Sa. 6:14, 16´

כַּר m. (p. כָּרִים).—I. *fatted lamb.*— II. *the pasture where lambs feed.* —III. *battering ram.*

כִּרְכָּרוֹת f. pl., *dromedaries,* Isa. 66:20.

כָּרֵשׂ m., *belly,* Jer. 51:34.

כֹּרֶשׁ p. n., *Cyrus* king of Persia.

כַּרְשְׁנָא p. n., a Persian prince.

כָּרַת (imp. כְּרָת־; with ה parag כָּרְתָה; fut. יִכְרֹת).—I. *cut off, down;* כָּרוּת and שָׁפְכָה כְּרוּת *eunuch.*— II. with or without בְּרִית *make a covenant* (ὅρκια τέμνειν), (lit. strike a bargain), with אֶת, עִם, לְ.—III. *kill men,* Jer. 11:19. Niph. *was cut down, cut off.* Pu. כֹּרַת, כָּרַת *cut off.* Hiph. הִכְרִית *cut off, destroy.* Hoph. הָכְרַת *was cut off,* Joel 1:9.

כְּרֻתוֹת f. pl., *beams* (things cut).

כְּרִית p. n. of the brook *Cherith,* which falls into the Jordan not far from Samaria.

כְּרִיתֻת, כְּרִיתֻת f., *divorce;* with סֵפֶר *bill of divorce.*

כְּרֵתִי p. n.—I. a tribe of the Phi-listir es of the south west coast of Judea, derived from the Island of *Crete.*—II. title of certain brave soldiers in David's army.

כֶּשֶׂב m., same as כֶּבֶשׂ *lamb.*

כִּשְׂבָּה *female-lamb.*

כֶּשֶׂד p. n., a son of Nahor; the pro-genitor of the Chaldees.

כַּשְׂדִּים pl.—I. *Chaldees,* inhabitants of Babylon.—II. *astrologer.*

כַּשְׂדָּי m. Ch., a *Chaldee.*

כָּשָׂה *covered with fat,* Deu. 32:15´

**כָּשַׁל** (fut. יִכְשׁוֹל).—I. *totter, stagger.*
—II. *stumble.*—III. *stumble to fall*
(part. כּוֹשֵׁל *weak, weary*), with בְּ.
Niph. נִכְשַׁל *be tottering from
weakness.* Pi. and Hiph. I. *cause
to stumble.*—II. *fail, become weak.*
Hoph. part. מָכְשָׁלִים *made to
stumble,* Jer. 18:23.

**כָּשִׁיל** m., *an axe,* Ps. 74:6.

**כִּשָּׁלוֹן** m., *ruin,* Pro. 16:18.

**מִכְשׁוֹל** m.—I. *offence, delusion.*—II.
σκάνδαλον, *cause of offence, place,
instrument* or *cause of sin.*

**מַכְשֵׁלָה** f., *fall, ruin,* Isa. 3:6; Zep.
1:3.

**כָּשַׁף** Pi. כִּשֵּׁף *used witchcraft,* 2 Ch.
33:6; part. מְכַשֵּׁף *magician, wi-
zard;* מְכַשֵּׁפָה *witch.*

**כַּשָּׁף** m., *magician,* Jer. 27:9.

**כְּשָׁפִים** m. pl., *magical rites, incan-
tations.*

**כָּשֵׁר** *do well, be acceptable,* Est. 8:5;
Ecc. 11:6. Hiph. *give prosperity,*
Ecc. 10:10.

**כִּשְׁרוֹן** f., pl. כִּשְׁרוֹת *great prosperity,
wealth,* Ps. 68:7.

**כִּשְׁרוֹן** *prosperity, profit,* Ecc. 5:10.

**כִּישׁוֹר** m., *distaff,* Pro. 31:19.

**כָּתַב** I. *write, engrave,* with בְּ, עַל
אֶל before the material written
upon; with עַל, אֶל, לְ before the
person to whom the writing was
addressed. Niph. *was written.* Pi.
*wrote,* Isa. 10:1.

**כְּתַב** Ch., *he wrote.*

**כְּתָב** m.—I. *writing.*—II. *epistle.*—
III. *record.*—IV. *Scripture.*

**כְּתָב** m. Ch., *writing, edict.*

**כְּתֹבֶת** f., *writing,* Lev. 19:28.

**מִכְתָּב** m.—I. *writing.*—II. *epistle,
ordinance* (thing written).

**כִּתִּיִּים**, כִּתִּים p.n. the *Chittim,* probably the inhabitants of Cyprus
and of some part of Asia Minor.

**כָּתִית** *beaten small;* see כתה.

**כֹּתֶל** m., *wall,* Cant. 2:9.

**כְּתַל** m. Ch., *wall;* pl. emph. כָּתְלַיָּא
Dan. 5:5.

**כִּתְלִישׁ** p.n. of a town in the tribe of
Judah.

**כָּתַם** Kal not used; (Arab. *treasure
up*). Niph. נִכְתָּם *treasured up,* or
as some interpret, *embroidered with
gold;* see the next word, Jer.
2:22.

**כֶּתֶם** m., *the purest gold.*

**מִכְתָּם** m., *Michtam,* a word of uncertain meaning, occurring in the
titles of Psalms 16, 56—60, probably the name of the tune or air
to which they were sung.

**כֻּתֹּנֶת, כְּתֹנֶת** (with suff. כֻּתָּנְתִּי;
pl. כֻּתֳּנוֹת; const. כָּתְנוֹת), *garment,
shirt,* χιτών.

**כָּתֵף** const. כֶּתֶף f.—I. *shoulder* (with
suff. כְּתֵפִי; pl. כְּתֵפִים).—II. *side*
(of a building, the sea, a town);
pl. כְּתֵפוֹת; const. כִּתְפוֹת; with
suff. כְּתֵפָיו *sides, jambs of doors,*
Eze. 41:2, 26.— III. *shoulders of
axles, pivots,* 1 Ki. 7:30, 34.

**כָּתַר** Pi. כִּתֵּר *surround, encompass.*
Hiph. I. *surround, come about.*—
II. *comprehend.*

**כֶּתֶר** m., *diadem, crown.*

**כֹּתֶרֶת** f. (pl. כֹּתָרוֹת), *cincture,
capital of a column.*

כָּתַשׁ break, bruise.

מַכְתֵּשׁ m.—I. mortar, Pro. 27:22.—II. p. n. of a place, Jud. 15:19; Zep. 1:11.

כָּתַת (fut. יִכֹּת; imp. pl. כֹּתּוּ).—I. break to pieces (as a vessel, &c.).—II. beat out (as iron).—III. beat down (as enemies); part. כָּתוּת θλαδίας, eunuch. Pi. כִּתֵּת same as Kal. Pu. was broken. Hiph. (fut. יַכְתּוּ) defeat. Hoph. (fut. יֻכַּתּוּ) pounded to dust.

כָּתִית m., fine, pure oil.

מְכִתָּה f., breaking, Isa. 30:14.

## ל

ל insep. pa.—I. to, towards.—II. at, in.—III. till, until.—IV. in order to, for the purpose of.—V. for, belonging to, with respect to: לְהֵן therefore; לָכֵן so, thus, therefore; לָמֶּה why? When joined with subs. and adjs. it sometimes admits of being translated adverbially: לְשֶׁקֶר falsely; לְצֶדֶק justly. It is also used in a sense allied to that of the Arab. ل, and very foreign to the idiom of any European language: e.g. וַיִּקַּח לְיִרְמְיָהוּ he took hold on Jeremiah, Jer. 40:2, where it is equivalent to אֶת; probably it corroborates the meaning like the Arabic. With suff. לִי; לָנוּ, לָהּ, לוֹ, (לְכִי) לָךְ, (לְכָה) לָךְ; לָמוֹ, לָהֶן, לָהֶם; לָהֵנָּה, לָכֶם, see מִן. ל Ch., to, in order to, &c., like the Hebrew.

לֹא sometimes לוֹא not, no; לֹא כֹל no one, none; לֹא אִישׁ no one; לֹא דָבָר nothing, used for בְּלֹא without, and הֲלֹא is it? with pref. בְּלֹא without, there is none; הֲלֹא is it not? ἰδού; לְלֹא without; לֹא...גַּם not even.

לָא, לָה Ch., not, nothing.

לָהֵן Ch., therefore, on that account (see ל), for לָא הֵן unless. לָכֵן therefore (see ל), for לָא כֵן but if. לוֹ דְבָר p. n., a town in Gilead. לֹא עַמִּי (not my people) mystic name given to the prophet Hosea, Hos. 1:9.

לָאָב (Arab. thirsted).

תַּלְאֻבוֹת, תַּלְאָבוֹת thirst, drought, Hos. 13.5.

לְהַאְדִיב for לְהַאְדִיב Hiph. inf. with pref., from אדב.

לָאָה I. be weary, faint, Job 4:2, 5.—II. be vexed, Gen. 19:11. Niph. נִלְאָה I. become weary, faint.—II. was vexed.—III. dislike. Hiph. הֶלְאָה I. make weary.—II. vex.—III. ruin.

לֵאָה p. n., Leah, one of Jacob's wives.

תְּלָאָה f., weariness, trouble, vexation.

לָאוֹר for לְהָאוֹר Niph. inf. with pref., from אור.

לָאַט same as לוּט vail, cover the face, 2 Sa. 19:5; see also לָאַט, אַט in לָאַט.

לָאַט same as לָט, בַּלָּאַט secretly, Jud. 4:21.

לָאַךְ root not used; (Ethiop. he sent ministered).

מַלְאָךְ m.—I. messenger.—II. angel (messenger of God).—III. the Word of God, Jesus Christ, Ex. 23:20, seq., &c.—IV. *prophet.*—V. *priest.*

מַלְאָךְ m. Ch., *angel.*

מְלָאכָה f. (const. מְלֶאכֶת; with suff. מְלַאכְתּוֹ; pl. const. מַלְאֲכוֹת).—I. *ministry.*—II. *work.*—III. *making, acquisition, wealth.*—IV. *flocks.*

מַלְאֲכוּת f., *message, embassy,* Hag. 1:13.

מַלְאָכִי p.n., *Malachi,* the prophet, Μαλαχίας.

לָאֵל p.n. of a man.

לְאֹם (Arab. *assemblage*).

לְאֹם m.(with suff. לְאֻמִּי; pl. לְאֻמִּים).—I. *family, tribe, nation.*—II. לְאֻמִּים p.n. of a people, Αλλουμαιῶται, Gen. 25:3.

לֵב, לֵב־ (with suff. לִבִּי; pl. לִבּוֹת)

לֵבָב (const. לְבַב; with suff. לְבָבִי; לְבַבְכֶם; pl. לְבָבוֹת) m.—I. *the heart of man or beast.*—II. *the seat of thought, affection,* &c., *in man;* בְּלֵב וָלֵב *with a double heart,* i.e. *deceitful,* Ps. 12:3.—III. *the middle or interior of any thing.*

לְבַב, לֵב m. Ch., *heart, mind,* as Heb.

לֵבָב Niph. *take heart, be bold, daring,* Job 11:12. Pi. לִבֵּב *give heart, encourage,* Cant. 4:9; see also in לְבִיבָה.

לִבָּה f., *heart, mind,* as לֵב.

לְבִיבָה f., pl. לְבִיבוֹת *pancakes* made of fine wheaten flour. Pi. לִבֵּב *he made such pancakes,* 2 Sa. 13:6—10, only.

לַבָּה for לֶהָבָה *flame,* Ex. 3:2.

לְבִיא, לְבָאוֹת; see לָבִיא.

לְבַד *alone;* see בַּד, בָּדָד.

לָבַט. Niph. נִלְבַּט *stumbled, fell,* Pro. 10:8, 10; Hos. 4:14.

לָבִיא *lioness;* perhaps also *lion.*

לָבִי m., pl. m. לְבָאִים.—I. *lions;* t לְבָאוֹת *lionesses.*—II. p. n. of town in the tribe of Simeon.

לְבִיָּא f., *lioness.*

לְבִיבוֹת; see in לֵב.

לָבַן (from לְבֵנָה) *make bricks,* Gen. 11:3. Hiph.—I. *was white, pure.*—II. *made white, clean,* Dan. 11:35. Hithp. *shall become white, clean,* Dan. 12:10.

לָבָן m.—I. *white.*—II. p. n., *Laban,* the father-in-law of Jacob.—III. a place in the desert.

לְבָנָה f.—I. *the moon* (from her whiteness).—II. p. n. of a man.

לָבָן, לְבֶן m., *white.*

לִבְנֶה m., *the white poplar.*

לְבָנָה f.—I. *whiteness, clearness,* Ex. 24:10.—II. p. n., a city in the tribe of Judah.—III. a station of Israel in the desert.

לְבֵנָה f. (pl. לְבֵנִים) *brick* or *tile.*

לְבוֹנָה f.—I. *pure frankincense,* λίβανος.—II. p. n. of a town near Shiloh.

הַלְּבָנוֹן, לְבָנוֹן p.n., *Mount Lebanon;* so called from the whiteness of the snow on its eastern peak.

לִבְנִי p.n. of a man.

מַלְבֵּן m., *brick kiln.*

לָבַשׁ, לָבֵשׁ (fut. יִלְבַּשׁ).—I. *put on clothing, cloak;* part. לָבוּשׁ *clothed*—II. used metaphorically for the possession of certain qualities, as *clothed with, glory, justice,* &c.,

*covered with flocks* (as a pasture); with many others. Pu. מְלֻבָּשִׁים *clothed.* — Hiph. I. *clothe, invest,* with עַל. — II. *cover* (as the sky with clouds).

לְבֵשׁ Ch., *clothe.* Aph. the same.

לְבֵשׁ, לְבוּשׁ m., *upper* or *outer garment, cloak.*

מַלְבּוּשׁ m., the same.

תִּלְבֹּשֶׁת f., the same.

לַבַּת, Ex. 3:2, for לַהֲבַת const., from לֶהָבָה.

לֹג m., *the log,* a liquid measure containing 24.3 solid inches.

לֹד p. n., a town in the tribe of Benjamin, *Lydda.*

לֵדָה Kal inf., from יָלַד.

לֶדֶת Kal inf., from יָלַד.

לְדִתְּנָה Kal inf. with suff. and ה parag., from יָלַד.

לָהַב root not used; (Arab. *tongue of fire, flame*).

לַהַב m. — I. *flame.* — II. *glitter* of a sword or other weapon. — III. the weapon itself.

לֶהָבָה f., *flame;* pl. לְהָבוֹת; const. לַהֲבוֹת; s. const. לַבַּת, Ex. 3:2.

לֶהָבֶת f., the same.

שַׁלְהֶבֶת *flame, destruction, fire.*

לְהָבִים same as לוּבִים *the Lybians,* Gen. 10:13.

לָהַג root not used; (Arab. *intense occupation*).

לַהַג m., *much study,* Ecc. 12:12.

לָהַד p. n. of a man.

לָהָה (fut. וַתֵּלַהּ) same as לָאָה *was faint, feeble,* Gen. 47:13.

לָהָה. Hithp. part. מִתְלַהְלֵהַּ *insane, mad person,* Pro. 26:18.

לָהַט *flaming,* Ps. 104:4; part. לֹהֲטִים *inflamed* (i.e. *furious*) *men,* Ps. 57:5. Pi. לִהֵט *set on fire, inflame.*

לַהַט m., *flame,* Gen. 3:24.

לְהָטִים lit. *flames:* hence, *dazzlings, delusions,* Ex. 7:11.

לָהַם. Hith. part. מִתְלַהֲמִים *enchanting, fascinating things, dainties,* Pro. 18:8; 26:22.

לֶהֵן, f. לְהֵוֶן (*that they may be*) Ch. fut., the preformant dropped with the pref. ל, from הָוָה, הוא.

לָהֵן; see לְ and לֹא.

לַהֲקָה (const. לַהֲקַת) trans. for מַהֲלָה *congregation,* 1 Sa. 19:20.

לוּ, לוּא I. *if,* εἰ, ἐάν. — II. *would that* (compound of לֹא, לוּ) לוּלֵי, לוּלֵא for לֹא) *unless.*

לוּבִים, לֻבִּים p.n., *the Lybians,* inhabitants of the deserts west of Egypt.

לוּד p. n. of a people descended from Shem, Gen. 10:22; pl. לוּדִים; they inhabited some part of Africa, and probably Asia Minor.

לָוָה I. *borrow at usury.* — II. *get, obtain.* Niph. נִלְוָה *become turned, attached, joined,* with עַל, אֶל, עִם. Hiph. הִלְוָה. — I. *cause to borrow.* — II. *lend.*

לֵוִי p.n. — I. *Levi,* one of the sons of Jacob and Leah. — II. and לֵוִיִּי *a Levite;* pl. לֵוִיִּם and לְוִיִּם בְּנֵי לֵוִי *Levites.*

לֵוִי Ch., *a Levite.*

לִוְיָה const. לִוְיַת *chaplet, garland,* Pro. 1:9, &c.

לִוְיָה f., pl. לִוְיֹת perhaps for לָוָה, לֻוָּה for לִיָּה

architectural ornaments like *gar-lands*, 1 Ki. 7:29, 30, 36.

לִוְיָתָן m.—I. any *sea monster.*—II. *the sea serpent*, Isa. 27:1.—III. one of the carnivorous whales, Job 3:8, &c.

לְוָת Ch., *with*, Ezr. 4:12.

לוּז *escape, depart from*, Pro. 3:21. Niph. part. נָלוֹז *perverse, incorrigible.* Hiph. fut. יָלִיז *escape, flee from.*

לוּז m.—I. *almond tree*, Gen. 30:37. —II. p. n. of the town afterwards called בֵּית־אֵל, in the tribe of Benjamin.

לָזוּת f., *perverseness*, Pro. 4:24.

לוּחַ m.—I. *tablet of stone* or *wood*.—II. metaphorically, *of the heart*.—III. *leaf of a folding-door*, Cant. 8:9; לֻחֹת הָעֵדוּת לֻחֹת הַבְּרִית *tables of the covenant, testimony*; dual לְחֹתַיִם *benches* for the rowers of a ship, Eze. 27:5.

לוּחִית p. n. of a town in Moab.

לוֹחֵשׁ הַלֹּחֵשׁ p. n. of a man.

לוּט *cover, conceal*; part. לוֹט *covering*; לוּטָה f., *concealed.* Hiph. *hid.*

לָט m., *covert*; בַּלָּט *secretly*; pl. לָטִים *secret parts.*

לוֹט m.—I. *veil, covering*, Isa. 25:7. — II. p. n., *Lot*, the nephew of Abraham.

לֹט m., *gum-ladanum.*

לוֹטָן p. n. of a man.

לִוְיָתָן, לִוְיָה, לֵוִי; see לוה.

לוּלִים m. pl., *winding-stairs*, 1 Ki. 6:8.

לֻלָאֹת const. לֻלְאֹת f. pl., *loops* or *eyes* for hooks.

לוּלֵי, לוּלֵא; see לֹא.

I. לוּן and לִין (fut. יָלִין; apoc. יָלֶן; with pause יָלַן, יָלֹן; imper. לִין).—I. *lodge, remain, pass the night*, with אֶת, בְּ. Hiph. הֵלִין *cause to remain*, Jer. 4:14. Hith. הִתְלוֹנֵן *lodge, remain*, Ps. 91:1; Job 39:28

מָלוֹן m.—I. *lodging-house, inn.*—II. *quarters* (as of soldiers).—III. *tent, cot, hut*; f. מְלוּנָה.

II. לוּן. Niph. נָלוֹן *complain, murmur*; with עַל *against*; fut. pl. יִלֹּנוּ Hiph. הֵלִין the same; fut. apoc. וַיָּלֶן; וַיָּלִינוּ part. מַלִּינִים.

תְּלֻנּוֹת f. pl. (with suff. תְּלֻנֹּתֵיכֶם), *murmurings.*

לוּעַ *swallow*, Obad. v. 16.

לֹעַ m., *throat*, Pro. 23:2.

לוּץ *deride, scorn*, Pro. 9:12; part. לֵץ *scorner.* Hiph. הֵלִיץ *derided*; part. מֵלִיץ *interpreter, orator, ambassador.* Hith. הִתְלוֹצֵץ *was mocking*, Isa. 28:22.

לָצוֹן m., *derision*, Pro. 1:22.

מְלִיצָה f.—I. *interpretation.*—II. *saying, parable, enigma*, Pro. 1:6; Hab. 2:6.

לוּשׁ *knead dough.*

לוּשׁ p. n. of a man, same as לַיִשׁ.

לָוָת, see לוה.

לָזוּת; see לוז.

לָחָה root not used; (Arab. *cheek-bone*).

לְחִי, with pause לֶחִי f. (dual לְחָיַיִם; const. לְחָיֵי).—I. *cheek, jaw.*—II. לְחִי and רָמַת לֶחִי p. n., a place on the borders of Philistia.

לָחַח root not used; (Arab *eyes wet with tears*).

לַח m., *moist, green, fresh, new.*

לֵחַ m. (with suff. לֵחֹה Deu. 34:7), *vigour of youth.*

לָחַךְ (inf. לְחֹךְ) and Pi. לִחֵךְ *licked*, Nu. 22:4, *lapped up* (as a dog); with עָפָר *lick the dust.*

לָחַם (fut. יִלְחַם; inf. לְחֹם; imp. לְחַם).—I. *eat, feast upon, devour;* with בְּ *of;* לַחֲמֵי רֶשֶׁף *consumed of fever.*—II. *make, wage war,* with לְ, אֶת. Niph. נִלְחַם (inf. abs. לְהִלָּחֵם; fut. pl. תִּלָּחֲמוּ).—I. *make war;* with בְּ, עַל עִם, אֶל *against;* with לְ *for.*—II. with בְּ, עַל *besiege.*

לָחוּם m.—I. *eating, feasting* (with suff. לְחוּמוֹ).—II. *flesh* (with suff. לְחֻמָם Zep. 1:17).

לֶחֶם com.—I. *provision;* עֵץ בְּלַחְמוֹ *tree with its provision,* i. e. fruit, Jer. 11:19.—II. *feast.*—III. *bread.*—IV. *bread-corn,* Isa. 28:28; לֶחֶם הַפָּנִים (ἄρτος τοῦ προσώπου) *shew-bread,* lit. bread of the presence.

לְחֵם m. Ch., *a feast,* Dan. 5:1.

לָחֶם m. (inf. Pi.), const. לְחֶם *war,* Jud. 5:8.

לַחְמִי p. n. of a man, 1 Chron. 20:5.

מִלְחָמָה f.—I. *battle, war.*—II. *instruments of war,* Ps. 76:4; עָשָׂה מִלְחָמָה with אֶת, עִם *made war;* אִישׁ מ׳ *warrior, soldier;* עַם מ׳ *the same.*—III. *event of war, victory,* Ecc. 9:11.

מִלְחֶמֶת f., the same; with suff. מִלְחַמְתּוֹ.

לַחְמָם p. n. of a place in the tribe of Judah.

לְחֵנָה f. Ch., *concubine,* Dan. 5:2, 3, 23.

לָחַץ (יִלְחַץ) *oppress, afflict;* part. לַחֲצִים *oppressors.* Niph. *was pressed, injured,* Nu. 22:25.

לַחַץ m. *oppression, affliction.*

לָחַשׁ. Pi. לִחֵשׁ; part. pl. מְלַחֲשִׁים *whisperers, pronouncers of charms* Hith. *muse of, secretly consider, discuss.*

לַחַשׁ m.—I. *whisper.*—II. *incantation, charm.*—III. pl. לְחָשִׁים *amulets,* Isa. 3:20.

לָט, לָאט; see לוּט.

לְטָא (Arab. *cleave to the ground*).

לְטָאָה f., *a kind of lizard.*

לָטַשׁ *sharpen.* Pu. part. מְלֻטָּשׁ *sharpened,* Ps. 52:4.

לִיוֹת; see לוּט.

לַיִל (const. לֵיל לֵיל) לַיְלָה (pl. לֵילוֹת) m.—I. *night.*—II. *time of adversity;* adv. בְּלֵילוֹת, לֵילוֹת, לַיְלָה *by night;* יוֹמָם וָלַיְלָה *day and night*

לֵיל m., *night,* Isa. 21:11.

לֵילְיָא m. Ch., *night.*

לִילִית f., *screech owl,* Isa. 34:14.

לִין; see לוּן.

לִיסוֹד Kal inf. with pref. and dag. euphon., from יסד.

לִיקְחַת for לְיִקְחַת; see יָקַח.

לַיִשׁ m.—I. *strong lion.*—II. p. n. of a man.—III. of a town in the north of Palestine.

לֵךְ, לְכָה, לֶךְ imp., from יָלַךְ, הָלַךְ.

לָכַד I. *take,* (as a beast in toils, captives in war, &c.)—II. *intercept*

Niph. *was taken.* Hith. וּ׳, *be-*
*came adhering,* Job 41:9.

לֶכֶד m., *capture,* Pro. 3:26.

מַלְכֹּדֶת f., *snare, trap,* Job 18:10.

לְכָה imp. of יָלַךְ; לְכָה for לֵךְ; see לְ.

לָכִישׁ p. n. of a city in the tribe of
Judah.

לָכֵן; see לְ, בֵּן. לֹא.

לָכֶת Kal inf., from יָלַךְ הָלַךְ.

לִלָּאוֹת; see לוּל.

לָמַד (fut. יִלְמַד).—I. *accustom to,*
with אֶל.—II. *learn,* with acc. inf.
Pi. לִמַּד.—I. *accustom to.*—II. *teach,*
with לְ of the person, and בְּ of
the thing taught. Pu. לֻמַּד.—I.
*was accustomed.*—II. *was taught.*

לָמֵד, לִמּוּד m.—I. *accustomed.*—II.
*trained, taught.*—III. *disciple.*

מַלְמָד m., *ox-goad,* Jud. 3:31.

תַּלְמִיד m., *learner,* 1 Ch. 25:8.

לָמָה, לִמָּה *why;* see מָה.

לְמוֹ; see לְ.

לְמוּאֵל, לְמוֹאֵל p. n. or title of king Solomon, Pro. c. 31.

לֶמֶךְ p. n. of a man, *Lamech*

לְמַעַן; see עָנָה.

לֵנָה Zec. 5:4, for לָנָה Kal pret. f., from
לוּן.

לָנוּ for לָנֵנוּ Kal pret. pl., from לוּן.
לָנִים Kal part. pl., from לוּן.

לֹעַ *throat;* see לוּעַ.

לָעֵב. Hiph. *ridiculing, deriding,* with
בְּ, 2 Chron. 36:16.

לָעַג (fut. יִלְעַג) *mock, deride, scorn.*
Niph. *stammer,* Isa. 33:19. Hiph.
*mock,* with בְּ, לְ, עַל.

לַעַג m.—I. *derision, ridicule.*—II
*cause of derision.*

לָעֵג m., *mocker,* Ps. 35:16.

לַעְדָּה p. n. of a man.

לַעְדָּן p. n. of a man.

לָעַע *was rash,* Job 6:3.

לָעַז *spoke barbarously,* Ps. 114:1.

לָעַט. Hiph. *feed, give to eat.*

לָעַן (Arab. *drove away*).

לַעֲנָה f.—I. *wormwood.*—II. metaph.
*distress.*

לַפִּיד m., *lamp or torch.*

לַפִּידוֹת p. n., *Lapidoth* the husband of
Deborah.

לִפְנֵי, לִפְנַי; see פָּנִים or פָּנָה.

לָפַת *turned to, towards,* Jud. 16:29.
Niph. *turned about.*

לְצַבּוֹת for לְהַצְבּוֹת Hiph. inf. with
pref., from צָבָה.

לָצוֹן *scorn;* see לוּץ.

לֵץ, part. לֵצִים *scorners,* Hos. 7:5.
לַקּוּם p. n., a town in the tribe of
Naphtali.

לָקַח (fut. יִקַּח; inf. abs. לָקוֹחַ; const.
קַחַת, imp. קַח, לְקַח; with pause
קָח; with ה parag. קְחָה).—I. *take,*
with בְּ.—II. idiom, like the English *take* and *do.*—III. *take away.*
—IV. *take possession of.*—V. *receive.* Niph. נִלְקַח *was taken.*
Pu. לֻקַּח same as Niph. Hoph.
(fut. יֻקַּח the same). Hith. part. f.
מִתְלַקַּחַת *being taken with,* i. e.
*mixed, mingled with* (of fire),
Ex. 9:24, Eze. 1:4.

לֶקַח m., *taking, receiving,* specially
*instruction in religion.*

**לְקָחִי** p. n. of a man.

**מַלְקוֹחַ** m., *capture, spoil*; dual מַלְקָחַיִם *the jaws.*

**מֶלְקָחַיִם** m. dual.—I. *tongs.*—II. *snuffers.*

**מַלְקָחַיִם** m. dual, the same.

**מִקָּח** m., *accepting* (of gifts), 2 Chron. 19:7.

**מַקָּחוֹת** f. pl., *merchandise*, Neh. 10:32.

**לָקַט** and Pi. לִקֵּט *collect, gather, glean.* Pu. and Hith. *was gathered.*

**לֶקֶט** m., *collecting, gleaning.*

**יַלְקוּט** m., *bag* or *purse*, 1 Sa. 17:40.

**לָקַק** *lick* (as dogs); fut. יָלֹק; pl. יָלֹקּוּ. Pi. part. מְלַקְקִים *licking.*

**לָקַשׁ** (Syr. *late*). Pi. *cut, crop*, Job 24:6.

**לֶקֶשׁ** m., *latter grass, aftermath*, Am. 7:1.

**מַלְקוֹשׁ** m., *the latter rain* (in March and April).

**לְרֹא** for לִירֹא Kal inf. with pref., from יָרא.

**לָשַׁד** (Arab. *sucking*).

**לְשַׁד** m. (with suff. לְשַׁדִּי) *moisture*, Ps. 32:4; לְשַׁד הַשָּׁמֶן perhaps *fluid oil*, Nu. 11:8.

**לָשׁוֹן** com.—I. *tongue*; אִישׁ לָשׁוֹן *calumniator.*—II. *language.*—III. *nation, community* (having one language).—IV. *tongue of flame*, Is. 5:24.—V. *tongue* (wedge) of gold, Jos. 7:21, 24.

**לָשֵׁן** Po. part. with י parag. מַלְשִׁנִי *calumniator*, Ps. 101:5. Hiph. the same, Pro. 30:10.

**לָשָׁן** com. Ch., *tongue, language.*

**לִשְׁכָּה** f., *chamber*, specially those attached to the temple; with ה parag. לִשְׁכָּתָה *to the chamber*; pl. לְשָׁכוֹת.

**לֶשֶׁם** m.—I. *ligure*, a precious stone; LXX. λιγύριον.—II. p. n. of a city called also לַיִשׁ and דָּן.

**לֶשַׁע** p. n. of a city not far from Sodom.

**לָת** for לֶדֶת with pref. לָלֶת Kal inf., from ילד.

**לֶתֶךְ** m., *measure* (of capacity), *the half-homer*, Hos. 3:2.

**לָתַע** (Arab. *he bites*).

**מַלְתָּעוֹת** f. pl., *teeth*, Ps. 58:7.

**מְתַלְּעוֹת** f. pl. (trans.), *teeth.*

## מ

**מ** pref. prep.; see מן.

**מָא** Ch., same as מה.

**מַאֲבוּס** m., *granary*, see אבס.

**מֵאד**; see אוד.

**מֵאָה** const. f.—I. *a hundred*; dual מָאתַיִם *two hundred*; pl. מֵאוֹת *hundreds*; שֵׁשׁ מֵאוֹת *six hundred*; שְׁמֹנֶה מֵאוֹת *eight hundred.*—II. *a hundred-fold.*—III. *a hundredth part*, Neh. 5:11.—IV. p. n. of one of the towers of Jerusalem, Neh. 3:1.

**מְאָה** f. Ch., *a hundred*; dual מָאתַיִן *two hundred.*

**מַאֲוַיִּים** *desires*; see אוה.

**מְאוּם**; see מום.

**מְאוּמָה**; see מה.

**מְאֵרָה, מָאוֹר** *curse*; see אור.

**מֹאזְנַיִן, מֹאזְנַיִם** *balances*; see אזן.

**מַאֲכֶלֶת, מַאֲכָל**; see אכל.

**מָאן** m. Ch., *vessel.*

מָאֵן or מָאֵן .Pi. מֵאֵן (inf. מָאֵן; fut. יְמָאֵן) refuse, be unwilling.

מָאֵן m., refusing.

מֵאֵן m., pl. מֵאֲנִים recusants.

מָאַס (inf. מָאוֹס; const. with suff. מָאָסְם; fut. יִמְאַס).— I. despise, reject.— II. set at nought, lightly esteem, with בְּ. Niph. I. was despised, rejected. — II. same as מָסַס. Niph. dissolve, waste, Ps. 58:8; Job 7:5.

מַאֲפֶה baked; see אפה.

מַאֲפֵלְיָה, מַאֲפֵל; see אפל.

מָאַר (Arab. irritate a wound). Hiph. הִמְאִיר irritated, pained; צָרַעַת מַמְאֶרֶת the inflamed leprosy.

מַאֲרָב ambush; see ארב.

מְאֵרָה curse, see ארר.

מֵאֵת from the; see אֵת.

מִבְדָּלוֹת separations; see בדל

מָבוֹא entry; see בוא.

מְבוּכָה confusion; see בוך.

מַבּוּל deluge; see יבל.

מְבוּסָה treading down; see בוס.

מְבוֹנִים understanding; see בון.

מַבּוּעַ spring; see נבע.

מְבוּקָה void; see בוק.

מְבֻשִׁים, מְבוּשִׁים prudence; see בוש.

מִבְחָר, מִבְחוֹר choice; see בחר.

מַבָּט, מֶבָּט hope; see נבט.

מִבְטָא rashness; see בטא.

מִבְטָח confidence; see בטח.

מֵבִי for מֵבִיא Hiph. part., from בוא.

מַבְלִינִית exhilaration; see בלג.

מִבַּלְעֲדֵי besides; see בלה in בַּלְעֲדֵי.

מִבְנֶה building; see בנה.

מִבְנַי for סִבְכַי, 2 Sa. 23:27.

מִבְעָתְךָ for מְבַעֶתְךָ Pi. part. f. with suff., from בעת.

מִבְצָר fortress; see בצר.

מִבְּרֹאשָׁה comp. of בְּ, מָה and רֹאשׁ.

מָג m., fire worshipper, magian, Jer 39:3.

מַגְבִּישׁ p. n. of a place or person.

מִגְבָּלוֹת devices; see נבל.

מִגְבָּעָה mitre; see נבע.

מָגֵד (Arab. glory).

מֶגֶד m., excellence, glory.

מְגִדּוֹן, מְגִדּוֹ p. n., a city of the Manassites in the tribe of Issachar. LXX. Μαγεδδώ; בִּקְעַת־מְגִדּוֹ valley of Megiddo; מֵי מְגִדּוֹ brook Kishon.

מְגָדָנוֹת f. pl., choice, precious things.

מַגְדִּיאֵל p. n. of a prince of the Edomites.

מִגְדּוֹל, מִגְדָּל p. n.; see גדל.

מָגוֹג p. n. of a people and country Magog.

מְגוּרָה, מְגוּרָה, מָגוֹר, מָגוֹר see גור.

מַגְזֵרָה axes; see גזר.

מַגָּל sickle; see נגל.

מִגְדָּלָה mound; see נלל.

מִגַּמָּה desire; see גמם.

מָגֵן Pi. מִגֵּן give, give freely

מָגִנָּה, מָגֵן; see גנן.

מִגְעֶרֶת rebuke; see נער.

מַגֵּפָה plague; see נגף.

מְנַפִּיעָשׁ p. n. of a man.

מָגָר, part. pl. const. מְגוּרֵי fallen, delivered up, Eze. 21:17. Pi. מִגֵּר cast down.

מְגַר Ch. Pa. מַגֵּר cast down, Ezr 6:12.

מִגְרוֹן p. n., a town in the tribe of Benjamin.

מְגֵרָה saw; see נרר.

**מָנְרְפָּה** *furrow*; see נרף.

**מְנֹרֵשׁ**; see נרשׁ.

**מִדְבָּר** *wilderness*; see דבר.

**מָדַד** (pret. מַדֹּתִי, מָדֹדוּ; fut. יָמֹד).
—I. *extend a line*.—II. *measure*.
—III. *apportion*, Isa. 65:7. Niph.
(fut. יִמַּד) *be, can be, measured*.
Pi. מִדֵּד *measure* (see also in נדד).
Po. מוֹדֵד the same, Hab. 3:6;
"*viewed*" (Lee); see מוּד. Hith.
הִתְמֹדֵד *extended, stretched out*.

**מַד** m.—I. *measure, extent*; with suff.
מַדּוֹ; pl. מַדִּים.—II. *upper garment, tunic*, with suff. מַדּוֹ;
pl. מַדִּים, מִדִּין.—III. *hammer-
cloth, covering for a throne*, Jud.
5:10.—IV. מַדִּין p.n., a city in the
desert of Judah.

**מִדָּה** f. (m. Neh. 3:30).—I. *extent,
measure*; אִישׁ מִדָּה *tall man*,
1 Chron. 11:23; בֵּית מִדּוֹת *spacious house*, Jer. 22:14; מִדַּת יָמַי
*measure of my days*.—II. *tribute*.
—III. *vesture*, Ps. 133:2.

**מִנְדָּה, מִדָּה** f. Ch., *tribute*.

**מְמַדִּים** m. pl., *extents, measure*, Job
38:5.

**מַדְו** m. (pl. with suff. מַדְוֵיהֶם), *garment*.

**מָדוֹן** m., *height, tallness*, 2 Sa. 21:20;
see also in דין.

**מַדְוֶה** *disease*; see דָּוָה.

**מַדּוּחִים** *drivings out*; see נדח.

**מַדּוּעַ** *why*; see ידע.

**מַדְחֵפוֹת**; see דחף.

**מָדַי** f., *Media, the Medes*; מָדַי Ch. a
*Median*, const. emph. מָדָאָה the
same.

**מַדַּי**; see מָה. **מִדַּי**; see דַּי.

**מִדְיָן** p.n., the son of Abraham and

Keturah; מִדְיָנִי m., מִדְיָנִית f., a
*Midianite*.

**מָדִין** in מַד; see מָדַד in מֻדָּד. pl. for מַדִּים; see מַד in מדד.

**מְדִינָה**; see דִּין.

**מְדֹכָה** *mortar*; see דּוּךְ.

**מַדְמַנָּה, מַדְמֵנָה, מַדְמֵן**; see דמן.

**מָדָן, מָדִין, מָדֹנִים**; see דִּין.

**מַדַּע, מַדָּע**; see ידע.

**מָדוֹר, מְדֹר** *habitation* Ch., same as
see דּוּר.

**מַדְרֵךְ**; see דרך.

**הַמְּדָתָא** with art. מְדָתָא p. n. the father
of Haman.

**מָה, מֶה, מַה** inter. pron.—I. *what?*
מַה־לְּךָ *what wilt thou?* מַה־לִּי
וָלָךְ *what have I to do with thee?*
—II. *how? how much?*—III. *for
what? why?*—IV. *what? what
sort?* — V. *something, anything,
anything whatever; ...*מָה שֶׁ *that
which, the thing which* (in the
book of Ecclesiastes only); מַה־
נּוֹרָא *how terrible;* מַה־זֶּה for מַה־זֶּה
*what is this?* מַלְּכֶם *what mean
ye?* Isa. 3:15; לְמַד־דִּי for לְמַדִּי
*sufficiently,* 2 Chron. 30:3. Compounds: בַּמָּה, בַּמֶּה *why? how?
wherefore?* כַּמֶּה, בְּכַמָּה *how many?
how long? how much?* לָמָה, לְמֶה
*why?* לְמָה זֶּה *why? wherefore?*
לְמַבְרֹאשֹׁנָה (לְמָה בּ' for) *because
at first,* 1 Chron. 15:13; עַד־מָה
*how long?* עַל־מֶה, עַל־מָה *wherefore?*

**מָה** (מָא) Ch., *why, wherefore?* מָה־שׁ
*that which,* Dan. 2:28, 29; לְמָה,
*wherefore?* כְּמָה *how?
how much? so much?* Dan. 3:33;
מָה דִי *that which.*

**מָאוּמָה** (comp. of מָה וּמָה or מָה אוֹ

(מָה) *any thing*; with לֹא, אֵין, אַל *nothing*.

מָהַהּ Hith. הִתְמַהְמַהּ *delay, tarry, wait*.

מְהוּמָה *tumult*; see הוּם.

מְהוּמָן p.n. of a Persian eunuch.

מְהֵיטַבְאֵל p. n.—I. of a man, Neh. 6: 10.—II. of a woman, Gen. 36:39.

מְהֵימַן Ch., Aph. part. pass.; see אמן.

מְהַחְתִין Ch. Aph. part.; see נחת.

מָהָךְ Ch. Pe. inf., from הוּךְ.

מָהֻל, part. מָהוּל *debased, adulterated*, Isa. 1:22.

מְהֵמָהֶם Eze. 7:11, from הֵם; see המה.

מַהְמְצָעוֹת for מִקְצָעוֹת Hoph. part. f. pl., from קצע.

I. מָהַר *hasten, hurry*, Ps. 16:4. Pi. מִהַר *hasten, hurry*; used as an auxiliary, e. g. מִהֲרוּ שָׁכְחוּ *they soon forgot*, Ps. 106:13, &c. Niph. נִמְהָר *was hasty, hurried, rash*.

מָהִיר m., *ready, quick, skilful, hasty, speedy*.

מְהֵרָה m., *quick, ready, hasty, speedy, speed*; עַד־מְהֵרָה, בִּמְהֵרָה, מְהֵרָה adv., *quickly, readily, speedily*.

II. מָהַר *endow* (a wife with a dowry), Ex. 22:15; or *buy* (a wife with a dowry).

מֹהַר m., *gift* or *dower* (present made by a suitor to the parents of a damsel).

מַהְרַי p. n., one of David's generals.

מוֹאָב p.n.—I. of a man, *Moab*, the descendant of Lot.—II. f., the land of *Moab*, situated between the Dead Sea and the river Arnon m. מוֹאָבִי, f. מוֹאָבִיָּה, מוֹאָבִית *Moabite*.

מוּאָל same as מוּל *over against*, Neh. 12:38.

מוֹבָא *entrance*; see בּוֹא.

מוּג (fut. יָמוּג).—I. *flow*.—II. *dissolve, melt* (indicating weakness). Niph. נָמוֹג *were dissolved, undone*. Pil. מוֹגֵג I. *dissolve*, Ps. 65:11.—II. *waste away*, Job 30:22. Hith. *was dissolved, undone*.

מוּד Kal not used; see מוט. Po. מוֹדֵד *moved*, Hab. 3:6.

תָּמִיד m.—I. *perpetuity.*—II. *perpetual.*—III. *continually;* עוֹלַת הַתָּמִיד *the continual*, i. e. *daily offering;* לֶחֶם הַתָּמִיד *the bread constantly placed in the temple.*

מוֹדַעַת, מֹדַע, מוֹדָע; see ידע.

מוּט (fut. יָמוּט) *totter* (to a fall), *fail*. Niph. נָמוֹט *be moved, tottering.* Hiph. fut. יָמִיטוּ *cause to fall, come down.* Hithpo. *be moved*, Isa. 24:19.

מוֹט m.—I. *tottering, vacillating.*—II. *pole, staff.*—III. *yoke* (for burdens), Nah. 1:12.

מוֹטָה f., *pole or staff.*

מוּךְ same as מָכַךְ *become indigent.*

מוּל *circumcise.* Niph. I. *was circumcised.*—II. *circumcise one's self.* Pil. מוֹלֵל *cut off*, Ps. 90:6. Hiph. *cut off, down*, Ps. 118:10-12. Hithpo. הִתְמוֹלֵל *is cut off, down*, Ps. 58:8.

מוֹאל, מוּל Deu. 1:1, מוּל Neh. 12: 38).—I. *near, with.*—II. *opposite, over against*, ἀντικρύ: compounds

אֶל *before, over against*; אֶל־מוּל
מִמּוּל פְּנֵי *in front of, before*; מִמּוּל
*from before, opposite.*

מוּלָה f. (pl. מוּלֹת), *circumcisions*, Ex.
4:26.

מוֹלִיד, מוֹלֶדֶת, מוֹלָדָה; see יָלַד.

מוּם (מְאוּם) m., *spot, blemish* from
disease.

מוּמָת Hoph. part., from מָת.

מוּן; see מִין.

מוּסָב Hoph. part.; see סָבַב.

מוֹסָדוֹת, מוּסָדָה, מוּסָד; see יָסַד.

מוּסָךְ *porch*; see סָכַךְ.

מוֹסֵר (from אָסַר), pl. מוֹסְרִים and
מוֹסְרוֹת *chains.*

מוֹסֵר and ־וֹת p. n. of a place in the
wilderness.

מוּסָר *bonds*; see יָסַר.

מוֹעֵד, מוֹעָדָה, מוֹעֵד; see יָעַד.

מוֹעֶדֶת *assembly*; see יָעַד.

מוּעֶדֶת for מוֹעֶדֶת Kal part. f., from
יָעַד.

מוּעָף *darkness*; see עוּף.

מוֹעֵצָה *counsel*; see יָעַץ.

מוּעָקָה *pain*; see עוּק.

מוֹפֵת *sign*; see יָפַת.

מוּץ, part. מֵץ *oppressor*, Isa. 16:4.
מוֹץ, מֹץ m., *chaff*.
מִיץ m., *pressing, squeezing* (cream to
make butter), Pro. 30:33.

מוֹצָא, מוֹצָאָה; see יָצָא.

מוּצָא Hoph. part., from יָצָא.

מוּצָק, מוּצָקָה *fused, cast*; see יָצַק.

מוּצָק, מוּצָק; see צוק.

מוּק, Hiph. הֵמִיק *mock, insult*, Ps.
73:8.

מוֹקֵד, מוֹקְדָה *burning*; see יָקַד.
מוֹקֵשׁ *snare*; see יָקֵשׁ.

מוּר Hiph. הֵמִיר ־ I. *change, alter*,

with בְּ. ─ II. *exchange.* Niph.
נָמַר *was changed*, Jer. 48:11.

תְּמוּרָה f.─I. *equivalent, recompense.*
─II. *restitution*, Job 20:18. ─ III.
*exchange*, Ru. 4:7.

מוֹרָא; see יָרֵא.

מוֹרָאִים for מוֹרִים Hiph. part. pl., from
יָרָה.

מוֹרַג or מֹרַג m. (pl. מֹרְגִים, מוֹרִגִּים)
*threshing wain.*

מוֹרָד *descent, declivity*; see יָרַד.

מוֹרָה, Ps. 9:21, same as מוֹרָא *fear*,
see also in מָרָה *teacher*;
see יָרָה.

מוֹרָט *ruin*; see יָרַט.

מוֹרִיָּה p.n., same as מֹרִיָּה.

מוֹרִיגִּים for מוֹרְגִּים pl., from מוֹרַג.

מוֹרָשָׁה, מוֹרָשׁ *possession, inheritance*
see יָרַשׁ.

I. מוּשׁ I. *move*. ─ II. *remove*, Zec.
3:9. Hiph. הֵמִישׁ I. *move, depart*.─II. *remove, put away*.─III.
*cease, desist*, Jer. 17:8, with מִן.

II. מוּשׁ same as מָשַׁשׁ *feel*, Gen.
27:21, &c. Hiph. the same, Ps.
115:7, &c.

מוּשִׁי, מֵשִׁי p. n. of a man.

מוֹשָׁב *dwelling*, &c.; see יָשַׁב.

מֹשְׂכוֹת; see מָשַׁךְ.

מֹשָׁעוֹת *salvation*; see יָשַׁע.

מוּת (pret. מֵת; 1. pers. מַתִּי; pl.
מֵתוּ; part. מֵת, f. מֵתָה; inf.
abs. מוֹת; const. מוּת; imp. מֵת;
fut. יָמוּת; apoc. יָמֹת, וַיָּמָת) *die*
(of man or beast). Pil. מוֹתֵת
*put to death, caused to die.* Hiph.
הֵמִית the same. Hoph. הוּמַת *was
caused to die.*

מָוֶת m. (with ה parag. מָוְתָה; const

מוֹת; with suff. מוֹתוֹ; pl. מוֹתִים.‎ —I. *death*; מִשְׁפַּט מָוֶת *sentence of death*, Deut. 19:6; בֶּן־מָוֶת or אִישׁ־מ׳ *one guilty of a capital crime*.—II. *the grave*; שַׁעֲרֵי מָוֶת *gates of death*.—III. *person dead*, Isa. 38:18.—IV. *pestilence*.—V. *destruction, ruin*.

מוֹת m. Ch., *death*.

מָמוֹת m., pl. מְמוֹתִים *deaths*, Jer. 16:4; Eze. 28:8.

תְּמוּתָה f., *death*; בֶּן־תְּמוּתָה *condemned to death*.

מוֹתָר *abundance*; see יתר.

מֵזָא with suff. מֵזְיֵהּ Ch. Pe. inf., from אזא.

מִזְבֵּחַ *altar*; see זבה.

מֶזֶג (Arab. *mixture*); see מסך.
מֶזֶג m., *mixed wine*, Cant. 7:3.

מָזֶה *exhausted, reduced* (by famine), Deut. 32:24.

מַזֶּה for מַה־זֶּה, from מָה.
מִזֶּה p. n. of a man.
מְזָוִים *cellar*; see זוה.
מְזוּזָה *door-post*; see זוז.
מָזוֹן *food*; see זוז.
מָזוֹר *bandage*; see זור.

מֵזִיחַ, מֵזַח m.—I. *a girdle*.—II. *pride*, Job 12:21.

מֵזִין for מַאֲזִין Hiph. part., from אזן.
מַזָּלוֹת; see נזל.
מִזְלָגָה, מַזְלֵג *fork*; see זלג.
מְזִמָּה *invention*; see זמם.
מִזְמוֹר, מַזְמֵרוֹת, מְזַמְּרוֹת; see זמר.
מְזָרֶה, מְזָרִים; see זרה.
מְזָרוֹת; see נזל.
מִזְרָח *east*; see זרח.
מִזְרָק *cup*; see זרק.
מֹח, מֵחַ; see מחה.

מָחָא *smite, clap*; with כַּף, יַד *hands*. Pi. the same, Eze. 25:6.

מְחָא Ch., *struck, smote*. Pa. *exult*, Dan. 4:32. Ithp. *was smitten*, Exr. 6:11.

מַחָא Ch. Aph. part., from חיא;see חיה.

מַחֲבֹאִים, מַחֲבֵא *hiding-place*; see חבא.

מַחְבָּרוֹת, מַחְבֶּרֶת; see חבר.
מַחֲבַת *frying-pan*; see חבת.

מָחָה I. *wipe away*,—II. *arrive at*, Nu. 34:11, with עַל. Niph. (fut. apoc. יִמַּח) *was blotted out*. Hiph. (fut. apoc. תֶּמַח) *blot out*.

מְחִי m., *striking*, Eze. 26:9.

מְחֻגָה *compasses*; see חגג.
מָחוֹן *harbour*; see חון.
מְחִיָּאֵל, מְחוּיָאֵל p. n., a descendant of Cain.

מָחֲוִים p. n. of a place unknown.
מָחוֹל, מְחֹלָה *dance*; see חול.
מַחֲזִיאוֹת, מֶחֱזָה, מַחֲזֶה; see חזה.

מָחֹחַ (Arab. *marrow*).
מֵחַ m., *fat, rich*.
מֹחַ m., *marrow*, Job 21:24.

מְחִידָא p. n. of a man.
מְחִיָה; see חָוָה, חיה.
מְחִיר *price*; see מחר.

מָחְלִי, מַחְלוֹן, מַחֲלֶה, מַחֲלָה, מַחְלָה; see חלה; מַחֲלַיִים; see חלה.
מְחִלָּה *hole*; see חלל.
מַחְלְפוֹת, מַחֲלָף; see חלף.
מַחְלְקוֹת, מַחֲלֹקֶת; see חלק.
מְחֹלַת, מַחֲלַת; see חלה.
מְחֹלָתִי *Meholathite*; see אבל
מַחֲמָאוֹת; see חמא.
מַחְמֶצֶת; see חמץ.
מְחֹן Ch. Pe. inf., from חנן.

מַחֲנֶה ,מַחֲנַיִם camp; see חנה.

מַחֲסֶה ,מַחֲסָה ,מַחְסִיָה; see חסה.

מַחְסוֹם curb; see חסם.

מְחַסְפַּס part. of the quadriliteral verb חַסְפַּס; see חסף.

מָחַץ (.fut יִמְחַץ).— I. dash violently (the head to pieces)—(the foot into blood), Ps. 68:22.—II. shoot arrows, Nu. 24:8.

מַחַץ m., contusion, bruise, Isa. 30:26.

מֶחֱצָה ,מַחֲצִית; see חצה.

מחצצרים: see in חצר.

מָחַק destroyed, Jud. 5:26.

מֶחְקָר; see חקר.

מָחַר same as מכר.

מְחִיר m.— I. price; בִּמְחִיר with a price.—II. p. n. of a man.

מָחָר m. — I. morrow, some future day; לְמָחָר to-morrow; בְּיוֹם מָחָר for the morrow; כָּעֵת מָחָר and מָחָר כָּעֵת הַזֹּאת about this time to-morrow; כָּעֵת מָחָר הַשְּׁלִישִׁית this time the day after to-morrow. —II. adv. hereafter, henceforward.

מִמָּחֳרָת,לְמָחֳרָת f., to-morrow; מָחֳרָת the day after; מִמָּחֳרַת הַשַּׁבָּת the day after the sabbath; עַד־מִמָּחֳרָת until the next day; לְמָחֳרָתָם adv. the day after.

מַחֲרֶשֶׁת ,מַחֲרֵשָׁה; see חרש.

מַחְשֹׂף; see חשׂף.

מַחֲשֶׁבֶת ,מַחֲשָׁבָה; see חשב.

מַחְשָׁךְ darkness; see חשׁך.

מַחַת p. n. of a man.

מַחְתָּה shovel, &c.; see חתה.

מְחִתָּה breaking, &c.; see חתת.

מַחְתֶּרֶת digging; see חתר.

מְטָא Ch., come on, to, arrive at, with עַל.

מַטְאֲמָא; see טוא.

מְטַהֵר for מִתְטַהֵר Hith. part.; see טהר.

מָטוֹת ,מַטֶּה ,מַטָּה ,מַטֶּה ,מַטָּה; see נטה.

מַטְוֶה yarn; see טוה.

מְטַל (Arab. forged iron): hence, the English word metal.

מְטִיל m., iron bar, Job 40:18.

מַטְמוֹן treasure; see טמן.

מַטָּע plant; see נטע.

מַטְעַמִּים dainties; see טעם.

מִטְפַּחַת mantle; see טפח.

מָטָר. Hiph. הִמְטִיר rain, cause, give rain; used also of lightning, hail, fire and brimstone, manna, bread. Niph. was rained on, Am. 4:7.

מָטָר m. (pl. מְטָרוֹת; const. מְטָרוֹת) rain, shower.

מַטְרִי p. n. of a man.

מַטְרֵד p. n. of a woman.

מִטְרָא ,מַטָּרָה; see נטר.

מִי interrog. pron.—I. who? בַּת־מִי whose daughter? לְמִי to whom? בְּמִי by whom? אֶת־מִי whom? מִי מָנָה who can number? מִי יִתֵּן would that it were! מִי יִתֵּן וְהָיָה עֶרֶב would that it were evening! —II. without interrog., who, every one; מִי אֲשֶׁר whoever.

מֵידְבָא p. n. of a city in the tribe of Reuben.

מֵידָד p. n. of a man.

מֵיטָב good; see יטב.

מִיכָא p. n. of a man, same as מִיכָיָא

מִיכָאֵל (who is like unto God?) p. n.

—I. *Michael* the archangel.—II. of a man.

מִיכָה, מִיכָא p. n.—I. *Micah* the prophet.—II. also of other men.

מִיכָיָהוּ p. n.—I. of a man.—II. of a woman.

מִיכָה, מִיכָיָהוּ p. n. of a man.

מִיכָל p. n.; see מכל.

מַיִם m. pl. (const. מֵי, מֵימֵי; with suff. מֵימָיו; with ה loc. (הַמַּיְמָה).—I. *water, waters*, used with pl. adj., with verb either pl. or sing.—II. *seed*; יָצָא מִמֵּי פ׳ *whose son, descendant he is*, Isa. 48:1.

מֵי־הַיַּרְקוֹן p. n., a city in the tribe of Dan.

מֵי־נִפְתּוֹחַ p.n., a fountain near Jerusalem.

מִין, מוּן (Syr. *family*).

מִין m., *kind, species*, always with ל pref.; פְּרִי לְמִינוֹ *fruit after his kind*.

תְּמוּנָה f., *resemblance, likeness*.

מֵינִיקוֹת, מֵינָקֶת; see ינק.

מֵיפַעַת, מֵיפָעַת p. n., a town of the Levites in the tribe of Reuben.

מִיץ *chaff*; see מוץ.

מֵישָׁא p. n. of a man.

מִישָׁאֵל p. n. of a man.

מִישׁוֹר; see ישר.

מֵישַׁךְ p. n., *Meshach*, one of the captivity, called also מִישָׁאֵל.

מֵישַׁע p. n., a king of Moab.

מֵישַׁע p.n., a son of Caleb.

מֵישָׁרִים; see ישר.

מֵיתָר *cord*; see יתר.

מַכְאוֹב *pain*; see כאב.

מְכַבְּנָא same as כָּבּוֹן.

סְכַבְּנַי p n. of a man.

מַכְבֵּר, מִכְבָּר *carpet*; see כבר.

מַכָּה *stroke*; see נכה.

מְכָוֶה *burning*; see כוה.

מְכוּנָה, מְכוֹנָה, מָכוֹן; see כון.

מְכוּרָה; see כור.

מָכִיר p. n., *Machir* the son of Manasseh, Gen. 50:23; perhaps for *a Manassite*, Jud. 5:14; patronymic מָכִירִי.

מָכַךְ. Niph. fut. יִמַּךְ *become weak*, Ecc. 10:18. Hoph. pl. הֻמְּכוּ for הֻמַּכּוּ *they perish*, Job 24:24.

מְכַל root not used; (Arab. *empty of water*).

מִיכַל m.; מִיכַל הַמַּיִם *brooks of water*, 2 Sa. 17:20. — II. p. n., *Michal*, the daughter of Saul and wife of David.

מִכְלָאוֹת, מִכְלָה, see כלא; מִכְלָה, see כלה.

מַכְלֻלִים, מִכְלָל, מִכְלוֹל; see כלל.

מַאֲכֶלֶת for מַאֲכֹלֶת *food*; see אכל.

מִכְמָס, מִכְמָשׁ, מִכְמַשׁ (see כָּמַס), p. n. a town in the tribe of Benjamin, Μαχμάς.

מִכְמֶרֶת, מַכְבֹּר, מִכְמָר *net*; see כמר.

מִכְמְתָת p. n., a town on the borders of Ephraim and Manasseh.

מַכְנַדְבַי p. n. of a man.

מִכְנָס *breeches*; see כנס.

מֶכֶס, מִכְסָה *price*; see כסס.

מְכַסֶּה, מִכְסָה; see כסה.

מַכְפֵּלָה p. n. of a district near Hebron.

מָכַר (fut. יִמְכֹּר; inf. with suff. מָכְרָהּ, מָכְרָם; imp. with ה parag. מִכְרָה).
—I. *he sold*, with בְּ of the price.
—II. *he gave a daughter in marriage* (in consideration of a gift).
—III. *he gave up men* into the

power of others. Niph. נִמְכַּר *was sold.* Hith. הִתְמַכֵּר I. *was sold.*— II. *was surrendered.*

מֶכֶר m. (with suff. מִכְרָם).—I. *value, price.*— II. *valuable article,* Neh. 13:16.

מִכְרִי p. n. of a man.

מִמְכָּר m., מִמְכֶּרֶת f.—I. *sale.*—II. *thing sold.*

מָכֵר *relative;* see נכר.

מִכְרֶה *pit of salt;* see כרה.

מְכֵרָה *sword;* see כּוּר.

מְכֵרָתִי *Macherathite,* patron. 1 Chron. 11:36.

מַכְשֵׁלָה, מִכְשׁוֹל; see כשל.

מִכְתָּב *writing;* see כתב.

מְכִתָּה *breaking;* see כתת.

מִכְתָּם; see כתם.

מַכְתֵּשׁ *mortar;* see כתש.

מָלֵא, מָלָא (fut. יִמְלָא; inf. מְלֹאת). —I. *fill;* מָלְאוּ הַשְּׁלָטִים *fill the shields,* i. e. enlarge them so as to cover you, Jer. 51:11; מָלֵא יָד *filled the hand,* i. e. conferred an office.—II. *fulfil, execute fully, thoroughly;* מָלְאָה צְבָאָהּ *her warfare is accomplished;* מָלְאָה נַפְשִׁי *my soul is full,* Ex. 15:9. Niph. נִמְלָא (fut. יִמָּלֵא) *is full, filled,* with מִן, לְ. Pi. מִלֵּא (inf. מַלֵּאת, מַלֹּאת; fut. יְמַלֵּא).—I. *fulfil* (of time, promise, &c.).— II. *fill the hand,* i. e. consecrate to the priest's office.—III. *fill as a vessel* (with accus. מִן), *insert,* i. e. *fill in,* of the stones in the breast-plate, Ex. 28:17.—IV. used with other verbs, &c., implying the completion of their action; מִלֵּא יָדוֹ בַקֶּשֶׁת *he fully drew the bow,* lit. filled his

hand with, 2 Ki. 9:24; קָרְאוּ מָלֵאוּ *cry out strongly;* מָלֵא אַחֲרֵי *fulfilled the followings,* i. e. followed fully. Pu. part. מְמֻלָּאִים *filled with gems,* Cant. 5:14. Hith. fut. יִתְמַלָּאוּן *they are fully set against me,* Job 16:10.

מְלָא Ch., *filled,* Dan. 2:35. Hith. *was filled,* Dan. 3:19.

מָלֵא m., מְלֵאָה f., *full* (used as מָלָא, see above Pi. IV.); כֶּסֶף מָלֵא *full* (i. e. *just*), *money;* מֵי מָלֵא *waters of fulness* (i. e. *ample*), *abundant;* מְלֵא יָמִים *full of days,* Jer. 6:11.

מְלֹא, מְלוֹא m.—I. *filling, fulness;* מְלֹא כַף *the filling of the palm, palm full;* מְלֹא חָפְנֵיכֶם פִּיחַ *both your closed hands full of ashes,* Ex. 9:8; מְלֹא קוֹמָתוֹ *his full stature,* 1 Sam. 28:20.—II. *multitude,* Gen. 48:19.

מְלֵאָה f., *overplus, excess of corn and wine* which was to be offered to the Lord, Ex. 22:28; Nu 18:27.

מְלֹאת for מְלֹאת Kal inf., from מלא.

מַלְאָכִים for מַלְכִים pl., from מֶלֶךְ.

מִלּוֹא m., p. n.—I. a certain part of the citadel of Jerusalem, called also בֵּית מִלּוֹא 2 Ki.12:21.—II. a castle of the Sichemites, Jud. 9:6, 20.

מִלֻּאָה, מִלּוּאָה f., *insertion of gems* (see above מִלֵּא Pi. III.).

מִלֻּאִים m. pl.—I. *inauguration, consecration* (of priests). — II. אַבְנֵי מִלֻּאִים *set* (inserted jewels); see מִלֻּאָה.

מַלֵּאת f., Cant. 5:12, *fulness,* perhaps *prominency,* some peculiar mode of setting jewels.

מַלְאָכִי, מְלָאכָה, מַלְאֲכוּת, מַלְאָךְ; see
לאך.

מַלְבּוּשׁ same as לְבוּשׁ clothing; see
לבשׁ.

מַלְבֵּן brick kiln; see לבן.

מִלָּה saying, see מלל.

מְלוּ for מִלְאוּ Kal pret. pl., from מלא.

מְלוּכָה, מְלוּכָה rule; see מלך.

מָלוֹן מְלוּנָה inn; see לון.

I. מָלַח Niph. נִמְלַח pass away,
vanish, Isa. 51:6.

מְלָחִים m. pl., rolling, passing away,
Jer. 38:11, 12.

II. מָלַח (from מֶלַח), salted, Ex. 30:
35. Pu. part. מְמֻלָּח. Hoph. salted,
Eze. 16:4.

מֶלַח m., salt; יָם־הַמֶּלַח the salt sea,
i. e. the Dead Sea; בְּרִית מֶלַח covenant of salt, i. e. perpetual, Nu.
18:19.

מְלַח m. Ch., salt.

מְלַח Ch., eat salt, Ezr. 4:14.

מַלּוּחַ m., ἅλιμος, salt plant, (halimus
atriplex—Linn.).

מַלָּח m., pl. מַלָּחִים sailors.

מְלֵחָה f., salt land, waste.

מִלְחָמָה war; see לחם.

מָלַט Pi. מִלֵּט, מִלַּט.—I. cause to
escape, slip.—II. deliver, save.—III.
hatch (of eggs), Isa. 34:15. Hiph.
same as Pi. Niph. was delivered,
set at liberty, saved. Hith. same
as Niph.

מֶלֶט m., clay.

מְלַטְיָה p. n. of a man.

מְלִילוֹת ears of corn; see מלל.

מְלִינִים Hiph. part. pl., from לון.

מְלִיצָה saying; see לון.

מָלַךְ reigned; with בְּ, עַל was made a
king. Hiph. make any one a king,
with לְ. Hoph. was made king.
Dan. 9:1. Niph. took, sought,
counsel.

מֶלֶךְ m. (with suff. מַלְכִּי; pl. מְלָכִים,
מַלְכֵי) king, applied to God and
also to idols; דֶּרֶךְ הַמֶּלֶךְ royal
way.—II. p. n. of a man.—III.
עֵמֶק הַמֶּלֶךְ p. n., a valley not far
from the Dead Sea.

מֶלֶךְ m. Ch., king.

מְלַךְ m. Ch., counsel, Dan. 4:24.

מֹלֶךְ, with art. הַמֹּלֶךְ Μολόχ, Moloch,
an idol of the Ammonites.

מַלְכָּה f., queen. Ch. the same.

מִלְכָּה p. n. of a daughter of Haran.

מְלֶכֶת f. מ׳ הַשָּׁמַיִם the queen of
Heaven, Ashtoreth, Astarte, an idol
of Canaan.

מֹלֶכֶת p. n. of a woman.

מַלּוּךְ (מְלִיכוּ, מַלּוּכִי) p. n. of a man.

מְלוּכָה f., rule, government, royalty.

מַלְכוּת f., rule, kingdom, royal dignity.

מַלְכוּ f. Ch., the same.

מַלְכִּיאֵל p. n. of a man; ‑י patron.

מַלְכִּיָּהוּ, מַלְכִּיָּה p. n. of a man.

מַלְכִּי־צֶדֶק p. n., Melchizedek, king of
Salem.

מַלְכִּירָם p. n. of a man.

מַלְכִּי־שׁוּעַ p. n. of one of Saul's sons.

מִלְכֹּם, מַלְכָּם same as מֶלֶךְ.

מֶלֶךְם for מַה־לָכֶם; see מה.

מַמְלָכָה f. (const. מַמְלֶכֶת; with suff
מַמְלַכְתּוֹ; pl. מַמְלָכוֹת rule, regal
government; בֵּית מ׳ seat of government   עִיר מ׳ capital city;
זֶרַע מ׳ royal family.

מַמְלָכוּת const. מַמְלְכוּת f., the same.

מַלְכֹּדֶת trap; see לכד.

מָלַל speaking. Pi. מִלֵּל announce, tell.

מְלַל Ch. Pa. מַלִּל speak, announce.

מִלָּה f. (pl. מִלִּין, מִלִּים) — I. saying, argument.—II. thing spoken of.

מִלָּה f. Ch. (pl. מִלִּין) saying, decree.

מְלָלַי p.n. of a man.

מַלּוֹתִי p.n. of a man.

מְלִילָה f., pl. מְלִילוֹת ears of corn, Deu. 23:26.

מַלְמָד goad; see למד.

מָלַץ Niph. נִמְלְצוּ are become smooth, agreeable, Ps. 119:103.

מֶלְצַר a certain office in the king of Babylon's palace; nature of the office unknown, Dan. 1:11, 16.

מָלַק break, bruise, Lev. 1:15; 5:8; LXX. ἀποκνίζειν.

מַלְקֹחַיִם, מַלְקָחַיִם, מַלְקוֹת; see לקח.

מַלְקוֹשׁ latter rain; see לקש.

מֶלְתָּחָה f., wardrobe, 2 Ki. 10:22.

מַלְתָּעוֹת jaws; see לתע.

מַמְּגֻרוֹת granary; see גור.

מְמַדִּים measures; see מדד.

מְמוּכָן p.n. of a prince of Persia.

מְמוֹתִים, מָמוֹת; see מות.

מַמְזֵר m.—I. foreigner.—II. bastard.

מִמְכֶּרֶת, מִמְכָּר sale; see מכר.

מַמְלָכוּת, מַמְלָכָה kingdom; see מלך.

מַמְרֹרִים, מֶמֶר; see מרר.

מַמְרֵא p.n.; see מרא.

מֶמְשֶׁלֶת, מֶמְשָׁלָה, מִמְשָׁל; see משל.

מָן manna; see מֶן; מָנִים; see מנן.

מָן, מֵן Ch. pron.—I. who?—II. what? מָן דִּי whoever.

מִן, מִנִּי, מִי, מַד, מִן (with suff. מִמֶּם, סָנְהוּ, מִנָּהּ; סָנִי, מִנִּי; מִהֶן, מִנְהֶם or מֶהֶם; see מֶן in מנן) prep.—I. from.—II. from out of.—III. of.—IV. by.—V. because of.—VI. besides.—VII. among; תִּשָּׁכַל מִנָּשִׁים she shall be barren among women.—VIII. some of, part of.—IX. more than; used also with inf.; הִשְׁחִיתוּ מֵאֲבוֹתָם they are worse than the fathers; מָתוֹק מִדְּבַשׁ sweeter than honey; אֶגְדַּל מִמֶּךָּ I shall be greater than thee; מִן...וְעַד; מִן...עַד from ...unto; לְמִן from thence.

מִן Ch., the same.

מְנָאוֹת; see מָנָה in מנה.

מִנְדָּה same as מִדָּה; see מדד.

מַנְדַּע knowledge, &c.; see ידע.

מָנָה I. number.—II. appoint, constitute, with לְ. Niph. נִמְנָה was numbered, with אֶת. Pi. מִנָּה appoint, constitute, with עַל, לְ. Pu. part. מְמֻנִּים persons appointed, 1 Chron. 9:29.

מְנָא, מְנָה Ch., numbered, tried. Pa. constituted, appointed.

מָנֶה m., a certain weight, perhaps of one hundred shekels.

מָנָה f. (pl. מָנוֹת) part, portion.

מְנָת f. (pl. מָנִיּוֹת, מְנָאוֹת) part, portion.

מֹנִים m. pl., times; עֲשֶׂרֶת מ׳ ten times, Gen. 31:7, 41.

מְנִי m., an idol, Isa. 65:11.

מִנְיָן m. Ch., number, Ezr. 6:17.

מִנְהָרוֹת; see נהר.

מָנוֹד refuge; see נוד.

מְנוּחָה, מָנוֹחַ; see נוח.

מָנַת ; see נון.

מָנוֹס, מְנוּסָה ; see נוס.

מָנוֹד ; see ניר.

מְנוֹרָה ; see נור.

מִנְּזָרִים same as נְזִירִים.

מִנְחָה (Arab. *he gave*).

מִנְחָר f. (pl. מִנְחוֹר ; with suff. מִנְחֹתֵיכֶם).— I. *gift to men.*— II. *to God, meat-offering.*

מִנְחָה f. Ch., *gift.*

מְנַחֵם p.n. of a man.

מָנַחַת p.n.—I. of a man.— II. of a place.

מִנִּי p.n. of a place, perhaps *Armenia*, Jer. 51:27; see also in מֶן, מִן, מֶנּוּ.

מִנְיָן, מָנְיוֹת, מֵנִי ; see מנה.

מִיָמִין, מִנְיָמִין p.n. of a man.

מָן m., *manna*, the food miraculously supplied to the Israelites in the wilderness.

מֶן m. with suff. מִנְּהוּ *part of him,* with prep. מִן and suff. ; מִמֶּנִּי *from me*; מִמְּךָ, מִמֶּךָּ f. מִמֵּךְ *from thee*; מִמֶּנּוּ *from him*; מִמֶּנָּה *from her*; see מִן.

מִנִּים, מֵנִי pl., *strings of an instrument*, Ps. 150:4; 45:9.

מֵנִית p.n., a place in Ammon.

מָנַע (fut. יִמְנַע) *keep back, withhold,* with מִן and לְ. Niph. נִמְנַע *was withholden, kept back.*

מִנְעָל, מַנְעוּל ; see נעל.

מַנְעַמִּים *delicacies*; see נעם.

מְנַעְנְעִים *cymbals*; see נוע.

מְנַקִּיּוֹת *bowls*; see מְנַקִית in נקה.

מִנְקֶת ; see ינק.

מְנַשֶּׁה (*that which is forgotten*), p.n.

— I. *Manasseh* the son of Joseph, Μανασσῆς; patron. מְנַשִּׁי. הַמְנַשֶּׁה.— II. given also to other men.

מְנָת *part*; see מנה.

מָס, מַס, מִסִּים ; see מסס.

מְסִבּוֹת, מִסְבֵּי, מֵסַב ; see סבב.

מִסְגֶּרֶת, מַסְגֵּר ; see סגר.

מַסַּד *foundation*; see יסד.

מִסְדְּרוֹן *portico*; see סדר.

מָסָה same as מסס. Hiph. הִמְסָה I. *dissolved, melted.*—II. *fainted.*

מִסָּה, see מסס; מַסָּה, see נסה.

מַסְוֶה m., *veil of Moses*, Ex. 34:33-35.

מְסוּכָה same as מְשׂוּכָה *hedge*; see שׂוּךְ.

מָסָח ; see נסח.

מִסְחָר *traffic*; see סחר.

מָסַךְ *mixed.*

מֶסֶךְ m., *mixture*, Ps. 75:9.

מִמְסָךְ *mixed wine.*

מַסֵּכָה, מָסָךְ ; see סכך.

מַסֶּכֶת, מַסֶּכָה ; see נסך.

מִסְכְּנוֹת, מִסְכְּנֻת, מִסְכֵּן ; see סכן.

מַסְלוּל, מְסִלָּה ; see סלל.

מַסְמְרוֹת, מַסְמְרִים, מַסְמְרִים ; see סמר.

מָסַס I. *dissolve, melt.*—II. *faint.* Niph. נָמֵס, with pause יִמַּס (fut. יִמַּס), inf. הִמֵּס).—I. *was dissolved, melted.* — II. *enervated by fear, grief, pain.* Hiph. pl. הֵמַסּוּ *cause to faint,* Deu. 1:28; see מאס.

מָס m., *wasting, miserable*, Job 6:14.

מַס m., *tribute, tax*; הָיָה לָמַס and הָיָה לָמַס עֹבֵד *became tributary*; שׂוּם לָמַס or נָתַן the same; אֲשֶׁר עַל הַמַּס *who was over the tribute*; pl. שָׂרֵי מִסִּים *chief collectors* (of tribute), Ex. 1:11.

מִסָּה f., const. מִסַּת tribute, offering, Deu. 16:10.

תָּמֵס m., melting, wasting away, Ps. 58:9.

מַסָּע, מַסַּע; see נסע.

מִסְעָד prop; see סעד.

מִסְפֵּד grief; see ספד.

מִסְפּוֹא provender; see אסם.

מִסְפַּחַת, מִסְפָּחוֹת; see ספח.

מִסְפָּר, מִסְפֶּרֶת number; see ספר.

מָסַר, inf. לִמְסֹר to stir up, wring out rebellion, Nu. 31:16. Niph. fut. וַיִּמָּסְרוּ were extracted, selected, Nu. 31:5.

מָסֹרֶת f., fetters, bonds, Eze. 20:37, from אסר.

מֹסֵר discipline; see יסר.

מִסְתָּר, מִסְתּוֹר; see סתר.

מַעְבָּד work, see עבד; מַעֲבֶה deep, see עבה.

מַעְבָּרָה, מַעְבָּר passage; see עבר.

מַעְגָּלָה, מַעְגָּל, מַעֲנָל; see ענל.

מָעַד vacillate. Hiph. cause to vacillate. Hoph. made to vacillate, Pro. 25:19.

מַעֲדַי p. n. of a man.

מֹעַדְיָה, מַעַדְיָה p. n. of a man.

מַעֲדַנִּים, מַעֲדַנּוֹת delicacies; see עדן.

מֵעָה (Arab. bowels)

מֵעִים const. מְעֵי m. pl. (with suff. מֵעַי, מֵעֶיךָ).—I. intestines.—II. belly.—III. womb.—IV. heart, mind.

מְעִין m. pl. Ch., belly.

מֵעָה f., מְעֹוֹתָיו "its extent" (Lee), Isa. 48:19.

מָעוֹג cake; see עוג.

מָעֹז, מָעוּז; see עזז.

מָעוֹךְ p. n. of a man, 1 Sa. 27:2.

מְעוֹנָתִי, מְעוֹנָה, מְעֹנִים, מָעוֹן; see מעון עון.

מָעוּף; see עוף.

מָעוֹר nakedness; see עור.

מַעֲנָיָה, מַעֲזְיָהוּ p. n. of a man.

מָעַט was, became, few, small. Pi. מֵעֵט the same, Ecc. 12:3. Hiph. הִמְעִיט I. make few.—II. give little.

מְעַט (מְעָט) a little, few; pl. מְעַטִּים few; מְעַט מַיִם a little water, Gen. 18:4; מְתֵי מְעַט few men, Deu. 26:5; מְעַט מְעַט by little and little, Ex. 23:23; בִּמְעַט I. within a little.—II. shortly, soon.—III. as a few, as nothing.

מָעֻט, f. מְעֻטָּה drawn, naked (lit. bald), of a sword, Eze. 21:20.

מַעֲטֶה garment; see עטה.

מַעֲטָפָה; see עטף.

מְעִי; see עוה.

מְעִי p. n. of a man.

מְעִיל cloak; see מעל.

מֵעִים bowels, &c.; see מעה.

מַעְיָן well; see עין.

מָעַךְ, part. מָעוּךְ I. pressed, 1 Sa. 26:7.—II. bruised, injured (θλα- δίας), Lev. 22:24. with בְּ. Pu. מֹעַךְ pressed, Eze. 23:3.

מַעֲכָת, מַעֲכָה p. n.—I. of a region and city near Mount Hermon.— II. a name applied both to men and women; מַעֲכָתִי a Maachathite.

מָעַל (inf. מְעֹל; fut. יִמְעַל, יִמְעֹל), do perversely, wickedly, rebel, with בְּ.

מַעַל m., perverseness, sin, Job 21:34; see also in עלה.

מְעִיל m., long upper garment worn by persons of rank.

מַעֲלֶה ,מַעֲלָה ,מֹעַל ,מֵעַל; see עלה.

מֵעֲלִיל ,מַעֲלָל ,מַעֲלִין; see עלל.

מַעֲמָד ,מָעֳמָד; see עמד.

מַעֲמָסָה; see עמס.

מַעֲמַקִּים depths; see עמק.

מַעֲנִית ,מַעֲנֶה ,מַעֲנָה (לְמַעַן) מַעַן; see ענה.

מְעוֹנָה same as מְעוֹנָה habitation; see עון.

מַעַץ p.n. of a man.

מַעֲצָבָה labour; see עצב.

מַעֲצָד axe; see עצד.

מָעֲצוֹר ,מַעֲצָר; see עצר.

מַעֲקֶה; see עקה.

מַעֲשִׂים; see עשׂ.

מַעַר ,מַעֲרָה ,מְעָרָה ,מַעֲרֹת ,מַעֲרַת; see ער.

מַעֲרָב ,מַעֲרָבָה; see ערב.

מַעֲרָךְ ,מַעֲרָכָה ,מַעֲרֶכֶת; see ערך.

מַעֲרֻמִּים; see ערם.

מַעֲרָצָה terror; see ערץ.

מַעֲשֶׂה ,מַעֲשֵׂי ,מַעֲשִׂיָּה; see עשׂה.

מַעֲשֵׂר ,מַעַשְׂרוֹת ,מַעֲשֵׂר; see עשׂר.

מַעֲשַׂקּוֹת; see עשׁק.

מֹף and נֹף p.n., a city of Egypt.

מַפַּח ,מַפָּח; see נפח.

מְפִיבֹשֶׁת ,מְפִבֹשֶׁת p.n.—I. a son of Saul.—II. a son of Jonathan.

מֵפִיץ; see פוץ.

מַפָּל ,מַפֶּלֶת ,מַפָּלָה; see נפל.

מִפְלָאָה; see פלא.

מִפְלַגָּה classes; see פלג.

מִפְלָט escape; see פלט.

מִפְלֶצֶת idol; see פלץ.

מִפְלָשׂ poising; see פלשׂ.

מִפְעָל ,מִפְעָלָה; see פעל.

שִׂימְפַּעַת same as מִפַּעַת.

מִפָּץ ,מַפֵּץ; see נפץ.

מִפְקָד; see פקד.

מִפְרָץ; see פרץ.

מַפְרֶקֶת vertebra; see פרק.

מִפְרָשׂ; see פרשׂ.

מִפְשָׂעָה buttocks; see פשׂע.

מִפְתָּח ,מַפְתֵּחַ; see פתח.

מִפְתָּן threshold; see פתן.

מֹץ chaff, same as מוֹץ.

מָצָא (fut. יִמְצָא; imp. מְצָא; pl. f. מְצֶאןָ; inf. מְצֹא; with suff. מֹצַאֲכֶם; part. מוֹצֵא ,מוֹצֵא, f. מֹצֵאת ,מֹצֵאת).—I. come to, arrive at.—II. obtain, acquire.—III. find, discover.—IV. find, i. e. meet with, discover.—V. be enough, with לְ, עַד. Niph. נִמְצָא (fut. יִמָּצֵא).—I. was obtained, acquired.—II. was found, arrived at.—III. was present, at hand, with לְ. Hiph. הִמְצִיא I. cause to come, deliver up, with בְּיַד into the power of any one.—II. recompense, repay.—III. present, offer up.

מַצֵּבָה ,מַצֵּבָה ,מַצָּב ,מַצָּב, מַצֶּבֶת; see נצב.

מִצְבָּיָה p.n. of an unknown place.

מְצוּדָה ,מְצוּדָה ,מָצוֹד ,מְצָד; see צוד.

מָצָה suck, drain, wring out, with מִן. Niph. נִמְצָה become sucked, drained, wrung out.

מַצָּה see in מצץ and נצה.

מֹצָה p.n., a town in the tribe of Benjamin.

מְצָהֲלָה neighing; see צהל.

מִצְוָה; see צוה.

מְצוֹלָה ,מְצוּלָה depth; see צול.

מְצוֹק ,מָצוֹק ,מְצוּקָה restraint; see צוק.

**מָצוֹר** p. n., *Egypt*; 'מ יְאֹרֵי *the river of Egypt, the Nile*; see also מָצוֹר, מְצֻרָה in צוּר.

**מִצְרַיִם** p. n.—I. *a son of Ham.*—II. *Egypt.*—III. *an Egyptian.*

**מִצְרִי** m.; pl. מִצְרִים; f. מִצְרִית; pl. מִצְרִיּוֹת *an Egyptian.*

**מַצּוּת** *contention*; see נצה.

**מֵצַח** m. (with suff. מִצְחוֹ; pl. const. מִצְחוֹת), *forehead.*

מִצְחָה f., *greaves* (guards for the legs), 1 Sa. 17:6.

**מְצֻלָה, מְצוֹלוֹת, מְצֹלְתַּיִם**; see צלל.

**מִצְנֶפֶת** *turban*; צנף.

**מַצָּע** *bed*; see יצע.

**מִצְעָד**; see צער.

**מִצְעָר, מִצְעִירָה** *little*; see צער.

**מִצְפֶּה, מִצְפָּה**; see צפה.

**מַצְפֻּנִים** *hidden places*; see צפן.

**מָצַץ** *suck* (as an infant), Isa. 66:11.

מַצָּה f., ἄζυμον, pl. מַצּוֹת *pure, unleavened bread*, τὰ ἄζυμα; חַג הַמַּצּוֹת ἡ ἑορτὴ τῶν ἀζύμων, *the feast of unleavened bread*; see also in נצה.

**מֵצֶר, מְצָרִים** *trouble*; see צרר.

**מִצְרַיִם** *Egypt, &c.*; see מָצוֹר.

**מַק** *rottenness*; see מקק.

**מַקֶּבֶת, מַקָּבָה**; see נקב.

**מַקֵּדָה** p.n., a town in the tribe of Judah.

**מִקְדָּשׁ**; see קדש.

**מַקְהֵלוֹת, מַקְהֵלִים** *assemblies*; see קהל.

**מִקְוֶה, מִקְנֶה** *hope*; see קוה.

**מָקוֹם** *place*; see קום.

**מָקוֹר** *fountain*; see קור.

**מַסָּחַת, מִפָּח**; see לקח.

**מַקְטֶרֶת, מִקְטָר**; see קטר.

**מַקֵּל** m. (const. מַקֵּל, מַקַּל; with suff. מַקְלִי, pl. מַקְלוֹת), *stick.*

---

**מִקְלֹת** p. n. of a man.

**מִקְלָט** *safety*; see קלט.

**מִקְלַעַת** *sculpture*; see קלע.

**מִקְנֶה, מִקְנָה, מִקְנְיָהוּ**; see קנה.

**מָקָץ** p. n. of a place.

**מַקְצֹעַ, מִקְצֹעוֹת, מְקֻצְעוֹת**; see קצע.

**מָקַק**. Niph. נָמַק *waste away, consume, fail*. Hiph. הֵמַק *cause to waste*, Zec. 14:12.

מַק m., *rottenness*, Isa. 3:24.

**מִקְרָא**; see קרא.

**מְקֵרָה, מִקְרֶה**; see קרה.

**מְקֵרָה** *coolness*; see קרר.

**מְמַרְקֵר** Pi. part., from קור.

**מִקְשָׁה, מְקֻשָּׁה**; see קשה.

**מָר, מוֹר, מֹר, מַר**; see מרר.

**מָרָא**, part. מוֹרָאָה *rebellious*, Zep. 3:1. Hiph. *put forth courage*, Job 39:19; see מָרָה.

**מְרִיא** m.—I. *fattened.*—II. specially *a fatted calf.*

**מָרֵא** m. Ch., *Lord.*

**מֻרְאָה** f., *crop* (of birds), Lev. 1:16.

**מַמְרֵא** p.n.—I. of a man, *Mamre.*—II. אֵלוֹנֵי מַמְרֵא (*oaks of Mamre*), and מַמְרֵא p. n. of a place near Hebron.

**מֵרָא** p. n. of a woman.

**בְּרֹאדַךְ בַּלְאֲדָן** 'מ p. n., *one of the kings of Babylon.*

**מַרְאֶה, מַרְאָה**; see ראה.

**מְרַאֲשׁוֹת, מַרְאֲשָׁה, מְרֵאשָׁה**; see ראש.

**מֵרָב** p. n., *Merab*, a daughter of Saul

**מַרְבַּדִּים** *coverlets*; see רבד.

**מַרְבִּית, מַרְבָּה, מִרְבָּה**; see רבה.

**מִרְבָּץ, מַרְבֵּץ**; see רבץ.

**מַרְבֵּק** *stall*; see רבק.

**מִרְגָּעָה, מַרְגֹּעַ**; see רגע.

מַרְגְּלוֹת at the feet; see רגל.

מַרְגֵּמָה heap of stones; see רגם.

מָרַד rebelled, with בְּ, עַל.

מְרַד Ch., rebellion, Ezr. 4:19.

מֶרֶד m.—I. the same, Jos. 22:22.—
II. p. n. of a man.

מָרָד Ch., f. מָרְדָא rebellious, Ezr. 4:
12, 15.

מַרְדּוּת f., rebellion, 1 Sa. 20:30.

מְרֹדָךְ m., perhaps the name of an idol
of Babylon, Jer. 50:2.

מָרְדְּכַי p. n., Mordechai, a Jew in
Persia, Μαρδοχαῖος.

מָרָה rebelled, rebelled against, dis-
obeyed, with בְּ; מ' אֶת־פִּי יְהֹוָה
they rebelled against the mouth (i. e.
words) of the Lord. Hiph. הִמְרָה
fought against, embittered, an-
gered, with בְּ, עִם.

מוֹרָה m., razor.

מְרִי m. (with pause מֶרִי; with suff.
מֶרְיְךָ, מֶרְיָם).—I. bitterness.—II.
rebellion.—III. rebellious.

מְרִיב בַּעַל (מְרִי בַעַל) p. n., the son
of Jonathan, called also מְפִיבֹשֶׁת.

מִרְיָה p.n. of a man.

מְרָיוֹת p. n. of a man.

מִרְיָם p. n., Miriam the sister of
Moses, Μαρία.

מְרָתַיִם dual f. (double rebellion), a
prophetic title of Babylon, Jer.
50:21.

מָרוֹת ,מֹרָה ,מָרָה ,מֹרָה; see מרד.

מָרוּד persecuted; see רוד.

מֵרֹת p. n., a town in the north of Palestine.

מָרוֹחַ; see מרח.

מָרוֹם ,מָרוֹם; see רום.

מְרוּצָה מָרוּץ; see רוץ.

מִרְזַח ,מַרְזֵחַ; see רזח.

מָרַח apply (as a plaster). Isa. 38:21,
with עַל.

מָרוֹחַ m., מְרוֹחַ אֶשֶׁךְ with crushed testicles, Lev. 21:20.

מֶרְחָב wide; see רחב.

מַרְחַקִּים ,מֶרְחָק; see רחק.

מַרְחֶשֶׁת pot; see רחש.

מָרַט I. pluck out hair; hence,— II.
made smooth, polished. Niph. became bald. Pu. polished, 1 Ki. 7:
45.

מְרַט Ch., plucked, Dan. 7:4.

מִרְיָם ,מְרִיּוֹת ,מְרִי; see מרה.

מְרִיא fat; see מרא.

מְרִיבָה strife; see ריב.

מוֹרִיָּה ,מֹרִיָּה f. p. n., Moriah, a hill in
Jerusalem.

מְרִידִי מְרִירוּת; see מרר.

מֹרֶךְ m., softness, cowardice, Lev. 26.
36; LXX. δειλία.

מֶרְכָּבָה ,מַרְכָּבָה ,מֶרְכָּב; see רכב.

מַרְכֹּלֶת merchandise; see רכל.

מִרְמָה deceit; see רמה.

מְרֵמוֹת p. n. of a man.

מֶרֶס p. n. of a Persian prince.

מַרְסְנָא p. n. of a Persian prince.

מַרְעִית ,מִרְעֶה ,מְרֵעַ; see רעה.

מְרֹנֹתִי m., a Maronothite.

מִרְעָלָה p. n., a town in the tribe of
Zebulun.

מַרְפֵּה ,מַרְפֵּא; see רפא, רפה.

מָרַץ. Niph. was, became, unsound,
weak, diseased. Hiph. urge to
folly, Job 16:3.

מַרְצֵעַ awl; see רצע.

מַרְצֶפֶת; see רצף.

מָרַק rubbed bright, polished. Pu. מֹרַק
was polished, Lev. 6:21.

מְרוּקִים m. pl., *purifications*, Est. 2:12.

מָרָק m., *broth*, Jud. 6:19, 20.

תַּמְרוּג m., *purification, cleansing*.

מִרְקַחַת, מֶרְקָחָה, מֶרְקָח see רקח.

מָרַר; מַר לִי *it is bitter to me*, with מָן Niph. נָמַר *was offensive* (an odour), Jer. 48:11. Pi. מֵרַר (fut. יְמָרֵר) *makes bitter, grieves*; מ' בַּבְּכִי *was bitter in weeping, wept bitter tears*. Hiph. הֵמַר (inf. הָמֵר) *make bitter*. Hithpalp. הִתְמַרְמַר *was angry*, Dan. 8:7; 11:11.

מַר m.— I. *a drop*, Isa. 40:15.— II. *bitterness*; adj. מַר (pl. מָרִים; f. מָרָה) *bitter, bitterly*.

מֹר, מוֹר, מָר m., *myrrh*.

מָרָה f.—I. *bitterness, sorrow*, 2 Sa. 2:26.—II. p. n., *a well in the desert of Sinai*.— III. *title which Naomi gave herself*, Ru. 1:20.

מֹרָה f., *sorrow*, Pro. 14:10.

מֹרָה f., *the same*, Gen. 26:35.

מָרוֹת p. n, *a town of Judah*.

מְרִירִי m., *bitter*, Deu. 32:24.

מְרִירוּת f., *bitter sorrow*, Eze. 21:11.

מְרֹרָה f.—I. *gall*.—II. *bitterness*.

מְרֵרָה f., *gall bladder*, Job 16:13.

מְרֹרִים m. pl., *bitter herbs*.

מְרָרִי p. n., *a son of Levi*.

מֶמֶר m., *bitterness*, Pro. 17:25.

מְמֵרָה f., *gall bladder*, Job 20:25.

מַמְּרֹרִים m. pl., *bitter things*, Job 9:18.

תַּמְרוּרִים m. pl., *bitterness, bitter sorrow*; see also תמר.

מַשָּׂאַת, מְשָׂאֵת, מַשְׂאָה, מַשָּׂא, מַשָּׂא; מַשֻּׂאֵת; see נשא.

מִשְׂגָּב; see שׂגב

שֹׂכֵךְ see מְשׂוּכָּה; שׂוּךְ see מְשׂוּגָּה, see מְשׂוּכָה, see שׂכך

מַשּׂוֹר *saw*; see נשׂר.

מְשׂוּרָה; see משׂר.

מָשׂוֹשׂ; see שׂושׂ.

מִשְׂחָק *object of laughter*; see שׂחק.

מַשְׂטֵמָה *hatred*; see שׂטם.

מַשְׂכִּיֹּות, מַשְׂכִּית; see שׂכה.

מַשְׂכֹּרֶת *wages*; see שׂכר.

מַשְׂמְרוֹת *nails*; see סמר.

מִשְׂפָּח; see שׂפח.

מָשַׂר (Arab. *divided*).

מְשׂוּרָה f., *measure for liquids*.

מִשְׂרָה *government*; see שׂרה.

מַשְׂרֵפוֹת *burning*; see שׂרף.

מַשְׂרֵקָה p. n., *a place in Edom*.

מַשְׂרֵת m., *frying-pan*, 2 Sa. 13:9.

מַשׁ p. n., *Mash*, Gen. 10:23, probably the district called Mount Masius, which separates Armenia from Mesopotamia.

מֵשָׁא p. n., *Mesha*, one of the boundaries of the district of the Joktanites, Gen. 10:30, not exactly known.

מַשָּׁאָה, מַשָּׂא, see נשׂר; מִשָּׁאוֹן, see נשׁא

מַשְׁאַבִּים *watering places*; see שׁאב.

מִשְׁאָלָה, מִשְׁאָל; see שׁאל.

מִשְׁאֶרֶת *kneading trough*; see שׁאר.

מִשְׁבְּצוֹת; see שׁבץ.

מִשְׁבָּר, מַשְׁבֵּר *pain*; see שׁבר.

מִשְׁבַּתִּים; see שׁבת.

מִשְׁנֶה *mistake*; see שׁנה

מָשָׁה *drew* (out of the water), Ex. 2:10. Hiph. the same.

מֹשֶׁה (*drawn out of water*, Ex. 2:10), p. n., *Moses*, the lawgiver, Μωϋσῆς (Josephus).

מֶשִׁי m. *figured silk*, Eze. 16:10,13.

מָשָׁה *debt*: see נשׁה.

מְשׁוּאָה *desolation*; see שׁוא.

מַשְׁאוֹת, מַשּׁוּאוֹת; see שׁאה.

מְשׁוּבָה, מְשֻׁגָה *apostasy*; see שׁוב.

מְשׁוּגָה *error*; see שׁגג.

מָשׁוֹט, מִשׁוֹט *oar*; see שׁוט.

מָשַׁח (inf. מְשֹׁחַ, with ה parag.
מָשְׁחָה; imp. מְשַׁח; fut. יִמְשַׁח).
—I. *anointed*.—II. *anointed to an
office*.—III. *set apart to an office*,
Isa. 61:1.—IV. *dedicate by anointing*.—V. *anoint oneself for a banquet*, Am. 6:6, const. with בְּ.
Niph. נִמְשַׁח *was anointed*.

מָשִׁיחַ m.—I. *anointed*.—II. *the anointed One*, Christ.

מְשַׁח m. Ch., *oil*.

מָשְׁחָה f.—I. *unction*.— II. *portion*,
Lev. 7:35.

מָשְׁחָה inf., see מָשַׁח, Nu. 18:8; לְמׇ
*for a dedication*, i. e. thing set
apart for them.

מִמְשַׁח m., *extension, stretching out*,
Eze. 28:14.

מָשְׁחָת, מָשְׁחָת, מָשְׁחָת, מַשְׁחִית; see
שׁחת.

מִשְׁחָר *dawn*; see שׁחר.

מְשִׁי; see above מָשׁה.

מְשֵׁיזַבְאֵל p. n. of a man.

מָשַׁךְ I. *stretched out the hand*, Hos.
7:5.—II. *took hold of*, Ex. 12:21.
—III. *seized as spoil.*—IV. *drew, a
bow, yoke, net. &c.*, with בְּ.—V.
מָשַׁךְ הַיּוֹבֵל *lengthened the sound
of the trumpet*, Ex. 19:13.—VI.
*scattered seed*, Am. 9:13.—VII.
*continued in a thing.*—VIII. *reckon
with* (עִם), Ps. 28:3.—IX. *cheered*,

Ecc. 2:3. Niph. *was protracted,
delayed.* Pu. I. *spoiled*, Isa. 18:2,
7.—II. *obtained*, Pro. 13:12.

מֶשֶׁךְ m.—I. *acquiring*, Job 28:18.
—II. מֶשֶׁךְ הַזָּרַע *scattering of seed*,
Ps. 126:6.

מֹשְׁכוֹת f. pl., *attractions, influences*,
Job 38:31.

מֶשֶׁךְ p. n.—I. one of the sons of Japhet.
—II. the people descended from him,
Gen. 10:2. They were probably
the Muscovites; LXX. Μοσόχ;
Vulg. *Mosoch*.

מִשְׁכָּב, מִשְׁכַּב *bed*; see שׁכב.

מִשְׁכָּן *dwelling*; see שׁכן.

מָשַׁל I. *ruled.*—II. *had power over*,
with בְּ.—III. *had power to do*, with
לְ.—IV. *assimilated, compared to*,
with בְּ, עַל. Niph. *became like*,
with בְּ, עִם, אֶל. Pi. *speaking pa-
rables*, Eze. 21:5. Hiph. I. *give
authority* (inf. הַמְשֵׁל)Dan. 11:39.
—II. *made like*, Isa. 46:5. Hith.
*become like*, Job 30:19.

מֹשֵׁל m.—I. *authority*, Zec. 9:10.—
II. *anything like*, Job 41:25.

מָשָׁל m.—I. *solemn declaration.*—II.
*decision, rule, proverb*, γνώμη.—
III. *bye word, subject of taunt*.

מְשֹׁל m., *taunting proverb*, Job 17:6.

מִמְשָׁל m., *dominion*; pl. *rulers*, 1 Ch.
26:6.

מֶמְשָׁלָה f., *dominion, rule.*

מֶמְשֶׁלֶת f. (pl. מֶמְשְׁלוֹת, מֶמְשְׁלֹת),
the same.

מְשֻׁלָּחַת, מִשְׁלוֹחַ, מִשְׁלָח, מִשְׁלָח; see
שׁלח.

מְשֻׁלָּשׁ; see שׁלשׁ.

מְשֻׁלָּם p. n. of a man.

שְׁלֵמָיָה ,מְשֶׁלֶמְיָה p. n. of a man.

מְשִׁלֵּמוֹת ,מְשִׁלֵּמִית p. n. of a man.

מְשֻׁלֶּמֶת p. n., *Meshullemeth*, the wife of Manasseh.

מְשַׁמָּה *desolation*, &c.; see שמם.

מִשְׁמָן ;מִשְׁמַנִּים ,מִשְׁמַנָּה; see שמן.

מִשְׁמָע ;מִשְׁמַעַת; see שמע.

שָׁמַר see ;מִשְׁמֶרֶת ,מִשְׁמָרוֹת; מִשְׁמָר.

מִשְׁנֶה; see שנה.

מְשִׁסָּה *prey*; see שסם.

מִשְׁעוֹל *narrow way*; see שעל.

מָשַׁע (Arab. *take pains*).

לְמִ' מָשֵׁעִי *carefully*, Eze. 16:4.

מֵישָׁע p. n. of a man.

מִשְׁעָן ;מִשְׁעֶנֶת ,מַשְׁעֵנָה ,מִשְׁעָן; see שען.

מִשְׁפַּחַת מִשְׁפָּחָה *family*; see שפח.

מִשְׁפָּט *judgment*; see שפם.

מִשְׁפְּתַיִם; see שפה.

מֶשֶׁק m., מֶשֶׁק־בֶּן, LXX. υἱὸς Μέσεκ, Gen. 15:2, probably the name of a tribe or district in Syria, whence דַּרְמֶשֶׂק *Damascus*.

מִמְשָׁק m., *overspreading*, Zep. 2:9; but LXX. read Damascus.

מָשָׁק *running about*; see שקק.

מַשְׁקֶה *drink*; see שקה.

מִשְׁקוֹל ,מִשְׁקָל ,מִשְׁקֶלֶת ,מִשְׁקָלֶת; see שקל.

מַשְׁקוֹף see שקף.

מִשְׁרָה *juice*; see שרה.

מַשְׁרוֹקִיתָא *flute*; see שרק.

מִשְׁרָעִי p. n. of a man.

מָשַׁשׁ same as מוּשׁ *touch, feel*, Gen. 27:12. Pi. מִשֵּׁשׁ I. *examine by feeling.*—II. *felt his way, groped.* Hiph. (fut. יָמֵשׁ) *that may be felt*, Ex. 10:21; see in מוּשׁ.

---

מִשְׁתַּחֲוִיתֶם Eze. 8:16. Hith. part. pl with pers. pron., from שׁחה.

מֵת or מַת m., pl. מְתִים ,מְתַם, const. מְתֵי *men*.

מֵת ,מָתָה ,מַתָּה ,מֻתִּי ,מֻתוּ מְתִים, from מוּת Kal.

מְתָא Ch. Pe.inf., from אתה.

מַתְבֵּן *heap of straw*; see תֶּבֶן.

מֶתֶג m. (with suff. מִתְגִּי), *bridle*.

מָתוֹק ,מִתְקָה; see מתק.

מְתוּשָׁאֵל p. n., *Methusael*, one of Cain's descendants.

מְתוּשֶׁלַח p. n., *Methuselah*, the patriarch, the son of Enoch.

מָתַח *stretched out* (as a curtain), Isa. 40:22.

אַמְתַּחַת f. (pl. const. אַמְתְּחֹת), *sack* or *bag*.

מָתַי pa.—I. *when?*—II. *when*; אַחֲרֵי מָתַי *after how long?* Jer. 13:27; עַד מָתַי *how long?*

מַתְכֹּנֶת; see תכן.

מַתְלָאָה for מָה־תְּלָאָה *what trouble*. see לאה.

מִתְלַהְלַהּ Hith. part., from לָהַהּ.

מְתַלְּעוֹת *teeth*; see לתע.

מְתֹם *soundness*; see תמם.

מָתַן root not used; (Arab. *was firm*).

מָתְנַיִם m. dual, *loins*.

אֲמְתָנִי Ch. f., *powerful, mighty*, Dan. 7:7.

,מַתַּנְיָה ,מַתְּנֵי ,מַתְּנָא ,מַתָּן מַתְּנֵיהוּ; see נתן.

מִתְנִי p. n. of a man.

מָתַק (fut. יִמְתַּק), *were, became sweet.* Hiph. הִמְתִּיק I. *was sweet*, Job 20:12.—II. *made sweet*, Ps. 55:15

**מָתוֹק** m. (pl. מְתוּקִים; f. מְתוּקָה).
—I. *sweet.*—II. *sweetness.*— III.
*pleasant.*

**מֶתֶק** m., *sweetness.*

**מֹתֶק** m., the same, Jud. 9:11.

**מִתְקָה** p.n., a station of the Israelites
in the desert.

**מַמְתַּקִּים** m., pl. מַמְתַקִּים *sweetness,*
Neh. 8:10; Cant. 5:16.

**מִתְרְדָת** p.n., *Mithridates* the Persian
(Μιθριδάτης).

**מַתִּתְיָהוּ, מַתִּתְיָה, מַתַּתָּה, מַתָּת**; see
נתן.

**מֹסַתִּי** Pil. pret. 1. pers., from מוּת.

---

# נ

**נָא** interj., *I pray!* used,—I. in supplication.—II. in exhortation.—
III. in irony or blame; בָּא־נָא
*go I pray!* אִמְרִי־נָא *speak I pray!*
אֵלְכָה נָא *let me go, I pray!*
אַל־נָא תַעֲבֹר *pass not over, I
pray!* יֵאָמֶר־נָא *let it be told, I
pray!* אַל־נָא *do not I pray!* with
particles: אִם־נָא *if indeed;* אַל־נָא
*not so, I pray!* הִנֵּה־נָא *behold!*
אוֹי־נָא *alas!* see also in נְיָא.

**נֹא אָמוֹן, נֹא** p.n.; Διόσπολις, μέ-
ρις Ἀμμών, perhaps the city of
Thebes in Egypt.

**נָאד** root not used; (Arab. *poured out
water*).

**נֹאד** (נֹאוד) m. *skin bottle;* pl. נֹאדוֹת
*bottles.*

**נָאוָה** (pl. const. נְאוּוּ), *became, was
fair,* Ps. 93:5; see אָוָה.

**נָאֶה** f., pl. const. נְאוֹת *the best, choice,
parts* of any thing; נְ דֶּשֶׁא *plea-*
*sant herbage,* Ps. 23:2; generally
translated *habitation,* Ps. 74:20,
and elsewhere; but the former
appears to give a better sense.

**נָאוֶה** m., נָאוָה—I. *becoming, seemly*
—II. *fair.*

**נָאוּ** for נָאוֶה, from נאה.

**נָאוֹת** Niph. fut. pl. 1. pers., from אות.

**נָאַם** *make a solemn declaration,* Jer.
23:31; part. נְאֻם; נְ יֵי *saith the
Lord,* passim: used of Agur, Pro.
30:1.

**נָאַף** (fut. יִנְאַף).—I. *committed adultery.*—II. *worshipped false gods,*
Jer. 3:9; part. נֹאֵף *adulterer,*
נֹאֶפֶת *adulteress.* Pi. נִאֵף the
same.

**נַאֲפִים** m. pl.—I. *adulteries.*—II. *acts
of idolatry.*

**נַאֲפוּפִים** m. pl., *repeated acts of
adultery,* Hos. 2:4.

**נָאַץ** (fut. יִנְאַץ) *turned away from,
despised, rejected.* Pi. נִאֵץ (fut.
יְנָאֵץ) the same. Hiph. fut. יִנְאַץ
*it is despised,* Ecc. 12:5. Hith.
part. מִנֹּאָץ *contemned,* Isa. 52:5.

**נְאָצָה** f., *reproach, insult,* 2 Ki. 19
3; Isa. 37:3.

**נֶאָצָה** f., pl. נְאָצוֹת (נֶאָצוֹתֶיךָ), the
same.

**נָאַק** same as אָנַק *cry out,* Job 24:12

**נְאָקָה** const. נַאֲקַת f., *cry of sorrow*

**נָאַר.** Pi. נִאֵר (pret. 2. pers. נֵאַרְתָּה)
*rejected as worthless,* Ps. 89:40;
Lam. 2:7.

**נֶאְשְׁאָר,** Eze. 9:8, perhaps comp. of
אֶשָּׁאֵר and נִשְׁאַר; see שאר.

**נֹב** p.n., a city of the Levites in the

tribe of Benjamin; with ה, נֹבָה towards Nob.

נָבָא. Niph. נִבָּא *announced as the will of God, prophesied.* Hith. הִתְנַבֵּא, (וְהִתְנַבּוֹת) (inf.).—I. *prophecy.*—II. *be mad.*

נְבָא Ch. Ithp. הִתְנַבִּי *prophesied,* Exr. 5:1.

נָבִיא m. (with suff. נְבִיאֲכֶם).—I. *a prophet,* one who declares future events.—II. probably one devoted to the study of the revealed will of God; whence בְּנֵי הַנְּבִיאִים *the sons,* i.e. *disciples of the prophets* who studied under them.

נְבִיא m. Ch., the same.

נְבִיאָה f.—I. *prophetess.*—II. *prophet's wife.*

נְבוּאָה f.—I. *prediction,* Neh. 6:12. —II. *prophetical book.*

נְבוּאָה f. Ch., the same.

נְבוֹ p. n., *Nebo.*—I. one of the idols of Babylon, Isa. 46:1.—II. a mountain and city in the land of Moab. —III. a town in the tribe of Judah.

נְבוּזַרְאֲדָן p. n., one of Nebuchadnezzar's generals.

נְבוּכַדְרָאצַר, נְבוּכַדְנֶצַר, נְבוּכַדְנֶאצַר p. n., *Nebuchadnezzar,* the king of Babylon; LXX. Ναβουχοδονόσορ.

נְבוּשַׁזְבָּן p. n., a prince of Assyria.

נְבוֹב *proud;* see בּוּב.

נָבוֹח p. n. of a man.

נְבְזָה, נִבְזְבָּה f. Ch., *gift, reward.*

נִבְעֹה, 1 Sa. 14:36, Kal fut. pl. 1. pers. with ה parag. and dag. f. dropped; see בזה.

נָבַח *bark* (as a dog), Isa. 56:10.

נֹבַח p. n. of a man; also of a town in Gilead, Nu. 32:42; Jud. 8:11.

נִבְחַז p.n., an idol of the Avites, 2 Ki 17:31.

נָבַט. Pi. נִבַּט and Hiph. הִבִּיט.—I. *looked.*—II. *look at, towards,* with אֶל, לְ; *looked after,* with אַחֲרֵי.— III. *looked favourably at,* with בְּ; same as רָאָה *perceived.* — IV. *attended to.*—V. *noticed,* Ps. 10: 14.

נְבָט p. n., *Nebat,* the father of Jeroboam.

מַבָּט m., *expectation, hope,* Isa. 20: 5:6.

מֶבָּט m., the same, Zec. 9:5.

נְבִיאָה, נָבִיא see נבא.

נְבָיוֹת p. n., *Nebaioth,* a people of the race of Ishmael, Gen. 25:13, &c.

נָבִיתָ for נִבֵּאתָ, נִבֵּאתִי Niph. pret., from נבא.

נֵבֶךְ "*mazes of the sea*" (Lee), Job 38:16.

נָבֵל (fut. יִבֹּל).— I. *became shrivelled and fell* (as flowers, &c.). — II. *wasted away.* — III. *crumbled to dust.*—IV. *acted foolishly,* Pro. 30: 32. Pi. נִבֵּל *treated as worthless, set at nought.*

נָבָל m., נְבָלָה f.—I. *foolish.*—II. *impious.*— III. p. n. of a man, 1 Sa. c. 25.

וַנַּבֶל נָבֵל, Isa. 64:5, Hiph. fut. pl. 1. pers. from בלל; or for וַנָּבֶל Kal fut., from נבל.

נִבְלָה for נָבְלָה Kal fut. pl. 1. pers, with ה parag.; see בלל.

נְבֵלָה f.—I. *disgraceful action.*— II. *punishment of such an action,* Jos

7:15.— III. *impiety*, Isa. 32:6.—
IV. *folly*, 1 Sa. 25:25.

נְבֵלָה f. (const. נִבְלַת; with suff.
(נְבְלָתוֹ, נְבְלָתִי).—I. *carcase of an
animal.*— II. *dead body of a man.*
—III. *idols*, Jer. 16:18; collect.
*carcases.*

נַבְלוּת f., *shame, nakedness*, Hos. 2:
12.

נֵבֶל, נֶבֶל m. (pl. נְבָלִים).—I. *bottle*
(of skin).— II. *earthen jar.*— III.
*lute*, νάβλιον·

נְבַלָּט p. n., a town in the tribe of Benjamin.

נֹבֵעַ, נָבַע *springing* (as a fountain),
Pro. 18:4. Hiph. הִבִּיעַ—I. *ut-
ters, declares*—II. *prepares.*

מַבּוּעַ m., *spring, fountain of water.*

נָבְקָה for נָבְקָה Niph. pret. f., from
בקק.

נָבַר Niph., from ברר·

נֶבְרַשְׁתָּא f. Ch., *lamp*, Dan. 5:5.

נִבְשָׁן p. n. of a town in the tribe of
Judah.

נֶאֶלוּ for נֶאֶלוּ Niph. pret. pl., from
נאל II.

נְגֵב (Ch. נְגַב *was dry.*)

נֶגֶב m. — I. *the arid desert to the
south of Judea.* — II. *the south*;
נֶגְבָּה *towards, on, the south*;
לַנֶּגְבָּה, בַּנֶּגְבָּה *towards the south*;
מִנֶּגֶב *from the south.*

נָגַד Hiph. הִגִּיד *brought before, told,
made known*; with לְ of the person to whom. Hoph. הֻגַּד *was
told.*

נְגַד Ch., *proceeding, flowing*, Dan.
7:10.

נֶגֶד subst. *fore part of the body*; prep
*before, in front of, opposite to*,
adv. *straight forwards*; נֶגְדּוֹ, כְּנֶגֶד
*opposite to him*; לְנֶגֶד *before, opposite to*; מִנֶּגֶד *in presence of, in
sight, out of sight, over against,
opposite to, against.*

נָגִיד m.—I. *leader.*—II. *prince.*—III.
*chief.*—IV. *one appointed to any
charge.*

נָגַהּ *shined.* Hiph. הִגִּיהַּ *caused to
shine*, Isa. 13:10, *made light.*

נֹגַהּ f. (with suff. נָגְהָם).—I. *the dawn.*
— II. *light.* — III. p. n. a son of
David.

נֹגַהּ f. Ch., *dawn*, Dan. 6:20.

נְגֹהָה f., *light*, Isa. 59:9.

נָגַח (fut. יִגַּח), *push with the horn.*
Pi. נִגַּח the same. Hith. הִתְנַגַּח
*entered into conflict*, Dan. 11:40.

נַגָּח m., *addicted to pushing with the
horn*, Ex. 21:29, 36.

נָגַל root not used; (Arab. *sickle*).

מַגָּל m., *sickle*, Jer. 50:16; Joel 4:13

נָגַן and Pi. נִגֵּן *performed music.*

נְגִינָה f.—I. *music.*—II. *a song.*—III.
*subject of a song.*

מַנְגִּינָה f., *song of ridicule*, Lam.
3:63.

נָגַע (inf. נְגֹעַ, גַּעַת; with suff. נָגְעוֹ;
imp. גַּע; fut. יִגַּע; part. f. נֹגַעַת).
—I. *touched*, with בְּ, אֶל, עַל.—II
*touched gently, awakened*, with בְּ.
—III. *touched the heart*, with בְּ,
1 Sa. 10:26.—IV. *touched so as to
injure*, with בְּ.—V. *struck*, with
בְּ, Job 1:19. — VI. *arrived.* —
VII. *arrived at, reached*, with
בְּ, עַד, אֶל.—VIII. *reached the*

ear of, with אֶל, Jon 3:6. Niph.
were beaten in battle, Jos. 8:15.
Pi. נִגַּע struck with disease. Pu. are
afflicted, Ps. 73:5. Hiph. הִגִּיעַ
I. made to touch, with עַד, לְ, אֶל,
עַל.—II. reached, with עַד, לְ, אֶל,
עַל.—III. reached the ears of, with
אֶל, Est. 9:26.—IV. reached its
proper time, with לְ, Est. 9:1.—V.
came near, with לְ, Ps. 88:4.—VI.
arrived (of time).—VII. arrived
at, with עַד, לְ, אֶל.

נֶגַע m. (with suff. נִגְעוֹ; pl. נְגָעִים,
נִגְעֵי).—I. stroke, blow.—II. infliction of evil.—III. affliction.—IV.
mark of a blow, spot.

נָגַף (fut. יִגֹּף).—I. struck.—II. wounded.
—III. killed. — IV. defeated. — V.
struck with disease.—VI. stumbled.
Niph. נִגַּף (inf. abs. נָגוֹף), was defeated, routed (of an army), with
לִפְנֵי of the enemy. Hith. stumble,
Jer. 13:16.

נֶגֶף m.—I. infliction of disease.—II.
act of stumbling, Isa. 8:14.

מַגֵּפָה, const. מַגֵּפַת f.—I. plague,
pestilence.—II. defeat.

נָגַר. Niph. נִגַּר I. was put forth (the
hand), Ps. 77:3.—II. overflowed,
was spilt.—III. was scattered, as
wealth, Job 20:28. Hiph. הִגִּיר
I. dragged away.—II. poured out,
Ps. 75:9.—III. scattered, Mic.1:6.
Hoph. poured out, Mic. 1:4.

נָגַשׂ (fut. יִגֹּשׂ; תִּנְגֹּשׂ) exacted a task,
debt or tax; part. נֹגֵשׂ exactor,
taskmaster, slave-driver. Niph.
נִגַּשׂ was pressed, vexed, fatigued.

נָגַשׁ (fut. יִגַּשׁ; inf. גֶּשֶׁת; with suff.

(גִּשָׁה, גֶּשׁ, גְּשׁוּ) and imp. גַּשׁ, גְּשׁוּ; גִּשְׁתּוֹ;
Niph. נִגַּשׁ I. came near to, up to,
touched, with בְּ, לְ, אֶל.—עַל.—
II. perhaps depart, go away, Gen.
19:9. Hiph. הִגִּישׁ I. brought near.
—II. offered, i. e. brought near (an
offering). Hoph. הֻגַּשׁ was brought,
placed. Hith. approach, Isa. 45:20.

נֵד heap; see נדר.

נָדָא, fut. וַיַּדֵּא drave away, 2 Ki.
17:21.

נָדַב I. rendered willing, with לֵב and
רוּחַ.—II. impelled. Hith. הִתְנַדֵּב
offered or performed willingly.

נְדַב Ch. Hith. was willing, gave
willingly.

נָדָב p. n., Nadab.—I. the son of
Aaron.—II. given also to other men.

נְדָבָה, const. נִדְבַת f.—I. voluntary
offering. — II. free-will (בִּנְדָבָה,
נְדָבָה of his own accord, willingly),
—III. pl. abundance; גֶּשֶׁם נְדָבוֹת
plenteous rain, Ps. 68:10.

נְדַבְיָה p. n. of a man.

נָדִיב m.—I. willing, liberal.—II. noble,
distinguished. — III. Job 21:28;
perhaps " a libertine" (Lee).

נְדִיבָה f., liberality.

נִדְבָּךְ הִתְנַדְּבוּת (inf. Hith.) f. Ch., free-
will offerings, Exr. 7:16.

נִדְבָּךְ m. Ch., layer, course of stones
Exr. 6:4.

נָדַד (inf. נְדֹד; fut. יִדַּד).—I. fled
—II. wandered, walked to and fro.
—III. flapped the wings, Isa. 10:
14; part. נוֹדֵד. Po. נוֹדַד was
driven away, Nah. 3:17. Hiph.
הִגֵּד cause to wander, Job18:18.
Hoph. הֻנַּד made to wander, Job

20:8; *driven about*, 2 Sa. 23:6. Hith. *was agitated.*

נְדַד Ch., *fled*, Dan. 6:19.

נְדֻדִים m. pl., *restlessness* (of body or mind), Job 7:4.

נֵד m.—I. *a heap*, Isa. 17:11.—II. *a mound.*

נִדָּה f.—I. *legal impurity.*—II. *a woman in that state.*—III. *moral impurity.*—IV. *that which is impure, worthless*, Eze. 7:19, 20; מֵי הַנִּדָּה *water of impurity*, i. e. for the cleansing of legal impurity

נִידָה f., *impurity*, Lam. 1:8.

מְדָד m., *flight*, Job 7:4.

נָדָה same as נוּד. Pi. נִדָּה *put aside, desired to avoid*, with לְ, Isa. 66:5; Am. 6:3.

נֶדֶה m., *present, gift*, Eze. 16:33.

נֵדָן m., the same; see also below.

נָדַח (fut. יִדַּח).—I. *drove an axe*, Deu. 20:19.—II. *drove away*, 2 Sa. 14:14. Hiph. הִדִּיחַ I. *brought with violence*, with עַל.—II. *drove away.*—III. *induced to any thing*, Pro. 7:21. Niph. נִדַּח I. *was impelled.*—II. *was driven away.*—III. *was induced to an action*; part. נִדָּח (with suff. נִדְּחָךָ; pl נִדְּחוֹ f. נִדָּחָה). Pu. part. מְנֻדָּח *driven*, Isa. 8:22. Hoph. part. מֻדָּח *driven astray*, Isa. 13:14.

מַדּוּחִים m. pl., *expulsions, drivings out*, Lam. 2:14.

נְדִיב, נְדִיבָה; see נדב.

נִדְמָה for נִדַּמָּה Niph. fut. pl. 1. pers. with ה parag., from דמם.

נֵדָן m., *sheath* (of a sword), 1 Chron. 21:27; see also in נִדָּה.

---

נִדְנֶה m. Ch., "*midst*," Eng. Ver.; "*sheath*," Marg., Dan. 7:15.

נָדַף (fut. יִדֹּף, יִנְדֹּף).—I. *scattered, drove about.*—II. *routed, conquered* (an enemy), Job 32:13. Niph. נִדַּף (inf. הִנָּדֵף) *driven away.*

I. נָדַר (fut. יִדֹּר) *made a vow.*

נֶדֶר נֵדֶר m. (with suff. נִדְרִי; pl נְדָרִים, נִדְרֵי).—I. *vow.*—II. *thing vowed.*

II. נָדַר root not used; (Arab. *thresh corn*).

אִדַּר Ch., *threshing-floor*, Dan. 2:35; (Arab. the same).

נֹהַּ *lamentation*, Eze. 7:11; see נָהָה.

נָהַג (imp. נְהַג; fut. יִנְהַג).—I. *led, conducted.*—II. *drave cattle, &c.* —III. *guided.*—IV. *commanded an army.* Pi. נִהַג (fut. יְנַהֵג) I. *brought on a wind:* hence—II. נָהַג *breathed*, Nah. 2:8.—III. *led.* IV. *drave.*

מִנְהָג m., *driving of horses*, 2 Ki 9:20.

נָהַד root not used; (Arab. *swelled, grew vigorous*).

הוֹד m.— I. *vigour*, Pro. 5:9.—II. *glory, majesty.*—III. p. n. of a man

הוֹדַוְיָהוּ, הוֹדַוְיָה p.n.; see ירה.

הוֹדְיָה p.n. of a man.

הוֹדִיָּה p.n. of a man.

נָהָה *lamented*, Mic. 2:4. Niph. fut. וַיִּנָּהוּ *mourn after the Lord*, 1 Sa. 7:2.

נְהִי, with pause נֶהִי m., *lamentation* נְהִי, וַנָּהִי fut. apoc. pl.1. pers., from היה נְהִיָּה Mic. 2:4; see הָוָה.

נָהַל Pi. נִהַל (fut. יְנַהֵל).—I. *led.*—

II. tended, fed.—III. gave rest to, 2 Chron. 32:22. Hith. proceed with a flock, Gen. 33:14.

נַהֲלָל m.—I. pasture, Isa. 7:19.—II. p. n., a town in the tribe of Zebulun, called also נַהֲלֹל.

נָהַם (fut. יִנְהֹם).—I. roared, Isa. 5:29,30.—II. groaned.

נַהַם m., roaring of a lion.

נְהָמָה, const. נַהֲמַת f., roaring of the sea, Isa. 5:30.—II. groaning, Ps. 38:9.

נָהַק (fut. יִנְהַק) brayed (as an ass), Job 6:5; 30:7.

נָהַר I. brighten (of the face), Isa. 60:5; Ps. 34:6.—II. (fut. יִנְהַר) flow unto, assemble in.

נָהָר m. (pl. נְהָרוֹת, נְהָרוֹת, נְהָרִים).—I. river, stream.—II. current of the sea, Jonah; הַנָּהָר הַגָּדוֹל same as נְהַר פְּרָת Euphrates; אֲרַם נַהֲרַיִם Aram (Syria) of the rivers, Mesopotamia.

נְהַר m. Ch., river.

(נְהִיר) נְהוֹר m. Ch., light, Dan. 2:22.

נְהִירוּ f. Ch., light, wisdom, Dan. 5:11,14.

נְהָרָה f., light of day, Job 3:4.

מִנְהָרוֹת f. pl., clefts in mountains, serving as channels for the rain, Jud. 6:2.

נוֹא or נוּא Hiph. הֵנִיא—I. discouraged, Nu. 32:7.—II. prohibited.—III. frustrated.

תְּנוּאָה f.—I. aversion, Nu. 14:34.—II. heavy things, Job 33:10.

נוּב (fut. יְנוּב).—I. threw out shoots, Ps. 92:15.—II. produced fruit, Pro.

10:31.—III. increased, Ps. 62:11. Pi. נוֹבֵב makes fruitful, Zec 9:17.

נִיב m., produce, fruit.

נֵיבַי p. n. of a man.

תְּנוּבָה f., produce, fruit.

נְגֻנוֹת Niph. part. pl. f. for נֹגְנוֹת, from ינה.

נוּגֵי Niph. part. pl. for נוֹגֵי, from ינה. נוּגִים; see ינה.

נוּד (fut. יָנוּד).—I. move to and fro.—II. wandered as a fugitive; part. נָד a fugitive.—III. departed.—IV. shook the head, expressing pity, condoled. Hiph. הֵנִיד—I. moved to and fro.—II. drove out.—III. disturbed.—IV. shake the head in pity, Jer. 18:16. Hoph. part. מֻנָּד expelled, 2 Sa. 23:6. Hithpol הִתְנוֹדֵד bemoan himself, Jer. 31:18.

נוּד Ch., departs, Dan. 4:11.

נוֹד m.—I. wandering, Ps. 56:9.—II. p. n. (exile), the country to which Cain was banished.

נִיד m., moving of the lips, Job 16:5.

מָנוֹד m., shaking the head, Ps. 44:15.

נְדָב p. n., a son of Ishmael.

נָוָה (fut. יִנְוֶה) dwelt, Hab. 2:5. Hiph. prepare a dwelling; fut. with suff. אַנְוֵהוּ, Ex. 15:2.

נָוֶה m. (const. נְוֵה; with suff. נָוֶךָ, נָוֵהוּ, נְוֵהֶם).—I. fold for cattle.—II. dwelling of men.—III. habitation of God.

נָוָה f., habitation, Job 8:6; נְוַת בַּיִת she that remaineth at home; οἰκουρός, Ps. 68:13.

נָוָה dwelt quietly, Jer. 6:2.

נָיוֹת, Ketib נְוָיוֹת (*habitations*), p.n., a place near Ramah.

נוּחַ (fut. יָנוּחַ, וַיָּנַח).— I. *lay down, rested.*— II. *halted, ceased.*— III. *abode in,* with בְּ.—IV. *alighted on.* — V. *came down and possessed,* with עַל.— VI. *settled on* (as on a shoal, of the ark), Gen. 8:4. Hiph. I. הֵנִיחַ:— 1. *gave rest to.* — 2. *comforted.* — 3. *let fall,* Ex. 17:11.— 4. *caused to rest upon.*— II. הַנַּח and הִנִּיחַ— 1. *placed.*— 2. *left, forsook, quitted.*—3. *let rest, remain.* — 4. *permitted, gave into the power of.* — 5. *left untouched,* 2 Kı. 23:18, with לְ. Hoph. הוּנַּח. I. *rest was given,* Lam. 5:5.—II. *was placed, left, remaining.*

נוֹחַ נֹחַ m. (with suff. נוּחֲךָ).— I. *rest,* Est. 9:16-18.— II. p. n., *Noah;* LXX. Νῶε.

נַחַת f., *being placed,* Job 36:16; see also נחת.

הֲנָחָה (verb. Hiph.) f., *rest, peace,* Est. 2:18.

מָנוֹחַ m. (pl. with suff. מְנוּחֹתַיְכִי).—I. *place of rest.*—II. p. n., *Manoah,* the father of Samson.

מְנוּחָה מְנֻחָה f.— I. *rest, quiet.*— II. *place of rest.*—III. metaphorically, the land of Canaan.

נִיחֹחַ נִיחוֹחַ m., *satisfaction, approbation;* רֵיחַ הַנִּיחֹחַ *a sweet* (pleasant) *savour.*

נִיחֹחַ m. Ch., *offerings to God or man.*

נוֹט same as מוֹט *agitate, shake,* Ps. 99:1.

נוּל root not used; Ch. Pa., *polluted.*

נְוָלִי נְוָלוּ Ch. f., *dunghill.*

נוֹלְדוּ Niph. pret. pl. with dag. euphon. for נוֹלְדוּ, from ילד.

נוּם *slept.*

נוּמָה f., *sluggishness,* Pro. 23:21.

תְּנוּמָה f., *sleep, slumber.*

נוּן. Niph. fut. יִנּוֹן (Ketib יָנִין Hiph. fut.) *drawn out, perpetuated,* Ps. 72:17.

נוּן p. n., *Nun,* the father of Joshua.

נִין m., *posterity.*

מָנוֹן m., *despiser,* Pro. 29:21.

נוּס I. *fled.*—II. *escaped.*—III. *passed away.* Pol. נוֹסֵס *drive away,* Isa. 59:19. Hiph. הֵנִיס *caused to flee, put to flight;* see נסס.

נִים m., *fugitive,* Jer. 48:44; Kri. נָס.

מָנוֹס m. (with suff. מְנוּסִי).—I. *flight.* —II. *refuge.*

מְנוּסָה, const. מְנֻסַת f., *flight.*

נְתוּסְרוּ, Eze. 23:48 for נְתוּסְרוּ Nith., from יסר.

נוּעַ (fut. יָנוּעַ).—I. *was shaken.*— II. *was disturbed.* — III. *wandered about.*—IV. *varied,* Pro. 5:6.—V. *staggered* (as one drunken).—VI. *moved* (as the lips), 1 Sa. 1:13. Niph. *was shaken;* fut. יִנּוֹעַ. Hiph. הֵנִיעַ.— I. *shook.* — II. *caused to wander,* πλάζειν.— III. *dispersed* (as fugitives), Ps. 59:12.

מְנַעְנְעִים m. pl., *a musical instrument,* allied to the tambourine; Vulg. " sistra."

נֹעַרְיָה p. n. of men and women.

נוּף *have sprinkled,* Pro. 7:17. Hiph. הֵנִיף I. *cause to sprinkle,* Ps. 68: 10.—II. *shake to and fro.*—III.

lifted up the hand, over, and against, with אֶל.—IV. lifted up an instrument, with עַל.—V. presented an offering. Hoph. הוּנַף was offered, Ex. 29:27. Pil. נוֹפֵף beckons with his hand, Isa. 10:32.

נוֹף m., elevated situation; יְפֵה נ' beautiful for situation, Ps. 48:3; see also נף in נף.

נָפָה f.—I. a sieve, Isa. 30:28.—II. נָפַת דּוֹר p. n. of a city.

נֶפֶת f., elevated district, Jos. 17:11.

נֹפֶת f., dropping liquid, honey.

תְּנוּפָה f.—I. lifting up the hand, Isa. 19:16.—II. agitation, tumult, Isa. 30:32.—III. an offering.

נָצַץ Hiph. הֵנֵץ blossomed; see נצץ.
נִיצוֹץ m., a spark, Isa. 1:31.
נוֹצָה crest; see נצה.

נוּק same as יָנַק. Hiph. fut. with suff. תְּנִיקֵהוּ gave him suck, Ex. 2:9.

נוּר f. Ch., fire.

נֵר m.—I. a light.—II. prosperity.—III. p.n. of a man.
נִיר same as נֵר.
נִיר m., a light, metaph. prosperity, rank; see also in נִיר.

נֵרִיָּה p. n. of a man.
מְנוֹרָה f., the candlestick used in the Jewish ritual.

נָשָׁה be diseased, Ps. 69:21, same as אָנַשׁ.

נָזָה (fut. יִזֶּה, יֵז, יַז), was sprinkled, with עַל and מִן. Hiph. הִזָּה (fut. יַזֶּה, יֵז), sprinkled, specially with blood, with עַל.

נָזִיד; see זוד.
נָזִיר; see נזר.

נָזַל (fut. יִזַּל).—I. sank down, Jud. 5: 5.—II. dropped, dropped down; part. נוֹזְלִים flowing streams. Hiph. הִזִּיל caused to flow, Isa. 48:21.

מַזָּלוֹת f. pl., the planets, 2 Ki. 23:5.

מַזָּרוֹת a constellation; according to some from נֵזֶר the northern crown. Others read מַאֲזָרוֹת a belt, the belt of Orion.

נֶזֶם m.—I. a nose-jewel.—II. an ear-ring, Gen. 35:4.

נְזַק Ch., suffered loss. Aph. caused loss.

נֵזֶק m., injury, loss, Est. 7:4.

נָזַר Niph. נִזַּר I. restricted himself.—II. devoted him to, with לְ.—III. withdrew from.—IV. abstained from, with מִן. Hiph. הִזִּיר I. set apart to, with אֶל, אֵת.—II. restrained from, with אֵת, מִן.—III. devoted himself to.

נָזִיר m.—I. a Nazarite, one precluded by a vow from certain things lawful to others.—II. Gen. 49:26, applied to Joseph as separate from his brethren.—III. Lev. 25:5, 11, vines not pruned.

נֵזֶר m. (with suff. נִזְרוֹ, נִזְרֶךָ).—I. state of separation and dedication.—II. mark of such separation, specially the plate of gold in the high priest's mitre.—III. diadem.—IV. sovereignty, Pro. 27:24.—V. hair of the head, as shorn by the Nazarites, Jer. 7:29.

נְזִדִים m. pl., nobles, princes, Nah. 3:17.

נָחְבִּי; see חבה.

נָחָה (pret. with suff. נָחָם; imp. נְחֵה; with suff. נְחֵנִי). Hiph. הִנְחָה (fut. with suff. יַנְחֵנִי), led, conducted, guided.

נָחוּם same as רָחוּם p. n. of a man.

נָחוּם, נִחוּמִים; see נחם.

נָחוֹר, נְחִירִים; see נחר.

נְחוּשָׁה, נָחוּשׁ; see נחשׁ.

נָחַל (inf. נְחֹל; fut. יִנְחַל).—I. took possession of.—II. possessed.—III. took, received, as his portion.—IV. apportioned, Nu. 34:17. Pi. נִחֵל gave settlement to. Hiph. הִנְחִיל I. caused to possess.—II. left as an inheritance to, 1 Chron. 28:8. —III. gave an inheritance, Eze. 46:18. Hoph. הָנְחַל was made to possess, Job 7:3. Hith. הִתְנַחֵל I. took for himself.—II. left as an inheritance, Lev. 25:46.

נַחֲלָה f.—I. settlement, dwelling.—II. possession.—III. assigned portion, share; נַחֲלַת יְהֹוָה the Lord's portion, i. e. Israel, his chosen people. —IV. inheritance.

נַחֲלָת f., portion, Ps. 16:6.

נְחִילוֹת f. pl. nom., flutes (root חָלַל), Ps. 5:1.

נַחַל Niph. pret., from חָלַל; also Pi. pret., from נָחַל.

נַחַל m. (dual נְחָלִים; pl. נְחָלִים, with ה loc. נַחְלָה).—I. stream; נַחַל מִצְרַיִם the stream that divides Egypt and Palestine.—II. torrent.—III. valley.

נַחֲלָה same as נַחַל stream, Ps. 124:4.

נַחֲלִיאֵל p. n., one of the stations of Israel in the wilderness.

נֶחֱלָמִי p. n., Nehelamite, a title.

נָחַם. Niph. נִחַם I. was grieved, repented, with עַל.—II. pitied, felt pity, with עַל, אֶל, לְ, מִן.—III. pitied and withdrew an infliction, with עַל.—IV. recovered from his grief, with עַל, אַחֲרֵי.—V. avenged, freed himself from one displeasing, with מִן.—VI. mourned over, with אֶל, לְ or עַל.—VII. changed his purpose, with עַל. Pi. נִחַם sympathised with, comforted, with עַל, מִן. Pu. נֻחַם comforted, appeased. Hith. הִתְנַחֵם, הֶחֱנַם I. comforted himself.—II. changed his purpose, with עַל, Nu. 23:19. —III. gratified his anger, with לְ.

נַחַם p. n. of a man.

נֹחַם m., pity, change of purpose, Hos. 13:14.

נִחֻמִים, נְחוּמִים m. pl.—I. consolations.—II. pity, Hos. 11:8.

נַחוּם p. n., Nahum the prophet, Ναούμ.

נֶחָמָה f., consolation.

נְחֶמְיָה p. n. of a man, Nehemiah, Νεεμία.

נַחֲמָנִי p. n. of a man.

תַּנְחוּמִים m. pl., consolations, comforts.

תַּנְחֻמוֹת f. pl., the same, Job 15:11; 21:2.

תַּנְחֶמֶת p. n. of a man.

נֶחָם pret. Niph. and Pi., from חמם.

נֵחָמִים Niph. part. pl., from חמם.

אֲנַחְנוּ we; see נַחְנוּ.

נֶחֱנְתִּי Niph. pret. f. 2. pers. with parag., from חנן.

נָחוּץ part. urgent, 1 Sa. 21:9.

נָחַר (Arab. snorted).

נַחַר m., snorting, Job 39:20

נַחֲרָה f., the same, Jer. 8:16.

נַחֲרִי, נַחֲרַי p. n. of a man.

נָחוֹר p. n., *Nahor*, the brother of Abraham.

נְחִירִים m. pl., *nostrils*, Job 41:12.

נִחַר Niph. pret., from חרר.

נָחָשׁ m.—I. *serpent.*— II. p. n. of a man.— III. עִיר נָחָשׁ p. n., a city in the tribe of Judah.

נִחֵשׁ Pi. (denom. from ὀφιομαντεία, *divination by serpents*).—I. *used divination.*—II. *watched, observed.*

נַחַשׁ m., *divination.*

נַחְשׁוֹן p. n., *Naashon*, the son of Amminadab.

נְחָשׁ m. Ch., *brass* or *copper.*

נְחֹשֶׁת com. (with suff. נְחֻשְׁתֶּךָ).— I. *brass.*— II. *chain*, Lam 3:7; dual נְחֻשְׁתַּיִם *fetters, shackles.*— III. *money*, Eze. 16:36.

נְחֻשְׁתָּא p. n. of a woman.

נְחֻשְׁתָּן m., *the brazen serpent idolized*, 2 Ki. 18:4.

נָחוּשׁ m., *copper* or *brass*, Job 6:12.

נְחוּשָׁה f., the same.

נָחַת (fut. יֵחַת, יִנְחַת) same as יָרַד.— I. *came down*, Job 17:16.—II. *came down violently*, with עַל.—III. *penetrated the mind*, with בְּ. Niph. נִחַת *penetrated* (of arrows), with בְּ, Ps. 38:3. Pi. נִחַת *brought down, levelled* (the bow), Ps. 65:11. Hiph.imp. הַנְחַת *depress*, Joel 4:11.

נְחַת Ch., *came down.* Aph. *placed.* Hoph. *made to descend*, Dan. 5:20.

נַחַת m.— I. *descent, lighting down*, Isa. 30:30. — II. *being placed*, Job 36:16; see also in נוּחַ.

נָחַת m., pl. נְחִתִּים *coming down* (of an army), 2 Ki. 6:9.

נַחַת p. n. of a man; same as נוּחַ.

נִחַת Niph. pret., from חתת.

נָטָה (inf. const. נְטוֹת; fut. יִטֶּה apoc. יֵט, וַיֵּט, יְט; וַיֵּט).— I. *stretch out, extend* (the hand, &c.).— II. *spread out, stretch, pitch a tent.*—III. *bowed, inclined.*—IV. *turn, lead to*, with אַחֲרֵי, אֶל, לְ; or *from*, with מִן.—V. *go, depart*, 1 Sa.14:7. Niph. נִטָּה *stretched out.* Hiph. הִטָּה (fut. יַטֶּה; apoc. יַט; imp. הַטֵּה; apoc. הַט).— I. *stretch out.*— II. *spread out.*—III. *incline, bend down, lower.*—IV. *turn away, put away.*—V. *wrest, pervert.* Hoph. part. מֻטֶּה s., *wresting, perversion.*

מַטֶּה, const. מַטֵּה m. (f., Mic. 6:9).— I. *branch of a tree.*— II. *staff*; שָׁבַר מַטֵּה-לֶחֶם *he brake the staff of bread*, i.e. support, that on which life leans.—III. *rod.*—IV. *sceptre.* —V. *tribe, government*, of which the sceptre was a symbol; pl. מַטּוֹת

מִלְמַטָּה, לְמַטָּה *downwards;* מַטָּה the same.

מִטָּה f.—I. *couch, bed.*— II. *bier* (for the dead), 2 Sa. 3:31.

נְטִיפוֹת *earrings;* see נטף.

נָטַל (fut. יִטּוֹל).—I. *lifted up*, Isa. 40:15.—II. *laid a burden on*, with עַל, Lam. 3:28. Hiph. *took up and removed.*

נְטַל Ch., *lifted up.*

נֵטֶל m., *burden*, Pro. 27:3.

נָטִיל m., *loaded*, Zep. 1:11.

נִטְמָתֶם for נִטְמְאתֶם Niph. pl., from טמא.

נֶטַע (fut. יִטַּע; inf. נְטֹעַ, נְטַעַת).—I. *planted.*—II. *pitched a tent.*—III. *set up an idol temple,* Deut. 16: 21.— IV. *drove a nail.* Niph. *planted,* Isa. 40:24.

נָטִיעַ m., pl. נְטִעִים *planted,* Ps. 144: 12.

נֶטַע m. (with suff. נִטְעֶךָ; pl. נְטָעִים, נִטְעַי).—I. *plant.*—II. *plantation.*

נֶטַע const. נֶטַע m., *plant,* Isa. 5:7. מַטָּע m., *planting.*

נָטַף (fut. יִטֹּף).—I. *drop,* Job 29:22.— II. *let drop.* Hiph. הִטִּיף.—I. *let drop* (water), Am. 9:13.—II. *let fall* (sentiments, prophetic declarations).

נָטָף m.— I. *drop,* Job 36:27.— II. στακτή, *myrrh,* Ex. 30:34.

נְטֹפָה p. n., a town near Bethlehem; נְטֹפָתִי a Netophathite.

נְטִיפוֹת f. pl., *earrings* or *drops,* Jud. 8:26; Isa. 3:19.

נָטַשׂ (fut. יִטֹּר) (יִנְטֹר) *watched,*—1. *for good.*—2. *for evil,* with לְ, אֵת. נְטַר Ch., *kept,* Dan. 7:28.

מַטָּרָא (מַטְרָא) Lam. 3:12 f.—I. *custody, prison.*—II. *mark, object, butt.*

נָטַשׁ (fut. יִטֹּשׁ).—I. *left.*—II. *forsook,* God, a law, &c.— III. *left.* — IV. *ceased to think of,* 1 Sa. 10:2.— V. *spread, scattered.* — VI. *drew a sword,* Isa. 21:15.— VII. *allowed.* Niph. I. *was forsaken.*—II. *spread itself.*—III. *became loose.* Pu. *was forsaken,* Isa. 32:14.

נְטִישׂוֹת f. pl.—I. *shoots of the vine.* —II. *small towns, shoots of the capital,* Jer. 5:10.

נִי, בָּ נִיהֶם an error for בְּנִיתָם, Eze. 27: 32.

---

נִיא (Arab *raw*). נָא m., *raw* (uncooked), Ex. 12:9 גִּיבַי, גִּיב; see נוּב. נִידָה, נִיד; see נוּד. נָיוֹת; see נוה. נִיחֹחַ; see נוח. נִין *posterity;* see נון.

נִינְוֵה p. n., *Nineveh,* a city of Assyria LXX. Νινευί.

נִינָם Kal fut. pl. 1. pers. with suff., from ינה.

נִיס; see נוס.

נִיסָן m., the first month of the Hebrew year, called also אָבִיב, which see.

נִיצוֹץ *sparks;* see נוץ. נִיר *light;* see נור.

נִיר I. *clear ground for cultivation.*— II. *cultivate ground.*

נִיר m., *field newly cultivated;* see also in נור.

מָנוֹר m.; מְנוֹר אֹרְגִים *weaver's beam,* 1 Sa. 17:7; 2 Sa. 21:19.

נִירָם וַיִּירָם Kal fut. pl. 1. pers. with suff., from ירה.

נַךְ וַךְ Hiph. fut. apoc. pl. 1. pers., from נכה.

נְכֵא, נָכָא, see נכה; נִכְאוּ, see כאב.

נְכֹאת f., *storax,* Gen. 37:25; 43:11; LXX. θυμίαμα; Aquila στύραξ.

נֶכֶד m. (with suff. נֶכְדִּי), *posterity,* always with נִין, which see.

נָכָה Hiph. הִכָּה (imp. הַךְ, הַכֵּה; fut. יַכֶּה; with parag. יַכְּבֶה).—I. *struck.*—II. *wounded.*—III. *killed.* — IV. *conquered.* — V. *taunted* (struck with the tongue).—VI. *struck the hands together.*—VII

וַיַּךְ לֵב *his heart smote him,* 1 Sa.
24:6. Hoph. הֻכָּה, הֻגְּרָה *was
smitten, &c.,* pass. of Hiph. Niph.
נִגָּה *was wounded,* 2 Sa. 11:15.
Pi. inf. נַכֵּה־נַכֵּה *smiting.* Pu.
נֻכָּה *smitten.*

נָכֵה m.—I. נְכֵה רַגְלָיִם *lame* (smitten
in the feet), 2 Sa. 4:4; 9:3.—
II. נְכֵה רוּחַ *afflicted in spirit,* Isa.
66:2.

נָכֶה m., pl. נָכִים *smiting* (with the
tongue), *calumniators,* Ps. 35:15.

נָכֵא m., f. נְכֵאָה רוּחַ *afflicted, broken
spirit,* Pro. 15:13, &c.

נָכֵא m., pl. נְכָאִים *smitten,* Isa. 16:7.

מַכָּה f. (pl. מַכּוֹת, מַכִּים).—I. *stroke,
blow.*—II. *wound.*—III. *slaughter.*
—IV. *calamity.*

נְכֹה p. n., Pharaoh *Necho,* king of
Egypt; LXX. Νεχαώ.

נָכוֹן (same as כִּידוֹן), p. n. of a place.

נֹכַח I. *straight forwards.*—II. *opposite, over against.*—III. *in sight
of;* אֶל־נֹכַח *towards;* לְנֹכַח *in
front of, in behalf of, straight
forwards,* עַד־נֹכַח *as far as.*

נֶכַח (with suff. נִכְחוֹ) *opposite to,
against.*

נָכֹחַ m. (f. נְכֹחָה; pl. נְכֹחוֹת).—I.
*straight forward, upright.*—II. *up-
rightness,* Isa. 57:2.

נִכְחַת Niph. part. f., from יכח.

נָכַל *withholding,* Mal. 1:14. Pi. *used
artifice,* with לְ, Nu. 25:18. Hith.
the same, with בְּ.

נֵכֶל m., pl. נְכָלִים *artifices,* Nu.
25:18.

כִּילַי, כֵּלַי m., *avaricious, oppressive,*
Isa. 32:5, 7.

נְכָסִים root not used; same as כֶּנֶם.
נְכָסִים m., pl. נְכָסִים *treasures, wealth.*
נִכְסִין m. Ch., pl. נִכְסִין *treasures,
wealth.*

כִּים m., *purse, bag.*

נִכְפַּר Nith., from כפר.

נָכַר. Pi. נִכֵּר I. *recognised.*—II. *considered.*—III. *acknowledged.*—IV.
*alienated,* Deu. 32:27.—V. *rejected,*
with בְּ, 1 Sa. 23:7. Niph. נִכַּר I.
*feigned himself unknown,* Pro. 26:
24.—II. *was recognised,* Lam. 4:8.
11.—Hiph. הִכִּיר I. *recognised,
knew, acknowledged.*—II. *was par-
tial in judgment,* with פָּנִים.—III.
*beheld.*—IV. *regarded.*—V. *esteemed, accounted.*—VI. *took judicial cognizance of.* Hith. הִתְנַכֵּר
*make one's self strange,* Gen.
42:7.

נֵכָר, const. נֵכַר m., *strange, foreign,
a foreigner;* בֶּן־נֵכָר *son of the
stranger, foreigner;* אֱלֹהֵי נֵכָר
*strange gods.*

נָכְרִי m. (pl. נָכְרִים; f. נָכְרִיָּה, pl.
נָכְרִיּוֹת).—I. *foreign.*—II. *a stranger.*—III. *strange, singular.*

נֵכֶר, נֹכֶר m., *treating as a stranger,
punishment.*

הַכָּרָה (verb Hiph.) f., *astonishment,
consciousness of guilt,* Isa. 3:9.

מַכָּר m., *relative, neighbour,* 2 Ki.
12:6, 8.

נְכֹת, בֵּית נְכֹתֹה 2 Ki. 20:13; Isa.
39:2, *treasury,* γαζοφυλάκιον.

נלה root not used; (Arab. *succeeded*)
Hiph. inf. with pref. and suff.
כְּהַנְלֹתְךָ for כְּהִנָּלוֹתְךָ *when thou
hast accomplished,* Isa. 33:1.

מֶנְלָה possession, wealth, Job 15:29.

נִמְבְזָה despised; see בָּזָה.

נְמוּאֵל p. n. of a man.

נָמַל (fut. יִמַּל; pl. יִמֹּלוּ).—I. circumcise, Gen. 17:11.— II. withered, Ps. 37:2; Job 14:2. (some derive it from מָלַל same as מוֹל). Niph. נִמּוֹל was circumcised; part. נִמּוֹלִים (some derive it from מוֹל). נָמְלָה f., ant, Pro. 6:6; pl. נְמָלִים, Pro. 30:25.

נָמֵר root not used; (Arab. was spotted). נָמֵר m., a panther, Jer. 5:6; Hab. 1:8. נְמַר m. Ch., the same, Dan. 7:6.

נָמַר Niph. pret., from מרר.

נִמְרֹד p. n., Nimrod, the builder of Babylon, Νεβρώδης; אֶרֶץ נִמְרֹד Babylon.

נִמְרִים, נִמְרָה p. n., same as בֵּית נִמְרָה; see בֵּית.

נִמְשִׁי p. n., father of Jehu.

נֵס, נִסִּי; see נסס.

נָסַבָּה for נְסַבָּה Niph. pret. fem., from סבב.

נְסִבָּה; see סבב.

נָסַג recoil, shrink back; inf. נָסוֹג, Isa. 59:13; fut. יִסַּג Mic. 2:6. Hiph. הִסִּיג I. remove a boundary.—II. carry away property, Mic. 6:14. Hoph. הֻסַּג was perverted, Isa. 59:14.

נָסָה imp. נַסֵּה; (see נָשָׂא). Pi. נִסָּה I. tried.—II. proved, made a trial. —III. found on trial, experienced. מַסָּה f.—I. trial.—II. temptation by trial.

נָסָּה, Ps. 4:7, for נָשָׂא imp., from נשא.

נָסַח (fut. יִסַּח) dispersed, scattered. Niph. was dispersed.

נְסַח Ch. Ith. was pulled down, Ezr. 6:11.

מַסָּח m., disperser, driver away, 2 Ki. 11:6.

I. נָסַךְ I. poured out, Isa. 29:10.—II. melted.— III. anointed, Ps. 2:6.— IV. poured out a libation. Niph. נִסַּךְ was anointed, Pro. 8:23. Pi. נִסֵּךְ and Hiph. הִסִּיךְ poured a libation.—Hoph. was poured out.

נְסַךְ Ch., Pa. made an offering, Dan. 2:46.

נָסִיךְ m. — I. libation. — II. molten image, Dan. 11:8.— III. anointed one, prince.

נֶסֶךְ m. (with suff. נִסְכָּה, נִסְכּוֹ; pl. נְסָכִים).— I. drink-offering.— II. molten image.

נְסַךְ m. Ch., drink-offering, Ezr. 7:17. מַסֵּכָה I. fusing; אֱלֹהֵי מ' molten images.—II. libation, Isa. 30:1.

II. נָסַךְ same as סָכַךְ covered, Isa. 25:7. מַסֵּכָה covering, Isa. 25:7; 28:20. מַסֶּכֶת f. (Arab. he wove), web, Jud. 16:13, 14.

נָסַס raised, bore a standard, Isa. 10:18; 59:19. Hithpo. הִתְנוֹסֵס I. rally round a standard, Ps. 60:6. —II. raise oneself as a standard, Zec. 9:16.

נֵס m. (with suff. נִסִּי).—I. banner.— II. flag-staff.— III. sail. — IV. example, warning.—V. the leader to whom the banner belongs, Isa. 11:10.

נָסַע (fut. יִסַּע; inf. נְסֹעַ; imp. pl. סְעוּ) —I. departed.— II. travelled.— III. arose (a wind), Nu. 11:31.— IV. removed. — V. pulled up or out.

Niph. נִסַּע was *pulled up.* Hiph. הִסִּיעַ I. *caused to depart, &c.*—II. *made to blow,* Ps. 78:26.—III. *quarried stone,* 1 Ki. 5:31.

מַסָּע m.—I. *missile weapon,* Job 41: 18.—II. *march, journey*; pl. מַסָּעִים.

נָסַק *go up,* Ps. 139:8.

נְסַק Ch., *go up.* Aph. *lifted up,* Dan. 3:22. Hoph. *was lifted up,* Dan. 6:24.

נִסְרֹךְ p. n., *Nisroch,* an idol of the Ninevites.

נַעָה p.n., a town in the tribe of Ze-bulon.

נֹעָה p n. of a woman.

נֵעוֹר for נֵעוֹר Niph. pret., from עוּר.

נְעוּרִים *youth*; see נַעַר.

נְעִיאֵל p.n., a town in the tribe of Naphtali.

נָעִים *pleasant*; see נעם.

נָעַל I. *put on sandals,* Eze. 16:10, lit. *latch them.*—II. *bolted, latched the door.* Hiph. fut. with suff. וַיַּנְעִלוּם *shod them,* 2 Chron. 28:15.

נַעַל f., *shoe, sandal*; dual נַעֲלַיִם *pair of sandals*; pl. נְעָלִים, נְעָלוֹת.

מַנְעוּל m., *bolt, lock of a gate.*

מִנְעָל m., *defence,* Deu. 33:25.

נָעֵם (fut. וּנְעַם) *was pleasant, agree-able,* with לְ.

נָעִים m.—I. *pleasant.*—II. *sweet mu-sic.*—III. *amiable.*—IV. *becoming.*—V. *prosperous*; pl. נְעִימִים.

נַעַם p. n. of a man.

נֹעַם m.—I. *pleasantness.*—II. *kind-ness, grace.*

נַעֲמָה p.n.—I. a town in the tribe of Judah.—II. the daughter of La-

mech.—III. the mother of Reho-boam.

נָעֳמִי p. n., *Naomi,* the mother-in-law of Ruth.

נַעֲמִי patron.; see נַעֲמָן.

נַעֲמָן m.—I. *pleasantness,* Isa. 17:10.—II. p. n. of a man.

נַעֲמָתִי p. n., *Naamathite,* a title.

מַנְעַמִּים m. pl., *delicacies,* Ps. 141:4.

נָעַץ (Arab. a *thorny bush* in the Hed-jaz).

נַעֲצוּץ m., a species of *thorn bush,* Isa. 7:19; 55:13.

נָעַר I. *roar as a lion,* Jer. 51:38.—II. *shook off, out.* Niph. *was shaken out.* Pi. נֵעַר *threw out.* Hithp. Isa. 52:2, *shake thyself,* with מִן.

נַעַר m., *straying, strayed* (cattle), Zec. 11:16; see also below.

נְעֹרֶת f., *tow,* Jud. 16:9; Isa. 1:31.

נַעַר m. (with suff. נַעֲרְךָ, נַעֲרוֹ; pl. נְעָרִים, נְעָרַי).—I. *infant.*—II. *boy.*—III. *youth.*—IV. *servant.*

נַעֲרָה f.—I. *girl.*—II. *young woman.*—III. *female servant.*—IV. p. n. of a woman.—V. p. n., a town in the tribe of Ephraim, also נַעֲרָן.

נֹעַר m., *childhood, youth.*

נְעוּרִים m. pl., *youth, early life.*

נְעוּרוֹת f. pl., the same.

נְעַרְיָה p.n. of a man.

נַעֲרָן p.n., same as נַעֲרָה.

נֻף same as נוּף.

נָפָן p.n. of a man.

נָפָה see נוּף.

נְפִישֶׁסִים, נְפִיסִים, נְפוּסִים p.n. of a m.

נָפַח I. *blew, blew upon,* with בְּ.—II. *blew a fire.*—III. with נֶפֶשׁ *ex-pired*; יְגֻר נָפוּחַ *seething pot* Jer.

15:9. Pu. נֻפַּח *was blown* (of a fire), Job 20:26. Hiph. *puffed at, despised.*

נֹפַח p. n., a town in Moab.

מַפֻּחַ m., *bellows*, Jer. 6:29.

מַפַּח m. נָפֶשׁ 'מ, Job 11:20, *expiring*, "giving up the ghost," Eng. Ver.

נְפִילִים; see נפל·

נָפִישׁ p. n., *Naphish,* a son of Ishmael.

נֹפֶךְ m., an unknown precious stone; LXX. ἄνθραξ.

נָפַל (fut. יִפֹּל· inf. נְפֹל; with suff. נָפְלִי, נָפְלוֹ).—I. *fell, fell down, was killed,* &c.; (נֹפֵל *one prostrate*).—II. *fell upon,* with עַל.—III. *fell to* (of an inheritance), with לְ.—IV. *fell on his face,* with or without פָּנָיו אֶל פָּנָיו עַל.—V. *fell on* (was confined to) *his bed,* Ex. 21:18.—VI. *deserted to, joined,* with עַל or אֶל.—VII. *fell into the hand of,* with בְּיַד.—VIII. *perished,* Pro. 11:5, &c.—IX. *fell into a pit, mischief,* with בְּ, לְ.—X. בְּעֵינָיו 'נ *sank in his own esteem,* Neh. 6:16.—XI. בְּנַחֲלָה 'נ *obtained an inheritance,* Eze. 47:22.—XII. *sank* (of the heart), 1 Sa. 17:32.—XIII. אַרְצָה 'נ *perished.* Hiph. הִפִּיל I. *caused to fall.*—II. *killed.*— III. *annihilated.* — IV. *threw down.*—V. *divide* (by lot), Jos.23: 4. with לְ.—VI. *knock out a tooth,* Ex. 21:27.—VII. *overcame.*—VIII. *cause to settle,* Ps. 78:55.—IX. *cast out, forsook.*—X. *threw into the fire,* with עַל or בְּ. Hith. I. *prostrate myself.* — II. *fell upon violently,* with עַל.

נְפַל Ch.—I. *fall, fell down.*—II. *prostrated.*—III. *was thrown down.*— IV. *descended,* Dan. 7:20.—V. *fell* (became needful) to one, Ezr 7:20.

נֵפֶל נָפֶל m., *abortion.*

נְפִילִים m. pl., a tribe of the first inhabitants of Canaan, who were of gigantic stature.

נִפְלָאתָה Niph. pret. f. with ה parag., from פלא.

נִפְלָל Eze. 28:23, probably an error for נָפַל.

מַפָּל m.—I. *that which falls out of the ear, the worst,* of the corn, Am. 8:6.—II. *pendulous, flaccid parts* (of the flesh), Job 41:15.

מַפָּלָה, מַפֵּלָה f., *ruins* of an edifice, Jeremiah only.

מַפֶּלֶת f.—I. *fall, ruin.*—II. *that which falls, leaf,* Eze. 31:13.—III. *carcase,* Jud. 14:8.

נָפַץ same as פּוּץ.—I. *broke, dashed down.*—II. *dispersed,* Isa. 11:12. —III. *dispersed itself.* Pi. same as Kal I., II. Pu. *was broken down,* Isa. 27:9.

נֶפֶץ m., *breaking forth, bursting.*

מַפֵּץ m., "*battle axe,*" Eng. Ver., Jer. 51:20.

מַפָּץ m., *bruising,* Eze. 9:2.

נְפַק Ch., *came forth.* Aph. *brought out.*

נִפְקָא Ch. f., *outgoings, expence,* Ezr. 6:4,8.

נָפַשׁ Niph. I. *had breathing time, rest,* Ex. 23:12.—II. *rested.*

נֶפֶשׁ f., seldom m. (with suff. נַפְשִׁי pl. נְפָשִׁים; const. נַפְשׁוֹת).

—I. *breath.*—II. *an animal* (that which breathes).—III. *a person;* שִׁבְעִים נֶפֶשׁ *seventy souls,* i.e. *persons;* כָּל נֶפֶשׁ *every one, whosoever.*—IV. *self;* נַפְשִׁי *myself;* נַפְשֶׁךָ *thyself.*—V. נֶפֶשׁ מֵת *dead body, carcase;* טָמֵא לָנֶפֶשׁ *polluted by a dead body.*—VI. *livelihood,* Deu. 24:6.—VII. *the feelings, desire, inclination.*

נֶפֶת ,נֹפֶת; see נוף.

נַפְתּוּלִים see פתל.

נַפְתֻּחִים p.n. of a people.

נַפְתָּלִי (*my wrestlings,* Gen. 30:8), p.n., *Naphtali,* the son of Jacob and Bilhah.

נֵץ *hawk;* see נצץ.

נָצָא ,נָצָה *flew away,* Jer. 48:9; Lam. 4:15.

נָצַב. Niph. נִצַּב I. *stood.*—II. *was placed, appointed,* with עַל; part. נִצָּב *one set over, officer.* Hiph. הִצִּיב I. *placed.*—II. *set up.*—III. *fixed, appointed.*—IV. *set a trap,* Jer. 5:26.—V. *uphold,* Ps. 41:13. Hoph. הֻצַּב *set up,* Gen. 28:12.

נְצִיב m.—I. *pillar,* Gen. 19:26.—II. *garrison.*—III. *chief commander,* 1 Ki. 4:19.—IV. p. n., *a town in the tribe of Judah.*

נְצָב m. (part. Niph.), *handle of a knife,* Jud. 3:22.

נִצְבָּא f. Ch., *firmness, strength,* Dan. 2:41.

מַצָּב, const. מַצַּב m.—I. *standing place.*—II. *station, dignity,* Isa. 22:19.—III. *station, column of soldiers.*

מֻצָּב m. (part. Hoph.), *the same.*

מַצֵּבָה ,מַצְּבָה f., *the same.*

מַצֵּבָה, const. מַצֶּבֶת f.—I. *pillar set up as a memorial.*—II. *image, statue of an idol.*

מַצֶּבֶת f.—I. *pillar.*—II. *monument.*—III. *stem, root,* Isa. 6:13.

נָצַג. Hiph. הִצִּיג *set up, make stand up.* Hoph. הֻצַּג *was stayed,* Ex. 10:24.

נָצָה. Kal *was laid waste;* fut תִּצֶּינָה, Jer. 4:7. Niph. נִצָּה I. *excited to quarrel.*—II. *was stopped;* (part. pl. נִצִּים). Hiphil הִצָּה *was desolate;* see also נָצָא.

נֹצָה f. affix נֹצָתָהּ *contents of a bird's crop, entrails,* Lev. 1:16.

נוֹצָה *a feather,* Eze. 17:3.

מַצָּה f., *quarrel, strife,* Pro. 13:10; 17:19; see also in מצץ.

מַצּוּת f., *the same,* Isa. 41:12.

נִצָּה *blossom;* see נצץ.

נָצַח Kal not used; (Arab. *was innocent*). Pi. נִצַּח *superintend, preside over;* part. מְנַצֵּחַ I. *leader, chief.*—II. *choragus, leader of music.*

נְצַח Ch. Ith. *superior,* with עַל.

נֵצַח ,נֶצַח m.—I. *a title of God;* נ׳ יִשְׂרָאֵל *strength of Israel,* 1 Sa. 15:29.—II. *perpetuity.*—III. *success;* לָנֶצַח and לְנֵצַח I. *according to truth.*—II. *entirely, wholly;* נֶצַח לָנֶצַח *continually, for ever.*

נֵצַח m., *juice of grapes,* Isa. 63:3,6; (Arab. *sprinkled*).

נִצָּח (part. Niph.) f. נִצַּחַת *was perfected, finished.*

נִצְטַדָּק Hith. fut. pl. 1. pers., from צדק.

נָצִיב; see נצב.

נָצַל Pi. נִצֵּל I. delivered, Eze. 14:14.
—II. plundered.—III. gained spoil,
2 Chron. 20:25. Hiph. הִצִּיל I.
delivered, rescued.—II. took away,
with מִן.—III. parted, with בֵּין—
IV. deliver himself. Hoph. part.
מֻצָּל rescued. Niph. נִצַּל I. was
delivered, escaped.— II. ran away
to, with אֶל. Hith. strip themselves, Ex. 33:6.

נְצַל Ch. Aph. rescued.

הַצָּלָה (verb Hiph.) f., deliverance,
Est. 4:14.

נָצַץ I. glittering, Eze. 1:7.—II. fled.

נֵץ m. (with suff. נִצָּהּ).—I. flower,
Gen. 40:10.—II. hawk.

נֹצָה f., blossom.

נִצָּן m., pl. נִצָּנִים flowers, Cant. 2:12.

נָצַר (fut. יִנְצֹר, יִצֹּר; inf. abs. נָצוֹר;
const. נְצֹר; imp. נְצֹר; with ה
parag. נִצְרָה; with suff. נִצְּרָה—
I. guarded. — II. preserved from
evil.—III. watched.—IV. besieged,
shut up.— V. observed; נֹצְרִים
keepers.

נֵצֶר m., shoot, branch; (Arab. shone).

נָצִיר m., pl. const. (נְצִירֵי) נְצִירִי preserved, liberated.

נִצְרָה Kal imp. with ה parag. and dag.
euphon., from נצר.

נָקָא white; see נקה.

נָקַב (fut. יִקֹּב, יַקֹּב).— I. pierced.—
II. bored through. — III. bored a
hole.— IV. broke the head with a
staff, Hab. 3:14.— V. marked.—
VI. named.—VII. pronounced un-
fortunate.— VIII. cursed. Niph.
were marked by name.

נֶקֶב m.— I. holes bored in precious
stones, Eze. 28:13.—II. הַנֶּקֶב p.n.,
a city in the tribe of Naphtali.

נְקֵבָה f., female.

מַקֶּבֶת f., hammer

מַקֶּבֶת f.—I. hammer.—II. hole, shaft
of a well, Isa. 51:1.

נָקֹד root not used; (Ch. נְקַד mark
with spots).

נָקֹד m. (pl. נְקֻדִּים; f. נְקֻדָּה) spotted
sheep or goats, Gen. 30:32, 33.

נְקֻדָּה f., studs of silver, Cant. 1:11.

נֹקֵד m., shepherd, 2 Ki. 3:4; Am.
1:1.

נִקֻּדִּים m. pl.—I. bread, Jos. 9:5, 12.
—II. cakes (probably pricked like
Passover cakes), 1 Ki. 14:3.

נְקוֹדָא p. n. of a man.

נָקָה inf. נָקֹה was pure, Jer. 49:12.
Niph. נִקָּה—I. was innocent, clear
—II. was made innocent, cleared
with מִן.— III. was swept away,
devastated. Pi. נִקָּה I. cleansed.
— II. treated as innocent, freed
from punishment, with מִן.

נְקָא Ch., Pe. part. נָקֵא pure, white,
Dan. 7:9.

נָקִי m. (pl. נְקִיִּים).—I. innocent.—II.
clear from guilt, an oath, &c., with
מִן—III. exempt, 1 Ki. 15:22.

נָקִיא the same, Joel 4:19; Jonah 1:
14.

נִקָּיוֹן m.—I. innocency.—II. cleanness
of teeth, i. e. hunger, Am. 4:6.

מְנַקִּית f., pl. מְנַקִּיּוֹת bowls for drink-
offerings.

נָקַט same as קוּט loathe, Job 10:1.

נָקַל Niph. pret., from קלל.

נָקַם (fut. יִקֹּם).—I. avenged, took revenge on, with מִיַּד, מֵאֵת, מִן, עַל, לְ—II. punished.—Niph. נִקַם I. revenged himself on.—II. was punished, with מִן, בְּ. Pi. נִקֵם I. revenged, with מִן and בְּ. Hoph. fut. יֻקַּם shall be avenged. Hith. I. revenged himself.—II. part. מִתְנַקֵּם desired vengeance.

נָקָם m., נִקְמָתִי f. (with suff. ; pl. נְקָמוֹת).—I. vengeance taken or inflicted; עָשָׂה לָקַח הֵשִׁיב נָתַן took vengeance, נָתַן נְקָמוֹת let vengeance come upon any one.—II. punishment.—III. thirst for revenge, Lam. 3:60.

נָקַע (fut. יֵקַע; see יָקַע) fell away, was estranged from, Eze. 23:18, 22, 28.

נָקַף חַגִּים יִנְקֹפוּ "let them kill sacrifices," Eng. Ver., Isa. 29:1. Pi. נִקֵּף I. cut down, Isa. 10:34.—II. pierced, Job 19:26. Hiph. הִקִּיף I. fixed, placed around, with עַל.—II. surrounded. — III. went round a place, Isa. 15:8.—IV. came round (of time), Job 1:5. — V. shaved the head in a circle, Lev. 19:27; inf. הַקֵּף הַקִּיף.

נֹקֶף m., shaking of an olive tree to make the fruit fall, Isa. 17:6; 24:13.

נִקְפָּה f., "a rent" (in a garment), Eng. Ver., Isa. 3:24.

נָקַק same as נָקַב.

נָקִיק m., fissure in a rock.

נָקַר (fut. יִקֹּר) and Pi. נִקֵּר.—I. pierced through.—II. pecked out (as a bird). —III. put out an eye. Pu. dug out, Isa. 51:1.

נְקָרָה f., cleft (of a rock).

נָקַשׁ snared (as a fowler). Niph. is ensnared, Deu. 12:30. Pi. spread a snare for, with לְ. Hith. the same, with בְּ.

נְקַשׁ Ch., struck each other (of knees), Dan. 5:6.

נֵר, נֵר, גְּרִיָה; see נוּר.

נֵרְגַל m., name of an idol, 2 Ki. 17:30 נֵרְגַל שַׁרְאֶצֶר p. n. of an Assyrian prince, Jer. 39:3, 13.

נִרְגָּן m., babbler, calumniator.

נֵרְדְּ m. (with suff. נִרְדִּי; pl. נְרָדִים). spikenard, Cant. 1:12; 4:13, 14.

נָשָׂא (fut. יִשָּׂא, יִשָּׂאוּ, יִשָּׂא; inf. abs. נָשֹׂא, נָשֹׂא, שְׂאֵת; const. נְשֹׂא, שְׂאוֹ; imp. נָשָׂא, נְשָׂא, שָׂא).—I. lifted up: (a) his hand; (b) with בְּ against; (c) beckoned; (d) lifted up his voice; (e) lifted up his feet; (f) lifted up his face, looked towards, with אֶל; (g) lifted up his eyes; (h) lifted up his soul (set his heart on, paid regard, with נֶפֶשׁ), (i) raised the head, elevated, with רֹאשׁ; (k) took the sum of, examined the case of, with רֹאשׁ.—II. took, took up: (a) took into hand; (b) took into the mouth; (c) uttered, offered a prayer; (d) received a precept; (e) took away, took hold of, obtained.—III. פָּנִים נ' accepted the person, acted with partiality. —IV. (a) עָוֹן נ' took away iniquity; (b) forgave (without עָוֹן, with לְ of the person).—V. (a) carried, brought; (b) carried away; (c) endured; (d) bore punishment; (e) supported dignity; (f) assisted:

(g) *bore fruit, &c.*; (h) *supported*, with בְ; (i) *laid upon*, with עַל; (k) *imposed an oath upon*, 1 Ki. 8:31; (l) *removed itself (of the earth)*, Nah. 1:5. Niph. נִשָּׂא I. *was lifted up*; part. נִשָּׂא *lifted up.*—II. *raised himself.*—III. *was carried.*—IV. *was carried away.* Pi. נִשֵּׂא, נִשָּׂא I. *took away.*—II. *presented a gift.*—III. *carried.*—IV. *assisted.*—V. *raised in rank*, Est. 3:1.—VI. נ׳ נֶפֶשׁ *set his heart.* Hiph. הִשִּׂיא I. *caused to bear.*—II. *brought*, 2 Sa. 17:13. Hith. הִתְנַשֵּׂא, הִנָּשֵׂא I. *arose.*—II. *exalted himself.*—III. *was exalted.*

נְשָׂא Ch.—I. *carried away*, Dan. 2: 35.—II. *took*, Ezr. 5:15. Ithpa. *exalted himself*, Ezr. 4:19.

נָשִׂיא m.—I. *chief.*—II. *chief of a tribe among the Israelites.*—III. *chief of a subdivision of a tribe.*—IV. *prince.*—V. pl. נְשִׂיאִים *vapours.*

נְשִׂיאָה f., *burden*, Isa. 46:1.

נְשֻׂאת (Niph. part.) *a gift*, 2 Sa. 19:43.

שִׂיא m., *elevation, dignity*, Job 20:6.

שְׂאֵת inf.—I. *lifting up, elevation*, Gen. 4:7.—II. *swelling in the skin.*—III. *exaltation, dignity.*—IV. *judgment, sentence*, Hab. 1:7.

שֵׂת same as שְׂאֵת *rising*, Job 41: 17.

מַשָּׂא m., מַשּׂא פָנִים *preference of persons*, 2 Chron. 19:7.

מַשָּׂא m.—I. *carrying.*—II. *a burden.*—III. *a load.*—IV. *that which is burdensome.*—V. *a tribute.*—VI. *calamity.*—VII. *lifting up the*

*voice to sing.*—VIII. *solemn declaration.*—IX. *prophecy.*

מַשְׂאָה f., *rising of flame, burning*, Isa. 30:27.

מַשְׂאֵת f. (const. מַשְׂאֵת; pl. מַשְׂאת). —I. *the act of lifting up.*—II. *a signal.*—III. *prophecy.*—IV. *gift.*—V. *tribute.*

I. נָשַׂג. Hiph. הִשִּׂיג I. *reached.*—II. *was able to reach.*—III. *attained, obtained, overtook.*—IV. *befel.*

II. נָשַׂג same as סוּג. Hiph. הִשִּׂיג *removed (land marks)*, Job 24:2.

נָשַׂק. Hiph. הִשִּׂיק *kindled a fire.* Niph. *was kindled.*

נָשַׂר root not used; (Arab. *saw*).

מַשּׂוֹר m., *a saw*, Isa. 10:15.

I. נָשָׁא. Hiph. הִשִּׁיא I. *caused to err, led astray.*—II. *deceived*, with אֶת, בְ, לְ.—III. *laid a burden on*, with בְ. Niph. *was deceived.*

מַשָּׁאוֹן m., *deceit*, Pro. 26:26.

II. נָשָׁא same as נָשָׁה which see.

נָשַׁב *blew*, Isa. 40:7. Hiph. הִשִּׁיב I. *caused to blow.*—II. *dispersed, as dust.*

I. נָשָׁה I. *forgot.*—II. *neglected*, Jer. 23:39. Niph. the same, Isa. 44: 21. Pi. *cause to forget*. Gen. 41: 51. Hiph. הִשָּׁה *cause to forget*, Job 11:6; 39:17.

II. נָשָׁה, נָשָׁא *lent money*, Jer. 15: 10, with בְ; נֹשֶׁה, נֹשָׁא *creditor*; נֹשֶׁה *money lender.* Hiph. the same, with בְ; fut. יַשִּׁיא.

נָשֶׁה m., *the ischiatic nerve*, Gen. 32: 33; (Arab. the same).

נְשִׁי m., *a debt*, 2 Ki. 4:7.

נְשִׁיָה f., *forgetfulness*, Ps. 88:13.

מַשֶּׁה m., *debt*, Deu. 15:2.

מַשָּׁא m., *interest*, Neh. 5:7.

מַשָּׁאָה const. מַשְׁאַת f., *debt*.

נְשׁוּא for נְשׁוּאִי, from נָשָׂא.

נְשֻׂא, Ps. 32:1. for נָשׂוּא Kal part. pass.,
from נָשָׂא.

נָשִׁים *woman*; see אִשָּׁה in אנש.

נַשֶּׁים for נַשִּׁים or נָשֵׁם Hiph. fut. pl.
1. pers., from שָׁמַם.

נָשַׁךְ (fut. יִשַּׁךְ יְשֹׁךְ) I. *bit.* — II. *an-
noyed.* — III. *was lent on interest*,
Deu. 23:20. Pi. *bit* (of a serpent).
Hiph. *lent on interest*, with לְ, Deu.
23:20, 21.

נֶשֶׁךְ m., *interest*.

נִשְׁכָּה f., (pl. נִשְׁכוֹת for לִשְׁכָּה) *chamber of the temple* (book of Nehe-
miah only).

נָשַׁל (fut. יִשַּׁל; imp. שַׁל). — I. *fell off.*
— II. *pulled off a shoe.* — III. *drove
out.* Pi. *drove out*, 2 Ki. 16:6.

נָשַׁם *snort*; fut. אֶשֹּׁם, Isa. 42:14;
see שָׁמַם.

נְשָׁמָה f. — I. *breath.* — II. *life.* — III. *a
human being.* — IV. *breath of God*:
(a) *his anger*; (b) *the life he gives.*
— V. *the wind.*

נִשְׁמָא f. Ch., *breath, life*, Dan. 5:23.

תִּנְשֶׁמֶת f. — I. *an unclean bird* (species uncertain), Lev. 11:18; Deu.
14:16. — II. *an unclean beast*, Lev.
11:30. (species unknown).

נָשַׁף I. *blew.* — II. *blew on*, with בְּ.

נֶשֶׁף m. (with suff. נִשְׁפּוֹ). — I. *dawn.*
— II. *evening, twilight.* — III. *darkness.*

יַנְשׁוּף יַנְשׁוֹף m., *bittern*; LXX. ἴβιϛ.

נָשַׁק (fut. יִשַּׁק, יְשֹׁק; imp. שַׁק, נַשְּׁקָה).
— I. *kissed*; with לְ and אֶל *kissed
each other.* — II. *adored*, with לְ. —
III. *rule, order*, Gen. 41:40. — IV.
*draw up in battle array*, with עַל.
Pi. *kissed.* Hiph. *joined, touched*,
Eze. 3:13.

נֶשֶׁק, נֵשֶׁק m. — I. *battle*, Ps. 140:8.
— II. *battle array*, Job 39:21. — III.
*arms.* — IV. *an armoury*

נְשִׁיקָה f., *kiss*.

נָשַׁר (Arab. *eagle*).

נֶשֶׁר m., *an eagle*.

נְשַׁר m. Ch., *an eagle*.

נָשַׁת I. *was parched*, Isa. 41:17. — II.
*wasted away*, Jer. 51:30. Niph.
*dried up*, Isa. 19:5.

נִשְׁתָּוָה Nith., from שׁוה.

נִשְׁתְּוָן m., *a letter.* Ch. the same
(book of Ezra only).

נָתַב (Arab. *was lofty, raised up*).

נָתִיב m., נְתִיבָה f. — I. *path.* — II.
*drift of a vein of metal*, Job 28:7.
— III. *course of life.*

נָתַח. Pi. נִתַּח *divided, cut in pieces*
(a slaughtered animal).

נֵתַח m., *joint, piece of flesh*; pl.
נְתָחִים.

נָתַךְ (fut. יִתַּךְ) *poured out.* Niph.
I. *was poured out.* — II. *was melted.*
Hiph. הִתִּיךְ I. *poured out.* — II.
*melted.* Hoph. הֻתַּךְ *be melted*,
Eze. 22:22.

הִתּוּךְ (verb Hiph.) m., *melting* (metal), Eze. 22:22.

נָתַן (fut. יִתֵּן, יִתֶּן; pl. נָתַן, נִתֵּן; inf.
abs. נָתֹן; const. תֵּת, נְתֹן; with

uff. תִּתִּי; imp. תֵּן, תְּנָה).—I. *gave*
(as a present, in marriage, &c.).—
II. *gave forth* (produced fruit,
emitted odour, &c.).—III. *ascribed.*
—IV. *sold.*—V. *offered,* Lev. 20:2,
3, with אֶת.—VI. *placed,* with אֶל,
בְּ, לְ, עַל.—VII. *appointed.*—VIII.
*imposed tribute,* with עַל.—IX. *inflicted.*—X. *wrought miracles.*—
XI. *rendered like, considered as,*
with כְּ.—XII. *made, rendered,*
with לְ; מִי יִתֵּן; see מִי. Niph.
נִתַּן pass. of Kal.—Hoph. fut. יֻתַּן
*shall be given, &c.*

נְתַן Ch., *gave.*

נָתָן p. n.—I. *Nathan,* the prophet.
—II. the name also of a son of
David and of other men.

נְתַנְאֵל (*gift of God*), p. n. of a man,
Ναθαναήλ.

נְתַנְיָהוּ, נְתַנְיָה (*gift of the Lord*), p. n.
of a man.

נְתַן־מֶלֶךְ p. n. of king Josiah's cham-
berlain, 2 Ki. 23:11.

נְתִינִים m. pl., (*devoted*), *Nethinim,*
servants of the Temple, waiting
upon the Levites; Ch. נְתִינִין.

מַתָּן m.—I. *gift.*—II. p. n. of a
man.

מַתָּנָה f.—I. the same.—II. p. n. of
a place between Moab and the
desert.

מַתְּנָא f. Ch., the same.

מַתְּנַי (for מַתַּנְיָה), p. n. of a man.

מַתַּנְיָה, מַתַּנְיָהוּ p. n. of a man.
מַתַּת f., *a gift.*

מַתִּתְיָה, מַתִּתְיָהוּ p. n. of a man,
Ματθαθίας.

מַתִּתָּה p. n. of a man.

נָתַם *break down, cut off,* Job 30:13.

נָתַע. Niph. *broken down, cut off,* Job
4:10, for נִתַּץ.

נָתַץ (fut. יִתֹּץ).—I. *broke down, destroyed.*—II. *ruined a person.*—III.
*struck out teeth,* Ps. 58:7. Pi.
נִתֵּץ *destroyed.* Niph. נִתַּץ, Pu.
נֻתַּץ and Hoph. הֻתַּץ *was destroyed.*

נָתַק I. *drew one away from* (a place),
Jud. 20:32.—II. *drew off* (a ring),
Jer. 22:24.—III. part. נָתוּק *cas-
trated,* Lev. 22:24. Niph. נִתַּק
I. *drawn away.*—II. *purged away,*
Jer. 6:29.—III. *broken* (of a shoe-
string, cord). Pi. נִתֵּק I. *removed
took off,* Isa. 58:6.-II. *pulled up,
uprooted.* — III. *broke a cord.*—
IV. *broke off, frustrated,* Job 17:
11, &c. Hiph. הִתִּיק *drew away*
Hoph. הָנְתַּק pass. of Hiph., Jud
20:31.

נֶתֶק m., *scalled head;* lit. plucking
off of hair, Lev. 13:30 — 37;
14:54.

נְתַקְנוּהוּ Jud. 20:32, Kal pl. 1. pers.
with suff. and dag. euphon., from
נתק.

נָתַר (fut. יִתַּר), *beat violently* (the
heart), Job 37:1. Pi. *leap* (as
locusts), Lev. 11:21. Hiph. הִתִּיר
I. *loosened,* Ps. 105:20, &c.—II.
*stretched out the hand,* Job 6:9.—
III. *straightened,* 2 Sa. 22:33.—
IV. *made vibrate, caused to tremble,* Hab. 3:6.

נְתַר Ch., *fell off.* Aph. *shake off,*
Dan. 4:11.

נֶתֶר m.—I. *nitre, natron,* Pro. 25:20.
—II. *soap made of natron and oil*
Jer. 2:22.

**נָתַשׁ** (fut. יִתּשׁ), with אֶת.—I. *expelled.*—II. *destroyed.* Niph. I. *was expelled, destroyed.*—II. *failed* (of waters). Hoph. הֻתַּשׁ *plucked up* (of trees), Eze. 19:12.

**נָתַתְּ** נָתַתִּי, נָתַתָּ, נָתַתְּ Kal pret., from נתן.

## ס

**סְאָה** f., *a dry measure,* containing one third of an ephah, σάτον; dual סָאתַיִם; pl. סְאִים.

**סַאסְּאָה** f., the same, Isa. 27:8.

**סְאָן**, part. סֹאֵן *having greaves,* Isa. 9:4.

**סְאוֹן** m., *greaves* (armour for the legs), Isa. 9:4.

**סָבָא** *drank wine, became drunk;* part. סוֹבֵא *drinker* (pl. סוֹבְאִים Ketib, סֹבְאִים Kri, Eze. 23:42).

**סֹבֶא** m. (with suff. סׇבְאֵךְ).—I. *wine.*—II. *the act of drinking wine,* Nah. 1:10.

**סְבָא** p. n.—I. *the son of Cush,* Gen. 10:7.—II. *the people descended from him;* סְבָאִים *the Sabeans.*

**סָבַב** (pret. סַבּוּ, סְבָבוּ, סַבֹּתִי; fut. יִסֹּב; pl. יָסֹבּוּ; inf. סֹב, יְסֹב; imp. סַב; part. סוֹבֵב, סֹבֵב).—I. *turned about.*—II. *made a circuit,* with אֶת, בְּ.—III. *reached round.*—IV. *surrounded,* with אֶת, עַל.—V. *ended a circuit at,* with אֶל or לְ.—VI. *an act overtaken in its consequences,* with אֶת.—VII. *circumvented, entrapped.*—VIII. *went round, examined in succession,* Ecc. 7:25.—IX. *arrived at a*

*conclusion* (after going round), Ecc. 2:20. Niph. נָסֵב (fut. יִסֹּב; pl. יִסַּבּוּ).—I. *turn about, make a circle, surround.*—II. *returned.*—III. *came round in turn.*—IV. *was changed, changed, changed his conduct.* Pi. סִבֵּב *brought to pass,* 2 Sa. 14:20. Poel סוֹבֵב I. *made a circuit,* with עַל.—II. *surrounded,* with עַל. Hiph. הֵסֵב (fut. יָסֵב; יָסֵבּוּ).—I. *caused to turn about, make a circuit, surround.* — II. *changed his name to.* Hoph. הוּסַב *was turned round, enclosed.*

**סָבִיב** m.—I. *a circuit;* adv. מִסָּבִיב, סָבִיב סָבִיב *around, from around,* סָבִיב לְ *around.*—II. pl. סְבִיבִים, סְבִיבוֹת *surrounding places, suburbs,* Jer. 17:26; 33:13; with suff. סְבִיבוֹתַי *around me.*

**סֹבֵב** for סָבִיב Kal part., from סבב.

**סִבָּה** f., *change, turn in affairs,* 1 Ki 12:15.

**נְסִבָּה** f., the same, 2 Chron. 10:15.

**מוּסָב** m., *the wall that surrounds a house,* Eze. 41:7.

**מֵסַב** m. (pl. const. מְסִבֵּי, מְסִבּוֹת). I. *sofas for reclining on* (ranged round), Cant. 1:12.—II. *places surrounding.* — III. adv. *round about,* 1 Ki. 6:29.

**סָבַךְ** *wrapped, folded, coiled, entangled,* Pu. סֻבַּךְ.

**סְבָךְ** m., *thicket, tangled place.*

**סֹבֶךְ** m., pl. const. סׇבְכֵי; the same.

**סְבֹךְ** m., the same; with suff. סֻבְכוֹ.

**סֻבְּכוֹ** with dag. euphon. for סֻבְכוֹ from סֹבֶךְ.

**סִבְּכַי** p. n., *Sibbeckai,* one of David's generals, 2 Sa. 21:18, &c.

שַׂבְּכָא, סַבְּכָא f. Ch., a certain musical instrument, σαμβύκη, of what kind is unknown, Dan. 3:5, 7,10.

סָבַל I. carried (a load), Isa. 46:4.—II. carried (as a child).—III. bore consequences of. Pu laden, Ps. 144:14. Hith. הִסְתַּבֵּל become a burden.

סְבַל Ch., the same. Po. brought, Ezr. 6:3.

סֵבֶל m., burden, task.

סַבָּל m., porter.

סֹבֶל m. (with suff. סֻבְּלוֹ), burden, Isaiah only.

סֻבְּלוֹ; see above.

סִבְלָה f., pl. const. סִבְלוֹת burdens, labours, tasks, Exodus only.

סִבֹּלֶת f. (in the dialect of the tribe of Ephraim, for שִׁבֹּלֶת), ear of corn, Jud. 12:6.

סְבַר Ch., hope, propose, Dan. 7:25.

סִבְרַיִם p.n., a city between Damascus and Hamath.

סַבְתָּה, סַבְתָּא p. n., Sabtah, one of the sons of Cush, Gen. 10:7, and the people descended from him.

סַבְתְּכָא, סַבְתְּכָה p. n., Sabtechah, one of the sons of Cush, Gen. 10:7.

סְגִנִים same as סִינִים; see סוּג.

סָגַד worshipped, with לְ.

סְגַד Ch., the same.

סָגַל root not used; סְגַל bought, acquired.

סְגֻלָּה f.—I. collection of valuables.—II. an object of special regard.

סָגָן m., pl. סְגָנִים—I. chiefs among the Babylonians and Persians.—

—II. chiefs among the Jews after the second captivity.

סְגַן m. Ch., pl. סִגְנִין the same.

סָגַר (fut. יִסְגֹּר).—I. shut a door, shut in.—II. closed a breach, 1 Ki. 11: 27, with בְּעַד, עַל; part. סָגוּר shut up; זָהָב סָגוּר pure gold, lit. such gold as is shut, hoarded up. Niph. נִסְגַּר was shut. Pi. סִגַּר, with בְּיַד delivered up, surrendered. Pu. סֻגַּר was shut up. Hiph. הִסְגִּיר I. shut up, with בְּיַד, אֶל, לְ.—II. delivered up; part. מַסְגִּיר.

סְגַר Ch., shut. Dan. 6:23.

סְגוֹר m.—I. enclosure, Hos. 13:8.—II. refined gold, Job 28:15.

סֻגַּר m., prison, Eze. 19:9.

סַגְרִיר m., rain, Pro. 27:15.

מִסְגֵּר (part. Hiph.) m.—I. confinement, prison.—II. joiner, i.e. closer.

מִסְגֶּרֶת f. (pl. מִסְגְּרוֹת).—I. inclosure.—II. border, moulding.

סָדַד root not used; (Arab. shut up).

סַד m., fetters.

סְדֹם p.n., Sodom, one of the cities of the plain, Σόδομα.

סָדַן root not used; (Arab. wool, covering).

סָדִין m.—I. fine cloth of Syrian manu facture.—II. a dress made of it, Isa. 3:23.—III. a piece of it used as a sheet, Jud. 14:12,13.

סָדַר root not used; (Syr. set in order).

סֵדֶר m., pl. סְדָרִים ranks, orderly arrangement, Job 10:22.

שְׂדֵרָה f., pl. שְׂדֵרוֹת the same.

מִסְדְּרוֹן m., portico, Jud. 3:23

סָהַר root not used (Samar. סהר), encompassed about, was round.

סַהַר m., *roundness* (like the full moon), Cant. 7 : 3.

סֹהַר m., בֵּית הַסֹּהַר *prison*, Gen. 39 & 40, only.

שַׂהֲרֹנִים m. pl., *small moons* (ornaments).

סוֹא p. n., *Sevechus* king of Egypt, 2 Ki. 17 : 4.

I. סוֹג *slid back from God*. Niph. נָסוֹג (fut. יִסּוֹג).—I. *driven back*.—II. *induced to go back*.

II. סוֹג *fenced*, Cant. 7 : 3.

סוּג m. (pl. סִינִים, סִיגִים), *dross* (of metals).

סוֹדִי, סוֹד ; see יסד.

סוּחַ root not used; same as סחה *cleanse*.

סוּחַ p. n. of a man.

סוּחָה f., *filth*, Isa. 5 : 25.

סוֹטַי (see שׁוּט) p. n. of a man.

סוּךְ same as נָסַךְ.—I. *anoint himself.*—II. *anoint another*, with בְּ. Hiph. *anointed himself*; fut. וַיָּסֶךְ.

אָסוּךְ m., *vessel for anointing oil*, 2 Ki. 4 : 2.

סוּמְפֹּנְיָה f. Ch., συμφωνία, a musical instrument, *the hautboy*, Ital. *zampogna*, Dan. 3 : 5, 15.

סְוֵנֵה p. n., *Syene*, a city of Egypt; (hierog. Soun).

סוּס m.—I. *a horse*.—II. *a swallow*, Isa. 38 : 14 ; Jer. 8 : 7.

סוּסָה f., *horses*, Cant. 1 : 9.

סוּסִי p. n. of a man.

סוּף *come to an end, perish.* Hiph. *cause to perish.*

סוּף Ch., *came to an end, was completed.* Aph. *destroyed.*

סוֹף m.—I. *end, termination, comple-*

tion, result.—II. *rear of an army*, Joel 2 : 20.

סוֹף m. Ch., the same.

סוּפָה f., *whirlwind, tornado*, with ה parag. סוּפָתָה.

סוּף m.—I. *sea weed*; יַם־סוּף *the Red Sea.*—II. p. n. of a man.

סוּר (fut. יָסוּר, וַיָּסַר).—I. *went, turned aside*, with מֵעַל, מִן, אֶל.—II. *went away*, with מִן.—III. *was removed.*—IV. *ceased.*—V. *rebelled against*, with בְּ. Pil. סוֹרֵר *turned away*, Lam. 3 : 11. Hiph. הֵסִיר (fut. יָסִיר, וַיָּסַר).—I. *removed*, Lev. 1 : 16.—II. *laid aside, gave up.*—III. *drew off* (a ring).—IV. *set aside.*—V. *destroyed.* ה׳ רֹאשׁ מֵעַל *cut off his head*; ה׳ מֵאַחֲרֵי יְהֹוָה *estranged him from following the Lord.* Hoph. הוּסַר *was removed, taken away.*

סוּר m.—I. *degenerate branch*, Jer. 2 : 21.—II. p. n., one of the gates of the temple, 2 Ki. 11 : 6, called יְסוֹד in the parall. pass., 2 Chron. 23 : 5.

סִיר com.—I. *a thorn*; pl. סִירִים.—II. pl. סִירוֹת *hooks*, Am. 4 : 2.—III. *pot, vessel*; pl. סִירוֹת.

סָרָה f.—I. *turning from God, rebellion.*—II. ... *from the truth, falsehood*, Deu. 19 : 16; see סָר.

סִרָה p. n. of a well or tank, 2 Sa. 3 26.

סוּת. Hiph. הֵסִית, הֵפִית (fut. יָסִית, וַיָּסֶת ;) part. (מֵסִית) *urged, excited, induced*, with אֶת and בְּ.

סוּת, Gen. 49 : 11, wrong reading for כְּסוּת *covering*; see כסה.

סָחַב 1. *drew along the ground*, 2 Sa.
17:13, &c.—II. *tore in pieces and
devoured*, Jer. 49:20, &c.

סְחָבָה f., *tearing to pieces*; בְּלֹיֵ
הַסְּחָבוֹת "old cast clouts;" Eng.
Ver., Jer. 38:11, 12.

סָחָה. Pi. סִחָה *swept away*, Eze.
26:4.

סְחִי m., *offscouring*, Lam. 3:45.

שָׂחִיש, סָחִים m., *spontaneous produce, that which comes without
sowing*, 2 Ki. 19:29; Isa. 37:30;
LXX. αὐτόματα; Aquila αὐτοφυῆ.

סָחַף *beat down, crush*, Pro. 28:3.
Niph. *beaten down*, Jer. 46:15.

סָחַר *travelled to a place*, with אֶל;
*over a country*, with אֶת; part.
סֹחֵר (pl. סֹחֲרִים) *traveller,
merchant*; f. סֹחֶרֶת. Pil.
סְחַרְחַר *was agitated* (the heart), Ps. 38:
11.

סַחַר m.—I. *commerce*.—II. *wealth
acquired by commerce*.—III. *seat
of commerce*, Isa. 23:3.

סַחַר m., *the same*.

סְחֹרָה f., *seat of commerce*, Eze. 27:
15.

סֹחֵרָה f., *tower*, Ps. 91:4; (Syr.
*tower*).

סֹחֶרֶת f., *black marble* or *tortoise-
shell* (uncertain which), Est. 1:6;
LXX. πάρινος λίθος.

מִסְחָר m., *traffic*, 1 Ki. 10:15.

סֵטִים *sinners*; same as שֵׁטִים; see
שׂוּט.

סִין *dross*; see סוּג.

סִיוָן m., name of the third month of
the Jewish year, Est. 8:9.

---

סִיחוֹן p. n.—I. *Sihon*, king of the Amorites.—II. the district over which
he ruled.

סִין p. n., a city of Egypt, "Pelusium,"
(Jerome); probably Syene; Eze.
30:15, 16; see סְוֵנֵה.

מִדְבַּר־סִין p. n., the wilderness of *Sin*.

סִינִי p. n.—I. a people of Canaan, Gen.
10:17; 1 Ch. 1:15.—II. אֶרֶץ
סִינִים the land of *Sin*.

סִינַי p. n., a mountain on the pro-
montory between Egypt and Canaan; its two summits are called
Sinai and Horeb.

סִים Jer. 8:7, same as סוּס a *swallow*.

סִיסְרָא p. n., *Sisera*, a Canaanitish
leader, and other men.

סִיעָהָא, סִיעָא p. n. of a man.

סִיר; see סוּג.

סָכַך I. *covered*.—II. *protected by covering*.—III. *placed as a covering*,
with עַל.—IV. *compacted, put together*, Ps. 139:13; part. סוֹכֵךְ *defence*. Hiph. הֵסֵךְ I. *covered*, with
עַל.—II. *protected*, with לְ.—III.
*dressed himself*, 2 Sa. 12:20.—IV.
*confined*, with בְּעַד. Hoph. הֻסַּךְ
*was covered*, with בְּ. Pilp. סִכְסֵךְ
*armed*, Isa. 9:10; 19:2.

סָךְ m., *multitude, crowd*, Ps. 42:5.

סֹךְ m. (with suff. סֻכּוֹ, סֻכֹּה), *thicket,
hiding-place, dwelling*.

סֻכָּה f.—I. *thicket*, Job 38:40.—II.
*hiding-place*, Ps. 31:21.—III. *hut*
(of branches or wattles).—IV.
*dwelling*; pl. סֻכּוֹת I. *tabernacles*;
חַג הַסֻּכּוֹת *feast of tabernacles*.—
II. סֻכּוֹת בְּנוֹת, 2 Ki. 17:30, probably a proper name.—III. p. n., a

station of the Israelites.— IV. a town of the Gadites.

סִכּוּת f., *shrine*, Am. 5:26.

סֻכִּיִּים p. n., *Sukkiims*, 2 Ch. 12:3, some part of the invading army of Shishak; meaning unknown.

סְכָכָה p. n., a town in the tribe of Judah.

מָסָךְ const. מֵסַךְ m.—I. *covering* (of tabernacle).— II. (with פָּרֹכֶת) a *veil*.—III. *curtain of a fortress*, Isa. 22:8.

מְסֻכָּה f., *covering*, Eze. 28:13.

מִיסָךְ (מֵיסַךְ) מוּסָךְ m., *covering, porch*, 2 Ki. 16:18.

סָכַל. Niph. *became foolish, acted foolishly*. Pi. *made foolish*. Hiph. *acted the fool*.

סָכָל m., *a fool, foolish*.

סֶכֶל m., *folly*, Ecc. 10:6.

שִׂכְלוּת, סִכְלוּת f., *folly*, book of Eccles. only.

סָכַן, with עַל, לְ.—I. *was prosperous*, Job 34:9.—II. *was beneficial*, Job 15:3.—III. part. סֹכֵן *a companion, counsellor*; f. סֹכֶנֶת. Hiph. *was familiar with, accustomed to*, with עִם. Pu. part. מְסֻכָּן *poor, needy* (Arab. *was poor*), Isa. 40:20. Niph. נִסְכַּן *exposed himself to danger* (Ch. סְכַן *was in danger*), Ecc. 10:9.

מִסְכֵּן m., *poor*.

מִסְכֵּנֻת f., *poverty*, Deu. 8:9.

מִסְכְּנוֹת f. pl. (same as מִכְנְסוֹת; see כָּנָס), *magazines, treasuries*.

I. סָכַר. Niph. *was shut*. Pi. (see סָגַר), *delivered up*, Isa. 19:4.

II. סָכַר same as שָׂכַר *hired*, Ezr. 4:5.

סָכַת. Hiph. הִסְכִּית *was silent*, Deu 27:9.

סָל, סַלָּא, סַלִּים; see סָלַל.

סָלָא. Pu. *valued*, Lam. 4:2

סָלַד. Pi. *harden oneself*, Job 6:10

סֶלֶד p. n. of a man.

סָלָה trampled on, Ps. 119:118. Pi. the same, Lam, 1:15. Pu. *valued, estimated*, Job 28:16, 19.

סֶלָה a musical note, in the Psalms and the prayer of Habakkuk.

סָלַח (fut. יִסְלַח), *forgave*. Niph. *was forgiven*.

סַלָּח m., *one who forgives, is placable*, Ps. 86:5.

סְלִיחָה f., *forgiveness*.

סַלְכָה p. n., a town in the land of Bashan.

סָלַל threw up an embankment, levelled, made a road. Pilp. סִלְסֵל exalt, Pro. 4:8. Hithpo. הִסְתּוֹלֵל opposing, exalting himself, with בְּ, Ex. 9:17.

סַל m. (pl. סַלִּים) *basket*.

סִלָּא p.n. of a place.

סַלּוּ p.n. of a man.

סַלָּא, סַלּוּא p.n. of a man.

סַלּוּא p.n. of a man.

סַלַּי p.n. of a man.

סִלּוֹן *a thorn*, Eze. 28:24.

סַלּוֹן m., the same; metaph. *wicked man*, Eze. 2:6.

סֹלְלָה f., *a mound*.

סֻלָּם m., *a ladder*, Gen. 28:12.

סַלְסִלּוֹת f. pl., *baskets*, Jer. 6:9.

מְסִלָּה f.—I. *raised highway*.—II. *road, path*.—III. *terraces* (Lee), *"steps"* (Gesenius), 2 Chron. 9: 11.

מַסְלוּל m., *highway*, Isa. 35:8.

סֶלַע m.— I. *cleft in a rock, cavern.*—II. *rock.*—III. p.n. of a city, perhaps *Petra* in Edom.

סָלְעָם m., *a kind of locust*, Lev. 11:22.

סָלַף Pi. סִלֵּף I. *perverts.*— II. *overthrows.*

סֶלֶף m., *capriciousness, perverseness.*

סְלֵק Ch., *came up, grew up.*

סֶלֶת root not used; (Arab. *shelled grain*).

סֹלֶת com., *shelled grain, fine flour.*

סַמִּים, סַם; see סמם.

סַמְגַּר־נְבוּ p.n. a prince of Babylon.

סְמָדַר m., *flower* (of the grape).

סָמַךְ I. (with אֶת יָדָיו, עַל) *laid his hands on.*— II. *supported.* — III. *pressed, weighed upon*, with עַל, Ps. 88:8.—IV. *advanced towards*, with אֶל, Eze. 24:2. Niph. I. *leaned on.*— II. *trusted in.* — Pi. *support*, Cant. 2:5,

שְׂמִיכָה f., *coverlet*, Jud. 4:18.

סְמַכְיָהוּ p. n. of a man.

סֶמֶל, סֵמֶל m., *figure, form.*

סָמַם (Arab. *exhaled perfume*).

סַם m., pl. סַמִּים *perfumes.*

סָמַן. Niph. part. נִסְמָן *"appointed"* Eng. Ver. (of barley), Isa. 28:25.

סָמַר *grew hard, rigid*, Ps. 119:120. Pi. the same, Job 4:15.

סָמָר m., *rough, bristly* (of a locust), ὀρθόθριξ, Jer. 51:27.

מַסְמְרִים, מַסְמְרוֹת m. pl., *nails.*

מַשְׂמְרוֹת, מַסְמְרוֹת, מִסְמְרוֹת f. pl. the same.

סְנָאָה p.n., a town of Judah.

סְנֻאָה p.n., probably of a woman, Neh. 11:9.

סַנְבַלָּט p.n. of a Persian governor of Samaria.

סְנֶה m., *the bush of Sinai*, Ex. 3: 2—4; Deu. 33:16.

סֶנֶּה p.n., a rock near Michmash, 1 Sa. 14:4.

סַנְוֵרִים m. pl., *blindness*, Gen. 19:11; 2 Ki. 6:18.

סַנְחֵרִיב p.n., *Sennacherib*, king of Assyria.

סַנְסִנִּים m. pl., *the plume of the palm-tree*, Cant. 7:9.

סַנְסַנָּה p.n., a city of the tribe of Judah.

סְנַפִּיר m., *fin of a fish*, Lev. 11:9; Deu. 14:9.

סָס m., *clothes-moth*, Isa. 51:8.

סִסְמַי p.n. of a man.

סָעַד (fut. יִסְעַד; imp. סְעַד, סְעָד; with ה parag. סְעָדָה).—I. *was prosperous*, Pro. 20:28.— II. *made prosperous*, Ps. 20:3.— III. *supported.*—IV. *cheered, refreshed*, with לֵב.

סְעַד Ch., *assisting*, Ezr. 5:2.

מִסְעָד m., *prop, support*, 1 Ki. 10:12.

סְעָה; רוּחַ סֹעָה *rapid wind*, Ps. 55:9.

סָעַף Kal not used; (Arab. *palm branch*). Pi. סֵעַף (perhaps from סָעִיף) *cut off branches*, Isa. 10:33.

סָעִיף m.— I. *cleft, cavern.*— II. *sect party*, 1 Ki. 18:21.—III. *a branch*

סְעַפּוֹת f. pl., *branches*, Eze. 31:6,8.

סַרְעֻפּוֹת f. pl., the same, Eze. 31:5.

סֵעֵף m., pl. סְעַפִּים *persons of divided minds*, Ps. 119:113.

שְׂעִפִּים *thoughts of the mind* (lit. *branches*).

שַׂרְעַפִּים m. pl., *thoughts*, Ps. 94:19; 139:23.

סָעַר I. *was tempestuous*, Jon. 1:11, 13, &c.—II. *tossed by calamity*, Isa. 54: 11. Niph. *was agitated* (the heart), 2 Ki. 6:11. Pi. סֵעַר *scattered*, Zec. 7:14. Po. *scattered*, Hos. 13:3; see שָׁעַר.

סַעַר m., *pestilential, violent wind, whirlwind*.

סְעָרָה, const. סַעֲרַת f., the same.

סַף with pause סָף m. (pl. סִפִּים, סִפּוֹת).—I. *dish, bason, goblet, bowl.*—II. *threshold.*—III. p. n. of a man.

הִסְתּוֹפֵף Hith. inf., *remain at the threshold*, Ps. 84:11.

סָפָא (Arab. *filled*).

מִסְפּוֹא m., *provender, fodder*.

סָפַד *lamented, bewailed*, with עַל, לְ, לִפְנֵי. Niph. *was lamented*.

מִסְפֵּד, const. מִסְפַּד m., *lamentation*.

סָפָה I. *came to an end, perished.*— II. *brought to an end, destroyed*; inf. סְפוֹת *increase*, Nu. 32:14. Niph. נִסְפָּה *was perished*. Hiph. הַסְפָּה *heap, accumulate* (trouble), Deu. 23:23.

סְפוּן; see ספן.

סְפוֹרָה; see ספר.

סָפַח *admitted*, 1 Sa. 2:36. Niph. *was admitted*, Isa. 14:1. Pi. *poured out*, Hab. 2:15. Pu. *scattered*, Job

30:7. Hith. הִסְתַּפֵּחַ *obtained admission*, 1 Sa. 26:19.

סָפִיחַ m.—I. *pouring out of water*, Job 14:19.— II. *spilt, self-sown grain*; pl. סְפִיחִים.

סַפַּחַת f., *a scar, scald*, Lev. 13:2; 14:56.

מִסְפַּחַת f., *scurf, scab*, Lev. 13:6—8. מִסְפָּחוֹת f. pl., *cushions, pillows*, Eze. 13:18, 21.

סַפִּי p. n., same as סַף.

סַפִּיר m., *a sapphire*.

סֵפֶל m., *a bowl*, Jud. 5.25; 6:38.

סָפַן I. *covered.*—II. *secured*, Deu. 33: 21.

סִפֻּן m., *ceiling*, 1 Ki. 6:15.

סְפִינָה f., *ship*, Jon. 1:5.

הַסְתּוֹפֵף, סָפַף; see סַף.

סָפַק I. *clapped the hands together.*— II. *smote upon the thigh.*—III. *expressed contempt for*.

סֵפֶק m., *abundance, sufficiency*, with suff. סִפְקוֹ, Job 20:22.

סָפַר (fut. יִסְפֹּר) *numbered, reckoned*, part. סֹפֵר (pl. סֹפְרִים) *writer, scribe*, γραμματεύς. Niph. *was numbered*. Pi. סִפֵּר I. *counted.* — II. *recounted.*—III. *talked.* Pu. סֻפַּר *was related, &c.*

סְפַר m. Ch., *scribe*.

סֵפֶר m., *enumeration*, 2 Chron. 2:16.

סֵפֶר m. (with suff. סִפְרְךָ; pl. סְפָרִים, סִפְרֵי).—I. *enumeration*, Gen. 5:1. —II. *register.*—III. *book.*—IV. *letter.*—V. *writing*.

סְפַר m. Ch., *book*.

סִפְרָה f., *book*, Ps. 56:9.

סֹפֶרֶת p.n. of a man.

מִסְפָּר f., *number*, Ps. 71:15.

מְסַפֵּר m.— I. *number;* אַנְשֵׁי מ׳ or
מְתֵי מ׳ *few men.*—II. *narrative,*
Jud. 7:15.—III. p. n. of a man;
מִסְפֶּרֶת the same.

סְפָר p. n. of a city, Gen. 10:30.

סְפָרַד p. n., a country into which
the Jews were carried, Obad. v. 20.

סְפַרְוַיִם p. n., *Sepharvaim,* a city of
Assyria; סְפַרְוִים *Sepharvites.*

סָקַל *stoned.* Pi.— I. as Kal.—II.
*cleared of stones.* Niph. and Pu.
*was stoned.*

סָרָב *rebellious,* Eze. 2:6.

סַרְבָּלִין m. pl. Ch., *drawers, trousers,*
Dan. 3:21, 27.

סַרְגּוֹן p. n., *Sargon,* king of Assyria.

סֶרֶד p. n. of a man; patron. סַרְדִּי.

סָרָה ,סֻרָה ;סרר ,סור see.

סָרַח I. *unconfined, loose,* Ex. 26:12,
13, &c.—II. *luxuriant* (of a vine),
Eze. 17:6.—III. *loose, dissolute,*
Am. 6:4, 7. Niph. *scattered, va-
nished* (of wisdom), Jer. 49:7.

סֶרַח m., *portion of a thing left loose,*
Ex. 26:12.

סִרְיוֹן *corslet,* same as שִׁרְיָה; see שׁרה.

סָרִים m. (const. סָרִיס; pl. סָרִיסִים
const. סָרִיסֵי).—I. *eunuch.*—II. any
*chief officer.*

סָרְכִין m. pl. Ch., *superintendants of
the whole empire,* Dan. 6:3.

סְרָנִים, const. סַרְנֵי m. pl.—I. *axles,*
1 Ki. 7:30.—II. the name of the
five princes of the Philistines.

סַרְעַפּוֹת *branches;* see סעף.

שָׂרַף same as שָׂרַף. Pi. part. מְסָרֵף
*burning, he who burns,* Am. 6:10.

סְרְפַד m., the name of an unknown
shrub; LXX. κόνυζα; Vulg. urtica.

סָרַר *was perverse, refractory,* Hos. 4:
16; part. סֹרֵר (pl. סוֹרְרִים; f.
סוֹרֶרֶת ,סוֹרְרָה) *perverse, rebellious*
סַר m., סָרָה f., *averse, disinclined, sad;*
see also another סָרָה in סור.

סְתָה root not used; (Arab. *winter*).
סְתָו (סְתָיו) m., *winter,* Cant. 2:11.

סָתַם I. *filled, blocked up.*—II. *repaired.*—III. *shut up, concealed*
Niph. *was repaired,* Neh. 4:1. Pi.
*blocked up,* Gen. 26:15, 18.

סָתַר *concealed,* Pro. 22:3. Niph.
נִסְתַּר I. *concealed himself.*—II.
*was concealed, unknown.*—III. *was
sheltered.*—IV. *was distant.*—V.
*was excluded;* part. נִסְתָּר *hidden,
hidden thing;* pl. נִסְתָּרוֹת *hidden
things.* Pi. *hide, shelter,* Isa. 16:3
Pu. *concealed,* Pro. 27:5. Hiph.
הִסְתִּיר I. *concealed.*—II. *sheltered*
—III. *placed for security,* Isa.
49:2.—IV. *turned his face from.*
Hith. הִסְתַּתֵּר I. *concealed, lost.*—
II. *hid himself.*

סְתַר Ch. Pa. סַתַּר *put out of sight,
destroyed.*

סִתְרִי p. n., a prince of Assher.

סֵתֶר m. (with suff. סִתְרִי).—I. *secresy*
—II. *secret place.*—III. בַּסֵּתֶר
*secretly.*—IV. *place of conceal-
ment.*—V. *place of security.*

סִתְרָה f., *shelter, protection,* Deu.
32:38.

סִתְרִי p. n. of a man.

מַסְתָּר m.—I. *ambush.*—II. *secret
place.*

מִסְתּוֹר *hiding place,* Isa. 4:6.

## ע

עֵב m., *epistyle, frieze* (in architecture), 1 Ki. 7:6; Eze. 41:25, 26; pl. עָבִּים; see also עוּב.

עָבַד (inf. and imp. עֲבֹד; fut. יַעֲבֹד).— I. *served* (God or man).— II. *worked, laboured.*—III. *tilled the ground.*—IV. *assented to,* 1 Ki. 12:7.—V. *performed a religious service.*—VI. *made to serve,* with בְּ of the person. Niph. נֶעֱבַד I. *became, was, served,* Ecc. 5:8.— II. *was tilled.* Pu. עֻבַּד *labour was imposed upon,* with בְּ. Hiph. הֶעֱבִיד I. *caused to labour.*—II. *caused to serve.*—III. *wearied,* Isa. 43:23, 24. Hoph. הָעֲבַד *was induced to worship.*

עֲבַד Ch.—I. *made.*—II. *performed, did,* with בְּ, עִם. Ith. *was made.*

עֶבֶד m. (with suff. עַבְדּוֹ; pl. עֲבָדִים).— I. *slave, servant.*—II. *vassal.*— III. עֶבֶד יְהוָֹה *servant of the Lord,* i. e. one who worships and serves him, or executes some special commission for him.—IV. a submissive epithet.—V. p.n. of a man.

עֲבַד m. Ch., the same.

עֹבֵד p.n. of a man.

עַבְדָּא p.n. of a man.

עַבְדְּאֵל p.n. of a man.

עַבְדּוֹן p.n., a city of the Levites in the tribe of Asher.

עַבְדִּי p. n. of a man.

עַבְדִּיאֵל p.n. of a man.

עֹבַדְיָה, עֹבַדְיָהוּ (*servant of the Lord,* ᾿Αβδίας), p.n., *Obadiah* the prophet and others.

עֶבֶד מֶלֶךְ p.n., an Ethiopian in the service of king Zedekiah, Jer. 38:7, &c.

עֲבֵד נְגוֹ (נְגוֹא) p.n., *Abednego,* one of the three holy children, Dan. chaps. I. II. III.

עֹבֵד m., *work,* Ecc. 9:1.

עֲבֹדָה f.—I. *servitude.*—II. *employment.*—III. *tillage.*—IV. *religious service, worship.*—V. *service* required by the king.—VI. לַעֲבֹדַת הָאָדָם *for the service* (use) *of man,* Ps. 104:14.

עֲבֻדָּה f., *slaves, gang of slaves,* Gen 26:14; Job 1:3.

עֲבִידָא f. Ch.—I. *work, building.*—II. *worship, service,* Ezr. 6:18.—III. *business,* Dan. 2:49; 3:12.

עַבְדוּת f., *slavery,* Ezr. 9:8, 9; Neh. 9:17.

מַעֲבָד m. (Heb. and Ch.), pl. מַעֲבָדִים *works, doings,* Job 34:25; Dan. 4:34.

עָבָה *became large, thick, heavy.*

עֳבִי m., *thickness.*

עֲבִי m., the same.

מַעֲבֶה m., *thickness,* 1 Ki. 7:46.

עָבַט *gave a pledge;* fut. יַעֲבֹט. Pi. יְעַבֵּטוּן *break ranks,* Joel 2:7. Hiph. הַעֲבִיט *lent on security,* Deu. 15:6, 8.

עֲבוֹט m., *pledge,* Deu. 24:10-13.

עַבְטִיט m., *accumulation of pledges* in the hands of an unfeeling usurer; "thick clay," Eng. Ver., Hab. 2:6.

עָבַר (inf. and imp. עֲבֹר; fut. יַעֲבֹר).— I. *passed on.*—II. *passed away, ceased.*—III. *passed a person, place, river, &c.*—IV. *passed a limit.*— V. *trespassed, transgressed;* עָבַר

בְּרִית transgressed a covenant.—
VI. exceeded, went beyond.—VII.
overflowed, overwhelmed, with עַל.
—VIII. passed through, with עַל,
מֵעַל ,עַל פְּנֵי ,לִפְנֵי.—IX. passed
away, disappeared.—X. passed
through, with בְּ.—XI. entered into,
with בְּ; בִּבְרִית עֹ' made a covenant.—XII. dropped (as liquid).—
XIII. עֹבֵר כֶּסֶף current money,
Gen. 23:16. Niph. can be passed,
Eze 47:5. Pi. עִבֵּר I. conceived,
Job 21:10.—II. caused to pass,
1 Ki. 6:21. Hiph. הֶעֱבִיר I. caused,
allowed to pass.—II. removed, took,
or put away.—III. removed guilt,
&c.—IV. destroyed.—V. trans-
ferred.—VI. offered presents to
God or idols; ה' לַמֹּלֶךְ caused to
pass through fire to Moloch.—VII.
שׁוֹפָר ה' blew a trumpet, lit. caused
the breath to pass through it.
Hith. הִתְעַבֵּר allowed himself beyond proper limits, was angry,
with עַל ,בְּ ,עִם.

עֲבוּר (only with pref.), בַּעֲבוּר I. prep.
because of, in return for; with suff.
בַּעֲבוּרִי on my account; בַּעֲבֻרֶךָ
because of thee.—II. conj. 1. for
the purpose that (בַּעֲבוּר אֲשֶׁר, בְּ
the same).—2. because, while.

עֲבוּר m., produce of the ground, Jos.
5:11, 12.

עֵבֶר m.—I. ford.—II. mountain pass.
—III. passage over.—IV. banks of
a river.—V. side; אֶל־עֵבֶר towards,
on the other side; אֶל־עֶבְרוֹ separately, alone; מֵעֵבֶר beyond, opposite to, across; מִכָּל־עֲבָרִים from
every side; עֵבֶר אֶחָד עֵבֶר אֶחָד

on this and on that side; עַל־עֵבֶר
פְּנֵי in front of it, Ex. 25:37; אֶל־
עֵבֶר פָּנָיו forwards, Eze. 1:9, 12.
—VI. p. n., Eber, the grandson of
Shem, Gen. 10:24, 25, and pro-
genitor of Abraham, whose descendants were called from him;
הָרֵי or הַר Hebrews; עֵבֶר ,בְּנֵי עֵבֶר
הָעֲבָרִים a range of hills beyond
Jordan.

עֲבַר Ch., beyond.

עִבְרִי m., a Hebrew; pl. עִבְרִים,
עִבְרִיּוֹת .f עִבְרִיָּה; pl. עִבְרִיִּים.

עֲבָרָה f., raft, passage boat, 2 Sa. 19:
19.

עֶבְרָה f., any unrestrained feeling,
specially, anger.

מַעֲבָר m.—I. ford.—II. mountain
pass.

מַעֲבָרָה f., pl. מַעְבְּרוֹת the same.

עַבְרוֹנָה p. n., a station of the Israelites.

עָבֵשׁ became shrivelled, worthless, Joel
1:17.

עָבַת Pi. confirm, establish, Mic. 7:3.
עָבֹת m., עֲבֻתָּה f., thick, entangled.
עֲבוֹת m. (pl. עֲבֹתִים, עֲבֹתוֹת).—I.
thick branches, Eze. 31:3, 10, 14.
—II. cord, rope.—III. twisted chain.
—IV. obligation, restraint.

עָגַב (fut. יֶעְגַּב) loved, fell in love with,
with אֶל ,עַל, Eze. c. 23.

עֲגָבָה f., love; with suff. עֲגָבָתָהּ, Eze
23:11.

עֲגָבִים m. pl., the same, Eze. 33:31, 32
עֻגָב ,עוּגָב m., a musical instrument,
probably, the pipe, Gen. 4:21, &c
עֲגָה עָנָה, see עוּג.

עָגוּר m., crane.

עֲגַל (Syr. turned round).

עֲגֹל m., עֲגֻלָּה f., round, circular.

עָגִיל m. ear-ring.

עֵגֶל m. (with suff. עֶגְלְךָ).— I. calf.— — II. image of one.— III. עֶגְלֵי עַמִּים princes, leaders, of the people, Ps. 68:31.

עֶגְלָה f.—I. she-calf, heifer.—II. p. n., one of the wives of David.

עֲגָלָה f. (with suff. עֶגְלָתוֹ; pl. עֲגָלוֹת עֲגָלֹת).—I. waggon drawn by two bullocks.—II. war chariot, Ps.46:10.

עֶגְלוֹן p. n.—I. a city in the tribe of Judah.—II. a king of Moab.

מַעְגָּל or מַעֲגָל m. (pl. מַעְגָּלִים, מַעְגָּלוֹת).—I. wheel.—II. track of a wheel.— III. way, path.— IV. way, manner.—V. waggon.—VI. barricade of waggons.

מַעְגָּלָה f., the same.

עָגַם despise. Job. 30: 25.

עָגַן. Niph. prevented from marrying, Ru. 1:13.

עֵד, see עֵדָה; עַד, עֹד, see עוּד.

עָדַד (Arab. numbered, computed).

עִדִּים menstruous, Isa.64:5; (Arab.the same).

עִדָּן m. Ch.—I. time.—II. a prophetic period of time.

עֵדָה; see יַעַד, עוּד.

עָדָה (fut. יַעֲדֶה).—I. passed through, with עַל, Job 28:8.— II. adorned. — III. put on as an ornament. Hiph. stripped off a garment, Pro. 25: 20.

עֲדָא, עֲדָה Ch.—I. passed upon, with בְּ.—II. passed away, with מִן.—III. was altered. Aph. removed.

עַד m.— I. spoil, Gen. 49:27; Isa 33:23; Zep. 3:8.— II. perpetuity, eternity. — III. antiquity; לָעַד, עוֹלָם וָעֶד ,לְעוֹלָם וָעֶד עֲדֵי עַד for ever; (pl. עֲדֵי) pa. unto, as far as, until, before, while, during, still; עַד־אֲשֶׁר while; (שֶׁ) while; עַד־אֲשֶׁר אִם until; עַד־לֹא, עַד־אֲשֶׁר לֹא before; with suff. עָדַי to me; עָדֶיךָ; עָדָיו, עֲדֵיכֶם; עֲדֵיהֶ.

עַד Ch. to, as far as, until; עַד־דִּי while.

עֶדֶן, Ecc. 4:3, same as עַד־הֵנָּה hitherto, as yet.

עֲדֶנָּה Ecc. 4:2, the same.

עָדָה p. n., Adah.—I. the wife of La. mech.—II. the wife of Esau.

עֲדִי m. (with pause עֶדִי; with suff. עֶדְיוֹ עֶדְיֵךְ; pl. עֲדָיִים).—I. ornaments.—II. trappings of a horse. —III. lot, appointment, Ps. 103:5.

עֲדִיאֵל p. n. of a man.

עֲדָיָה, עֲדָיָהוּ p. n. of a man.

עֲדִיתַיִם p. n., a town in the tribe of Judah.

עַדּוּא, עִדּוֹ p.n. of a man.

עֶדְרָת; see עוּד.

עַדְלַי p. n. of a man.

עֲדֻלָּם p. n., a cave and city of the tribe of Judah; עֲדֻלָּמִי an Adullamite.

עָדַן. Hith. live luxuriously, Neh. 9:25. עָדִין, f. עֲדִינָה luxurious, delicate, Isa. 47:8; (s. smiling, perhaps), 2 Sa.23:8; a very difficult place, see Ges. Thes.

עֲדִינָא p. n. of a man.

עֵדֶן m.— I. pleasure.— II. Eden, the abode of our first parents.

עֵדֶן p. n., a district of Mesopotamia; בֵּית ע׳ see בֵּית.

עֶדְנָה f., *pleasure*, Gen. 18:12.

עַדְנָא p. n. of a man.

עַדְנָה p. n. of a man.

מַעֲדַנּוֹת, מַעֲדַנִּים, מַעֲדַנִּים pl., *delicacies, delights*; adv. *willingly*; מַעֲדַנּוֹת trans. for מַעֲדַנּוֹת *bands*, i.e. *influences*, Job 38:31; see עָנַד.

עִדָּן *time*; see with עַד.

עֲדְעָדָה p.n., a town in the tribe of Judah.

עָדַף I. *was superfluous.*—II. *exceeded,* with עַל. Hiph. הֶעְדִּיף *allowed to exceed.*

עָדַר *arranged, set in order.* Niph. נֶעְדַּר I. *was missing, left behind.* —II. *was dilatory, delayed,* Zep. 3:5.—III. *was cleared out.* Pi. עִדַּר *omitted, neglected,* 1 Ki. 5:7.

עֵדֶר m. (with suff. עֶדְרוֹ; pl. עֲדָרִים (עֲדָרֵי).—I. *flock or herd.*—II. p.n., a town in the tribe of Judah.— III. p. n. of a man.

עֶדֶר p. n. of a man.

עַדְרִיאֵל p.n., *Adriel,* son-in-law of Saul, 1 Sa. 18:19, &c.

מַעְדֵּר m., *rake,* Isa. 7:25.

עֲדָשִׁים m. pl., *lentiles.*

עַוָּה, עַוָּא p. n. of an ancient unknown city; עַוִּים *the Avims,* either the inhabitants of this city, or the early settlers in Canaan.

עוּב Hiph. הֶעִיב *treated as worthless, rejected,* Lam. 2:1.

עָב com. (pl. עָבוֹת, עָבֵי, עָבִים).—I.

*cloud.*— II. *covering,* Ex. 19:9 see also עַב in its place.

עֵיבָל, עוֹבָל p. n. of a people descended from Shem.

עוּג *bake cakes,* Eze. 4:12.

עֻגָּה, עֻגָּה, f., *cakes,* ἐγκρυφίας.

מָעוֹג m., *round cake of bread.*

עוֹג p. n., *Og,* king of Bashan.

עוּד *testified,* Lam. 2:13, Ketib. Pi. עוֹדֵד *surrounded,* Ps. 119:61. Hiph. הֵעִיד I. *called witnesses, to, for, or against.*— II. *called as a witness* with אֶת and בְּ.—III. *made a declaration.* — IV. *enjoined, commanded, reproved,* with בְּ, עַל הֵעִיד עֵדוֹת בְּ *gave commandment to, &c.* Hoph. הוּעַד *information was given,* Ex. 21:29, with בְּ. Pil. עוֹדֵד *raised up, confirmed,* Ps. 146: 9; 147:6. Hithpo. הִתְעוֹדֵד *stood upright,* Ps. 20:9, &c.

עֵד m.—I. *witness.*— II. *testimony.*— III. *proof,* עָנָה עֵד בְּ *gave testimony against.* — IV. *commander,* Isa. 55:4.

עֵדָה f.—I. *eye or ear witness.*—II *proof;* see also in יָעַד.

עֵדָת, עֵדוּת f. (pl. עֵדְוֹת).—I. *covenant* —II. *the law.*—III. *the book of the law.* — IV. *the decalogue.* — V. *religious ordinance,* Ps. 122:4; אֹהֶל אֲרוֹן הָעֵדוּת, לֻחֹת הָעֵדוּת הָעֵדוּת *the tables, the ark, the tabernacle of the covenant.*—VI. Ps. 60:1; 80:1, the name of some unknown musical instrument.

עוֹד, עֹד I. *again.*— II. *besides.*— III *still.*—IV. *any longer;* with suff עוֹדֶנִּי *I (am) still;* עוֹדְךָ *thou (art,* still; עוֹדֶנּוּ עוֹדֶנָּה he, she (is) still; עוֹדָם they (are) still, &c.; בְּעוֹד, מְעוֹד בְּעֹד as yet, while, within; מְעוֹדִי since I (am).

עוֹדֵד p.n., Oded.—I. the father of Azariah the prophet, 2 Chron. 15:1, 8.—II. another prophet, 2 Chron. 28:9.

תְּעוּדָה f.—I. institution, custom, Ru. 4:7.—II. law, oracle, Isa. 8:16, 20.

עָוָה עָוִים p.n.; see עַוָּא.

עָוַד was crooked, perverse, did wrong, Est. 1:16; Dan. 9:5. Niph. I. נַעֲוָה bent with pain, Isa. 21:3. — II. bowed with sorrow, Ps. 38:7.—III. perverse in mind, Pro. 12:8. Pi. עִוָּה I. made crooked, Lam. 3:9.—II. overturned, Isa. 24:1. Hiph. הֶעֱוָה I. made crooked, Jer. 3:21.—II. perverted, Job 33:27.— III. walked perversely.

עָוָה f., being overturned, Eze. 21:32.
עֲוָיָא f. Ch., iniquities, Dan. 4:24.
עֲוֹנָה for עֲוֹנָה Kal imp. with ה parag., from עָוָה.

עָוֹן עָוֹן m. (const. עֲוֹן; with suff. עֲוֹנָה; pl. עֲוֹנִים, עֲוֹנוֹת).— I. sin, iniquity.—II. guilt.—III. punishment.

עֲיָּת עַיּוּת p.n., a town of Edom.
עִי m. (pl. עִיִּים).—I. ruin, heap of ruins, heap. — II. עִיִּים p.n.—1. a part of Mount Abarim.—2. a town in the tribe of Judah.

עַי עַיָּה, עַיָּא, עַיָּת p.n., a city of the Canaanites in the tribe of Benjamin.

עִיּוֹן p.n., a strong city in the tribe of Naphtali.

עַוְעִים m. pl., giddiness; Vulg. vertigo, Isa. 19:14.

מְעִי m., heap of ruins, Isa. 17:1.

עָוַז took refuge with, Isa. 30:2. Hiph. הֵעִיז I. took refuge, Isa. 10:31.— II. caused to take refuge, collected in a place of safety.

עָוֹז; see עֹז.

עוּט (Arab. dug into any thing).
עֵט m.—I. graver.—II. pen.

עוֹל part. f. pl. עֹלוֹת.—I. being with young.—II. suckling.

עֹל m., infant at the breast.
עֲוִיל m., suckling, Job 21:11; see also עוּל.

עָוַל. Pi. עִוֵּל acts unjustly.
עַוִּיל wicked.
עַוָּל m., one habitually unfair, unjust wicked.

עָוֶל, עֶוֶל m.—I. unfairness.—II. injustice.—III. iniquity.

עוֹלָה f., the same; with ה parag. עוֹלָתָה.

עוֹלָה f., the same; with ה parag. עֹלָתָה; pl. עוֹלוֹת; see also in עֹלָה.

עוֹלֵל, עוֹלֵל, עוֹלוֹת; see עלל.
עוֹלָם; see עלם.

עָוָן (Arab. to live with).
עֹנָה f., conjugal rites, Ex. 21:10.
מָעוֹן m.—I. habitation.—II. refuge.—III. den of wild beasts.—IV. p.n.: (a) of a town in the tribe of Judah; (b) of a strange people, Jud 10:12, &c.; (c) of a man.

מְעוֹנָה, מְעֹנָה f., the same.
מְעוּנִים p.n., the inhabitants of the city of Meon.
מְעוֹנֹתַי p.n. of a man
עָוִים, עָוָן; see עוה.

I. עוּף (fut. יָעוּף). — I. flew.—II. flew

away.—III. *flew upon* (as a bird of prey). Pil. עוֹפֵף I. *flew.* — II. *brandished* (a sword), Eze. 32:10. Hiph. *turned the eyes on*, Pro. 23:5. Hithpo. same as Kal II., Hos. 9:11.

עוֹף m. collect., *birds.* Ch. the same.

II. עוּף (fut. וַיָּעַף) *fainted.*

עֵיפָה f.—I. *darkness*, Am. 4:13. (with ה parag. עֵיפָתָה) *great darkness*, Job 10:22.—II. p. n.: (a) of a son of Midian and the people descended from him; (b) of a man; (c) of a woman.

עַפְעַפִּי, const. עַפְעַפֵּי m. dual. — I. *eyelids.*—II. synec. *eyes.*

מְעוּף m., *darkness*, Isa. 8:22.

מוּעָף m., the same, Isa. 8:23.

עוּץ (imp. pl. עֻצוּ) *consult ye*, Jud. 19:30; Isa. 8:10.

עוּץ p.n., a district of Arabia, Αὐσῖτις.

עוּק. Hiph. הֵעִיק *presses, rushes*, Am. 2:13.

עָקָה f., *pressure, oppression*, Ps. 55:4.

מוּעָקָה f., *pressure, pain*, Ps. 66:11.

עוּר *aroused, awoke, arose* (imp. עוּרָה, עוּרִי *arise!*) Niph. נֵעוֹר I. *was awakened.* — II. *was raised to strike* (shoot), Hab. 3:9. Pil. עוֹרֵר. —I. *roused.*—II. *excited, stirred up.* —III. *raised a spear, scourge, cry.* Hiph. הֵעִיר I. *roused, excited.*—II. *awoke*, Ps. 57:9; 108:3. Hith. הִתְעוֹרֵר *awoke.*

עִיר m. Ch., *watcher*, probably an angel, Dan. 4:10, 14, 20.

עוֹר m. (pl. עוֹרֹת) *the skin of man* or *animals;* עוֹר שִׁנָּיִם *skin of his teeth*, Job 19:20, i.e. *gum.*

מְעָרָה f., *cave;* (Arab. *went under ground*).

מְעוֹרִים m. pl., *nakedness*, Hab. 2:15

עוּר. Pi. עִוֵּר *blinded.*

עוּר m. Ch., *chaff*, Dan. 2:35.

עִוֵּר m., עִוְּרָה f.—I. *blind.*—II. *mentally blind.*

עִוָּרוֹן m., *blindness.*

עַוֶּרֶת f., the same, Lev. 22:22.

עוּשׁ *assemble yourselves*, Joel 4:11.

עוּת *aid, help*, Isa. 50:4.

עוּת. Pi. עִוֵּת I. *made crooked.* — II. *perverted.*— III. *treated unfairly, unjustly.* Pu. part. מְעֻוָּת *bowed down.* Hith. *bowed himself*, Ecc. 12:3.

עַוָּתָה f., *oppression*, Lam. 3:59.

עַוְתַי p.n. of a man.

עֵז f. (pl. עִזִּים).—I. *goat.*—II. *she goat* —III. pl. *goats' hair.*

עֵז f. Ch., the same, Ezr. 6:17.

עַז, עֹז, עָזָּא; see עזז.

עֲזָאזֵל m. (lit. *goat of departure;* see אָזַל) *the scape-goat*, Lev. 16:8, 10, 26; LXX. ἀποπομπαῖος.

עָזַב (fut. יַעֲזֹב). — I. *left behind.*—II. *allowed to remain.*—III. *went away from.*—IV. *forsook, neglected.*— V. *failed, allowed to fail.*— VI. *took away.*—VII. *gave loose to.*— VIII. with אֶל, לְ *entrusted to, left with;* also with עַל. Niph. נֶעֱזַב *was forsaken, entrusted, &c.*, with לְ. Pu. עֻזַּב *was forsaken.*

עֲזוּבָה f.—I *ruins*, Is. 17:9.—II. p.n. of a woman.

עִזְבוֹנִים I. *merchandise.*—II. *a market*, Eze. c. 27.

עֲזְבּוּק p. n. of a man.

עָזְגָּד p. n. of a man.

עָזַז (fut. יָעֹז, וַיָּעָז; inf. עֲזוֹז).—I. was strong.—II. prevailed.—III. considered himself strong, Ps. 52:9.—IV. showed himself strong, Ps. 68:29. Hiph. הֵעַז made bold; ה' פָּנָיו or בְּפָנָיו put on a bold face, Pro. 7:13; 21:29.

עַז with pause עָז m. (pl. עַזִּים, f. עַזָּה, pl. עַזּוֹת).—I. strong.—II. harsh.—III. strength.—IV. עַז־פָּנִים bold.

עַזָּה p. n., Gaza, a city of the Philistines; עַזָּתִי a Gazathite.

עֹז עוֹז m. (with suff. עֻזִּי, עָזִּי, עֻזֵּנוּ).—I. strength, power, might. —II. ascription of power, praise, Ps. 8:3.—III. source of strength, refuge.—IV. עַז פָּנִים impudence.

עַזָּא עֻזָּה p. n. of a man.

עֻזִּי m.—I. might of God.—II. might in war, Isa. 42:25.

עִזּוּז m.—I. mighty, Ps. 24:8.—II. mighty men, Isa. 43:17.

עֻזִּי p. n. of a man.

עֻזִּיָּהוּ p. n. of a man.

עֻזִּי p. n. of a man.

עֻזִּיאֵל p. n. of a man.

יַעֲזִיאֵל same as.

עֻזִּיָּה עֻזִּיָּהוּ (the strength of the Lord), p. n., Uzziah, king of Judah; LXX. Ὀζίας; elsewhere עֲזַרְיָה; applied also to other men.

עַזִּיזָא p. n. of a man.

עַזְמָוֶת p. n. of a man; בֵּית ע' a place in Judah or Benjamin.

מָעוֹז מָעֹז m. (with suff. מָעוּזִּי, מָעֻזִּי; pl. מָעֻזִּים) place of strength, munition; often applied to persons.

עָזְנִיָּה f., the sea-eagle, Lev. 11:13 Deu. 14:12.

עָזַק. Pi. עִזֵּק digged, Isa. 5:2.

עִזְקָא f. Ch., engraved ring, seal, Dan. 6:18.

עֲזֵקָה p. n., Azekah, a city in the tribe of Judah.

עָזַר (fut. יַעְזֹר; pl. יַעְזְרוּ; imp. with suff. עָזְרֵנִי; pl. עָזְרֻנִי) helped, assisted, with אַחֲרֵי, עִם, לְ; part. עֹזֵר helper, patron, companion Niph. נֶעֱזַר was holpen. Hiph. helped, 2 Ch. 28:23.

עֵזֶר m. (with suff. עֶזְרוֹ).—I. help.—II. helper.—III. p. n. of a man.

עֵזֶר p. n. of a man.

עֶזְרָה עֶזְרָת f. (with ה parag. עֶזְרָתָה). —I. help.—II. p. n. of a man; same as עֵזֶר.

עֶזְרָא p. n., Ezra; LXX. Ἔσδρας.

עַזּוּר עָזָר p. n. of a man.

עַזְרִיאֵל p. n. of a man.

עֲזָרָה f.—I. court of the temple.—II. border, moulding.

עֶזְרִי p. n. of a man.

עֶזְרִיאֵל p. n. of a man.

עֲזַרְיָה עֲזַרְיָהוּ p. n., Azariah.—I. king of Judah; called also עֻזִּיָּה—II used also for other men.

עַזְרִיקָם p. n. of a man.

עָט, see עוּט; עָטָא, see יָעַט.

עָטָה I. put on, wore.—II. covered, with עַל.—III. invested.—IV. took possession of, invested with, Jer. 43:12. with אֶת. Hiph. הֶעְטָה placed as a covering, Ps. 89:46, with עַל.

מַעֲטֶה m., garment (of praise), Isa. 61:3.

עֲטַלֵּף m., *bat*.Lev. 11 : 19 ; Isa.2 : 20.

עָטַן (Arab. *prepared skin*).

עָטִין m., pl. עֲטִינִים *water or milk skin*, Job 21 : 24.

עָטַף (fut. יַעֲטֹף).—I. *covered*, with לְ. —II. *covered himself.*—III. *covered his face, was exhausted*; part. עָטוּף *worn out, weak.* Niph. *was exhausted*, Lam. 2 : 11. Hiph. הֶעֱטִיף the same, Gen. 30 : 42. Hith. הִתְעַטֵּף the same.

מַעֲטָפָה f., *mantle*, Isa. 3 : 22.

עָטַר I. *surrounded.*— II. *covered*, Ps. 5 : 13. Pi. עִטֵּר I. *crowned*, Cant. 3 : 11.— II. *adorned, blessed*, with לְ. Hiph. part. f. מַעֲטִירָה *giving crowns*, Isa. 23 : 8.

עֲטָרָה (const. עֲטֶרֶת; pl. עֲטָרוֹת) f. —I. *crown, royal diadem.*—II. p.n. of a woman.

עֲטָרוֹת p.n., a city in the tribe of Gad; עֲטָרוֹת אַדָּר and עֲטָרוֹת a city in the tribe of Ephraim; ע׳ בֵּית יוֹאָב a place in Judah; ע׳ שׁוֹפָן a place in Gad.

עָטַשׁ (Arab. *sneezed*).

עֲטִישָׁה f., *sneezing*, Job 41 : 10.

עֲי, עֵי, עַיָּה, עַיִּים, עַיָּא, עַיּוֹן, עִיּוּת; see עוה.

עֵיבָל p.n.—I. same as עוֹבָל.—II. a rock in the northern range of Mount Ephraim; LXX. Γαιβάλ.

עִיט I. *was angry with*, with בְּ.—II. *rushed on with anger, pounced on*, with אֶל; fut. וַיַּעַט.

עַיִט, const. עֵיט m., *rapacious bird or beast.*

עֵיטָם p.n., a town and hill in the tribe of Judah.

עֵילוֹם same as עוֹלָם; see עלם.

עִילַי p.n., one of David's generals.

עֵילָם p.n., a people and district, situation uncertain; עֵלְמָיֵא pl. Ch., *the Elamites.*

עַיִם m., *drought*, Isa. 11 : 15.

עַיִן f. (const. עֵין; with suff. עֵינוֹ; dual עֵינַיִם, עֵינֵי).— I. *an eye.*— II. *the sight.* — III. *the judgment.* — IV. *appearance in the eye.*— V. עֵינַיִם *outward appearance*, 1 Sa. 16 : 7 ; לְעֵינֵי פ׳ *in the sight of*; בְּעֵינֵי *in the judgment of*; מֵעֵינֵי *without the knowledge of*; בֵּין עֵינַיִם *between the eyes, on the forehead*, עַיִן בְּעַיִן *eye to eye.*—VI. *fountain, spring*; with ה parag. עַיְנָה *to the fountain*; pl. עֲיָנוֹת, const. עֵינוֹת: hence many p.n.:—I. עַיִן a town of the Levites in the tribe of Simeon. —II. a town in the north of Canaan.— III.עֵינַיִם a town of Judah.— IV. עֵין גֶּדִי a town of Judah.—V. עֵין גַּנִּים a town of Judah.— VI. a town of Issachar. — VII. עֵין דֹּאר a town of the Manassites.—VIII. עֵין חַדָּה a town of Issachar.—IX. עֵין חָצוֹר a town of Naphtali.—X. עֵין חֲרֹד a *well* near the town of *Charod.* —XI. עֵין מִשְׁפָּט a well in Kadesh. —XII. עֵין עֶגְלַיִם a town of Moab. —XIII. עֵין רֹגֵל a well on the confines of Judah and Benjamin.— XIV. עֵין רִמּוֹן a town in the tribe of Judah.—XV. עֵין שֶׁמֶשׁ a town on the confines of Judah and

Benjamin.—XVI. עֵין תַּנִּים a well near Jerusalem.—XVII. עֵין תַּפּוּחַ a town of Manasseh.

עַיִן com. Ch., *eye.*

עָיִן m., *watching with an evil eye,* 1 Sa. 18:9.

עֵינָן p. n. of a man.

מַעְיָן m. (with ו parag. מַעְיָנוֹ ; with suff. מַעְיָנוֹ ; pl. מַעְיָנִים, מַעְיְנֵי, מַעְיְנוֹת, מַעְיָנוֹת (מַעְיָנוֹת *fountain, well of water.*

עָיֵף *is weary,* Jer. 4:31 ; וַיַּעַף, see עוּף.

עָיֵף m., עֲיֵפָה f. — I. *weary.* — II. *parched.*

עֵיפִי p. n. of a man.

עֵיפָה *darkness;* see עוּף.

עַיִר m. (with suff. עֵירֹה; pl. עֲיָרִים). —I. *ass.*—II. *young ass.*

עִיר m.—I. *heat, anger, fear,* Ps. 73: 20; Jer. 15:8; Hos. 7:4; 11:9; Ges.)—II. *a city, town, settlement;* עִירָה *towards the city;* pl. עֲרִים see next word.

עָר m. — I. *an enemy.* — II. *city;* pl. עָרִים, עָר־מוֹאָב *Ar of Moab,* otherwise *Rabbah,* the chief city of Moab.

עָר m. Ch., *an enemy.*

עִיר Ch.; see עוּר.

עִירָא p. n. of a man.

עִירוּ p. n. of a man.

עִירָם p. n., a prince of Edom.

עִירָד p. n. of a man.

עֵירִים, עֵירֻמִּים; see ערם.

עַיִשׁ; see עָשׁ.

עַיִת same as עַי; see עוה.

עַכָּבִישׁ m., *a spider.*

עַכְבָּר *the jerboa;* "dipus jaculus" (Linn.)

עַכְבּוֹר p. n. of a man.

עַכּוֹ p. n., a city in the tribe of Asher, Ἀκη, "Ptolemais."

עָכָן (עָכָר) p. n. of a man.

עֶכֶס m.—I. *fetter,* Pro. 7:22.—II. pl עֲכָסִים *anklets, rings for the feet,* Isa. 3:18.

עָכַס Pi. *wear anklets,* Isa. 3:16.

עַכְסָה p. n., the daughter of Caleb.

עָכַר (fut. with suff. יַעְכָּרְךָ) *caused sorrow, vexation, disgrace.* Niph. נֶעְכַּר *was irritated, excited.*

עָכוֹר p. n., a valley near Jericho.

עֶכְרָן p. n. of a man.

עַכְשׁוּב m., *an asp,* Ps. 140:4.

עַל, עַלָּא, עַל, see עלה.

עַל, עָלָה, עַלָּא; see עלל.

עִלֵּג m., *foreigner, stammerer,* Isa. 32:4.

עָלָה (fut. יַעֲלֶה, apoc. יַעַל) const. with עַל, אֶל, לְ, בְּ. — I. *went up, came up.*—II. *arose* (of the dawn).— III. *grew up, grew.*—IV. *increased.* — V. *produced,* Pro. 24:31.— VI. *was put upon.* Niph. נַעֲלָה I. *is exalted* (God).— II. *was lifted up,* Eze. 9:3.—III. *was led away,* 2 Sa. 2:27.—IV. *was taken up,* Eze. 36: 3. Hiph. הֶעֱלָה (pret. הַעֲלִית, הֶעֱלִיתָ; imp. apoc. הַעַל; fut. apoc. יַעַל).—I. *caused to go up.* — II. *offered a burnt-offering.*— III. *placed a thing on another.* — IV. *placed, set up,* Nu. 8:2. Hoph. הָעֳלָה I. *was offered,* Jud. 6:28.— II. *was brought up*

Nah. 2:8.— III. *was placed upon, inscribed*, 2 Chron. 20:34. Hith. fut apoc. יִתְעַל *lifts up himself*, Jer. 51:3.

עַל m., *the Lofty One, the Most High*; adv. *on high*, 2 Sa. 23:1; מֵעַל I. *from above*, Gen. 27:39; 49:25.—II. *above*, Ps. 50:4, &c.

עֲלֵי עַל; (with suff. עָלֶיךָ, עָלַי, עָלֶיהָ, עֲלֵיכֶם, עֲלֵיהֶם, עָלֵימוֹ) עָלָיו prep. (ὑπὲρ, ἐπί).—I. *upon, on.*—II. *above, over.*— III. *beside, near, before.*— IV. *besides, over and above.* — V. *in reference to, towards, against.*— VI. *for, on account of, in behalf of*; עַל לָתֵת *it is mine to give* (the kingdom); חָיָה עַל, ζῆν ἐπί, *live by* (bread), Deu. 8:3.

מֵעַל (with suff. עָלָיו מֵעָלֶיךָ, מֵעֲלֵיכֶם, &c.).—I. *from upon.*—II. *from above.*—III. *above.*

עַל Ch. same as Heb., *upon, above, besides, for.*

עֵלָּא Ch., with מִן *above*, Dan. 6:3.

עָלֶה, const. עֲלֵה m. (with suff. עָלֵהוּ; pl. const. עֲלֵי).— I. *leaf.*—II. *foliage.*

עוֹלָה, עֹלָה f.—I. *a step.*—II. *a burnt-offering.*

עֲלָתָא, עֲלָה f. Ch., *burnt-offering.*

עֶלְיוֹן, f. עִלִּית *upper*, Jos. 15:19; Jud. 1:15; pl. עֲלִיּוֹת.

עִלָּי m. Ch.— I. *high, supreme* (of God).—II. *the Most High.*

עִלִּית f. Ch., *upper room, chamber*, Dan. 6:11.

עֵלִי p.n., *Eli*, 'Ηλί, *the priest.*

עֱלִי m., *pestle*, Pro. 27:22.

עֲלִיָּה f.—I. *upper room, chamber.*— II. *ascent, staircase*, 2 Chron. 9:4.

עֶלְיוֹן עֶלְיוֹנָה m., f.— I. *lofty.*— II. *higher, upper* (in place).—III. *high* (in rank).— IV. *the Supreme, the Most High* (of God).

עֶלְיוֹן m. Ch., *the Most High.*

מַעֲלֶה m.—I. *ascent.*—II. *mount.*

מַעַל m., with ה מַעֲלָה.— I. *over against, near*, Isa. 6:2, &c.— II. *above*; לְמַעְלָה *upwards, onwards, over, above*; מִלְמַעְלָה *from above, upward*; מִמַּעַל *from above*, with לְ *over, above.*

מֹעַל m., *elevating, lifting up of*, Neh. 8:6.

מַעֲלָה f.—I. *ascent.*—II. *step of stairs.* —III. *graduated face of a sun-dial.*—IV. *mental suggestions*, Ezr. 7:9.—V. an unknown title of some of the Psalms.

תְּעָלָה f.— I. *channel for water.*— II. *recovery from illness*, Jer. 30:13; 46:11.

עַלְוָה f.—I. same as עוֹלָה.—II. p.n., *a tribe of the Edomites.*

עֲלוּמִים *youth*, see עֶלֶם.

עַלְוָן, עַלְיָן p.n. of an Edomite.

עֲלוּקָה f., *a leech*, Pro. 30:15.

עָלַז (fut. יַעֲלֹז; pl. יַעֲלֹזוּ) *rejoiced, exulted*, with עַל or בְּ (of the subject of joy).

עַלֵּז m., *rejoicing*, Isa. 5:14.

עָלִיז m., *rejoicing, expressing joy.*

עָלַט (Arab. *was covered with clouds*).

עֲלָטָה f., *darkness.*

עֶלְיוֹן, עַלְוָה, עֲלִיָּה, עֲלִית, עֶלְיוֹן; see עלה.

עֲלִיצוּת; see עלץ.

עָלַל (Syr. *entered*). Po. עוֹלֵל I. *made to enter*, Job 16:15.— II. *treated*,

acted towards, with לְ. — III. affected. — IV. gleaned. — V. part.
מְעוֹלֵל babyish boy, Isa. 3:12.
Poa. was done, caused, Lam.1:12.
Hith. I. exerted himself against.
—II. insulted. Hithpo. practised,
Ps. 141:4

עֲלַל Ch., entered. Aph. הַנְעֵל brought
in. Hoph. הֻעַל was brought in.

עֹל, עוֹל m. (with suff. עֻלּוֹ).— I. yoke,
—II. servitude.

עִלָּא p. n. of a man.

עִלָּה f. Ch., pretext, ground for complaint, Dan. 6:5, 6.

עָלִיל m., crucible, Ps. 12:7.

עוֹלֵל, עוֹלָל m. (pl. עוֹלִים, עוֹלְלִים)
infant, young child, child.

עוֹלֵלוֹת, עֹלֵלוֹת f. pl., gleanings.

עֲלִילָה f.— I. action.— II. an action
(good- or bad).

עֲלִילִיָּה f., action, Jer. 32:19.

מֵעָל m. Ch., setting (of the sun), Dan.
6:15.

מַעֲלָל m., pl. מַעֲלָלִים habitual doings
(good or bad).

תַּעֲלוּל m., pl. תַּעֲלוּלִים.— I. children,
Isa. 3:4.—II. vexations, calamities,
Isa. 66:4.

עָלַם, part. עֹלְמִים hidden things, sins,
Ps. 90:8. Niph. נֶעְלַם was hidden; part. נַעֲלָמִים hidden (crafty)
men. Hiph. הֶעְלִים hide, conceal;
ה' עֵינָיִם מִן turned his eyes away
from, Pro. 28:27. Hith. הִתְעַלֵּם
was hidden, with מִן.

עֹלָם, עוֹלָם m.— I. antiquity.— II.
eternity.—III. duration of the earth.
— IV. whole life.— V. unlimited,
future time; מֵעוֹלָם from of old;

יְמוֹת עוֹלָם the ancient days,
עוֹלָם, עַד־עוֹלָם, לְעוֹלָם, עוֹלָמִים for
ever; future duration, unlimited,
but not endless.

עֵילוֹם m., eternity, 2 Chron. 33:7.

עָלַם m. Ch., eternity.

עֶלֶם m., a young man.

עַלְמָה f., damsel, virgin, ἡ παρθένος.

עֲלוּמִים m. pl., youth.

עַלֶמֶת p. n. of a town in the tribe of
Benjamin; עֲ' דְּבִלָתָיְמָה p.n., a
station of Israel.

עֲלָמוֹת f. pl., an unknown title of
Psalm 46.

עַלְמוּת f., the same, Ps. 9:1; 48:15.

עָלֶמֶת p. n. of a man.

עַלְמוֹן p.n., same as עֲלֶמֶת.

תַּעֲלֻמָה f., any thing hidden, secret;
pl. תַּעֲלֻמוֹת.

עֵלְמָיֵא Elamites; see עֵילָם.

עָלַם exult, rejoice, Job 20:18. Niph.
is exulting, Job 39:13. Hith. be
exulting, Pro. 7:18.

עָלַע gulped, swallowed down, Job 39:
30.

עֲלַע com. Ch., rib, Dan. 7:5.

עָלַף Pu. I. fainted, Isa. 51:20.—
II. covered, overlaid, Cant. 5:14.
Hith. was clothed, Gen. 38:14,
fainted.

עֻלְפֶּה m., languor, fainting, Eze. 31:
15.

עָלַץ (fut. יַעֲלִץ) exult, rejoice; with בְּ
in, לְ against, לִפְנֵי before.

עֲלִיצוּת f., rejoicing, Hab. 3:14.

עֶם, עַם, עִם; see עמם.

עָמַד (fut. יַעֲמֹד).—I. stood fast, still.
— II. stood over, overlooked, with

לִפְנֵי — III. *stood over, presided,*
with עַל.—IV. *stood before,* with
עַל, אֵת.—V *ceased,* with מִן.—VI.
*stood before,* with מִן, לִפְנֵי, בִּפְנֵי,
נֶגֶד—VII. *persevere, remain in any
occupation,* with בְּ.—VIII. *stood
against, opposed,* with עַל. Hiph.
הֶעֱמִיד I. *cause to stand.*—II. *set
up, raise.*—III. *establish.*—IV. *appoint.* — V. *confirm, accomplish.*
(הֶעֱמַדְתָּ, Eze. 29:7, a wrong reading for הִמְעַדְתָּ *thou madest to
tremble.*) Hoph. הָעֳמַד *made to
stand.*

עֹמֶד m., *standing-place, station.*

עַמּוּד m., *pillar.*

עֶמְדָּה f., *station, standing.* Mic. 1:11.

מַעֲמָד m.— I. *standing, order.*— II.
*station.*

עֹמֶר, עָמוּ, see עֲמָה; עַמּוֹן see עמם.
עֲמֹם, see עמם; עֲמֹק, see עמק.
עֲמִיר; see עמר.

עֲמִית *society, company.*

עָמַל *wrought, laboured.*

עָמֵל m.—I. *working, labouring;* pl.
עֲמֵלִים *labourers.* — II. *weary,
wretched.*

עָמָל m.—I. *labour.*—II. *sorrow, vexation.*— III. *sorrow brought on by
sin.*— IV. *weariness.*—V. *fruit of
labour.*—VI. p. n. of a man.

עֲמָלֵק p.n., *Amalek,* a people inhabiting the south of Palestine and
the borders of the desert of Sinai;
עֲמָלֵקִי *Amalekite;* הַר הָעֲמָלֵקִי *hill
of the Amalekites* in the tribe of
Ephraim.

עָמַם *concealed,* Eze 28:3; 31:8.

Hoph. הוּגַם *was obscured,* Lam.
4:1.

עַם, עָם com. (with suff. עַמִּי), *people,
nation;* בְּנֵי עַמִּי *the children of
my people;* pl. עַמִּים, עֲמָמִים.

עַם m. Ch., *people;* pl. עַמְמִין.

עִם prep. (with suff. עִמְּדִי, עִמִּי;
עִמְּךָ; עִמָּכֶם; עִמּוֹ, עִמָּנוּ; עִמָּם,
מֵעִם (עִמָּהֶם) *with, along with;*
*from with,* (like the French *de
par*).

עִם Ch., the same.

עֻמָּה f.—I. …כָּל־עֻמַּת שֶׁ *in the same
way as;* לְעֻמַּת *near, towards, like,
opposite to;* pl. לְעֻמּוֹת *like;*
מִלְּעֻמַּת *near.*—II. p.n., a town of
Asher.

עַמּוֹן p.n., *Ammon,* the son of Lot's
daughter, and his descendants,
בְּנֵי עַמּוֹן; pl. עַמֹּנִים; f.
עַמֹּנִית; pl. עַמֹּנִיּוֹת *Ammonites.*

עַמִּיאֵל p. n. of a man.
עַמִּיהוּד p. n. of a man.
עַמִּינָדָב p. n. of a man.
עַמִּיחוּר p. n. of a man.
עַמִּינָדָב p. n. of a man.
עַמִּישַׁדַּי p. n. of a man.
עַמְעָד p. n., a town in the tribe of
Asher.
עַמְרָמִי p. n. of a man; patron. עַמְרָמִי
עִמָּנוּאֵל (*God with us*), *Immanuel*
one of our Lord's prophetic titles,
Ἐμμανουήλ, Isa. 7:14.

עָמַס, עָמַשׂ (fut. יַעֲמֹס) *load, lay a
burden upon.* Hiph. הֶעֱמִיס *caused
to be laden,* 1 Ki. 12:11; 2 Chron.
10:11.

עָמוֹס p.n., *Amos,* the prophet.
עֲמַסְיָה p.n. of a man.
מַעֲמָסָה f., *burden,* Zec. 12:3.

עָמֹק *was very deep*, Ps. 92:6. Hiph. הֶעֱמִיק *make deep*, Isa. 30:33.

עָמֹק m., עֲמֻקָּה f.—I. *deep.*—II. *subtle, unsearchable.*

עֹמֶק or עָמֶק m., *the same*; pl. const. עָמְקֵי

עָמוֹק p. n. of a man.

עֵמֶק m. (with suff. עֶמְקְךָ; pl. עֲמָקִים).—I. *deep place.*—II. *unintelligible.*

עֹמֶק m., *depth*, Pro. 25:3.

עַמִּיק m. Ch., *deep, profound thing*, Dan. 2:22.

מַעֲמַקִּים m. pl., *depths.*

עָמַר. Pi. עִמֵּר *binding-sheaves*, Ps. 129:7. Hith. הִתְעַמֵּר *treat as a slave*, with בְּ.

עָמִיר m., *sheaf of corn.*

עֹמֶר m.—I. *sheaf*; pl. עֳמָרִים.—II. *omer*, a dry measure, the tenth part of an ephah.

עֲמֹרָה p. n., *Gomorrah*, one of the cities of the plain; LXX. Γομόρρα.

עָמְרִי p. n.—I. *Omri*, king of Israel.—II. of other men.

עֲמַר m. Ch., *wool*, Dan. 7:9.

עַמְרָם p. n.; see עמם.

עָמַשׂ *same as* עָמַס *carried.*

עֲמָשָׂא p. n. of a man.

עֲמָשַׂי p. n. of a man.

עֲמַשְׂסַי p. n. of a man.

עֵנָב (Arab. *grapes*).

עֵנָב p. n., a town in the tribe of Judah.

עֵנָב m. (pl. עֲנָבִים, עִנְּבֵי), *grapes.*

עָנוּב p. n. of a man.

עִנְּבֵי pl. const. with dag. euphon., from עֵנָב.

עֻנַּג Pu. *delicately brought up*, Jer.

---

6.2. Hith. *delighted himself in*, with עַל, מִן.

עָנֹג m., עֲנֻגָּה f., *delicate, tender.*

עֹנֶג m., *delight, pleasure.*

תַּעֲנוּג m., *delight, pleasure, enjoyment, luxury.*

עָנַד *bound*, Job 31:36; Pro. 6:21.

I. עָנָה (fut. יַעֲנֶה, וַיַּעַן).—I. *spoke* —II. *celebrated.*—III. *shout.*—.V. *bellow, bleat.*—V. *answer.* Niph. נַעֲנָה *was answering, answered.* Pi. עִנָּה *answered, sang in response.* Hiph. *answer favorably*, Ecc. 5:19.

עֲנָה Ch.—I. *answered, spoke, began to speak.*—II. *was afflicted*; see below.

II. עָנָה I. *was humbled.*—II. *was afflicted.* Niph. *was humbled, afflicted*, with מִפְּנֵי. Pi. I. *humbled, subdued.*—II. *afflicted*; with אִשָּׁה *had connexion with a woman* with נֶפֶשׁ *fasted.* Pu. *was afflicted, humbled*; inf. עֻנֹּתוֹ *his suffering affliction*, Ps. 132:1. Hiph. *oppressed.* Hith. הִתְעַנָּה I. *was afflicted*, 1 Ki. 2:26.—II. *was humbled*, with לִפְנֵי.

עֲנָה p. n.—I. the son of Seir, and his descendants.—II. the son of Zibeon.

עָנָו m. (pl. עֲנָוִים, עֲנָיו), *humble, meek, poor, afflicted.*

עֲנָוָה f., *meekness, humility.*

עֲנָוָה f., *the same.*

עֱנוּת f., *affliction of the humble* (Lee., Ps. 22:25.

עָנִי adj.m. (pl. עֲנִיִּים; f. עֲנִיָּה), *afflicted, miserable, poor.*

עֳנִי, with pause עֹנִי m., *misery.*

עֻנִּי p. n. of a man.

עֲנָיָה p. n. of a man

עִנְיָן m., *thing, matter.*

עֲנָת p. n. of a man; see בֵּית

עֲנָתוֹת p.n.—I. a city of the Levites in Benjamin; עֲנָתֹתִי *inhabitant of Anathoth.*—II. of a man.

עֲנָתֹתִיָה p. n. of a man.

יַעַן pa., *because;* יַעַן כִּי, יַעַן אֲשֶׁר *because, because of;* יַעַן וּבְיַעַן the same.

יַעֲנָי p. n. of a man.

מַעֲנֶה m.—I. *answer.*— II. *answer to prayer,* Pro. 16:1.

לְמַעַן, מַעַן *intent, purpose.* — I. *because.*—II. *thence, so, accordingly;* לְמַעַן אֲשֶׁר *in order that, because that.*

מַעֲנָה f., *furrow,* Ps. 129:3.

מַעֲנִית Kri, the same.

תַּעֲנִית f., *self-humiliation,* Ezr. 9:5.

עֵנָיִם p.n., a town of Judah.

עֵנָם p.n., a town of Issachar; elsewhere עֵין-גַּנִּים.

עֲנָמִים p.n., a foreign people unknown.

עֲנַמֶּלֶךְ p.n., an idol of the Sepharvites.

עָנַן (part. עֹנֵן; f. עֹנְנָה) and Po. עוֹנֵן (fut. יְעוֹנֵן; part. מְעוֹנֵן) *divined, used auguries,* Isa. 2:6, &c. Pi. (inf. with suff. עֲנָנִי *my bringing on a cloud,* Gen. 9:14; see עָנָן.

עָנָן, const. עֲנַן m.—I. *a cloud.*— II. p. n. of a man.

עֲנָנָה f., *cloud,* Job 3:5.

עֲנַן m. Ch., *cloud,* Dan. 7:13.

עֲנָנִי p.n. of a man.

עֲנָנְיָה ('Ανανίας) p.n.—I. of a man. —II. of a place in Benjamin.

עָנָף, const. עֲנַף m. (pl. with suff. עֲנָפֵיהֶם, עֲנָפֶיהָ) *a branch.*

עֲנַף m. Ch., *a branch.*

עֲנֵף, f. עֲנֵפָה *branching out,* Eze. 19:10.

עָנָק m. (pl. עֲנָקִים, עֲנָקוֹת).—I. *a chain* (collar for the neck).—II. p.n., הָעֲנָק, יְלִידֵי עֲנָק (הָעֲנָק), עֲנָקִים בְּנֵי עֲנָקִים *the Anakims,* the first inhabitants of Canaan, who were giants.

עָנַק *put on a collar,* i.e. *exalted, lifted up,* Ps. 73:6. Hiph. הֶעֱנִיק *place on the neck* like a collar, Deu 15:14.

עָנֵר p.n.—I. a man of Canaan, Gen. 14:13, 24.—II. p.n., 1 Chron. 6:55, probably a wrong reading for תַּעֲנָךְ.

עָנַשׁ (fut. יַעֲנֹשׁ).—I. *taxed.*—II. *fined in money,* with לְ. Niph. *was fined, mulcted.*

עֹנֶשׁ m., *mulct, fine, tax*

עֲנָשׁ m. Ch., *tax.*

עֲנָתֹתִיָה עֲנָתוֹת עֲנָת; see עָנָה.

כְּעֵנֶת עֲנֵת; see עֵת.

עָסַס *tread* (as grapes), Mal. 3:21.

עָסִיס m. — I. *new wine-juice.* — II. *juice of the pomegranate,* Cant.8:2.

יַעְרְעוּ for יְעַרְעֲרוּ *raised a cry,* Isa. 15:5; see עוּר Pil.

עֶפְתָּה, עֻפָה; see עִיפָה in עוּף.

עָפָה root not used; (Syr. *flourished.*)

עֳפִי m., pl. עֳפָאִים *leaves,* Ps. 104:12.

עֳפִי m. Ch., *leaves.*

עָפַל. Pu. *swollen, inflated,* Hab. 2:4. Hiph. *raised themselves,* Nu 14:44.

עֹפֶל m. — I. *swelling tumour.* — II *mount, hill.*

הָעֹפֶל p.n. of a peak of Mount Zion, to the east.

עֳפָלִים, pl. const. עָפְלֵי hæmorrhoids, emerods; see also מְחוֹרִים.

עָפְנִי p.n., a city of Benjamin, Jos. 18:24.

עַפְעַפִּי, עַפְעַפַּיִם; see עוּף.

עָפַר Pi. עִפֵּר dashed with dust, 2 Sa. 16:13. with בֶּעָפָר.

עֹפֶרֶת f., lead.

עָפָר, const. עֲפַר m.—I. earth, mould, clay.—II. dust.—III. the earth.— IV. depth of the earth; pl. const. עֲפָרוֹת dusts, i.e. small dust, molecules.

עֹפֶר m., kid, young goat.

עֵפֶר p. n. of a man.

עָפְרָה p. n.—I. a city of Benjamin. —II. a city of Manasseh.—III. of a man.

עֶפְרוֹן (עֶפְרָיִן) p.n.—I. a town on the borders of Ephraim.—II. a mountain between Judah and Benjamin. —III. the name of a Hittite, Gen. 23:8, &c.

עֵץ, עֵצִי, עֵצִים; see עצה.

עָצַב pained, grieved, thwarted. Niph. was pained, grieved, with בְּ, עַל, אֶל. Pi. I. bound together, Job 10: 8.—II. pained, thwarted. Hiph. I. grieved, thwarted, Ps.78:40.—II. worship, Jer. 44:19; (see Lee). Hith. was grieved.

עֲצַב Ch., grieved.

עָצָב m., pl. עֲצַבִּים idols.

עֶצֶב, עֹצֶב m.—I. tendon, sinew, Jer. 22:28.—II. labour.—III. pain.

עֹצֶב m.—I. idol.—II. pain, grief.

עֹצֶב m. (pl. with suff. עֲצְבֵיכֶם) your labours, Isa. 58:3.

עַצֶּבֶת, עֲצָבָה f. (const. עַצֶּבֶת; pl. with suff. עַצְּבוֹתָם).—I. pain, grief. —II. "sorrows," Eng. Ver.; perhaps idols, Ps. 16:4.

עִצָּבוֹן m., painful, great, labour, Gen 3:16, 17.

מַעֲצֵבָה f., labour, affliction, Isa. 50: 11.

עָצַד (Arab. axe).

מַעֲצָד m., axe.

עָצָה close the eyes, Pro. 16:30.

עֵץ m. (pl. עֵצִים).—I. a tree עֵץ פְּרִי fruit-tree.—II. wood.—III gallows.

עֵצָה f., wood, Jer. 6:6; see also in יַעַר.

עָצֶה m., spine of the back, Lev. 3:9.

עֶצְיוֹן גֶּבֶר p.n., a sea-port, probably on the eastern coast of the Red Sea.

עָצֵל Niph. be sluggish, Jud. 18:9.

עָצֵל m., sluggard; book of Proverbs only.

עַצְלָה sloth, Pro. 19:15, עַצְלוּת f., Pro. 31:27; dual עַצְלְתַּיִם great sloth, Ecc. 10:18.

עָצַם, עָצֵם I. was numerous.—II. was strong.—III. was great. Pi. עִצֵּם I. bind the eyes, Isa. 29:10.—II. break the bones, Jer. 50:17, from עֶצֶם. Hiph. strengthens, Ps 105:24.

עָצוּם m.—I. numerous.— II. strong. —III. great; pl. עֲצוּמִים great ones, Ps. 10:10.

עֶצֶם f. (pl. עֲצָמִים, עֲצָמוֹת).—I. bone —II. body.—III. self-same (never of persons); בְּעֶצֶם הַיּוֹם הַזֶּה or this very day —IV. p.n., a city of Judah.

עֹצֶם m., עָצְמָה f.—I. *strength.*—II. *power.*—III. *multitude,* Nah. 3:9.

עַצְמוֹן p. n., a town in the southern borders of Canaan.

עֲצֻמוֹת f. pl., *defence in argument,* Isa. 41:21.

תַּעֲצֻמוֹת f. pl., *strength,* Ps. 68:36.

עֵצֶן m., p. n. of a place, 2 Sa. 23:8.

עָצַר (fut. יַעֲצֹר).—I. *shut up, restrain, detain,* with לְ.—II. with כֹּחַ *retain power, reign.* Niph. נֶעְצַר *was shut up, detained.*— II. *was assembled.*

עֶצֶר m., *rule, supreme power,* Jud. 18:7.

עֹצֶר m.—I. *shutting up the womb from child-bearing,* Pro. 30:16.—II. *in prison,* Isa. 53:8

עֲצֶרֶת, עֲצָרָה f.—I. *day of assembly.* —II. *restraint.*

מַעְצָר m., *restraint, hindrance,* Pro. 25:28.

מַעְצוֹר m., the same, 1 Sa. 14:6.

עָקַב (fut. יַעֲקֹב).—I. *take by the heel,* Hos. 12:4; see עָקֵב.—II. *circumvent, defraud;* part. עֲקֻבָּה *traced, marked,* Hos. 6:8. Pi. *trace,* Job 37:4.

עָקֵב m.— I. *heel.*— II. *impression of the heel, track;* pl. עֲקֵבִים *heels;* עִקְּבוֹת *footsteps.*—III. *rear of an army,* Gen. 49:19, &c.— IV. עֲוֹן עֲקֵבַי *iniquity of my tracks,* i. e. ways, Ps. 49:6.

עָקֹב m., *steep place,* Isa. 40:4; see above.

עֵקֶב m.—I. *in consequence that, for the sake of.*—II. *consequence, fruit;* עֵ, רַב, Ps. 19:12, "great reward,"

Eng. Ver.; עֵקֶב, עַל עֵקֶב *in consequence, because, for that reason,* with כִּי אֲשֶׁר the same.

עָקְבָה f., *fraud, deceit,* 2 Ki. 10:19.

עָקוּב p. n. of men.

יַעֲקֹב (*took by the heel*), p. n., Jacob, the son of Isaac, afterwards Israel; קְהִלַּת יְ׳, בֵּית יְ׳, בְּנֵי יַעֲקֹב זֶרַע יְ׳ I. his descendants, the Israelites.—II. the name also of their land and national polity.

יַעֲקֹבָה p. n. of a man.

עָקַד (fut. יַעֲקֹד) *he binds, ties,* Gen. 22:9.

עָקֹד m. (pl. עֲקֻדִּים) *stripe, streak on cattle.*

עָקָה s., *oppression;* see עוק.

מַעֲקֶה m., *parapet, battlement;* LXX στεφάνη, Deut. 22:8.

עָקַל. Pu. part. מְעֻקָּל *became perverted,* Hab. 1:4.

עֲקַלָּתוֹן m., *very crooked,* Isa. 27:1.

עֲקַלְקַל m., עֲקַלְקַלּוֹת f. pl., *very crooked, perverted.*

עָקַר *eradicate,* Ecc. 3:2. Niph. *was rooted up, destroyed,* Zep. 2:4. Pi. עִקֵּר *hough, cut the hamstring.*

עֲקַר Ch. Ith. *was rooted,* Dan. 7:8.

עָקָר m., עֲקֶרֶת, עֲקָרָה f., *barren, sterile.*

עֵקֶר m.—I. *root,* i. e. head of a strange family, Lev. 25:47.—II. p. n. of a man.

עֲקַר m. Ch., *nerve, stump,* Dan. 4:12

עֶקְרוֹן p. n., one of the five principal cities of the Philistines, Ἀκαρών; עֶקְרֹנִי an Ekronite.

עַקְרָב m.—I. *a scorpion.*—II. *some implement of torture.*—III. *a war-*

*like engine.*—IV. מַעֲלֵה עַקְרַבִּים
p. n., a place in the south of
Palestine, 'Ακραβίν.

עָקַשׁ *convict of perverseness*, Job 9:20.
Niph. *is perverse*, Pro. 28:18. Pi.
*made crooked.*

עִקֵּשׁ m.—I. *perverse, tortuous.*—II.
p. n. of a man.

עִקְּשׁוּת m., *perverseness.*

מַעֲקַשׁ m., pl. מַעֲקַשִּׁים *unlevel, abrupt
places*, Isa. 42:16.

עָר; עָרִים; see עִיר.

עֵר p. n., *Er*, the son of Judah, and
other men.

עָרַב I. *was agreeable, sweet.*—II.
*agreed, made compact.*—III. *became surety, pledged*, with לְ.—
IV. *became dark;* imp. עֲרֹב; fut.
יֶעֱרַב. Hith. הִתְעָרֵב I. *intermixed
with*, with בְּ, לְ, עִם.—II. *agreed,
made compact with*, with אֶת.
Hiph. inf. הַעֲרֵב *growing
late* (of the day), 1 Sa. 17:16.

עֲרַב Ch., *mixed.* Ith. *was mixed,
associated.*

עֲרָב, עֲרַב *Arabia;* עַרְבִי *an
Arab;* pl. עַרְבִיאִים עַרְבִים *Arabs.*

עֹרֵב m.—I *a raven.*—II. p. n., a
prince of Midian.—III. *Oreb, a
rock beyond Jordan.*

עָרֵב m., *agreeable, sweet*, Pro. 20:
17, &c.

עָרֹב m., *gad-fly;* LXX. κυνόμυια.

עֵרֶב m. (with art. הָעֵרֶב).—I. *foreigner,
stranger, mixed multitude.* — II.
*woof in weaving.*

עֶרֶב m. (f. 1 Sa. 20:5).—I. *evening,
in the evening;* לָעֶרֶב, בָּעֶרֶב עֶרֶב
pl. עֲרָבוֹת; dual הָעַרְבַּיִם בֵּין *from*

*evening to evening,* i. e. a whole
day.—II. pl. עַרְבֵי עֲרָבִים *oziers,
willows.*—III. נַחַל עֲ' *a stream in
Moab*, Isa. 15:7.

עֲרָבָה f.—I. *plain, open country.*—
II. *desert.*—III. הָעֲרָבָה *the country
between Jericho and the gulf of
Akabah, called by the Arabs El
Arabah;* יָם הַעֲ' *Sea of Arabah,
Dead Sea;* נַחַל הַעֲ' *brook Kedron.*
—IV. p. n., a town in Benjamin;
עַרְבָתִי *an Arbite.*

עֲרֻבָּה f., *pledge, surety.*

עֵרָבוֹן m. (ἀρραβών), *security, pledge,*
Gen. 38:17, &c.

מַעֲרָב m.—I. *the west.*—II. *merchandise*, Eze. c. 27; מַעֲרָבָה *towards the west.*

מַעֲרָבָה f., *the west.*

תַּעֲרוּבָה f., *security, hostages.*

עָרַג *bleat, cry as an animal from desire*, with עַל, אֶל; fut. יַעֲרֹג.

עֲרוּגָה f., *raised bed in a garden,
parterre.*

עָרַד *root not used;* (Arab. *fled away*)

עָרוֹד m., *wild ass*, Job 39:5.

עֲרָד m. Ch.—I. *wild ass*, Dan. 5:21.
—II. p. n., a place in the wilderness of Judah.—III. p.n. of a man.

עָרָה Pi. עֵרָה (inf. עָרוֹת; fut. apoc.
תְּעַר).—I. *make naked.*—II. *empty,
pour out.* Hiph. הֶעֱרָה I. *make
bare, expose*, Lev. 20:18, 19.—II.
*pour out*, Isa. 53:12. Niph. נֶעֱרָה
*was poured out*, Isa. 32:15. Hith.
הִתְעָרָה I. *was stripped, exposed,*
Lam. 4:21.—II. *was spread abroad,*
Ps. 37:35.

שָׂדֶה f., pl. עָרוֹת bare places, pastures, Isa. 19:7.

עֶרְוָה f.—I. unfortified country, Gen. 42:9, 12.—II. nudity.—III. shame, disgrace.

עַרְוָה f. Ch., loss, Ezr. 4:14.

עֶרְיָה f., nakedness.

מַעֲרֶה m., bare place, moor, Jud. 20: 33.

מַעַר m., nudity.

מַעֲרוֹת f. pl., plains, suburbs, 1 Sa. 17:23.

מַעֲרָת p. n., a town in Judah.

תַּעַר m. (with suff. תַּעְרָה).—I. razor. — II. penknife, Jer. 36:23. — III. scabbard of a sword.

עָרוֹם, עֲרוּמִים, עֲרֹם; see ערם.

עֲרוֹעֵר p. n.; see ערר.

עֵרִי p. n., one of the sons of Gad.

עֲרִיסוֹת dough; see ערם.

עֲרִיפִים nobles; see ערף.

עָרִיץ; see ערץ.

עֲרִירִי, עֲרִירִים; see ערר.

עָרַךְ (fut. יַעֲרֹךְ).—I. set in order, arrange, dispose; with or without מִלְחָמָה set in battle array; with or without מִלִּים prepared an address, speech; with לְ to any one; with אֶל against any one; with or without מִשְׁפָּט prepared a cause for judgment; עָ' בְּרִית prepare a covenant. — II. compared together, valued, estimated, with לְ. Hiph. הֶעֱרִיךְ valued, set a tax on.

עֵרֶךְ m.—I. order, arrangement, system.—II. value, estimation.

מַעֲרָךְ m., disposings (of the heart), Pro. 16:1.

מַעֲרָכָה f., disposition, arrangement.

מַעֲרֶכֶת f., the same.

עָרֵל esteem profane, Lev. 19.23. Niph. appeared uncircumcised, Hab. 2:16.

עָרֵל, const. עֲרַל m., uncircumcised person; עֲ' שְׂפָתַיִם hesitating of speech; עֲרַל לֵב uncircumcised of heart; לִבְּכֶם הֶעָרֵל their heart uncircumcised; עֲרֵלָה אֹזֶן uncircumcised of ears.

עָרְלָה f., foreskin; עֲ' לֵב uncircumcised of heart; עָרְלָתוֹ פִּרְיוֹ uncircumcision of its fruits, i. e. first fruits of a tree, Lev. 19:23; pl. עֲרָלוֹת, const. עָרְלוֹת I. foreskins. — II. p. n., a hill not far from Gilgal.

עָרַם was cunning, subtle. Hiph הֶעֱרִים I. act cunningly.—II. act prudently, wisely. Niph. נֶעֱרַם became swollen, heaped, Ex. 15:8.

עָרוּם m.— I. cunning.— II. prudent, cautious.

עָרֹם, עָרוֹם m. (pl. עֲרוּמִּים; f. עֲרֻמָּה), —I. naked.—II. exposed, spoiled.

עֵירֹם, עֵרֹם m.—I. nakedness.— II. naked; adj. pl. עֵירֻמִּים.

עָרְמָה m., craftiness, cunning, Job 5: 13.

עָרְמָה f.—I. cunning.—II. prudence.

עֲרֵמָה f., pl. —ת —ים — heap (of ruins of corn, &c.).

עַרְמוֹן m., the plane tree.

מַעֲרֻמִּים m., pl. מַעֲרֻמִּים nudities 2 Chron. 28:15.

עֵרָן p. n. of a man.; patron. עֵרָנִי.

עָרַם rootnotused; (Ch. עֲרַם mixed).

עֲרִיסָה f., pl. עֲרִיסוֹת dough; LXX φύραμα.

עַרְעָר, עֲרָעָר, עַרְעָר; see עָרַר.

עָרַף (fut. יַעֲרֹף).—I. behead, Ex. 13:13, &c.— II. destroy, ruin, Hos. 10:2. —III. drop (as blood from a decapitated bird); applied to speaking.

עֹרֶף m., neck; פָּנָה ע or נָתַן עֹרֶף he turned the back, turned from any one, with אֶל; הָפַךְ ע, פָּנָה ע turned the back, fled; נָתַן אוֹיְבִים עֹרֶף gave him the back of his enemies, i.e. made them flee before him, Ps. 18:41, with לְ or אֶל.

עָרְפָּה p.n., Orpah, a woman of Moab.

עֲרִיפִים m.pl., clouds; metaph. nobles, Gen. 37:9.

עֲרָפֶל m., thick darkness.

עָרַץ (fut. יַעֲרֹץ).—I. feared, trembled. — II. affrighted, alarmed. — III. shook, with acc. מִפְּנֵי. Niph. part. נַעֲרָץ terrible, Ps. 89:8. Hiph. הֶעֱרִיץ causing to fear, Isa. 8:13.

עָרוּץ m., abrupt, fearful place, Job 30:6.

עָרִיץ m.—I. strong, mighty.—II. violent, cruel.

מַעֲרִיץ m., terrible, fearful one, Isa. 8:13.

מַעֲרָצָה f., fearfulness, terror, Isa. 10:33.

עָרַק fled, escaped, Job 30:3.

עֹרְקַי my nerves, Job 30:17.

עַרְקִי p.n., the Arkites, a people of Canaan.

עָרַר (imp. עֹרָה) was naked, Isa. 32:11. Po. עוֹרֵר I. stir up.—II. make

naked. Pil. עִרְעֵר and Hithpa. הִתְעַרְעֵר was, became, exposed.

עֲרִירִי m. (pl. עֲרִירִים) childless.

עַרְעָר m., naked, destitute, poor.

עֲרֹעֵר, עֲרוֹעֵר I. perhaps stump, dead tree, Jer. 48:6.—II. p.n., Aroer, a town on the river Arnon, called also עֲרוֹעֵר.— III. a town near Rabbath Ammon. — IV. p.n., a town in Judah; עֲרֹעֵרִי an inhabitant of Aroer.

עֶרֶשׂ f. (pl. עֲרָשׂוֹת) couch, bed.

עֵשֶׂב m. (with suff. עֶשְׂבָּם; pl. const. עִשְׂבוֹת) green herb (considered as food).

עֲשַׂב m. Ch., the same.

עָשָׂה (fut. יַעֲשֶׂה; inf. abs. עָשֹׂה, עָשׂוֹ; const. עֲשׂוֹת, עֲשׂוֹתֵ).—I. wrought, laboured in, with בְּ.—II. made, fabricated, produced, constituted, appointed, with לְ.— III. did, performed, made, exercised.— IV. passed time, Ecc. 6:12. Niph. נַעֲשָׂה (pret. f. נֶעֶשְׂתָה; fut. f. תֵּעָשֶׂה; apoc. תֵּעַשׂ).—I. was made. —II. was done; יֵעָשֶׂה to be done. Pu. עֻשֵּׂיתִי I was made, Ps. 139:15. Pi. עִשָּׂה pressed, injured, Eze. 23:3, 8.

עֲשַׂהְאֵל p.n. of a man.

עֲשִׂיאֵל p.n. of a man.

עֲשָׂיָה p.n. of a man.

מַעֲשֶׂה m. (pl. מַעֲשִׂים).—I. work (of an artificer).—II. labour, business, occupation.

מַעֲשַׂי p.n. of a man.

מַעֲשֵׂיָהוּ, מַעֲשֵׂיָה p.n. of a man.

עֵשָׂו (hairy), p.n., Esau, the son of Isaac; בֵּית ע, בְּנֵי עֵשָׂו the *sons of Esau, Edomites;* see אֱדֹם; הַר עֵשָׂו *mountains of Edom.*

עֲשׂוֹר, עֲשִׂירִי; see עֶשֶׂר.

עָשַׁק. Hithp. *contend with,* Gen. 26: 20.

עֵשֶׂק (*strife*), p.n. of a fountain.

עֶשֶׂר f., עֲשָׂרָה m., *ten;* pl. עֶשְׂרֹת *tithes.*

עָשָׂר m., עֶשְׂרָה f. (used only in composition with the other numbers), *ten;* אַחַד עָשָׂר *eleven, the eleventh;* f. אַחַת עֶשְׂרֵה; שִׁשָּׁה עָשָׂר m., שֵׁשׁ עֶשְׂרֵה f., *sixteen;* pl. עֶשְׂרִים *twenty.*

עָשַׂר v. (fut. יַעֲשֹׂר) *decimate, tithe,* 1 Sa. 8:15, 17. Pi. עִשֵּׂר *take or pay tithe.* Hiph. inf. with pref. לַעְשֵׂר *to pay tithe.*

עָשׂוֹר m., *ten;* בֶּעָשׂוֹר לַחֹדֶשׁ *the tenth (day) of the month;* נֶבֶל עָשׂוֹר *a lute of ten strings.*

עֲשַׂר f., עֶשְׂרָה m. Ch., *ten;* עֶשְׂרִין *twenty.*

עֲשִׂירִי m., *tenth;* f. עֲשִׂירִיָּה, עֲשִׂירִית.

עִשָּׂרוֹן m. (pl. עֶשְׂרֹנִים) *a dry measure, the tenth part of an ephah.*

מַעֲשֵׂר m. (const. מַעְשַׂר; with suff. מַעֲשְׂרוֹ) pl. מַעַשְׂרוֹת) *tithe.*

עָשְׁתָ for עֶשְׂתָה Kal pret. f., from עָשָׂה.

עָשׁ m., name of a constellation, probably the great bear, Job 9:9; (38: 32;) see also עַיִשׁ.

עַיִשׁ m.; בְּנֵי עַיִשׁ *the three stars in the tail of the bear,* Job. 38:32.

עָשָׁן p.n. of a man.

עָשַׁן (fut. יֶעְשַׁן).—I. *smoked.*—II. metaphorically, of the divine wrath.

עָשֵׁן n., *smoking,* Ex. 20:18.

עָשָׁן m. (const. עֲשַׁן; with suff. עֲשָׁנוֹ).

—I. *smoke.*—II. *fierce anger.*—III. *cloud.*—IV. p.n. of a town, same as כּוֹר עָשָׁן.

עָשֵׁן m., the same, Ex. 19:18.

עָשַׁק (fut. יַעֲשֹׁק).—I. *oppressed, injured, wronged, defrauded.*—II. *press upon.* Pu. part. f. מְעֻשָּׁקָה *one oppressed,* Isa. 23:12.

עָשׁוֹק m., *fraudulent, oppressive person,* Jer. 22:3.

עֲשׁוּקִים m. pl., *frauds, oppressions.*

עֵשֶׁק p.n. of a man.

עֹשֶׁק m.—I. *oppression, injury.*—II. *that which is obtained thereby.*

עָשְׁקָה f., *oppresses, ruins me,* Isa. 38:14.

מַעֲשַׁקּוֹת f. pl., *oppressions.*

עָשַׁר (fut. יֶעְשַׁר) *was rich.* Hiph. הֶעְשִׁיר I. *made rich.*—II. *was, became, rich.* Hith. part. מִתְעַשֵּׁר *becomes rich,* Pro. 13:7.

עָשִׁיר m.—I. *rich.*—II. *proud.*—III. *rich* (in grace), Ecc. 10:6.

עֹשֶׁר m., *riches.*

עָשֵׁשׁ *became old, wasted.*

עָשׁ m., *moth* (that which wastes, eats).

עָשַׁת *was made smooth, shone,* Jer. 5:28. Hith. *remember,* Jon. 1:6.

עֲשִׁית, עֲשֵׁת Ch., *thought, designed,* Dan. 6:4.

עֶשֶׁת m.—I. *net-work* of ivory, Cant. 5:14.—II. עֶשֶׂר with עֶשְׂרֵה, עַשְׁתֵּי (perhaps *excess beyond ten*) *eleven.*

עַשְׁתוּת f., *taunting,* Job 12:5.

עֶשְׁתֹּנוֹת f. pl., *devices, machinations,* Ps. 146:4.

עַשְׁתֹּרֶת f., 'Αστάρτη, perhaps the deified planet Venus. It is probably the feminine of אֲשֵׁרָה;

pl. עַשְׁתָּרוֹת *statues of Ashtoreth.*
—II. p. n. of a city of Bashan, called also עַשְׁתָּרוֹת קַרְנַיִם *Ashtoreth with horns;* עַשְׁתְּרָתִי *an inhabitant of Ashtoreth;* עַשְׁתְּרוֹת צֹאן *produce of the flock;* LXX. ποιμνία τῶν προβάτων, Deu. 7: 13, &c.

עֵת, עֵת־ com. (with suff. עִתִּי), *time, season,* ὁ καιρός; כָּעֵת הַזֹּאת *about this time;* כָּעֵת מָחָר *about this time to-morrow;* כָּעֵת חַיָּה *this time next year, or, as in the times of a vigorous woman* (Lee), Gen. 18: 10, 14; כָּעֵת *as at this time;* בָּעֵת הַהוּא *in that time;* בְּעִתּוֹ *in his time;* לְעֵת עֶרֶב *in the evening;* מֵעֵת עַד עֵת *from time to time, always;* עֵת *adv. now, sometimes;* pl. עִתִּים *times, vicissitudes;* רַבּוֹת עִתִּים *many times, on many occasions,* Neh. 9: 28.

עַתָּה (with pause עָתָּה) adv. νῦν, νύν).—I. *now, shortly, speedily.*—II. *then;* מֵעַתָּה *from this time;* עַד עָתָּה *until this time.*

עִתִּי m., *seasonable,* Lev. 16: 21.

עִתַּי p. n. of a man.

עֵת קָצִין p. n. of a man; with ה loc. עִתָּה קָצִין p. n., a city of Zebulon.

עָתַד Pi. *prepare,* Pro. 24: 27. Hith. *have become prepared,* Job 15: 28.

עָתִיד m., *prepared, ready.* Pl. עֲתִידוֹת I. *things ready to take place.*—II. *wealth.*

עֲתִיד m. Ch., *ready,* Dan. 3: 15.

עַתּוּד m.—I. *he-goat.*—II. *leader, governor.*

עֲתָיָה p. n. of a man.

עָתָךְ p. n., a town of Judah.

עַתְלַי p. n. of a man.

עֲתַלְיָהוּ, עֲתַלְיָה p. n.—I. *Athaliah, the wife of Joram.*—II. used also for men.

עָתַם. Niph. נֶעְתַּם *is burnt, consumed,* Isa. 9: 18.

עָתְנִי p. n. of a man.

עָתְנִיאֵל p. n., *Othniel, a judge of Israel;* LXX. Γοθονιήλ.

עָתַק (fut. יֶעְתַּק).—I. *remove quickly, hurry from,* with מִן.—II. *grow old.* Hiph. הֶעְתִּיק I. *cause to remove.*—II. *transcribe,* Pro. 25: 1.—III. *put away, silenced,* Job 32: 15.

עָתָק m., *insolent, biting word.*

עֹתֶק m., *freedom, liberty,* Pro. 8: 18.

עָתִיק m., *freely,* Isa. 23: 18.

עַתִּיק m.—I. *ancient,* 1 Chron. 4: 22.—II. *removed,* with מִן, Isa. 28: 9.

עַתִּיק m. Ch., *ancient,* Dan. 7: 9, 13, 22.

עָתַר (fut. יֶעְתַּר), *prayed, supplicated,* with אֶל, לְ. Niph. נֶעְתַּר (inf. נַעְתּוֹר) I. *was prevailed upon by prayer, was made propitious.*—II. נַעְתָּרוֹת *seemingly propitious* (false), Pro. 27: 6, with לְ. Hiph. הֶעְתִּיר I. *prayed,* with לְ.—II. בְּעַד *multiplied,* Eze. 35: 13.

עָתָר m.—I. *suppliant,* Zep. 3: 10.—II. *abundance,* Eze. 8: 1.

עֶתֶר p. n., a town of Simeon.

עֲתֶרֶת f., *riches, abundance,* Jer. 33: 6.

## פ

פֹּא *here,* Job 38: 11, for פֹּה.

פָּאָה. Hiph. fut. with suff. אַפְאֵיהֶם *I will scatter them far and wide* Deu. 32: 26.

פֵּאָה, const. פְּאַת f.—I. corner, angle (of a field, table, &c.).—II. קְצוּצֵי פֵאָה having the hair clipped or shaven in angles; a Canaanitish custom forbidden to the Israelites; פַּאֲתֵי מוֹאָב, Nu. 24:17, the clipped cornered ones of Moab, i. e. who trim their hair thus.

פֶּה m. (const. פִּי; with suff. פִּיךָ, פִּיהֶם, פִּיהוּ, פִּיו; pl. פִּים, פִּיּוֹת).—I. mouth; פֶּה אֶל פֶּה mouth to mouth, without intervention, Nu. 12:8; פֶּה אֶחָד unanimously.—II. mouth of a sack, aperture in anything.—III. edge of a sword, &c.—IV. border of the sea, Pro. 8:29.—V. פֶּה לָפֶה from end to end.—VI. share, portion; פִּי שְׁנַיִם two parts.—VII. word, command.—VIII. expression, tenor; with pref. כְּפִי as, according to; כְּפִיךָ as thou (art); כְּפִי אֲשֶׁר so as; לְפִי according to; עַל פִּי according to.

פֵּיָה f., edge of a sword; pl. פֵּיוֹת Jud. 3:16.

פִּיפִיּוֹת f. pl., edges, two-edged, Ps. 149:6; Isa. 41:15.

פִּי־בֶסֶת p.n., a city of Egypt, Bubastis.

פִּי־הַחִירוֹת הַחִירוֹת p.n., a place on the Red Sea.

פִּיכֹל p.n. of a man.

פִּינְחָם p. n. of a man.

פָּאַר. Pi. פֵּאֵר I. adorned, made beautiful.—II. went over the branches accurately, Deu. 24:20. Hith. הִתְפָּאֵר I. felt complacency, with בְּ—II. boasted himself, with עַל.

פְּאֵר m. (pl. פְּאָרֵי, פְּאָרִים) ornamental head-dress.

פֹּארָה, פְּאֹרָה f., a branch.

פָּארוּר m., blackness, paleness (of face) Joel 2:6; Nah. 2:11.

תִּפְאֶרֶת, תִּפְאָרָה f.—I. beauty, ornament.—II. glory.—III. boast, subject of glorying.

פָּארָן p. n., Paran, the wilderness between Egypt and Palestine.

פַּגֵּג (Arab. unripe fig).

פַּג m., pl. פַּגִּים unripe figs, Cant. 2:13.

פִּגּוּל m., pl. פִּגֻּלִים impure, disgusting (thing).

פָּגַע I. came to a place, reached, with בְּ—II. met, fell in with, with אֶל, בְּ—III. met hostilely, fell upon, with בְּ—IV. waited on in prayer, entreated.—V. admitted favourably. Hiph. הִפְגִּיעַ I. cause to come, fall in with, wait upon.—II. fell upon.—III. entreated.

פֶּגַע m., occurrence, accident.

פַּגְעִיאֵל p. n., a prince of Asher.

מִפְגָּע m., object of attack, butt, Job 7:20.

פָּגַר. Pi. פִּגַּר became languid, unable to proceed, 1 Sa. 30:10, 21, with מִן.

פֶּגֶר m. (pl. פְּגָרִים) dead body of man or beast.

פָּגַשׁ I. met, with בְּ—II. met hostilely, Hos. 13:8, &c. Niph. נִפְגַּשׁ met each other. Pi. stumble against Job 5:14.

פָּדָה I. redeemed, with בְּ (of the price)—II. delivered. Niph. נִפְדָּה was redeemed, delivered. Hiph. הִפְדָּה allowed to be redeemed, Ex. 21:8

Hoph. inf. הָפְדֵּר same as Niph., Lev. 19:20.

פְּדַהְאֵל p. n. of a man.

פְּדַהְצּוּר p.n. of a man.

פְּדוּיִים m. pl., λύτρον.—I. redemption price, ransom.— II. redeemed, delivered persons.

פְּדוֹן p. n. of a man.

פְּדוּת f.— I. redemption.— II. פְּדוּת separation, Ex. 8:19.

פְּדָיָהוּ‎, פְּדָיָה p. n. of a man.

פְּדִיוֹם‎, פִּדְיוֹן m., ransom.

פַּדָּן m., plain, Gen. 48:7; פַּדַּן אֲרָם Padan-Aram; with ה, פַּדֶּנָה אֲרָם towards Padan-Aram.

אַפֶּדֶן Ch., palace, camp, Dan. 11:45.

פָּדַע redeem, deliver, Job 33:24.

פֶּדֶר m. (with suff. פִּדְרוֹ) fat.

פֶּה; see פאה.

פֹּה (פָּא, פּוֹ).— I. here.— II. hither; מִפֹּה hence; עַד פֹּה thus far; אֵיפֹה where?

פּוּאָה (פֻּנָּה) p. n. of a man.

פּוּג (fut. יָפֻן‎, יָפוּג) became chilled, languid, ceased to act. Niph. the same, Ps. 38:9.

פּוּגָה f., intermission, Lam. 2:18.

הַפֻּגָה f., intermission, Lam. 3:49.

פּוּחַ I. blew.— II. became cool by a breeze. Hiph. הֵפִיחַ I. inflamed, Pro. 29:8.—II. blew, blew a fire, with בְּ.—III. puffed at (scornfully), with בְּ.—IV. uttered.— V. (from פַּח) ensnared, Ps. 12:6.

פִּיחַ m., ashes, Ex. 9:8, 10.

פּוּט p. n., one of the sons of Ham, and his descendants.

פּוּטִיאֵל p. n. of a man.

פּוֹטִיפַר p. n. (πετεφρη, he who is devoted to the sun), an officer in Pharaoh's household.

פּוֹטִי פֶרַע (the same); p. n., Joseph's father-in-law.

פּוּךְ m.—I. stibium, powdered antimony.—II. אַבְנֵי פוּךְ; LXX. λίθοι πολυτελεῖς, a precious stone; קֶרֶן הַפּוּךְ p. n. of a woman.

פּוֹל m., beans.

פּוּל p.n.—I. a people and nation of Africa.—II. a king of Assyria.

פֻּם‎, פֹּם m. Ch., mouth, aperture.

פּוּן, fut. אָפוּנָה; LXX. ἐξηπορήθην; Vulg. conturbatus sum, I pine away, Ps. 88:16.

פּוּנָה p.n., a gate of Jerusalem.

פּוּנִי p.n. of a man.

פּוּנֹן p.n., a town on the borders of the desert.

פֻּעָה p.n. of a woman.

פּוּץ I. dispersed themselves, were scattered.—II. overflowed. Niph. were scattered. Pil. פֹּצֵץ and Pilp. פִּצְפֵּץ shatter, shake to pieces. Hiph. הֵפִיץ I. scattered, confused. —II. poured out.— III. was scattered. Hithpo. are shattered, Hab. 3:6. Tiphel תְּפוֹצֹתִיכֶם I will scatter you, Jer. 25:34.

מֵפִיץ m.—I. disperser.—II. club, Pro. 25:18.

I. פּוּק stagger, stumble, Isa. 28:7. Hiph. stagger, stumble, Jer. 10:4.

II. פּוּק Hiph. הֵפִיק 1. supplied, Isa. 58:10.—2 obtained.—3. prospered, Ps. 140:9.

פּוּקָה f., *cause of stumbling*, 1 Sa. 25:31.

פִּים m., *staggering*, Nah. 2:11

I. פּוּר (Arab. *bubbled*); see פָּרַר.

פּוּרָה f., *wine-press*.

פָּרוּר m., *pot for boiling*.

II. פּוּר m., a Persian word.—I. *lot*; pl. פּוּרִים.—II. *the feast of Purim*.

פּוּרָתָא p.n., *a son of Haman*.

פּוּשׁ (pret. פְּשָׁתֶּם).—I. *became numerous, flourished.* — II. *spread themselves*, Hab. 1:8. Niph. *were scattered*, Nah. 3:18.

פַּשׁ m., *extent*, Job 35:15.

פִּישׁוֹן p.n., *one of the rivers of Paradise*.

פּוּת (Arab. *interstice*).

פֹּת m., Isa. 3:17; pl. פֹּתוֹת *hinges*, 1 Ki. 7:50.

פּוּתִי p. n. of a man.

פָּז (fut. pl. יָפֹזּוּ) *are strong and active*, Gen. 49:24. Pi. פִּזֵּז *dancing*, 2 Sa. 6:16. Hoph. part. מוּפָז *purified*, 1 Ki. 10:18.

פָּז m.—I. *refined gold.* — II. *refined*, Cant. 5:11.

פָּזַר *dispersed*, Jer. 50:17. Pi. פִּזַּר I. *dispersed.*—II. *distributed liberally.* Niph. and Pu. *was scattered.*

פַּח m. (pl. פַּחִים).—I. *snare, gin.*—II. *any concealed danger.*—III. *plate of metal*, Ex. 39:3; Nu. 17:3.

פָּחַד (fut. יִפְחַד).—I. *feared*, with מִן, מִפְּנֵי.—II. *was agitated.*—III *hastened.* Pi. *feared greatly, continually.* Hiph. *caused to shake, tremble*, Job 4:14.

פַּחַד m. (with suff. פַּחְדְּכֶם; pl. פְּחָדִים).—I. *fear, dread, reverence*—II. *object of fear.*—III. *thigh*, Job 40:17; פּ' אֱלֹהִים *fear of God.*

פַּחְדָּה f., *fear*, Jer. 2:19.

פֶּחָה m. (const. פַּחַת; with suff. פֶּחָם, פֶּחָתְךָ; pl. פַּחוֹת; const. פַּחֲווֹת).—I. *governor of a province.*—II. *captain;* Ch. the same; hence the modern word *Pacha.*

פָּחַז (*swelling like boiling water*).—I. *was dissolute*, Jud. 9:4.—II. *was proud*, Zep. 3:4.

פַּחַז m., *wantonness, pride*, Gen. 49:4.

פַּחֲזוּת f., *pride*, Jer. 23:32.

פָּחַם root not used; (Arab. *charcoal*).

פֶּחָם m., *charcoal.*

פָּחַר root not used; (Syr. *he founded*).

פֶּחָר m. Ch., *potter*, Dan. 2:41.

פַּחַת m. (pl. פְּחָתִים).—I. *a pit, well.*—II. *destruction.*

פַּחֶתֶת f., *corrosion, fretting into a garment*, Lev. 13:55.

פַּחַת־מוֹאָב p.n. of a man.

פַּחַת Kal inf., from נפח.

פִּטְדָה f., *a precious stone, topaz or emerald.*

פָּטַר (fut. יִפְטֹר).—I. *slipped out, or away.*—II. *let out* (of water).—III. *expand* (of flowers), 1 Ki. c. 6.—IV. *exempt from duty*, 1 Chron. 9:33. Hiph. *open wide* (the mouth), Ps. 22:8.

פָּטִיר Ketib, same as פָּטוּר (part. see פָּטַר), *exempt from duty*, 1 Chron 9:33.

פֶּטֶר m., *opening, beginning*; פֶּטֶר רֶחֶם *first-born*.

פִּטְרָה f., the same, Nu. 8:16.

פָּטַשׁ root not used; (Arab. *beat out iron with a hammer, spread out*).

פַּטִּישׁ m., *a hammer*.

פְּטִישׁ m. Ch., *a tunic*, Dan. 3:21.

פִי with comp. פֶּיהָ; see פֶּה in פָּאָה.

פִּיד root not used; (Arab. *disappeared, died*).

פִּיד m., *destruction*.

פִּיחַ; see פּוּחַ.

פִּילֶגֶשׁ; see פִּלֶגֶשׁ.

פִּים root not used; (Arab. *was fat*).

פִּימָה f., *fatness, food, strength*, Job 15:27.

פִּינֹן p. n., *a prince of Edom*.

פִּיפִיּוֹת; see פָּאָה.

פִּיק; see פּוּק.

פִּישׁוֹן; see פּוּשׁ.

פִּיתֹן p. n. of a man.

פָּכָה Pi. *flowing out*, Eze. 47:2.

פַּךְ m., *flask, cruse*.

פֹּכֶרֶת הַצְּבָיִים p. n. of a man.

פָּלָא Niph. נִפְלָא I. *was marvellous*.—II. *appeared marvellous*, with בְּעֵינֵי—III. *was concealed*, with מִן—IV. *was struck with wonder*; part. pl. נִפְלָאִים, נִפְלָאוֹת *wonderful things, wonderfully*. Pi. פִּלֵּא *set apart*; פִּלֵּא נֶדֶר *set apart by vow, devoted*. Hiph. הִפְלִיא I. *set apart*.—II. *made wonderful*.—III. *acted wonderfully*. Hith. *show one's self wonderful*, with בְּ, Job 10:16.

פֶּלֶא m. (with suff. פִּלְאֲךָ).—I. *sepa-*

ration, *peculiarity*.—II. *marvellousness*.—III. *a miracle*; pl. פְּלָאִים adv. *wonderfully*; פְּלָאוֹת *wonderful things*.

פִּלְאִי or פֶּלִי m., *wonderful*, Jud. 13. 18; Ps. 139:6.

פְּלִיאָה f., or פְּלִאיָה the same.

פְּלָיָה p. n. of a man.

פְּלָיָה p. n. of a man.

פַּלּוּא p.n., *a son of Reuben*; patron. פַּלֻּאִי.

מִפְלָאָה f., *miracle*, Job 37:16.

פָּלַג. Niph. *was divided*. Pi. I. *cut out, formed*, Job 38:25.—II. *divided*, Ps. 55:10.

פְּלַג Ch., *divided*, Dan. 2:41.

פְּלַג m. Ch., *half*, Dan. 7:25.

פֶּלֶג m.—I. *channel, stream*.—II. p.n., *a son of Eber*.

פְּלַגּוֹת f. pl., *brooks*.

פְּלֻגָּה f., pl. פְּלֻגּוֹת *divisions*, 2 Chron. 35:5.

מִפְלַגָּה f., pl. מִפְלַגּוֹת the same, 2 Chron. 35:12.

פִּילֶגֶשׁ, פִּלֶגֶשׁ f. (pl. פִּילַגְשִׁים, פִּלַגְשֵׁי), *concubine*, παλλακή.

פְּלָדָה f., pl. פְּלָדוֹת *iron of chariots*, perhaps *scythes*, Nah. 2:4.

פִּלְדָּשׁ p. n. of a man.

פָּלָה same as פָּלָא. Niph. *are separated*, Ex. 33:16. Hiph. הִפְלָה I. *separated*.—II. *set apart*, Ps. 4:4.

פְּלֹנִי m.—I. with אַלְמֹנִי ὁ δεῖνα, *a certain one*.—II. p. n. of a man.

פַּלְמֹנִי m., *this particular one*, Dan 8:13.

פָּלַח *cut*, Ps. 141:7. Pi. פִּלַּח I. *cut to*

*pieces*, 2 Ki. 4:39.—II. *disentangle*, Job 39:3. - III. *pierce through*, Pro.7:23.—IV. *harrow*, Job 16:13.

פֶּלַח m.—I. *piece, part.*—II. *mill-stone*; פֶּלַח רֶכֶב *upper mill-stone*; פֶּ תַחְתִּית *nether mill-stone.*

פִּלְחָא p. n. of a man.

פְּלַח Ch., *served, worshipped.*

פָּלְחָן m. Ch., *service, worship*, Ezr. 7:19.

פָּלַט *escaped*, Eze. 7:16. Pi. I. *delivered.*—II. *bring forth safely*, Job 21:10. Hiph. *delivered.*

פָּלִיט, פָּלֵיט m., *fugitive, one escaped.*

פְּלֵטָה, פְּלֵיטָה f., *the escaped, remnant.*

פֶּלֶט m., *deliverance.*

פֶּלֶט p. n. of a man.

פַּלְטִי p. n. of a man.

פַּלְטִי p. n. of a man.

פַּלְטִיאֵל p. n. of a man.

פְּלַטְיָהוּ p. n. of a man.

מִפְלָט m., *escape, safety*, Ps. 55:9.

פְּלָיָה, פְּלִיאָה, פְּלִיא, פְּלִי; see פלא.

פְּלִילִי, פְּלִילָה, פְּלִילִי; see פלל.

פָּלַךְ root not used; (Arab. *was round*).

פֶּלֶךְ m.—I. *spinning distaff.*—II. *circuit, district.*

פָּלַל Pi. פִּלֵּל I. *judged*, 1 Sa. 2:25. —II. *adjudged punishment*, with לְ, Eze.16:52.—III. *inflicted punishment*, Ps. 106:30.—IV. *expected*, Gen. 48:11. Hith. *prayed* (lit. *appealed to a judge*), with בְּעַד, לִפְנֵי, אֶל, לְ, עַל.

פָּלִיל m., *a judge*; pl. פְּלִילִים.

פְּלִילָה f., *justice*, Isa. 16:3.

פָּלִיל m., *judicial*, Job 31:28.

פְּלִילִיָּה f., *judgment*, Isa. 28:7.

פָּלָל p. n. of a man.

פְּלַלְיָה p. n. of a man.

תְּפִלָּה f.—I. *prayer.*—II. *intercession.*—III. *hymn*, Ps. 72:20.

פַּלְמֹנִי, פְּלֹנִי; see פלה.

פָּלַס Pi.—I. *pondered*, Isa. 26:7.— II. *approved.*—III. *planned.*

פֶּלֶס m., *balance, steel-yard.*

מִפְלָשׂ m., *poising, balancing*, Job 37:16.

פָּלַץ Hith. *shook, trembled*, Job 9:6.

פַּלָּצוּת f., *trembling, fear.*

מִפְלֶצֶת f., *idol, image.*

תִּפְלֶצֶת f., *terror*, Jer. 49:16.

פָּלַשׁ Hith. *rolled themselves in dust.*

פְּלֶשֶׁת p. n., *Philistia*, the sea-coast of the south of Palestine; it was divided into five provinces. פְּלִשְׁתִּי *a Philistine*, pl. פְּלִשְׁתִּים; פְּלִשְׁתִּיִּים *Philistines*; LXX. Ἀλλόφυλοι.

פֶּלֶת p. n. of a man.

פְּלֵתִי m., *mercenary soldier, Pelethite.*

פֶּן, פֶּנָּה, see פנן; פֶּן, see פנה.

פַּנַּג, perhaps *millet*, in English, *panic*, Eze. 27:17.

פָּנָה (fut. יִפְנֶה, תֵּפֶן, וַיִּפֶן, עֹרֶף).—I. *turn himself to go away.*—II. *turned towards.*— III. *changed, declined, began*; לִפְנוֹת בֹּקֶר *at the turn of the morning*, i.e. in the morning; לִפְנוֹת עֶרֶב *in the evening.* Pi. פִּנָּה I. *removed.* — II. *cleared a road or house.* Hiph. הִפְנָה (fut. apoc. וַיִּפֶן).—I. *turned.*—II. *turned himself.* Hoph. *were made to turn themselves*, Jer. 49:8.

פָּנֶה m., pl. פָּנִים; const. פְּנֵי I. *face*

פָּנִים בְּפָנִים, פָּנִים אֶל־פָּנִים face to face.—II. person, presence; שׂוּם פָּנִים, with אֶל or עַל he set his face toward; שׂוּם פ׳, נָתַן, with לְ and inf. he designed to do; פְּנֵי my person, i.e. I; פְּנֵיךָ thy person, i.e. thou, &c.— III. surface.—IV. front; פָּנִים in front; לְפָנִים before, formerly; מִפָּנִים in, from the presence of; מִלְפָנִים from ancient time; with prefixes אֶל־פְּנֵי before, in presence of; אֶת־פְּנֵי before; מֵאֵת פְּנֵי from before; בִּפְנֵי before; לִפְנֵי in the sight of, before, preceding, against, in time; with suff. לְפָנַי, לְפָנֶיךָ, לְפָנָיו, מִלְפָנַי from, because of; מִפְּנֵי אֲשֶׁר because of; עַל־פְּנֵי in presence of, in preference to, towards; מֵעַל־פְּנֵי from before.

פֶּן, part. μή, lest.

פְּנִיאֵל, פְּנוּאֵל p.n.—I. a place beyond Jordan.—II. of a man.

פְּנִים m., within; פְּנִימָה to, on, the inside; לִפְנִימָה within, on the inside; מִפְּנִים, מִפְּנִימָה within.

פְּנִימִי m., פְּנִימִית f., inner.

פְּנִינִים m. pl., pearls.

פֵּן m. (with suff. פִּנָּהּ; pl. פִּנִּים) corner.

פִּנָּה f.—I. corner; אֶבֶן פ׳, רֹאשׁ פ׳ chief corner-stone.—II. battlement, parapet.—III. dignitary, prince.

פְּנֻנָּה p.n. of a woman.

פָּנַק. Pi. brought up delicately, Pro. 29:21.

פַּס, פַּסָּה, פִּסִּים; see ססס.

פָּסַג. Pi. count, observe, Ps. 48:14.

פִּסְגָּה p.n., a peak on the mountains of Moab.

פָּסַח passed over for defence, defended, protected. Niph. was lamed, 2 Sa. 4:4. Pi. leaped about, 1 Ki. 18:26.

פֶּסַח p.n. of a man.

פֶּסַח m.—I. feast of the Passover.—II. the paschal lamb; עָשָׂה פ׳ keep the Passover.

פִּסֵּחַ m. (pl. פִּסְחִים) lame.

תִּפְסַח p.n., a city on the Euphrates, Thapsacus.

פָּסַךְ p.n. of a man.

פָּסַל hewed, carved.

פָּסִיל m., pl. פְּסִילִים carved images, idols.

פֶּסֶל m. (with suff. פִּסְלִי) an idol.

פְּסַנְתֵּרִין, פְּסַנְטֵרִין m. Ch., ψαλτήριον, a musical instrument.

פָּסַס ceased to exist, disappeared, Ps. 12:2.

פַּס m. כְּתֹנֶת פַּסִּים coat of many colours, Gen. 37:3; long cloak, covering the hands and feet (Ges. and Lee); but Jacob knew Joseph's coat when torn and dipped in blood; it was the quality or colour of the cloth, therefore, not the shape that distinguished it; LXX. χιτὼν ποικίλος.

פַּס m., palm of the hand.

פִּסָּה f., abundance, Ps. 72:16

פַּס דָּמִים p.n., same as אֶפֶס דַּמִּים.

פִּסְפָּה p.n. of a man.

פָּעָה cry out, Isa. 42:14.

אֶפְעֶה com., adder, viper.

אָפַע the same.

פָּעוּ , פָּעִי p.n., a city of Edom. פָּעוֹר; see פְּעֹר.

פָּעַל v. (fut. יִפְעַל יִפְעֹל).—I. worked. —II. made, formed.—III. did, performed.—IV. practised, with לְ or בְּ of the person for whom the action is performed.

פֹּעַל m. (with suff. פָּעֳלֶךָ, פָּעֳלוֹ, פָּעֳלָךְ; pl. פְּעָלִים).—I. work, action, practice.—II. wages.—III. acquisition, Pro. 21:6.

פְּעֻלָּה f.—I. work, employment.—II. wages, Lev. 19:13.—III. reward or punishment.

פֹּעֲלוֹ for פָּעֳלוֹ, from פֹּעַל. פְּעֻלְּתָי p.n. of a man.

מִפְעָל m., מִפְעָלָה f., } work, doings.

פָּעַם moved, excited to action, Jud. 13:25. Niph. was moved, disturbed. Hith. same as Niph., Dan. 2:1.

פַּעַם f. (m. Jud. 16:28).—I. pl. פְּעָמִים footsteps, feet.—II. progress.—III. an anvil, Isa. 41:7.—IV. pl. פַּעֲמוֹת feet of the ark (Lee).—V. an act, and the time of its performance, a time, once; dual פַּעֲמַיִם twice; שֶׁבַע פְּעָמִים seven times; פַּעַם וּשְׁתַּיִם once or twice, Neh. 13:20; בְּפַעַם הַזֹּאת, הַפַּעַם בַּפַּעַם הַהִיא now, at the present time; כְּפַעַם בְּפַעַם even so as before; פַּעַם...פַּעַם sometimes.

פַּעֲמֹן m., bell, Ex. chapters 38 and 39 only.

פֻּעֲנֵחַ; see צָפְנַת פּ'.

פָּעַר open the mouth, gape, with פֶּה בָּפֶּה.

פְּעוֹר p.n. of a mountain of Moab;

בַּעַל־פְּעוֹר and פְּעוֹר an idol of Moab.

פָּעֲרַי p.n., one of David's generals; elsewhere נַעֲרַי.

פָּצָה I. opened the mouth.—II. rescued.

פָּצַח broke forth into singing, with רִנָּה. Pi. broke to pieces, Mic. 3:3. פְּצִירָה; see פצר.

פָּצַל Pi. פִּצֵּל peeled, Gen. 30:37, 38. פְּצָלוֹת f. pl., the parts peeled, stripped of bark, Gen. 30:37.

פָּצַם broke the earth, Ps. 60:4.

פָּצַע wounded; פְּצוּעַ דַּכָּה eunuch. פֶּצַע m. (with suff. פִּצְעִי; pl. פְּצָעִים), a wound.

פָּצַץ Hithpo.; see פוץ. פָּצֵץ p.n. of a man.

פָּצַר (fut. יִפְצַר).—I. pressed upon to injure, Gen. 19:9.—II. urged to consent, with בְּ. Hiph. inf. הַפְצֵר was too urgent, obstinate, 1 Sam. 15:23.

פְּצִירָה f., a file, 1 Sam. 13:21.

פָּקַד I. visited, enquired for.—II. enquired for without finding, missed. —III. enquired into or after, cared for.—IV. punished, with אֶל of the crime, or עַל of the person, and בְּ of the punishment.—V. examined and arranged—VI. numbered, took account of.—VII. placed, appointed, set over, with אֶת, עַל, (פְּקֻדִים officers).—VIII. laid a charge upon any one, with עַל. Niph. I. was missed.—II. was punished.—III. was numbered.— IV. punishment was inflicted.—V. was visited with evil. Pi. ex-

*amined, numbered.* Pu. I. *was taken account of,* Ex. 38:21.—II. *was deprived of,* Isa. 38:10. Hiph. I. *placed, appointed,* with עַל or לְ.—II. *committed to some one,* with עַל־יְדֵי, בְּיַד, אֶת. Hoph. I. *was punished,* Jer. 6:6.—II. *placed, appointed;* part. מֻפְקָדִים *officers.* Hith. *was examined, numbered.* Hoth. pl. הָתְפָּקְדוּ the same.

פְּקֻדָּה f.—I. *providence,* Job 10:12.—II. *office.*—III. *government.*—IV. *class,* 1 Chron. 23:11.—V. *treasure,* Isa. 15:7.—VI. *punishment;* בֵּית הַפְּקֻדּוֹת *prison.*

פִּקָּדוֹן m., *deposit.*

פְּקִדֻת f., *captain of the guard,* Jer. 37:13.

פְּקוֹד m.—I. *punishment,* an allegorical name of Babylon, Jer. 50:21.—II. *dominion,* Eze. 23:23.

פִּקּוּדִים m. pl., *precepts of God.*

פָּקִיד m., *officer, chief, superintendent.*

מִפְקָד m.—I. *arrangement,* 2 Chron. 31:13.—II. *census publicly appointed,* 2 Sa. 24:9.—III. שַׁעַר הַמִּפְקָד *one of the gates of Jerusalem,* Neh. 3:31.

פָּקַח (fut. יִפְקַח) *opened the eyes* or *ears.* Niph. *was opened.*

פֶּקַח p.n., *Pekah, king of Israel.*

פְּקַחְיָה p.n., *Pekahiah, king of Israel.*

פִּקֵּחַ m., *having the eyes opened, able to see.*

פְּקַח־קוֹחַ m., *complete opening, opening of the prison,* Isa. 61:1.

פָּקִיד *officer;* see פקד.

פַּקֻעוֹת f. pl., *the fox-grape,* 2 Ki. 4:39.

פְּקָעִים m. pl., *architectural ornaments of a globular form,* 1 Ki. 6:18; 7:24.

פַּר, פָּר m., *young bull.*

פָּרָה f.—I. *young cow, heifer.*—II. הַפָּרָה p.n., *a town in the tribe of Benjamin.*

פָּרָא same as פָּרָה Hiph., *propagate,* Hos. 13:15.

פֶּרֶא, פֶּרֶה com. (pl. פְּרָאִים), *wild ass.* פִּרְאָם p.n., *a king of Canaan.*

פֹּראת same as פֹּארת; see פֵּארָה.

כַּרְוָר, פַּרְבָּר m., *suburb.*

פָּרַד *separated, spread* (of wings). Niph. *separated himself,* with מֵעַל, מִן. Pi. *go aside,* Hos. 4:14. Pu. part. מְפֹרָד *separate,* Est. 3:8. Hiph. *same as Kal.* Hith. same as Niph.

פֶּרֶד m. (with suff. פִּרְדּוֹ; pl. פְּרָדִים), *a mule.*

פִּרְדָּה f., *she-mule.*

פְּרֻדֹת f. pl., *seeds scattered, corn sown,* Joel 1:17.

פַּרְדֵּס m., παράδεισος, *enclosure, park,* Neh. 2:8; Cant. 4:13; Ecc. 2:5.

פָּרָה *heifer;* see פָּר; פֶּרֶה same as פֶּרֶא *wild ass.*

פָּרָה *bore fruit, was fruitful* (of trees, plants, men, animals, &c.); part. f. פֹּרִיָּה, פֹּרָת *fruit tree.* Hiph. הִפְרָה (fut. apoc. וַיֶּפֶר) *made fruitful.*

פְּרִי m. (with pause פֶּרִי; with suff. פִּרְיָם, פֶּרְיְךָ, פִּרְיְכֶם, פִּרְיָהֶם). I. *fruit of a tree;* עֵץ פְּרִי *fruit tree.*—II. *produce of the ground;* אֶרֶץ פְּרִי *a fruitful land.*—III. *fruit of the womb, offspring.*—IV *result of actions, reward* or *punishment.*

פָּרָה p. n. of a man.

פְּרִידָא, פְּרוּדָא p.n. of a man.

פַּרְוָיִם p. n. of a country, same as
סְפַרְוַיִם, which see.

פַּרְוָר *suburb;* see פַּרְבָּר.

פָּרוּר *pot;* see פּוּר.

פָּרַן (Arab. *separated*). see פָּרַץ.

פְּרָז m., *ruler,* Hab. 3:14.

פְּרָזוֹן m., *justice;* with suff. פִּרְזוֹנוֹ,
Jud. 5:7, 11.

פְּרָזוֹת f. pl., *unwalled towns, villages.*

פְּרָזִי m., *one living in a village;*
pl. פְּרָזִים; Ketib פְּרוֹזִים.

פְּרִזִּי p. n., *the Perizzite,* a people of
Canaan.

פַּרְזֶל m. Ch., *iron;* Heb. בַּרְזֶל.

פָּרַח (fut. יִפְרַח).—I. *budded.*—II. *shot
up, flourished.*—III. *spread, extended
itself.* Hiph. *caused to bud, budded.*

פֶּרַח m. (with suff. פִּרְחָם; pl. פְּרָחִים).
—I. *young shoot.*— II. *bud.*—III.
*the artificial representation of a
bud.*

פַּרְוַח p.n. of a man.

פַּרְחָה m., *insolent, with insult,* Job
30:12.

אֶפְרֹחַ m., pl. אֶפְרֹחִים *young of birds.*

פָּרַט *abounded* or *sang;* LXX. ἐπικρο-
τοῦντες, Am. 6:5.

פֶּרֶט m., *omission, what is omitted,*
Lev. 19:10.

פְּרִי *fruit;* see פרה.

פָּרִיץ *wild beast;* see פרץ.

פֶּרֶךְ m., *harshness, oppression.*

פָּרֹכֶת f., *the veil which separates the
holy place from the holy of holies.*

פָּרַם (fut. יִפְרֹם) *rent, torn* (of garments), Leviticus only.

פַּרְמַשְׁתָּא p.n., a son of Haman.

פַּרְנָךְ p.n. of a man.

פָּרַס *broke, distributed, bread.* Hiph.
*dividing the hoof;* see פַּרְסָה.

פְּרַס Ch., *divide.*

פֶּרֶס m., *the osprey,* Lev. 11:13; Deu
14:12.

פַּרְסָה f., *a hoof;* pl. const. פַּרְסוֹת,
פַּרְסֵי.

פָּרַס; פָּרְסִי *a Persian, Parsee*

פָּרַע I. *uncovered the head.*—II. *placed
in a state of disorder,* Ex. 32:25.
III. *was disregarded.*— IV. *left a
road,* Pro. 4:15.— V. *exempted,*
Eze. 24:14.—VI. *avenged,* Jud. 5:
2. Niph. *became lawless,* Pro. 29:
18. Hiph. I. *made idle,* Ex. 5:4.—
II. *brought vengeance on,* 2 Chron.
28:19.

פֶּרַע m., *head of hair;* pl. פְּרָעוֹת,
פְּרָעוֹת, *vengeance,* Deu. 32:42;
Jud. 5:2.

פִּרְעָתוֹן p.n., *a town of Ephraim;*
פִּרְעָתֹנִי *a Pirathonite.*

פַּרְעֹה *title of all monarchs of Egypt*
(lit. φρη *the sun*); Φαραώ.

פַּרְעֹשׁ m.—I. *a flea.*—II. p. n. of a
man.

פַּרְפַּר p.n., *a small river which joins
the Amana near Damascus,* 2 Ki.
5:12.

פָּרַץ (fut. יִפְרֹץ).—I. *broke down, made
a breach in, a wall.*— II. *burst
forth, overflowed* (of water).—III.
*broke in pieces, afflicted.*—IV. *urged*
(a person).—V. *dispersed an enemy*

**VI.** *distributed* persons, 2 Chron. 11:23. Niph. part. נִפְרָץ *much, frequent* (Lee), 1 Sa. 3:1. Pu. *broken down*, Neh. 1:3. Hith. *breaking loose*, 1 Sa. 25:10.

פָּרִיץ m.—**I.** *violent, lawless, person.* —**II.** *wild beast*, Isa. 35:9.

פֶּרֶץ m. (pl. פְּרָצוֹת, פְּרָצִים).—**I.** *breach in a wall.*—**II.** *overflowing of water.*—**III.** *sudden calamity.* —**IV.** p. n. of a man; patron. פַּרְצִי.

מִפְרָץ m., probably, *creek*, marg. (*breach*, Eng. Ver.), Jud. 5:17.

פָּרַק **I.** *pulled off*, with מֵעַל, Gen. 27: 40.—**II.** *tore in pieces*, Ps. 7:3.— **III.** *rescued*. Pi. פֵּרַק **I.** *tore in pieces.* — **II.** *pulled off*, Ex. 32:2. Hith. הִתְפָּרֵק **I.** *was broken off*, Eze. 19:12. — **II.** *pulled off from himself.*

פְּרַק Ch., *break off*, Dan. 4:24.

פֶּרֶק m. (Kri מָרֶק without authority), *fragments*, Isa. 65:4.

פֶּרֶק m.—**I.** *tearing in pieces, prey*, Nah. 3:1.—**II.** *cross way*, Obad. v. 14.

מַפְרֶקֶת f., *vertebræ of the neck*, 1 Sa. 4:18.

פָּרַר *cleft, divided*; inf. abs. פּוֹר. Pil. פּוֹרֵר *cleft*, Ps. 74:13. Hithpo. *was cloven*, Isa. 24:19. Pilp. פִּרְפֵּר *shattered, agitated, the mind*, Job 16:12. Hiph. הֵפֵר, הֵפִיר; with pause הֵפַר **I.** *broke a covenant or command.*—**II.** *frustrated.* — **III.** *annulled.* — **IV.** *withdrew, broke off*. Hoph. הֻפַר *was disannulled.*

פָּרַשׂ (fut. יִפְרֹשׂ).— **I.** *spread.*— **II.** *stretched out the hands.*—**III.** *gave, assisted*, Pro. 31:19.— **IV.** *seized*, Lam. 1:10.— **V.** *broke*, like פָּרַס. Niph. *was scattered*, Eze. 17:21. Pi. פֵּרֵשׂ, with pause פֵּרָשׂ **I.** *spread out the hands.*—**II.** *scattered.*

מִפְרָשׂ m.—**I.** *expansions of*, Job 36: 29.—**II.** *sail of a ship*, Eze. 27:7.

פָּרַשׁ *mark distinctly*, Lev. 24:12. Niph. *scattered*, Eze. 34:12; see פָּרַשׂ. Pu. פֹּרַשׁ **I.** *was marked out distinctly*, Num. 15:34.—**II.** *made clear*, Neh. 8:8. Hiph. *stung*, Pro. 23:32.

פְּרַשׁ Ch., *the same*. Pa. part. מְפָרַשׁ *made clear.*

פֶּרֶשׁ m. (with suff. פִּרְשׁוֹ) *dung.*

פָּרָשָׁה f., *distinct account*, Est. 4:7 , 10:2.

פָּרָשׁ m., pl. פָּרָשִׁים *horses*; בַּעֲלֵי הַפָּרָשִׁים *horsemen.*

פָּרָשׁ, const. פָּרַשׁ m., *horseman*; pl. פָּרָשִׁים.

(פִּתְשֶׁגֶן), (פַּרְשֶׁגֶן) m. Heb. and Ch., *copy of a writing*, Ezra only.

פַּרְשְׁדֹנָה or פַּרְשְׁדוֹן *dung*, as some render, *podex*, as others, Jud. 3:22.

פַּרְשֵׁז *spreading*, Job 26:9

פַּרְשַׁנְדָּתָא p.n., *a son of Haman.*

פְּרָת p.n., *the river Euphrates*, Εὐφράτης.

פָּרָה; see פְּרָת.

פַּרְתְּמִים m. pl., *chiefs, nobles.*

פָּשָׂה *spread itself* (an eruption), Leviticus only.

פָּשַׂע *stepped, trod*, with בְּ, Isa. 27:4

פֶּשַׂע m., a step, 1 Sa. 20:3.

מִפְשָׂעָה f., buttocks, 1 Chron. 19:4

פָּשַׂק opened, expanded, Pro. 13:3.
Pi. the same, Eze. 16:25.

פָּשׂ spreading; see פּוּשׂ·

פָּשַׁח Pi. tore to pieces, Lam. 3:11.
פַּשְׁחוּר p.n. of a man.

פָּשַׁט (fut. יִפְשֹׁט).—I. stripped off his
dress.— II. spread, extended itself,
with אֶל, בְּ, עַל Pi. stripped another. Hiph. I. stripped another.
II. skinned, with מֵעַל. Hith. stripped himself, 1 Sa. 18:4.

פָּשַׁע I. rebelled, rebelled against, with
מִתַּחַת and בְּ. — II. transgressed.
Niph. transgressed against, Pro.
18:19.

פֶּשַׁע m. (with suff. פִּשְׁעִי; pl. פְּשָׁעִים).
—I. rebellion. — II. transgression,
sin.— III. injury (by loss), Ex.
22:8.

פְּשַׁר Ch., interpreted, explained. Pa.
the same.

פְּשַׁר m. Ch., interpretation.

פֵּשֶׁר m. Heb., the same, Ecc. 8:1.

פִּשְׁתָּה m.—I. flax.—II. linen.
פִּשְׁתּוֹ f., a lamp-wick of flax, Isa.
42:3; 43:17; (pl. פִּשְׁתִּים) linen,
Ex. 9:31.

פַּת, פִּתִּים, see פָּתַת; פַּת, see פּוּת·
פְּתָאִים; see פְּתִי·
פִּתְאֹם suddenly; see פֶּתַע·

פַּתְבַּג m. Heb. and Ch., portion of
food, mess.

פִּתְגָּם m. Ch.—I. decree.— II. royal
letter.— III. epistle; Heb. decree,
sentence.

פָּתָה was silly, Deu. 11:16, Job 31:
27. Niph. was persuaded, enticed.
Pi. I. led to folly, persuaded, enticed.—II. deceived.—III. used fair
words to. Pu. pass. of Pi. Hiph.
(fut. apoc. יַפְתְּ) declared foolish,
idolatrous, with לְ, Gen. 9:27.

פְּתוּאֵל p.n. of a man.

פֶּתִי, with pause פֶּתִי m. (pl. פְּתָיִים,
פְּתָאִים).—I. ignorant.—II. foolish
—III. folly, Pro. 1:22.

פְּתַי m. Ch., breadth.

פְּתַיּוּת f., folly, Pro. 9:13.

פָּתוֹר, see פתר; פְּתוֹת, see פתת.

פָּתַח (fut. יִפְתַּח).—I. opened.—II.
uttered, opened his mouth.—III.
opened the ears, Isa. 50:5.—IV.
cleft a rock, Ps. 105:41.— V.
loosened, untied, Isa. 14:17.—VI.
brought out for sale.—VII. drew
a sword, Ps. 37:14. Niph. was
opened, unloosed. Pi. I. opened, &c.,
as Kal.—II. carved, engraved.
Pu. engraven. Hith. loose thyself, Isa. 52:2.

פְּתַח Ch., opened.

פֶּתַח m. (with suff. פִּתְחוֹ; pl. פְּתָחִים,
פְּתָחֵי). — I. opening, gateway,
entrance.—II. door or gate; בְּפֶתַח,
הַפֶּתְחָה, פֶּתַח to the gate.

פֵּתַח m., opening, laying open, Ps.
119:130.

פְּתִיחוֹת f. pl., drawn swords, Ps.
55:22.

פִּתּוּחַ m., engraving, carving.

פִּתְחוֹן, const. פִּתְחוֹן m., opening of
the mouth.

פְּתַחְיָה p.n. of a man.

מַפְתֵּחַ m., key.

מִפְתָּה m., *opening the lips*, Pro. 8 : 6.

פְּתִיגִיל m., "stomacher," Eng. Ver., Isa. 3 : 24, meaning uncertain.

פָּתַל Niph. *was twisted with, struggled together*, Gen. 30 : 8. Hith. *struggled against*, Ps. 18 : 27; תִּתְפַּל for תִּתְפַּתָּל the same, 2 Sa. 22 : 27.

פָּתִיל m.—I. *lace, thread, cord.*—II. *string* for a signet-ring.—III. *plate of gold.*—IV. *cloth for a cover*, Nu. 19 : 15.

פְּתַלְתֹּל m., *perverse*, Deu. 32 : 5.

נַפְתּוּל m., *struggles*, Gen. 30 : 8.

פִּתֹם p. n., a city of Egypt in the vicinity of Goshen, probably Damietta.

פֶּתֶן m., *an asp*.

מִפְתָּן m., *threshold of a door, gate, &c.*

פֶּתַע m.—I. *suddenness.*—II. adv. *suddenly*; בְּפֶתַע the same.

פִּתְאֹם adv., *suddenly, immediately*; בְּפִתְאֹם the same; בְּפֶתַע פִּתְאֹם 'פ, לְפֶתַע and לְפֶתַע 'פ the same; פַּחַד פּ' *sudden fear*.

פָּתַר (fut. יִפְתֹּר) *interpreted, explained*, Gen. chaps. 40 and 41 only.

פִּתְרוֹן m., *interpretation*, Gen. chaps. 40 and 41 only.

פְּתוֹר p. n., the country of the prophet Balaam, probably *Petra*.

פַּתְרֹס p. n., some nation bordering upon Egypt; פַּתְרֻסִים its inhabitants.

פַּתְשֶׁגֶן same as פַּרְשֶׁגֶן.

פָּתַת *broke to pieces*, Lev. 2 : 6.

פַּת f. (with suff. פִּתִּי; pl. פִּתִּים), a *piece, piece of bread*.

פִּתּוֹת m., the same, Eze. 13 : 19.

---

## צ

צֵא, with ה parag. צֵאָה Kal imp, from יצא.

צֵאָה *excrement*; see צוֹא.

צֶאֱלִים m., pl., *trees in dry places, shady bushes*, Job 40 : 21, 22.

צֹאן (צָאוֹן) com.—I. coll. *sheep or goats.*—II. *a flock of sheep or goats.*—III. *a people* (the flock of God).

צַעֲנָן p. n., a city in the tribe of Judah; called also צְנָן.

צֶאֱצָאִים; see יצא.

צֵאת Kal inf., from יצא.

צָבִים ; see צבב.

צָבָא I. *assembled for war, fought.*—II *assembled for a service, performed it.* Hiph. *marshalled an army.*

צָבָא m. (pl. צְבָאוֹת, צְבָאִים Ps. 103 : 21).—I. *an army.*—II. *any multitude*; אַנְשֵׁי הַצָּבָא *soldiers*; שַׂר הַצָּבָא *commander in chief.*—III *warfare, military service.*—IV. *any appointed service* or *trial*, צְבָא הַשָּׁמַיִם *the host of heaven*, i. e.—1. *the stars.*—2. *the angels*; יְהֹוָה צ', אֱלֹהֵי צְבָאוֹת *the Lord of Hosts*, one of the titles of God; see also צְבָאוֹת, צְבָאִים in צְבִי under צְבָה.

צְבוֹיִם, צְבֹאִים p. n., one of the cities of the plain destroyed with Sodom.

צְבָא Ch., *wished, was willing*.

צְבוּ f. Ch., *determination, resolution*, Dan. 6 : 18.

צָבַב (Arab. *hid, concealed*).

צָב m.—I. *a covered waggon*; pl. צַבִּים.—II. *a kind of lizard*, Lev. 11 : 29.

צִבְכָּה p. n. of a woman.

צָבָה I. same as צָבָא; part. צֹבֶה. *waging war.*—II. *burst*, Nu. 5:27. Hiph. *caused to burst*, Nu. 5:22.

צָבֶה m., צָבָה f., *swelling*, Nu. 5:21.

צְבִי m.—I. *beauty, ornament, honour.* — II. *an antelope*; pl. צְבָיִים, צְבָאוֹת; f. צְבָאוֹת.

צְבִיָּה f., *she antelope.*

צִבְיָה p. n. of a woman.

צְבִיָּא p. n. of a man.

צָבַט *took up in his hand*, Ru. 2:14.

צָבַע (Arab. *dyed*).

צְבַע Ch. Pa. *dyed, made wet.* Hith. *was dyed.*

צֶבַע m., *a dyed dress*, Jud. 5:30.

צָבוּעַ m., *hyæna*, Jer. 12:9 (Arab. *hyæna*).

צְבֹעִים p. n., a valley and town of Benjamin.

צִבְעוֹן p. n., a son of Seir.

אֶצְבַּע f. (with suff. אֶצְבָּעוֹ; pl. אֶצְבָּעוֹת).—I. *a finger.*—II. *a toe.* —III. *the hand.*—IV. *a digit.* Ch. the same.

צָבַר (fut. יִצְבֹּר).—I. *heaped up.*—II. *laid up, treasured up.*

צִבֻּרִים m. pl., *heaps*, 2 Ki. 10:8.

צָבַת (Arab. *took in his hand*).

צְבָת m., pl. צְבָתִים *handfuls*, Ru. 2:16.

צָדַד (Arab. *turned the face away*).

צַד m. (with suff. צִדָּה; pl. צִדִּים). —I. *side*, with ה parag. צִדָּה *to the side*; מִצַּד *at the side*; עַל צַד the same.—II. *adversary*, Jud. 2:3.

צַד m. Ch. *side*; מִצַּד *at the side*; לְצַד *against*.

צֵדָד p. n., a town in the north of Palestine.

צִדִּים p. n., a town of Naphtali.

צָדָה *laid wait for*, Ex. 21:13. Niph. *was destroyed*, Zep. 3:6.

צְדָא m. Ch., *perverseness*, Dan. 3:14.

צְדִיָּה f., *lying in wait*, Nu. 35:20, 22.

צָדַק (fut. יִצְדַּק).—I. *was righteous, equitable.*—II. *acted justly.*—III. *was in the right.*—IV. *was acknowledged to be just, in the right.* Niph. *was purified, exculpated*, Dan. 8:14. Pi. *justified, cleared, himself or another.* Hiph. — I. *did justice.*—II. *gave judgment in favour of, acquitted.*—III *justified before God*, Ex. 23:7. Hith. fut. pl. נִצְטַדָּק *cleared himself*, Gen 44:16.

צֶדֶק m. (with suff. צִדְקוֹ).—I. *truth.* —II. *fairness, equity.*—III. *a just cause.*—IV. *acquittal, justification.* V. *righteousness.*

צְדָקָה f.—I. *truth, equity.*—II. *a just cause or claim.*— III. *righteousness.*—IV. *favor, approbation.*

צִדְקָה f. Ch., *equity, righteousness.*

צַדִּיק m.—I. *righteous.*—II. *having a just cause.*— III. *innocent.*—IV *true*, Isa. 41:26.

צָדוֹק p. n. of a man.

צִדְקִיָּה, צִדְקִיָּהוּ p. n.—I. *Zedekiah king of Judah.*—II. also of other men.

צִדְקָתֶךָ Eze. 16:52. Pi. inf., with suff. and f. termination, from צָדַק.

צָהֵב. Hoph. part. מֻצְהָב *of a gold colour*, Ezr. 8:27.

צָהֹב m., *red.*

*I.* צָהַל 1. *neighed.* — 2. *shouted for joy.* Pi. *shouted for joy or sorrow,* with קוֹל. — II. *same as* זָהַר. Hiph. הִצְהִיל *caused to shine,* Ps. 104: 15.

צָהֲלָה f., *neighing.*

צָהַר *same as* זָהַר. Hiph. *made the fine oil called* יִצְהָר, Job 24:11.

צֹהַר m. — I. *a light, window, &c.* — II. *noon.*

יִצְהָר m. — I. *fine olive oil.* — II. p.n. *of a man; patron.* יִצְהָרִי

צַו, צֵו; *see* צָוָה.

צֹא m., *filthy,* Zec. 3:3, 4.

צוֹאָה f., *filth, dung.*

צֵאָה f., *excrement.*

צַוָּאר, צַוָּר, *const.* צַוַּאר m. (pl. צַוָּארֹת; צַוָּארֵי, צַוָּארִים) *neck, shoulder, back;* Ch. *the same.*

צַוְּרֹנִים m. pl., *the neck,* Cant. 4:9.

אֲרַם צוֹבָה *or* צ' צוֹבָא, צוֹבָה p. n., *a city and district of Syria.*

צוּד *hunted, pursued, watched for, men or animals.* Pil. צוֹדֵד *ensnare, beguile.* Hith. הִצְטַיָּד (see צַיִד) *furnished with provisions,* Jos. 9:12.

צַיִד, *const.* צֵיד m. — I. *hunting.* — II. *game, prey.* — III. *provisions (of any kind).*

צֵדָה, צֵידָה f., *provisions.*

צַיָּד m., *hunter,* Jer. 16:16.

צִידוֹן p.n., *Zidon, a city of Phenicia;* צִידֹנִי m., צִידֹנִית f., *a Zidonian.*

מָצָד m. (pl. מְצָדוֹת) *fortress, strong place.*

מָצוֹד m. }
מְצוֹדָה f. } — I. *prey.* — II. *net.* — III. *fortress.*

מָצוֹד m., *hunter's net,* Job 19:6.

מְצֹדָה, מְצוֹדָה f. — I. *prey.* — II. *net* — III. *fortress.*

צָוָה. Pi. צִוָּה (fut. יְצַוֶּה; apoc. יְצַו; imp. צַוֵּה; apoc. צַו). — I. *commanded, gave orders,* with אֶל, עַל, לְ. — II. *appointed.* — III. *caused,* i.e *appointed a thing;* צַוֵּה אֶל בֵּיתוֹ *he gave his last orders to his house,* 2 Sa. 17:23. Pu. צֻוָּה *was commanded.*

צַו, צֵו m., *precept, command.*

צִיּוּן m. — I. *sepulchral monument.* — II. *waymark,* Jer. 31:21.

מִצְוָה f. (pl. מִצְוֹת) *command, precept.*

צָוַח *shouted for joy,* Isa. 42:11.

צְוָחָה f., *cry of sorrow.*

צוּל (Arab. *lay hid*); *see* צָלַל *sank.*

צוּלָה f., *the deep,* Isa. 44:27.

מְצוֹלָה, מְצוּלָה f., *depth (of the sea, &c.)*

צוּם *fasted.*

צוֹם m. (pl. צוֹמוֹת) *fasting.*

צוּע (Arab. *formed, designed*).

מַעֲשֵׂה צ' צַעֲצֻעִים m. pl., *carvings,* 2 Chron. 3:10.

צוֹעֵר, צֹעֵר; *see* צָעַר.

צוּף *flowed,* Lam. 3:54. Hiph. הֵצִיף I. *caused to flow.* — II. *caused to float.*

צוּף m. — I. *honey-comb.* — II. צוּף, צוֹפַי, צִיף p.n., *the son of Elkanah.*

צָפָה f., *overflowing,* Eze. 32:6.

צַפְצָפָה f., *a willow,* Eze. 17:5.

צוּץ; *see* צִיץ.

*I.* צוּק *same as* יָצַק *pour,* Job 28:2; 29:6.

II. צוּק *was in difficulty*, Dan. 9:25. Hiph. הֵצִיק I. *urged, constrained.* —II. *distressed.*

צוּקָה f., *distress.*

מָצוֹק m., *restraint, difficulty, trouble.*

מָצוּק m.— I. *pillars, supports.* — II. *peaks, projections of rocks,* 1 Sa.14:5.

מוּצָק with pause מוּצָק m., *constraint;* see also in יצק.

מְצוּקָה f., *restraint, difficulty, trouble.*

צוּר I. *formed, fashioned.*—II. *tied up money.* — III. *surrounded.* — IV. *overlaid.*—V. *acted hostilely.*—VI. *besieged,* with עַל אֶל.

צוּר m. (pl. צוּרִים, צוּרוֹת).— I. *a rock.* —II. *a refuge* (applied to God).— III. *a stone,* Isa. 8:14. — IV. *a sharp stone used as a knife,* Jos. 5:2, 3.—V. *edge of a sword,* Ps. 89:44.— VI. *form, figure,* Ps. 49: 15.—VII. p. n. of a man.

צֻר m.— I. *a rock,* Eze. 3:9. — II. *a knife,* Ex. 4:25.

צוֹר, צֹר p. n., *Tyre,* the capital of Phenicia, Τύρος; צֹרִי *a Tyrian.*

צוּרָה f., *form, figure,* Eze. 43:11.

צוּרִיאֵל p. n. of a man.

צוּרִישַׁדָּי (*my rock is the Almighty*), p. n. of a man.

צִיר m.—I. *figure, image,* Isa. 45:16. —II. *hinge,* Pro. 26:14. — III. *pangs of a woman in labour;* see also in loc.

צַר m., צָרָה f., *narrow, small, close;* see also in צרר.

צֵר p. n., a town in the tribe of Naphtali.

מָצוֹר m.— I. *restraint.*—II. *siege.* —III. *mound of besiegers.*—IV. *munition, citadel.* — V. p. n., *Egypt,* same as מִצְרַיִם, which see.

מְצוּרָה f., *fortress, citadel, mound.* צֻרוֹתִים ,צֻר; see צָוָּאר.

צוּת. Hiph. הִצִּית *set on fire,* Isa. 27: 4; same as יצת.

צָחֶה root not used; Ch. *thirsted.*

צָחֶה m., *parched,* Isa. 5:13.

צָחָא p. n. of a man.

צָחַח *was white,* Lam. 4:7.

צַח m., צָחָה f.— I. *hot, burning.*— II. *bright, white.* — III. *distinctly, plainly,* Isa. 32:4.

צָחִיחַ m.—I. *dry, bare.*—II. *open, exposed,* Neh. 4:7.

צְחִיחִי m., pl. צְחִיחִים *dry places,* Neh. 4:7.

צְחִיחָה f., *a parched land,* Ps. 68:7.

צַחְצָחוֹת f. pl., *dry places,* Isa. 58: 11.

צָחַן (Arab. *was hot*).

צַחֲנָה f., *the heat of putrefaction, stench,* Joel 2:20.

צָחַק *laughed,* with לְ. Pi. צִחֵק I. *made laughter, joked.*—II. *laughed at, insulted,* with בְּ.

צְחֹק m., *laughter, ridicule.*

יִשְׂחָק, יִצְחָק p. n., *Isaac,* the son of Abraham and Sarah; LXX Ἰσαάκ.

צָחַר m., *whiteness,* Eze. 27:18.

צָחֹר m., *white,* Jud. 10:5.

צֹחַר p. n. of a man.

צִיבָא p. n. of a man.

צִידוֹן ; see צוד. צַיִד ,צֵידָה ,צַיָּד

צִיָּה root not used; (Arab. *drought*).

צִי m. (see צִיָּה), *a ship;* pl. צִיִּים צִים.

צִיָּה f.—I. *drought,* Job 24:19.—II. *parched land, wilderness.*

צִיִּים m. pl., *inhabitants of the desert, men or beasts.*

צִיּוֹן m., *parched land.*

צִיּוּן; see צוה.

צִיּוֹן f. (*citadel*), p. n., *Zion*, the well known hill on and around which Jerusalem was built.

צִין, צִן p.n., *the desert between Canaan and the land of Edom.*

צִינק *fetters*; see צנק.

צִיעַ p. n., *a town of Judah.*

צִיץ (pret. צָץ; fut. יָצִיץ).—I. *flowered.* —II. *flourished.* Hiph. *looked cheerfully*, Cant. 2:9.

צִיץ m.—I. *a flower*; pl. צִצִּים.—II. *anything shining, plate of metal.*— III. *plumage, wings.*—IV. p. n. of a place.

צִיצָה f., *flower*, Isa. 28:4.

צִיצִת f.—I. *lock of hair*, Eze. 8:3.— II. *fringe*, Nu. 15:38,39.

צִקְלַג, צִיקְלַג, צִיקְלָג p.n., *a city of the Philistines in the land of Simeon.*

צִיר Kal not used; (Arab. *went*). Hith. הִצְטַיֵּר *prepared for a journey*, Jos. 9:4.

צִיר m., *person sent on a journey, messenger*; see also in צור.

צְלָגֶל, צְלָה, אֵל; see צלל.

צְלָא Ch. Pa. *prayed.*

צָלָה *roasted*, Isa. 44:16,19.

צָלִי m., *roasted.*

צָלַח, צָלֵחַ (fut. יִצְלַח).—I. *crossed a river.*—II. *fell upon, descended*, with עַל, אֶל — III. *advanced, flourished.*—IV. *was useful, fit*, with לְ. Hiph. הִצְלִיחַ I. *made to pros-*

per, with לְ.—II. *accomplished.*— III. *was prosperous.*

צְלַח Ch. Aph. הַצְלַח I. *made prosperous.*—II. *was prosperous.*

צֵלָחוֹת f. pl., *dishes.*

צְלֹחִית f., *a dish*, 2 Ki. 2:20.

צַלַחַת f., *the same.*

I. צָלַל I. *sank in the water*, Ex. 15: 10.—II. *became shaded*, Neh.13:19. Hiph. part. מֵצֵל *giving shade*, Eze. 31:3.

צְלוּל (צָלִיל) m., *a barley cake*, Jud. 7:13.

צֵלֶל m. (with suff. צִלְלוֹ; pl. צְלָלִים, צִלְלֵי), *a shadow.*

צֵל m. (with suff. צִלֹּה).—I. *a shadow.* —II. *dusk.*—III. *shelter, protection.*

צִלָּה p.n., *Zillah*, the wife of Lamech.

צַלְמָוֶת m., *shadow of death*, applied to any thick darkness.

צַלְמֻנָּע p.n., *a king of the Midianites.*

צַלְפוֹנִי (with art.), p. n. of a man.

מְצִלָּה f., *shady place.*

II. צָלַל I. *tingled (of the ears).*—II. *quivered (of the lips)*, Hab. 3:16.

צְלָצַל, const. צִלְצַל m.—I. *a cymbal.*— II. *a species of locust*, Deu. 28:42. — III. *tumult of an army or shadowing*; see I. צָלַל Isa. 18:1. —IV. *harpoon*, Job 40:31.

צֶלְצְלִים, pl. const. צִלְצְלֵי *cymbals.*

מְצִלָּה f., pl. מְצִלּוֹת.—I. *cymbals.*— II. *bells.*

מְצִלָּה f., dual מְצִלְתַּיִם *pair of cymbals.*

צָלַם root not used; (Arab. *was dark*).

צֶלֶם m.—I. *a shadow*, Ps. 39:7.—II. *an imagination*, Ps. 73:20.—III

representation, picture, image.—
IV. resemblance.

צֶלֶם m. Ch., an image.

צַלְמוֹן (shady ?) p. n., a mountain of
Ephraim.

צַלְמוֹנָה p. n., one of the stations in
the wilderness.

צַלְמָוֶת; see in I. צלל.

צֹלֵעַ part. צֹלֵעַ; f. צֹלֵעָה halting,
lame.

צֶלַע m., limping, falling.

צֵלָע f. (const. צֶלַע, צֵלַע; with suff.
צַלְעוֹ).—I. a rib.—II. a plank
for wainscoting.—III. a side.—IV.
side chamber; pl. צְלָעוֹת; const.
צַלְעוֹת side planks, side chambers;
צְלָעִים folding doors.—V. p. n.,
the town of Benjamin where Saul
was buried.

צֶלַף p. n. of a man.

צְלָפְחָד p. n. of a man.

צֶלְצַח p. n., a piace in Benjamin.

צְלָצַל, צֶלְצָל, צִלְצְלִים; see II. צלל.

צֶלֶק p. n., one of David's captains.

צִלְּתִי p. n. of a man.

צָמֵא, fut. יִצְמָא.—I. thirsted.—II.
earnestly desired.

צָמֵא m., צְמֵאָה f., thirsty.
צָמָא m., thirst.

צִמְאָה f., thirst, Jer. 2:25.
צִמָּאוֹן m., thirsty land.

צָמַד. Niph. was bound, yoked (to
idolatry). Pu. tied, fastened, 2 Sa.
20:8. Hiph. contrived, Ps. 50:19
צָמִיד m.—I. tied, fastened, Nu. 19:15.
—II. a band, bracelet.
צֶמֶד m. (with suff. צִמְדּוֹ; pl. צְמָדִים,

(צְמָדִי).—I. a pair, yoke (of oxen,
&c.).—II. the quantity of land
ploughed in a day by a yoke of
oxen.

צָמוּק; see צמק.

צָמַח (fut. יִצְמַח).—I. shot, grew up.
—II. flourished.—III. sprang up,
arose, began.—IV. produced. Pi.
grew (of hair). Hiph. (fut. יַצְמִיחַ
וַיַּצְמַח) caused to grow, produced.

צֶמַח m. (with suff. צִמְחָהּ).—I. shooting.—II. a shoot.—III. plants.—
IV. the Branch (a title of Christ).

צְמִיתַת; see צמת.

צָמַם root not used; (Arab. tied); Ch.
covered.

צַמָּה f., a woman's veil.

צַמִּים m.—I. noose, snare.—II. destruction.

צָמֵק dry (of the breasts), Hos. 9:14
צִמּוּק m., dry grapes; Ital. simmuki.

צֶמֶר m. (with suff. צַמְרִי), wool.

צַמֶּרֶת f., foliage.

צְמָרִי p. n., an unknown people, Gen.
10:18.

צְמָרַיִם p. n., a town of Benjamin.

צָמַת silenced, destroyed, Lam. 3:53.
Niph. was put to silence. Pi. and
Hiph. put to silence, destroyed.
Pilp. צָמְתֵת the same.

צְמִתֻת f., perfect silence; לִצְמִתֻת,
לִצְמִיתֻת completely (without power
of redemption), Lev. 25:23, 30.

צִמְּתֻתֻנִי Ps. 88:17. Pil. pret. pl.,
with suff., from צמת.

צֵן; see צין.

צִנָּה, צְנֵא; see צאן.

צֶנָה, צֹנִים, צֵנִים ;צִנִּים; see צנן.

צִנּוֹר m., watercourse, cataract.

צָנַח I. dismounted.—II. went down, Jud. 4:21.

צָנַם part., f. pl. צְנֻמוֹת "withered," Eng. Ver.; Gen. 41:23 (meaning not very certain).

צִנִּים m. pl., fence of thorns, thorns.

צְנִינִים m. pl:, thorns.

צִנָּה f.—I. barb of hook, Am. 4:2.—II. a shield.—III. a shield-shaped vessel used for snow, Pro. 25:13.

צִנְצֶנֶת f., a basket, Ex. 16:33.

צָנַן same as צָאַנָן.

צָנַע ready, prepared, Pro.11:2. Hiph. being ready, Mic. 6:8.

צָנַף I. bound, wrapped round, Isa. 22:18.—II. wrapped round the head, Lev. 16:4.

צָנִיף (צָנוֹף) m., turban.

צְנֵפָה f., wrapping, Isa. 22:18.

מִצְנֶפֶת f., turban worn by the high priest.

צָנַק root not used; (Arab. fetters).

צִינֹק m., fetters, Jer. 29:26.

צַנְתָּרוֹת f. pl., pipes, tubes, Zec.4:12.

צָעַד (fut. יִצְעַד; inf., with suff. צַעְדְּךָ). —I. walked, advanced.—II. went over a country.—III. shot up, Gen. 49:22. Hiph. caused to walk, brought over, Job 18:14.

צַעַד m.—I. stepping, Pro. 30:29.—II. a step, 2 Sa. 6:13.—III. progress, action, conduct.

צְעָדָה f., marching; pl. צְעָדוֹת anklets, Isa. 3:20.

אֶצְעָדָה f., bracelet.

מִצְעָד m., step, proceeding.

צָעָה wandering for plunder, losing one's way, perishing. Pi. צָעָה plundered, Jer. 48:12.

צָעִיף m., woman's veil.

צָעִירָה, צָעִיר little; see צער.

צָעַן removed, Isa. 33:20.

צַעֲנַנִּים p. n., a city of the Kenites in Naphtali.

צֹעַן p. n., Zoan, a city of Lower Egypt; possibly Tanis.

צַעֲצֻעִים ;see צוּג.

צָעַק (fut. יִצְעַק) cried out for help, with אֶל, לְ. Pi. cried vehemently, 2 Ki. 2:12. Hiph. cause to be summoned, 1 Sa. 10:17. Niph. I. were called, summoned.—II. assembled themselves.

צְעָקָה const. צַעֲקַת f., a cry for help.

צָעַר was small, of little importance

צֹעַר, צֹעַר p. n., one of the cities of the plain, formerly בֶּלַע.

צָעִיר m., צְעִירָה f.—I. small.—II. young.—III. p. n. of a place, 2 Ki. 8:21.

צָעוּר Ketib, same as צָעִיר, Jer. 14:3; 48:4.

צְעִירָה f., smallness, inferiority in age. מִצְעָר m., little, small; לְמִצְעָר for a little time.

מִצְעִירָה f., of a small kind, Dan. 8:9.

צָפַד adhered, cleaved to, Lam. 4:8.

I. צָפָה I. kept watch.—II. looked for, expected; צֹפֶה observer, watchman.—III. watched, observed, with בְּ, בֵּין.—IV. plotted against, with

ל. Pi. צָפָה I. kept watch.—II. looked, expected help.

צְפִיָּה f., watch-tower, Lam. 4:17.

צָפִית f., watch-tower, Isa. 21:5.

צְפַת p. n., a town of Canaan, afterwards called חָרְמָה.

צְפָתָה p. n., a valley near Maresha in Judah.

מִצְפֶּה m.—I. watch-tower.—II. p. n., a town in Judah.—III. in Moab.—IV. in Gad.—V. in Benjamin.—VI. a valley in the north of Palestine.

מִצְפָּה p. n.—I. a town in Gilead, same as מִצְפֵּה־גִלְעָד.—II. a town in Benjamin, same as מִצְפֶּה.

II. צָפָה covered, overlaid with wood or metal, with בְּ, אֶל. Pu. was overlaid.

צִפָּה s. f.; see צוּף.

צְפוֹ צְפִי p. n., a son of Eliphaz.

צִפּוּי m., covering, coat.

צָפוֹן צְפִיוֹן p. n. of a man; patron. צְפֹנִי.

צְפוֹן צְפוֹנִי; see צפן.

צִפֳּרִים צִפּוֹר; see צפר.

צָפָה (Arab. made broad).

צוֹפַח צֹפַח p. n. of a man.

צַפַּחַת f., a dish, vessel.

צַפִּיחִית f., flat cake, cake.

צָפוֹעַ צְפִיעוֹת; see צפע

צָפִיר צְפִירָה; see צפר.

צָפִית; see צפה.

צָפַן I. hid, concealed. — II. excluded, Job 17:4.—III. laid up, treasured up.—IV. lay hid, lay in wait, with ל: part. צָפוּן a secret, treasure, one hidden (of God). Niph. I. was

hidden, with מִן.—II. was laid up, destined for, with ל. Hiph. hid.

צָפוֹן com. (hidden, dark quarter).—I. the north. — II. the north wind; מִצָּפוֹן לְ, צָפוֹן לְ northward of any where; צָפוֹנָה towards the north; לַצָּפוֹנָה the same; מִצָּפוֹנָה from the north; with ל from the north of any where.—II. p. n., a town of Gad; see also צָפוֹן same as צְפִיּוֹן in II.; צְפַת; see also in בַּעַל.

צְפוֹנִי m., northern, Joel 2:20.

צָפִין (צָפוּן) m., treasure.

צְפַנְיָהוּ, צְפַנְיָה (whom the Lord hath hidden), p. n.—I. Zephaniah, the prophet; LXX. Σοφονίας. — II. other men.

מַצְפּוּן m., hidden place, Obad. v. 6.

צָפְנַת פַּעְנֵחַ the Egyptian title of Joseph; its meaning altogether unknown, Gen. 41:45.

צֶפַע m., basilisk, Isa. 14:29.

צִפְעוֹנִי m. (pl. צִפְעֹנִים) the same.

צָפִיעַ m., pl. צָפִיעִים dung, Eze. 4:15
צְפִיעָה f., pl. צְפִיעוֹת, "issue," Eng. Ver., Isa. 22:24.

צָפַף Pil. צִפְצֵף I. chirped (as a bird), Isa. 10:14, &c.—II. spoke in a low voice.

צַפְצָפָה; see צוּף.

צָפַר hastened (fut. יִצְפֹּר), Jud. 7:3.

צָפִיר m., goat, he-goat.

צְפִיר m. Ch., the same.

צְפִירָה f.—I. a crown, Isa. 28:5.—II. "morning," Eng. Ver., Eze. 7:7, 10; sense uncertain.

צִפּוֹר com. (pl. צִפֳּרִים).—I. a bird.—II. specially, a sparrow.—III. p. n. the father of Balaam the prophet.

צִפּר com. Ch., *a bird.*

צִפּרָה p.n., *the wife of Moses.*

צְפַרְדֵּעַ com., *a frog.*

צִפּרֶן m.—I. *nail of the finger.*—II. *point of the graver.*

צְפָתָה, צְפַת; see צפה.

צֶפֶת f., *capital of a pillar,* 2 Chron. 3:15.

צִצִּים; see צִיץ.

צַק Kal imp., from יצק.

צִיקְלָג same as צְקְלָג.

צִקָלוֹן m., *husk,* 2 Ki. 4:42.

צֶקֶת Kal inf., from יצק.

צַר, צֵר, צֹר, see צור; צָרִי, צֵר, see צרר.

צָרַב. Niph. *was scorched,* Eze. 21:3.

צָרֶבֶת f.—I. *burning,* Pro. 16:27.—II. *inflammation,* Lev. 13:23, 28.

צְרֵדָה p.n., *a town of Manasseh;* צָרְתָן, צְרֵדָה the same.

צֶרָה s. f.; see צרר.

צֳרִי, צֳרֵי, with pause צֳרִי m., *mastich, the gum from the pistachia lentiscus.*

צֹרֵר p.n., same as יִצְרִי; see יָצַר.

צְרוּיָה, צָרְיָה p.n., *the mother of Joab.*

צָרוֹר same as צְרֹר.

צָרַח *shouted,* Zep. 1:14. Hiph. the same, Isa. 42:13.

צְרִיחַ m., *a high tower.*

צֹרֶךְ m., *need, necessity,* 2 Chron. 2:15.

צָרַע, part. צָרוּעַ and Pu. part. מְצֹרָע m., מְצֹרַעַת f., *struck with leprosy.*

צְרוּעָה p.n., *the mother of Jeroboam.*

צָרְעָה p.n., *a town of the Danites in Judah;* צָרְעִי, צָרְעָתִי *a Zarachite.*

צִרְעָה f., coll. *wasps, hornets.*

צָרַעַת f. (with suff. צָרַעְתּוֹ) *the leprosy.*

צָרַף (fut. יִצְרֹף).—I. *refined metals.*—II. *purified a person's character.*—III. *tried a person's character;* part. צֹרֵף *refiner, goldsmith, silversmith;* צָרוּף *purified, pure.* Niph. *shall be purified,* Dan. 12:10. Pi. part. מְצָרֵף *goldsmith,* Mal. 3:2, 3.

צָרְפִי (with art.), p. n. of a man.

צָרְפַת p.n., *a town between Tyre and Zidon,* Σάρεπτα, with ה loc. צָרְפָתָה.

מַצְרֵף m., *crucible.*

צָרַר I. *tied or bound up.*—II. *acted hostilely to.*—III. *was straitened;* part. צֹרֵר *an adversary;* impers. צַר לִי *I am distressed, grieved, concerned for some one,* with עַל. Niph. הֵצַר (inf. הָצֵר) *distressed.* Pu. part. מְצֹרָר.

צַר, with pause צָר m.—I. *difficulty, adversity, distress;* f. צָרָה; בַּצַּר לִי *when I am in distress.*—II. *enemy, besieger.* —III. *rival;* with art. הַצַּר; with suff. צָרִי; pl. צָרִים.—IV. *rock;* see צוּר.

צָרָה f., *enemy, adversary;* with ה parag. בְּצָרָתָה לִי *when I am in trouble.*

צְרֹר, צָרוֹר m. (pl. צְרֹרוֹת) — I. *a bundle.*—II. *a bag of money.*—III. *a small stone, a particle, grain.*—IV. p. n. of a man.

מֵצַר m., *restraint, trouble.*

צְרֵדָה; see צְרֵדָה.

צָרַת p.n. of a man.

**צָרַת הַשַּׁחַר** p. n., a town of Reuben.
**צְרֵתָן**; see **צְרֵדָה**.

# ק

**קֵא** vomit; see **קִיא**.
**קָאם** for **קָם** Kal pret., from **קוּם**.
**קָאֵם** Ch. Pe. part., from **קוּם**.
**קָאַת** (with art. **הַקָּאָת**; const. **קְאַת** f.), a pelican or heron, not certain which.

**קָבַב** cursed; imp. with suff. and נ epenth. **קָבְנוּ**; with ה parag. **קָבָה**.
**קַב** m., a measure, the sixth part of **סְאָה**, 2 Ki. 6:25.
**קֻבָּה** f., alcove, tent, Nu. 25:8, again in the same verse **אֶל קֻבָּתָהּ** "in her alcove" (Lee), generally interpreted of the person of the woman.
**קֻבָּתָהּ, קֵבָה**; see **נקב**.
**קֵבָה** root not used; (Arab. stomach).
**קֵבָה** f., the stomach, Deut. 18:3.
**קֵבָה** (pronounced kŏbāh), Kal imp. with ה parag., from **קבב**.

**קָבַל** Pi. **קִבֵּל** I. accepted.—II. took. — III. undertook, Est. 9:23, 27. Hiph. taking hold of.
**קַבֵּל** Ch. Pa., received, took.
**קָבָל** prep., before, the front, 2 Ki. 15:10.
**לְקָבָל** m. (with suff. **קְבֵלּוֹ** or **קָבֳלוֹ**), opposing, Eze. 26:9.
**קָבֵל, קְבֵל** m. Ch., the front; **לָקֳבֵל** 1. in front of.—2. in consideration of; with **דִּי** in consequence of; **כָּל קֳבֵל דְּנָה** all before that, i. e. for this reason, therefore; **כָּל קֳבֵל דִּי** because.

**קָבְנוּ** Kal imp. with suff. and נ epenth., from **קבב**.

**קָבַע** forsook, neglected.
**קוֹבַע** m., a helmet.
**קֻבַּעַת** f., a drinking cup, Isa. 51: 17, 22.

**קָבַץ** collected, gathered together. Niph. were assembled, assembled themselves. Pi. I. collected.—II. acquired. Pu. was gathered together, Eze. 38:8. Hith. assembled themselves.
**קְבֻצָה** f., collection, heap, Eze. 22:20.
**קִבּוּץ** m., company, troop, Isa. 57:13.
**קִבְצַיִם** (two heaps), p. n., a town in Ephraim.
**יָקְבְצְאֵל, קַבְצְאֵל** p. n., a town of Judah.

**קָבַר** (fut. **יִקְבֹּר**) and Pi. **קִבֵּר** buried. Niph. and Pu. was buried.
**קֶבֶר** m., burial place, sepulchre, with suff. **קִבְרוֹ**; pl. **קְבָרִים, קִבְרֵי**, **קְבָרוֹת, קִבְרוֹת**.
**קִבְרוֹת הַתַּאֲוָה** (the graves of lust), p. n., a place in the wilderness of Sinai, Nu. 11:34.
**קְבֻרָה** const. **קְבֻרַת** f.—1 burial.—II. burial place.

**קָדַד** bowed his head; fut. **יִקֹּד**.
**קִדָּה** f., cassia.
**קָדְקֹד** m. (with suff. **קָדְקֳדוֹ**), crown of the head.
**קָדֹשׁ**; see **קדש**.

**קָדַח** I. struck, kindled a fire.—II. a fire was kindled.
**קַדַּחַת** f., a fever.
**אֶקְדָּח** m., a precious stone, the carbuncle, Isa. 54:12.

**קָדַם** Pi. קִדֵּם I. *preceded, came before.* — II. *came upon, against.* — III. *hastened, was early,* Ps. 119: 147. Hiph. I. *anticipate,* Job 41:3. — II. *come upon any one of* misfortune, Am. 9:10.

קֶדֶם m. (*that which precedes*) — I. adv., *before, in place.* — II. s., *the east*; אֶרֶץ קֶדֶם and קֶדֶם *the east,* i. e. *eastern country*; קֵדְמָה *towards the east*; מִקֶּדֶם *from the east*; with לְ *from the eastward of any place*; בְּנֵי קֶדֶם *those to the east of Palestine.* — III. *antiquity*; מִקֶּדֶם *from of old*; adv. *formerly*; קַדְמֵי אֶרֶץ *the ancient ones of the earth.*

קָדִים m. — I. *the east.* — II. *the east wind*; קָדִימָה *eastward.*

קַדְמֹנִים m. pl., *the ancients,* Jud. 5:21.

קֳדָם,קְדָם Ch. — I. *before.* — II. מִן קֳדָם *from the presence, power of, by order of.*

קַדְמָה f. — I. *former condition.* — II. *origin,* Isa. 23:7. — III. const. קַדְמַת *before* (in time), Ps. 129:6.

קַדְמָה f. Ch., *former state or time;* מִן קַדְמַת דְּנָה *before.*

קִדְמָה f., const. קַדְמַת *eastward of any place.*

קֵדְמָה p. n., *a son of Ishmael.*

קְדֵמוֹת p. n., *a town of the Reubenites.*

קַדְמִי m. Ch., *first, former.*

קַדְמִיאֵל p. n. of a man.

קַדְמֹן m., קַדְמוֹנָה f., *eastern,* Eze. 47:8.

קַדְמֹנִי m. — I. *eastern.* — II. *former, ancient*; pl. קַדְמֹנִים *ancestors*; f.

קַדְמֹנִיּוֹת *former things.* — III. p. n. of a man.

קָדְקֹד *crown of head*; see קדד.

קָדַר I. *was dark, black, darkened.* — II. *was gloomy, distressed*; קֹדֵר *darkening, mourning.* Hiph. *made dark,* Eze. 31:15; 32:7, 8. Hith *became dark,* 1 Ki. 18:45.

קֵדָר (*blackness*), p. n., *Kedar, the son of Ishmael and his descendants*; בְּנֵי קֵדָר *the sons of Kedar.*

קִדְרוֹן p. n., *Kedron, a brook which* flows by Jerusalem.

קַדְרוּת f., *darkness,* Isa. 50:3.

קְדֹרַנִּית adv., *mournfully,* Mal. 3:14.

קָדַשׁ,קָדֵשׁ (fut. יִקְדַּשׁ). — I. *hallowed, consecrated.* — II. *rendered sacred, set apart from,* Isa. 65:5. Niph. I. *was made holy,* Ex. 29:43. — II. *was reverenced,* with בְּ. Pi. קִדֵּשׁ I. *hallowed, set apart.* — II. *reverenced,* Deu. 32:51. — III. *kept holy.* — IV. *rendered sacred by contact,* Eze. 44:19. — V. *purified by rites.* — VI. *appointed a religious service.* — VII. *prepared,* Mic. 3:5. Pu. *was consecrated, &c.* pass. ot Pi. Hiph. I. *hallowed.* — II. *reverenced.* — III. *purified.* — IV. *prepared.* Hith. I. *made himself to be reverenced.* — II. *was celebrated* (a festival). — III. *purified himself.* — IV. *kept himself pure.*

קָדֵשׁ, קָדֹשׁ m. — I. *holy, pure* (of God, angels, and men). — II. *sacred, set apart to God*; pl. קְדֹשִׁים.

קַדִּישׁ m. Ch., *holy.*

קֹדֶשׁ, קוֹדֶשׁ m. (with suff. קָדְשִׁי; pl. קֳדָשִׁים or קָדָשִׁים, const. קָדְשֵׁי). — I. *holiness.* — II. *that which is*

consecrated to God, holy; קֹדֶשׁ
קָדָשִׁים Holy of Holies (the place
within the vail of the tabernacle
and temple).

קָדֵשׁ m. (one devoted to an idol).—I.
Sodomite or, perhaps, priest of
Baal-peor.—II. f. קְדֵשָׁה a harlot.
III. קָדֵשׁ, קָדֵשׁ בַּרְנֵעַ p. n., a city
of the wilderness, between Edom
and Egypt.

קֶדֶשׁ p. n.—I. a town of Judah.—II.
of Naphtali.—III. of Issachar,
called also קִשְׁיוֹן.

מִקְדָּשׁ (מִקְדָּשׁ) m.—I. sanctuary (the
tabernacle or temple).—II. sacred
thing, part, Nu. 18:29.—III. asy-
lum (place of safety).

קָהָה were set on edge (of teeth).
Pi. קֵהָה became blunt (of an instrument), Ecc. 10:10.

קְהָת p. n., Kohath, the son of Levi;
patron. קְהָתִי.

קָהַל Hiph. הִקְהִיל called together,
summoned. Niph. assembled themselves.

קָהָל m.—I. a meeting.—II. assemblage, multitude.—III. הַקָּ׳ the congregation of Israel.

קְהֵלָה p. n., a station of Israel in the
wilderness.

קְהִלָּה f., assembly.

קֹהֶלֶת m. (f., Ecc. 7:27), p. n.
(preacher), applied to Solomon in
the book of Ecclesiastes; LXX.
ἐκκλησιαστής.

מַקְהֵלִים m. pl., congregations, assemblies.

מַקְהֵלוֹת f. pl.—I. the same.—II.
p. n., a station in the wilderness.

קוּ, קַו; see קוה.

קוֹא I. vomited.—II. expelled with disgust. Hiph. הֵקִיא the same.

קָא m., a vomit, Pro. 26:11

קִיא m., the same.

קִיקָלוֹן m., "shameful spewing," Eng
Ver.; Hab. 2:16.

קוֹבֵע; see קבע.

קָוָה hoped in, waited for; part. קֹוֶה.
Pi. קִוָּה (inf. קַוֵּה, קַוֹּה; fut. יְקַוֶּה,
יְקַו).—I. trusted in, expected, with
אֵל, לְ.—II. watched for evil,
plotted against. Niph. assembled
themselves.

קַו, קָו m.—I. a measuring line.—II.
a boundary line.—III. a limit, rule,
direction, Ps. 19:5; with suff
קַוָּם.

קָוֶה m., 1 Ki. 7:23, Ketib for קָו.

מִקְוֶה m.—I. expectation, confidence,
hope.—II. one confided in.—III. collection, assemblage.

מִקְוָה f., collection, repository, Isa.
22:11.

תִּקְוָה f.—I. hope, expectation.—II. a
cord, thread.—III. p. n. of a man.

קוֹחַ; see פקח.

I. קוּט (fut. יָקוּט), was wearied,
loathed, scorned, with בְּ. Niph.
were loathed. Hith. הִתְקוֹטֵט same
as Kal, with בְּ.

II. קוּט (Arab. was broken); fut. יָקוּט
will be broken, Job 8:14.

קוֹל (Arab. he said).

קוֹל m. (with suff. קֹלְךָ, קֹלוֹ; pl.
קֹלוֹת).—I. voice.—II. cry of animals.—III. any sound; קוֹל יְהוָה
the voice of the Lord, thunder.

קוּלְיָה p. n. of a man.

קָל m. Ch., *voice, sound.*

קוּם (fut. וַיָּקָם, יָקָם, יָקוּם).—I. *rose up.*—II. *arose from bed.*—III. *arose from an ambush.*—IV. with עַל, אֶל, בְּ *arose against in anger* (abs. קָמַי *they that rise up against me*).—V. *stood up.*—VI. *began anything.*—VII. *came into being, appeared.*—VIII. *took place.*—IX. *stood, stood firm.*—X. *was permanent* (an office).—XI. *was fixed* (of the eyes). Pi. קִיֵּם I. *strengthened, supported.*—II. *kept a resolution.*—III. *fixed a time.* Pil. קוֹמֵם I. *set up, restore.*—II. *set himself up*, Mic. 2:8. Hiph. הֵקִים (fut. וַיָּקֶם, יָקֶם, יָקִים).—I. *caused to rise up.*—II. *raised up.*—III. *strengthened.*—IV. *set up, fixed.*—V. *raised up, appointed.*—VI. *made or confirmed a covenant, or other engagement.*—VII. *put in force.* Hoph. הוּקַם I. *was set up.*—II. *was appointed.*—III. *was confirmed.* Hith. הִתְקוֹמֵם *arose against*, with לְ.

קוּם Ch. I. *arise.*—II. *stand up.*—III. *stand.* Pa. קַיֵּם *confirmed an engagement.* Aph. הֲקֵים, אֲקֵים (fut. וִיהָקִים, יָקִים).—I. *set up.*—II. *established.*—III. *appointed.*—IV. *confirmed.* Hoph. הֲקִים *was set up*, Dan. 7:4.

קוֹמָה f., *height, stature.*

קִים *an adversary*, Job 22:20.

קִימָה f., *the act of rising up*, Lam. 3:63.

קְיָם m. Ch., *a decree*, Dan. 6:8, 16.

קַיָּם m., קַיָּמָה f. Ch., *enduring, steadfast.*

קָמָה f. (pl. קָמוֹת), *standing corn,* specially *in the ear.*

קָמוֹן p. n., *a town of Gilead.*

קוֹמְמִיּוּת adv., *at full height, erect,* Lev. 26:13.

יְקוּם m., *all that lives,* i.e. *has been raised up*, Gen. 7:4, 23; Deu. 11:6.

מָקוֹם com. (pl. מְקוֹמוֹת).—I. *place.*—II. *habitation, residence.*—III. *room, space.*—IV. *place, country, neighbourhood;* בִּמְקוֹם אֲשֶׁר *in the place where.*

תְּקוּמָה f., *power of resisting*, Lev. 26:37.

תְּקוֹמֵם m., *an adversary*, Ps. 139:21.

קוּן. Pil. קוֹנֵן *uttered a lamentation, lamented*, with עַל, אֶל.

קִינָה f.—I. *lamentation;* pl. קִינִים קִינוֹת.—II. p. n., *a city of Judah.*

קוּס or קָסַם. Pil. קוֹסֵם *cut off*, Eze. 17:9, same as קָצַץ.

קוֹעַ m., *prince*, Eze. 23:23; etymon unknown.

קוֹף *ape*, 1 Ki. 10:22; 2 Chron. 9:21.

קוּף *go round*, like נָקַף; not used.

תְּקוּפָה f.—I. *orbit of the sun*, Ps. 19:7.—II. *circle of the year.*

קוּץ I. *loathed*, with בְּ.—II. *feared*, with מִפְּנֵי.—I. Hiph. הֵקִיץ *besieged*, Isa. 7:6.—II. Hiph.—1. *awoke.*—2. *arose from the dead, came to life.*—3. *was vigilant, active;* קָיַץ from קַיִץ *pass the summer*, Isa. 18:6.

קוֹץ m.—I. *a thorn bush;* pl. קֹצִים, קוֹצֵי.—II. p. n. of a man.

קַיִץ m.—I. *summer.*—II. *summer fruits.*

קְוֻצּוֹת f. pl., *locks of hair*, Cant. 5:2.

קוּר *dig a well.* Pil. קִרְקֵר I. *dug down*, Num. 24:17.—II. *destroyed a people*, Isa. 22:5. Hiph. הֵקִר *threw up water* (a well), Jer. 6:7.

קוּר m., *thread*, Isa. 59:5, 6.

קוֹרַת; see קרה.

מָקוֹו I. *spring.*—II. *origin.*—III. *wife.*

קשׁ (fut. pl. יְקוֹשׁוּן) *ensnared*, Isa. 29:21.

קֵשׁ p.n. of a man.

קִישִׁי, קוּשָׁיָהוּ p.n. of a man.

קִישׁוֹן p.n., *Kishon.*—I. a river of Palestine.—II. a town in Issachar.

קֶשֶׁת com. (pl. קְשָׁתוֹת).—I. *a bow.*—II. *the rainbow.*

קַשָּׁת m., *an archer*, Gen. 21:20.

קַח, in pause קָח, with ה parag. קָחָה Kal imp., from לקח.

קַח for לָקַח, Eze. 17:5; with suff. קָחָם for לְקָחָם, Hos. 11:3.

קַחַת קַחַת, מַחַת Kal inf., from לקח.

קֶטֶב, קֶטֶב m. (with suff. קֶטְבְּךָ) *cutting down, destruction.*

קָטַט same as קוט.

קָטַל *slew.*

קְטַל Ch., *slew.* Pa. קַטֵּל the same. Ithpe. and Ithpa. *was slain.*

קֶטֶל m., *slaughter*, Obad. v. 9.

קָטֹן (fut. יִקְטַן) *was small, of little importance.* Hiph. *made small*, Am. 8:5.

קָטָן קָטֹן m. (pl. קְטַנִּים; f. קְטַנָּה).—I. *small, in size, quantity or importance.*— II. *young.*— III. s. *the little finger*; with suff. קָטְנִי or קְטָנִי.—IV. הַקָּטֹן p.n. of a man.

קָטַף *plucked off.* Niph. *was cut off, withered*, Job 8:12.

קְטַר. Pi. קִטֵּר I. *burnt incense.*—II. *fumigated.*—III. *burnt fat*; part. f. pl. מְקַטְּרוֹת *altars of incense* Pu. part. f. מְקֻטֶּרֶת *was perfumed*, Cant. 3:6. Hiph. הִקְטִיר I. *burnt incense.*—II. *burnt sacrifice.* Hoph. הָקְטַר *was burnt in sacrifice*; part מֻקְטָר *offering of incense*, Mal. 1:11.

קְטוֹרָה f., *incense*, Deu. 33:10.

קְטוּרָה p.n., *Keturah*, one of Abraham's wives.

קְטֹר, pl. חֲצֵרוֹת קְטֻרוֹת "*courts joined*," Eng. Ver.; "*with chimneys*," marg.; *covered* (Ges.), Eze. 46:22.

קְטֹרֶת f., *incense.*

קִיטוֹר m.—I. *smoke.*—II. *vapour*, Ps. 148:8.

מִקְטָר m., *incense*, Ex. 30:1.

מְקְטֶרֶת f., *a censer.*

קְטַר (Syr. *bound*).

קְטַר m. Ch., pl. קִטְרִין—I. *joints, ligatures.*—II. *difficulties.*

קִטְרוֹן p.n. of a place in Zebulun, called also קַטָּת.

קִיא; see קוא.

קָיָה *vomited*; imp. pl. קִיא, Jer. 25:27.

קַיִט m. Ch., *summer*, Dan. 2:35.

קִיטוֹר; see קטר.

קִימָה, קִים, קִים, קִים; see קום.

קִימֹשׁ same as קִמֹּשׁ; see קמשׁ.

קִין root not used; (Arab. *cane, a spear*).

קַיִן m.—I. *a spear made of cane*, 2 Sa 21:16.—II. p.n., *Cain*, the son of Adam.—III. p.n., the *Kenites*, a

tribe of Canaan.—IV. הַקַּיִן a town of Judah.

קֵינִי, קֵנִי, קִינִי the *Kenites*, one of the tribes inhabiting Canaan.

קִינָה; see קוּן.

קֵינָן p. n. of a man.

קַיִץ *summer, &c.*; see קוּץ.

קִיצוֹן, קִיצוֹנָה; see קצץ.

קִיקָיוֹן m., the shrub *palma Christi, ricinus comm.*, κίκι.

קִיקָלוֹן; see קוֹא.

קִיר, קִר com. (pl. קִירוֹת).—I. *a wall.* —II. *side of the altar.*—III. *sides of the heart*, Jer. 4:19.—IV. *city*, Isa. 15:1; 16:7.—V. קִיר מוֹאָב, קִיר חֲרֶשֶׂת, קִיר חֶרֶשׂ p. n., a city of Moab.—VI. p. n., a part of Assyria.

קֵירֹס, קֵרֹס p. n. of a man.

קִישׁ, קִישׁוֹן; see קוּשׁ.

קִיתָרֹס m. Ch., κίθαρις, *a harp.*

קַל, קַלָּה; see קלל.

קָל Ch., קֹל *voice*; see קוֹל.

I. קָלָה I. *roasted.*—II. *burnt alive*, Jer. 29:22. Niph. part. נִקְלֶה *burning disease*, Ps. 38:8.

קָלִי, קָלִיא m., *corn roasted in the ear.*

II. קָלָה same as קָלַל. Niph. *was despised*; part. *despised, mean.* Hiph. *despised*, Deu. 27:16.

קָלוֹן m.—I. *worthlessness.*—II. *shame.* —III. *contempt.*—IV. *pudenda.*

קַלַּחַת f., *a caldron.*

קָלַט (Arab. *deformity*); part. קָלוּט *dwarfish.*

מִקְלָט *asylum, place of refuge.*

קְלִיטָה, קְלָיָה p.n. of a Levite.

קָלַל (fut. יֵקַל, יִקַּלּוּ).—I. *was diminished, became shallow.*—II. *was swift.*—III. *was worthless, unworthy.* Niph. נָקַל, נְקַל (fut. יֵקַל, יִקַּלּוּ).—I. *was thought a small, easy thing*; impers. נָקֵל מִן *it is a small thing that*; עַל־נְקַלָּה *lightly, easily.*—II. *was despised.* —III. *lowered himself*, 2 Sa. 6:22. —IV. *became easy*, Pro. 14:6. Pi. קִלֵּל *revile, wished ill to*, with בְּ. Pil. קִלְקֵל I. *shook arrow in divination*, Eze. 21:26 (like the Arab. *removed, shook*). Hiph. הֵקַל I. *slighted.*—II. *lightened, removed a load*, with מֵעַל, מִן. Hithpal *was shaken*, Jer. 4:24.

קַל m. (pl. קַלִּים; f. קַלָּה).—I. *swift.* —II. *swiftly.*—III. *swift-footed.*

קַלַּי p. n. of a man.

קָלָל m., *polished, shining.*

קְלָלָה, const. קִלְלַת f.—I *reviling.*— —II. *a curse.*—III. *object of reviling.*

קְלֹקֵל m., *worthless food*, Nu. 21:5.

קָלַס. Pi. and Hith. *mocked, scorned.*

קֶלֶס m., *scorn, contempt.*

קַלָּסָה f., the same, Eze. 22:4.

קָלַע I. *cut out, carved.*—II. *slung*, Jud. 20:16.—III. *expelled*, Jer. 10:18; קֹלֵעַ *a slinger.* Pi. *slung a stone.*

קֶלַע m. (with suff. קַלְעוֹ; pl. קְלָעִים) —I. *a sling.*—II. *a curtain*, from its tremulous motion.

קַלָּע m., pl. קַלָּעִים *slingers*, 2 Ki. 3:25

מִקְלַעַת f., *carving, sculpture*, 1 Ki only.

קַלְקַל; see קלל.

קַלְּשׁוֹן m., 'קִ שִׁלֹשׁ three pronged pitch-fork, 1 Sa. 13:21.

קְמוּאֵל p.n. of a man.

קָמוֹן, see קוּם; קָמוֹשׁ, see קמשׁ.

קֶמַח m., flour.

קָמַט (Arab. bound with a rope), bound as a captive, Job 16:8. Pu. was seized and carried off, Job 22:16.

קָמֵל, קָמַל withered.

קָמַץ grasped, took up in the hand.

קֹמֶץ m. (with suff. קֻמְצוֹ).— I. the hand, fist.— II. abundance.— III. pl. קְמָצִים handfuls.

קמשׁ root not used.

קִמּוֹשׁ, קִימוֹשׁ, pl. קִמְּשׂוֹנִים m., nettles.

קֵן, קֵן, קֵנִים; see קנן.

קָנָא. Pi. קִנֵּא I. was jealous for, with לְ (ζηλοῦν).—II. emulated, with בְּ; envied, with בְּ, לְ.—III. was jealous of, with בְּ. Hiph. הִקְנִיא made jealous, angry.

קַנָּא m., jealous (of God against idols only).

קַנּוֹא m., the same.

קִנְאָה f.—I. jealousy.—II. envy.—III. anger.—IV. zeal.

קָנָה (fut. apoc. וַיִּקֶן).— I. make.— II. acquire, appropriate to one-self. Niph. was acquired, pur-chased, Jer. 32:15, 43. Hiph. I. appropriated as a slave, Zec. 13: 5.—II. provoked to jealousy, Eze. 8:3.

קְנָא Ch., acquired, procured, Ezr. 7: 17.

קְנָת p.n., a town of Manasseh.

קִנְיָן m., possession, wealth.

מִקְנֶה m. (with suff. מִקְנֵהוּ; pl. מִקְנִים) possession, wealth of land, flocks, cattle; אַנְשֵׁי מ' possession of cattle; אֶרֶץ מ' land full of cattle.

מִקְנָה f., acquirement, purchase, pos-session.

מִקְנֵיָהוּ p. n. of a man.

קָנֶה m. (const. קְנֵה; with suff. קָנֶה; pl. קָנִים, קְנוֹת).— I. reed, cane.— II. sweet cane. — III. measuring reed of six cubits.— IV. beam of the balance.—V. stalk of wheat.— VI. branch of candlestick.— VII. arm-bone above the elbow, Job 31: 22.—VIII. a staff to lean upon.

קָנָה p.n.— I. a place on the borders of Ephraim and Manasseh.—II. a town in Asher.

קַנּוֹא same as קַנָּא; see קנא.

קֵנַז p.n.— I. of a man; קְנִזִּי patron.— II. of a people of Canaan.

קֵנִי same as קֵינִי.

קִנָּמוֹן, const. קִנְּמָן m., cinnamon.

קָנַן. Pi. קִנֵּן built a nest. Pu. part. מְקֻנַּנְתִּי(ב)was built (of a nest).

קֵן, const. קַן־ m. (with suff. קִנּוֹ; pl. קִנִּים).— I. a nest.—II. a dwelling —III. a family.—IV. cells, cham-bers.

קַנְצֵי for קַצֵּי, Job 18:2; see קֵץ in קצץ.

קָסַם divine with arrows, &c.; part. קֹסֵם diviner.

קֶסֶם m.— I. divination, enchant-ment.—II. the reward of divina-tion.

מִקְסָם m., *divination*, Eze. 12:24; 13:7.

קָסַם; see קוס.

קֶסֶת; see קשה.

קְעִילָה p. n., a city of Judah.

קַעֲקַע m., *mark, impression*, Lev. 19:28.

קָעַר root not used; (Arab. *being deep*). קְעָרָה f. (const. קַעֲרַת; pl. קְעָרֹת, מְעָרוֹת; with suff. קְעָרוֹתָיו) *deep saucer, dish*.

קָפָא I. *congealed* (of waters).— II. *hardened* (of men), Zep. 1:12. Hiph. *condense*, Job 10:10.

קִפָּאוֹן m., *congealing, denseness*, Zec. 14:6.

קָפַד (Arab. *finished his work*). Pi. *finished, cut short*, Isa. 38:12.

קְפָדָה, with ה parag. קִפָּדָה m., *destruction*, Eze. 7:25.

קִפֹּד m., *a hedge-hog*; (Arab. the same).

קִפּוֹז (Arab. *springing serpent*). קִפּוֹז m., *one of the springing snakes*, Isa. 34:15.

קָפַץ *shut up, close, constrict* (the hand, &c.)— Niph. *are shut up*, Job 24:24. Pi. *leaping*, Cant. 2:8.

קֵץ *end*; see קצץ.

קָצַב I. *cut wood*, 2 Ki. 6:6.—II. *shear sheep*, Cant. 4:2.

קֶצֶב m., *clefts of the mountains*.—II. *form, character*, Jon. 2:7.

קָצָה I. *cut off, destroy*.—II. *cut down*. Pi. *cutting off, down*, 2 Ki. 10:32; Pro. 26:6. Hiph. *cut, scraped, off*; inf. הַקְצוֹת.

קָצֶה m. (const. קְצֵה; with suff. קָצֵהוּ; pl. קְצָיִם, קְצֵי) *end, extremity, limit*; הָעָם מִקְצֵה *men from all parts*; מִקְצֵה שְׁלֹשֶׁת יָמִים *at the end of three days*.

קֵצֶה m., the same.

קָצָה f., *extremity, border, limit*; מִקְצָה *from the extreme parts*; pl. קָצוֹת, with הָעָם *the extremities of the people*, i. e. any of them.

קְצָה f. Ch., *end*.

קָצְוּ m., pl. const. קַצְוֵי *extremities, borders*.

קְצָווֹת f. pl., the same.

קְצָת f.—I. *end, limit*; מִקְצָת יָמִים עֲשָׂרָה *at the end of ten days*.— II. Ch. *a part*.

קָצִין m.—I. *judge*.—II. *governor*.—III. *prince*.

מִקְצָת f., *part, limit*.

קֶצַח m., *black pepper*, Isa. 28:25, 27.

קָצִיר *harvest*; see קצר.

קָצַע Hiph. הִקְצִיעַ *scrapes off*, Lev. 14:41. Pu. part. מְקֻצָעוֹת and Hoph. part. מְהֻקְצָעוֹת *small courts*, Eze. 46:22.

קְצִיעָה f., κασσία.—I. *cassia*, Ps. 45:9. —II. p. n., a daughter of Job, *Keziah*.

מִקְצוֹעַ m., *corner, angle*; pl. מִקְצֹעִים, מִקְצֹעוֹת.

מַקְצֻעָה f., "*planes*," Eng. Ver., Isa. 44:13.

קָצַף *was angry, wroth, enraged*, with אֶל, עַל. Hiph. *made angry*, with אֶת. Hithp. *became wroth*, Isa. 8:21.

קְצַף Ch., *was angry*.

קֶצֶף m.—I. *a broken branch, stick*,

Hos. 10:7. — II. *anger, wrath of God*, with suff. קִצְפּוֹ, קִצְפִּי.

קְצַף m. Ch., *anger.*

קְצָפָה f., *fracture, wasting*, Joel 1:7.

קָצַץ *cut off.* Pi. קִצֵּץ, קִצֵּץ *cut off.* Pu. part. מְקֻצָּצִים, Jud. 1:7.

קְצַץ Ch. Pa. *cut off.*

קֵץ m. (with suff. קִצּוֹ; pl. קָצִים, קִצֵּי).
—I. *end, limit.*—II. *end, cessation.*
—III. *end, ruin;* מִקֵּץ *from the end* (of the earth), *at the end* (of a time);* לְקֵץ *the same;* עֵת קֵץ, קֵץ הַיָּמִים, מוֹעֵד קֵץ *the time of the end*, i.e. of our Lord's first and second advent.

קִיצוֹן m., קִיצוֹנָה f., *the last*, Exodus only.

I. קָצַר (fut. יִקְצֹר), *cut down, reap;*
*part. reaper.* Hiph. *reaped*, Job 24:6.

קָצִיר I. *crop.* — II. *harvest.* — III. *branches.*

II. קָצַר (fut. יִקְצַר).—1. *short, deficient, unable for.*—2. with רוּחַ or נֶפֶשׁ *unable to bear up, discouraged.* Pi. קִצֵּר *made short*, Ps. 102:24. Hiph. *made short*, Ps. 89:46.

קָצֵר m., *short, cut off;* קְצַר אַפַּיִם, ק' רוּחַ *angry.*

קֹצֶר m., with רוּחַ *impatience*, Ex. 6:9.

קָר, קָרִים, קַר; *see* קָרַר.
קַר *same as* קִיר.

I. קָרָא (inf. קְרֹא, קְרֹאות with suff. קָרְאִי; imp. קְרָא; fut. יִקְרָא).—
1. *cried, called, shouted.*—2. *called to or for*, with אֶל.—3. *called after*, with אַחֲרֵי.—4. *call upon* in *prayer.*—5. *celebrate.*—6. *call*

*by name, name*, with לְ.—7. *call together, assemble, invite*, with אֵת, אֶל.—8. *called into question litigation.*—9. *appointed to an office.*—10. *called forth soldiers*, Isa. 13:3. — 11. *proclaim, publish, preach.*—12. *read from a book, read aloud.* Niph. נִקְרָא 1. *called for, summoned.*—2. *called together, assembled*, with בְּ or בְּשֵׁם פ' *in the name of some one.*—3. *named*, with עַל, שֵׁם פ' *the name of some one is upon thee*, with שֵׁם יְהוָה עַל *the name of the Lord is named upon thee*, Deu. 28:10. Pu. קֹרָא *called, named*, with לְ.

קְרָא Ch., *read, recited, proclaimed.* Ithp. *was called*, Dan. 5:12.

קֹרֵא m.—I. *partridge.*—II. p. n. of a man.

קָרִיא m., *called, sent*, Numbers only.

קְרִיאָה f., *cry, proclamation*, Jon. 3:2.

מִקְרָא m.—I. *act of assembly.*—II. *convocation.*—III. *reading, reciting*, Neh. 8:8.

II. קָרָא *same as* קָרָה 1. *approached, met hostilely.*—2. *met.*—3. *happened;* inf. קִרְאָה, לִקְרַאת *to meet, meeting with;* with suff. לִקְרָאתֶךָ *over, against thee;* לִקְרָאתְכֶם *over against you.* Niph. 1. *met, happened to meet*, with עַל.—2. *happened;* fut. יִקָּרֵא; inf. נִקְרָא. Hiph. *cause to happen to*, Jer. 32:23.

קִרְאָן for קִרְאֶנָּה Kal imp. pl. f., Ex. 2:20, from I. קרא

קְרֹאות Kal inf., with ו quiescent, Jud 8:1, from I. קרא

קָרֵב, קָרַב (fut. יִקְרַב; inf. קְרֹב; קָרְבָה; imp. קְרַב).—I. *approached drew near*, with לִפְנֵי, בְּ, לְ, אֶל.—II. *attacked*, with עַל.—III. *keep by thyself*, with אֶל. Isa. 65:5. Niph. *should, ought to draw near*. Pi. קֵרֵב *made, caused to draw near*. Hiph. I. *made approach.*— II. *presented.*—III. *removed*, with בְּ, מִן.

קְרֵב Ch., *came to*. Pa. *offered*. Aph. *brought to, offered*.

קָרֵב m., *approaching, drawing near*.

קָרוֹב m., קְרוֹבָה f., *near, at hand*, with אֶל, לְ (*of time, place, things*, &c.); מִקָּרוֹב adv., *short, shortly, soon*.

קְרָב m., *contest, battle, war*; pl. קְרָבוֹת.

קְרָב m. Ch., *the same*.

קֶרֶב m. (with suff. קִרְבִּי; pl. with suff. קְרָבַי).—I. *inward part, entrails.*—II. *amidst, among*, often מִקֶּרֶב, בְּקֶרֶב *the same*.

קִרְבָה const. קִרְבַת f., *approach, access*.

קָרְבָּן const. קָרְבַּן m., *offering*.

קֻרְבָּן m., *the same*.

קָרְבָתָם Kal inf., with ה parag. and suff., from קְרַב.

קַרְדֹּם (with suff. קַרְדֻּמּוֹ; pl. קַרְדֻּמִּים, קַרְדֻּמּוֹת), *an axe*.

קָרָה s. f.; see קרר.

קָרָה (וַיִּקֶּר, יִקְרֶה; see קָרָא II. (fut. *met, happened*, with לְ. Niph. *met with persons only*, with לִפְנֵי, אֶל, עַל *met accidentally, dropped in with*. Pi. קֵרָה *framed together, made to join*. Hiph. I. *made, caused to meet with him*, Gen. 27:20.—II. הִקְרָה לוֹ *made convenient for him*, Nu. 35:11.

קֶרֶה m., קְרֵה־לָיְלָה *accidental pollution during sleep*, Deu. 23:11.

קוֹרָה f.—I. *a beam.*—II. *a roof*, Gen 19:8.

קְרִי in pause קֶרִי m., *meeting, opposing*; בִּקְרִי or הָלַךְ קְרִי עִם *he opposed, resisted*.

קִרְיָה f., *a town* or *city*, combined in the names of many cities.—I. קִרְיַת in the tribe of Benjamin.—II. קִרְיַת אַרְבַּע in the tribe of Judah, afterwards Hebron.—III. ק' בַּעַל same as ק' יְעָרִים.—IV. ק' חֻצוֹת in Moab.—V. ק' עָרִים, ק' יְעָרִים in Judah.—VI. ק' סֵפֶר, ק' סַנָּה in Judah, called also ק' דְּבִיר — VII. קִרְיָתַיִם 1. in Reuben.—2. in Naphtali, called also קַרְתָּן.—VIII. קְרִיּוֹת in Moab. קִרְיָא, קִרְיָה Ch.

קֶרֶת f.—I. *a city.*—II. *a pulpit*, Job 29:7.

קַרְתָּה p. n., a town of Zebulun.

מִקְרֶה m.—I. *accident.*—II. *event, result*.

מְקָרֶה m., *building, edifice*, Ecc.10:18.

קָרַח and Hiph. הִקְרִיחַ *shaved, made bald*. Niph. and Hoph. *have made themselves, become, bald*.

קֹרַח p. n. of a man.

קֵרֵחַ m., *bald* (on the crown of the head).

קֶרַח m.—I. *cold.*—II. *frost, ice.*—III. *crystal*, Eze. 1:22.

קֹרַח m.—I. *frost, ice*, Ps. 147:17.— II. p. n., *Korah*, a son of Esau.— III. a son of Eliphaz.—IV. the Levite who conspired against Moses, patron. קָרְחִי.—V. applied to other men.

קָרְחָה, קָרְחָא f., *baldness*.

קָרַחַת f., *thread bare* (of cloth), Lev. c. 13 only

קְרִיּוֹת ,קִרְיַת ,קִרְיָה ,קְרִי; see קרה.
קִרְיָה ,קְרִיאָה; see קרא.

קָרַם overlaid, cased, with עַל; fut. יִקְרַם Eze. 37:6, 8.

קֶרֶן f. (dual. קַרְנַיִם, pl. קְרָנוֹת, קְרָנוֹת).—I. the horn of an animal.—II. used as a vessel for oil. —III. used as a trumpet, Jos. 6:5. —IV. Isa. 5:1, " a very fruitful hill," Eng. Ver.; " a horn, the son of oil ;" marg. perhaps Mount Tabor.—V. metaphorically, power, strength, in men or states.—VI. probably the name of a weapon, 2 Sa. 22:3.—VII. the ornaments at each corner of the altar.—VIII. rays of light, Hab. 3:4.

קֶרֶן com. Ch., horn.

קָרַן v. denom., emitted rays, shone (the face of Moses), Exodus c. 34 only. Hiph. produced horns, Ps. 69:32.

קָרַס became bent, bowed down, Isa. 46:2.

קֶרֶס m., hook, link, loop.

קֶרֶס same as קֶרֶם.

קַרְסֻלַּיִם m. dual, ankles.

קָרַע tore, rent (as a garment, &c.); once, of the eyes, Jer. 4:30, "thou rendest thine eyes with stibium," i. e. givest them an enlarged appearance as if they were torn open; this is the effect of it. Niph. was torn, rent.

קְרָעִים m. pl., rendings, pieces, rags.

קָרַץ closed, pressed together (the lips or eyes, denoting fraud or cunning). Pu. was cut, hewn out, Job 33:6.

קָרֶץ m., destruction, Jer. 46:20.

קְרַץ m. Ch., rending.

קַרְקַע m.—I. basis, foundation of the Tabernacle.— II. p.n., a town of Judah.

קַרְקֹר p. n. of a place.

קָרַר (Arab. was cold, quiet).

קַר or קָר m., cold water; pl. קָרִים cool, quiet, Pro. 17:27.

קֹר m., cold (season), Gen. 8:22.

קָרָה f., cold, chilliness.

מְקֵרָה f., coolness, refreshing, Jud. 3: 20.

קָרַשׁ (Arab. he cut).

קֶרֶשׁ m.—I. plank or board.—II. bench of a ship, Eze. 27:6.

קַרְתָּן ,קַרְתָּה ,קָרֶת; see קרה.

קָשָׂה (Arab. wicker basket).

קְשָׂוֹת, קְשָׂווֹת f. pl., small vessel, patten, phial, or the like.

קֶסֶת f., inkhorn carried in the girdle, Eze. 9:2, 3, 11.

קַשְׂקֶשֶׂת m., pl. קַשְׂקַשִׂים.—I. scales of a fish.— II. scale armour, 1 Sa. 17:5.

קַשְׂקֶשֶׂת f., the same.

קֶשֶׁט (Arab. pair of scales).

קְשִׂיטָה f., a piece of silver, weighed out to pass for a given value as money.

קֹשׁ; see קושׁ.

קְשָׂאִים; see קשה.

קָשַׁב (fut. יִקְשַׁב) attend, listen, Isa. 32:3. Hiph. attended to, regarded with בְּ, לְ, עַל, אֶל.

קֶשֶׁב m., attention, hearkening.

קַשָּׁב, f. קַשֶּׁבֶת attentive, Neh. 1:6, 11.

קָשֻׁב, f. pl. קַשֻּׁבוֹת attentive.

קָשָׁה I. was hard, grievous.—II. was difficult, Deu. 1:17. Niph. part. נִקְשֶׁה subject to difficulty, Isa. 8:21. Pi. hardened (fut. apoc. וַתְּקַשׁ). Hiph. הִקְשָׁה (fut. apoc. וַיֶּקֶשׁ).—I. hardened.—II. made grievous, difficult.—III. made refractory, Pro. 28:14; Job 9:4.

קָשֶׁה m., קָשָׁה f.—I. obdurate, unyielding, cruel.—II. with עֹרֶף stiff-necked, obstinate.—III. with פָּנִים impudent, Eze. 2:4.—IV. hard, grievous (of servitude).—V. with רוּחַ overwhelmed, depressed, 1 Sa. 1:15.

קְשִׁי m., obstinacy, Deu. 9:27.

קִשְׁיוֹן p.n., a place in Issachar; קֶדֶשׁ the same.

קִשֻּׁאִים m. pl., cucumbers, Nu. 11:5.

מִקְשֶׁה m., wreathed work.

מִקְשָׁה f.—I. wreathed work.—II. place, garden, of cucumbers, Isa. 1:8.

קָשַׁח. Hiph.—I. made obdurate, Isa. 63:17.—II. treated hardly, Job 39:16.

קֹשֶׁט קֹשְׁט m., religious truth.

קְשׁוֹט m. Ch., truth.

קָשַׁר (fut. יִקְשֹׁר).—I. tied, bound; part. קָשׁוּר bound, firm.—II. conspired against. Niph. bound, made firm, sure, Neh. 3:38; metaph., 1 Sa. 18:1. Pi. I. bind on (as ornaments), Isa. 49:18.—II. secure to thyself, Job 38:31. Pu. part. f. מְקֻשָּׁרוֹת compact, Gen. 30:41. Hith. conspired.

קֶשֶׁר m. (with suff. קִשְׁרוֹ) conspiracy, treason.

קְשֻׁרִים m. pl., bandages, belts.

קָשַׁשׁ collect, assemble together, Zep. 2:1. Po. קֹשֵׁשׁ collect, gather. Hithpo. assemble yourselves, Zep. 2:1.

קַשׁ m.—I. stubble.—II. chaff.

קֶשֶׂת קָשֶׂת; see קוּשׁ.

קִיתָרֹס same as קַתְרֹס.

## ר

רָאָה (inf. abs. רָאֹה, רָאוֹ; const. רְאוֹת, רְאֵה; imp. רְאֵה; fut. יִרְאֶה; apoc. וַתֵּרֶא, וַיַּרְא, וַיֵּרֶא).—I. saw, viewed, observed, with לְ.—II. looked out, provided, chose, cared for, with עַל, בְּ, אֶל.—III. visited (a sick person, &c.).—IV. saw the sun, lived, Ecc. 7:11.—V. perceived, found, felt, with בְּ.—VI. discern, discriminate (as a soothsayer). Niph. נִרְאָה (inf. הֵרָאֹה, הֵרָאוֹת; imp. הֵרָאֵה; fut. יֵרָאֶה; apoc. וַיֵּרָא).—I. was seen, apparent, appearing, with אֶת־פְּנֵי, לְ, אֶל.—II. was provided. Pu. רֹאוּ were seen, Job 33:21. Hiph. הֶרְאָה, הִרְאָה (fut. וַיַּרְא, יַרְאֶה).—I. showed.—II. see, experience, evil, with בְּ. Hoph. הָרְאָה.—I. was seen.—II. was shown. Hith. הִתְרָאָה looked at each other.

רָאָה, Deu. 14:13, an incorrect reading for דָּאָה, a vulture or kite.

רֹאֶה m., seer, prophet.

רַאֲוָה, Eze. 28:17, Kal inf., from ראה.

רְאוּת, רְאִית seeing, viewing, Ecc. 5:10.

רְאוּבֵן (behold a son!), p.n., Reuben, Jacob's eldest son; patron. רְאוּבֵנִי a Reubenite.

רְאִי m., mirror, Job 37:18

רֳאִי with pause רֹאִי m.—I. vision, revelation.—II. appearance, sight.—III. monstrosity, Nah. 3:6.

רְאָיָה p.n. of a man.

רֵוּ m. Ch., aspect, appearance.

מַרְאֶה m.—I. vision, appearance.—II. view, sight.

מַרְאָה f.—I. vision (seen by a seer).—II. mirror, Ex. 38:8.

רָאַם was raised, elevated, Zec. 14:10.

רְאֵם m. (pl. רְאֵמִים, רְאָמִים, רֵמִים) buffalo, wild ox; LXX. unicorn, μονόκερως.

רָאמוֹת f. pl.—I. things high, sublime, Pro. 24:7.—II. most precious.—III. p.n.: (a) a town of Issachar; (b) of Gilead.

רְאוּמָה p. n. of a woman.

רָאמַת נֶגֶב p.n., same as רָמוֹת נֶגֶב; see רוּשׁ.

רֹאשׁ, רֵאשׁ m. (pl. רָאשִׁים; with suff. רָאשֵׁיהֶם.(רֹאשׁוֹ, רָאשָׁיו—I. head of man or beast.—II. chief, leader.—III. metropolis, chief city.—IV. top of a mountain, &c.—V. first, chief, principal of any thing; רֹאשׁ שִׂמְחָה chief joy.—VI. capital, amount, sum (of numbers, money, &c.).—VII. source, commencement (of a river).—VIII. an unknown poisonous plant, poison. Phrases: נָשָׂה רֹאשׁ מֵרֹאשׁ appointed a chief; from the beginning; רֹאשׁ חֳדָשִׁים the first month (of the year); רֹאשׁ

פִּנָּה head stone of the corner; רֹ דֶּרֶךְ a cross way, Eze. 16:25; רֹ חוּצוֹת the head of the streets, רָאשִׁים sources of rivers, Gen. 2:10

רֹאשׁ m. Ch. (pl. רֵאשִׁין, רָאשִׁין)—I. head.—II. chapter, summary, Dan. 7:1.

רֹאשָׁה f., אֶבֶן הָרֹאשָׁה head stone, Zec. 4:7.

רֵאשָׁה f., beginning, Eze. 36:11.

רַאֲשֹׁתָי pl. const. רַאֲשׁוֹת the part about the head (of Saul), 1 Sa. 26:12.

רִישׁוֹן (for רִאישׁוֹן), רִאשׁוֹן m.—I. first, former, foremost (in time, place, dignity, &c.); pl. רִאשֹׁנִים ancestors; מֵרִאשׁוֹן from the beginning; f. רִאשֹׁנָה the same.—II. adv. formerly; בָּרִאשֹׁנָה in front; כְּבָרִאשֹׁנָה as formerly, Isa. 1:26; לָרִאשֹׁנָה formerly; pl. רִאשֹׁנוֹת former things.

רִאשֹׁנִי, f. רִאשֹׁנִית first, Jer. 25:1.

רֵשִׁית, רֵאשִׁית f.—I. first, former, in state or time.—II. firstfruits, firstborn.—III. first of way, beginning.

מַרְאֲשֹׁות f. pl., places or things where the head is.

מַרְאֲשֹׁות f. pl., the same; with suff. מַרְאֲשֹׁתָיו at his head.

מָרֵשָׁה, מַרְאֵשָׁה p. n.: (a) a fortress of Judah, Μαρισά; (b) of a man.

רֹשׁ, רֹאשׁ m., poison; see רֹאשׁ.

רֹאשׁ p.n., a northern nation: probably the Ῥῶς of the Byzantine authors; now Russia.

רֵב same as רִיב.

רָבַב (pret. רַב, inf. רֹב).—I. became many, numerous. Pu. see רְבָבָה.

רַב m. (in pause רָב, pl. רַבִּים; f. רַבָּה, pl. רַבּוֹת).—I. much, many. — II. abundant, enough. — III. great, vast, in extent, station, dignity, &c.

רַבָּה (metropolis) p. n. — I. the chief city of Ammon.—II. a city of Judah.

רַב m. Ch. (pl. רַבְרְבִין). — I. great, large.—II. s., great men, nobles.

רֹב, רוֹב, רָב־ m. (with suff. רֻבְּכֶם) multitude, abundance. לָרֹב abundantly.

רְבָבָה f., ten thousand, myriad; pl. רִבָּבוֹת, רְבָבוֹת myriads. Pu. denom. part. מְרֻבָּבוֹת increased to myriads, Ps. 144:13.

רִבּוֹא, רִבּוֹ f., the same; dual רִבּוֹתַיִם two myriads; pl. רִבֹּאוֹת, רִבּאוֹת, רִבּוֹת myriads.

רִבּוֹ Ch., the same; pl. רִבְוָן (רִבְבָן).

רְבִיבִים m. pl., showers.

רַבִּית p. n., a city of Issachar.

רַבְרְבָן m. Ch., a prince.

רַבְשָׁקֵה p. n., Rabshakeh, leader of the Assyrians.

II. רָבַב shot, as arrows, &c. Pret. pl. רֹבּוּ.

רָבַד spread, strewed, made up, Pro. 7:16; (Arab. tied, bound).

רָבִיד m., collar, neck-chain; (Arab. the same.)

מַרְבַדִּים m. pl., coverlets.

רָבָה (fut. יִרְבֶּה, apoc. יֵרֶב, יֵרְבְּ). — I. became many, multiplied. — II. grew. — III. was great, powerful. Pi. רִבָּה made much, Ps. 44:13. Hiph. הִרְבָּה (fut. יַרְבֶּה, apoc. יֶרֶב; imp. הֶרֶב; inf. abs. הַרְבֵּה, הַרְבָּה;

const. הַרְבּוֹת).—I. multiplied, increased.—II. extended, made large. — III. made great. Inf. הַרְבֵּה, sometimes הַרְבּוֹת adv. much, very much; לְהַרְבֵּה plentifully.

רְבָה Ch., grew great, Dan. 4:8, 19. Pa. became great, Dan. 2:48.

רְבִיבִים, רְבוֹת, רְבוּא, רַבָּה; רַבִּית; see רבב.

רְבוּ, רְבוּת f. Ch., greatness.

אַרְבֶּה m., a species of locust, so called from the multitudes of them.

מַרְבֶּה m., greatness, abundance.

מַרְבָּה f., much, too much, Eze. 23:32.

מַרְבִּית, f. — I. abundance. — II. increase, interest.—III. offspring.

תַּרְבּוּת f., progeny, Nu. 32:14.

תַּרְבִּית f., usury.

רָבִיד; see רבד.

רְבִיעִי, רְבִעִית; see רבע.

רָבַךְ (Arab. mixed). Hoph. part. מֻרְבֶּכֶת mixed, saturated.

רִבְלָה p. n., Riblah, a city to the north of Palestine.

I. רָבַע lying with (carnally). Hiph. cause to lie with.

רֹבַע m., lying down, with suff. רִבְעִי Ps. 139:3; see also below.

II. רָבַע from אַרְבַּע, רֶבַע; part. רָבוּעַ four-sided; pl. רְבֻעִים. Pu. part. מְרֻבַּעַת m., מְרֻבַּעַת f., made four-sided.

רֶבַע I. fourth part of anything, side of anything square.—II. p. n., a king of Midian.

רֹבַע m., fourth part.

רְבִיעִי m., the fourth, רְבִיעִית f., fourth part; בְּנֵי רִבֵּעִים children of the fourth generation.

רְבִיעַ m. Ch., *fourth.*

רִבְּעִים m. pl., *posterity in the fourth degree.*

אַרְבַּע f., אַרְבָּעָה, אַרְבַּעַת m. — I. *four;* with suff. אַרְבַּעְתָּם *they four;* dual אַרְבַּעְתַּיִם *fourfold;* pl. אַרְבָּעִים *forty.*—II. p. n. of a giant.

אַרְבַּע f., אַרְבָּעָה m. Ch., *the same.*

רָבַץ (fut. יִרְבַּץ). — I. *lie down* (of beasts, &c.)—II. *lie upon the conscience, soul,* of sin, Gen. 4:7, &c. Hiph. I. *cause to lie down.*—II. *set* (of precious stones), Isa. 54:11.

רֶבֶץ m.—I. *crib, lying place of cattle.*—II. *resting place* (for man), Pro. 24:15.

מַרְבֵּץ m., *a resting place, for cattle or wild beasts,* Zep. 2:15.

מִרְבָּץ m., *the same,* Eze. 25:5.

רָבַק (Arab. *tied up to fatten.*)

רִבְקָה p.n., *Rebecca,* the wife of Isaac, Ρεβέκκα.

מַרְבֵּק m., *stall for feeding cattle.*

רַבְשָׁקֵה רַבְרְבָן רַבְרְבִין; see I. רבב.

רֶגֶב m., pl. רְגָבִים.—רִגְבֵי—I. *clods of earth,* Job 38:38.—II. *stones set up as monuments,* Job 21:33.

רָגַז (imper. רְגַז, רְגָזָה pl. רִגְזוּ; fut. יִרְגַּז).—I. *shook, trembled.*—II. *became disturbed, agitated.* Hiph. I. *move.*—II. *agitate, disturb,* with לְ. Hith. *thy commotion, excitement,* with אֶל.

רְגַז Ch. Aph., *provoked, excited to anger.*

רֹגֶז m. — I. *vexation. trouble.* — II. *neighing,* Job 39:24. — III. *fury,*

anger, Hab. 3:2. — IV. *roar of thunder,* Job 37:2.

רְגַז m. Ch., *anger,* Dan. 3:13.

רַגָּז m., *trembling,* Deu. 28:65.

רָגְזָה f., *perturbation,* Eze. 12:18

אַרְגָּז m., "*coffer,*" Eng. Ver., 1 Sa 6:8, 11, 15 ; (Arab. *a panier,* on one side of a camel's pack saddle: also, the sack of stones hung on the other side when but one panier is used.)

רָגַל *go about speaking evil, backbite,* Ps. 15:3. Pi. I. *goes about calumniating,* with בְּ, 2 Sa. 19:28. — II. *explore as a spy;* part מְרַגְּלִים *spies,* Gen. 42:9. Tiphel תִּרְגַּל *was near* (at foot, i. e., at hand), Hos. 11:3.

רֶגֶל com. (dual רַגְלַיִם, רַגְלֵי) *the foot,* בְּרַגְלֵי פ׳ *at the feet of any one ;* לְרַגְלֵי פ׳ *on account of any one.* (For many other idiomatic usages of רֶגֶל see Fürst's Concordance.) Pl. רְגָלִים *strokes of the feet, times, repetitions.*

רְגַל, רְגַל com. Ch., *foot.*

רַגְלִי m., *foot soldier* ; pl. רַגְלִים *infantry,* Jer. 12:5.

דִּגְלַיִם p.n.—I. see עַיִן.—II. pl. רֹגֵל a place in Gilead.

מַרְגְּלוֹת f. pl., *at the feet, anything at the feet.*

רָגַם *stone to death,* with בְּ, עַל.

רִגְמָה f., *stone of defence,* Ps. 68:28

מַרְגֵּמָה f., *heap of stones,* Pro. 26:8

רֶגֶם p.n. of a man.

רֶגֶם מֶלֶךְ p.n. of a man.

רָגַן and Niph. נִרְגַּן *murmuring;* with בְּ *against.*

רָגַע. I. *hastens to decay* (the skin), Job 7:5.—II. *calms* (the sea), Job 26:12. Niph. *rested*, Jer. 47:6. Hiph. I. *rested, found rest*. — II. *give, restore to, make to, rest*.

רָגֵעַ m., *quiet, peaceable*, Ps. 35:20.

רֶגַע m., *instant, moment of time*; רֶגַע בְּרֶגַע, כְּרֶגַע adv., *in a moment, suddenly*; לִרְגָעִים *moment after moment, incessantly*.

מַרְגּוֹעַ m., *rest, quiet*, Jer. 6:16.

מַרְגֵּעָה f., the same, Isa. 28:12.

רָגַשׁ *are tumultuous, in uproar*, Ps. 2:1.

רְגַשׁ Ch., the same. Aph. *assembled tumultuously*.

רֶגֶשׁ m., *tumult, multitude shouting*, Ps. 55:15.

רִגְשָׁה f., the same, Ps. 64:3.

רֵד, Isa. 45:1, Kal inf., from רדד; Jud. 19:11, for יָרַד.

רֵד Kal imp., from ירד.

רָדַד *brings down, subdues*, Ps. 144:2; Isa. 45:1. Hiph. *lays down on*, 1 Ki. 6:32.

רַדַּי p.n. of a man.

רָדִיד m., *loose mantle, veil*, Cant. 5:7; Isa. 3:23.

רָדָה (fut. apoc. יֵרֵדְ; pl. יִרְדּוּ). — I. *subdue, rule, govern*, with בְּ; of fire, Lam. 1:13. — II. *took down*, Jud. 14:9. Hiph. *cause to rule, govern*; fut. apoc. יַרְדְּ, Isa. 41:2.

רְדָה I. in pause רֵדָה Kal imp. with ה parag.—II. Gen. 46:3, inf. with ה parag., from ירד.

רָדַם Niph. נִרְדָּם *be insensible, as in deep sleep, fast asleep*.

תַּרְדֵּמָה f., *deep sleep, stupor, trance*.

רֹדֵם Kal part. with suff., from רדה.

רוֹדָנִים p.n., 1 Chron. 1:7, an unknown people to the west of Canaan.

רָדַף I. *followed after*.—II. *pursued as an enemy*, with אֶל, לְ, אַחֲרֵי. Pi. *followed, pursued*. Hiph. *chased*, Jud. 20:43. Niph. and Pu. I. *was pursued*. — II. *succeeded*, Ecc. 3:15.

מֻרְדָּף m. (Hoph. part.) *pursued, chased*, Isa. 14:6.

רֶדֶת Kal inf., from ירד.

רָהַב I. *deal with as fearing*, Pro. 6:3.—II. *insult*, with בְּ. Hiph. *embolden*, Cant. 6:5.

רַהַב m.—I. *insolence*, Job 9:13; 26:12. — II. *a prophetic name for Egypt*.

רָהָב m., *insolent*, Ps. 40:5.

רֹהַב m., *pride, insolence*, Ps. 90:10

רְהָנָה p. n. of a man.

תִּרְהוּ, רָהָה; see ירה.

רַהַט (Syr. *stream*; Arab. *strap, thong, household goods*).

רַהַט m., pl. רְהָטִים.—I. *watering trough*. — II. *thongs*, Cant. 7:6; *"like a king bound in thongs"* (Lee).

רָהִיט m., pl. רָהִיטִים *furniture, furnishing* (of a house), φατνώματα, Cant. 1:17.

רָו *aspect*; see ראה.

רוּב *strife*; see ריב.

רוֹב *same as* רֹב *many*; see רבב.

רוּד *walked with* (God), Hos. 12:1. Hiph. I. *wander* (mentally), Ps. 55:3.—II. *wander, be a nomade people*, Gen. 27:40.

סָרוּד m., *one persecuted*, Lam. 3:19; מְרוּדִים *persecuted ones*, Lam. 1:7.

רָוָה *was satiated* (with anything), with מִן. Pi. רִוָּה I. *was satiated, filled.* — II. *fill, delight, satisfy.* Hiph. הִרְוָה *satiate, fill.*

רָוֶה m., רָוָה f.—I. *soaked, satiated.*— II. *drunken*, Deu. 29:18.

רִי m., *irrigation*, Job 37:11.

רְוָה f., *abundance, plenty of water.*

רָז m. Ch., *a secret.*

רִיחַ, רוּחַ. Hiph. הֵרִיחַ I. *smell* (sweet odour).—II. *was satisfied, appeased.* —III. *was inspired with*, with בְּ, Isa. 11:3.—IV. *feel the fire*, Jud. 16:9. —V. *perceive*, Job 39:25.

רוּחַ com. (pl. רוּחוֹת, רְחוֹת).—I. *air, breeze, cool breeze.*— II. *breath.*— III. *spirit, soul of man.*—IV. *mind, spirit, disposition.* — V. *spirit of God.*—VI. *the wind.*—VII. *anger, wrath.*— VIII. *vanity, folly* (used idiomatically in many ways; see Concordance).

רוּחַ com. Ch.—I. *the wind.*—II. *spirit, mind.*

רַחַת f., *winnowing fan*, Isa. 30:24.

רֵיחַ m., *odour, smell;* Ch. the same.

רָוַח (fut. יִרְוַח) *there was relief*, with לְ 1 Sa. 16:23; Job 32:20. Pu. part. מְרֻוָּחִים *spacious, ample*, Jer. 22:14.

רֶוַח m. — I. *space, distance.*—II. *deliverance, quiet.*

רְוָחָה, רַוְחָה f., *the same.*

רוּם (fut. יָרוּם, יָרֹם, וַיָּרָם).—I. *was high, lofty.* — II. *raised himself, was raised.*—III. *was high in rank or power.* — IV. *was lifted up, haughty* (fut. וַיָּרָם); part. רָם m.,

רָמָה f. — I. *high.*—II. *loud*, Deu. 27:14.— III. *high in rank.* — IV. *haughty;* pl. רָמִים *the heights of heaven.*—V. p.n. of a man.. Pil. רוֹמֵם I. *lifted up, raised.*—II. *made to grow.* —III. *brought up* (children).—IV. *exalted with praise.*— V. *raised a building.* Pul. רֹמַם *was lifted up, raised, high.* Hiph. הֵרִים I. *lifted up.*—II. *took up.*— III. *took out for an offering.*—IV. *offered.*—V. *removed.*—VI. *set up.* Hoph. הוּרַם I. *was offered.* — II. *was removed.* Hithpal. *raised, exalted himself*, Dan. 11:36.

רוּם Ch., *was lifted up*, Dan. 5:20. Pil. *exalting with praise*, Dan. 4: 34. Aph. *exalting in power*, Dan. 5:19. Ithpal. *exaltest thyself*, Dan. 5:23.

רָמָה f.—I. *high place for idolatry*, Eze. c. 16.—II. p.n. *Ramah:* (a) a town of Benjamin; (b) a town of Ephraim, called also רָמָתַיִם צֹפִים; (c) a town of Naphtali; (d) רָמַת הַמִּצְפֶּה a town in Gilead, called also רָאמוֹת, רָמוֹת *Ramoth Gilead;* (e) רָמַת לְחִי same as לְחִי; רָמָתִי *a Ramathite.*

רָמוּת f., *pile, heap of dead bodies*, Eze. 32:5.

רוּם m. — I. *height*, Pro. 25:3. — II. *haughtiness.*

רוּם m. Ch., *height.*

רוֹם m., רוֹמָה f.—I. *height*, Hab. 3: 10.— II. *on high, haughtily*, Mic. 2:3.

רוּמָה p.n. of a place.

רוֹמֵם m., *extolling praise;* pl. const. רוֹמְמוֹת, Ps. 149:6.

רוֹמֵמֻת f, *exaltation, majesty*, with suff. רֹמְמָתְךָ, Isa. 33:3.

רְמַמְתִּי־עֶזֶר p. n. of a man.

רֶמֶת p.n., *a town of Issachar.*

מָרוֹם m.—I. *high, on high, height.*— II. *a high place.*—III. *haughtiness; adv. haughtily.*

מֵי מָרוֹם p.n. *a lake in the north of Canaan,* Σαμοχωνιτις.

תְּרוּמָה f.—I. *contribution, gift.*— II. *offering to God.* — III. *sacrificial gift, heave-offering.*

תְּרוּמִיָּה f., *offering,* Eze. 48:12.

רוּן (Arab. *conquer*). Hithpa. part. מִתְרוֹנֵן *overcome* (of wine), Ps. 78: 65.

I. רוּעַ (pret. רַע; inf. רֹעַ) *was evil,* with בְּעֵינֵי *displeased.* Niph. (fut. יֵרֹעַ).—I. *got worse,* Pro. 13:20.— II. *suffer evil, injury,* Pro. 11:15. Hiph. הֵרַע I. *did evil.* — II. *did evil to, afflicted;* part. מֵרַע, מֵרֵעַ *evil doer,* with בְּ, עִם, עַל, לְ. Hith. הִתְרוֹעַ *suffered injury,* Pro. 18:24.

רַע in pause רָע m., רָעָה f.—I. *wicked.* II. *fatal, deadly.*—III. *calamitous.* IV. *sad.*—V. *ill-favoured.*—VI. s.: (a) *wickedness;* (b) *harm, injury, calamity.*

רֹעַ, רוֹעַ m.—I. *badness, evil condition.* —II. *sadness of countenance,* Ecc. 7:3.

II. רוּעַ *shout, call together,* רֵעַ, Isa. 8:9. Hiph. הֵרִיעַ (pl. הָרֵעוּ).— I. *shouted.*—II. *sounded a trumpet.* Pil. fut. יְרֹעַע *there shall be shouting,* Isa. 16:10. Hithpal. *shouted.*

רֵעַ m., *shouting, crying out* see also רֵעָה.

תְּרוּעָה f.—I. *shout of joy.*—II. *shout of battle.*—III. *sound of a trumpet.*

רוּץ I. *ran, ran to, after.* — II. *rushed upon,* with עַל, אֶל.—III. *ran into for a refuge,* with בְּ.—IV. *hastened.* —V. *did a thing readily,* Hab. 2: 2. Part. pl. רָצִים *runners, couriers.* Pil. רוֹצֵץ *ran swiftly,* Nah. 2:5. Hiph. I. *caused to run.*—II. *brought quickly.*—III. *stretched out his hands quickly,* Ps. 68:32.

מֵרוּץ m., *a race,* Ecc. 9:11.

מְרוּצָה f.—I. *mode of running.*—II. *course of life.* See also רָצַץ.

רִיק; see רוּק.

רוּר *spat,* Lev. 15:3.

רִיר m.—I. *spittle,* 1 Sa. 21:14.—II. *whey,* Job 6:6.

רֹאשׁ; see רֹאשׁ.

רוּשׁ *was poor, in want,* Ps. 34:11; part. רָשׁ, רָאשׁ *poor, a poor man.* Hith. הִתְרוֹשֵׁשׁ *feigned himself poor,* Pro. 13:7.

רָאשׁ, רִישׁ, רֵישׁ m., *poverty.*

רוּת p. n. of a woman, *Ruth.*

רָזָה *diminished, brought low,* Zep. 2: 11. Niph. *was wasted away,* Isa 17:4.

רָזֶה m.—I. *lean* (of cattle), Eze. 34 20.—II. *barren* (of land), Nu. 13 20.

רָזִי m., *destruction;* רָזִי לִי *woe is me* רָזוֹן m., *wasting, destruction.* See also in רָזָה.

רָזַח root not used ; Arab. *cried out*) מַרְזֵחַ m., *lamentation,* Jer. 16:5. מִרְזַח *cry of merriment,* Am. 6:7.

רָזַם laid hold on, Job 15:12.

רָזַן (Arab. weighty); part. רוֹזְנִים chiefs, princes.

רָזוֹן m., prince; see also רָזָה.

רְזוֹן p.n., Rezon, king of Damascus.

רָחַב was widened, enlarged, opened. Niph. part. enlarged, extended, Isa. 30:23. Hiph. הִרְחִיב I. made broad.—II. with נֶפֶשׁ extended his desires, enlarged itself.—III. opened the heart, mouth, &c.—IV. with לְ, liberated, made room for, gave way.

I. רָחָב m., רְחָבָה f., broad, large, extensive, capacious; with יָדַיִם broad on both hands, very broad; with לֵב of unlimited desires.

II. רָחָב p.n., Rahab, the woman of Jericho.

רַחַב m., plenty, Job 36:16; 38:18.

רֹחַב m. (with suff. רָחְבּהּ).—I. breadth, width.—II. extent, expanse, Job 37:10.—III. with לֵב extent of understanding, 1 K. 5:9.

רְחוֹב, רְחֹב f. (pl. רְחֹבוֹת).—I. broad, open place in a town, square, street, market-place.—II. בֵּית רְחֹב and רְחֹב p.n., a town in the north of the tribe of Asher; a Syrian city near it was called אֲרַם בֵּית רְחוֹב and אֲרַם רְחֹב.—III. רְחֹבוֹת p.n., (a) the name of a well; (b) עִיר רְ a town in Assyria; (c) הַנָּהָר רְ a town on the Euphrates.

רְחַבְיָהוּ p.n. of a man.

רְחַבְעָם p.n., Rehoboam, the son of Solomon, king of Judah. LXX. Ῥοβοάμ.

מֶרְחָב m.—I. wide places.—II prosperity, considered as freedom.

רָחִיק, רָחוֹק see רחק.

רָהִיטִים Ketib for רָהִיטִים; see רהט.

רֵחַיִם m. dual, pair of millstones.

רָחֵל f.—I. a ewe.—II. any sheep—III. p.n., Rachel, the wife of Jacob; LXX. Ῥαχήλ.

רָחַם or רָחֵם loved, Ps. 18:2. Pi. רִחַם loved, pitied, had mercy on, with accus. עַל. Pu. רֻחַם obtained mercy.

רָחָם, רָחָמָה m., the aquiline vulture; vultur percnopterus (Linn.), Lev. 11:18; Deu. 14:17.

רַחוּם m., merciful (of God only).

רְחוּם p. n. of a man.

רֶחֶם, רַחַם m. (f. Jer. 20:17).—I. the womb.—II. a girl; dual רַחֲמָתַיִם—III. רַחַם p. n. of a man.

רַחֲמִים m. pl.—I. the viscera.—II. pity, mercy.

רַחֲמִין m. pl. Ch., mercy.

רַחְמָנִי m., f. pl. רַחֲמָנִיּוֹת tender, merciful, Lam. 4:10.

רָחַף shook, trembled, Jer. 23:9. Pi. רִחֵף fluttered, hovered, Deu. 32: 11; part. מְרַחֶפֶת hovering, brooding (of the Spirit of God), Gen. 1:2.

רָחַץ (fut. יִרְחַץ; imp. רְחַץ, pl. רַחֲצוּ; inf. רָחְצָה, רְחֹץ) washed himself or another; washed away. Pu. was washed. Hith. washed himself, Job 9:30.

רַחַץ m., washing, Ps. 60:10.

רַחְצָה f., washing-place for sheep, Cant. 4:2; 6:6.

רְחַץ Ch. Ith. *depend on, trust to,* Dan. 3:28.

רָחַק (fut. יִרְחַק; inf. רְחָקָה) I. *was distant.*—II. *kept at a distance, withdrew himself.* Pi. רִחַק *placed at a distance, forsook.* Hiph. הִרְחִיק I. *caused to be distant.*—II. *went to a distance;* inf. הַרְחֵק adv., *afar off.*

רָחֵק m., *one who forsakes,* Ps. 73:27.

רָחוֹק m., רְחוֹקָה f.—I. *a distance, interval.*—II. *distant.*—III. *out of reach.* — IV. *difficult,* Pro. 31:10 (i. e., *brought from afar, precious);* בְּרָחוֹק *afar off;* מֵרָחוֹק *from, at a distance* (of time or space); לְמֵרָחוֹק *at a distance* (time or space); עַד־רָחוֹק *to a distance.*

רַחִיק m. Ch., *distant,* Ezr. 6:6.

מָרְחָק m. (pl. מֶרְחַקִּים), *distance, distant part.*

מַרְחָק m., *the same;* pl. מַרְחַקִּים.

רָחַשׁ *threw up, bubbled up* (as a spring), Ps. 45:2.

מַרְחֶשֶׁת f., *pot for boiling.*

רַחַח; see רוּחַ.

רָטֹב (fut. יִרְטַב) *was wet* (with rain), Job 24:8.

רָטֹב m., *moist, fresh,* Job 8:16. (Arab. the same).

רְטָה, יִרְטְנוּ; see יָרַט.

רָטַט root not used; Ch. *trembled;* Syr. the same.

רֶטֶט m., *trembling,* Jer. 49:24.

רֻטֲפַשׁ *grew fresh, moist,* Job 33:25.

רָטַשׁ Pi. רִטֵּשׁ *smote, killed.* Pu. *were killed.*

רִי; see רָוָה.

רִיב (pret. רָב, רַבְתָ, רִיבוֹת; inf. abs רֹב; inf. const. and imp. רִיב; fut. יָרִיב).—I. *disputed, quarrelled with,* with בְּ, אֶל, עִם.—II. *defended,* with לְ.—III. *opposed,* with עַל.—IV. *decided a cause favourably.* Hith. part. מֵרִיב *opposed, contended with.*

רִיב m. (pl. רִיבִים, רִיבוֹת).—I *controversy, suit.* — II. *quarrel, strife.*

רִיבַי p. n. of a man.

יָרֵב m., *an adversary,* Hos. 5:13, 10:6.

יָרִיב m.—I. *the same.*—II. p. n. of a man.

יְרִיבַי p. n. of a man.

יְרֻבֶּשֶׁת, יְרֻבַּעַל p. n., titles of Gideon.

מְרִיבָה f.—I. *strife, contention.* — II. p. n., a spring in the desert of Sinai.

רִיחַ, הָרִיחַ, רֵיחַ; see רוּחַ.

רֵים same as רְאֵם.

רָעָה, רֵיעַ; see רוּעַ; הָרִיעַ, רֵיעַ, see רָעָה.

רִיפוֹת f. pl., *grain.*

רִיפַת p. n., *one of Japhet's sons, and his descendants.*

רִיק. Hiph. הֵרִיק — I. *emptied.* — II. *made empty, poured out.*—III. *drew a sword, made ready for war,* Gen. 14:14. Hoph. הוּרַק *was poured out.*

רִיק m.—I. *empty.*—II. *an empty, vain thing.*—III. *in vain.*—IV. adv. רִיק, לָרִיק *in vain.*

רֵיק, רֵק m., רֵקָה f.—I. *empty.* — II. *hungry, poor.* — III. *unimportant,* Deu. 32:47. — IV. *worthless in character.*

רֵיקָם adv. — I. *emptily.* — II. *empty*

handed.—III. *without cause.*—IV. *without effect.*

רִיו ran; see רוּר.

רֵישׁ, רֵישׁ *poverty*; see רוּשׁ.

רֵישָׁן Job 8:8; same as רִאשׁוֹן *first.*

רַדּ רֹך; see רכך.

רָכַב (fut. יִרְכַּב; inf. רְכֹב).—I. *rode on a horse, ass,* or *camel.*—II. metaph. of God on the clouds or wind, with בְּ, עַל, accus.; part. רֹכֵב *a horseman.* Hiph. I. *caused to ride.*—II. *carried in a chariot.*—III. *placed upon.* — IV. *caused to be ridden,* Hos. 10:11.

רֶכֶב m. (f. Nah. 2:5). — I. *riding, a rider.* — II. *the upper millstone* (that which rides).—III. *a chariot, chariots.*

רֵכָב p. n. — I. *Rechab,* the father of Jonadab, from whom the Rechabites (רֵכָבִים) were descended. — II. used also of other men.

רְכוּב m., *vehicle, chariot,* Ps. 104:3.

רַכָּב m.—I. *horseman.*—II. *charioteer.*

מֶרְכָּב m.—I. *any carriage to ride in,* Lev. 15:9.—II. *chariots,* 1 K. 5:6.

מֶרְכָּבָה f. (with suff. מֶרְכַּבְתּוֹ; pl. מֶרְכְּבוֹת, מַרְכָּבוֹת), *a chariot.*

מֶרְכֶּבֶת f., *the same.*

רֵכָה p. n. of a place unknown.

רְכוּשׁ *wealth*; see רכשׁ.

רָכִיל *slander*; see רכל.

רָכַךְ *was timid, gentle.* Niph. *was timid*; fut. יֵרַךְ. Pu. *was softened,* Isa. 1:6. Hiph. הֵרֵךְ *rendered timid,* Job 23:16.

רַךְ m., רַכָּה f. — I. *tender, young.* — II. *object of care.*—III. *effeminate.* — IV. *weak, timid, gentle.* — V.

*tender-eyed,* i. e. having sore eyes. Gen. 29:17.

רֹךְ f., *effeminacy,* Deu. 28:56.

רָכַל *went to and fro, travelled as a merchant*; part. רֹכֵל, f. רֹכֶלֶת *a merchant, dealer.*

רָכָל p. n., a town of Judah.

רָכִיל m.—I. *a busy body.*— II. *slanderer*; הָלַךְ רָכִיל *he went about tale bearing.*

רְכֻלָּה f., *merchandise* (Ezekiel only).

מַרְכֹּלֶת f., *merchandise,* Eze. 27:24

רָכַס *tied, fastened.* Ex. 28:28; 39:21.

רֹכֶס m., רִכְסֵי אִישׁ *combinations, artifices,* Ps. 31:21.

רֶכֶס m., pl. רְכָסִים *rugged places,* Isa. 40:4.

רָכַשׁ *acquired, gained* (Genesis only).

רְכֻשׁ, רְכוּשׁ m., *property, wealth.*

רֶכֶשׁ m., *swift species of horse.*

רֵם; רֶם, רָמָה, see רום; רְאֵם same as רֵם

רָמָה I. *threw.*—II. *shot with a bow.* Pi. רִמָּה *deceived,* lit. threw down. רְמָא, רְמָה Ch. — I. *threw.*—II. *imposed tribute.* Ithpe. *were thrown placed.*

רִמּוֹן, רִמָּה; see רמם.

רָמוֹת, רָמוּת; see רום.

רְמִיָּה f.—I. *deceit.*—II. *negligence.*

רְמְיָה p.n. of a man.

מִרְמָה f.—I. *deceit, artifice.*—II. p.n. of a man.

תַּרְמָה f., *deceit, craft,* Jud. 9:31.

תַּרְמִית (תַּרְמוּת) f., *the same.*

רֹמַח m. (pl. רְמָחִים; with suff. רָמְחֵיהֶם) *a spear.*

רַמִּי pl. הָרַמִּים same as הָאֲרַמִּים *the Syrians.*

רֶמֶךְ f., a mare, Est. 8:10.

רְמַלְיָה p. n., Remaliah, the father of Pekah, king of Israel.

רָמַם (pret. pl. רֹמּוּ, רָמוּ) was high, lofty; part. f. רוֹמֵמָה high. Niph. (imp. pl. הֵרֹמּוּ; fut. pl. יֵרֹמּוּ) was raised, Eze. 10:15, 17, 19.

רִמָּה f., a worm, worms

רִמּוֹן m.—I. a pomegranate fruit or tree.—II. an artificial imitation of the fruit.—III. p. n.: (a) a city of Simeon; (b) a city near Gibeah; (c) an idol of the Syrians; (d) רִמּוֹן הַמְּתֹאָר a town of Zebulun; (e) רִמּוֹן פֶּרֶץ one of the stations of the Israelites.

רָמַס I. trampled on, trod on. — II. walked in; part. רֹמֵס an oppressor, Isa. 16:4. Niph. was trodden down, Isa. 28:3.

מִרְמָס m., that which is trampled under foot.

רָמַשׂ I. move (as a quadruped).—II. creep (as a reptile).

רֶמֶשׂ m. collec.—I. reptiles.—II. small land animals.— III. sea creatures, perhaps seals, Ps. 104:25.

רֶמֶת; see רום.

רָנָה rang, rattled, Job 39:23.

רָנַן (fut. יָרֹן).—I. sung.—II. shouted.—III. invited.—IV. called for help. Pi. רִנֵּן I. sung, rejoiced, with עַל, בְּ.—II. sung of, celebrated, with לְ, אֶל. Pu. fut. יְרֻנַּן there shall be singing, Isa. 16:10. Hiph. הִרְנִין I. caused to sing. — II. rejoiced. Hith. see in רון.

רָנֵן m., pl. רְנָנִים ostriches Job 39:13.

רְנָנָה f., singing, rejoicing.

רֹן m., pl. רָנִּים songs, Ps. 32:7.

רִנָּה f.—I. singing, shout of joy.—II. a shout or cry of any kind.—III. a cry for help.—IV. p. n. of a man.

רֶסֶן m.—I. bridle, halter.— II. p. n. a city of Assyria.

רָסַס sprinkled, Eze. 46:14.

רִסָּה p.n., one of the stations in the wilderness.

רְסִיסִים m. pl. — I. sprinkling, drop, Cant. 5:2.—II. fractures, Am. 6:11.

רָעָה, רוּעַ, see רֵעַ, רֵעַ, see רֵעַ, רַע, רֵעַ

רָעֵב (fut. יִרְעַב).—I. was hungry.—II. hungered for, was famished.—III. suffered from famine, with לְ. Hiph. הִרְעִיב allowed, caused to suffer hunger.

רָעֵב m., רְעֵבָה f., hungry, famishing.

רָעָב m.—I. hunger.—II. famine.

רַעֲבוֹן, const. רַעֲבוֹן m., the same.

רָעַד (fut. יִרְעַד) trembled, Ps. 104:32. Hiph. the same.

רַעַד m.,  } trembling, awe.
רְעָדָה f., }

רָעָה (fut. יִרְעֶה; apoc. יִרַע).— I. fed. —II. consumed. — III. devastated. — IV. fed on, delighted in. — V. associated with.—VI. fed cattle.—VII. governed a people. — VIII. nourished. — IX. for רַע injured, oppressed; part. רֹעֶה a shepherd. Pi. רֵעָה became a companion, Jud. 14:20. Hiph. pres. aff. יִרְעֵם ruled them, Ps. 78:72. Hith. הִתְרָעָה was intimate with, became a companion, with אֶת.

רֵעֵהוּ m. (pl. with suff. רֵעַ, רֵעֶה, רֵעַ

**רֵעַ** (רֵעֶיהוּ)—I. *a friend, neighbour, companion, lover;* רֵעַ ... אִישׁ *one ... the other.*— II. *thought, will,* Ps. 139:2, 17; see also רוּעַ·

**רֵעָה** f., pl. רֵעוֹת *female friend, companion.*

**רָעָה** f., *evil, &c.;* see רַע in רוּעַ·

**רֵעָה** *breaking;* see רעע·

**רְעוּת** f.— I. *friend, neighbour.*— II. with רוּחַ *feeding on the wind.*

**רְעוּת** f. Ch., *wish, will.*

**רְעוּ** p. n. of a man.

**רְעוּאֵל** p. n. of a man.

**רְעִי** m., *pasture,* 1 Ki. 5:3.

**רֹעִי** m., *a shepherd.*

**רֵעִי** p. n. of a man.

**רַעְיָה** f., *female companion, friend.*

**רַעְיוֹן** m., *desire, pursuit.*

**רַעְיוֹן** m. Ch., *desire, purpose, thought.*

**מֵרֵעַ** m. (with suff. מֵרֵעֵהוּ; pl. מֵרֵעִים) *desire, purpose, thought.*

**מִרְעֶה** m., *pasture.*

**מַרְעִית** f.—I. *pasturing, feeding cattle.* —II. *a flock.*

**רָעַל** Hoph. הָרְעַל *were thrown* (of javelins), Nah. 2:4.

**רַעַל** m.—I. *trembling, giddiness,* Zec. 12:2.—II. pl. רְעָלוֹת *veils,* Isa. 3:19.

**רְעֵלָיָה** p. n. of a man.

**תַּרְעֵלָה** f., *trembling, staggering.*

**רָעַם** (fut. יִרְעַם).—I. *resounded, roared* (of the sea).—II. *was excited,* Eze. 27:35. Hiph. הִרְעִים I. *thundered.* —II. *caused anger, vexation.*

**רַעַם** m.—I. *thunder.* — II. *tumult, rage,* Job 39:25.

**רַעְמָה** f.—I. *rage,* Job 39:19.— II. p. n. of a city of Cush.

**רַעְמְסֵס, רַעַמְסֵס** (*born of the sun*),

p. n.—I. *the district which forms the eastern boundary of Egypt, called also Goshen.* — II. *a city built there by the Israelites.*

**רָעַן.** Pil. רַעֲנַן *was green.*

**רַעֲנָן** m. — I. *green, flourishing.* — II. *prosperous.* — III. *surrounded with foliage,* Cant. 1:16.—IV. *anointed,* Ps. 92:11.

**רַעֲנָן** m. Ch., *green, flourishing.*

**רָעַע** (fut. יֵרַע; inf. רֹעַה).— I. *broke, broke to pieces.*—II. *crushed.* Niph. fut. יֵרוֹעַ and Hiph. הָרַע; see in רוּעַ· Hith. הִתְרוֹעֵעַ *was broken to pieces, ruined.*

**רְעַע** Ch. (fut. f. תְּרֹעַ), *broke.* Pa. the same.

**רֹעָה** f., *breaking;* שֵׁן רֹעָה *a broken tooth.*

**רָעַף** and Hiph. הִרְעִיף *flowed, let drop.*

**רָעַץ** *crushed, overpowered, oppressed.*

**רָעַשׁ** (fut. יִרְעַשׁ), *was shaken, trembled.* Niph. *quaked* (of the earth), Jer. 50:46. Hiph. I. *shook.*—II. *filled with eagerness* (of a horse), Job 39:20.

**רַעַשׁ** m.—I. *shaking.*—II. *an earthquake.*—III. *rumbling of wheels.*— IV. *rattling of a horse's hoofs,* Job 39:24.— V. *any tumult* Job 41: 21.—VI. *the rattling of a spear.*

**רָפָא** (imp. רְפָא, רְפָה; fut. יִרְפָּא; pl. f. תִּרְפֶּנָה).— I. *healed.* — II. *restored to prosperity, delivered from calamity.* — III. *healed,* i. e., *removed transgressions;* part. רֹפֵא *a physician.* Niph. נִרְפָּא (pret. f. הָרְפָּה, הֵרָפֵא; inf. הֵרָפֵה, נִרְפָּתָה; *fut.*

pl. (יְרֻפּוּ).—I. *was repaired* (a vessel).
— II. *was healed* (a person or wound).—III. *was rendered wholesome* (water), Eze. c. 47.—IV. *was restored to prosperity*, Isa. 53:5. Pi. רִפָּא (fut. pl. יְרַפּוּ).—I. *repaired*, 1 Ki. 18:30.—II. *healed.*—III. *caused to be cured*, Ex. 21:19. —IV. *made wholesome*, 2 Ki. 2:21. Hith. *get himself cured*.

רְפָאֵל p. n. of a man.

רְפָיָה p. n. of a man.

רְפָאִים p. n., the name of a people inhabiting the country on the east of the Dead Sea, supposed to have been giants; called also יְלִידֵי הָרָפָה. עֵמֶק רְפָאִים *the valley of the Rephaims*, close to mount Moriah.

רִפְאוּת f., *health*, Pro. 3:8.

רְפֻאוֹת f. pl., *bandages, remedies.*

רְפוּא p.n. of a man.

מַרְפֵּא, רִפְאָה m.—I. *remedy.*—II. *healing.*—III. *soundness.* See also in רָפָה.

תְּרוּפָה f., *healing*, Eze. 47:12.

רָפַד *supported himself*, Job 41:22; fut. יִרְפַּד. Pi. I. *constructed a couch*, Job 17:13.—II. *refreshed*, Cant. 2:5.

רְפִידָה f., *a throne*; Vulg. reclinatorium, Cant. 3:10.

רְפִידִים p.n., *Rephidim*, a station in the wilderness.

רָפַף (fut. יִרְפֶּה, יִרָף).—I. *hung down* (the hands).—II. *declined* (the day). —III. *sank down* (fuel in the fire), Isa. 5:24.—IV. *gave way* (to anger), Jud. 8:3; with מִן.— V. *became weak*, Jer. 49:24. — VI. *desisted.*

Niph. part. נִרְפִּים *became, were idle*, Ex. 5:8, 17, &c. Pi. רִפָּה I. *allowed to hang down*, Eze. 1:24, 25. — II. *weakened* (part. מְרַפֵּא). Hiph. הִרְפָּה (imp. apoc. הֶרֶף; fut. apoc. יֶרֶף) I. *ceased from*, with מִן.—II. *withheld.*—III. *gave up.*—IV. *let go.*—V. *ceased.* Hith. *relaxed himself, was slothful.*

רָפֶה m. (pl. f. רָפוֹת), *weak.*

רָפֶה p. n.; see in רפא.

רִפְיוֹן m., *weakness*, Jer. 47:3.

מַרְפֵּא m., *yielding*, Ecc. 10:4; see also in רפא.

רֶפַח p. n. of a man.

רָפַשׂ, רָפַס *trampled down.* Niph. part. נִרְפָּשׂ *disturbed by trampling.* Hith. הִתְרַפֵּס *submitted, humbled himself.*

רְפַס Ch., the same.

מִרְפָּשׂ *water made muddy by trampling*, Eze. 34:19.

רַפְסֹדוֹת f.pl., *floats, rafts*, 2 Ch. 2:15.

רָפַף. Po. רוֹפַף *trembled.*

רָפַק. Hith. *trembled*, Cant. 8:5.

רָפַשׂ; see רפס.

רֶפֶשׁ m., *mud*, Isa. 57:20.

רְפָתִים m. pl., *stalls for oxen*, Hab. 3:17.

רָצִים, see רוּץ; רֵץ, רָצִי, see רצץ.

רָצָא, Eze. 1:14; same as רוּץ *he ran.*

רָצַד Pi. *he laid wait for*, Ps. 68:17.

רָצָה (וַתִּרֶץ, יִרְצֶה).—I. *approved of, took pleasure in*, with בְּ.—II. *received favourably.*—III. *loved.*—IV. *fulfilled.*—V. *associated with*,

with עִם.—VI. *was received favourably*; (part. רָצוּי *accepted*). Niph. נִרְצָה I. *was received favourably*.—II. *was fulfilled*, Isa. 40:2. Pi. *satisfied by restitution*, Job 20:10. Hiph. *fulfilled*, Lev. 26:34. Hith. *made himself acceptable*, 1 Sa. 29:4.

רָצוֹן m. — I. *approbation, favour* (עַל רְ, לִרְצוֹן *acceptable, well-pleasing*).—II. *object of approbation*.—III. *will, pleasure, choice*.—IV. *uncontrolled will, violence*, Gen. 49:6.—V. *enjoyment*.

רָצַח (fut. יִרְצַח) *struck fatally, killed*; with or without נֶפֶשׁ; part. רֹצֵחַ *homicide*. Niph. *was killed*. Pi. *killed habitually, was a murderer by profession*. Pu. *be killed*, Ps. 62:4. תֵּרָצְחוּ for תְּרָצְּחוּ. רֶצַח m. — I. *crushing*, Ps. 42:11. — II. *slaughter*, Eze. 21:27.

רְצִיָא p. n. of a man.

רְצִין p.n., *Rezin*, king of Syria.

רָצַע *pierced, bored*, Ex. 21:6.

מַרְצֵעַ m., *an awl*.

רָצַף *covered, overlaid*, Cant. 3:10.

רֶצֶף m.—I. *burning coals*, 1 Ki. 19:6.—II. p. n., *a city of some country subdued by the Assyrians*.

רִצְפָּה f.—I. *burning coal*, Isa. 6:6.—II. *an inlaid pavement*.—III. p. n., *Rizpah, the concubine of Saul*.

מַרְצֶפֶת f., *the pavement on which the brasen sea stood*, 2 Ki. 16:17.

רָצַץ (fut. תָּרָץ, יָרוּץ).—I. *bruised, broke, crushed*.—II. *oppressed*.—III. *became broken, burst*.—IV. *relaxed*

*himself*, Isa. 42:3. Niph. נָרוֹץ *was bruised*. Pi. רָצַץ I. *bruised*.—II. *oppressed*. Po. רוֹצֵץ the same; see also in רוּץ. Hiph. *bruised*; fut. וַתָּרָץ. Hithpo. *struggled together*, Gen. 25:22.

רַץ m. (pl. const. רָצֵי), *small piece of silver*, Ps. 68:31.

מְרוּצָה f., *oppression*, Jer. 22:17; see also in רוּץ.

רְקִי, רֹק, רַק; see רקק.

רִיק; see רִיק.

רָקַב (fut. יִרְקַב) *became rotten, decayed*

רָקָב m , *decay, rottenness*.

רִקָּבוֹן m., the same, Job 41:19.

רָקַד *leaped, danced*. Pi. the same. Hiph. *made to leap*, Ps. 29:6.

רַקּוֹן, רַקָּה; see רקק.

רָקַח (fut. יִרְקַח) *compounded, prepared*, Ex. 30:33; part. רֹקֵחַ *a compounder of drugs and aromatics*. Pu. part. מְרֻקָּחִים *compound, ointment*, 2 Chron. 16:14. Hiph. *threw in spices*, Eze. 24:10.

רֶקַח m., *perfuming, the preparing of perfumes*, Cant. 8:2.

רֹקַח m., *ointment*, Ex. 30:25, 35.

רַקָּח m., *apothecary, perfumer*; f. pl. רַקָּחוֹת.

רִקֻּחִים m. pl., *perfumes*, Isa. 57:9.

מֶרְקָח m., pl. מֶרְקָחִים *perfumes*, Cant. 5:13.

מֶרְקָחָה f.—I. *a pot of ointment*, Job 41:23.—II. *spices eaten as condiments*, Eze. 24:10.

מִרְקַחַת f., *perfumery*.

רָקִיע, see רקע; רָקִיק, see רקק.

רָקַם *streaked*; part. רֹקֵם s. *an embroid*

*erer*. Pu. *wrought with art* (met. of Christ's mystical body), Ps. 139:15.

רִקְמָה f.—I. *embroidery.*—II. *variety of colours*, Eze. 17:3; dual רִקְמָתַיִם *embroidered on both sides*, Jud. 5:30.

רֶקֶם p. n.—I. *a town of Benjamin.*—II. *of a man.*

רָקַע I. *stretched out* (of God in creation). — II. *stamped on*, 2 Sa. 22:43. — III. *stamped with the feet*, Eze. 6:11. Pi. I. *beat into thin plates.* — II. *covered with a thin plate of gold*, Isa. 40:19. Pu. part. *overlaid*, Jer. 10:9. Hiph. *stretched out*, Job 37:18.

רָקִיעַ m.—I. *the expanse of heaven, atmosphere, sky*, Vulg. firmamentum.—II. *a canopy* (Ezekiel only).

רְקֻעִים m. pl., *plates of metal*, Nu. 17:3.

רָקַק same as יָרַק *spit*, with בְּ; fut. יָרֹק, Lev. 15:8.

רָקִיק m., *a thin cake.*

רֹק m. (with suff. רֻקִּי) *spittle.*

רַק m., רַקָּה f. (Arab. *was thin*) *thin, lean*, Gen. c. 41.

רַק adv. — I. *only.*—II. *certainly*, i. e. *this only.* — III. *except*, with a negative.

רַקָּה f.—I. *the temple* (of the head), Jud. 4:21, 22; 5:26.—II. *the cheek*, Cant. 4:3; 6:7.

רַקּוֹן p.n., *a town of Dan.*

רַקַּת p. n., *a town of Naphtali.*

רָשׁ; see רוּשׁ.

רֵשׁ, רָשׁ Kal imp., from יָרַשׁ

רָשָׁה root not used ; (Syr. *he gave*).

רִשְׁיוֹן m., *grant, permission*, Ezr. 3:7.

רֵשִׁית *beginning*; see רֵאשִׁית in רֹאשׁ.

רָשַׁם *wrote, decreed*, Dan. 10:21.

רְשַׁם Ch., the same.

רָשַׁע *was, acted, wickedly, unjustly impiously.* Hiph. הִרְשִׁיעַ I. *condemned.* — II. *declared, proved guilty.*—III. *acted wickedly.*

רָשָׁע m., רִשְׁעָה f.—I. *wicked.* — II. *guilty, faulty.*

רֶשַׁע m. (with suff. רִשְׁעוֹ) *wickedness, impiety, injustice* ; pl. רְשָׁעִים.

רִשְׁעָה f. — I *wickedness.* — II. *fault*, Deu. 25:2.

רִשְׁעָתַיִם p.n.; see כּוּשַׁן.

מִרְשַׁעַת f., *wickedness*, 2 Chron. 24:7.

רֶשֶׁף m. (pl. const. רִשְׁפֵי).—I. *a burning coal*, Cant. 8:6.—II. *lightning.* III. בְּנֵי ר׳ *burning arrows*, Job 5:7; רִשְׁפֵי קֶשֶׁת the same, Ps. 76:4.—IV. *burning disease*, Deu. 32:24.—V. *lust*, Cant. 8:6.—VI. p. n. of a man.

רָשַׁשׁ. Po. רֹשֵׁשׁ *reduced, subdued*, Jer. 5:17. Pu. רֹשַׁשׁ *was subdued*, Mal. 1:4.

תַּרְשִׁישׁ I. p.n., *Tarshish*, some country far distant from Canaan; אֳנִיּוֹת 'תַּ probably *merchant ships.*— II. *a precious stone*, probably *the topaz.*—III. p. n. of a man.

רֶשֶׁת Kal inf., from יָרַשׁ.

רָתַח. Pi. and Hiph. *boil, caused to boil.* Pu. *was boiled, agitated*, Job 30:27.

רֶתַח m., *boiling*, Eze. 24:5.

רָתַם *bind, yoke*, Mic. 1:13.

רֹתֶם m. (pl. רְתָמִים), *the broom;* in Spanish, *retama.*

רִתְמָה p. n., one of the stations in the wilderness.

רָתַק (Arab. *joined*). Niph. *was bound,* Ecc. 12:6, Kri. Pu. the same, Nah. 3:10.

רַתּוֹק m., *a chain,* Eze. 7:23.

רַתּוּקוֹת (רְתִיקוֹת) f. pl., *chains,* 1 Ki. 6:21.

רְתֻקוֹת f. pl., the same, Isa. 40:19.

רָתַת (Syr. *he trembled*); see רטט.

רְתֵת m., *trembling,* Hos. 13:1.

## שׁ

שָׂא Kal imp. and inf. from נשׂא.

שְׂאֹר m., *leaven.*

שְׂאֵת from נשׂא.

שָׂבַךְ same as סָבַךְ, *twist.*

שׂוֹבֶךְ m., *entangled branch,* 2 Sa.18:9.

שְׂבָךְ m., pl. שְׂבָכִים *ornaments of wreathing,* 1 Ki. 7:17.

שְׂבָכָה f.—I. *network* on the capitals of pillars.—II. *lattice,* 2 Ki. 1:2.—III. *a net,* Job 18:8.

שְׂבָכָא same as סַבְּכָא.

שֶׂבֶם, שְׂבָמָה p. n., a city of the Reubenites.

שָׂבַע, שָׂבֵע *was full, satisfied, sur-feited,* with בְּ, מִן. Pi. *satisfied.* Hiph. *filled,* with לְ *of the person;* with בְּ, מִן *of the thing.*

שָׂבֵעַ m., שְׂבֵעָה f., *full, satisfied, sur-feited.*

שָׂבָע m., *abundance.*

שֹׂבַע m., the same; לְשֹׂבַע *to the full.*

שָׂבְעָה, שִׂבְעָה f., the same, Eze. 16:49.

שָׂבַר *looked at, examined,* Neh. 2:13, 15; with בְּ. Pi. *looked to, hoped for* or *in,* with אֶל, לְ.

שֵׂבֶר m. (with suff. שִׂבְרִי), *hope.*

שָׂנָא same as שָׂנָה. Hiph. I. *increased,* Job 12:23. — II. *magnified,* Joh 36:24.

שְׂנָא Ch., *increased, became great.*

שַׂנִּיא m., *the Great One* (of God), Job 36:26; 37:23.

שַׂנִּיא m., שַׂנִּיאָה f. Ch.—I. *great.*—II. *much, many.*—III. *greatly.*

שָׂנַב *was exalted.* Niph. I. *was lofty, exalted.* — II. *was secure,* Pro. 18:10. Pi.I. *raised, placed in security.*—II. *made powerful,* Isa. 9:10. Pu. pass. of Pih., Pro. 29:25. Hiph. *was lofty,* Job 36:22.

שָׂנִיב, שָׂנוּב p. n. of a man.

מִשְׂנָב m. (with suff. מִשְׂנַּבִּי).—I. *a hill, strong place.*—II. *refuge* (of God).

שָׂנַג same as שָׂנָא. Pil. שִׂנְשֵׂנ *cause to grow;* according to others, from סוּנ *he fences,* Isa. 17:11.

שָׂנָה *increased, became great.* Hiph *increased,* Ps. 73:12.

שָׂדַד. Pi. *harrowed.*

שִׂדִּים p. n., the valley of the Dead Sea, *Siddim.*

שָׂדֶה m. (with suff. שָׂדֵהוּ; pl. שָׂדוֹת; const. שְׂדֵי, שְׂדוֹת).—I. *a field.*—II. *the country.*—III. *any country;* אִישׁ שָׂדֶה *husbandman;* חַיַּת הַשָׂדֶה *the beasts of the field;* שְׂדֵה מוֹאָב *the land of Moab;* שְׂדֵה אֲרָם *Mesopotamia.*

שָׂדַי sing., the same.

שְׁדֵרוֹת ; see סדר.

שֶׁה same as שִׁיָה.

שָׂהֵד (Syr and Ch. סְהַד bare witness).

שָׂהֵד m., eye witness, Job 16:19.

שָׂהֲדוּת f. Ch., testimony, Gen. 31:47.

שַׂהֲרֹנִים crescents; see סהר.

שׂוֹא Kal inf., from נשׂא.

שׁוּב ; see שׁיב.

שׁוֹבֵךְ ; see שׂבך.

שׁוּג same as סוּג drove back, 2 Sa. 1: 22.

שׁוּחַ same as שׁיחַ to meditate, Gen. 24:63.

שׁוּם turn aside, Ps. 40:5.

שָׂטִים, סָטִים m. pl., they who turn aside to, Ps. 101:3; Hos. 5:2.

שׂוּךְ hedged with thorns. Pil. שׂוֹכֵךְ the same, Job 10:11.

שׂוֹךְ m.,
שׂוֹכָה f., } a bough, Jud. 9:48, 49.

שׂוֹכֹה p. n., a town of Judah.

שׂוּכָתִי a Succothite.

מְשֻׂכָה, מְשׂוּכָה f., a thorn hedge.

שׂוּם, שׂים (fut. יָשׂוּם, יָשִׂים; apoc. וַיָּשֶׂם יָשֶׂם; inf. aos. שׂוֹם; const. שׂים, שׂוּם; imp. שִׂים. שִׂימָה).—I. placed, set.— II. set up.— III. set in array.— IV. placed aside.—V. with עַל, set over.—VI. with עַל, place upon.—VII. with עַל, ב, ל, impute to any one.—VIII. with לְ שֵׁם named.—IX. with שְׁמוֹ placed His name (of the Lord), i. e. the true worship.—X. with or without לִבּוֹ set his heart, considered, regarded, with עַל, אֶל, לְ.—XI. with עַל לֵב or אֶל לֵב or בְּלֵב considered laid

to heart. — XII. שׂוּם עַל לֵב he considered.—XIII. with לְנֶגְדּוֹ considered, set before him.—XIV. with בְּאָזְנֵי פּ' he told.— XV. שׂוּם אַף heaped up wrath. (For other idiomatic usages of שׂוּם see concordance.) Hiph. (imp. הָשִׂימִי; part. מֵשִׂים) place, set. Hoph. was placed; fut. יוּשַׂם.

שׂוּם Ch.—I. appointed.—II. with טְעֵם made a decree.—III. with טְעֵם עַל לֵב regarded. — IV. with בָּל לְ endeavoured. — V. שֵׁם דִּי פּ' named. Ithpe. אִתְּשַׂם I. was made, placed. —II. with טְעֵם was decreed.

תְּשׂוּמֶת f., with יָד a deposit, Lev. 5: 21; [6:2.]

שׂוּר I. governed; fut. וַיָּשַׂר, Jud. 9: 22. Hiph. הָשִׂיר appointed princes, Hos. 8:4.—II. same as שָׂרָה strove, contended, Hos. 12:5. — III. same as סוּר departed. — IV. same as Ch. נְסַר he sawed, 1 Chron. 20:3; fut. וַיָּשַׂר.

שׂוֹרָה f., a row, in rows, Isa. 28:25; (Arab. the same).

שׂיש, שׂוּשׂ, שׂוּשׂ (fut. יָשִׂישׂ; inf. abs. שׂוֹשׂ; const. שׂוּשׂ; imp. שִׂישׂ) rejoiced, exulted in, with בְּ, עַל.

שָׂשׂוֹן m., joy, rejoicing.

מָשׂוֹשׂ m., joy.

שָׂח ; see שׂיחַ.

שָׂחָה swam, Isa. 25:11. Hiph. overflowed, Ps. 6:7.

שָׂחוּ m., swimming, Eze. 47:5.

שָׂחַט squeezed, crushed, Gen. 40:11.

שָׂחַק I. laughed.—II. with אֶל approved.—III. with עַל laughed at.—IV

with לְ *despised.* — V. *caused laughter.* Pi. שִׂחֵק (inf. שַׂחֵק; fut. יְשַׂחֵק).
— I. *rejoiced, sported.* — II. *played on an instrument,* 2 Sa. 6:21. — III. *made sport,* Jud. 16:25. — IV. *skirmished,* 2 Sa. 2:14. Hiph. *derided,* with עַל, 2 Chron. 30:10.

שְׂחוֹק ,שְׂחֹק m. — I. *laughter.* — II. *subject or object of laughter.*

מִשְׂחָק m., *object of laughter,* Hab. 1:10.

שָׂטָה (fut. יִשְׂטֶה; apoc. יֵשְׂטְ). — I. *went aside,* Pro. 7:25. — II. *went astray,* Nu. c. 5.

שֵׂטִים; see שׂוּם.

שָׂטַם *acted fiercely, hardly towards, was hated.*

מַשְׂטֵמָה f., *hatred,* Hos. 9:7, 8.

שָׂטַן *was an adversary to, opposed;* part. שֹׂטֵן *an adversary,* Ps. 71:13.

שָׂטָן m. — I. *an adversary.* — II. הַשָּׂטָן *the devil, the great adversary.*

שִׂטְנָה f. — I. *accusation,* Ezr. 4:6. — II. p. n. of a well.

שִׂיא; see נשׂא.

שִׂיאוֹן p. n., one of the peaks of Hermon.

שִׂיב *was grey-headed.* Part. שָׂב, Job 15:10; Ch. the same.

שִׂיב m., *grey hairs, old age,* 1 K. 14:4. שֵׂיבָה f., the same.

שִׂיג m., *retirement,* 1 K. 18:27.

שִׂיד *plastered,* Deu. 27:2, 4.
שִׂיד m., *plaster.*

שֶׂה ,שֶׂיֶה com. (const. שֵׂה, with suff. שִׂיוֹ ,שֵׂיֵהוּ), *a sheep or goat.*

שִׂיח I. *meditated,* with בְּ. — II. *spoke,*

with לְ *with,* or בְּ *of.* — III. *composed a psalm, sung,* with בְּ. Pil. I. *uttered,* Isa. 55:8. — II. *meditated,* Ps. 143:5.

שֶׂחַ m., *purpose, design,* Am. 4:13.

שִׂיחַ m. — I. *a plant, bush.* — II. *speech, message.* — III. *a complaint.* — IV. *sorrow,* Job 7:13.

שִׂיחָה f., *complaint, prayer, meditation.*

שִׂים; see שׂוּם.

שָׁךְ ,שָׂכִים ,שֹׂךְ ,שְׂכוֹת; see שׂכך.

שָׂכָה root not used; (Syr. *expected*)

שֵׂכוּ p. n., a place near Ramah.

שֶׂכְוִי m., "*a thunderstorm*" (Lee), Job 38:36.

שְׂכִיָּה f., *objects* (of sight or thought), Isa. 2:16.

מַשְׂכִּית f. (pl. מַשְׂכִּיוֹת). — I. *figure, external image.* — II. *imagination internal image.*

שַׂכִּין m., *a knife,* Pro. 23:2; (Arab. the same).

שָׂכִיר ,שְׂכִירָה; see שׂכר.

שָׂכַךְ *placed as a covering,* Ex. 33:22.
שֵׂךְ m., pl. שִׂכִּים *thorns,* Nu. 33:55.
שָׂךְ m. (with suff. שְׂכּוֹ), *a fence,* Lam. 2:6.
שִׂכָּה f., pl. שֻׂכּוֹת *spears,* Job 40:31.
מְשׂוּכָה f., *a fence,* Pro. 15:19; Isa. 5:5; see שָׂךְ.

שָׂכַל *was wise, careful, skilful,* 1 Sa. 18:30. Pi. *acted wisely, designedly,* Gen. 48:14. Hiph. I. *looked at.* — II. *reflected.* — III. *cared for.* — IV. *acted wisely, was wise.* — V *prospered.* — VI. *made wise, taught,* with בְּ, עַל, אֶל; part. מַשְׂכִּיל 1 *thoughtful, prudent.* — II. *a didactic*

poem (title of Psalms); inf. הַשְׂכֵּל.
הַשְׂכִּיל understanding, wisdom,
with accus. לְ.

שְׂכַל Ch. Ith. part. מִשְׂתַּכַּל considered,
looked at, with בְ.

שֵׂכֶל, שֶׂכֶל m. (with suff. שִׂכְלוֹ).—I.
understanding, skill. — II. estimation, esteem, Pro. 3:4. — III. sig-
nification, Neh. 8:8.

שִׂכְלוּת; see סכל.

שָׂכְלְתָנוּ f. Ch., understanding, skill,
Dan. 5:11, 12, 14.

שָׂכַר I. hired. — II. bribed. Niph.
hired himself, 1 Sa. 2:5. Hith.
הִשְׂתַּכָּר the same, Hag. 1:6.

שָׂכָר m.—I. reward, hire.—II. p. n.
of a man.

שֶׂכֶר m., hire.

שָׂכִיר m., hired person or thing.

שְׂכִירָה f., the act of hiring, τὸ μι-
σθοῦν, Isa. 7:20.

מַשְׂכֹּרֶת f. (with suff. מַשְׂכֻּרְתִּי).—I.
wages.—II. reward, Ru. 2:12.

שְׂלָו f. (pl. שְׂלָוִים), a quail.

שַׂלְמָה trans. for שִׂמְלָה f.(pl. שְׂלָמוֹת).
—I. a garment.— II. any cloth.—
III. clothing.—IV. p. n., the father
of Boaz, who was called also
שַׂלְמוֹן.—V. p. n. of a man.

שַׂלְמַי p. n. of a man.

שְׂמֹאל, שְׂמֹאול m., the left hand
or side; מִשְׂמֹאל on the left or
north; עַל שׂ׳ or שֶׁל שׂ׳ on or to
the left or north.

הַשְׂמִיל, הִשְׂמִיל, הַשְׂמִאיל Hiph.—
I. went to the left. — II. used the
left hand.

שְׂמָלִי, שְׂמֹאלִי m., שְׂמָאלִית f., be
longing to the left, on the left.

שָׂמַח, שָׂמֵחַ I. was glad. — II. expressed joy.—III. burned brightly,
with בְּ, עַל. לְ. Pi. שִׂמַּח made to
rejoice, with עַל, לְ, מִן. Hiph. the
same.

שָׂמֵחַ m. (pl. const. שִׂמְחֵי; f.
שְׂמֵחָה).—I. joyful.—II. expressing
joy. — III. rejoicing in or at, with

שִׂמְחָה f. (pl. שְׂמָחוֹת).—I. joy.—II.
a festival.—III. merriment.

שְׂמִיכָה; see סמך.

שְׂמֹאל; see in הִשְׂמִיל.

שִׂמְלָה f. (pl. שְׂמָלוֹת), garment; see
שַׂלְמָה I.

שַׂמְלָה p. n., a king of Edom.

שְׂמָמִית f., a species of lizard, Pro.
30:28.

שָׂנֵא (fut. יִשְׂנָא; inf. abs. שָׂנֹא, const.
שְׂנֹא, שְׂנֹאת, שִׂנְאָה) hated, with
לְ; part. שֹׂנֵא hater, enemy. Niph.
was hated. Pi. part. מְשַׂנֵּא an
enemy.

שְׂנֵא Ch. part. שָׂנְאִין, haters.

שִׂנְאָה f., hatred.

שָׂנִיא m., שְׂנִיאָה f., hated, Deu. 21:15.

שְׂנִיר p. n., the name of mount Hermon
among the Amorites.

שְׂעַפִּים; see סעף.

שָׂעַר I. shuddered. — II. feared, Deu.
32:17, with עַל.—III. swept, tore
away as a tempest, Ps. 58:10.
Niph. a tempest raged, Ps. 50:3.
Pi. swept away with a tempest, Job
27:21. Hith. raged like a tempest, Dan. 11:40.

שָׂעִיר m., שְׂעִירָה f.—I. hairy, Gen. 27:
11, 23. — II. a goat (always with
עִזִּים). Pl. שְׂעִירִים I. probably

*wild goats*, Isa. 13:21; 34:14.—II. *showers*, Deu. 32:2.

שֵׂעִיר p.n., *Seir*.—1. the district between the Dead Sea and the gulf of Akabah.—II. a mountain of Judah.

שְׂעִירָה p.n., a district unknown.

שְׂעַר const. שְׂעַר m., *the hair*.

שְׂעַר m. Ch., *the hair*.

שַׂעַר m.—I. *a storm, tempest.* — II. *shuddering, horror*; same as סַעַר.

שְׂעָרָה f., *a tempest*.

שַׂעֲרָה f.—I. *a hair*.—II. *the hair*.

שְׂעֹרָה f., *barley* (the plant); pl. שְׂעֹרִים *barley* (the grain).

שְׂעָרִים p.n. of a man.

שָׂפָה f. (dual שְׂפָתַיִם, שִׂפְתֵי; with suff. שְׂפָתָיו; pl. const. שִׂפְתוֹת).—I. *a lip*.—II. *a language.* — III. *words.*—IV. *brim of a vessel.*—V. *shore of the sea, bank of a river.* —VI. *edge, edging.* — VII. *border of a country*, Jud. 7:22.

שָׂפַח. Pi. *struck with baldness*, Isa. 3:17.

מִשְׂפָּח "oppression," Eng. Ver., Isa. 5:7.

שָׂפָם m., *the chin, the beard*.

שָׂפַן *hid, concealed*, Deu. 33:19.

שָׂפַק I. *clapped the hands*, Job 27:23. —II. *sufficed*, 1 Ki. 20:10. Hiph. *bargained with*, Isa. 2:6; with בְּ.

שֶׂפֶק m., *contempt*, Job 36:18.

שַׂק m. (with suff. שַׂקּוֹ; pl. שַׂקִּים).—I. *sack-cloth*.—II. *a sack*.

שָׂקַד. Niph. *was bound, tied*, Lam. 1:14.

שָׂקַד. Pi. *painted the eyes with stibium* (a black powder), Isa. 3:16.

שֵׁר; see שׁוּר.

שָׂרַג. Pu. *was interwoven*, Job 40: 17. Hith. the same, Lam. 1:14.

שָׂרוּג p.n. of a man.

שָׂרִיגִים m. pl., *branches of a vine*.

שָׂרַד *fled, escaped*, Jos. 10:20; (Arab the same.)

שָׂרִיד m., *one that escapes*.—II. *a remnant*, Isa. 1:9.

שְׂרָד m., *colour*; בִּגְדֵי שְׂ׳ *coloured garments* (Exodus only).

שְׂרָד m., *only*.

שָׂרָה *was a prince, prevailed*, with אֶת, עִם; see שָׂרַר.

שָׂרָה s. f.; see שַׂר.

שָׂרַי p.n., *Sarai* (afterwards *Sarah*), the wife of Abraham.

שְׂרָיָהוּ, שְׂרָיָה p.n. of a man.

מִשְׂרָה f., *government*, Isa. 9:5, 6.

שָׂרַח p.n. of a man.

שָׂרַט *cut, made incisions*. Niph. *was crushed*, Zec. 12:3.

שֶׂרֶט m., *an incision*, Lev. 19:28.

שָׂרֶטֶת f., the same, Lev. 21:5.

שָׂרִינִים, see שׂרג; שָׂרִיד, see שׂרד.

שָׂרַךְ. Pi. part. f. מְשָׂרֶכֶת *twisting its course, wandering in all directions*, Jer. 2:23.

שְׂרוֹךְ m., *shoe latchet*.

שַׂרְסְכִים p. n. of an Assyrian eunuch.

שָׂרַע, part. שָׂרוּעַ *stretched out, monstrously prolonged* (of a limb). Hith. *stretched himself out*, Isa. 28:20.

שַׂרְעַפִּים *thoughts*; see סעף.

שָׂרַף I. *burned, consumed.*—II. *burned spices at a funeral.* — III. *baked bricks*, Gen. 11:3. Niph. and Pu. *was burnt.*

שָׂרָף m.—I. *a venomous serpent*, probably the coluber cerastes — II. p. n. of a man.

שְׂרָפִים m. pl., *seraphim, six-winged spirits*, Isa. 6:2, 6.

שְׂרֵפָה f.—I. *burning fire.*—II. *a funeral burning.*

מִשְׂרְפוֹת f. pl.—I. *burning.*—II. מִשְׂרְפוֹת מַיִם p. n., *a place near Sidon.*

שָׂרַק *combed, hackled flax*, Isa. 19:9.

שׂרֵק m., שֹׂרֵקָה f.—I. *a vine of a choice quality.*—II. שֹׂרֵק p. n., a valley between Askelon and Gaza.

שְׂרוּקִים m.pl., *shoots of the vine*, Isa. 16:8.

שָׂרֹק m., pl. שְׂרֻקִּים *bay* (colour of a horse), Zec. 1:8.

שָׂרַר *acted as a prince.* Hith. הִשְׂתָּרֵר *made himself a prince.*

שַׂר m. (pl. שָׂרִים), *prince, ruler, chief, captain.*

שָׂרָה f.—I. *a princess, a woman of rank.* — II. p.n., *Sarah*, the wife of Abraham; see שָׂרַי.

שִׂשׂוֹן; see שׂוּשׂ.

שֵׂת for שְׂאֵת; see נשׂא.

שׂתַם *shut out*, Lam. 3:8.

שָׂתַר. Niph. *were concealed*, 1 Sa.5:9.

## שׁ

שֶׁ‍...‍שָׁ‍... an abbreviation of אֲשֶׁר, prefixed to every part of speech.

שָׁאַב (fut. יִשְׁאַב) *drew water.*
מַשְׁאָב m., pl. מַשְׁאַבִּים *watering places*, Jud. 5:11.

שָׁאַג (fut. יִשְׁאַג).—I. *roared as a lion.* —II. *shrieked for anguish*, Ps. 38:9.

שְׁאָגָה const. שַׁאֲגַת f.—I. *roar of a lion.* — II. *groan, shriek of anguish.*

שָׁאָה *was desolate* (a city), Isa. 6:11. Niph. I. *was desolate* (a city), Isa. 6:11. — II. *were dashed together*, Isa. 17:12, 13. Hiph. *lay waste*, Isa. 37:26. Hith. הִשְׁתָּאֵה *wondered, was in astonishment*, with לְ.

שְׁאָוה f., Pro. 1:27, Ketib *a storm*; same as שֹׁאָה.

שְׁאִיֶּהֶם; see שֹׁוא.

שְׁאִיָּה f., *crash, destruction*, Isa. 24:12.

שְׁאֵת f., *desolation*, Lam. 3:47.

שֵׁת f., *noise, tumult of war*, Num. 24:17.

שָׁאוֹן m. — I. *shouting, the noise of waves.*— II. *desolation, ruin.*

מַשּׁוּאוֹת, מַשְׁאוֹת f. pl., *desolations, a desolate place.*

שָׁאָט contempt; see שׁוּט.

שָׁאט part. from II. שׁוּט.

שָׁאַל, שָׁאֵל (fut. יִשְׁאַל).—I. *questioned, enquired.* — II. *requested, prayed for.* — III. *borrowed*, with מֵאֵת, מִן, מֵעִם, or לְ; שָׁאַל לְשָׁלוֹם *enquired of his welfare, saluted*; שָׁאַל בֵּאלֹהִים *enquired of God.* Niph. *requested for himself.* Pi. שִׁאֵל *asked earnestly*, with בְּ. Hiph. *gave in answer to a request, gave.*

שְׁאֵל Ch., *asked, enquired.*

שָׁאָל p. n. of a man.

שָׁאוּל p. n. of a man, *Saul.* Patron שָׁאוּלִי

שְׁאֹל, שְׁאוֹל com., *the abode of the*

*soul after death* (see אֲבַדּוֹן), with loc. ה שְׁאֵלָה.

שְׁאֵלָה f. (with suff. שְׁאֵלָתִי, שְׁאֵלָתְךָ, שְׁאֵלָתָם), *asking, a request.*

שֵׁלָה I. same as שְׁאֵלָה. — II. p.n., one of the sons of Judah; patron. שֵׁלָנִי.

שְׁאֵלָא f. Ch., *demand*, Dan. 4:14.

שַׁלְתִּיאֵל, שְׁאַלְתִּיאֵל p.n. of a man.

מִשְׁאָל p.n., a town of the Levites in the tribe of Asher.

מִשְׁאָלָה f., *prayers.*

שָׁאַן. Pil. שַׁאֲנַן *was quiet, secure, wanton.*

שַׁאֲנָן m., שַׁאֲנַנָּה f. — I. *quiet.* — II. *wanton, luxurious.* — III. *wantonness, pride.*

שָׁאסַיךָ, שָׁאס; see שסס.

שָׁאַף I. *panted, gasped*, Ps. 119:131. — II. *panted for, desired eagerly.* — III. *swallowed up, destroyed.*

שָׁאַר *was left*, 1 Sa. 16:11. Niph. the same. Hiph. *left, had left.*

שְׁאָר m., *the remainder, remnant.*

שְׁאָר m. Ch., *the same.*

שְׁאָר יָשׁוּב (*a remnant shall return*). Prophetic name of the son of Isaiah, Isa. 7:3.

שְׁאֵר m. — I. *flesh.* — II. *any near relation.*—III. *a right arising from marriage*, Ex. 21:10.

שַׁאֲרָה f., *near, relation, relationship*, Lev. 18:17.

שַׁאֲרָה p.n. of a woman.

שְׁאֵרִית, שְׁאֵרִית f., *remainder, remnant.*

מִשְׁאֶרֶת f., *kneading trough.*

שְׁאָת; see שאה.

שֵׁב, with ה parag. שְׁבָה Kal imp. from ישׁב.

שְׁבָא p.n. of a country, probably Arabia Felix.

שָׁבַב (Arab. *kindled*).

שָׁבִיב m., *flame*, Job 18:5.

שְׁבִיב m. Ch., *the same.*

שְׁבָבִים m. pl., *fragments*, Hos. 8:6.

שָׁבָה (imp. וּשֲׁבֵה; fut. apoc. וַיִּשְׁבְּ) *carried captive, took prisoners, carried off*; part. שָׁבוּיִם m., שְׁבִיּוֹת f., *captives.* Niph. *was led captive.*

שְׁבוּאֵל p.n. of a man; written also שׁוּבָאֵל.

שְׁבִי, with pause שֶׁבִי m. (with suff. שֶׁבְיְךָ, שִׁבְיוֹ, שִׁבְיְכֶם); f. שִׁבְיָה I. *captive.* — II. *troop of captives.* — III. *captivity.*

שִׁבְיָה f. — I. *troop of captives, spoil.* — II. *captivity.*

שְׁבִית, שְׁבוּת f. — I. *captivity.* — II. *captives.* שׁוּב שׁ׳ I. *turned from captivity.* — II. *restored to prosperity.*

שְׁבוּ m., *an agate*; LXX. ἀχάτης.

שָׁבַח. Pi. שִׁבַּח I. *praised, commended.* — II. *quieted, restrained, kept back.* Hiph. *quieted*, Ps. 65:8. Hith. *boast of, glory in*, with בְּ.

שְׁבַח Ch. Pa. *praised.*

שֵׁבֶט, שָׁבַט com. (with suff. שִׁבְטִי). — I. *staff.*—II. *rod* (for punishment).— III. *sceptre.* — IV. *dart, short spear.*—V. *tribe.*

שְׁבַט com. Ch., *a tribe*, Ezr. 6:17.

שְׁבָט m., *the eleventh month of the Jewish year, corresponding to our February and March.*

שַׁרְבִּיט m., *a sceptre* (Esther only).

שְׁבִי, שִׁבְיָה *captive, &c.*; see שבה.

שְׁבִי and שְׁבִי p. n. of a man.

שְׁבִיסִים m. pl., "*sun-like ornaments of the neck*," (Schrœder); "*cauls*," Eng. Ver., Isa. 3:18; sense uncertain.

שְׁבִיעַ, שְׁבִיעִית; see שׁבע.

שְׁבִירָה; see שׁבה.

שְׁבִיל m., *a path, mode of conduct*; (Arab. the same).

שְׁבָל m., "*locks*" (of hair), Eng. Ver., Isa. 47:2.

שְׁבֵל or שֶׁבֶל f., pl. const. שִׁבְּלֵי *a branch*, Zec. 4:12.

שִׁבֹּלֶת f. (pl. שִׁבֳּלִים).—I. *a stream of water*.—II. *an ear of corn*.

שַׁבְלוּל m., *a snail*, Ps. 58:9.

שֶׁבְנָה, שֶׁבְנָא p. n., Shebna, the scribe.

שְׁבַנְיָה p. n. of a man.

שֶׁבַע, const. שְׁבַע, f. שִׁבְעָה, const. שִׁבְעַת m., *seven, the seventh*; adv. *seventh, sevenfold*; שִׁבְעָה שִׁבְעָה *by sevens*; שִׁבְעָה עָשָׂר m., שִׁבְעָ עֶשְׂרֵה f., *seventeen*; dual שִׁבְעָתַיִם I. *sevenfold*. — II. *seventimes*. Pl. שִׁבְעִים *seventy*.

שִׁבְעָנֶה m., *seven*, Job 42:13.

שָׁבוּעַ m. (dual שְׁבֻעַיִם; pl. שָׁבֻעִים, שְׁבֻעוֹת).—I. *a week*; חַג שָׁבֻעוֹת *the feast of weeks*.—II. *a week of years*, Dan. c. 9 & 10.

שְׁבִיעִי m., שְׁבִיעִית f., *seventh*.

II. שֶׁבַע p. n., (a) *a town of Simeon*; (b) *of a man*; (c) שִׁבְעָה *name of a well*.

שָׁבַע *bound by oaths*, Eze. 21:28. Niph. נִשְׁבַּע *swore*, with לְ; *swore to*, with בְּ; *swore by*. Hiph. I. *caused to swear*.—II. *adjured*.

שְׁבֻעָה, שְׁבוּעָה f., *an oath*.

שָׁבַץ. Pi. "embroider," Eng. Ver., Ex. 28:39; sense doubtful. Pu. *set* (of a precious stone), Ex. 28:20.

שָׁבָץ m., *perplexity*, 2 Sa. 1:9.

מִשְׁבְּצוֹת f. pl.—I. *gold settings* (for stones).—II. *cloth of gold*, Ps. 45:14.

תַּשְׁבֵּץ m., *embroidery*, Ex. 28:4.

שְׁבַק Ch. *left*. Ith. *was left*.

שָׁבַר fut. (יִשְׁבֹּר).—I. *broke to pieces*. —II. *tore* (as a wild beast).—III. *broke the heart*.—IV. *broke the power of, destroyed*.—V. *quenched thirst*.—VI. *assigned*, with חֹק.— VII. from שֶׁבֶר *sold corn*, Gen. 41:56.—VIII. *bought corn*. Niph. I *was broken*.—II. *was torn*.—III. *was broken* (the heart). —IV. *was destroyed*. Pi. שִׁבֵּר *broke with violence*. Hiph. I. *caused to suffer labour pains*, Isa. 66:9. — II. *sold corn*. Hoph. *was broken-hearted*, Jer. 8:21.

שֶׁבֶר, שֵׁבֶר (with suff. שִׁבְרוֹ) I. *breaking, fracture*. — II. *vexation, sorrow*. — III. *calamity, ruin*. — IV. *provision, corn*.—V. *interpretation*, Jud. 7:15.—VI. p. n., *a place near Ai*.

שִׁבָּרוֹן m.—I. *breaking*, i.e. pain, sorrow, Eze. 21:11. — II. *calamity, ruin*, Jer. 17:18.

מַשְׁבֵּר m. — I. *pains of childbirth*. — II. *violent pains* (of any kind), 2 Sa. 22:5.—III. *breakers* (of the sea). מִשְׁבָּר m., *the same*.

שְׁבַשׁ Ch. Ith., *perplexed*, Dan. 5:9.

שָׁבַת (fut. יִשְׁבֹּת ,יִשְׁבַּת).—I. *ceased.*—
II. *rested;* with מִן *from.*—III. *was
interrupted,* Neh. 6:3.—IV. *ceased
to exist, came to an end.*—V. with
שַׁבָּת *kept the sabbath.* Niph.
*came to an end.* Hiph. I. *caused
to cease.* — II. *interrupted.* — III.
*brought to an end.*

שֶׁבֶת m.—I. *ceasing.* — II. *intermission;* see also in יָשַׁב.

שַׁבָּת com. (with suff. שַׁבַּתּוֹ; pl.
שַׁבָּתוֹת; const. שַׁבְּתוֹת) *cessation, time of rest, sabbath;* שַׁבַּת
שָׁנִים *a sabbath of years.*

שַׁבָּתוֹן m., *rest, a time of rest.*

שַׁבְּתַי p. n. of a man.

מִשְׁבָּת m., pl. מִשְׁבַּתִּים *cessations,*
Lam. 1:7.

שֶׁבֶת Kal inf., from יָשַׁב.

שָׁבַת Ch. Kal pret. f., from שׁוּב.

שָׁנָא same as שָׁנָה.

שָׁגַג *erred, committed an error,* Lev.
5:18; inf. בְּשִׁגָּם *because of their
sin.*

שְׁגָגָה f., *error, unintentional fault.*

שָׁגָה *erred, went astray,* with מִן.
Hiph. I. *allowed to err,* Ps. 119:
10.—II. *caused to go astray.*

שָׁגָא p. n. of a man.

שְׁגִיאָה f., *error,* Ps. 19:13.

שִׁגָּיוֹן m. (pl. שִׁגְיוֹנוֹת) *a doleful song,
lament,* Ps. 7:1; Hab. 3:1.

מִשְׁגֶּה m., *mistake, inadvertency,* Gen.
43:12.

שָׁגַח. Hiph. *looked to.*

שָׁגַל *lay with a woman;* fut. יִשְׁגַּל.
Niph. and Pu. pass. of Kal.

שֵׁגָל f., *a queen.*

שֵׁגַל f. Ch., the same.

שַׁגָּם Kal inf. with suff., from שָׁגַג.

שָׁגַע. Pu. part. מְשֻׁגָּע *maddened, mad.*
Hith. *acted like a madman.*

שִׁגָּעוֹן m., *madness, impetuosity.*

שֶׁגֶר ,שֶׁגַר m., *offspring, progeny,*
Exod. 13:12.

שַׁד, see שָׁדָה; שֹׁד, see שׁוּד; שַׂד,
see שָׂדָה ,שָׂדַד.

שָׁדַד (fut. with suff. יְשָׁדֵּם ,יִשְׁדָּדֵם).—
I. *attacked, invaded.*—II. *plundered,
laid waste, ruined;* part. שֹׁדֵד *in-
vader, plunderer;* שָׁדוּד *destroyed.*
Niph. *was laid waste.* Pi. *laid waste,
ruined utterly.* Pu. שֻׁדַּד ,שֹׁדַד
*was laid waste.* Po. *laid waste.*
Hoph. הֻשַּׁד *was laid waste.*

שֹׁד m.—I. *destruction, ruin.*—
II. *violence, oppression.*—III. *ex-
torted property,* Am. 3:10.

שַׁדַּי m., *the Almighty* (the name of
God as revealed to the Patriarchs); LXX. παντοκράτωρ.

שָׁדָה root not used; (Arab. *was well
watered*).

שַׁד m.—I. *teats of an animal.*— II.
*breast of a woman;* dual שָׁדַיִם,
שְׁדֵי *the breasts.*

שֹׁד m., the same.

שִׁדָּה f., שִׁ׳ וְשִׁדּוֹת, Ecc. 2:8, "musical instruments and that of all
sorts," Eng. Ver.—*pleasures of
every kind* (Ges. and Lee).

שְׁדֵיאוּר p. n. of a man.

שְׁדֵמָה f., *blighted corn;* pl. שַׁדְמוֹת,
שְׁדֵמוֹת.—I. *fields.*—II. *corn fields,*
Hab. 3:17.—III. *vineyards.*

שָׁדַף *blighted.*

שְׁדֵפָה f., *blight in corn*, 2 Ki. 19:26.

שִׁדָּפוֹן m., the same.

שְׁדַר Ch. Ithp. *exerting himself*, Dan. 6:15.

שַׁדְרַךְ p.n., *Shadrach*, one of the three holy children.

שֹׁהַם m.—I. *onyx* or *sardonyx*.—II. p. n. of a man.

שׁוֹא m. (pl. with suff. שֹׁאֵיהֶם) *ragings*, Ps. 35:17.

שָׁוְא m.—I. *guilt.*-II. *calamity.*-III. *worthlessness, vanity.*— IV. *falsehood.*

שָׁו same as שָׁוְא.

שׁוֹאָה f.—I. *a storm.*—II. *destruction.* —III. *a desolate place.*

מְשׁוֹאָה f., *desolation, a desolate place.*

תְּשֻׁאָה f., pl. תְּשֻׁאוֹת *tumult, shouting.*

שׁוֹב, Jer. 42:10, for שׁוֹב Kal inf., from יָשַׁב.

שׁוּב (fut. וַיֹּשֶׁב יָשָׁב יָשׁוּב).—I. *went or came back*; with מִן *from*; *turned to, returned*, with עַל, לְ, אֶל, עַד *to.* — II. *turned himself about*, 1 Chron. 21:20. — III. *changed his course of life.* (For many uses with other words which slightly modify these primary meanings, see Concordance.) Pil. שׁוֹבֵב I. *led back.*—II. *restored.*— III. *led astray*, Isa. 47:10. — IV. *refreshed*, Ps. 23:3. Pul. שׁוֹבַב *was brought back.* Hiph. הֵשִׁיב (fut. וַיֹּשֶׁב יָשֵׁב יָשִׁיב).—I. *brought back.*—II. *restored.*—III. *requited.* —IV. *brought upon a person.*—V. *sent as a tribute or atonement.*—

VI. *distributed, assigned.* — **VII.** *moved away, put aside.*—**VIII.** *repelled, hindered.*— IX. *recalled, revoked a declaration.*—X. *caused to turn from sin.*— XI. *withheld, withdrew.*—XII. *brought down, reduced.*— XIII. *caused to answer*, Job 20:2. With דָּבָר *answered*; with פָּנָיו *turned away his anger;* with (עַל) אֶל־לֵב *laid to heart, considered;* with פ' פְּנֵי *turned away, refused.* Hoph. הוּשַׁב *was returned, brought back.*

שׁוּבָה f., *returning*, Isa. 30:15.

שִׁיבָה f., *returning*, Ps. 126:1; see another meaning in יָשַׁב.

שׁוֹבָב m.—I. *a rebellious person.*—II. p.n. of a man.

שׁוֹבֵב m., שׁוֹבֵבָה f., *a rebel.*

שׁוּבָאֵל p. n., same as שְׁבוּאֵל.

מְשׁוֹבָב p.n. of a man.

מְשׁוּבָה, מְשֻׁבָה f.—I. *turning away* (from God). — II. *rebellious, back sliding.*

תְּשׁוּבָה f.—I. *return.*—II. *an answer.*

שׁוֹבָךְ p. n. of a man.

שׁוֹבָל p. n. of a man.

שׁוֹבֵק p. n. of a man.

שָׁוּג same as שָׂגָה, שָׁנָה.

מְשׁוּגָה f., *error*, Job 19:4.

שׁוּד same as שָׁדַד *laid waste*; fut. יָשׁוּד, Ps. 91:6.

שׁוֹד same as שֹׁד; see שָׁדַד.

שֵׁד m., pl. שֵׁדִים *idols*, Deu. 32:17; Ps. 106:37; LXX. δαιμόνια.

שָׁוָה I. *was equal to, resembled.*—II. *was of equal value or importance.* —III. *was fitting, proper*, Est. 3:8. —IV. *was sufficient*, Est. 7:4. With

בְּ, לְ, אֶל. Pi. שִׁוָּה I. *made level, smoothed,* Isa. 28:25. — II. *made similar,* Ps. 131:2. — III. *made himself like,* Isa. 38:13. — IV. *placed, proposed.* — V. *produced fruit,* Hos. 10:1. Hiph. *made like, compared.* Nithpa. נִשְׁתַּוָּה *being made like,* Pro. 27:15.

שְׁוָא Ch. Pa., *placed, made equal,* Dan. 5:21, with עִם. Ithpa. *was made into,* Dan. 3:29.

שָׁוָה f., *equity,* Job 33:27.

שָׁוֵה p. n., *a plain to the north of Jerusalem;* שָׁוֵה קִרְיָתָיִם *a city of Moab.*

שׁוּחַ *went down, sank.*

שׁוּחַ p. n. of one of Abraham's sons; patron. שׁוּחִי.

שׁוּחָה f.—I. *a pit, pitfall.*—II. p.n. of a man.

שִׁיחָה f., *a pit,* Ps. 119:85.

שֻׁחָם p. n. of a man.

שַׁחַת f.—I. *a pit.* — II. *a dungeon.*—III. *a grave;* see also in שָׁחַת.

I. שׁוּט 1. *spread like water, went to and fro.*—2. *struck, struck into the water,* i.e. *rowed.* Pil. שׁוֹמֵט *ran far and wide.* Hithpal. הִתְשׁוֹטֵט *same as Pil.*

שׁוֹט m.—I. *a whip, scourge.*—II. *calamity.*

שַׁיִט m., *an oar, oars,* Isa. 33:21.

שֹׁטֵט m., *a whip, scourge,* Jos. 23:13.

מָשׁוֹט m., *an oar, rudder,* Eze. 27:29.

מִשׁוֹט m., *the same,* Eze. 27:6.

II. שׁוּט (Syr. *despised*); part. שָׁאט *despised* (Ezekiel only).

שְׁאָט m. (with suff. שְׁאָטְךָ), *contempt* (of another), Ezekiel only.

---

שׁוּגָל m., *skirt* (of a garment), *train.*

שׁוֹלָל *spoil;* see שָׁלַל.

שׁוּלַמִּית; see שָׁלֵם.

שׁוּם m., *garlick,* Nu. 11:5.

שׁוּנִי p. n., *a son of Gad.*

שׁוּנֵם p. n., *a town of Issachar;* שׁוּנַמִּי m., שׁוּנַמִּית f., *a Shunemite.*

שׁוַע, שָׁוַע. Pi. שִׁוַּע *cried out for help, implored,* with אֶל. Pil. and Hiph. see in יָשַׁע.

שֶׁוַע m. (with suff. שַׁוְעִי), *a cry for help,* Ps. 5:3.

שׁוֹעַ m.—I. *affluent,* Job 34:19.—II. *liberal,* Isa. 32:5.

שֶׁוַע m.—I. *safety,* Job 30:24. — II. *affluence,* Job 36:19 —III. p.n. of a man.

שַׁוְעָה f., *cry for help.*

שׁוּעָא p. n. of a man.

תְּשׁוּעָה, תְּשֻׁעָה f., *freedom, safety, salvation, deliverance.*

שׁוּעָל; see שָׁעַל.

שׁוֹעֵר; see שָׁעַר.

שׁוּף (fut. יְשׁוּף).—I. *bruised, shattered,* Gen. 3:15; Job 9:17. — II. *concealed,* Ps. 139:11.

שׁוֹפָךְ p. n., *same as* שׁוֹבָךְ.

שֻׁפָמִי p. n. of a man.

שׁוֹפָר *trumpet;* see שָׁפַר.

שׁוּק *same as* שָׁקַק. Hiph. הֵשִׁיק I. *caused to run over,* Joel 2:24. — II. *overflowed,* Joel 4:13. Pil. שׁוֹקֵק *cause to overflow,* Ps. 65:10.

שׁוּק m. (pl. שְׁוָקִים), *a street.*

שׁוֹק com. (dual שֹׁקַיִם), *leg* (of a man or animal); trop. שׁוֹקֵי הָאִישׁ *perhaps infantry,* Ps. 147:10

שָׁק m. Ch., *leg.*

תְּשׁוּקָה f., *desire.*

שׁוּר (fut. יָשׁוּר). — I. viewed, beheld, perceived. — II. watched (for good or evil). — III. went, Is. 57:9; part. f. pl. שָׁרוֹת travellers, Eze. 27:25. See also in שִׁיר.

שׁוּר m. — I. an enemy (one who watches for evil), Ps. 92:12. — II. a wall; pl. שׁוּרוֹת. — III. p. n., a place in the wilderness; מִדְבַּר שׁוּר the wilderness of Shur, between Egypt and Palestine.

שׁוּר m. Ch., a wall.

שׁוּרוֹת f. pl., walls, Jer. 5:10.

שׁוֹר m. (pl. שְׁוָרִים).—I. an ox.—II. a herd of oxen.

תְּשׁוּרָה f., a present, 1 Sa. 9:7.

שַׁיִשׁ root not used ; (Syr. alabaster).

שַׁיִשׁ m., white marble, 1 Ch. 29:2.

שֵׁשׁ m.—I. white marble, Est. 1:6.— II. very fine linen. (See also in its place.)

שׁוּשַׁן m.—I. a lily.—II. an artificial lily.—III. שׁוּשַׁן עֵדֻת probably the name of a musical instrument.— IV. שׁוּשַׁן p. n.: (a) the city of Susa in Persia; (b) a place unknown.

שׁוֹשׁ m., a lily; pl. שׁוֹשַׁנִּים. — I. lilies.—II. musical instruments.

שׁוֹשַׁנָּה f., the same.

שׁוּשַׁנְכוּא Ch., an inhabitant of Susa.

שׁוֹשַׁתִּי Po. pret. from שָׁסָה; same as שׁסה.

שׁוּת; see שִׁית.

שׁוּתֶלַח p. n. of a man. Patron. שׁוּתַלְחִי.

שֵׁזַב Ch. Pe. שֵׁיזִב, שֵׁיזִיב delivered, rescued.

שָׁזַף beheld, saw. (See also in שָׂרַף.)

שָׁזַר Hoph.part. שֵׁשׁ מָשְׁזָר fine twined

linen (probably wrung out for the purpose of bleaching it).

שַׁח; see שׁחח.

שָׁחַד bribed.

שֹׁחַד m.—I. a present.— II. a bribe. —III. bribery, Job 15:34.

שָׁחָה bowed himself, Isa. 51:23. Hiph. הִשְׁחָה bowed down, Pro. 12:25. Hith. הִשְׁתַּחֲוָה (inf. הִשְׁתַּחֲוֹת; Ch. הִשְׁתַּחֲוָיָה; imp. f. הִשְׁתַּחֲוִי; fut. יִשְׁתַּחֲוֶה; apoc. וַיִּשְׁתָּחוּ) I. prostrated himself; with לְ, לִפְנֵי, before.—II. worshipped.

שַׁחֲנוּת f., a pit, Pro. 28:10.

שַׁחִית f., the same.

שָׁחוֹר same as שִׁיחוֹר; see שׁחר.

שָׁחַח (pret. שַׁחוּ, שָׁחוּ; fut. יִשַּׁח). — I. bowed himself, stooped. — II. was brought low, humbled. Niph. the same. Hiph. הֵשַׁח brought low, humbled. Hithp. הִשְׁתּוֹחֵחַ brought low, broke.

שַׁח m., having downcast eyes, meek, Job 22:29.

שָׁחַט (fut. יִשְׁחַט; inf. שְׁחָטָה). — I. slaughtered (an animal).—II. slew (a person).—III. זָהָב שָׁחוּט " alloyed gold" (Lee). Niph. was slaughtered.

שְׁחִיטָה f., slaughtering, sacrifice, 2 Ch. 30:17.

שִׁחִין; see שׁחן.

שְׁחִים spontaneous; see סָחִישׁ.

שְׁחִית, see שׁחח; שְׁחִיתָה, see שׁחת.

שַׁחַל m., a lion.

שְׁחֵלֶת f., some kind of perfume, or pastil; LXX. ὄνυξ, Ex. 30:34.

שָׁחַן (Arab. fever).

שַׁחַן m., *inflammation, any burning disease*; שׁ מִצְרַיִם *the ulcer of Egypt.*

שָׁחַף *root not used* ;(Arab. *was thin*).

שָׁחִיף m., *thin covering of wood*, Eze. 41:16.

שַׁחַף m. LXX. λάρος; *a sea gull*, Lev. 11:16; Deu. 14:15.

שַׁחֶפֶת f., *consumption.*

שָׁחַץ (Arab. *was lifted up*).

שַׁחַץ m., *mightiness, fierceness.*

שַׁחֲצִים p. n., *a place in the tribe of Issachar.*

שָׁחַק *reduced to dust, crushed, wasted away.*

שַׁחַק m.—I. *dust*, Isa. 40:15.—II. *a cloud*; pl. שְׁחָקִים *clouds.*—III. *the sky.*

שָׁחַר I. *was black*, Job 30:30.—II. *did a thing early, sought early.* Pi. שָׁחַר *sought early*, with אֶל.

שָׁחֹר, שְׁחוֹרָה m., שְׁחוֹרָה f., *black*;

שְׁחוֹר m., *blackness*, Lam. 4:8.

שַׁחַר m.—I. *the dawn*; בֶּן־שַׁחַר *lucifer*, "the morning star." — II. adv. *in the morning.* — III. *rise, origin*, Isa. 47:11.

שַׁחֲרוּת f., *dawn of life, youth*, Ecc. 11:10.

שְׁחַרְחֹרֶת f., *very black*, Cant. 1:6.

שְׁחַרְיָה p. n. of a man.

שְׁחָרַיִם p. n. of a man.

מִשְׁחָר m., *the dawn*, Ps. 110:3.

שִׁחֹר, שְׁחוֹר, שִׁיחוֹר m.—I. the name of a river of Egypt, probably the *Nile.* —II. שִׁיחוֹר לִבְנָת *a river in Asher.*

שָׁחַת. Niph. I. *was spoilt.*— II. *was corrupted*, Gen. 6:11, 12. — III. *was destroyed*, Ex. 8:20. Pi. שִׁחֵת

I. *acted corruptly.*—II. *destroyed* — III. *broke a covenant*, Mal 2:8. —IV. *laid aside* (of pity), Am. 1:11. Hiph. הִשְׁחִית same as Pi.; with or without דַּרְכּוֹ *corrupted his way.* Hoph. הָשְׁחַת; part. מָשְׁחָת I. *injured*, Mal. 1:14. —II. *polluted*, Pro. 25:26.

שְׁחַת Ch., part. שְׁחִיתָה *a fault.*

שַׁחַת m.—I. *corruption.*—II. *destruction*; see also שׁוּחָה.

מַשְׁחִית m. (Hiph. part.).—I. *destroyer*, Ex. 12:23—II. *plunderer*.

מִשְׁחָת m., *defilement*, Lev. 22:25.

מַשְׁחֵת m., *destruction*, Eze. 9:1.

מִשְׁחָת m., *disfigured*, Isa. 52:14.

שִׁטָּה f.—I. *the pea-thorn*; (Arab. שנט ; Egypt. *shont*); pl. שִׁטִּים *shittim wood, the wood of the pea-thorn.*—II. p. n., a valley of Moab.

שָׁטַח *spread abroad, strewed.* Pi. שִׁטַּח *spread abroad* (the hands in prayer), Ps. 88:10.

מִשְׁטוֹחַ, מִשְׁטָח m., *place for spreading nets*, Eze. 26:5, 14; 47:10.

שָׁטַם; see שׂוּט.

שָׁטַף I. *washed off* or *away.*—II. *cleansed by washing.* —III. *swept away* (of a torrent). Niph. I. *was cleansed*, Lev. 15:12. — II. *was swept away*, Dan. 11:22. Pu. *was cleansed*, Lev. 6:21.

שֶׁטֶף, שָׁטֶף m., *washing away, overflowing, inundation.*

שָׁטַר; part. שֹׁטֵר *magistrate, ruler*, Ex. 5:10, 14; Deu. 1:15

שִׁטְרַי p. n. of a man.

מִשְׁטָר m., *authority, influence*, Job 38:33.

שְׁטַר m. Ch., *sovereignty* (if the reading be correct; some suppose an error for שְׂטַר side), Dan. 7:5.

שַׁי m., *offering, present* (always with יוֹבִלוּ *bring ye*).

שִׂיאֹן p n., a name of Hermon.

שִׁיבָה; see יָשַׁב, שׁוּב.

שָׁיָה, fut. apoc. תֵּשִׁי *thou forgettest*; LXX. ἐγκατέλιπες, Deu. 32:18; see נָשָׁה.

שִׁינָא p. n. of a man

שֵׁיזִיב; see שׁוּב.

שַׁיִט; see שׁוּט.

שִׁיחָה; see שׁוּחַ.

שִׁילֹנִי, שִׁילֹה; see שׁלה.

שׁוּן, שִׁין (Syr. minxit).

שַׁיִן or שֵׁין m., pl. שֵׁינִים *urine*.

שֵׁיצָא Ch.; see יצא.

שׁוּר, שִׁיר (שָׁר, וַיָּשַׁר, יָשִׁיר fut.).— I. *sung*; with לְ *to*.—II. *sung of*; part. שָׁרִים, שָׁרוֹת *singers*. Pil. שׁוֹרֵר *sounded*, Zep. 2:14; part. a *singer*. Hoph. הוּשַׁר *was sung*.

שִׁיר m.—I. *singing*.—II. *a song*.—III. *instrumental music*; כְּלֵי שִׁיר *musical instruments*.

שִׁירָה f., *a song*.

שַׁיִשׁ; see שֵׁשׁ.

שִׁישַׁק p.n., *Shishak*, king of Egypt; LXX. Σεσογχις.

שׁוּת, שִׁית (וַיָּשֶׁת, יָשֶׁת, יָשִׁית fut.; inf. abs. שֹׁת; inf. const. and imp. שִׁית) same as שׂוּם — I. *placed, laid*; with לְ, עַל *upon*; with עָלָיו *decorated himself*:— also II. *set over, appointed*.—III. *set together, compared*, with עִם.—IV. שִׁ פָּנָיו *looked towards*.—V. עֵינָיו שִׁ

*looked out after*, Ps. 17:11. — VI. שִׁי לֵב *set his heart upon, regarded*, with אֶל, לְ — VII. שִׁי יָד עִם *assisted*.—VIII. לְנֶגְדּוֹ שִׁי *looked at, examined*, Ps. 90:8.—IX. *laid up treasure*.—X. *rendered*. Hoph. הוּשַׁת *was required*, with עַל, Ex. 21:30.

שַׁיִת m. (with suff. שִׁיתוֹ) *thorn* (Isaiah only).

שִׁית m., *putting on a dress*.

שֵׁתוֹת m. pl., *foundations*.

שֵׁת p. n.—I. *Seth*, the son of Adam. —II. an epithet of the Moabites, Nu. 24:17.

שֹׁךְ, שֵׁךְ Kal inf., from שָׁכַךְ.

שָׁכַב (fut. יִשְׁכַּב; inf. שְׁכַב, שְׁכֹב; imp. שְׁכַב, שִׁכְבָה.— I. *lay down*. —II. *slept*.—III. *kept his bed*.—IV. *slept with his fathers, died*.—V *rested* (of the head).—VI. *lay with* (carnally). Pu. *to be laid, to lie*. Niph. I. *placed*.—II. *caused to rest, stopped*. Hoph. *was placed, laid*.

שְׁכָבָה, const. שִׁכְבַת f.—I. *the act of lying with*.— II. *covering of dew*, Ex. 16:13, 14.

שְׁכֹבֶת f., *act of lying with*.

מִשְׁכָּב m. (pl. מִשְׁכָּבִים, מִשְׁכְּבוֹת).— I. *a bed*.—II. *a bier*, 2 Chron. 16: 14.—III. *lying in bed*.— IV. *lying with*.

מִשְׁכַּב m. Ch., *a bed*.

שָׁכָה. Hiph. part. מַשְׁכִּים *wandering about lasciviously*, Jer. 5:8.

שָׂכוּל, שַׁכּוּל; see שׁכל.

שִׁכּוֹר; see שׁכר.

שָׁכַח, שָׁכֵחַ (fut. יִשְׁכַּח) *forgot, disregarded, neglected*, with מִן. Niph. *was forgotten, neglected*. Pi. and

Hiph. *cause to forget.* Hithpa. same as Niph., Ecc 8:10.

שָׁכֵחַ m. (pl. const. שְׁכֵחֵי) *forgetting, neglecting.*

שְׁכַח Ch. Ithp. הִשְׁתְּכַח *was found, was.* Aph. הַשְׁכַּח *found, discovered.*

שְׁכַיָה p.n. of a man.

שָׁכַךְ (inf. שֹׁךְ, שֵׁךְ; fut. pl. וַיִּשְׁכּוּ). I. *stooped.* — II. *abated.* Hiph. הֵשֵׁךְ I. *placed.* — II. *emptied.*

שָׁכַל (fut. יִשְׁכַּל) *lost children, became childless.* Pi. I. *made childless.* — II. *stripped of inhabitants.* — III. *destroyed* (of a sword), Deu 32:25. — IV. *produced an abortion.* — V. *lost fruit, &c., was barren;* part. מְשַׁכֵּלֶת *an abortion.* Hiph. *lost its inhabitants* (a land).

שְׁכוֹל m. — I. *privation of children.* — II. *destitution.*

שַׁכּוּל m., שַׁכֻּלָה f. — I. *childless.* — II. *deprived of, without young.*

שִׁכֻּלִים m. pl., *loss of children,* Isa. 49:20.

אֶשְׁכּוֹל m. (pl. const. אֶשְׁכְּלוֹת, אַשְׁכְּלוֹת) — I. *a cluster, bunch of grapes* or *flowers;* (Arab. bound). — II. p. n.: (a) of a valley in the south of Palestine; (b) of a man.

שַׁכְלֵל; see כָּלַל.

שָׁכַם. Hiph. הִשְׁכִּים I. *arose in the morning.* — II. *as soon as he arose.* — III. *came in the morning.*

שְׁכֶם with pause שָׁכֶם m. (with suff. שִׁכְמוֹ). — I. *shoulder, shoulders.* — II. *a load, portion,* Gen. 48:22. — III. p. n., *Shechem,* a city of the Levites in Ephraim; with ה loc.

שֶׁכְמָה, with pause שֶׁכְמָה — IV p.n. of a man.

שֶׁכֶם p.n. of a man; patron. שִׁכְמִי

שִׁכְמָה f., *the shoulder-blade,* Job 31:22.

שָׁכֵן, שָׁכַן (fut. יִשְׁכֹּן). — I. *lay down to rest, rested.* — II. *continued* — III. *dwelt.* — IV. *inhabited, was inhabited;* part. שֹׁכֵן *inhabiting.* Pi. I. *caused to dwell.* — II. *placed;* שִׁכֵּן שְׁמוֹ *placed his name.* Hiph. I. *caused to dwell.* — II. *fixed.*

שְׁכֵן Ch. Pa., same as Pi. Heb.

שָׁכֵן, const. שְׁכַן m., שְׁכֵנָה, שְׁכֶנֶת f. — I. *inhabitant.* — II. *neighbour, neighbouring people.*

שֶׁכֶן m., *a dwelling;* with suff. שִׁכְנוֹ, Deu. 12:5.

שְׁכַנְיָה p.n. of a man.

שְׁכַנְיָהוּ p.n. of a man.

מִשְׁכָּן m. — I. *habitation, dwelling.* — II. *the Tabernacle and Temple.* — III. *lair of beasts.*

מִשְׁכָּן m. Ch., *habitation.*

שָׁכַר (fut. יִשְׁכַּר). — I. *drank wine* or *strong drink.* — II. *was exhilarated, intoxicated.* — III. *became giddy.* Pi. and Hiph. *made drunken.* Hith. *made himself drunken,* 1 Sa 1:14.

שִׁכּוֹר, שִׁכֹּר m., שִׁכֹּרָה f., *drunken, a drunkard.*

שֵׁכָר m. — I. *strong drink* (not wine) — II. *wine,* Nu. 28:7.

שִׁכָּרוֹן m., *drunkenness* (Ezekiel only)

שִׁכְרוֹן p.n., a place of Judah.

אֶשְׁכָּר m., *rich gift, present.*

שֶׁל; see אֲשֶׁר.

שִׁלְאָנָן, שַׁל; see שָׁלָה.

שָׁלַב. Pu. part. מְשֻׁלָּבֹת *joined together* (Ex. 26 : 17 ; 36 : 22).

שְׁלַבִּים m. pl., *edges, borders,* 1 Ki. 7 : 28, 29.

שֶׁלֶג m., *snow.*

הִשְׁלִיג Hiph. "was white as snow," Eng. Ver., Ps. 68 : 15.

שָׁלָו, שָׁלָה (pret. שָׁלַוְתִּי, שָׁלוּ ; fut. יִשְׁלָיוּ ; fut. apoc. יֶשֶׁל).— I. *was prosperous, at ease.*—II. *made prosperous, gave ease to.* Niph. *became negligent,* 2 Ch. 29 : 11. Hiph. *flattered, deceived,* 2 K. 4 : 28.

שְׁלָה Ch., *was at rest,* Dan. 4 : 1.

שָׁל m., *fault, error,* 2 Sa. 6 : 7.

שָׁלָה f. Ch., *error;* same as שָׁלוּת, Dan. 3 : 29. Ketib.

שִׁלָה, 1 Sa. 1 : 17, same as שְׁאֵלָה ; see שָׁאַל.

שָׁלֵו m. (pl. const. שַׁלְוֵי) שַׁלְוָה f.— I. *prosperous, at ease.* — II. *unmindful of God,* Eze. 23 : 42.

שְׁלֵיו, שָׁלֵיו m. — I. *prosperous.* — II. *prosperity.*

שָׁלֵו m. (with suff. שַׁלְוִי), *prosperity,* Ps. 30 : 7.

שַׁלְוָה f.—I. *prosperity, ease.*—II. *negligence of God.*

שְׁלֵוָה f. Ch., *prosperity,* Dan. 4 : 24.

שָׁלוּ, שָׁלוּת f. Ch., *error, fault, trespass.*

שֶׁלִי m. בְּשֶׁלִי *quietly, privately,* 2 Sa. 3 : 27.

שִׁלְיָה f., *the after-birth,* Deu. 28 : 57.

שַׁלְאֲנַן (from שַׁאֲנַן and שָׁלָה) m., *wholly at rest,* Job 21 : 23.

שִׁילֹה, שִׁלֹה, Gen. 49 : 10 ; *quasi* אֲשֶׁר לוֹ, i. e., *he whose it is* ; "Shiloh," Eng. Ver.

שִׁילֹו, שִׁילֹה, שִׁלֹה, שִׁילֹה p. n., a city of Ephraim, where the tabernacle stood ; שִׁילֹנִי *a native of Shiloh.*

שַׁלְהֶבֶת *flame;* see לָהַב.

שָׁלוֹם, שִׁלּוּם, שִׁלּוּם ; see שָׁלַם.

שִׁלּוֹן p. n. of a man.

שָׁלוֹשׁ ; same as שָׁלֹשׁ.

שָׁלַח (fut. יִשְׁלַח ; inf. שְׁלֹחַ, שָׁלֹחַ ; שָׁלַח ; imp. שְׁלַח, שִׁלְחָה).—I. *sent* (a person or thing), with לְ, or אֶל, sometimes עַל — II. *sent word, charge;* with לְ *to* ; and בְּיַד *by, by the hand of.*—III. *sent a message to,* with or without דְּבַר.—IV. יָד or בְּ *put forth his hand* (to injure), *laid his hand on,* with אֶל. It has the same meaning without יָד, 2 Sa. 6 : 6.— V. *shoot out arrows* (For other modifications of the primary senses, see Concordance.) Niph. inf. נִשְׁלוֹחַ *to be sent,* Est. 3 : 13. Pi. שִׁלַּח I. *sent.*—II. *sent away.*—III. *allowed to depart, dismissed.* — IV. *set at liberty.* — V. *gave in marriage.*—VI. *sent away, divorced* (a wife). — VII. *put in a place.*—VIII. *put forth* (his hand). —IX. with בָּאֵשׁ *set on fire.* — X. *inflicted a calamity.* — XI. *caused,* Pro. 16 : 28.—XII. *threw, threw off.* —XIII. *cast out, shoot forth.* (See also Concordance.) Pu. שֻׁלַּח *was sent, dismissed, set at liberty, divorced, thrown.* Hiph. with בְּ I. *sent.*—II. *inflicted a calamity.*

שְׁלַח Ch.—I. *sent word, orders.* — II. *put forth* (his hand).

שִׁלּוּחִים m. pl., *divorce* (of a wife), Ex. 18 : 2. — II. *renunciation* (of a claim), Mic. 1:14. — III. *presents, dowry,* 1 Ki. 9:16.

שֶׁלַח m. (with suff. שִׁלְחוֹ).—I. *missile.*—II. *rejection, contempt.*—III. pl., *shoots, produce.*—IV. *p.n. of a man.*—V. *p.n., Siloah,* a stream which ran through Jerusalem; called also שֶׁלַח.

שִׁלְחוֹת f. pl., *shoots,* Isa. 16:8.

שִׁלְחִי *p.n. of a man.*

שִׁלְחִים *p.n., a town of Judah.*

שֻׁלְחָן m. (pl. שֻׁלְחָנוֹת), *table;* עֲרֹךְ שֻׁלְחָן *spread, provided, a table;* שֻׁלְחַן הַמַּעֲרֶכֶת שׁ' הַפָּנִים *the table of shew-bread.*

מִשְׁלָח m.—I. *the sending forth of cattle* (to graze).—II. (with יָד) *the putting out the hand.*

מִשְׁלוֹחַ, מִשְׁלָח m., the same; I. and II.

מִשְׁלַחַת f., the same as II.

שָׁלַט (fut. יִשְׁלָט) *ruled, had power over,* with עַל, בְּ. Hiph. I. *allowed to rule.*—II. *gave authority to, permitted,* with בְּ and לְ.

שְׁלֵט Ch., with בְּ.—I. *ruled.*—II. *had power over.*— III. *seized.* Aph. *caused to rule.*

שֶׁלֶט m., pl. שְׁלָטִים *shields.*

שַׁלֶּטֶת f.—I. *ruler, prince.*—II. *violent,* Eze. 16:30.

שַׁלִּיט m. Ch.—I. *a ruler.*—II. *that which is permitted, lawful;* לֹא שַׁלִּיט *it is not lawful,* Ezr. 7:24.

שִׁלְטוֹן m., *power, authority,* Ecc. 8:4, 8.

שִׁלְטוֹן m. Ch., *authority, ruler,* Dan. 3:2, 3.

שָׁלְטָן m. Ch., *authority, empire.*

שֶׁל, שֶׁלָּיו, שֶׁלֹּה; see שׁלה.

שְׁלִישִׁי, שְׁלִישִׁית; see שׁלשׁ.

שָׁלַךְ. Hiph. הִשְׁלִיךְ I. *threw into,* אֶל; on, בְּ; to, לְ; from, מִן.—II. *threw down, out, away.*—III. *cast off* (as a plant its leaves).—IV. *expelled* (a people).—V. with אַחֲרָיו *cast behind him, despised.*—VI. with עַל יְהוָה *committed to the Lord.* Hoph. הֻשְׁלַךְ, הָשְׁלַךְ I. *was thrown down, out.*—II. *was thrown upon the Lord* (for help), with עַל

שָׁלָךְ m., *the gannet;* LXX. καταράκτης, Lev. 11:17; Deu. 14:16

שַׁלֶּכֶת f.—I. *felling a tree,* Isa. 6:13. II. *p.n., a gate of the temple.*

שָׁלַל (pret. שַׁלּוֹתִי, שָׁלַלְתָּ; inf. שָׁלֹל, fut. תִּשְׁלָל, with suff. וְשֹׁלֲלֻ).—I. *plundered, spoiled.*—II. *carried off spoil.*— III. *scattered,* Ru. 2:16. Hith. אֶשְׁתּוֹלָל (Ch. for הִשְׁתּוֹלָל) *spoiled.*

שָׁלָל m.—I. *spoil, plunder.*—II. *gain,* Pro. 31:11.

שׁוֹלָל m., (spoiled) *a captive, captives.*

שָׁלֵם (fut. יִשְׁלַם).—I. *was at peace,* Job 9:4.—II. *was completed.* Part. שֹׁלְמִי *one at peace with me,* Ps. 7:5; שָׁלוֹם *peaceable,* 2 Sa. 20:19. Pi. שִׁלֵּם I. *completed.* — II. *restored.*—III. *gave in return, requited.*—IV. *performed a vow.* Pu. I. *was requited.*—II. *was performed* (a vow). Part. *made perfect,* Isa. 42:19. Hiph. I. *made peace with* — II. *made at peace with,* with אֶת, עִם, אֶל.—III. *completed.*— IV. *brought to an end.* Hoph. *was made at peace,* Job 5:23.

שְׁלֵם Ch., *completed.* Aph. I. *terminated,* Dan. 5:26.—II. *restored,* Ezr. 7:19.

שָׁלֵם m., שְׁלֵמָה f.— I. *perfect, complete, full.* — II. אֲבָנִים שְׁלֵמוֹת *rough, unhewn stones.* — III. אֶבֶן שְׁלֵמָה *hewn, prepared stone,* 1 Ki. 6:7.—IV. *peaceable, at peace,* with עִם.—V. *at peace with God,* with עִם יְהוָֹה. — VI. p.n. of a place, Gen. 33:18.—VII. p.n., *Jerusalem,* Σόλυμα.

שָׁלוֹם m.—I. *peace.*—II. *public quiet.* —III. *prosperity.*—IV. *safety.*—V. *soundness of body.*—VI. *friendship.* Phrases : הֲשָׁלוֹם לְ *is he well?* שָׁאַל לְשָׁלוֹם *enquired after their welfare;* עֲשֵׂה שָׁלוֹם *farewell!* עָשָׂה שׁ' לְ *made peace with them;* קָרָא לְשָׁלוֹם *named peaceable proposals;* עָנָה שָׁלוֹם אֶת *gave a peaceable answer.*

שְׁלָם m. Ch., *peace, safety.*

שֶׁלֶם and pl. שְׁלָמִים m. — I. *peace offering.*—II. *thank offering.*—III. *offering in completion of a vow.*

שִׁלֵּם m.— I. *retribution,* Deu. 32:35. —II. p.n., *a son of Naphtali;* patron. שִׁלֵּמִי.

שִׁלֻּם, שִׁלּוּם m., *retribution.*

שִׁלֻּמָה f., *the same,* Ps. 91:8.

שַׁלּוּם, שַׁלֻּם p.n.—I. *Shallum, king of Israel.*—II. *used for other men.*

שְׁלֹמֹה p.n., *Solomon, king of Israel;* LXX. Σαλωμών.

שְׁלֻמִי p.n. of a man.

שְׁלֻמִיאֵל p.n. of a man.

שֶׁלֶמְיָהוּ p.n., *same as* מְשֶׁלֶמְיָה

שְׁלֹמִית p.n. of a man.

שְׁלֹמִית p.n. of a woman.

שַׁלְמוֹן m., pl. שַׁלְמֹנִים *bribes, penalties,* Isa. 1:23.

שַׁלְמַנְאֶסֶר, שַׁלְמַן p.n., a king of Assyria.

שָׁלַף I. *drew a sword.*—II. *took off a shoe,* Ru. 4:7, 8. — III. *plucked up grass,* Ps. 129:6; אִישׁ שֹׁלֵף חֶרֶב *a man drawing the sword;* i.e., *armed.*

שֶׁלֶף p.n. of some foreign nation, perhaps Σαλαπηνοί.

שָׁלֹשׁ, שָׁלוֹשׁ const. שְׁלֹשׁ, שְׁלָשׁ; f. שְׁלֹשָׁה, const. שְׁלֹשֶׁת m., *the numeral three;* with suff. שְׁלָשְׁתְּכֶם *ye three;* שְׁלָשְׁתָּם *they three,* שְׁלֹשׁ עֶשְׂרֵה *thirteen;* pl. שְׁלֹשִׁים *thirty, thirtieth.*

שִׁלֵּשׁ Pi. I. *divided into three parts.*— II. *did a thing the third time.*— III. *did a thing on the third day.* Pu. part. I. *threefold.* — II. *three years old,* Gen. 15:9.

שָׁלֵשׁ p.n. of a man.

שְׁלִישִׁי m., שְׁלִישִׁיָּה, שְׁלִישִׁית f., pl. שְׁלִישִׁים I. *third parts.*—II. *chambers third in order, third stories;* f. *a third part;* בַּשְּׁלִישִׁית, שְׁלִישִׁיתָהּ *the third, on the third;* הַשְּׁלִישִׁית; see מָחָר.

שָׁלִישׁ, שְׁלִישׁ m.—I. *a measure,* probably *the third part of an Ephah.* —II. *abundantly;* pl. שְׁלִישִׁים.— III. *a musical instrument, a trichord* (either *harp* or *lute*).— IV. *officers of high rank.*— V. *a peculiar class of soldiers,* LXX. ἀναβάται ριστάται; *their commander was called* רֹאשׁ הַשָּׁלִישִׁים הַשָּׁלִישׁ *and* רֹאשׁ הַשָּׁלִשִׁי.

שָׁלִשִׁים m. pl., *descendants of the*

third generation, *great grandchildren.*

שֶׁלְשָׁה p.n., *a region of Palestine.*

שִׁלְשָׁה p. n. of a man.

שִׁלְשׁוֹם, שִׁלְשֹׁם adv. *three days ago;* תְּמוֹל שִׁלְשׁוֹם *yesterday and the day before,* i.e. *formerly;* כִּתְמוֹל שִׁ׳ *as before;* מִתְּמוֹל שִׁ׳ *heretofore, previously.*

כְּמִשְׁלֹשׁ חֳדָשִׁים m., *a triad; a triplicity of,* i.e. *three months,* Gen. 38:24.

שְׁאֵלָתֵךְ 1 Sa. 1:17, for שְׁאֵלָתֵךְ; see שְׁאֵלָה in שאל.

שָׁם adv., *there, thither;* אֲשֶׁר...שָׁם *where;* שָׁם...שָׁם *here...there;* שָׁמָּה *thither, there;* אֲשֶׁר..שָׁמָּה *whither...where;* מִשָּׁם *thence;* אֲשֶׁר...מִשָּׁם *whence.*

שֵׁם, שֶׁם־ m. (with suff. שְׁמִי, שִׁמְךָ; pl. שֵׁמוֹת).—I. *a name;* בְּשֵׁם פּ׳ *in the name of any one.*—II. *fame, reputation* (good or bad).—III. *memory.*—IV. p. n., *Shem* the son of Noah.

שֻׁם m. Ch. (with suff. שְׁמֵהּ; pl. שְׁמָהָן), *a name.*

שְׁמֶאֵבֶר p.n., *a king of Zeboim.*

שְׁמוּאֵל (perhaps for שְׁמוּעָאֵל *heard of God*), p. n.—I. *Samuel,* the judge of Israel.—II. used also of other men.

שְׁמִידָע p. n., *a son of Gilead;* patron. שְׁמִידָעִי.

שַׁמָּא p. n. of a man.

שִׁמְאָה p.n. of a man; שִׁמְאָם *the same.*

שַׁמְגַּר p. n., *Shamgar,* a judge of Israel.

שָׁמַד. Hiph. *destroyed;* inf. *destruction.* Niph. *was destroyed.*

שְׁמַד Ch. Aph. *to destroy.*

שָׁמָה *root not used;* (Arab. *heaven*).

שָׁמַיִם, const. שְׁמֵי m. pl.—I. *heaven, the sky.*—II. *towara heaven, the sky.*

שְׁמַיִן emph. state, שְׁמַיָּא m. pl. Ch., *heaven.*

שְׁמָהוּת, שַׁמָּה; see שמם.

שַׁמּוּעַ p. n., same as שִׁמְעָא.

שְׁמוּעָה; see שמע.

שָׁמוֹת Eze. 36:3, Kal inf., from שמם.

שָׁמַם I. *gave up a debt.*—II. *left the land to itself.*—III. *threw down.*—IV. *stuck fast.* Niph. *was thrown down,* Ps. 141:6. Hiph. *gave up, forgave,* Deu. 15:3.

שְׁמִטָּה f., *release, acquittal;* שְׁנַת הַשְּׁמִטָּה *year of release.*

שָׁמַיִם *heavens;* see שמה.

שְׁמִינִי, שְׁמִינִית; see שׁמֹנֶה.

שָׁמִיר; see שמר.

שְׁמִירְמוֹת p. n. of a man.

שַׁמְלַי p. n. of a man.

שָׁמֵם (fut. יִשֹּׁם; pl. יִשַּׁמּוּ; imp. שֹׁם). I. *was desolate, laid waste.*—II. *was astonished;* part. שׁוֹמֵם *desolate, solitary;* שׁוֹמֵמוֹת *desolate places.* Niph. נָשַׁם *was desolate, astonished.* Po. part. מְשׁוֹמֵם I. *a desolator.*—II. *astonished,* Ezr. 9:3, 4. Hiph. הֵשַׁם (fut. יָשִׁים; inf. הַשַּׁם; part. מַשִּׁים) I. *made desolate, laid waste.*—II. *astonished* —III. *was astonished.* Hoph. הֻשַׁם or הָשַׁם (pl. הֻשַּׁמּוּ) *was made desolate.* Hith. הִשְׁתּוֹמֵם (fut. תִּשׁוֹמֵם, יִשְׁתּוֹמֵם) I. *was dis-*

*consolate* (of the heart).—II. *wondered.*—III. *destroyed himself*, Ecc. 7:16.

שְׁמֵם Ch. Ith., *was astonished*, Dan. 4:16.

שָׁמֵם m., שְׁמֵמָה f., *desolate*.

שְׁמָמָה f.—I. *desolation.*—II. *astonishment.*—III. *a desolate place*.

שְׁמֵמָה f.—I. *desolation*, Eze. 35:7, 9.

שַׁמָּה f.—I. *desolation* (pl. שַׁמּוֹת).—II. *astonishment.*—III. p.n.: (a) a brother of David, called also שִׁמְעָא; (b) used also for other men.

שְׁמָמוֹת, שַׁמְהוּת p.n.; same as שַׁמָּה.

שִׁמָּמוֹן m., *astonishment, terrors*, Eze. 4:16; 12:19.

מְשַׁמָּה f.—I. *astonishment*, Eze. 5:15. —II. *desolation*.

שָׁמֵן or שָׁמַן (fut. יִשְׁמַן) *was fat, prosperous*. Hiph. I. *became fat*, Neh. 9:25. — II. *made fat*, Isa. 6:10.

שָׁמֵן m., שְׁמֵנָה f.—I. *plump* (of an animal). — II. *robust, stout* (of a man).—III. *nourishing* (of food). —IV. *rich, fertile, abundant*.

שֶׁמֶן m.—I. *oil.*—II. *ointment.*—III. *richness, delicacy of food*, I 25: 6. — IV. *fertility.*—V. *prosperity*, Isa. 10:27. (עֵץ שֶׁמֶן *any resinous tree*.)

שְׁמָנִים m. pl., *fatness*, Gen. 27:28, 39.

אַשְׁמַנִּים m. pl., "*desolate places,*" Eng. Ver., Isa. 59:10.

מִשְׁמָן m., *fatness*; pl. מִשְׁמַנִּים *fertile places*.

מַשְׁמַנִּים m. pl., *rich food*, Neh. 8:10.

מִשְׁמַנָּה p.n. of a man.

שְׁמֹנֶה־ f., שְׁמֹנָה const. שְׁמֹנַת m., *eight*; pl. שְׁמֹנִים *eighty*.

שְׁמִינִי m., *eighth*; שְׁמִינִית a musical instrument, probably *with eight strings*.

שָׁמַע, שֵׁמַע (fut. יִשְׁמַע; inf. שְׁמֹעַ; const. שְׁמֹעַ, with ה parag. שָׁמְעָה, with suff. שָׁמְעוֹ; imp. שְׁמַע, with ה parag. שִׁמְעָה).—I. *heard.*—II. *hearkened*, with בְּ, אֶל, לְ.—III. *understood*. Niph. I. *was heard.*—II. *was hearkened to*. Pi. I. *caused to hear, summoned*. Hiph. הִשְׁמִיעַ (fut. apoc. תַּשְׁמַע).— I. *caused to hear, be heard.*—II. *proclaimed.*—III. *summoned*.

שְׁמַע Ch., *he heard*. Ith. *he obeyed*.

שֶׁמַע p.n. of a man.

שֵׁמַע, שֵׁמַע m. (with suff. שִׁמְעִי, שִׁמְעֲךָ).—I. *the act of hearing.*— II. *report, fame.*—III. *sound*.

שָׁמָע p.n. of a man.

שֶׁמַע p.n., a town of Judah.

שֹׁמַע m. (with suff. שָׁמְעוֹ), *fame*.

שִׁמְעָא p.n. of a man; see שַׁמָּה.

שִׁמְעָה p.n., same as שַׁמָּה; patron. שִׁמְעָתִי.

שִׁמְעָה (with art.) p.n. of a man.

שִׁמְעוֹן p.n.—I. *Simeon*, the son of Jacob and Leah (LXX. Συμεών). —II. used also of his descendants, שִׁמְעֹנִי *a Simeonite*.

שִׁמְעִי p.n. of a man, *Shimei*.

שְׁמַעְיָהוּ, שְׁמַעְיָה p.n. of a man.

שְׁמַעַן Kal imp. pl. f. for שְׁמַעְנָה from שָׁמַע.

שִׁמְעַת p.n. of a woman.

שְׁמֻעָה, שְׁמוּעָה f.—I. *a report.*—II. *a message*.

הַשְׁמָעוּת f., *a hearing*, Eze. 24:26.

מִשְׁמָע m.—I. *act of hearing*, Isa. 11:3 —II. p.n. of a man.

מִשְׁמַעַת f. — I. *court of hearing, council.*—II. *subjects,* Isa. 11:14.

שָׁמַן root not used; (Arab. *hastened*).

שֶׁמֶץ m., *a small portion, a hint,* Job 4:12; 26:14.

שִׁמְצָה f., *defeat,* Ex. 32:25.

שָׁמַר (fut. יִשְׁמֹר).—I. *kept watch over, watched.*—II. *guarded, preserved.* —III. *kept in mind.*—IV. *attended to an office.*—V. *took heed.*—VI. *observed, remembered.* — VII. *regarded, reverenced.*—VIII. *guarded against, avoided.* Niph. I. *noticed, was aware of, perceived.*—II. *was preserved, delivered.* — III. *took heed.* — IV. *guarded himself, abstained,* with מִן and מִפְּנֵי; imp. הִשָּׁמֶר. Pi. *regarded,* Jon. 2:9. Hith. הִשְׁתַּמֵּר *kept, guarded himself.*—II. *was observed.*

שָׁמִיר m.—I. *a thorny shrub,* "spina Egyptiaca."—II. *a diamond.*—III. p.n.: (a) a town of Judah; (b) a town of Ephraim; (c) of a man.

שְׁמָרִים m., pl. שְׁמָרִים.—I. *sediment, lees, dregs.*—II. שׁ׳ מְזֻקָּקִים *clear wine.*—III. p.n. of a man.

שֶׁמֶר p.n. of a man, and of a woman.

שְׁמֻרָה f., *a watch,* Ps. 141:3.

שְׁמֻרוֹת f. pl., the same, Ps. 77:5.

שִׁמֻּרִים m. pl., *observance of a festival,* Ex. 12:42.

שִׁמְרוֹן p.n.—I. a town of Zebulun. — II. a son of Issachar. Patron. שִׁמְרֹנִי.

שֹׁמְרוֹן p.n.—I. Samaria (Σεβάστη). —II. the land of Israel; שֹׁמְרֹנִי *a Samaritan.*

שָׁמְרַיִן Ch., p.n., *Samaria.*

שְׁמָרִי p.n. of a man.

שְׁמַרְיָה p.n. of a man

שְׁמַרְיָהוּ p.n. of a man.

שְׁמָרִית p.n. of a woman; same as שֶׁמֶר

שִׁמְרָת p.n. of a man.

אַשְׁמוּרָה f., *night-watch;* const. אַשְׁמֹרֶת; pl. אַשְׁמֹרוֹת.

מִשְׁמָר m. — I. *the act of guarding, watching.* — II. *keeping guard.* — III. *imprisonment.* — IV. *a prison.* —V. *an appointed duty.*

מִשְׁמֶרֶת f. (pl. מִשְׁמְרוֹת).—I. *guarding, watching.*—II. *imprisonment.*

שְׁמַשׁ Ch. Pa., *attended, served,* Dan. 7:10.

שֶׁמֶשׁ com. (with suff. שִׁמְשֵׁךְ), *the sun,* pl. שְׁמָשׁוֹת *thy pinnacles,* Isa. 54:12; עִיר שֶׁמֶשׁ *a city of* Dan.

שִׁמְשׁוֹן p.n., *Samson.* (LXX. Σαμψών.)

שִׁמְשַׁי p.n. of a man.

שַׁמְשְׁרַי p.n. of a man.

שִׁמְשָׁתִי p.n. of a man.

שֵׁן, שַׁנּוּ, שְׁנָאָב; see שׁן.

שֵׁנָא, שֵׁנָן; see שׁנה.

שֵׁנָא *sleep,* Ps. 127:2; see יָשַׁן.

שַׁנְאַצַּר p.n. of a man.

שָׁנַב (Arab. *had a cool mouth*).

אֶשְׁנָב m., *a latticed window.*

שָׁנָה (fut. יִשְׁנֶא, יִשְׁנֶה).—I. *repeated an action.*—II. *was different,* with מִן—III. *was changed.*—IV. *was disobedient* (part. שֹׁנִים *rebellious*). Niph. *being repeated,* Gen. 41:32. Pi. שִׁנָּה, שִׁנָּא I. *changed.* — II. *violated a promise.*— III. *removed a person to another place,* Est. 2:9:

with אֶת־טַעְמוֹ *changed his mind, feigned himself mad.* Pu. fut. יְשֻׁנֶּא *was changed,* Ecc. 8 : 1. Hith. *changed, disguised himself,* 1 Ki. 14 : 2.

שְׁנָא Ch.—I. *was changed.* — II. *was different from,* with מִן. Pa. I. *changed.*—II. *made different;* part. pass. *different.* Ith. *was changed.* Aph. *changed.*

שָׁנָה f. (pl. שָׁנוֹת, שְׁנֵי, שָׁנֵי). —I. *a year.*—II. *the produce of a year;* שָׁנָה בְּשָׁנָה, שְׁנֵי מִדֵּי, בִּשְׁנַת שְׁתַּיִם *yearly;* בִּשְׁנַת שְׁתַּיִם לְיוֹאָשׁ *in the second year of Joash;* בִּשְׁנַת שֵׁשׁ מֵאוֹת שָׁנָה *in the six hundredth year.* Dual שְׁנָתַיִם *two years;* שְׁנָתַיִם יָמִים *for two years.*

שְׁנָא, שְׁנָה f. Ch., *year;* pl. שְׁנִין.

שֵׁנָה, שְׁנָת *sleep;* see יָשֵׁן.

שֶׁנְהַבִּים *ivory;* see שֵׁן.

שָׁנִי m., *bright, scarlet colour;* pl. שָׁנִים.

שְׁנַיִם const. שְׁנֵי m., שְׁתַּיִם const. שְׁתֵּי f. dual, *the numeral two;* שְׁנַיִם שְׁנַיִם *apiece;* with suff. שְׁנֵיהֶם *both of them;* f., *twice, again;* בִּשְׁתַּיִם *again.* שְׁנֵים עָשָׂר m., שְׁתֵּים עֶשְׂרֵה f., *twelve.*

שֵׁנִי m., שֵׁנִית f., *second;* f., *again.* Pl. שְׁנַיִם.

שַׁנְאָן m., "*angels,*" Eng. Ver.; אַלְפֵי שִׁנְאָן *thousands repeated* (Ges.), Ps. 68 : 18.

מִשְׁנֶה const. מִשְׁנָה m.—I. *second.*— II. *the second rank, second in rank.* III. *double.*—IV. *a copy.*—V. *of an inferior kind,* 1 Sa. 15 : 9. — VI. *a division of Jerusalem.*

שָׁנַן (pret. שַׁנּוֹתִי, שִׁנְּנוּ).—I. *sharpened*

*a sword, &c.*— II. *sharpened the tongue* (of slanderers), Ps. 64 : 4 140:4. Pi. *taught assiduously,* with לְ, Deu. 6 : 7. Hithpo. הִשְׁתּוֹנָן *was pained acutely,* Ps. 73 : 21.

שֵׁן, שֵׁן com. (with suff. שִׁנִּי; dual שִׁנַּיִם, שֶׁן).—I. *a tooth.*—II. *ivory* —III. *the ridge of a rock;* שֵׁן סֶלַע. — IV. *the prong of a fork.* — V. p. n. of a place.

שֶׁנְהַבִּים m. pl., *elephant's tooth, ivory.* (The word is probably a compound of שֵׁן *a tooth,* and הָב *an elephant;* from the Sanscrit *ibha*.)

שְׁנִינָה f., *pointed saying, taunt;* הָיָה לִשְׁנִינָה *he was for a taunt.*

שִׁנְאָב p. n. of a king.

שָׁנַס. Pi. שִׁנַּס *girded his loins,* 1 Ki. 18:46.

שִׁנְעָר p. n., one of the names of Babylon and its vicinity.

שָׁסָה *plundered;* part. שֹׁסִים *spoilers.* Po. שׁוֹסֵה *the same,* Isa. 10:13.

שָׁסַס (fut. יָשֹׁס) *the same;* part. שֹׁאֵס, with suff. שֹׁאסֶיךָ. Niph. נָשַׁס *was plundered.*

מְשִׁסָּה f., *prey.*

שֶׁסַע שְׁסַע *having a division;* פַּרְסָה שְׁסַעַת or פַּרְסָה הַשְּׁסוּעָה *having divided hoofs;* Pi. I. *clove,* Lev. 1: 17. — II. *tore asunder,* Jud. 14:6, &c.—III. *withheld,* 1 Sa. 24:8.

שֶׁסַע m., *division in a hoof.*

שָׁסַף. Pi. שִׁסֵּף *cut down,* 1 Sa. 15:33.

I. שָׁעָה (fut. apoc. וַיִּשַׁע) *looked at favourably, approved,* with אֶל.—II. *looked at with attention,* with בְּ

- III. *looked to for help*, with אֶל,
עַל. — IV. *looked away from, re-
spited*, with מִן, Job 7:19. Hiph.
imp. הָשַׁע I. *looked away from*,
with מִן, Ps. 39:14.—II. *turn away
the eyes*, Isa. 6:10. See also in
שָׁעַע. Hith. fut. apoc. תִּשְׁתָּע *look
about with alarm*, Isa. 41:10; pl.
with ה parag. נִשְׁתָּעֶה *we may look
with alarm, be dismayed*, Isa. 41:23.

II. שָׁעָה *same as* שָׁעַע; imp. שְׁעוּ *be
blinded* (Ges.); " *cry*," from שׁוּעַ,
Eng. Ver., Is. 29:9.

שָׁעָה f. Ch., *an hour*; בַּהּ שַׁעֲתָא *immediately.*

שַׁעֲטָה f., *stamping of hoofs*, Jer. 47:
3. (Arab. *pounded.*)

שַׁעַטְנֵז m., *cloth of a mixture of wool
and flax*, Lev. 19:19; Deu. 22:11.

שַׁעַל, שֹׁעַל (with suff. שָׁעֳלוֹ; pl.
שֳׁעֳלָי, שְׁעָלִים). — I. *palm of the
hand*, Isa. 40:12.—II. *a handful.*

שׁוּעָל m.—1. *a fox.* — II. p. n. of a
man.

שַׁעַלִים p. n. of a district.

שַׁעֲלַבִּים, שַׁעַלְבִּין p. n., *a town of the
Danites*; שַׁעַלְבֹנִי *a Shaalbonite.*

מִשְׁעוֹל m., *a narrow way*, Nu. 22:24.

שָׁעַן, Niph. נִשְׁעַן I. *leaned on*, with
עַל.—II. *reclined.*—III. *touched a
boundary* with לְ, Nu. 21:15.—
IV. *depended on*, with בְּ, אֶל, עַל.

מִשְׁעָן m., *a support.*

מַשְׁעֵן m., מַשְׁעֵנָה f., the same, Isa.
3:1.

מִשְׁעֶנֶת f. (pl. מִשְׁעֲנוֹת), *walking
stick, staff.*

שָׁעַע Pil. שִׁעֲשַׁע I. *delighted.* — II.

*played*, Isa. 11:8. Pul. שֻׁעֲשַׁע *was
fondled*, Isa. 66:12. Hiph. imp
הָשַׁע *cover the eyes, make blind*,
Isa. 6:10; see in שָׁעָה. Hithpal.
הִשְׁתַּעֲשַׁע *delighted himself*, with
בְּ.

שַׁעֲשֻׁעִים m. pl., *delights, source of
delight.*

שֶׁעַע p. n. of a man.

שָׁעַר Pro. 23:7, " thinketh," Eng
Ver.; meaning uncertain.

שַׁעַר m.—I. *value, measure*, Gen. 26:
12. — II. m. (f. Isa. 14:31). — 1.
*opening, gate of a city.* — 2. *the
people assembled at the gate*, Ru.
3:11.— 3. *the city itself*; with ה
loc. שַׁעְרָה; pl. שְׁעָרִים, שַׁעֲרֵי.

שַׁעֲרַיִם p. n., *a town of Judah.*

שׁוֹעֵר m., *a porter.*

שֹׁעָר m., pl. שֹׁעָרִים *blighted figs*, Jer
29:17.

שַׁעֲרוּר m., f. שַׁעֲרוּרָה *causing to shud-
der, horrible.*

שַׁעֲרוּרִי m., f. שַׁעֲרוּרִיָּה, שַׁעֲרִירִת *horrible*, Jer. 18:13.

שְׁעַרְיָה p. n. of a man.

שַׁעַשְׁגַּז p. n. of a man.

שַׁעֲשֻׁעִים, שִׁעֲשֵׁעַ; see שׁעע.

שָׁפָה (Arab. *became visible*). Niph.
הַר נִשְׁפֶּה *a lofty, conspicuous
mountain*, Isa. 13:2. Pu. שֻׁפּוּ
*became prominent* (the bones), Job
33:21.

שְׁפָה or שָׁפָה f., *cheese*; pl. const.
שְׁפוֹת, 2 Sa. 17:29.

שְׁפִי in pause שֶׁפִי m. (pl. שְׁפָיִים,
שְׁפָיִם) *elevated, conspicuous place.*

שְׁפִי, שְׁפוֹ p. n. of a man.

שִׁפְחָה f. (pl. שְׁפָחוֹת) *female servant or slave.*

מִשְׁפָּחָה const. מִשְׁפַּחַת f. (with suff. מִשְׁפַּחְתִּי; pl. מִשְׁפָּחוֹת).— I. *a household.* — II. *a family or clan.* —III. *a race or kind*

שָׁפַט I. *judged.*—II. *decided a cause.* —III. *defended the right of.* — IV. *decided between,* with בֵּין...וּבֵין, בֵּין...לְ.—V. *punished.*—VI. *ruled;* part. שֹׁפֵט *a judge, ruler.* Niph. שְׁנִשְׁפַּט I. *was judged,* Ps. 9:20.—II. *reasoned with another, disputed,* with עַל, לְ, עִם, אֶת. Po. part. מְשֹׁפְטִי *my judge.*

שְׁפַט Ch. part. שָׁפֵט *judge,* Ezr. 7:25.

שָׁפוֹט m. (pl. שְׁפוֹטִים) *judgments.*

שֶׁפֶט p. n. of a man.

שֶׁפֶט m., pl. שְׁפָטִים *judgments, punishments.*

שְׁפַטְיָה p. n. of a man.

שְׁפַטְיָהוּ p. n. of a man.

שִׁפְטָן p. n. of a man.

מִשְׁפָּט m.—I. *deciding, decision, sentence.* — II. *punishment.* — III. *a court of justice.* — IV. *a cause for trial.* — V. *justice, equity.* — VI. *any positive institution; the right claimed upon such institution.*— VII. *custom.* — VIII. *manner, appearance.*

שְׁפִי, שֶׁפִי, שְׁפָיִם; see שפה.

שְׁפִים, שְׁפִיפֹן; see שפף.

שָׁפִיר, שַׁפִּיר; see שפר.

שָׁפַךְ I. *poured out.*—II. *shed blood.*— III. *threw up a mound.* — IV. *uttered a prayer.* — V. metaph. *poured out his soul, his heart, his*

*anger.* — VI. *gave abundantly* Niph. trop. *was poured out, was shed.* Pu. I. *was poured out.*—II. *slipped.* Hith. הִשְׁתַּפֵּךְ *was shed.*

שֶׁפֶךְ m., *the place of pouring out,* Lev. 4:12.

שָׁפְכָה f., *membrum virile,* Deu. 23:2.

שָׁפֵל (fut. יִשְׁפַּל; inf. שְׁפַל).— I. *was low, was lowered.*—II. *was humbled.* Hiph. I. *brought low.*—II. *sent down,* Isa. 57:9.—III. *cast down, humbled;* שׁ' רוּחַ *humble in spirit.*

שְׁפַל Ch. Aph. *humbled, brought low.*

שָׁפָל m., שְׁפָלָה f.—I. *low.*—II. *low in rank or importance.*—III. *humble.*

שְׁפַל m. Ch., *low in rank,* Dan. 4:14.

שֵׁפֶל m. (with suff. שִׁפְלֵנוּ), *lowly place, condition.*

שִׁפְלָה f., the same, Isa. 32:19.

שְׁפֵלָה f., *low country;* הַשְּׁפֵלָה *the low country,* i. e. the plain between Joppa and Egypt.

שִׁפְלוּת f., *lowness of the hands, inactivity,* Ecc. 10:18.

שָׁפָם p. n. of a man.

שְׁפָם, שִׁפְמוֹת p.n., *a town of Judah;* שִׁפְמִי *a Shiphmite.*

שָׁפָן m.—I. *the jerboa;* LXX. χοιρο-γρύλλιος, Lev. 11:5; Deu. 14:7. —II. p. n. of a man.

שָׁפַע (Syr. *inundated*).

שֶׁפַע m., *overflowing, abundance,* Deu. 33:19.

שִׁפְעָה f.—I. *inundation.*—II. *multitude.*

שִׁפְעִי p. n. of a man.

שָׁפַף (Syr. *he crept;* Arab. *a speckled make*).

שְׁפִיפֹן m., a species of serpent, Gen. 49:17.

שֻׁפֻּפָּם p.n., a son of Benjamin.

שְׁפוּפָן p.n. of a man.

שֻׁפִּים p.n. of a man.

שָׁפַר was pleasing, with עַל, Ps. 16:6.

שִׁפְרָה f., beauty, Job 26:13.

שְׁפַר Ch., was fair, pleasing, with עַל אֲדָם.

שׁוֹפָר m. (pl. שׁוֹפָרוֹת), trumpet, curved horn.

שֶׁפֶר m.—I. pleasantness, beauty, Gen. 49:21.—II. p.n., a mountain in the wilderness.

שִׁפְרָה p.n. of a woman.

שָׁפִיר p.n., an unknown place.

שַׁפִּיר m. Ch., pleasing, fine.

שַׁפְרוּר (שַׁפְרִיר) m., royal canopy, Jer. 43:10.

שְׁפַרְפָּרָא m. Ch., the dawn, Dan. 6:20.

שָׁפַת fixed, placed.

שְׁפַתַּיִם m. dual, cooking vessels.

מִשְׁפְּתַיִם dual, the same.

שֶׁצֶף m., overflowing, Isa. 54:8.

שָׁק Ch., leg, same as שׁוֹק.

שָׁקַד I. was sleepless, awake.—II. watched, kept watch for, with עַל. Pu. see next word.

שָׁקֵד I. almond tree.—II. almond. Hence denom. Pu. part. מְשֻׁקָּדִים formed like almonds.

שָׁקָה. Niph. was overflown (see שׁקע), Am. 8:8. Hiph. הִשְׁקָה (fut. apoc. יַשְׁקְ) I. gave drink to any one.—II. watered the ground; part. מַשְׁקֶה giving water, Ps. 104:13. Pu. watered, refreshed, Job 21:24.

שֹׁקֶת f., drinking-trough; pl. const שִׁקְתוֹת.

שִׁקּוּי m. (pl. with suff. שִׁקּוּיַי).—I. refreshment.—II. drink.

שִׁקּוּי or שִׁקּוּ m. (pl. with suff. שִׁקּוּיַי), drink.

מַשְׁקֶה m.—I. cup-bearer.—II. drink.—III. a watered country.

שָׁקָה Kal imp. with ה parag., from נשק שִׁקּוּץ; see שׁקץ.

שָׁקַט I. was quiet, undisturbed.—II. ceased.—III. remained inactive.—IV. was silent. Hiph. I. caused to cease.—II. was quiet, ceased, with לְ and מִן; inf. הַשְׁקֵט rest, tranquillity.

שֶׁקֶט m., rest, quiet, 1 Chron. 22:9.

שָׁקַל I. weighed.—II. weighed in payment, paid.—III. estimated, judged.—Niph. 1. was paid.—II. was judged.

שֶׁקֶל m. (pl. שְׁקָלִים, שִׁקְלֵי).—I. a certain standard weight, the shekel.—II. a silver coin of that weight.

מִשְׁקָל m., act of weighing, weight.

מִשְׁקוֹל m., weight, Eze. 4:10.

מִשְׁקֶלֶת f., balance, Isa. 28:17.

מִשְׁקֹלֶת f., the same, 2 Ki. 21:13

שִׁקְמָה f., pl. שִׁקְמִים, שִׁקְמוֹת sycamore tree, a species of fig.

שָׁקַע I. sank.—II. was overflown.—III. abated (of fire). Niph. was overflown, Am. 8:8 (Ketib נִשְׁקָה) which see in שׁקה.

מַשְׁקָע m., a pond, Eze. 34:18.

שְׁקַעְרוּרֹת f. pl., hollows, parts corroded, κοιλάδες, Lev. 14:37.

שָׁקַף. Niph. and Hiph. I. looked.—

II. *looked down, through, towards.*
—III. *threatened.*

שֶׁקֶף m., *covering, coping,* 1 Ki. 7:5.

שְׁקֻפִים m. pl., *coped, having copings,*
1 Ki. 6:4.

מַשְׁקוֹף m., *lintel, beam over a doorway.*

שָׁקַץ Pi. I. *regarded with disgust.*
—II. *loathed,* Ps. 22:25.—III. *polluted.*

שֶׁקֶץ m., *abominable thing.*

שִׁקּוּץ m., *an abomination.*

שָׁקַק (fut. יָשֹׁק).—I. *ran to and fro.*—
II. *was eager.* Hithpal. *ran to
and fro;* fut. pl. יִשְׁתַּקְשְׁקוּן, Nah.
2:5.

מַשָּׁק m., *running to and fro,* Isa.
33:4.

שָׁקַר (fut. יְשַׁקֵּר) *acted falsely towards,*
with לְ. Pi. שִׁקֵּר with בְּ.—I. *uttered a falsehood.*—II. *acted falsely.*

שֶׁקֶר m.—I. *falsehood.*—II. *a deceitful thing.*—III. עֵד שֶׁ *false
witness;* לַשֶּׁקֶר *in vain, falsely;*
בַּשֶּׁקֶר, בְּשֶׁקֶר *falsely;* שֶׁקֶר adv.
*in vain.*

שְׁקָתוֹת, שֹׁקֶת; see שׁקה.

שֹׁר, שֵׁרֵךְ; see שׁרר.

שְׁרָא; see שׁרה.

שַׁרְאֶצֶר p. n. of an Assyrian prince;
see נֵרְגַל שׁ.

שָׁרָב m.—I. *drought,* Isa. 49:10.—II.
*the mirage,* Isa. 35:7 (Arab. the
same).

שְׁרֵבְיָה p. n. of a man.

שַׁרְבִיט same as שֵׁבֶט *a sceptre* (Esther
only).

שָׁרָה *set at liberty,* Job 37:3. Pi.
שָׁרָה the same, Jer. 15:11.

שְׁרָא Ch.—I. *untied.*—II. *solved.*—III.
*halted, dwelt.* Pa. I. *untied.*—II.
*began.* Ithpa. *was loose.*

שֵׁרוֹת, שָׁרוֹת *walls;* see שׁוּר.

שְׁרִי p. n. of a man.

שִׁרְיָה f., *coat of mail,* Job 41:18.

שִׁרְיָן m., the same.

שִׁרְיוֹן, סִרְיֹן m. (pl. שִׁרְיֹנִים, שִׁרְיֹנוֹת
סִרְיֹנוֹת).—I. *a coat of mail.*—II.
שִׁרְיוֹן p. n., a part of Mount Hermon.

מִשְׁרָה f., *juice;* מִשְׁרַת־עֲנָבִים *juice
of grapes,* Nu. 6:3.

שֵׁרוֹת, שָׁרוֹת; see שׁרר.

שָׁרוּחֶן p. n., a city of the tribe of
Simeon.

שָׁרוֹן p. n., the plain between Joppa
and Cesarea.

שְׁרִיקוֹת; see שׁרק.

שְׁרִירוּת, שָׁרִיר; see שׁרר.

שְׁאֵרִית same as שְׁאֵרִית; see שׁאר.

שָׁרַץ (fut. יִשְׁרַץ). — I. *became numerous.* — II. *produce in great
numbers, swarm.*—III. *creep, crawl,*
Eze. 47:9.

שֶׁרֶץ m. col., *small creatures, whether
insects, reptiles, or fishes.*

שָׁרַק (fut. יִשְׁרֹק)—I. *whistle, or hiss
for, call by whistling,* with לְ.—II.
*hiss at in contempt,* with עַל.

שְׁרֵקָה f., *derision, scorn.*

שְׁרִיקוֹת f., *hissing, derision,* Jer. 18:16.
—II. *whistling, piping,* Jud. 5:16.

מַשְׁרוֹקִית m. Ch., "flute," Eng. Ver.;
LXX. σύριγγος, Dan. 3:5—15.

I. שָׁרַר (Arab. *made wicked*); part.
שֹׁרֵר *adversary.*

שָׁרָר p. n. of a man.

II. שָׁרַר (Syr. *was firm*).

שֵׁר m. (with suff. שָׁרְרֵךְ), *the navel,* Cant. 7:3.

שֹׁר m. (with suff. שָׁרֶךָ), *the same.*

שָׁרִיר m., pl. שְׁרִירִים *firm, solid parts,* Job 40:16.

שְׁרִירוּת f. with לֵב, *firmness, obstinacy of heart.*

שֵׁרָה f., pl. שֵׁרוֹת *chains, bracelets,* Isa. 3:19.

שַׁרְשָׁרָה f., *a chain.*

שַׁרְשְׁרָה f., pl. const. שַׁרְשְׁרוֹת *chains, small bracelets,* Ex. 28:22.

שֹׁרֶשׁ m. (with suff. שָׁרְשָׁם; pl. שָׁרָשִׁי, שָׁרָשִׁים).—I. *a root.*—II. *shoot, suckers,* Isa. 11:10; 53:2.—III. *lowest part of any thing;* e.g., *sole of the foot, bottom of the sea,* &c.—IV. *foundation, groundwork;* שׁ דָּבָר *ground of complaint,* Job 19:28.

שֵׁרֵשׁ Pi. denom. *rooted up.* Pu. *was rooted up.* Poel שֹׁרֵשׁ and Poal שֹׁרַשׁ *took root.* Hiph. הִשְׁרִישׁ the same.

שֹׁרֶשׁ m. Ch., *a root.*

שֶׁרֶשׁ p. n. of a man.

שְׁרֹשׁוּ (שְׁרֹשִׁי) f. Ch., *rooting up, banishment,* Ezr. 7:26.

שַׁרְשְׁרוֹת שָׁרְשׁוֹת, see שרר.

שֵׁרֵת. Pi. שֵׁרֵת.—I. *waited on,* with אֵת.—II. *attended to,* with accus.—ל.— III. שׁ or שׁ בְּשֵׁם יְהֹוָה *performed the service of the sanctuary.*—IV. *worshipped,* Eze. 20:32. Part. מְשָׁרֵת m., מְשָׁרֶת f., *minister.*

שָׁשָׁה Po. שׁוֹשָׁה; see שָׁסָה.

שֵׁשׁ f., שִׁשָּׁה const., שֵׁשֶׁת m., *six;* pl. שִׁשִּׁים *sixty;* see also in שׁוּשׁ

שִׁשָּׁה Pi. *gave a sixth part of,* Eze. 45:13.

שִׁשִּׁי m., שִׁשִּׁית f., *the sixth;* in f. *a sixth part.*

שֵׁשָׁא Pi. שֵׁשָׁא *caused to walk, led,* Eze. 39:2.

שֵׁשְׁבַּצַּר p. n., the Persian name of Zerubbabel.

שֵׁשַׁי p. n. of a man.

שִׁשַׁי p. n. of a man.

שֵׁשַׁךְ p. n., a prophetic title of Babylon.

שֵׁשָׁן p. n. of a man.

שָׁשָׁק p. n. of a man.

שָׁשֵׁר with pause שָׁשֵׁר m., *red ochre* or *red lead;* LXX. μίλτος.

שֵׁת, שָׁתָה שָׁתִי pret. from שִׁית.

שֵׁת *tumult,* see שָׁאָה.

שֵׁת p. n., שֵׁתוֹת, see שִׁית.

שֵׁתוֹת שֵׁת, see שתת.

שֵׁת Ch., *six;* pl. שִׁתִּין *sixty.*

שָׁתָה (inf. שָׁתֹה שָׁתוֹ שְׁתוֹת; fut יִשְׁתֶּה; apoc. שֵׁתְּ (יֵּשְׁתְּ).—I. *he drank*—II. *sat at table, banqueted,* Est. 7:1.—III. met., *experienced.*—IV. *consumed.* Niph. fut. יִשָּׁתֶה, *was drunk,* Lev. 11:34.

שְׁתָא Ch., *he drank;* pret. with א pros. אֶשְׁתִּיו.

שְׁתִי m.—I. *drinking.*—II. *the warp of a well.*

שְׁתִיָּה f., *drinking,* Est. 1:8.

מִשְׁתֶּה m.—I. *the act of drinking.*—II. *a banquet.*—III. *the drink itself.*

מִשְׁתְּיָא emph. m. Ch., the same.

שָׁתֻּ Ps. 73:9, pret. pl., from שתת

שְׁתַּיִם see שְׁנַיִם.

שָׁתַל *planted a tree.*

שָׁתִיל m., pl. שְׁתִלֵי זֵיתִים olive shoots, branches, Ps. 128:3.

שָׁתַם (Copt. to close); שְׁתֻם הָעַיִן "whose eyes were opened," Eng. Ver., Nu. 24:3, 15.

שָׁתַן. Hiph. made water; מַשְׁתִּין בְּקִיר that ... against the wall; i. e., a very mean man.

שָׁתַק I. became still, was at rest. — II. ceased (of strife), Pro. 26:20.

שְׁתָר p. n., a prince of Persia.

שְׁתַר בּוֹזְנַי p. n. of a Persian.

שָׁתַת same as שִׁית placed.

שֵׁת m. (pl. with suff. שְׁתוֹתֵיהֶם), the buttocks.

## ת

תָּא m., a room or chamber; pl. תָּאִים, תָּאוֹת; (Arab. habitation).

תָּא; see תָּוָה.

I. תָּאַב desired, longed for, with לְ, Ps. 119, 40, 174.

תַּאֲבָה f., desire, Ps. 119:20.

II. תָּאַב same as תָּעַב. Pi. part. מְתָאֵב abhorring, Am. 6:8.

תָּאָה Pi. mark, mark out; fut. pl. תְּתָאוּ, Nu. 34:7, 8.

תְּאָהֲבוּ for תֶּאֱהָבוּ Kal fut. pl., from אהב.

תּוֹא, תְּאוֹ m., the Egyptian antelope; antelope oryx (Linn.).

תַּאֲוָה desire; see אוה.

תֹּאכְלֵהוּ Pi. fut. with suff. for תְּאַכְּלֵהוּ, or Kal fut. with suff. for תֹּאכְלֵהוּ, from אכל.

תַּאֲלָה cursing; see אלה.

תָּאַם was double, part. תְּאֹמִים twins. Hiph. produced twins.

תָּאַם m., pl. תְּאוֹמִים, תּוֹמִים twins, pl. const. תָּאֳמֵי.

תַּאֲנִיָּה, תֹּאֲנָה, תַּאֲנָה; see אנה.

תְּאֵנָה, תְּאֵנִים; see און.

תַּאֲנַת שִׁלֹה p. n., a town of Ephraim.

תָּאַר I. turned, made a circuit. — II. was formed, drawn, used in both senses of a boundary only. Pi. delineated, marked the form of.

מְתֹאָר p. n. of a place, Jos. 19:13.

תֹּאַר m. (with suff. תָּאֳרוֹ, תָּאֳרוֹ).—I. form, personal appearance. — II beauty.

תֶּאְרֵעַ p. n. of a man.

תְּאַשּׁוּר; see אשר.

תָּאֵבָה for תֹּאבֶה Kal fut. 2. pers., from אבה.

תָּבֹאינָה Kal fut. pl. f., from בוא.

תֵּבָה const. תֵּבַת f. (Coptic an ark, chest; Hierog. the same). — I. Noah's ark. — II. the basket in which Moses was exposed.

תְּבוּאָה; see בוא.

תְּבֹאתִי; תְּבֹא for תָּבֹאתָה, תְּבֹאָה for תָּבֹאי Kal fut. with ה parag., and with suff. תְּבֹאָתְךָ for תְּבֹואֲךָ, from בוא.

תְּבוּנָה, תָּבוּן; see בין.

תְּבוּסָה; see בוס.

תָּבוֹר p. n. — I. a mountain of Galilee on the borders of Zebulun and Naphtali. — II. a city of the Levites in Zebulun. — III. a grove of oaks in Benjamin.

וַתֵּבְךְ, תֵּבְךְ Kal fut. apoc., from בכה.

תֵּבֵל see יבל; תָּבֵל, see בלל.

תֵּבֵל same as תּוּבָל.

תַּבְלִית; see בלה.

תבל 280 תוך

תְּבַלֺל; see בלל.

תֶּבֶן m., *straw.*
תִּבְנִי p. n. of a man.
מַתְבֵּן m., *heap of straw,* Isa. 25:10.

תַּבְנִית; see בנה.

תִּבְעָיוּן Kal fut. pl. with נ parag. from בעה.

תַּבְעֵרָה; see בער.

תֵּבֵץ p. n., a place not far from Sichem.

תְּבַר Ch. part., f. תְּבִירָה *brittle,* Dan. 2:42.

תִּנְבְּהֵינָה for תִּנְבַּהְנָה Kal fut. pl. f. from נבה.

תִּנְיוּן Hiph. fut. pl. with נ parag. from ינה.

תִּנַּל Niph. fut. apoc. from נלה.

תִּ׳ פִּלְנְאֶסֶר,תִּלְנַת פִּלֶסֶר,תִּנְלַת פִּלְאֶסֶר תִּ׳ פִּלְנֶסֶר p. n., a king of Assyria.

תַּנְמוּל; see נמל.

תִּנְרָה; see נרה.

תּוֹנַרְמָה, תּוֹגַרְמָה p. n., some country to the north of Palestine.

תְּדְהָר; see דהר.

תְּדִירָא; see דור.

תְּדַמְּיוּנִי Pi. fut. pl. with suff. from דמה.

תַּדְמֹר p. n., a city in the Syrian desert, *Palmyra.*

תִּדְעָל p. n. of a king, Gen. c. 14.

תָּהָה (Arab. *a desert*).
תֹּהוּ m. — I. *emptiness.* — II. *a vain thing, nothing.* — III. *desolation.* — IV. *a desert, wilderness.* — V. adv. *in vain.*

תְּהוֹם *the deep;* see הום.

תְּהִי, תֶּהִי, וַתְּהִי, in pause תֶּהִי, fut. apoc. from היה.

תְּהִימֶנָּ for תְּהִימִינָה Hiph. fut., from הום.

הלל; see תְּהִלָּה, תְּהִלָּה.

תְּהִלָּתֶיךָ for תְּהִלָּתֶךָ; see הלל in הלל.

תַּהֲלוּכָה *procession;* see הלך.

תַּהְפֵּכוֹת, תַּהְפּוּכָה; see הפך.

תְּהַתֵּלּוּ Pi. fut. pl. with dag. euphon., from התל.

תֶּו; see תוה.

תֹּוא same as תְּאוֹ.

תּוּב Ch., *returned.* Aph. I. הָתִיב *returned, carried back.* — II. *answered,* with פִּתְנָם.

תְּבַל, תֻּבַל p. n. of some northern nation, perhaps the *Tibarenes.*

תּוּבַל קַיִן p. n., a son of Lamech, the first artificer in iron.

תּוּגָה; see ינה.

תּוֹדָה; see ידה.

תְּוַהּ Ch., *was amazed,* Dan. 3:24

תָּוָה Pi. תִּוָּה *made marks, scrabbled,* 1 Sa. 21:14. Hiph. l. with תָּו *made a mark,* Eze. 9:4. — II. metaph. *provoked,* i.e. made a painful mark, scratch, wound, Ps. 78:41; Vulg *exacerbaverunt.*

תָּו m., *a mark* or *sign,* Eze. 9:4; (Arab. *a mark in the form of a cross,* put upon the necks of camels; hence the Phœnician and Greek letters τ tau).

תּוֹחַ p. n. of a man.

תּוֹחֶלֶת; see יחל.

תָּוֶךְ, const. תּוֹךְ m., *the middle;* בְּתוֹךְ *in the middle, among, within, through;* מִתּוֹךְ *from the midst of;* אֶל־תּוֹךְ *into the midst of;* תּוֹךְ *oppression;* see in תָּכַךְ.

תִּיכוֹן m., תִּיכוֹנָה f., *middle.*

תּוֹכֵחָה, תּוֹכַחַת; see יכח.

תּוֹלֵד, תּוֹלֶדֶת; see ילד.

תּוֹלָל; see ילל.

תּוֹלָע, תּוֹלֵעָה, תּוֹלַעַת; see תלע.

תּוֹמִים same as תְּאוֹמִים; see תאם.

תּוֹמִיךְ for תֹּמֶךְ Kal part., from תמך.

תּוֹעֵבָה, תּוֹעֵבָה; see תעב.

תּוֹעָה; see תעה.

תּוֹעָפוֹת; see יעף.

תּוּף (Arab. *spit through detestation*).

תֹּפֶת f.—I. לְפָנִים 'ת *object of detestation* (one in whose face they spit), Job 17:6.—II. תֹּפֶת, with ה parag. תָּפְתֶּה p.n., a place in the valley of Hinnom, near Jerusalem.

תּוֹצָאוֹת; see יצא.

תּוּר I. *go about as a spy, spy out.*— II. *search out, explore.*—III. *travel about*, 1 Ki. 10:15.—IV. *seek after the heart, go astray*, Nu. 15:39, with אַחֲרֵי· Hiph. I. *send spies*, Jud. 1:23.—II. *direct aright*, Pro. 12:26.

תּוֹר m.—I. *turn, order*, Est. 2:12, 15. —II. *row, string of beads*, Cant. 1:10, 11.— III. *a turtle dove.*— IV. same as תּוֹרָה *way, manner*, 1 Chron. 17:17.

יָתוּר m., "*that which one discovers*" (Ges.); "*abundance*," see יֶתֶר (Lee); "*range*," Eng. Ver., Job 39:8.

תּוֹרָה; see ירה

תּוֹר m. Ch., *an ox*.

תּוֹשָׁב; see ישב.

תּוּשִׁיָּה f.—I. *abundance, wealth.*—II. *abundantly, entirely*, Job 30:22.— III. *security.*—IV. *wisdom.*

תּוֹתָח; see יתח.

---

הֵתַז, תָּזַז; see תזז.

תָּאֱלִי, תָּאֱלִי for תָּאֱלִי Kal fut. 2. pers. from אזל.

תַּזְנֻת; see זנה.

תָּאָזְרֵנִי for תְּאַזְּרֵנִי Pi. fut. with suff. from אזר.

תַּחְבֻּלוֹת, תַּחְבּוּלוֹת; see חבל.

תָּחוּ p.n., same as תּוֹחַ.

תַּחַז Kal fut. apoc. from חזה.

תַּחֵז for תֹּאחֵז Kal fut. from אחז.

תְּחִי fut. apoc. from חיה.

תַּחְכְּמֹנִי p.n. of a man.

תֵּחֵל for תֵּחַל Niph. fut. from חלל.

תְּחִלָּה; see חלל.

תַּחֲלֻאִים; see חלה.

תַּחְמָס; see חמס.

תַּחֲנוֹת, תַּחַן; see חנה.

תַּחֲנוּנוֹת, תַּחֲנוּנִים, תְּחִנָּה; see חנן.

תַּחְפַּנְחֵס, תְּחַפְנְחֵס (תַּחְפְּנֵס), p. n.— I. a city of Egypt.—II. תַּחְפְּנֵיס a queen of Egypt.

תַּחֲרָה, תַּחְרָא; see חרה.

תַּחְרֵעַ p.n. of a man.

תַּחַשׁ m. עוֹר תַּחַשׁ תְּחָשִׁים עֹרֹת. —I. a colour of which skins were dyed, probably *blue*; "badgers' skins," Eng. Ver. — II. p. n. of a man.

וַתַּחַשׁ, תָּחַשׁ, Job 31:5; Kal fut. apoc. (חָשָׁה); see חוּשׁ.

תָּחַת root not used; (Ethiop. "cast down").

תַּחַת m., *that which is under, below*. Adv. *below*; prep. ὑπό.—I. *under.*— II. *instead of.*—III. *in return for*; תַּחַת אֲשֶׁר *whereas, because that*; 'ת כִּי *because*; (also without כִּי). With suff. תַּחְתֶּיךָ (תַּחְתֵּנִי); תַּחְתָּיו; תַּחְתֵּינוּ (תַּחְתֵּנָה) תַּחְתֶּיהָ, תַּחְתָּיו;

תְּחֻתֵּיהֶם, תַּחְתֵּיכֶם, תַּחְתָּם, Comp.
מִתַּחַת from under, under; מְתַּחַת
under, beyond; אֶל־תַּחַת under. לְ

תַּחַת p. n.—I. one of the stations of
Israel in the wilderness.—II. name
of a man.

תַּחַת Ch.,
תְּחוֹת Ch., } under.

תַּחְתִּי m., תַּחְתִּיָּה תַּחְתִּית f., lower,
lowest; pl. m. תַּחְתִּיִּים, f. תַּחְתִּיּוֹת
lowest parts or places.

תַּחְתּוֹן m., תַּחְתּוֹנָה f., lower, lowest.

תַּחַת Ch. Aph. fut. from נחת.

תֵּחַת Kal fut. f. from נחת.

תֵּט Kal fut. apoc. from נטה.

תִּיז Hiph. הֵתַז, with pause הֵתָז cut
off.

תִּיכוֹן; see תָּוֶךְ.

תִּילוֹן, תִּלּוֹן p. n. of a man.

תֵּימָא p. n. of a people of
Arabia, and of their country.

תֵּימָן; see ימן.

תִּימָרוֹת; see תמר.

תֵּיעָשֶׂה, Ex. 25:31, for תֵּעָשֶׂה Niph.
fut. from עשׂה.

תִּירוֹשׁ, תִּירֹשׁ; see ירשׁ.

תִּירְיָא p. n. of a man.

תִּירָם p. n., one of the sons of Japhet.

תַּיִשׁ m. (pl. תְּיָשִׁים), he-goat or ram.

תָּכָה Pu. תֻּכּוּ were seated, sat down,
Deu. 33:3.

תֵּכֶּה, וַתֵּכַהּ Kal fut. apoc. from כהה.

תְּכוּנָה; see תכן, כון.

תֻּכִּיִּים, תֻּכִּיִּים m. pl., probably
peacocks, 1 Ki. 10:22; 2 Ch. 9:21.

תְּכַךְ Ch., injured, hurt.

תּוֹךְ, תֹּךְ m., craft, oppression; see
also תָּוֶךְ in תּוֹךְ.

תְּכָכִים m. pl., oppressions, injuries,
Pro. 29:13.

תַּכְלִית, תִּכְלָה; see כלה.

תְּכֵלֶת f., violet blue.

תָּכַן I. weighed. — II. pondered, examined. Niph. I. was measured,
examined.—II. was of just measure,
fair, equal. Pi. תִּכֵּן I. measured.
—II. fixed, Ps. 75:4.—III. directed,
Isa. 40:13. Pu. measured, reckoned, 2 Ki. 12:12.

תֹּכֶן m.—I. fixed quantity, Ex. 5:18.
—II. measure, standard, Eze. 45:11.
—III. p. n., a town of the Simeon-
ites.

תְּכוּנָה f. — I. arrangement, order,
structure. — II. costly thing, Nah.
2:10; see also in כּוּן.

תָּכְנִית f., measure, standard.

מַתְכֹּנֶת f. (with suff. מַתְכֻּבְנְתּוֹ), measure, proportion.

תֵּכַס Pi. fut. apoc. from כסה.

תִּכַּסֶּה Hith. fut. from כסה.

תַּכְרִיךְ; see כרך.

תִּלָּה, תֵּל; see תלל.

תְּלָאִים, תְּלָא; see תלה.

תְּלָאָה; see לאה.

תְּלָאֹבוֹת, תַּלְאוּבֹה; see לאב.

תְּלַאשָּׂר, תְּלַאשָּׂר p. n., a city of Syria
or Mesopotamia.

תִּלְבֹּשֶׁת; see לבשׁ.

תְּלַג m. Ch., snow.

תִּלְגַּת; see תְּגָלַת.

תָּלָה (part. תְּלוּי; pl. תְּלוּאִים, תְּלוּיִם,
תְּלָאִים).—I. hung, with בְּ, עַל upon
(a tree). — II. "made dependent,"
Job 26:7 (Lee).—III. placed in sus

*pense.* Niph. *was hanged.* Pi. *hung,* Eze. 27:10, 11.

תָּלָה, וַתֵּלַא Kal fut. apoc., from לתה.

תְּלִי m. (with suff. תֶּלְיֶךָ) *quiver (that which is suspended),* Gen. 27:3.

תְּלֻנּוֹת; see לון.

תֶּלַח p. n. of a man.

תָּלַל *raised a mound;* part. תָּלוּל *elevated, thrown up,* Eze. 17:22; (הֵתֵל, see הֵתַל).

תֵּל m. (with suff. תִּלָּה) (תִּלָּם).—I. *heap of ruins.*—II. *hill, mound.*—III. תֵּל אָבִיב p. n. of a town of Babylonia. —IV. תֵּל חַרְשָׁא p.n.; see חֲרָשׁ. —V. תֵּל מֶלַח (*hill of salt*), p.n., a place in Babylonia.

תֶּלֶם m., *furrow.*

תַּלְמִי p. n. of a man.

תַּלְמִיד; see למד.

תָּלַן Kal fut. apoc., from לון.

תָּלַע Pu. part. מְתֻלָּעִים *clothed in scarlet,* Nah. 2:4.

תּוֹלָע m. (pl. תּוֹלָעִים)—I. *worm* of any kind.—II. *the worm used in dying scarlet.*—III. *scarlet cloth.* —IV. p.n., *Tolah:* (a) a son of Issachar; patron. תּוֹלָעִי.—(b) a judge of Israel.

תּוֹלֵעָה f., *a worm.*

תּוֹלַעַת f.(with suff. תּוֹלַעְתָּם) *a worm;* שָׁנִי תוֹ׳, תּו׳ שָׁנִי I. *scarlet or crimson.*—II. *the kermes insect whence it was dyed.*

תַּלְפִּיּוֹת f. pl., "an armoury," Eng. Ver.,Cant.4:4; meaning uncertain.

תִּלְאשָׁר same as תְּלַאשַּׂר.

תְּלָת f., תְּלָתָא m. Ch., *three;* pl. תְּלָתִין *thirty.*

תְּלָת m. Ch., the same; שַׁלִּיט תַּלְתָּא and תַּלְתָּא *prince third in rank.*

תַּלְתִּי m. Ch., *third.*

תְּלִיתָי Ch., f. תְּלִיתָאָה the same.

תַּלְתַּלִּים m. pl., *hanging, flowing of hair;* LXX. ἐλάται, Cant. 5:11.

תָּם Ch., with ה parag. תַּמָּה *there.*

תָּמָּה, תָּם, תַּמָּה, תֹּם; see תמם.

תֵּימָא same as תֵּימָא.

תָּמַהּ *wondered, was amazed.* Hith. imp. הִתַּמְּהוּ *be astonished,* Hab. 1:5.

תְּמַהּ m. Ch., *wonder, miracle.*

תִּמָּהוֹן m., *astonishment, terror.*

תַּמּוּז p. n. a Syrian idol, perhaps *Adoni*

תְּמוֹל adv., *yesterday;* אֶתְמוֹל, אֶתְמוֹל, אֶתְמוּל the same.

תְּמוּנָה; see מין.

תְּמוּרָה; see מור.

תְּמוּתָה; see מות.

תֶּמַח p. n. of a man.

תָּמַח Hiph. fut. apoc., with י parag. תֶּמְחִי, from מחה.

תָּמִיד; see מוד.

תָּמִים; see תמם.

תָּמַךְ I. *took hold of,* with בְּ.—II. *held, held up, supported.*—III. *obtained.* —IV. *apprehended.*—V. *arrived at, reached.* Niph. *was holden,* Pro. 5:22.

תָּמַם (fut. תָּתֹּם, יִתֹּם, יִתּוֹם; pl. יִתַּמּוּ, with pause יִתָּמּוּ).—I. *was completed, ended.*—II. *was perfec. in character, upright.*—III. *ceased, came to an end, finished.* — IV. *wasted away, consumed, destroyed;* עַד תֻּמָּם *until they were destroyed*

Niph. (fut. pl. יִתַּמּוּ).— I. *was finished.*—II. *was consumed.* Hiph. הֵתַם (fut. יַתֵּם; inf. with suff. הֲתִימְךָ).—I. *finished, consumed.*—II. *declared perfect.*—III. *took the sum of, counted,* 2 Ki. 22:4.—IV. *cause to cease, remove,* with מִן, Eze. 22:15. Hithpa. *showed himself perfect;* fut. תִּתַּמָּם, 2 Sa. 22:26; Ps. 18:26.

תָּמִים m., תְּמִימָה f.— I. *complete.*— II. *whole, entire.*—III. *free from fault, defect.*—IV. *integrity.*

תָּם m., תַּמָּה f., *blameless, honest, virtuous, pious.*

תֹּם, תּוֹם, ־תָּם m. (with suff. תֻּמּוֹ).—I. *completeness.*—II. *security, peace, prosperity.*—III. *innocence, integrity;* pl. תֻּמִּים probably *truth;* see אוּרִים.

תֻּמָּה f., *innocence, integrity.*

תָּאֳמִים double, contr. for תָּאֳמִים.

מְתֹם m., *unhurt, sound, soundness.*

תִּמְנָה p.n., *a city of Judah.*

תִּמְנָתָה p.n., *a town of the Philistines;* תִּמְנִי *a Timnite.*

ת׳ סֶרַח תִּמְנַת חֶרֶס p.n., *a town in Mount Ephraim.*

תִּמְנָע p.n.—I. *of a woman.*—II. *of one of the tribes of Edom.*

תָּמָס; see מסס.

תַּמָּס, וַתָּמָס Hiph. fut. apoc., from מסה.

תָּמָר m.—I. *a palm tree;* pl. תְּמָרִים.—II. p.n. of a woman.—III. p.n. of a town in south Palestine.—IV. p.n., same as תַּדְמֹר.—V. עִיר הַתְּמָרִים (*city of palms*), a name of Jericho.

תֹּמֶר m. *palm-tree,* Jer. 10:5.

תִּמֹרָה f. (pl. תִּמֹּרִים, תִּמֹרוֹת), *artificial palm tree.*

תַּמְרוּרִים m. pl., *columns,* Jer. 31:21; see also in מָרַד.

תִּימָרָה f., pl. const. תִּימֲרוֹת *pillars of smoke.*

תָּמֹר Ex. 23:21, for תָּמַר Hiph. fut., from מרר (same as מרה).

תֹּאמְרוּ for תֹּאמְרוּ Kal fut. pl., from אמר.

תַּמְרוּק; see מרק.

תַּנִּים, תַּן; see תנן.

תְּנָה, תֵּן Kal imp., from נתן.

תִּנְדַּע Ch. Pe. fut., from ידע.

תָּנָה hired, Hos. 8:10. Pi. I. *ascribed praise to,* Jud. 5:11.— II. *celebrated an action,* Jud. 11:40. Hiph. same as Kal, Hos. 8:9.

תַּנּוֹת f. pl., *habitations,* Mal. 1:3; see also in תַּנִּים.

אֶתְנָה f., *gift, wages of prostitution,* Hos. 2:14.

אֶתְנִי p.n. of a man.

אֶתְנַן m. (with suff. אֶתְנַנָּה).—I. *fee, gift, wages of prostitution.*—II. p.n. of a man.

תִּנְיָן m. Ch., *the second:* f. תִּנְיָנָה Dan. 7:5.

תִּנְיָנוּת Ch. adv., *a second time, again,* Dan. 2:7.

תְּנוּאָה; see נוא.

תְּנוּבָה; see נוב.

תְּנוּךְ; see תנך.

תְּנוּמָה; see נום.

תְּנוּפָה; see נוף.

תַּנּוּר m., *a furnace, oven.*

תַּנְחֻמֹת, תַּנְחוּמוֹת, תַּנְחוּמִים; see נחם.

תְּנוּךְ m., with אֹזֶן *the lower part of the ear.*

תַּן or תָּן m., pl. תַּנִּים, תַּנִּין *jackals, or*

*other wild animals of the desert;* the precise meaning unknown.

תַּנִּים m. sing., for תַּנִּין Eze. 29:3; 32:2.

תַּנִּין m. (pl. תַּנִּינִים).—I. *a serpent.*—II. *any large marine animal.*—III. *a crocodile.*

תִּנְשֶׁמֶת; see נשם.

תֹּסֶף for תֹּאסֵף Kal fut., from אסף.

תָּעַב Pi. תִּעֵב I. *abhorred.* — II. *rendered loathsome.* — III. *was abominable.* Hiph. הִתְעִיב I. *acted abominably.*—II. adv. *abominably.* Niph. נִתְעַב *was abhorred.*

תּוֹעֵבָה const. תּוֹעֲבַת f.—I. *abomination.*—II. *impure detestable action.*—III. *anything polluting.*—IV. *an idol.*

תֵּעֲנֶגְנָה for תֵּעֲנַגְנָה Niph. fut. pl., from ענג.

תָּעָה (fut. apoc. תֵּתַע).—I. *wandered, went astray.*—II. *staggered through drunkenness.* — III. *was in confusion, disorder.*—IV. with מֵעַל, מִן, מֵאַחֲרֵי *departed from the true worship.* Niph. נִתְעָה I. *was led astray.*—II. *was made to stagger.* Hiph. הִתְעָה (fut. apoc. יַתַע) I. *caused to wander, go astray.*—II. *deceived, led astray.*—III. *acted deceitfully.*

תּוֹעָה f.—I. *apostacy,* Isa. 32:6.—II. *hurt, injury,* Neh. 4:2, 8.

תֹּעוּ, תֹּעִי p. n. of a man.

תְּעוּדָה; see עוד.

תְּעָלָה, תְּעָלַת; see עלה.

תַּעֲלוּלִים; see עלל.

תַּעֲלֻמָה; see עלם.

תַּעֲנוּג; see ענג.

תַּעֲנִית; see ענה.

תַּעְנָךְ, תַּעֲנָךְ p. n., *a city of the Manassites in the tribe of Issachar.*

תָּעַע Pil. part. מְתַעְתֵּעַ *mocking,* Gen. 27:12. Hith. part. pl. מִתְעַתְּעִים *mocked,* 2 Chron. 36:16.

תַּעְתֻּעִים m. pl., *mockeries, deceptions,* Jer. 10:15; 51:18.

תַּעֲצֻמוֹת; see עצם.

תַּעַר; see ערה.

תַּעֲרוּבָה; see ערב.

תֻּפִּים, תֹּף; see תפף.

תִּפְאֶרֶת, תִּפְאָרָה; see פאר.

תַּפּוּחַ m.—I. *apple-tree.*—II. *apple.*—III. p.n.: (a) *a town of Judah;* (b) *a town of Ephraim;* (c) *a town between Ephraim and Manasseh;* (d) *the name of a man.*

תְּפוֹצוֹתֵיכֶם Thiphel 1. pers. with suff., from פוץ.

וַתִּפְהוּ, תִּפְהוּ for תֹּאפְהוּ Kal fut. with suff., from אפה.

תְּפִינִים; see אפן.

תָּפֵל (Arab. *was unseasoned*).

תָּפֵל m.—I. *that which is insipid, unsavoury,* Job 6:6. — II. *insipid, foolish,* Lam. 2:14. — III. *lime, lime-wash for walls* (Eze. only).

תֹּפֶל p. n., *a place in the wilderness*

תִּפְלָה f., *insipidity, folly.*

תְּפִלָּה; see פלל.

תִּפְלֶצֶת; see פלץ.

תִּפְסַח; see פסח.

תֹּפֵף part. f. pl. תֹּפֵפוֹת *beat the tambourine or drum,* Ps. 68:26. Pi *smite the bosom,* Nah. 2:8.

תֹּף m. (pl. תֻּפִּים), *tambourine, drum*

תָּפַר *sew, join together.* Pi. the same, Eze. 13:18.

תָּפַשׂ I. *laid hold of, seized, with* בְּ

—II. *took in war.*—III. *handle, manage the bow, &c.*—IV. *carry on war.*—V. *set, enchase,* Hab. 2:19.—VI. *administer the law,* Jer. 2:8.—VII. *used the name of God irreverently, perjured himself,* Pro. 30:9. Niph. *was taken, caught.* Pi. *took hold,* Pro. 30:28.

תָּפַת ,תִּפְתָּה; see תּוּף.

תִּפְתָּיֵא Ch. m. pl. emph. *lawyers or judges,* Dan. 3:2, 3.

תִּצְלֶנָה for תֶּצֱלֶינָה Kal fut. pl., from צלל.

תִּקְוָה; see קוה.

תְּקוֹמֵם ,תְּקוּמָה; see קום.

תָּקוֹעַ; see תקע.

תְּקוּפָה, see קוף; תַּקִּיף, see תקף.

תְּקַל Ch., *weighed;* part. pass. תְּקִל; *weighed;* pret. תְּקַלְתָּ *thou art weighed.*

תָּקַן *was arranged, straight.* Pi. I. *set in order.* — II. *made straight* (Ecclesiastes only).

תְּקַן Ch., the same. Hoph. הָתְקַן *was set in order, established.*

תָּקַע I. *smote the hands together* (for joy, &c.).— II. *thrust in, stabbed* (of a weapon).—III. *fixed, fastened.*—IV. *pitched a tent.*—V. *threw into the sea,* Ex. 10:19.—VI. with שׁוֹפָר ,בַּשּׁוֹפָר *blew a trumpet;* with תִּרְגֹּעַ *blew a horn.* Niph. I. with לְיָד *strikes hands, becomes a surety,* Job 17:3.—II. with שׁוֹפָר *a trumpet is blown.*

תָּקוֹעַ m., *blast with a trumpet,* Eze. 7:14.

תֶּקַע m., the same, Ps. 150·3.

תְּקוֹעַ p.n., *Tekoa,* a town of Judah, whence the name מִדְבַּר תְּקוֹעַ *the wilderness of Tekoa;* m. תְּקֹעִי, f תְּקֹעִית *a Tekoite.*

תָּקַף *overpower, prevail over.*

תְּקֵף Ch.—I. *was strong.*—II. *was violent.* Pa. *made strong.*

תֹּקֶף m., *might, power.*

תְּקֹף m. Ch., the same.

תְּקוּפָה *circuit;* see קוף.

תַּקִּיף m., *strong, powerful,* Ecc. 6:10.

תַּקִּיף m. Ch., *strong, powerful.*

תִּרְאֲלָה p.n., a town of Benjamin.

וַתֶּרֶב ,תֵּרַב Kal fut. apoc., from רבה.

תַּרְבִּית ,תַּרְבּוּת; see רבה.

תַּרְגֵּל; see רָגַל.

תַּרְגֵּם Ch. quadrilitt., *interpreted, translated;* part. pass. מְתַרְגַּם, Ezr. 4:7.

תַּרְדֵּמָה; see רדם.

תִּרְהָקָה p.n., *Tirhakah,* king of Egypt and Ethiopia.

תְּרוּמִיָּה ,תְּרוּמָה; see רום.

תְּרוּעָה; see רוע.

תְּרוּפָה; see רפא.

תֵּרוֹץ Niph. fut., from רצץ.

תִּרְזָה f., name of a tree, *the holly.*

תֶּרַח p.n.—I. a station of Israel in the wilderness.—II. the father of Abraham.

תִּרְחֲנָה p.n. of a man.

תְּרֵין const. תְּרֵי m., תַּרְתֵּין f. Ch., *two.*

תַּרְמִית ,תַּרְמָה; see רמה.

תֹּרֶן I. *mast of a ship.*—II. *flag or banner.*

תְּרַע m. Ch.—I. *entrance, door.*— II *palace* (the porte).

תָּרָע m. Ch., *door keeper.*

תַּרְעֵלָה; see רעל.

תִּרְעָתִי p. n. of a man.

תְּרָפִים m. pl., *Teraphim*; idols of some kind.

תִּרְפֶּינָה Job 5:18, Kal fut. pl., from רפה.

תִּרְצָה p.n.—I. one of the royal cities of Israel.—II. the name of a woman.

תֶּרֶשׁ p.n. of a Persian.

תַּרְשִׁישׁ; see רשׁשׁ.

תִּרְשָׁתָא, with art., a title of Nehemiah.

תַּרְתָּן p.n., a chief of the Assyrians.

תַּרְפָּס p.n., an idol of the Arvadites.

תִּשָּׁאֶינָה for תִּשָּׂאנָה Kal fut. pl., from נשׂא.

תְּשֻׂמֶת; see שׂים.

תְּשֻׁאוֹת; see שׁוא.

תִּשְׁבִּי p. n. of a man.

תִּשְׁבֵּץ; see שׁבץ.

תְּשׁוּבָה; see שׁוב.

תְּשׁוּעָה; see ישׁע.

תְּשׁוּקָה; see שׁוק.

תְּשׁוּרָה; see שׁאר.

תֵּשִׁי, Deu. 32:18, fut. apoc., from שׁיה.

תֵּשַׁם fut., from ישׁם.

תֵּשַׁע const. תְּשַׁע, f. תִּשְׁעָה const. תִּשְׁעַת m., *nine, the ninth*; pl. תִּשְׁעִים *ninety*.

תְּשִׁיעִי m., תְּשִׁיעִית f., *the ninth*.

תֵּשְׁתְּ Kal fut. apoc., from שׁתה.

תִּשְׁתַּחֲוּ Hith. fut. apoc. sing. for תִּשְׁתַּחֲוֶה, from שׁחה.

תִּשְׁתָּעַ Hith. fut. apoc. for תִּשְׁתָּעֶה, from שׁעה.

תֵּת, with suff. תִּתִּי Kal inf., from נתן.

תִּתְבָּרַר for תִּתְבָּרֵר Hith. fut., from ברר.

תִּתָּה for נָתַתָּה Kal pret., from נתן.

תִּתְחַר Hith. fut. apoc., from חרר.

תִּתַּם תְּתָם Kal fut., from תמם.

תִּתְנַי p.n., a Persian noble.

וַתֵּתַע תֵּתַע Kal fut. apoc., from תעה.

תִּתְפַּל, 2 Sa. 22:27, transpos for תִּתְפַּתָּל Hith. fut., from פתל.

תִּתְיָצָּב, Ex. 2:4, for תִּתְיָצֵּב Hith. fut., from יצב.

וַתֹּתַר אֹתָר Hiph. fut. in pause from יתר.